About the Author

Raymond Buckland has been studying and practicing Spiritualism, fortune-telling, Witchcraft, Gypsy magic, and other aspects of the supernatural for fifty years. He has had nearly forty titles published, with translations in seventeen languages, including *The Witch Book, The Fortune-Telling Book,* and the classic *Buckland's Complete Book of Witchcraft.* Of Romany (Gypsy) descent, Buckland was born in London, where he obtained a doctorate in anthropology. In 1962 he moved to the United States and became affiliated with Wicca pioneer Dr. Gerald Gardner. Buckland has been the subject of and has written countless newspaper and magazine articles, appeared on many television and radio shows, served as technical advisor for several movies, and lectured on college campuses nationwide.

THE
SPIRIT
BOOK

THE ENCYCLOPEDIA OF
CLAIRVOYANCE, CHANNELING,
AND SPIRIT COMMUNICATION

THE SPIRIT BOOK

THE ENCYCLOPEDIA OF CLAIRVOYANCE, CHANNELING, AND SPIRIT COMMUNICATION

RAYMOND BUCKLAND

Detroit

THE SPIRIT BOOK

THE ENCYCLOPEDIA OF CLAIRVOYANCE, CHANNELING, AND SPIRIT COMMUNICATION

Visible Ink Press®
43311 Joy Rd. #414
Canton, MI 48187-2075

Visible Ink Press is a registered trademark of Visible Ink Press LLC.

Most Visible Ink Press books are available at special quantity discounts when purchased in bulk by corporations, organizations, or groups. Customized printings, special imprints, messages, and excerpts can be produced to meet your needs. For more information, contact Special Markets Director, Visible Ink Press, at www.visibleink.com or (734) 667-3211.

Art Director: Mary Claire Krzewinski
Typesetting: The Graphix Group

ISBN   978-1-57859-790-1

CIP on file with the Library of Congress

Front cover image:
I-D-O Psy-ch-i-deo-graph, 1919, by Theodore H. White.
Collection of Louis Wildfong,
Cultural Relics and Artifacts Place,
Ferndale, Michigan.

Back cover images courtesy Fortean Picture Library.

CONTENTS

Introduction [xiii]
Acknowledgments [xix]

Raps, Taps, and Spirit Voices:
An Introduction

It all officially began on the night of Friday, March 31, 1848. That was the night when two frightened children and their mother "spoke" with the spirit of a dead (murdered) peddler.

The episode occurred at the Fox homestead in Hydesville, Wayne County, New York. Hydesville was a small community founded by Dr. Henry Hyde in 1815. The Fox family rented and moved into a small cabin in the community on December 11, 1847. For several weeks, strange, unexplained taps and knocks were heard in various parts of the house. John Fox and his wife, Margaret, would move from room to room, carefully examining both the outside and the inside of the building, searching for the source of these noises. They ensured that shutters were tightly fastened and that no tree limbs rattled against the structure; that cupboard doors were fixed firmly and animals safely penned. Yet night after night the noises continued. It was usually during the hours of darkness that the raps and taps were heard, causing John and Margaret to prowl the house through the night, with lanterns in hand.

As the weeks passed, the noises continued, and the Fox's two young daughters became more and more distraught. Margaretta was seven and Cathie, or Kate, was ten years of age. They were disturbed by the noises but also upset by their mother's reactions. Margaret Fox was losing sleep and her nerves were frayed. The children begged and were allowed to sleep in a bed in the same room as their parents. On the night of Friday, March 31, 1848, the noises were especially loud, even in the early evening before it really got dark. As the raps and thumps continued, young Cathie—on impulse—sat up, clapped her hands three times, and said aloud, "Mr. Splitfoot, do as I do." (The children, thinking of a cloven-hoofed imp, had dubbed the perpetrator "Mr. Splitfoot.") Immediately there came three raps on the wall. Cathie repeated her claps and the spirit repeated the raps. Then the girl sat silent and no noise was heard. Cathie's sister Margaretta cried out, "Do just as I do. Count one, two, three, four." She clapped her hands together to that count. Again, the raps echoed her, coming once, twice, three times, and four times. Margaretta fell silent, in awe of the phenomenon.

Margaret Fox then had an idea. She spoke out and asked that the ages of her children be rapped out. Immediately it happened. Each one of her seven children's ages was sounded. There was a slight pause at the end and then three more loud raps were given, for the youngest child who had died at that age. Margaret was dumbfounded. In a statement made later, she said,

> I then asked, "Is this a human being that answers my questions so correctly?" There was no rap. I asked, "Is it a spirit? If it is, make two raps." Two sounds were given as soon as the request was made. (*History of Spiritualism*, Arthur Conan Doyle)

So began the first recorded intercourse between the living and the dead. The Foxes went on with their questions and slowly learned that the spirit was a thirty-one-year-old man, a peddler named Charles B. Rosna, who had been murdered in the house.

John Fox was not entirely satisfied and had his wife ask, "Will you continue to rap if I call in my neighbors, that they may hear it too?" The raps were affirmative. Margaret Fox called in her neighbor, Mrs. Redfield. In her testimony, Margaret recalled,

> Mrs. Redfield is a very candid woman. The girls were sitting up in bed clinging to each other and trembling in terror ... Mrs. Redfield came immediately (this was about half past seven), thinking she would have a laugh at the children. But when she saw them pale with fright and nearly speechless, she was amazed and believed there was something more serious than she had supposed. I asked a few questions for her and she was answered as before. He told her age exactly. She then called her husband, and the same questions were asked and answered. (*History of Spiritualism*, Arthur Conan Doyle)

The Foxes went on to call in the Dueslers, the Hydes, the Jewells, and several others. All had their questions answered quickly and accurately. While this episode at Hydesville was certainly not the first example of spirit contact, it was the first to be recorded and made public, and the first contact to feature a "conversation" developing between spirit and living being. It led to public demonstrations of spirit communication by the Fox sisters, feeding popular interest in the phenomena.

From that beginning, the whole Modern Spiritualist movement came into being, sweeping this country and eventually reaching out around the world. The ground had been laid for the movement by such figures as the mystic Emmanuel Swedenborg in the eighteenth century, and also with the Shaker movement (an earlier nineteenth century splinter group of the Quakers). The complete story of the Fox sisters and the development of the Spiritualist movement are described in this in-depth look at the events, related movements, personalities, beliefs, techniques, and practices.

The Spirit Book is broad in scope, dealing not only with the history of spirit communication but also of the various adjunct subjects such as channeling, ESP, ghosts,

and electronic voice phenomena. The encyclopedia provides full biographies of prominent mediums and other people connected to the field, virtually around the world.

The *Spirit Book* provides a comprehensive introduction to the myriad facets of
spirit communication. From earliest times humans have made occasional contact with
apparent spirits of the dead, usually in the form known as "ghosts." Shakespeare gave a
number of examples, such as Hamlet's encounter with the ghost of his father, and the
ghost of Banquo, which appeared to Macbeth. In the Bible, the woman of Endor (1
Samuel 28)—who was, in effect, a medium—clairvoyantly saw Samuel and materialized him to the point where Saul was able to speak with him through her. In the Middle Ages, access to the spirits of the dead was obtained through the art of necromancy.
In eighteenth- and early nineteenth-century Haiti, the followers of Vodoun were able
to speak with their deceased ancestors through the Vodoun priesthood.

Mediumship is an aspect of spirit communication that can be fraudulently
duplicated with ease. In fact the history of Spiritualism is replete with imposters—
those who preyed upon the bereaved. But just because mediumship can be done fraudulently does not mean that *all* mediums are frauds. Far from it. The history is also filled
with wonderful examples of the most amazing people who have demonstrated time
and again, in front of the most intense investigations, that contact with the spirits of
the deceased is not only possible but is certain. Such mediums as Leonora Piper,
Eileen Garrett, Leslie Flint, Gordon Smith, and many more are sufficient to prove, as
the old saying goes, that it only takes one white blackbird to prove that not all blackbirds are black.

In his foreword to *The Mediumship of Jack Webber*, Harry Edwards writes of the
more than four thousand persons who witnessed Webber's physical mediumship. He
writes of the caliber of the investigators, and of the photographers "representing
national newspapers who have provided their own cameras and plates and undertaken
all process work in their own studios." Edwards goes on to say,

> A skeptical mind has to face the fact that the photographs and reports are true.
> Otherwise there must have been a gigantic conspiracy embracing many hun-
> dreds of people, including organizations and newspapers of note, all actively par-
> ticipating in fraudulent acts to deceive the public without motive or reward.
> Newspapers and their critical representatives are only too willing to expose
> fraudulent mediums; yet all, without exception, have testified to the medi-
> umship under review. No critic worthy of the name would classify all the alert,
> questioning minds that have testified to the mediumship of Jack Webber as
> dupes or simpletons.

So Jack Webber must be one of the white blackbirds ... one of many, in fact.

In the February 12, 2005, issue (No. 3787) of the British weekly newspaper
Psychic News, a front-page story reports that Professor David Fontana, former President of the prestigious Society for Psychical Research, wrote a foreword thoroughly
endorsing the physical mediumship of Minnie Harrison, as reported in her son Tom's
book *Life After Death—Living Proof*. Such brilliant minds as those of Sir William F.
Barrett, Sir William Crookes, Sir Arthur Conan Doyle, Dr. Richard Hodgson,
William James, Sir Oliver Lodge, and many more, spent years investigating medi-

umship and similarly arrived at the conclusion that there is solid evidence for a continuation of existence of the spirit after the death of the physical body.

The encyclopedia sorts through fraudulent mediums and psychics as well as fraudulent skeptics. There are those who are so intense in their prejudice against a belief in Spiritualism, channeling, or any form of psychism, that they will stop at nothing to disprove the possibility of spirit communication and allied practices. In early 2004 a young Russian girl, Natalia Demkina, visited Britain and appeared on British television. She had what was described as X–ray vision, or X–ray clairvoyance. Seventeen-year-old Natalia traveled from Saransk, 400 miles east of Moscow, to appear on the program where she was faced with four complete strangers. She proceeded to describe their medical conditions—which included the fact that one of them had only one kidney—in accurate detail. Of one she said that there had been surgery on the spleen. The woman showed the scar. Of another Natalia said, "There is damage to three areas of the spine. The major problem is where the chest part of the spine meets the waist part. Something is probably inserted there. It is something traumatic." The woman agreed. She said that she had "metal rods in my back for many years. They were taken out but there was a broken screw which remained there. It was not removed because it would have caused damage." Of the last person, Natalia said that there was a right shoulder problem. The woman explained, "I smashed my shoulder into twelve pieces." (*Psychic News* #3735, Feb. 7, 2004)

Such was the impression that Natalia made, that the skeptics wanted to carry out their own tests. The Committee for the Scientific Investigation of Claims of the Paranormal arranged for testing to be shown on television's Discovery Channel. However, the designers of the experiment "falsely represented to the viewers that they were the world's 'top' objective, impartially unencumbered 'scientists' and that Natalia would be subjected to legitimate 'scientific scrutiny'," according to psychical researcher and investigator Victor Zammit. This claim was repeated throughout the documentary. Yet actually the testing had been designed by Andrew Skolnick, a debunking journalist and extreme skeptic. Natalia was asked to identify which patients had undergone which operations. The Russian girl was correct four out of the seven tries—odds of one in fifty against chance. Because the skeptics had determined that they wanted her to score *five* out of the seven, they dubbed her a failure, in spite of the fact that statisticians state her results were extremely significant (successes have been hailed with results of only one in nineteen against chance) and in spite of the fact that in an earlier test she had scored five out of six. Natalia herself said of the test, "The atmosphere of the testing was unfriendly. The conditions I was looking for were in some cases dubious. Why is it that if I get five out of seven I pass, but if I get four I'm [regarded by the CSICP as] a total failure?" (*Psychic News* #3735, Feb. 7, 2004)

A man who came to spend most of his time exposing fraudulent mediums was Harry Houdini (Ehrich Weiss). In fact he did Spiritualism a great service by weeding out the imposters. Yet after Houdini's death it was a medium, Arthur Ford, who broke the "Houdini code," thereby proving that the magician himself had survived bodily death. Houdini had left a message with his wife, Beatrice, and told her that only a true medium would be able to give her his message. Many tried, and then Arthur Ford came along and was successful. Ford gave Beatrice the message "Rosabelle, believe," which was done in the long, complicated code which the two Houdinis had used in a vaudeville act they had done many years before.

Channeling seems to be a relatively modern practice, yet it too has roots in history. The sibyls of ancient Greece and Rome would channel the teachings and predictions of the deities, those deities not being of "this world." In modern day channeling, the entity speaking, or lecturing, may or may not have lived previously on Earth. He or she (it seems to be predominantly a he) may claim to come from "a galaxy far, far away" or even to be a combination of many entities.

Channeling differs from mediumship in that where a medium is allowing the living to communicate with their deceased loved ones on a very personal level, the channeler is acting as a pipeline for an entity that offers teachings in the form of lectures. These might be on an individual basis but are more often presented in a large auditorium, with no exchange with the audience other than, perhaps, a short question and answer period at the end. The messages so presented are usually positive, though some seem to be of the "doom and gloom" variety and suggest that we poor earthlings are an inferior people who desperately need the given guidance.

A form of spirit communication that has come very much to the fore in recent years is Electronic Voice Phenomena (EVP), together with Instrumental Transcommunication (ITC). In the 1920s Thomas Alva Edison said,

> If our personality survives, then it is strictly logical or scientific to assume that it retains memory, intellect, other faculties, and knowledge that we acquire on this Earth. Therefore … if we can evolve an instrument so delicate as to be affected by our personality as it survives in the next life, such an instrument, when made available, ought to record something. (*Scientific American*, Oct. 1920)

Today there is in fact a lot of recording done of surviving personalities. Tape recorders are used, as are video cameras. Voices from spirits are received over telephones, radios, television sets, fax machines, computers, cell phones, and satellite dishes. Not only are voices received, but visual images as well. Two of the first serious investigators were Friederich Juergenson and Dr. Konstantin Raudive, recording spirit voices in the 1950s and 1960s. Since then a tremendous interest has developed in the subject, with Tom and Lisa Butler—directors of the American Association of Electronic Voice Phenomenon—leading the research.

Spirits are around us all of the time. It is possible, by a wide variety of means, to speak to them and to have them speak to us. This book looks at the methods of communication, the history of it, and the personalities who have developed throughout the past three hundred years. Some of the details are almost unbelievable: the case of Carlos Carmine Mirabelli, for example, and of Daniel Dunglas Home. There are well-known names here, from Abraham Lincoln to Mark Twain to Mae West. There are stories and explanations of ghosts and of hauntings, of levitation and meditation, of astral projection, psychic surgery, self-painting portraits, crystal gazing, predictions, and poltergeists. There are stories of fakes and frauds as well as of psychics and mediums that have never been found in question. *The Spirit Book* is very much an encyclopedia of clairvoyance, channeling, spirit communication … and more.

ACKNOWLEDGMENTS

Many thanks to my agent, Agnes Birnbaum, and to the staff and associates of Visible Ink Press, including Marty Connors, Roger Jänecke, Roger Matuz, Mary Beth Perrot, Christa Gainor, Terri Schell, Christopher Scanlon, John Krol, Mary Claire Krzewinski, Robert Huffman, Peggy Daniels, and Marco Di Vita. My thanks also to Rebecca Weller of *Psychic News* and Ron Nagy of the Lily Dale Museum.

Special thanks to Theresa K. Murray, who completed her part of this project under the most trying of circumstances. Her indexing work is dedicated to the memory of her parents, Mary (Evy) (November 21, 1924–June 25, 2005) and Lee (December 22, 1922–July 7, 2005) Kuhn, who made contact at a difficult time.

Although my personal library was able to furnish most of the research material, I would be remiss if I did not acknowledge the part that the World Wide Web now plays in bringing material straight to the writer's computer. Hours of laborious study are cut short with the click of a few keys.

Finally, my deepest thanks to my wife, Tara, for her continual encouragement, constructive criticism, and constant support over a period of concentrated writing. In this instance I owe her an additional special debt of gratitude for nursing me through the aftereffects of open heart surgery.

I GREET YOU

A

Absent Healing *see* Distant Healing

ACORAH, DEREK

British psychic/**medium** Derek Acorah had many **psychic** experiences as a child—his first at age six when the **spirit** of his deceased grandfather visited him—but he grew up to play professional soccer with Bill Shankly's Liverpool Football Club and the Australian USC Lion team. In 1980 he became a professional psychic and medium and eventually had a television show called *Most Haunted* and another called *Antiques Ghost Show*. In the latter an expert examined articles such as old family heirlooms brought in by their owners. Acorah then handled the object and relayed information about the ancestors who had owned the artifact. For this he used a combination of **psychometry**, **clairvoyance**, and **clairsentience**. Acorah communicates with the **spirit world** through his **spirit guide** Sam. Describing Acorah's presentations, genealogist Anthony Adolph, writing in *Family History Monthly*, said, "Dozens of volunteers, a modest sized production team and a small army of camera and sound men all focused their attention on Derek's readings of the heirlooms and the subsequent discovery of how much—if any—of his statements were verifiable. The conclusion to which I have been drawn is

that psychics really can get things right … if subterfuge was involved, the sheer volume of deception and skullduggery required would scarcely have been justified for a million-pound bank heist, let along making a satellite TV program."

On a visit to the Granada television studios in Manchester in 2004, Acorah was called in to get rid of some negative spirit energy that seemed to be "**haunting**" the set of the long-running series *Coronation Street*. This he was able to do, with one of the actors later saying, "The problems have been sorted out and all is peaceful and harmonious once more." Acorah visits **Spiritualist** churches across Britain and Europe, demonstrating also in the Middle East and America. Acorah lives in Southport, Merseyside, England, with his wife Gwen and two children.

Sources:

Acorah, Derek: *The Psychic World of Derek Acorah.* London: Piatkus Books, 1999
Derek Acorah Homepage: http://www.derekacorah.org
Psychic News #3720, October 18, 2003. Stansted, Essex
Psychic News #3769, October 2, 2004. Stansted, Essex

ADARE, LORD (1841–1926)

Lord Adare, son of the Earl of Dunraven, was a close friend of **Daniel Dunglas Home**. Adare met the **medium** in 1867 at a hydropathic establishment run by a Dr. Gully. Hydropathy is the treatment of disease by water. As a formal system it came into vogue about 1829 and was popular both in Europe and America. The men, both "taking the water cure," became firm friends and, by 1869, shared an apartment in London. Because of his close contact with the medium, Adare was in a position to ascertain that there was no trickery involved in Home's performances. Home, as reported elsewhere in this volume, was possibly the world's greatest **physical medium**. At his **séances** the sitters experienced strong winds, phantom hands, **music** produced without instruments, **levitation**, **materializations**, and more. Most, if not all of these, if produced theatrically, would have required considerable apparatus. Adare testified that this was not the case.

Adare's father, the Earl of Dunraven, was a devout Roman Catholic but also a believer in Home and in spirit communication. In 1869, at his father's urging, Lord Adare wrote and published a book, *Experiences in Spiritualism with D. D. Home*, which was a detailed and most remarkable record of the medium's many phenomena. The book was first privately printed because of the Earl's religious affiliation, but in 1925, after his father's death, Adare agreed to its reprinting by the **Society for Psychical Research**. Much of the book is in the form of letters that Adare wrote to his father, reporting in detail on the séances he had attended. In his preface to the book, Lord Adare wrote:

> "We have not, on a single occasion, during the whole series of séances, seen any indication of contrivance on the part of the medium for producing or facilitating the manifestations which have taken place."

Sources:
Fodor, Nandor: *Encyclopedia of Psychic Science*. London: Arthurs Press, 1933

AFFIRMATIONS

Affirmations are positive statements that are repeated by an individual, usually at intervals throughout the day. They are focused on betterment of the mind or body. For example, they may aid memory, give self-confidence, or promote health. By repetition, the statement becomes established in the unconscious mind.

Affirmations can be single words or short phrases; usually the shorter and more succinct, the better. They can be made up or can be quotations. Affirmations may be slanted in any direction, depending upon where the need is greatest. For example, to aid memory you might regularly repeat the phrase, "I am easily able to remember everything I see, read, and hear." More specifically—if there is a problem with remembering names, for example—an affirmation might be, "I can easily remember the names of everyone I meet" or "I have no problem remembering people's names." It is best, however, if you can avoid the negatives; avoid saying "no" or "not." In other words, instead of saying you will have "*no* problem," you say that you "*will* easily ... (do whatever)." Always use the positive.

Some suggested affirmations for promoting your psychic abilities are:

- "**Psychic** powers are natural powers that I possess strongly."
- "My psychic abilities flow naturally."
- "I am easily able make contact with the **spirit world**."
- "The more I practice, the more my **mediumistic** abilities progress."

Place your affirmation(s) where you will constantly encounter it. Use stick-on note sheets to place the words on your bathroom mirror, on your computer screen, on the refrigerator door ... all the places where you are bound to see it. Every time you see it, you will read it and repeat it. In this way the phrase—and the suggestion—reinforces the conscious mind and you not only start to believe what you say, but you find that it is actually manifesting.

Sources:
Wilde, Stuart: *Affirmations*. Taos: White Dove, 1987

ÂKÂSA

Âkâsa, or Akasha, is equated with the element of air and is a term denoting pure **spirit**. It is sometimes referred to as "the breath of god" or "ether-space," incorporating sound in its qualities. The *Ramayana*, II. 110. 5 makes Brahma spring from this ether. Âkâsa is called the fifth cosmic element; the subtle spiritual essence that pervades all space. The *Bhagavad-Gita* says that *prakriti* (primal nature or substance) manifests in eight portions: air, earth, fire, water, ether (âkâsa), mind, understanding, self-sense.

Sources:

Gaskell, George Arthur: *Dictionary of All Scriptures and Myths*. New York: Avenel, 1981

AKASHIC RECORDS

A term from **Theosophy** applied to an astral filing system of all thoughts, words, actions, and events that have ever taken place anywhere in the world. The belief is that all things make an impression on the **âkâsa**, or soniferous ether. The Akashic Records are akin to the Collective Unconsciousness, or Universal Mind, as postulated by Carl Jung. **Helena Blavatsky** refers to the âkâsa as "the subtle, supersensuous spiritual essence which pervades all space; the primordial substance erroneously identified with Ether. But it is to Ether what Spirit is to Matter ... the Universal Space in which lies inherent the eternal Ideation of the Universe...."

Certain adepts may tap into these impressions in order to review such things as past lives. It is akin to having a computer that contains all the details of everyone and everything from the beginning of time. In pre-computer days the Akashic Records were likened to a vast library containing the collective records of the ages. Some early writers even believed that such a library actually existed (physically or astrally) beneath the Sphinx, or some such place. **Edgar Cayce**, the "Sleeping Prophet," received much of his information from the Akashic Records. According to Dr. **Wesley Ketcham**, who worked with him, Cayce was "in direct communication with all other subconscious minds, and is capable of interpreting through his objective mind and imparting impressions received to other objective minds."

Sometimes referred to as the "Book of Life," the Akashic records have special importance to some sects and religions that believe in reincarnation. Some **Spiritualist mediums** and **psychics** claim that they access this Book of Life, in much the same way as did Cayce, when doing psychic and past life **readings**. One concept of the Akashic records is that they may not be used for self gain, other than spiritual advancement.

Sources:

Blavatsky, Helena Petrovna: *The Theosophical Glossary*. London: Theosophical Publishing Society, 1892

Bonnell, Gary: *Your Book of Life: Accessing the Akashic Records*. Taos, Societas res Divina, 1996

Cayce, Edgar: *Edgar Cayce on the Akashic Records: The Book of Life*. Virginia Beach, A.R.E. Press, 1997

ALDEN, WILLARD (1800–1878)

Willard Alden owned land beside **Lake Cassadaga** in upstate New York, where **Spiritualists** first started holding regular meetings in 1871. He married Corintha Wilcox on September 27, 1832, in Cassadaga, Chautauqua, New York. They had two children: Theodore Cleremont (b. 1833) and Theodosia Augusta (b. 1835).

The Spiritualist meetings started as simple picnics to which Alden invited fellow Spiritualists. They were for fun and socializing, but soon grew more serious. Willard Alden became more and more serious about Spiritualism and engaged **Lyman C. Howe**, a prominent proponent of and lecturer on Spiritualism, to speak at a meeting on Sunday June 15, 1873. At that time Alden's Grove was dedicated to the special care of the Spiritualists. A series of popular one-day events featuring lectures and discussions with prominent speakers continued for four years.

In 1877 **Jeremiah Carter**, at the behest of a **spirit** voice he kept hearing, prevailed upon

Alden to arrange a camp meeting, which was held from Tuesday, September 11 until Sunday, September 16, 1877. Annual camp meetings followed, with the second one running for an additional ten days. At that time Alden's Grove was fenced in and a cottage was built on the property. The camp meetings ran regularly until Alden's death in 1878 and then continued under the aegis of his son Theodore Alden.

Sources:

Buckland, Raymond: *Buckland's Book of Spirit Communications*. St. Paul: Llewellyn, 2004

Vogt, Paula M. and Joyce LaJudice: *Lily Dale Proud Beginnings: A Little Bit of History* Lily Dale: Lily Dale Museum, 1984

ALLISON, LYDIA WINTERHALTER (1880–1959)

Lydia Allison, an ardent **psychical researcher** in both America and Great Britain, helped found the **Boston Society for Psychical Research** in 1925. From 1921 through 1927 Allison made frequent trips to England in order to sit with various **mediums** including the famous **Gladys Osborne Leonard.**

Allison served as a Trustee of the **American Society for Psychical Research** from 1941 until her death in 1959, chairing its committee on publication from 1943 to 1959. She was also a member of the International Committee for the Study of Parapsychological Methods, part of the **Society for Psychical Research** in London. She attended the First International Conference of Parapsychological Studies in Utrecht, Holland, in 1953.

Sources:

Shepard, Leslie A: *Encyclopedia of Occultism & Parapsychology*. New York: Avon Books, 1978

AMERICAN ASSOCIATION OF ELECTRONIC VOICE PHENOMENA

The American Association of Electronic Voice Phenomena (AA-EVP) was founded by Sarah Estep in 1982 "to provide objective evidence that we survive death in an individual conscious state." Estep published a quarterly newsletter that contained ideas on experiments and equipment and reported on developments in **electronic voice phenomena** (EVP) and **instrumental transcommunication** (ITC). She authored a book on her personal experiences, titled *Voices of Eternity* (1988).

Members of AA-EVP experiment with a wide variety of devices, testing different concepts. These include radios, telephones, **tape recorders**, video equipment, **computers**, still cameras, and answering machines. They maintain that the **spirits** of the dead can, and have, communicated through all of these devices. Estep rates the voices at three levels. Class A are clear, can be duplicated onto other tapes, and can even be heard without headphones. Class B can sometimes be heard without headphones but are not as clear and constant as Class A. Class C are very faint and can easily be overlooked, often being lost in background sound.

The association stresses that any "objective evidence" must be based on good science. Consequently the members take great care to maintain an objective view of the phenomena and to thoroughly examine all possible explanations to ensure that any messages are truly nonphysical in origin.

After running AA-EVP for eighteen years, Estep handed over leadership to Lisa and Tom Butler, who have developed and expanded the association. Pioneers instrumental in leading Sarah Estep to create the society include **Friedrich Jürgenson, Konstantin Raudive, Franz Seidl, Scott Rogo, Raymond Bayless, Klaus Schreiber,** and others.

Sources:

American Association of Electronic Voice Phenomenon: http://aaevp.com

Butler, Tom and Lisa: *There Is No Death and There Are No Dead*. Reno: AA-EVP, 2003

Estep, Sarah: *Voices of Eternity*. New York: Ballantine, 1988

Sherman, Harold: *You Can Communicate With the Unseen World.* New York: Fawcett, 1974

World ITC Organization: http://www.worlditc.org

AMERICAN PSYCHICAL INSTITUTE AND LABORATORY

In 1920 distinguished British **psychical research** investigator and author **Hereward Carrington** founded the American Psychical Institute and Laboratory for specialized research. Sigmund Freud was invited to become a member in 1921 but declined, saying that he wanted to keep psychoanalysis distinctly apart from the **occult**. Freud did, however, admit to his fascination for the field. He is reported to have said, "I am not one of those who, from the outset, disapprove of the study of so-called occult psychological phenomena as unscientific, as unworthy or even dangerous. If I were at the beginning of a scientific career, instead of, as now, at the end of it, I would perhaps choose no other field of work, in spite of its difficulties."

The Institute existed for only two years, but in 1933 it was resurrected, reorganized, and incorporated. Originally headquartered at 20 West 58th Street, New York, by 1937 it had moved to 247 Park Avenue, New York. Carrington was Director of the Institute and his wife, Marie Sweet Carrington, its Secretary. An advisory council made up of a number of men of distinction in the field helped lead the association, which published a quarterly journal titled *Bulletins*.

Sources:

Fodor, Nandor: *Encyclopedia of Psychic Science.* London: Arthurs Press, 1933

Spark Online: http://www.spark-online.com

AMERICAN SOCIETY FOR PSYCHICAL RESEARCH

The oldest **psychical research** organization in the United States, the American Society for Psychical Research (ASPR) was founded in

Boston in 1885, by Sir **William Fletcher Barrett** of the British **Society for Psychical Research** (SPR). The initial directors included astronomer Professor Simon Newcombe, President; N.D.C. Hodges, Secretary; and Vice Presidents Professors Stanley Hall, George S. Fullerton, Edward C. Pickering, and Charles S. Minot. Renowned Harvard psychologist and philosophy Professor **William James** was a founding member. The society aimed to investigate **apparitions, hypnosis, mediumship, telepathy,** and all other fields of **parapsychology.**

In 1887 Dr. **Richard Hodgson**, the British SPR's chief investigator, came to America to act as Secretary to the ASPR. He continued in this position until he suffered a fatal heart attack while playing handball at the Boat Club in Boston, Massachusetts on December 20, 1905.

In 1889, under Professor S. P. Langley's presidency, the American society affiliated with its British counterpart due to financial problems. After Hodgson's death in 1905, the society dissolved but reemerged the following year, as a separate entity from the British SPR. Dr. **James Hervey Hyslop** became President and took over where Hodgson had left off as Chief Investigator for the society.

On Hyslop's death in 1920, Dr. **Walter Franklin Prince** assumed the presidency and served until he resigned five years later. The society has enjoyed active participation from a number of outstanding scientists and philosophers, among them the physicists Sir William Barrett and Sir **Oliver Lodge**. By 1940 **Gardner Murphy** had become a Vice President and he assumed the presidency in 1962. He initiated the first wireless **electronic voice phenomena** telepathic experiments in Chicago and New Jersey. He also focused the research of the society on scientific experiments, especially in **extrasensory perception**, working with Dr. **J. B. Rhine**, and on altered states of consciousness and survival after death.

Today the American Society for Psychical Research is headquartered in New York and maintains one of the world's largest libraries of books on parapsychology.

Sources:

Buckland, Raymond: *The Fortune–Telling Book: The Encyclopedia of Divination and Soothsaying*. Detroit: Visible Ink Press, 2004

Guiley, Rosemary Ellen: *The Encyclopedia of Ghosts and Spirits*. New York: Facts On File, 1992

Shepard, Leslie A: *Encyclopedia of Occultism & Parapsychology*. New York: Avon Books, 1978

ANDERSON, GEORGE

George Anderson is the youngest child of George and Eleanor Anderson, who lived on New York's Long Island. His brothers and sister are Alfred, Dolores, and James. At age six, George Jr. had a near fatal bout with chicken pox that led to encephalomyelitis (inflammation of the spinal cord and brain). He was temporarily paralyzed and unable to walk for several months. Perhaps this illness in some way brought about George's **psychic** and **mediumistic** abilities, for it was shortly after his recovery that he correctly predicted the death of a friend's grandmother.

Anderson attended a parochial Roman Catholic school on Long Island, where the nuns were aghast as he began to display his psychic powers. One nun reportedly threatened to "beat him insane," and there was talk of committing him to a psychiatric institution. He was misdiagnosed as a passive schizophrenic but quickly rejected the sedative medications pushed at him.

After leaving school, Anderson worked for a while as a switchboard operator. In 1973 he joined a local psychic group, and he gradually allowed his mediumship to mature. In 1978 a good friend, Eileen Maher, encouraged Anderson to commit seriously to developing his psychic and mediumistic abilities and to work more with the general public. This he did. He was also encouraged and counseled by his friend Monsignor Thomas Hartman. Anderson worked seriously at his calling for eight years. In 1980 he met Joel Martin, host of a successful late night radio show, and appeared on the show in October of that year. Martin had been introduced to Anderson by

a young production assistant who worked at the radio station., who pleaded with Martin to have Anderson on the show. Though Martin felt sure he would simply expose the man as a phony, he was greatly surprised when Anderson began to give him intimate details of his life—things which no one else could possibly know.

Over the next several years Anderson and Martin worked together compiling records of tests they did of Anderson doing both public and private **readings**. All readings done on the radio shows involved anonymous callers, who limited their responses to no more than "yes" and "no." In Martin's words:

> "Invariably the results are the same: George reveals to his subjects information—about events, experiences, trivia, even nicknames—for which the only possible source is the living consciousness, the **spirit**, of the deceased. In some cases, the spirits give forth information about events that occurred during and after their own physical death, or that will occur in the future."

The two men kept notes, and audio and video tapes, with full details from the day they first met. This information eventually developed into a book written by Martin with a co-author, Patricia Romanowski, and published in 1988 (*We Don't Die*, G. P. Putnam's Sons). The book was an immediate success and was followed three years later with a second book (*We Are Not Forgotten*) and other subsequent titles.

As Martin noted, "People need to know not only that their loved ones continue to exist in some form and dimension, but that they still play a role in their lives here on earth." This is the essence of **Spiritualism**. Information received by mediums, from the spirits of the deceased, show that there *is* continuation of "life" after the transition known as "death." These experiences invariably provide details that are far from earth-shattering in themselves but that prove, beyond a shadow of a doubt, to the sitters, that the spirit coming through is indeed the same person they knew and loved when alive. Verification that the spirit is truly who it claims to be brings tremendous comfort to the sitters. On the television show *Larry King Live*, on March 6, 2001, Rabbi Shmuley Boteach asked of psychic medium **James Van Praagh**, "Aren't you a bit surprised that the only message that the dead seem to be able to give us is someone had a nickname Miss Piggy? And they can only tell us that, you know, I had a heart condition?.... I want to hear just one of the psychics today tell me when is there going to be the next bus bombing in Tel Aviv so we can avoid going on that bus." Obviously the good Rabbi had not thought through what he was saying. If a psychic gave such a prediction, there would be no reason for the Rabbi, or anyone else, to pay him or her any heed. Where would be the proof? But when the deceased indicates to a bereaved relative information that may seem frivolous to the Rabbi or others, details such as a family nickname or the specific details of a medical condition, the experience is incredibly evidential to the bereaved, proving beyond doubt that the spirit is present and that life does indeed continue beyond death. George Anderson and other such mediums work with anonymous sitters to obtain this verification through correct information known only to the sitters and the deceased relative. Occasionally the deceased reveals information that even the sitters don't know, and research is necessary to the accuracy of the message. In such cases, the possibility of **telepathy** between medium and sitter is ruled out as an explanation.

After the appearance of the first book, Anderson did a nationwide tour. He also demonstrated his abilities on such television shows as *Donahue*, *Live with Regis & Kathie Lee*, and *Larry King Live*, plus numerous regional shows on both television and radio. Many of the shows aligned him with dyed-in-the-wool skeptics who would never be convinced no matter the weight of the evidence. As Martin put it, "George decided that sparring with skeptics, convincing reporters and talk show hosts that he is for real, and seeking out the next scientist with the next theory about what makes him tick stole time from helping the bereaved."

At the end of the year's tour, therefore, Anderson concentrated on doing readings that would bring comfort to those who had lost loved ones. In 1991 he published his second book with Martin and Romanowski, in 1994 the third, and in 1997 a fourth, all of which have now been translated into many different languages. Anderson found himself in constant demand for readings. Today he works tirelessly at comforting the bereaved. He is popular throughout Europe and in South Africa and parts of Asia.

Sources:

Anderson, George: *Lessons From the Light*. New York: Putnam's, 1999

Anderson, George: *Walking in the Garden of Souls*. New York: Putnam's, 2001

George Anderson Grief Support Programs: http://www.georgeanderson.com

Martin, Joel and Patricia Romanowski: *Love Beyond Life*. New York: Putnam's, 1997

Martin, Joel and Patricia Romanowski: *Our Children Forever*. New York: Putnam's, 1994

Martin, Joel and Patricia Romanowski: *We Are Not Forgotten*. New York: Putnam's, 1991

Martin, Joel and Patricia Romanowski: *We Don't Die*. New York: Putnam's, 1988

ANDREWS, MARY

Mary Andrews, of Moravia, New York, was one of the earliest **materialization mediums**. Described as "a plain, uneducated peasant woman," she held her **séances** in the home of a neighboring farmer named Keeler. Starting in 1871, she conducted two types of séances: "dark-room séances" and "light-room séances." The former was held in total darkness and the latter in only slightly diminished light.

In the dark-room séances, questions asked by the sitters were answered by **spirit lights**. There was a lot of physical phenomena, including the playing of a piano that was in the séance room, the sprinkling of water into the faces of the sitters, the sound of spirit voices, and touching by spirit hands. In the light-room séances, Mary

Andrews sat in a **cabinet**. Hands, arms, and busts materialized outside the cabinet. When spirit faces appeared, their lips were seen to move as they spoke and many of the sitters recognized departed relatives. Andrews did not go into **trance**, though she sat in séances almost every day for an extended time.

Another phenomenon at materialization séances that pleased many was the perceived scent of a perfume-like fragrance (**clairalience**). Sometimes it was recognizable as a flower, such as a rose, and sometimes as a particular lady's perfume. It was impossible to gauge the origin of the fragrance.

There is little record of Mary Andrews in **Spiritualist** literature, though she is mentioned briefly in T. R. Hazard's *Eleven Days in Moravia*, in Epes Sargent's *Proof Palpable of Immortality*, and in Eugene Crowell's *The Identity of Primitive Christianity and Modern Spiritualism*.

Sources:

Awtry-Smith, Marilyn: *"They" Paved the Way*. New York: Spiritualism & More, nd

Crowell, Eugene: *The Identity of Primitive Christianity and Modern Spiritualism*. New York: 1875

Fodor, Nandor: *Encyclopedia of Psychic Science*. London: Arthurs Press, 1933

Sargent, Epes: *Proof Palpable of Immortality*. Boston: 1880

ANGEL

A ngel is from the Latin *angelus*, and the Greek *aggelos*, meaning "a messenger." The Hebrew word for angel is *malak*, a "person sent." In the **Bible**, in Mark 1:2, it is applied to John the Baptist: "Behold I send my messenger (*angel*) before thy face...." In the corresponding prophecy of Malachi the word is the same (*malak*). It was applied to such men as ambassadors and other representatives. In Judaism the "angel of the congregation" was the chief of the synagogue, according to Lewis Spence. Belief in angels is an essential tenet of Islam. In ancient **Greece** they were known as *daimons*, which could be good or evil. In **Buddhism** they would be the *devas*, or "shining ones."

In **Christianity** and Judaism, and those religions influenced by them, the term "angel" has come to be used for a **spirit** inferior to the deity yet superior, in intellect and will, to humankind. References to angels—as messengers of God—are found in the Bible mainly in the Old Testament in areas where it has been said that the writings derive from more ancient documents. Belief in intermediaries between God and the visible universe was common to most primitive religions, according to the *Encyclopedia Britannica* (1964). Although the Church spoke of the creation of angels by God, the time of their creation is glossed over. There was some fear of confusion with Gnostic and pagan doctrines of demigods. It was only very gradually that Christianity arrived at the concept of angels as pure spirits, because that concept seemed too close to divinity.

A hierarchy of angels developed, with specific names being given to certain major angel figures: Michael, Raphael, Gabriel, etc. There was also an early belief that each person had his or her own personal angel as a guardian. Although many speak of angels and archangels, the latter term is only used twice in the Bible, in Jude 9 and in I Thessalonians 4:16. As Lewis Spence points out, "there is nothing in the whole of Scripture ... to show that intelligent beings exist who have other than human attributes."

It is generally accepted that the ancient **Egyptian** and Assyrian depictions of winged beasts associated with royalty influenced the graphic representations of angels, particularly the cherubim of the Old Testament. In Christianity, it wasn't until the end of the fourth century that wings started to be depicted on angels, and it wasn't until the Renaissance that child angels began to appear in illustrations, echoing early classical depictions of Eros or Cupid. Many of the angels either appear in white tunics or are naked.

There seems to be a common origin for Persian, Jewish, and Mohammedan accounts of angels, as both males and females. In the

Mohammedan writings there is an angel of death, Azreal, and an angel of destruction, Asrafil. There are also angels armed with whips of iron and fire (Moukir and Nakir). The Koran speaks of there being two angels for every person; one to record the good deeds and one the bad. In the New Testament Lucifer, an angel, defied God and was cast out of heaven. One third of the other angels went with him. They became known as the demons of hell, with Lucifer renamed Satan.

In early Church writings, angels would be mistaken for men (not having yet acquired their wings). In fact in Daniel 8:16 and 9:21 Gabriel is actually referred to simply as a man ("the man Gabriel, whom I had seen in the vision"). Today, there seems a throwback to that idea, with many people claiming to talk with angels and to see angels in human form. On the Internet there is a site dedicated to stories of angel encounters, at http://www.angels-online.com. One typical story is of a woman's recollection of going to church with her father when she was twelve years old. Her father usually sang at the church but had missed a performance because of having the flu. He went there wanting to test his voice in the empty church. As he strained to sing, the daughter saw what she took to be an angel "dressed in a white robe" walk forward from the altar and place his hands on the father's shoulder. His voice immediately changed and became strong and full again. The angel disappeared. The daughter told the father what she had seen and he admitted to having felt a sudden warmth envelop him. This is typical of the stories of angel encounters.

Many **mediums** and **psychics**, as well as ordinary people, say they have had this kind of experience. Sometimes, as in the above story, there is a report of a visible manifestation. Mediums experience the contact through **clairvoyance** and **clairaudience**. In Spiritualism there is a belief in a **Spirit Guide**, or Guardian Spirit. Most mediums have one, who acts as a "doorkeeper" during **séances**. This could certainly be viewed as a **Guardian Angel**. During World War II, in Budapest, a group of Hungarian artists claimed to have been in contact with a number of angels.

Angels surround a crucified Christ in "Vision of the Cross" from Dante's *Paradiso*. *Courtesy Fortean Picture Library.*

They described their experiences in a book *Talking with Angels* (Watkins). Their medium was West German Gabriele Wittek.

Sources:

Angels Online: http://www.angels-online.com

Burnham, Sophy: *A Book of Angels*. New York: Ballantine, 1990

Encyclopedia Britannica. Chicago: William Benton, 1964

Godwin, Michael: *Angels*. New York: Simon & Schuster, 1990

Spence, Lewis: *An Encyclopedia of the Occult*. London: George Routledge & Sons, 1920

ANKA, DARRYL

Darryl Anka is a **channeler** for the entity Bashar. Bashar claims to be from the planet Essassani, which he describes as being 500 light years away. Anka is a special effects designer. The entity he channels provides some of the most technical and analytical material channeled today, according to Jon Klimo, a former Rutgers University professor.

Sources:

Klimo, Jon: *Channeling: Investigations on Receiving Information from Paranormal Sources.* Los Angeles: Jeremy P. Tarcher, 1987

ANNALI DELLO SPIRITISMO

see also Italy

The "Annals of Spiritualism," or *Annali Dello Spiritismo*, was the first major **Spiritualism** journal published in **Italy**. It appeared in Turin in 1863 and continued in print until 1898, under the editorship of Signor Niceforo Filalete, a pseudonym of Professor Vincenzo Scarpa.

Daniel Dunglas Home had visited Italy in 1852 and when he returned to England left a violent controversy amongst the Italian journalists. Home's enthusiasm had brought about the formation of a large number of **development circles** throughout the country. This led to the publication of *Il amore del Vero*, in Geneva, edited by Dr. Pietro Suth and Signor B. E. Manieri. It contained accounts of Spiritualist activities in other parts of Europe and in the United States and was circulated in Italy, despite the protests of the Church.

At the same time that *Annali Dello Spiritismo* first appeared, a Spiritualist society was formed in Palermo, named *Il Societa Spiritual di Palermo*, with Signor J. V. Paleolozo as president and with members of the caliber of Paolo Morelle, professor of Latin and philosophy.

Sources:

Spence, Lewis: *An Encyclopedia of the Occult.* London: George Routledge & Sons, 1920

ANTHONY, SUSAN BROWNELL (1820–1906)

Born in Adams, Massachusetts, on February 15, 1820, to a **Quaker** family, Susan B. Anthony spent fifteen years teaching before becoming active in temperance. Her family had a long activist tradition that gave her a sense of justice and moral fervor. In 1845 the family moved to Rochester, New York. There they became very active in the anti-slavery movement, with like-minded Quakers meeting at their home on a weekly basis. The year after moving to Rochester, she was appointed head of the girls' department at Canajoharie Academy and taught there for two years, earning $110 per year. While at the academy, she joined the Daughters of Temperance and campaigned for stronger liquor laws.

As a woman, she was not allowed to speak at temperance rallies; a situation that led her, in 1852, to join the women's rights movement. She was encouraged in this by one of the leaders of the women's rights movement, Elizabeth Cady Stanton. Anthony was introduced to Stanton by Amelia Bloomer. In 1853 Anthony asked, at the state teachers' convention, for women to have a voice at the convention, to take committee positions, and to receive better pay. In 1856 Anthony became an agent for the American Anti-Slavery Society. Despite verbal and physical abuse, she made speeches, organized rallies, placed posters, and distributed leaflets. She became well enough known that she was hung in effigy and, in Syracuse, her image was dragged through the streets.

In 1863, together with Elizabeth Stanton, Anthony organized a Women's National Loyal League to petition for the abolition of slavery. Five years later she encouraged New York women in the sewing and printing trades to form their own union. In 1868, with Stanton, in Rochester, she started a newspaper titled *The Revolution.* In 1870 she formed, and became President of, the Workingwomen's Central Association, which kept reports on working conditions and provided advancement opportunities for women.

It was in 1891 that Anthony first appeared at **Lily Dale**, the New York **Spiritualist** community. The *Post Journal* of Jamestown, New York, reported "Susan B. Anthony, with Elizabeth Cady Stanton, decided to visit Chautauqua Institution

Susan Brownell Anthony (1820–1906), American feminist leader and campaigner for women's rights, c. 1890. *Hulton Archive/Getty Images.*

in the interest of the founding of the National Women's Suffrage Institution. Upon their arrival in Chautauqua, the (antagonistic) feeling was so great that it was decided that no meeting could be held there. As a result, the ladies came over the hills to Lily Dale where they held their meeting." Anthony herself recorded the event: "People came from far and near. Finally three thousand were assembled in that beautiful amphitheater, decorated with yellow, the suffrage color, and the red, white, and blue. There hanging by itself, was our national flag ten by fourteen feet, with its red and white stripes, and in the center of the blue corner just one golden star, Wyoming, blazing out alone. [Wyoming was the first U.S. state to recognize women's suffrage.] Every cottage in the camp was festooned with yellow, and when at night the Chinese lanterns were lighted on the plazas, it was as gorgeous as any Fourth of

July celebration, and all in honor of Woman's Day and her coming freedom."

Susan B. Anthony continued to spend time at Lily Dale for a number of years after that initial visit. She was not herself a Spiritualist but in her later years she did visit a **medium** at Lily Dale. She received a message from her aunt. Anthony's reported response was "I didn't like her when she was alive, and I don't want to hear from her now. Why don't you bring someone interesting like Elizabeth Cady?"

Women got the vote with the Nineteenth Amendment to the Constitution in 1920. This became known as the Susan B. Anthony Amendment. Anthony didn't live to see it—she died at her home in Rochester, New York on March 13, 1906.

Sources:

The Susan B. Anthony House: http://www.susanbanthonyhouse.org

Vogt, Paula M. and Joyce LaJudice: *Lily Dale Proud Beginnings: A Little Bit of History.* Lily Dale: Lily Dale Museum, 1984

Wicker, Christine: *Lily Dale: The True Story of the Town That Talks to the Dead.* San Francisco: HarperSanFrancisco, 2003

APPARITION

Another name for a **ghost**, an apparition is the appearance of persons or animals when they are not physically present. Contrary to popular opinion, apparitions are not always of the dead; they can also be of the living. Where a ghost is thought of as a vague shadowy figure or a transparent figure in white, apparitions generally seem solid like a normal living being. As many as one person in sixteen sees an apparition at least once in his or her lifetime, according to a survey taken in 1899.

During all the major wars, many people have reported seeing apparitions of fighting men and women appearing many miles from the battle scene. These appearances frequently coincided with the actual person's sudden death, wounding, or traumatic event.

Shortly after the founding of the **Society for Psychical Research** in 1882, there was a systematic attempt to collect firsthand reports of apparitions. The vast majority of these were of the "crisis" variety mentioned above; the appearance of a loved one at the moment of crisis. The full report was published in book form as *Phantasms of the Living* (1886). Typical was one such report from a Mrs. Taunton, of Birmingham, England:

> On Thursday evening, 14 November, 1867, I was sitting in the Birmingham Town Hall with my husband at a concert, when there came over me the icy chill which usually accompanies these occurrences. Almost immediately, I saw with perfect distinctness, between myself and the orchestra, my uncle, Mr. W., lying in bed with an appealing look on his face, like one dying. I had not heard anything of him for several months, and had no reason to think he was ill. The appearance was not transparent or filmy, but perfectly solid-looking; and yet I could somehow see the orchestra, not through, but behind it. I did not try turning my eyes to see whether the figure moved with them, but looked at it with a fascinated expression that made my husband ask if I was ill. I asked him not to speak to me for a minute or two; the vision gradually disappeared, and I told my husband, after the concert was over, what I had seen. A letter came shortly after telling of my uncle's death. He died at exactly the time when I saw the vision.

Her husband verified the report. Another similar report came from the Rev. F. Barker, Rector of Cottenham, Cambridge, England:

> At about 11 o'clock on the night of December 6, 1873, I had just got into bed, and had certainly not fallen asleep, or even into a doze, when I suddenly startled my wife by a deep groan, and when she asked the reason, I said, 'I have just seen my aunt. She came and stood beside me, and smiled with her old kind smile, and disappeared.' A much-loved aunt, my mother's sister, was at that time in Madeira for her health, accompanied by my cousin, her niece. I had no reason to think that she was critically ill at this time, but the impression made upon me was so great that the next day I told her family (my mother among them) what I had seen. Within a week afterwards we heard that she had died on that very night, and, making all allowance for longitude, at about that very time. When my cousin, who was with her to the last, heard what I had seen, she said, 'I am not at all surprised, for she was calling out for you all the time she was dying.' This is the only time I have experienced anything of this nature. I think, perhaps, this story firsthand may interest you. I can only say that the vivid impression I received that night has never left me.

Rev. Barker's wife, verifying his account, added the details that "He said she had 'something black, it might have been lace, thrown over her head.'" These and similar reports seem to indicate that the majority of apparitions are there for the purpose of giving a message—of a death or accident, for example.

The story of Rev. Russell H. Conwell, founder of Philadelphia's Temple University, is given in the Reader's Digest book *Quest For the Unknown—Life Beyond Death*. Shortly after his wife's death in the early 1900s, Conwell would see his deceased wife standing at the foot of his bed every morning. He said that she seemed completely real and solid and that she even spoke to him. He decided to put the apparition to a few tests. He asked it where his army discharge papers were kept. The figure answered correctly. Then he had his housemaid hide a pen, without telling him where. The next day the apparition of his wife told him, correctly, where it had been placed. Eventually he said to the figure "I know you aren't really there." His ghostly wife replied, "Oh, but I am!"

Apparitions have been seen by a number of people at the same time. Frequently when this happens the observers see the apparition from different viewpoints, depending upon where they are standing at the time. It is, therefore, as though there is an actual person present, rather than something similar to a projected figure. One may see the full face, another the side of the face, and another the back of the head.

Apparitions of long-dead people have been seen, often on a regular or irregular basis. Also, some apparitions speak (or the observer "hears" words in his or her head) and even responds to questions and observations. Not all apparitions are visual. It is not uncommon to hear sounds or voices, to smell particular scents, and to be touched by invisible hands. These latter points tie in with the experiences of **Spiritualist mediums**, when they contact **spirits** of deceased persons. **Clairvoyants** usually "see" the spirit as though a solid person. **Clairaudiants** hear the voice.

Apparitions of religious figures are often reported by devout followers. As many as one in thirty apparitions are of the religious type, and generally referred to as "visions." The Roman Catholic Church, however, is slow to accept such sightings on faith. A.R.G. Owen (*Man, Myth & Magic—Visions*) points out that there are "fashions" in visions: "In the Middle Ages visionaries saw saints and martyrs and, in certain limited circles, apparitions of the child Jesus were extremely frequent. Later, visions of the suffering and wounded Jesus or of his Sacred Heart were favored. In recent times the Virgin Mary has almost monopolized the field." Despite the number of reported visions—some by saints and other holy persons—the Roman Catholic Church only accepts the *possibility* of their being true.

Apparitions have appeared in a large number of photographs. They have not been visible to the people present but have shown up in photographs developed later. In 1865, after the assassination of President Lincoln, his widow Mary Todd Lincoln went incognito to a Boston photographer named William Mumler. He took her photograph and when developed it showed a clear image of her late husband standing behind her chair (see Spirit Photography).

Sources:

Auerbach, Lloyd: *ESP, Hauntings and Poltergeists: A Parapsychologist's Handbook*. New York: Warner Books, 1986

Gurney, Edmund; Frederick W. H. Myers; and Frank Podmore: *Phantasms of the Living*. London: The Society for Psychical Research and Trubner & Co., 1886

Leonard, Sue (ed): *Quest For the Unknown—Life Beyond Death*. Pleasantville: Reader's Digest, 1992

Owen, A. R. G.: *Man, Myth & Magic: Visions*. London: BPC Publishing, 1970

Steiger, Brad: *Real Ghosts, Restless Spirits, and Haunted Places*. Detroit: Visible Ink Press, 2003

APPORTS

The word is from the French *apporter*, meaning "to bring." In **Spiritualism**, an apport is something that has been brought into the **séance** room by a **spirit**—usually the **spirit guide** of the **medium**. It appears "out of thin air" and is sometimes initially hot to the touch. The explanation is that the object has dematerialized, been transported (or "**teleported**") through space, and then rematerialized in the séance room. Some apports suddenly appear on the table in the middle of the circle of sitters. Some actually materialize in the hands of one or more of the sitters. Some materialize in the **trumpet**, if there is one, and are then tipped out of either the bell end or the mouthpiece end. Interestingly, **Maurice Barbanell**, the **psychic** investigator, spoke of some apports appearing this way and added that although they were tipped out of the small mouthpiece end of the trumpet, the objects were actually larger than the diameter of that end.

The apport itself can be anything. Small precious and semiprecious stones are common, but it could be a piece of jewelry, a vase, a book, or even a living thing such as a flower, bird, or small animal. (In the case of **Eusapia Paladino**, she once apported a dead rat!) In fact apports

Photograph of a golden lily, which appeared at a séance in June, 1890. *Courtesy Fortean Picture Library.*

are not restricted to small items. There is a wonderful story of the two mediums **Charles Williams** and **Frank Herne** who specialized in apport séances. They were giving a séance and someone jokingly suggested that they should apport the famous medium Mrs. **Agnes Guppy**, who lived only a short distance from their séance room in High Holborn, London. This suggestion was greeted with laughter since Mrs. Guppy was a very large woman. But within a matter of minutes, a very large figure suddenly appeared, with a thump, on the top of the table. It was Mrs. Guppy, wearing a dressing gown, holding a pen wet with ink, and looking very startled. **Frank Podmore** (*Modern Spiritualism*, 1902) repeats an account that appeared in the *Echo* of June 8, 1871, written by one of the sitters at the séance, which says "From the joking remark about bringing Mrs. G. to the time that she was on the table three minutes did not

elapse. The possibility of her being concealed in the room is as absurd as the idea of her acting in collusion with the media." W. H. Harrison, the man who had originally suggested her for an apport, together with another of the sitters, escorted Mrs. Guppy the two miles back to her home. There they found that the servants could attest to the fact that one minute Mrs. Guppy had been sitting in her study doing the household accounts, and the next she had disappeared. In fact her friend Miss Neyland had been in the room with her, reading a newspaper. When she happened to look up she found that Mrs. Guppy had disappeared, leaving a slight haze near the ceiling. Mr. Guppy, on being told that his wife had disappeared, commented that the spirits must have taken her and went off to eat his supper! He was about eighty years old at the time.

White Hawk, the guide of medium **Kathleen Barkel**, frequently had apport "parties," as he called them. He thought they were a lot of fun, and the sitters usually agreed with him. At one of Barkel's séances, a ring materialized between the cupped hands of Maurice Barbanell. When he examined it, he found it to be a plain nine-carat gold ring with the words *Per ardua ad astra—B* engraved on the inside. White Hawk explained that the ring came from the late author Dennis Bradley. Barbanell immediately recognized that *Per ardua ad astra*—meaning "through difficulties towards the stars"—was the motto of the Royal Air Force, in which Bradley had served. Also, Bradley's first book about Spiritualism had been titled *Towards the Stars*. The letter B was appropriate both for Bradley and for Barbanell.

The Australian medium known as **Charles Bailey**, through his guide Abdul, apported such items as live fish, crabs and turtles, live birds sitting on eggs in their nests, rare antiques and coins, a stone from beneath the sea still dripping with salt water, a human skull, and ancient clay cylinders with Babylonian inscriptions. Many apports produced by Bailey, for his sponsor Thomas Welton Stanford, are now to be seen at the Leland Stanford University in California. On occasion Bailey was suspected of fraud, though he usually was able to explain away any ambiguities.

The famous medium **Estelle Roberts**, and her guide Red Cloud, also produced apports. Kenneth Evett, Roberts's son-in-law, once asked if he might receive an apport from **Egypt**. Red Cloud agreed. Some time later, after a large number of the sitters had received apports, Evett got his wish. It was a beautiful scarab talisman edged with gold. Red Cloud said it came from Abydos, though Evett was unfamiliar with the place name. Later he took the scarab to the British Museum to get an expert's opinion on it. He was told it was indeed a genuine specimen, and was typical of the scarabs from Abydos.

One of the best known apport mediums was **"Madame d'Esperance"** (Elizabeth Hope), whose spirit guide was a young girl named Yolande. At one séance Yolande presented her medium with a huge golden lily, as tall as the medium herself. This was similar to an apport produced at one of Mrs. Guppy's sittings when a friend of the naturalist Alfred Russel Wallace asked for a sunflower. No sooner had he done so than a huge, six-foot specimen, with clumps of earth still clinging to it, thumped down on the séance table.

Sources:

Barbanell, Maurice: *This Is Spiritualism*. Oxshott: The Spiritual Truth Press, 1959

Guiley, Rosemary Ellen: *The Encyclopedia of Ghosts and Spirits*. New York: Facts On File, 1992

Podmore, Frank: *Modern Spiritualism*. London: 1902; reprinted as *Mediums of the Nineteenth Century*. New York: University Books, 1963

ARIGÓ, JOSÉ (1918–1971)

José Pedro de Freitas, later known as José Arigó, was born in Congonhas do Campo, Brazil, in 1918. As a child he had many **psychic** experiences, seeing lights and hearing voices that spoke to him in a variety of languages he did not understand. When he was in his early thirties, he discovered that he had a **spirit guide** who called himself Dr. Adolphus Fritz. This guide claimed to have been a German surgeon in World War I. He would take control of Arigó's body, with Arigó going into a **trance**, and would operate on sick people.

Arigó first became aware of his **healing** talent shortly after finding a crucifix lying in the street. He picked it up and took it home. At that time he ran a restaurant and, out of the kindness of his heart, he would feed an old man who frequently came in at closing time. One day he asked the man to arrive earlier if he wanted to eat. The man suggested that instead Arigó might bring the food to him at the local cemetery. Arigó refused and the man told him that it was he who had left the crucifix for Arigó to find. The man said that if Arigó held it in his hand and said a prayer, he could cure the sick. Arigó was skeptical but tried it out on a sick neighbor. It worked, and she was cured. From then on he devoted part of every day to healing the sick.

When confronted with a dying relative whom the doctors said they could not cure, Arigó grabbed a knife from the kitchen and, before he could be stopped, cut into the woman's stomach and removed a huge tumor. Pressing the sides of the wound together, they healed and the woman recovered. Arigó came out of a trance that he had gone into. This was when he first became aware of the deceased German doctor operating through him. Arigó went on to perform other such "operations" using unsterilized instruments such as kitchen knives, scissors, tweezers, and similar. He always worked in trance and without giving his patients any form of anesthetic. News of these unconventional cures quickly spread and soon Arigó was being asked to treat hundreds of desperate people. At one time a group of doctors from South America watched as Arigó removed a tumor from a young woman's womb, using an ordinary pair of scissors. The woman was conscious throughout the entire operation and experienced no pain.

In 1956 Arigó was finally arrested for illegally practicing medicine. Following the announcement of an eight-month sentence and fine, in response to a public outcry the Brazilian president issued a pardon. However, Arigó did have to serve a sentence on a similar charge eight years later, despite impressing a visiting judge with his talents. He served sixteen months in prison and did not perform any more psychic surgery on his release. But while in prison he was permitted to continue to operate. The judge who presided over Arigó, Judge Filippe Immesi, wrote the following report after his visit to Joseacute; in prison:

> "I saw him pick up ... a pair of nail scissors. He wiped them on his shirt and used no disinfectant. I saw him then cut straight into the cornea of the patient's eye. She did not flinch, although perfectly conscious. The cataract was out in seconds ... Arigó said a prayer and a few drops of liquid appeared on the cotton in his hand. He wiped the women's eye with it and she was cured."

Sources:

King, Francis: *The Supernatural: Wisdom From Afar.* London: Aldus, 1975

Wilson, Colin: *The Supernatural: Healing Without Medicine.* London: Aldus Books, 1975

ART, AUTOMATIC

An aspect of **automatic writing**, automatic art is produced with the **medium** unaware of what is being painted. In this instance the "medium" is not necessarily a professional (although in fact we all have mediumistic abilities latent within us). Just as virtually anyone can operate a **talking board**, so can anyone do automatic writing, drawing and painting. Some people go into **trance** when doing automatic art, but most remain fully conscious, if unaware of what it is their hand is about to reveal.

Some **automatists** are not aware that their hands are moving and are surprised when they see the results of their unconscious actions. Others are aware but feel that they have absolutely no control over what is being drawn

or painted. Just as automatic writing is often produced at incredibly high speed—far faster than one could normally write—so is automatic art produced that way by many of its practitioners. Heinrich Nusslein, a German automatic artist, painted in total darkness, producing small pictures in three or four minutes, totaling 2,000 pictures in two years. In the late nineteenth century Marjan Gruzewski of Poland and David Duguid of Glasgow, Scotland, also painted in total darkness. **John Ballou Newbrough**, the automatist who produced *Oahspe*, was also an automatic artist who could paint with both hands at once in total darkness. Susannah Harris would complete an oil painting in two hours when blindfolded and painting it upside down. Augustine Lesage painted from the top of the canvas working his way down. A Captain Bartlett similarly produced detailed architectural drawings of Glastonbury Abbey, as it was originally, working from the top left hand corner and coming down, giving verified archeological details with incredible precision.

Emily A Tallmadge, of New York City (who died in 1956 at the age of 82), produced thousands of intricate drawings and paintings, many of them done with colored pencils. Most were similar to mandalas. She claimed that they were inspired by her spirit guides. Of the thousands she produced, no two were the same. Automatic drawing does not always develop into automatic painting. Generally, the painting seems to develop independently.

Toward the end of the nineteenth century observation of hysterical and brain-damaged patients indicated that some people could exhibit unusual artistic talent that they did not have in their normal state. The **Spiritualist** community therefore decided that true automatic writing and art should show some evidence of connection to the **spirit world**. In other words, a piece of writing or art should in some way reveal correct information that was not previously known to the entranced artist, be it unknown information of a **spirit** or of the artist him or herself. Alan Gauld (*Man, Myth &*

Example of automatic art in the style of Cezanne by trance artist Luiz Gasparetto. *Courtesy Fortean Picture Library.*

Magic: Automatic Art, 1970) gives the example of Frederic L. Thompson, a goldsmith who in 1905 felt a strong urge to paint a series of pictures of trees and landscapes. In 1906 he happened to go to an exhibit of paintings by the recently deceased Robert Swain Gifford (1840–1905). Most of these paintings were landscapes and pictures of trees. While there, Thompson heard in his head the voice of Gifford telling him to, "take up and finish my work." He seemed to do just that. He produced a large number of paintings that turned out to be not copies of Gifford's works but exact renderings of actual scenes that had been known to the dead painter. So similar were the paintings that it seemed they were scenes that Gifford *would* have painted had he lived. Yet Thompson had never actually visited these places and had only seen the scenes in his head.

In 1978 a Brazilian artist named Luiz Antonio Gasparetto appeared on television and in 75 minutes produced 21 paintings. He worked in trance and sometimes worked with both hands at the same time. The paintings were varied, being done in the vastly different and distinctive styles of Toulouse-Lautrec, Degas, Gaugin, Modigliani and Renoir. British automatic artist **Matthew Manning** began producing similar work in the 1970s when only in his teens. He did not go into trance but simply watched his hands producing drawings and paintings as though from the hands of Picasso, Aubrey Beardsley, Paul Klee, Albrecht Dürer, and Leonado da Vinci, among others.

Sources:

Gauld, Alan: *Man, Myth & Magic: Automatic Art*. London: BPC Publishing, 1970

Leonard, Sue (ed): *Quest For the Unknown—Life Beyond Death*. Pleasantville: Reader's Digest, 1992

Myers, Frederick W. H.: *Human Personality and Its Survival of Bodily Death*. London: Longmans, 1903

ASPORT

The opposite of **apport**. Where apports are brought *into* the **séance** room, asports are taken *from* the sitting. Sometimes an apport disappears just as quickly as it appeared, and is found later in another room. The famous **medium Eusapia Paladino** was well known for making the valuables of some of her sitters disappear. The sitters would usually find them later when they returned home—though not always! In July, 1928, at one of the séances attended by Madame Fabian Rossi and the Marquis Centurione Scotto, the sitters were tapped on their heads by a small parchment drum. Also, the Marquis and Madame Rossi felt their hands squeezed by iron mittens. These objects were no longer in the room at the end of the sitting. The drum was found in another room and the iron mittens found lying at the foot of a suit of armor.

Sources:

Fodor, Nandor: *Encyclopedia of Psychic Science*. London: Arthurs Press, 1933

Guiley, Rosemary Ellen: *The Encyclopedia of Ghosts and Spirits*. New York: Facts On File, 1992

ASSOCIATION OF PROGRESSIVE SPIRITUALISTS OF GREAT BRITAIN

This was the first representative organization of **Spiritualists** in Great Britain. It was founded in 1865 and held its first convention in Darlington, Yorkshire. The members were later attacked by other Spiritualists and charged with being "anti-Christian." The organization suffered to the point where it died out after only three years. In 1873 the **British National Association of Spiritualists** formed in the London area as another attempt at a national organization, but that too had a difficult beginning, eventually reforming in 1883 as the London Spiritualist Alliance.

There is little record of other "Progressive Spiritualist" groups today. There was the Portsmouth Progressive Spiritualist Church in Portsmouth, Hampshire, and there are a few groups scattered across the United States. In San Francisco, the Society of Progressive Spiritualists was incorporated in 1883 under the leadership of H. C. Wilson and with financial backing from Mrs. Eunice Sleeper. There were also the People's Progressive Spiritualists' Society of Hollister, the First Progressive Spiritual Society of San Francisco, and the First Society of Progressive **Mediums**, also of San Francisco. Meanwhile, on the east coast there was the Working Union of Progressive Spiritualists in Boston. An impressive temple was designed by Hartwell and Richardson in 1884 and built on Exeter Street in Boston. In 1885 this group was renamed The Spiritual Fraternity.

Sources:

Ephemera—SpiritHistory.com: http://www.spirithistory.com

Fodor, Nandor: *Encyclopedia of Psychic Science*. London: Arthurs Press, 1933

Nelson, Geoffrey K.: *Man, Myth & Magic: Spiritualism*. London: BPC Publishing, 1970

ASSOCIATION FOR RESEARCH AND ENLIGHTENMENT

The Association for Research and Enlightenment (ARE) is the official organization for preserving, researching, and disseminating the psychic work of **Edgar Cayce**, considered the best-documented **psychic** in America. ARE was founded in 1931, in Virginia Beach, Virginia, where the association still maintains its international headquarters. The offices have grown to include an impressive conference center and library. The association offers lectures and workshops throughout the year and its **Meditation** Room is a popular site for visitors. The bookstore carries all of the ARE publications plus other selected works of **metaphysics**. The library is one of the finest of its sort in the country. Members of the association have access to *The Circulating Files*, a collection of nearly 14,000 topically arranged transcripts of Cayce's original **trance readings** covering matters of religious, philosophical, and medical nature. It was after Cayce's death in 1945 that the transcripts were sorted, indexed, and later made accessible to members.

The original Edgar Cayce hospital is still on the site, and is used for massage therapy and other services and activities. Today there are ARE Centers in more than 25 countries around the world, with many more countries holding activities associated with the ARE. The association is currently headed by Hugh Lynn Cayce, one of Edgar Cayce's sons. Subjects of interest to members include **reincarnation**, **auras**, **Atlantis**, the Ascended Masters, **dreams**, and holistic health.

Sources:

Edgar Cayce Homepage: http://www.edgarcayce.org

Shepard, Leslie A: *Encyclopedia of Occultism & Parapsychology*. New York: Avon Books, 1978

ASTRAL BODY

The astral body is an invisible double of the physical body and functions on the **astral plane**. It is also known as the etheric double, and sometimes even as the **spirit**. It is this double that leaves the physical body during sleep, in **trance**, or under anesthetic. It also leaves the physical body permanently at death. According to **Nandor Fodor**, the astral body is "an exact replica of the physical body but composed of finer matter." He said that the etheric body is distinct from the astral body in **theosophy**, but in **Spiritualist** literature they are often interchanged. There is an infinitely elastic "silver cord" that always connects the astral body to the physical, no matter how far away the astral body should travel. But at death that cord separates. In the **Bible**, Ecclesiastes 12:6 refers to the silver cord and to its breaking at death. Also, in I Corinthians 15:44 there is the statement "There is a natural body, and there is a spiritual body," and in II Corinthians 12:3 it says "whether in the body, or out of the body, I cannot tell." The astral body is what is seen as an **apparition**, when the deceased needs to appear to the living.

The concept of the astral double is a very old one. There are descriptions, in ancient Indian writings, of the eight *siddhis*, or supernatural powers. These can be acquired through the yoga practice known as *Pranayama*. The sixth siddhi is astral projection or, as described, "flying in the sky." To the Hebrews, this astral body was the *ruach*. To the ancient **Egyptians** it was the *ka*. To the **Greeks** it was the *eidolon*. It is the etheric double, or astral body, which finally leaves the physical body and breaks the silver cord at death.

Some sensitives can actually see the astral body as a thin, dark line around the physical body. Interestingly, if the person being studied has a missing limb, the sensitive sees the outline of that limb as though it were still in place. The English painter **William Blake's** painting, *The Soul Hovering Above the Body*, shows the astral body leaving the physical body at death. It is thought to be based on Blake's own experiences of astral projection.

Some believe that **dreams** are memories of journeys that the astral body has had while the physical body was asleep (*see* **Astral Projection**).

Dreams can take the spirit anywhere in the world, and on those journeys the silver cord stretches as far as necessary but remains attached. There are stories of "evil spirits" trying to break the cord to kill the sleeping person, but such stories are pure fantasy. *Anything* affecting the astral body and the cord would cause the immediate awakening of the physical body.

The leader of Britain's Royal Air Force through World War II, Air Chief Marshall Lord Dowding, was a **Spiritualist**. In his book *God's Magic* (London, 1955), he said, "Everything in nature has, I believe, what is called an etheric double. Man and animals and plants certainly have. This body is actually material, though invisible and impalpable. In a normal 'natural death,' the etheric double and higher bodies are slowly withdrawn from the physical, a process which can be seen by some clairvoyants."

Sources:

Crookall, Robert: *The Study and Practice of Astral Projection*. London: Aquarian, 1960

Fodor, Nandor: *Encyclopedia of Psychic Science*. London: Arthurs Press, 1933

Fox, Oliver: *Astral Projection: A Record of Out-of-Body Experiences*. London: Rider, 1939

Hart, Hornell: *The Enigma of Survival*. London: Rider, 1959

Monroe, Robert A.: *Journeys Out of the Body*. New York: Doubleday, 1971

ASTRAL PLANE; ASTRAL WORLD

The Astral Plane, or Astral World, is described by **Nandor Fodor** as "the first sphere after bodily death. It is said to be material but of a refined texture. There are many speculations concerning this world of existence. Theosophy claims definite knowledge of its conditions and denizens. Many descriptive accounts are to be found in **Spiritualistic** after-death communications."

Many believe that there are seven planes of existence, or seven "**spheres**." The physical world is the lowest plane. The second plane is where we go at death. As Fodor said, Spiritualist literature gives descriptions of this second plane, which seems to be, in many ways, similar to our present world. Lewis Spence describes it as "the world of emotions, desires, and passions." He also states that the "lower order of the *devas* or **angels** and nature-spirits or elementals, both good and bad, such including **fairies** which are just beyond the powers of human vision...." all exist in this world.

Whatever its true description, it seems certain that the astral plane, or astral world, is where the **spirit** or soul proceeds at death. Although it is a **Theosophical** concept, it is also a universal one, found among primitives and with many mystic religions around the world.

Sources:

Fodor, Nandor: *Encyclopedia of Psychic Science*. London: Arthurs Press, 1933

Spence, Lewis: *An Encyclopedia of the Occult*. London: George Routledge & Sons, 1920

ASTRAL PROJECTION

The physical body has an invisible double known variously as the spirit, ethereal body, or **astral body**. Astral projection (or OOBE—Out-Of-Body Experience) is the ability to send out this etheric double, causing it to travel elsewhere without the physical body. The ability is inherent in most individuals and frequently occurs spontaneously. However, the majority of recorded cases of astral projections have occurred after development of the skill by long and assiduous cultivation.

In astral projection, your physical body relaxes and rests while your etheric double departs from it, maintaining an apparently tenuous yet surprisingly strong connection in the form of an infinitely elastic **silver cord**. This silver cord is what draws you back to your physical body in case of any emergency.

Some say that the astral body emerges from the physical body through the solar plexus. Oth-ers say it is from the position of the **Third Eye** or from the crown **chakra**. The person projecting often experiences what feels like a rapid shaking or vibration of the physical body at the moment of departure. From whatever point it leaves, the astral body floats up and away from the physical body so that it is possible for one versed in the art to look back down at their own sleeping form. Then the etheric double moves away rapidly to wherever it wishes to go. It travels with the speed of thought. If you decide you'd like to be half way around the world, you will be there immediately; and can return just as fast.

Many **dreams** may be the remembrance of astral journeys undertaken while asleep. All people dream, though not everyone remembers his or her dreams. Frequently dreams seem ridiculously involved and mixed up. This is because only the highlights of several dreams are remembered. The average person experiences a large number of dreams during the course of a normal night's sleep. Suppose that in the dream state—more correctly, on the astral plane—you take a trip to Scotland and do some salmon fishing. From there you travel to the Orient and have a pleasant journey in a sampan. Then you may visit the pyramids in **Egypt** before rounding out the night re-enacting a battle of the Civil War. On waking, you may have only a confused recollection of what seemed like one long, very strange dream. In it, you were drifting down the Nile River in a Chinese junk that suddenly disappeared and left you fighting Confederate soldiers with nothing more than a salmon-fishing pole!

The steps to remembering astral journeys, and later actually *directing* them, start with simply remembering the dreams. These should be written down in as much detail as possible *immediately* upon waking. You may remember very little to start with, but should persevere. Slowly more and more dreams will be remembered until each can be separated and all of the details noted. The next step is to decide, before going to sleep, what dream you would like to have. More exactly, where you would like your etheric double to travel on the **astral plane**. Tell yourself exactly where you want

Representation of an out-of-body experience (OOBE) in which the astral body hovers over the physical body yet remains connected. From *Projection of the Astral Body* by Sylvan Muldoon and Hereward Carrington (1929). *Courtesy Fortean Picture Library.*

to go, and what or whom you want to see. The following morning again record the details of your dreams, and see if there is any connection between them and what you wanted to do. After a very short period of training you will find that you can, in fact, go where you want to go.

A number of astral projection cases involving surgery patients have been reported.

After submitting to the anesthesia, the patient has astrally projected to watch the operation take place. Floating at ceiling level, the person has seen their own body being operated on and has given the full details to the surgeon on recovering.

There are hundreds of cases on record of people who have astrally traveled to a house they

have never been to before, and later have given accurate details of the rooms, decorations, people and actions taking place. Sylvan Muldoon was an accomplished projector. In 1924 he went to sleep and felt his etheric double take off, passing through the walls of his house. He was brought into a house he had never seen before and in it discovered an attractive young woman who was sewing a black dress. He stood for a while and studied her, before returning to his physical body. Six weeks later he happened to see the same girl get out of an automobile. He approached her and asked where she lived. She told him it was none of his business, but he explained to her why he asked. He went on to describe the room where he had seen her sitting, and other members of her family. She confirmed all he said, and that was the start of a long friendship and even astral projection projects, which they did together.

Robert Monroe, a Virginia businessman who is very accomplished at astral projection, has religiously kept a journal of his astral experiences over many years. This is one of the best documented records. Professor Charles Tart, a psychologist at the University of California, Davis, worked with Monroe on several documented laboratory experiments. In his introduction to Monroe's book (*Journeys Out of the Body*, 1971), Tart says:

> If we look to scientific sources for information about OOBEs we shall find practically none at all. Scientists have, by and large, simply not paid any attention to these phenomena. The situation is rather similar to that of the scientific literature on **extrasensory perception** (ESP). Phenomena such as **telepathy**, **clairvoyance**, **precognition**, and **psychokinesis** are 'impossible' in terms of the current physical world view. Since they can't happen, most scientists do not bother to read the evidence indicating that they do happen; hence, not having read the evidence, their belief in the impossibility of such phenomena is reinforced. This kind of circular reasoning in support of one's comfortable belief system is not unique to scientists by any means, but it has resulted in very little scientific research on ESP or OOBEs.

One way some people first experience and experiment with astral projection is through what is known as the "false awakening." Most people have had the experience of half-waking in the morning and knowing, or being told, that it is time to get up and get dressed. They get out of bed and sleepily start to dress. They may ponder what to wear, reach a decision, and then fully dress. They may even go into the kitchen to make a cup of coffee. Suddenly the alarm clock goes off again, or someone calls, and they realize they are still in bed! Yet they could have sworn they had actually got up and got dressed. This is a case of the astral body acting out the getting up

and getting dressed. If you can realize, at the time, that this is only your astral body operating, and that your physical body is still asleep, then you can go on from there and direct yourself where you will.

Sources:

Buckland, Raymond: *The Fortune–Telling Book: The Encyclopedia of Divination and Soothsaying*. Detroit: Visible Ink Press, 2004

Crookall, Robert: *The Study and Practice of Astral Projection*. London: Aquarian, 1960

Crookall, Robert: *The Techniques of Astral Projection*. London: Aquarian, 1964

Fox, Oliver: *Astral Projection: A Record of Out-of-Body Experiences*. London: Rider, 1939

Hart, Hornell: *The Enigma of Survival*. London: Rider, 1959

Monroe, Robert A.: *Journeys Out of the Body*. New York: Doubleday, 1971

ATLANTIS

Many believe that Atlantis once existed as a huge island in the middle of the Atlantic Ocean. Yet research done by Dr. W. Maurice Ewing, oceanographer and professor of geology at Columbia University, seemed to show that the floor of the Atlantic has never been above water. Ewing made the statement after an expedition aboard the *Devin Moran* in 1953. He said, "The rocks under every part of the ocean are completely different from those under the continents ... The continents are distinct entities and the ocean floor was never above water." Despite this, a few years later Dr. Rene Malaise of the Riks Museum in Stockholm, Sweden, and his colleague Dr. P. W. Kolbe, presented evidence to prove the sinking of the Atlantic Ridge. A core sample taken from a depth of 12,000 feet showed evidence—in the form of the tiny shells of diatoms; miniscule marine animals—that what was now the ocean floor had once been a fresh water lake above sea level. Certainly the Atlantic seabed is notoriously unstable. There are many recorded instances of islands appearing (e.g. Surt-

Painting representing the submerged, lost city of Atlantis. *Courtesy Fortean Picture Library.*

sey, just west of Iceland, in 1963) and disappearing (e.g. Sambrina, in the Azores, in 1811).

The debate continued and still continues. In 1963, Professor Georgly Lindberg of the former Soviet Union's Zoological Institute of the Academy of Sciences, issued the statement, "The hypothesis that there is a North Atlantic continent presently submerged beneath 4,500 to 5,000 meters of water is confirmed by new findings."

The classic work on Atlantis, *Atlantis, the Antediluvian World*, was published in 1882 by Ignatius Donnelly, a former Lieutenant-Governor of Minnesota, and revised and edited by Egerton Sykes in 1949. In this work, Atlantis is presented as having been a huge island continent where humanity rapidly developed from primitive life to sophisticated civilization. It was, in fact, the cra-

dle of civilization as we know it today. The theory is that Atlantis was destroyed in three cataclysms, with the final one occurring about 10,000 BCE. Many Atlanteans escaped the destruction by fleeing in boats to the surrounding lands. It is said that this explains the many similarities found today in places geographically distant from one another: for example, the pyramids of Egypt and South America, with both peoples practicing mummification. Donnelly makes the point that the same folk traditions, arts, religious beliefs, sciences, personal habits and social customs can be found in cultures on both sides of the Atlantic.

About 600 BCE, an Athenian named Solon visited Egypt and spent a lot of time discussing the history of the region with priests and philosophers. The wise men claimed that there had once existed a great kingdom to the west of Egypt, beyond the

Pillars of Hercules. They said it was "a land larger than Asia Minor and the whole of Libya—in other words, larger than the continent of Africa and the Middle East combined. Solon started to put all this information into verse form on his return to Athens, but died before completing it. Two hundred years later, Plato put Solon's verse into narrative form. Two of these dialogues, *Critias* and *Timæus*, speak of a land that was far advanced as a civilization but which was destroyed by the forces of nature. Plato's work sparked a great interest in this long-lost continent; an interest that still exists and even burgeons. Lewis Spence founded and for several years edited *The Atlantis Quarterly*, reporting on archaeological findings, occult studies, evidence, and folklore.

Plato identified the destruction of Atlantis as "the great deluge of all." It certainly seems to explain many of the flood legends—for example, the **Bible**'s Noah and his ark (Genesis 6-8), the earlier Chaldeo-Babylonian Gilgamish epic, the Arameans, various ancient **Egyptian** tales, the Satapatha Brahmana version in the Rig-Veda, and so on.

Evidence of the existence of this lost continent has been discovered in many places. None seems conclusive but, taken together, there seems a strong argument for the truth of the legend. German archaeologist Jurgen Spanuth found what he described as a "walled city" under 50 feet of water five miles off Heligoland in 1954. Gaston Jondet, an engineer, discovered a complete harbor, approximately 250 acres in size, off the mouth of the Nile River, during World War I. The French bathyscaphe *Archimède* reported seeing what seemed to be a flight of steps carved in the continental shelf off Puerto Rico. In 1968 a commercial pilot spotted from the air what appeared to be several underwater buildings near the Bahamas. This led to the discovery of the "Bimini Road," some three quarters of a mile long and composed of huge stone blocks fitted together. In 1975, the **Association for Research and Enlightenment** (ARE) sponsored the Poseidia 75 expedition to investigate this find. The ARE had a special interest in it because they are dedicated to the study of **Edgar Cayce's** teach-

ings. Cayce mentioned Atlantis in a large number of his **readings** given between 1923 and 1944. He predicted that Atlantis would "rise again" in 1969.

Cayce was not the only **psychic** to connect with Atlantis. **Judy Knight** (Judith Darlene Hampton) claims that the entity she **channels**, "Ramtha," lived thirty-five thousand years ago on the lost continent of Lemuria, a sort of Pacific Ocean equivalent to Atlantis. The well known and respected author **Dion Fortune** (Violet Mary Firth) believed that she had—and through regression exhibited memories of—a past life in Atlantis, where she was a priestess. Certain of the Theosophical information taken from the **Akashic Records** give details of Atlantis. **Helena Blavatsky** claimed that *The Book of Dyzan* was an Atlantean work that had somehow survived the destruction and found its way to Tibet. Philosopher Rudolf Steiner agreed with Blavatsky in believing that the Atlanteans were descendants of the earlier Lemurians. The journalist and automatist **Ruth Montgomery** has produced information about Atlantis through her **automatic writing**.

Sources:

Blavatsky, Helena Petrovna: *The Secret Doctrine*. London: Theosophical Publishing Society, 1888

Cayce, Edgar: *Edgar Cayce on Atlantis*. New York: Paperback Library, 1968

Donnelly, Ignatius: *Atlantis, the Antediluvian World*. New York: Gramercy, 1949

Earll, Tony: *Mu Revealed*. New York: Paperback Library, 1970

Scott-Elliot, W.: *The Story of Atlantis and the Lost Lemuria*. London: Theosophical Publishing House, 1968

Steiger, Brad: *Atlantis Rising*. New York: Dell, 1973

Stemman, Roy: *The Supernatural: Atlantis and the Lost Lands*. London: Aldus, 1975

AURA

see also Odic Force

According to metaphysics, the human body is composed of seven distinct elements. The first three—solid, liquid, and gas—form the physical body. The fourth is the **etheric** body and interpenetrates the physical body. Then there is the **astral body**, the mental body, and finally the spiritual body. The last two are virtually impossible to see because they vibrate at rates too high for normal detection by the physical eye, but the others can be seen by sensitives. These energy patterns are termed the *aura*.

The etheric body, or inner aura, extends slightly beyond the physical, appearing to the adept as a thin, dark line no more than an inch thick. Beyond it extends the astral body, which may be several inches in thickness. The aura extends around the whole body, but is most easily seen around the head, where it is termed the *nimbus*. The aura around the whole body is the *aureola*. The nimbus is what is shown in Christian art—especially from the fifth to the sixteenth centuries—as "halos" or "glorias." In paintings of Moslem prophets, the aura is often shown as a ring of flames. Crowns and priests' headdresses symbolize the aura. Some art of Ceylon, Mexico, Peru, and of Japanese **Buddhism** show light extending around the whole body of a holy person. Paracelsus, in the sixteenth century, said "The vital force is not enclosed in Man, but radiates round him like a luminous sphere."

The aura changes color with the person's health, mood, etc., and so can be used by the sensitive as an instrument of **divination**. A person with a blue or lavender aura, for example, will be in a deeply spiritual state. Love shows as a pink aura, and anger as a vibrant red. Vortexes and holes in the aura or the aureola may indicate health problems and a need for attention. Seeing a change of color, for example from dark pink to vibrant red, would indicate that the person's anger was increasing and could explode in the near future.

Sources:
Buckland, Raymond: *Color Magic—Unleash Your Inner Powers*. St. Paul: Llewellyn, 2002
Butler, William E.: *How to Read the Aura*. New York: Samuel Weiser, 1971
Cayce, Edgar: *Auras*. Virginia Beach: ARE Press, 1973
Spence, Lewis: *An Encyclopedia of the Occult*. London: George Routledge & Sons, 1920

Autography *see* **Writing, Slate**

Automatic Art *see* **Art, Automatic**

Automatic Writing *see* **Writing, Automatic**

AUTOMATISM

Automatism covers acts that are automatic in so far as they are not consciously produced. This would cover such things as **automatic writing**, drawing, painting, playing musical instruments, singing, and dancing. **Frederick W. H. Myers** divided automatism into two main types: motor automatism (active) and sensory automatism (passive). Motor automatism is movement of the tongue, head, or limbs, without guidance by the conscious mind. Sensory automatism is the external presentation of information received **clairvoyantly** or **clairaudiantly**. Rosemary Ellen Guiley points out that since ancient time automatisms have been attributed to **spirits** and to the gods.

The spirit paintings such as those done by the **Bangs sisters** are examples of automatism in which paintings were produced directly onto the canvases. The music of deceased masters played by **Rosemary Brown** is another example. Many such occurrences have been viewed by skeptics as examples of **extrasensory perception** or of secondary personalities coming through and producing information that has been long suppressed and forgotten. However, there are numerous cases of automatic writing which refute this explanation, producing material totally foreign to the automatist. A good example of this is the material that was produced by **Pearl Curran**, first by **Ouija®** board and then by automatic writing. Mrs. Curran, a St. Louis housewife, had sparse education and yet produced writings—over a period of more than seven years—which displayed detailed knowledge of life in the mid-1600s, both in England and in the American colonies. This was dictated by the spirit of a seventeenth century English woman named Patience Worth. It has been viewed as one of the finest examples ever of spirit contact.

Sources:

Buckland, Raymond: *Buckland's Book of Spirit Communications*. St. Paul: Llewellyn, 2004

Guiley, Rosemary Ellen: *The Encyclopedia of Ghosts and Spirits*. New York: Facts On File, 1992

BUSINESS

B

BABBITT, ELWOOD (B. 1922)

Elwood Babbitt was born in Orange, Massachusetts, on November 26, 1922. His father was Roy S. Babbitt, a toolmaker for the Starnett Tool Company and a **Spiritualist** who sometimes had **psychic** experiences. From early childhood, Elwood saw **spirit** people and was frequently unable to distinguish them from ordinary living people. Elwood also experienced spontaneous **astral projection** on many occasions.

When he was sixteen, Babbitt had a serious accident, being pushed off the road by an oncoming car that had lost control. As Babbitt swerved off the road into a driveway, a chain across the road struck him in the throat causing multiple injuries. Doctors gave him only a few hours to live but Babbitt's deceased grandmother appeared to him and assured him that he would be all right.

In 1941 Babbitt joined the Marines and was stationed in the Pacific. After the war he returned to Orange. While working as a bus driver, he began to concentrate on his spiritual development. He developed his **clairvoyance** and started to give what he termed "life readings" to people. In 1966, he started working with Charles H. Hapgood, of the Keene State College Society for **Psychical Research**. Babbitt began a series of readings in which it was claimed that he channeled the Christ Spirit and the spirits of various other **Biblical** figures. Hapgood described the energy which came through Babbitt not as **Jesus** himself but as "a universal force that can manifest through anyone." Babbitt also claimed to channel such entities as **Nostradamus**, Vishnu, Pontius Pilate, and others.

Sources:

Hapgood, Charles H.: *Voices of Spirit: Through the Psychic Experience of Elwood Babbitt*. New York: Delacourt Press, 1975

The Sites of Ledash: http://www.cosmosite.net

BAILEY, CHARLES

Born in Melbourne, Australia, Charles Bailey was a bootmaker who became one of the most famous **apport mediums** of his time. His first public appearance was in 1889. His **spirit guide** was named Abdul. Bailey traveled around the world and opened himself to all sorts of tests to prove his **mediumship**. He cooperated with virtually everyone who wanted to investigate his mediumship. Sir **Arthur Conan Doyle** was very impressed with him, to the point where he said he had "no confidence" in a claimed exposure of the medium.

Through his guide Abdul, Bailey apported such items as live fish, crabs and turtles, live birds sitting on eggs in their nests, rare antiques and coins, a stone from beneath the sea still dripping with salt water, a human skull, and ancient clay cylinders with Babylonian inscriptions. Many apports produced by Bailey, for his sponsor Thomas Welton Stanford, are now to be seen at the Leland Stanford University in California.

Although Bailey was suspected of fraud on a number of occasions, he was usually able to explain away any seeming irregularities. Doyle said that "Bailey's own account is that he was the victim of a religious conspiracy, and in view of his long record of success it is more probable than that he should, in some mysterious way, have smuggled a live bird into a séance room in which he knew that he would be stripped and examined." Doyle backed up his confidence in the medium in his historical work *The History of Spiritualism*. In that book he describes a séance with Bailey:

> "We then placed Mr. Bailey in the corner of the room, lowered the lights without turning them out, and waited. Almost at once he breathed very heavily, as one in a **trance**, and soon said something in a foreign tongue...the voice then said that he was a Hindoo [sic] control who was used to bring apports for the medium, and that he would, he hoped, be able to bring one for us. "Here it is," he said, a moment later, and the medium's hand was extended with something in it. The light was turned full on and we found it was a very perfect bird's nest, beautifully constructed of some very fine fibre mixed with moss. It stood about two inches high and had no sign of any flattening which would have come with concealment. The size would be nearly three inches across. In it lay a small egg, white, with tiny brown speckles."

The guide went on to explain that it came from India and that the bird was the Jungle Sparrow.

Bailey underwent a long series of tests in Milan. Without his knowledge, some of the inves-

tigators—nine business men and doctors—secretly spied on him in his bedroom. In the course of seventeen sittings with the medium, they could find no flaw in his performances, even though for some of them he was placed in a sack. The investigation lasted from February to April, 1904.

Sources:

Awtry-Smith, Marilyn: *"They" Paved the Way*. New York: Spiritualism & More, nd

Doyle, Sir Arthur Conan: *The History of Spiritualism*. New York: Doran, 1926

BAILEY, LILIAN

Lilian Bailey was a twentieth century English deep trance **medium** who was invited to give **séances** for much of European royalty plus such dignitaries as Canadian Prime Minister MacKenzie King. Bailey also had sittings with movie stars Mary Pickford, Merle Oberon, **Mae West**, and others. On one occasion, after agreeing to sit with "a group of VIPs," she was blindfolded and taken to a building. She quickly went into **trance** and afterward found her audience included Queen Elizabeth, the Queen Mother. Apparently while Bailay was in trance the **spirit** of the late King George VI came through to speak to his widow. The Queen Mother gave Bailey a personal brooch as a token of gratitude.

Bailey was awarded the Order of the British Empire medal for her services during World War I. She joined the Queen Mary's Army Auxiliary Corps, assigned to the Director General of Transport's Department, and worked not far behind the front lines.

Bailey had three main **spirit guides**: a young soldier named William Hedley Wootton (a Grenadier Guards' captain who had been killed in France in World War I), a Scottish doctor named Thomas Adamson, and a young Cingalese girl who called herself Poppet. On one ocaasion Bailey obtained a photograph of her guide Wootton through the **spirit photographer William Hope**. Once, when asked what her mediumship meant to her, Bailey replied: "I am so sure that life goes on after death. It is not a hope—it is an absolute conviction. There is no question in my mind that we shall meet and be with those whom we love."

Sources:

Aarons, Marjorie: *The Tapestry of Life: Teachings Through the Mediumship of Lilian Bailey.* London: Psychic Press, 1979

Lilian Bailey Biography: http://website.lineone.net/~ enlightenment/lilian_bailey.htm

Neech, W. F.: *Death Is Her Life.* London: Psychic Press, 1957

BALFOUR, ARTHUR JAMES, FIRST EARL OF (1848–1930)

Arthur James Balfour was born in Whittinge-hame, East Lothian, Scotland, on July 25, 1848. He was the eldest son of James Maitland Balfour and Lady Blanche Gascoyne-Cecil (sister of the third Marquess of Salisbury). He was educated at Eton and at Trinity College, Cambridge. According to the *Encyclopedia Britannica*, in the great Victorian struggle between science and religion, Balfour was on the side of religion.

The Earl of Balfour was one of England's most prominent researchers of **psychic** and **Spiritualist** phenomena. He was a British statesman and considered a brilliant aristocratic intellectual. He was Prime Minister of England from 1902 to 1905. In 1882, his sister introduced him to Spiritualism, and his brother, the Rt. Hon. Gerald W. Balfour, was also very much interested in psychic research. His sister was married to Professor **Henry Sidgwick** who was the first president of the **Society for Psychical Research**. The Earl himself later came to serve as president of the society.

Balfour had been very much in love with Alfred Lyttleton's sister, Catherine Mary Lyttleton, who died suddenly of typhus on Palm Sunday, 1875, a month after they became engaged. Balfour never again seriously considered marriage. Many years later the medium Winifred Margaret Tennant—known in psychical research

literature as "Mrs. Willett"—played an important part in **cross correspondent** spirit communications that came from the then deceased **Edmund Gurney** and **Frederick. W. H. Myers**. These were received by **automatic writing** and by **trance** utterances, between 1912 and 1929. In them Mrs. Willett revealed intimate details of the relationship between Balfour and Catherine Mary Lyttleton. These became known as the "Palm Sunday" case.

Nandor Fodor states that Balfour's paper on the Ear of Dionysius cross correspondence, attributed to the discarnate minds of Professors Butcher and Verrall, which Balfour read before the Society for Psychical Research in November 1916, "is a most constructive presentation of an excellent piece of evidence for survival."

Sources:

Broad, C. D.: *Man, Myth & Magic: Mrs. Willett.* London: BPC Publishing, 1970

Encyclopedia Britannica. Chicago: William Benton, 1964

Fodor, Nandor: *Encyclopedia of Psychic Science.* London: Arthurs Press, 1933

BALLOU, ADIN (1828–1886)

Adin Ballou was a Universalist minister who helped prepare the way for **Spiritualism** in America. In 1842 he formed the Hopedale Community, near Milford, Massachusetts. The community did a lot of good public relations work for the burgeoning Spiritualist movement, and from 1850 onward various **spirit** manifestations were produced there. Ballou proclaimed his conversion to Spiritualism in 1852, with the publication of his book *Modern Spirit Manifestations*. In that year he also received the first of several communications from his deceased son. He became one of Spiritualism's staunchest supporters.

Sources:

Shepard, Leslie A: *Encyclopedia of Occultism & Parapsychology.* New York: Avon Books, 1978

BANGS SISTERS: ELIZABETH S. (1859–1922) AND MAY EUNICE (B. 1853)

The early 1900s paintings of Lizzie and May Bangs are perhaps the most amazing examples of spiritual or **automatic art**. The portraits materialized on blank canvases, gradually taking form and color. The end result is similar to a modern airbrushed picture but with detail, especially in the eyes, unknown in portraits of that period. Examples can be seen at the **Lily Dale Museum**—where historian **Ron Nagy** is one of the country's leading expert on the phenomena—and in Lily Dale's Maplewood Hotel. Some of the Bangs sisters' paintings are also in **Camp Chesterfield**, Indiana, **Harmony Grove**, California, and elsewhere.

May was born in 1853 and Elizabeth in 1859. Their parents were Edward and Meroe Bangs. Edward was a tinsmith. The sisters had two brothers, Edward and William. Originally from Maine, Edward and Meroe moved to Kansas and then on to Chicago, where the two sisters were born.

Elizabeth (Lizzie) S. and May Eunice Bangs were known as the Bangs Sisters and became extraordinary **Spiritualist mediums**. They were able to produce amazing spirit portraits in full color. They also did **slate writing**. They did everything in broad daylight and invariably were very carefully observed and investigated. Their production of phenomena had started when they were extremely young children, with the moving of heavy furniture and coal falling from the ceiling of their parents' home. The production of spirit portraits did not begin until the fall of 1894.

Initially, two blank paper "canvases" mounted on frames were placed face-to-face on a table. The canvases were upright, leaning against a window. The sitter would sit beside the table, holding the edge of the canvases with one hand. The Bangs Sisters would be on the other side of the table, not touching the canvases. Curtains were drawn across the window on either side, up to the edges of the canvases, and a blind pulled

down to the tops. This ensured that the only light coming into the room filtered in through the paper canvas. After a while, shadows appeared on the translucent surface, as though an artist was doing preliminary sketches. Then color would be seen rapidly covering the canvas. When the canvases were separated, there would be a beautiful portrait on one, with no smudges of paint on the other still-plain one. The painting would be an extremely lifelike portrait of a deceased relative of the sitter.

In a letter to a Mr. James Coates, dated September 17, 1910, May Bangs wrote:

> The room is shaded sufficiently to cause all the light from the window to pass through the canvas, thus enabling the sitter to witness the development and detect the least change in the shadows. No two sittings are exactly alike. Usually in the development of a portrait the outer edges of the canvas become shadowed, showing different delicately colored lines, until the full outline of the head and shoulders is seen. When the likeness is sufficiently distinct to be recognized, the hair, drapery and other decorations appear. In many cases, after the entire portrait is finished, the eyes gradually open, giving a life-like appearance to the whole face.

Later the portraits were produced in full daylight, often on a stage with a single canvas propped up facing the audience. The sitter, often picked at random from the audience, would sit on one side, not touching the table. One or both of the Bangs Sisters would sit on the other side, some distance from the table and canvas and never touching or even approaching them. The painting would manifest fairly quickly, much like a Polaroid photograph develops, and would be a portrait of a relative of the randomly chosen audience member.

Art experts have examined the portraits and cannot explain the media used. It is not paint, ink, pastel, nor any known substance. The media looks as though it has been applied with a modern airbrush and has the consistency of the powder on butterfly wings. Admiral W. Usborne Moore, in *Glimpses of the Next State* (London, 1911), said: "The stuff of which the picture is composed is damp, and rubs off at the slightest touch, like soot, it comes off on the finger, a smutty oily substance." The portraits were produced in a matter of minutes when artists who have studied them have stated they should have taken many hours, if not days, to complete. Some sitters would mentally request that such an item as a flower in the hair be added, and it would appear. Eyes in the portraits would often be closed at first and then open later. Although most sitters were requested to bring with them a photograph of the deceased, they were never asked to actually produce it and the portraits were not copies of those photographs, in style or pose. The subject in the portrait would be wearing different clothing, have a different facial expression and even be at a different age from that in the photograph. Lyman C. Howe, a writer and lecturer, said that he had placed an envelope behind the canvases. The envelope contained two photographs of his loved one Maude. The Bangs sisters had never seen the woman or the photographs. The envelope was not opened. Yet the finished portrait—unlike either photograph—was more lifelike than any photograph Howe had ever seen. He mentally asked that Maude have a yellow rose in her hair and her name written at the foot of the picture. Although he told no one of these requests, both were carried out.

In the early 1900s the Bangs Sisters also produced amazing spirit writing, which was scrutinized and analyzed by Sir **William Crookes**, the physicist. Many frauds tried, unsuccessfully, to duplicate the performances of the Bangs Sisters and many skeptics tried to explain away the phenomena, but without success.

An interesting characteristic of the paintings was that they might change in detail after initially being produced. As **Elizabeth Owens** reports: "When Mrs. Gertrude Breslan Hunt, an economic and social lecturer from Norwood Park, Illinois, visited the Bangs sisters in 1909, she requested several changes during her sitting.

Here's what happened: While the painting was in process, Mrs. Hunt kept her eyes on the canvas so she could verify that no human hand had ever touched it. The background of the painting appeared first, then the whole face. Mrs. Hunt objected to the pose and asked that it be full face. The entire face obediently faded away and was rapidly resketched. Mrs. Hunt then commented that the hair was too light and the cheeks should be more colorful. As she sat observing, the shadows began to intensify in the waves of the hair until it darkened, the cheeks gained more color and the sleeves of the robe were also altered." It took only a few hours for Mrs. Hunt's painting to be completed, yet the quality was such that an artist later examining it said that he could not have finished a picture of the same excellence in less than three days, even if he worked on it for eight hours per day.

Sources:

Buckland, Raymond: *Buckland's Book of Spirit Communications*. St. Paul: Llewellyn, 2004

Heagerty, N. Riley: *The Physical Mediumship of the Bangs Sisters*. Swadlincote: Noah's Ark Society Newsletter, 1997

Moore, W. Usborne: *Glimpses of the Next State*. London: Watts, 1911

Owens, Elizabeth: *The Phenomena of Psychic Art*. Lakeville: FATE Magazine, April 2004

BARBANELL, MAURICE (1902–1981)

Maurice Barbanell was a British author, lecturer, and **medium**. He was the founder of the weekly **Spiritualist** newspaper *Psychic News*, and was its editor for two decades. He was also the editor of *Two Worlds*, the magazine founded in 1887 by **Emma Hardinge Britten**.

Although he was of Jewish heritage, as a young man Barbanell claimed to be an atheist. He was born on May 3, 1902. In the 1930s, he worked as a journalist. During this time, he was attracted to Spiritualism only because he thought he might be able to write a number of stories exposing it as fraudulent. However, at the second **séance** he attended he fell asleep ... or so he thought. When he woke up he was told that a **spirit** identifying itself as Silver Birch had been speaking though him.

For more than sixty years Barbanell was the medium at the **Hannen Swaffer** Home Circle. The teachings of Silver Birch—published in a dozen or more books—are read by people around the world. They were first published shortly after World War II and brought comfort to a tremendous number of people. The books are still in print and in demand. Barbanell's **spirit guide** has been described as "an old soul who took the guise of a humble **Native American** in order to be readily accepted."

Sources:
Barbanell, Maurice: *This Is Spiritualism*. Oxshott: The Spiritual Truth Press, 1959

BARKEL, KATHLEEN

Kathleen Barkel was a British **trance** and **apport medium**. Her **spirit guide** was White Hawk, who claimed to have been chief of the Sioux approximately 800 years ago. Kathleen started to display **psychic** gifts as a child but serious mediumship did not develop until 1922. For some years she worked at the **British College of Psychic Science**, giving **séances** and doing **healings** with her husband.

Maurice Barbanell claimed that White Hawk treated apport séances as a party with himself giving out gifts. Barbanell described the guide as "breezy and genial, with a characteristic laugh." Barbarnell also wrote: "The only physical indication that Mrs. Barkel had that an apport séance would shortly take place was the curious fact that for days beforehand her figure began to swell. At the end of the séance her body resumed its normal size. I do not know the explanation. My theory is that in some way or other her body was used to store the **ectoplasm** required to rematerialise the objects after they had been brought through the atmosphere, doubtless in their atomic form."

Nandor Fodor stated that the usual apports were beautifully cut precious and semiprecious stones. The guide placed the medium's hand over that of the sitter and the apport "formed," or materialized, between the two hands.

Sources:
Barbanell, Maurice: *This Is Spiritualism*. Oxshott: The Spiritual Truth Press, 1959

Fodor, Nandor: *Encyclopedia of Psychic Science*. London: Arthurs Press, 1933

BARRETT, SIR WILLIAM FLETCHER (1845–1926)

Sir William Fletcher Barrett was Professor of Physics at the Royal College for Science, Dublin, from 1873 to 1910. He was also one of the distinguished early pioneers of **psychical research**.

In 1874, at the age of 29, he started his first investigation of **mesmerism** and the mesmeric **trance**. From there his interest turned to **Spiritualism** and its physical phenomena. Initially, he thought phenomenon such as **levitation** must be due to hallucination. He later admitted that he had personally experienced phenomena in conditions where fraud was impossible, such as outdoors. In 1876 he submitted a paper, *Some Phenomena Associated with Abnormal Conditions of the Mind*, to the British Association for the Advancement of Science. The paper was rejected by the Biological Committee but accepted by the Anthropological Sub-section, with the casting vote of chairman Dr. Alfred Russel Wallace. The paper dealt with Barrett's own investigations and experiences, and ended with the recommendation that a committee be formed for the systematic investigation of the phenomena of mesmerism and Spiritualism. Several prominent members, including Dr. Wallace and **Sir William Crookes**, applauded the recommendation but no action was taken on it.

In 1882, Barrett instigated a meeting in the office of the **British National Association of Spiritualists**, which led to the founding of the **Society for Psychical Research**. Over the years

Sir William Barrett, early psychical researcher and founder of both the American and British Society for Psychical Research. *Courtesy Fortean Picture Library.*

he wrote a number of books, including *On the Threshold of a New World of Thought* (1908), *Psychical Research* (1911), *Swedenborg: the Savant and the Seer* (1912), *On the Threshold of the Unseen* (1917), *Au Seuil de l'Invisible* (1923), *The Divining Rod* (1926), and *Death-Bed Visions* (1926). One of his main interests was the **divining rod** and the art or science of dowsing.

Barrett visited the United States and founded the **American Society of Psychical Research** in Boston in 1885. One of the founding members was the renowned Harvard psychologist and professor of philosophy, **William James**.

After many years of research, Barrett concluded that there was a spiritual world of existence, there was survival of the **spirit** after death, and occasional communication between the worlds was possible.

Sources:

Awtry-Smith, Marilyn: *"They" Paved the Way.* New York: Spiritualism & More, nd

Fodor, Nandor: *Encyclopedia of Psychic Science.* London: Arthurs Press, 1933

BAYLESS, RAYMOND

Raymond Bayless wrote *Phone Calls From the Dead* (1979) with **D. Scott Rogo**, after a two-year investigation into phantom phone calls. The authors were surprised to find that a large number of people had received phone calls from friends and relatives who had died. In some cases the call was received before the recipient knew of the death of the caller. In other cases, the caller was long deceased.

In 1956, Bayless became interested in the work of Attila von Szalay, who had done extensive work on **spirit** voices. The two worked together and in 1959 published their initial findings in *The Journal of the **American Society for Psychical Research***. According to Tom and Lisa Butler (*There Is No Death and There Are No Dead*, 2003),

The two constructed a **cabinet** that von Szalay sat in while trying to generate voices. A microphone was placed in the opening of a **trumpet**, a device used by **Spiritualist mediums** to amplify spirit voices, and then placed in the cabinet. A tape recorder was placed outside the cabinet and connected to a speaker so that any voices or noises developed within the enclosure could be heard. Whistles, whispered voices and rapping were heard coming from the speakers whether von Szalay was in the cabinet or outside of it several feet away. The voices could be recognized as male and female and often sounded mechanical.

Voices recorded by Bayless and von Szalay gave verifiable information. Initially the messages were brief but as the research continued the messages increased in length, up to forty-five seconds. The results of these experiments met with criticism, including the charge that the "spirit voices" were random radio broadcasts that had been accidentally picked up. This criticism was easily answered when it was shown that some of the messages contained profanity that would not be heard on the radio and the voices would frequently answer specific questions and provide asked-for information about deceased relatives.

Sources:

Butler, Tom and Lisa: *There Is No Death and There Are No Dead.* Reno: AA-EVP, 2003

Rogo, D. Scott and Raymond Bayless: *Phone Calls From the Dead.* New Jersey: Prentice-Hall, 1979

BELK PSYCHIC RESEARCH FOUNDATION

Founded in the 1950s by Henry Belk, the Belk Psychic Research Foundation was established to investigate the phenomena of **extrasensory perception** (ESP). Belk spent some years working with Harold Sherman investigating the **psychic surgery** of Tony Agpaoa and other Philippine **healers**.

Sources:

Shepard, Leslie A: *Encyclopedia of Occultism & Parapsychology.* New York: Avon Books, 1978

BERRY, CATHERINE (1813–1891)

Catherine Berry was a British **medium** who discovered her talent as a "developing medium" at the age of fifty. She could imbue with power any other mediums who sat with her. Many well known mediums of the time sat with her in order to be charged with her power. According to *Human Nature*,

"After sitting with Mrs. Berry a medium has more power to cause the phenomena at any other circle he may have to attend. Messrs. Herne and Williams have been known to visit this lady for the purpose of getting a supply of power when they had a special séance to give. Mrs. Berry is, therefore, suc-

cessful in developing mediums, and has conferred the **spirit** voice manifestation, as well as other gifts, upon several mediums … These facts have not been arrived at hastily, but after years of patient investigation."

Berry's teacher was Mrs. Marshal. She also sat with **Agnes Guppy**, **Frank Herne**, **Charles Williams**, and Mrs. Everitt—all well known mediums of their time. She recorded these **séances** in her book *Experiences in Spiritualism.* Accounts were also published in the journal *The Medium*.

Berry was especially good at **automatic writing**, drawing, and painting. Five hundred of her unusual watercolors were exhibited at Brighton, Sussex. She also made **prophecies**, many of which came to be. She foresaw the Franco-Prussian war, for example, based on a **Bible** text that she felt was pertinent. It has also been said that she could throw sitters to the ground by a wave of her hand.

Sources:

Awtry-Smith, Marilyn: *"They" Paved the Way.* New York: Spiritualism & More, nd

Fodor, Nandor: *Encyclopedia of Psychic Science.* London: Arthurs Press, 1933

Betty Books *see* **White, Stewart Edward**

BIBLE

The Christian Bible is full of references to **psychic** and **Spiritualist** activities, to **materializations**, **healings**, **apparitions**, and **spirit** contact of all kinds. In 1 Corinthians there are exhortations for all to use their gifts of **prophecy** and other spiritual gifts. 1 Corinthians 12:8-10 says, "For to one is given, by the Spirit, the word of wisdom; to another the word of knowledge by the same Spirit; to another faith by the same Spirit; to another the gifts of healing by the same Spirit; to another the working of miracles; to another prophecy; to another discerning of spirits; to another diverse kinds of **tongues**; to another the interpretation of tongues." Also, 1 Corinthians 14:31 says: "For ye may all prophesy one by one, that all may learn, and all may be comforted."

There are a number of references to materializations in the Bible: Genesis 3:8, 18:1, 32:24, Exodus 24:10, 24:11, Ezekiel 11:9, Daniel 5:5, Luke 24:15, 16, 29-31, John 20:12, 14, 19, 26. In John 20:19 the Bible says: "Then the same day at evening, being the first day of the week, when the doors were shut where the disciples had assembled for fear of the Jews, came Jesus and stood in the midst, and saith unto them, Peace be unto you." This verse is describing an event that was supposed to have taken place two days after the crucifixion, which was carried out on the eve of the Jewish Sabbath. This is described as being on "the first day of the week." Jesus, early in the day, had appeared to Mary Magdalene in the garden of the sepulcher where his body had been laid, and told her to tell his brethren that he had not yet ascended to the Father, whom he described as "my Father and your father." When the disciples assembled in a room, with the door closed "for fear of the Jews," then suddenly Jesus appeared standing in the middle of them. Apparently it was a solid materialization for he showed them his hands and his side, to verify that it really was him, thus proving that there is indeed life after death and that communication is possible.

Independent spirit **writing** is found in Exodus 24:12, 31:18, 32:16, 34:1, Deuteronomy 5:22, 9:10. Independent spirit voices are mentioned in Deuteronomy 9:12, 13, 1 Samuel 3:3, 3:9, Ezekiel 1:28, Matthew 17:5, John 12:28-30, Acts 9:4, 9:7, 11:7-9. There are examples of healings in both the Old and the New Testaments, in Numbers 21:8, 9, 1Kings 16:17, 16:24, 2 Kings 4:18, 4:37, 5:1, 5:14, Matthew 6:5, 6:13, 7:10, 7:13, Luke 5:47, 5:54, Luke 9:11, 14:2, 14:4, Mark 3:2, 3:5, John 4:47, 4:54, 1 Corinthians 12:9, 12:28, Acts 3:1, 3:8, 16:8, 16:10. **Trance** is encountered in Genesis 15:2, 15:17, Daniel 8:18, 10:9, Acts 9:3, 9:9, 22:17, 2 Corinthians 12:2. There is spirit communication through **dreams** found in Job 33:15, Genesis 28:12, 31:24, 37:5, 41, and dream interpretation in Genesis 40:1-23, Genesis 41:14-36, Judges 7:13-14.

Spiritualism does not accept the Christian Bible as the infallible word of God. Rather, it recognizes that it is the product of a number of different authors writing at different times with material slanted to their particular conditions and circumstances. Regardless of the inspiration that moved the various authors, there is always what today is known as the "hidden agenda"— the slant or "spin" that is the author's individualism, promoting what he feels is important. Such writings cannot be relevant to all people at all times under all circumstances. Added to this is the confusion and inaccuracy that has grown from translations of translations together with a wide variety of interpretations and presentations, many of which were personally or politically motivated. Due to the numerous translations and the actions of the Council of Nicæa, a great deal of original meaning has been lost.

Spiritualism's recognition of the Bible's background is an important endorsement of Spiritualism's search for the truth and its ongoing investigation, analysis, and classification of psychic facts and spiritual values. Spiritualism believes that everyone is free to interpret according to their own understanding. Spiritualism acknowledges the history, prophecy, and spiritual phenomena which are spread throughout the Bible.

Modern Spiritualism's regard for the Bible was expressed by Moses Hull, who inspired the first Training School for Modern Spiritualism at Matua, Ohio, in July of 1897. He said the Bible is "one of the best of the sacred books of the ages," yet he acknowledged that it is far from infallible. The Bible is the basis for the Hebrew religion— with the Old Testament—as well as the Christian one—in the New Testament—and much of its teachings may also be found in the Koran. While not living up to all that is sometimes said of it, the Bible is accepted by Spiritualists as a book of history written by many different authors.

Sources:

Asimov, Isaac: *Asimov's Guide to the Bible*. New York: Avon, 1968

Buckland, Raymond: *The Fortune-Telling Book: The Encyclopedia of Divination and Soothsaying*. Detroit: Visible Ink Press, 2004

Holy Bible: various editions

Scott's Bible: Old and New Testaments with Notes, Observations, and References. New York: Samuel T Armstrong, 1827

BILLETS AND BILLET READING

Billet reading is frequently done by **mediums** on public platforms and by **Spiritualist** ministers in Spiritualist churches. Billets, from the French *billet* meaning "note," are pieces of paper usually about the size of a playing card. People are asked to write a name on the piece of paper—the name of the deceased, perhaps—or they might be asked to write any question they have. The papers are then folded up, collected, and handed to the medium, who will go on to name the name (and, perhaps, contact the spirit of the person named) or answer the question. This is done without the medium opening the folded billet. Billet reading is a development of **psychometry**, picking up the feelings of the person and other information from the paper.

Sources:

Buckland, Raymond: *Buckland's Book of Spirit Communications.* St. Paul: Llewellyn, 2004

BIOFEEDBACK

Biofeedback is the measurement of brain wave activity indicative of the depth of a **trance**, among other things. The principle behind biofeedback is that by providing the individual with knowledge of his or her internal body processes, these processes can be consciously controlled. Using biofeedback instruments, the operator can consciously modify his or her brainwave activity, heart rate, blood pressure, and skin resistance. This can be useful in relaxing into a deeper state of trance. The practice of using biofeedback machines was first introduced in the United States by Joe Kamiya, as reported in *Psychology Today* (April 1968, v. 1, no. 11). Biofeedback can use many tools: EEGs (electroencephalograms) to measure brain waves, EKGs (electrocardiograms)

A woman wears a biofeedback monitor at her temple. Biofeedback is a technique in which people are trained to gain awareness and insight using signals from their own bodies. *Michael Nemeth/The Image Bank/Getty Images.*

to graph heart processes, GSRs (galvanic skin responses) to measure skin responses, and EMGs (electromyographs) to check muscle tensions.

Biofeedback deals with the alpha waves (8-13 cycles per second frequency), beta waves (14-50 cycles), theta waves (4-8 cycles), and delta waves (0.5-4 cycles). The **American Society for Psychical Research** found that biofeedback can be effective in bringing the **psi** faculty under control. The beta frequency is the normal waking state but by relaxing—using such techniques as **meditation**, massage, yoga, or **hypnosis**—it is relatively easy to descend into the alpha state. Psychologists use biofeedback to help their patients cope with pain. Physical therapists use it to help stroke victims regain movement in paralyzed muscles.

In a typical biofeedback session, the subject has electrodes connected to the back of the head, the right forearm, and two fingers of the right hand. A respiration gauge may also be worn. These electrodes detect any changes in internal states and relay them back to the subject by way of lights, moving needles, or sounds. The Silva Mind Control organization, founded by José Silva (1914–1999) in the 1960s, conducted sessions leading to what they termed "functioning in the alpha." It emphasized positive thinking, self-hypnosis, and **visualization**.

Sources:

Holroyd, Stuart: *The Supernatural: Minds Without Boundaries*. London: Aldus, 1975

Karlins, Marvin and Lewis M. Andrews: *Biofeedback; Turning on the Power of Your Mind*. New York: Lippincott, 1972

Lawrence, Jodi: *Alpha Brain Waves*. New York: Avon, 1972

BIRD, MALCOLM J.

Malcolm J. Bird was the research officer of the **American Society for Psychical Research** from 1925 until 1931. Prior to that, he was the associate editor for *The Scientific American*'s investigation of the **physical phenomena** of **Spiritualism**. On the suggestion of Sir **Arthur Conan Doyle**, Bird traveled to Europe to investigate **mediums** including **Ada Emma Deane, William Hope, Gladys Osbourne Leonard, Evan Powell**, John C. Sloan, and Maria Vollhardt. In his book *My Psychic Adventures* (1924), Bird stated that he believed the phenomena were due neither to hallucination nor collective **hypnosis**. He went so far as to say that he thought that a good degree of probability existed for the genuineness of much of the psychic phenomena he witnessed.

Bird also published *Margery the Medium* (1925), in which he traced the development of **Margery Crandon** from 1923 through 1925. This book detailed *The Scientific American* investigation of her mediumship. Bird himself, along with fellow investigator **Hereward Carrington**, became completely convinced that Margery's mediumship was authentic.

Sources:

Doyle, Sir Arthur Conan: *The History of Spiritualism*. New York: Doran, 1926

Fodor, Nandor: *Encyclopedia of Psychic Science*. London: Arthurs Press, 1933

BLAKE, ELIZABETH (D. 1920)

Born in Bradrick, Ohio, Elizabeth Blake displayed mediumistic abilities from childhood. She was a strongly religious member of the Methodist Church but was expelled from it because of her **mediumship**. Blake specialized in **direct voice** séances. For these she used a long **trumpet**, two feet in length. The small end of the trumpet was placed against her ear and the large, bell end at the sitter's ear. The voices that came from the trumpet were very loud and often could be heard from as far away as a hundred feet.

Blake had no hesitation in submitting herself for testing by researchers. Professor **James Hyslop** investigated Blake and quickly became convinced of her genuineness. Hyslop said of Blake's voice **séances**, "The loudness of the sounds in some cases excludes the supposition that the voices are conveyed from the (medium's) vocal cords to the trumpet. I have heard the sounds twenty feet away, and could have heard them forty or fifty feet away, and Mrs. Blake's lips did not move." Hyslop gave details of a case where the **spirit** voice gave the correct solution for opening a combination lock to a safe, the combination being unknown to the sitter.

Sir **Arthur Conan Doyle** referred to her as "one of the most wonderful voice mediums of whom we have any record, and perhaps the most evidential, because in her presence the voices were regularly produced in broad daylight." Doyle described her as a poor, illiterate woman living on the shore of the Ohio River opposite the town of Huntingdon, in West Virginia.

Blakes's medical doctor, who was also the superintendent of the West Virginia Asylum at Huntingdon, Dr. L. V. Guthrie stated, "I have had sittings with her in my office, also on the front porch in the open air, and on one occasion in a carriage as we were driving along a road. She has repeatedly offered to let me have a sitting and use a lamp chimney instead of a tin horn (trumpet), and I have frequently seen her produce the voices with her hand resting on one end of the horn." Dr. Guthrie, in his writings, gave a number of instances of Blake's mediumship. One instance was when the grandfather of the sitter came through to give details of his death. It had been presumed that the old man had been drunk and fallen from a bridge, but the spirit described how he had been bludgeoned by two men, robbed, and thrown from the bridge. The details given of the two men enabled the police to find, arrest, and convict them.

Sources:

Awtry-Smith, Marilyn: *"They" Paved the Way*. New York: Spiritualism & More, nd

Doyle, Sir Arthur Conan: *The History of Spiritualism*. New York: Doran, 1926

BLAKE, WILLIAM (1757–1827)

William Blake was an English mystic, artist, and poet. He was born in London on November 28, 1757. His father James was a hosier. His mother was Catherine Harmitage. William had three brothers and a sister; he was the second eldest son. James Blake recognized his son William's artistic talents and encouraged him. At the age of ten Blake went to Henry Pars' drawing school and in August 1772, he was apprenticed to the engraver James Basire. At the end of his apprenticeship Blake entered the Royal Academy School and was taught by the chaser and enameller George Moser.

At the age of 21, having left the school, Blake set up as an engraver himself and made a good living for the next twenty years, working for publishers and booksellers. In 1780 he first exhibited at the Royal Academy. Blake was greatly influenced by the Gothic style, regarding it as the ideal. His first book of poems was *Poetical Sketches* and its publication was financed by Mr. Matthew, a clergyman and admirer.

Blake met Catherine Boucher, the illiterate daughter of a market-gardener, in 1781 and married her the following year. She learned to draw and paint well enough to help with her husband's work. In 1788, Blake started experimenting with a new method of printing using acid-etched copper plates. It is said that the method had been revealed to him in a **dream** by the **spirit** of his dead brother Robert. Robert was the youngest of the Blake boys and had been very artistic himself; he died at the age of twenty-one. The first examples of printing from these etched plates were in the two works *There Is No Natural Religion* and *All Religions Are One*. Together with Blake's *Songs of Innocence*—lyrical poems etched on copper with decorations colored by hand—these were a prelude to "the remarkable series of books in 'illuminated printing' which occupied Blake in some degree for the remainder of his life" (*Encyclopedia Britannica*).

Blake was a prolific painter. In 1797 alone he produced a series of 537 watercolor designs. He worked in tempera as well as water color but never painted in oils. Blake wrote that from a very early age he saw visions of angels and **ghostly** monks and that he saw and conversed with the Virgin Mary, the **angel** Gabriel, and various historical figures. According to Kathleen Raine, W. B. Yeats thought of Blake as a Rosicrucian initiate, while Swinburne "praised him as the champion of evil." Raine also said that Blake believed that much of his visionary poetry was "dictated" to him: "the authors are in eternity." Raine states, "Blake's genius was perhaps principally that of a creator of myths. When we think of Blake, we think of a living world of gods and demons in the continuous activity of their uninhibited energy. His pantheon of spiritual beings, or energies, whose names he himself invented, seems to exist in its own right no less than the pantheons of **Greece** or of **Egypt**, independently of those works in which the gods are depicted."

Engraving by William Blake, depicting the soul embracing the dying body, already sinking into its grave. *Courtesy Fortean Picture Library.*

Blake had many **visions** that have been described as perceptions of the collective unconscious. He claimed that these visions came to him spontaneously. They also came with a speed and energy which he said was far beyond his ability to adequately record them. He read as much as possible of the alchemical, Hermetic, and Neoplatonic texts, and as a young man Blake was a member of the **Swedenborgian** New Church. He was familiar with the works of Paraclesus, Fludd, Thomas Vaughan, Cornelius Agrippa, and of the mystic Jacob Boehme. He worked on the engravings of Jacob Bryant's *New System of Mythology.*

In 1717, John Toland assembled a line of delegates from Bardic and Druidic circles to form the Universal Druid Bond and from this, he formed what was known as the line of Chosen Chiefs. These chiefs were to include Toland himself, Dr.

William Stukeley the antiquary, Lewis Spence, and William Blake. There is evidence of a profound knowledge of English history and poetry to be found throughout Blake's work. William Butler Yeats believed that Blake had access to the secrets oral traditions of the Rosicrucians and brief extracts from Blake's works were included in the rituals of the Hermetic Order of the Golden Dawn (of which Yeats was a member).

Famous among Blake's "Prophetic Books" are *The Book of Thel* (1789), *The Marriage of Heaven and Hell* (1790), *The Book of Urizen* (1794), *America* (1793), *Milton* (1804–8), and *Jerusalem* (1804–20). Among Blake's later artistic works are drawings and engravings for Dante's *Divine Comedy* and the 21 illustrations to the *Book of Job,* which was completed when he was almost 70 years old. Blake died on August 12, 1827, leaving behind no debts. He was buried in an unmarked grave at the public cemetery of Bunhill Fields. Though generally dismissed as an eccentric during his lifetime, today he is highly rated both as a poet and an artist.

Sources:

Encyclopedia Britannica. Chicago: William Benton, 1964

Raine, Kathleen: *Man, Myth & Magic—Blake: Maker of Myths* London: BPC Publishing, 1970

Shepard, Leslie A: *Encyclopedia of Occultism & Parapsychology.* New York: Avon Books, 1978

BLAVATSKY, HELENA PETROVNA (1831–1891)

Helena Petrovna Blavatksy was born on August 12, 1831, in Ekaterinoslav, a town on the river Dnieper in southern Russia. She became one of the best known and most influential **occultists** in the world and was considered by many to be an excellent **Spiritualist** medium.

Helena's father was Colonel Peter Hahn, a Russian officer and member of the Mecklenburg family. Her mother was Helena de Fadeyev, a well-known novelist who died young. Helena's maternal grandmother was Princess Helena Dolgorukov, a gifted writer and botanist. Count Sergei Yulievich Witte, a Tsarist prime minister, was Helena's cousin. After the early death of her mother in 1842, Helena was brought up by her maternal grandparents, at their house in Saratov. Her grandfather was Civil Governor there.

An exceptional child, at an early age Helena was aware of being deeply sensitive and of possessing certain **psychic** powers. She could see **spirits** that were invisible to her friends and could foresee certain future events through various forms of **divination**. She was a natural linguist, a talented pianist, and a fine artist. She was also a fine horsewoman. According to her sister's memoirs, Helena had frequent bouts of somnambulism, walking in her sleep and speaking in unknown tongues (**glossolalia**). She could also cause **hallucinations** in her playmates with her vivid storytelling. Helena received no formal education and at the age of seventeen she married a much older man, Nikifor (or Nicephore) Blavatsky, Vice Governor of the Province of Erivan in Transcaucasia.

Within a few months of her marriage, Helena ran away to adopt a nomadic existence—a life that has been compared to the Victorian equivalent of a hippie—moving through **Egypt, Greece**, and Turkey. In London by the time she was twenty, Helena met an individual whom she claimed to have known from her childhood visions. He was the Mahatma Morya (or "M," as he became known among **Theosophists**, in later years), an Eastern Initiate of Rajput birth. He told Helena of the spiritual work that lay ahead of her, and from then on she fully accepted his guidance.

Later in 1851, Helena embarked for Canada. She traveled to various parts of the United States, Mexico, South America and the West Indies. In 1852 she went to India, traveling by way of the Cape and Ceylon. She was prevented from entering Tibet; in 1853 she returned to England. In the summer of the following year she again went to America, where she crossed the Rocky Mountains with a caravan of emigrants. In late 1855 she returned to India, this time going by way of Japan. On this attempt she succeeded in entering Tibet,

doing so through Kashmir and Ladakh. By 1858 she was in France and then Germany, finally returning to Russia in the late fall of that year. She stayed a short time with her sister Vera at Pskov.

By this time Helena had developed strong mediumistic abilities and achieved considerable fame as a Spiritualist **medium**, with a **spirit guide** named John King. It was said that whisperings, **rappings**, and other strange phenomena were heard all over her house. From 1860 to 1865, she traveled through the Caucasus and then left Russia again in the fall of 1865, going on to the Balkans, Egypt, Syria, Greece, and Italy.

In 1868 Helena again went to Tibet, this time via India. On this trip she met "the Master Koot Hoomi" (K.H.) for the first time, and stayed in Little Tibet and also in Great Tibet. She then underwent part of her occult training with her Master. She later reported that she had been initiated by the "Hidden Masters," who were to become her driving force for the rest of her life. By late 1870, she was back in Cyprus and then Greece. En route to Egypt, Helena sailed aboard the *Eumonia*, which was shipwrecked on July 4, 1871, near the island of Spetsai. Helena was saved from drowning. She went on to Cairo, where she tried unsuccessfully to form the *Société Spirite*. After further travels through the Middle East, she returned for a short time to her relatives at Odessa, Russia, in July of 1872.

In the spring of 1873, Helena was instructed by her Teacher to go to Paris. From there, on further direct orders from him, she left for New York City, arriving on July 7, 1873. Then forty-two years old and in possession of many spiritual and occult powers, she worked for a while as a dressmaker to earn a living. A year later, on a whim, she traveled to Vermont to witness the much-publicized **Eddy Brothers**, William and Horatio, two Spiritualists who produced a variety of phenomena. It was there that she met Colonel Henry Steele Olcott, a man with a reputation for honesty. He had served in the Civil War and later worked for the U.S. Government. Fodor says of her psychic abilities at this time: "Whereas there is a limit to

Madame Blavatsky, occultist, writer and founding member of the Theosophical Society. *Courtesy Fortean Picture Library.*

the phenomena of every Spiritualist medium, Mme. Blavatsky apparently knew none. From the **materialization** of grapes for the thirsty Colonel Olcott in New York to the duplication of precious stones in India, or the creation of toys for children out of nothingness, she undertook almost any magical task and successfully performed it to the stupefaction of her coterie."

Helena launched into journalism, translating Olcott's articles into Russian and writing her own articles on Spiritualism. In the opinion of the "Mahatmas," or Adepts, Helena Blavatsky was the best available instrument for the work they had in mind, namely to offer to the world a new presentation of the age-old *Theosophia*—"The accumulated Wisdom of the ages, tested and verified by generations of **Seers** ...." Her task was to challenge both the entrenched beliefs and dogmas of Christian Theology and the equally dogmatic materialistic view of the science of her day.

On September 7, 1875, Blavatsky and Olcott, together with several others, founded the **Theosophical Society**. The inaugural address by the President-Founder Colonel Olcott was delivered November 17, 1875, which is considered to be the official date of the founding of the Society. They stated the aims of the society to be:

1. To form a nucleus of the Universal Brotherhood of Humanity, without distinction of race, creed, sex, caste or color.

2. To encourage the study of Comparative Religion, Philosophy and Science.

3. To investigate unexplained laws of Nature, and the powers latent in man.

In September 1877, Blavatsky's first monumental work, *Isis Unveiled*, was published. It was her book on the divine wisdom, or body of truth, concerning god, man, and the universe. She claimed that, while writing it, she had glimpsed the goddess Isis herself. The first printing of 1,000 copies sold out within ten days.

On July 8, 1878, Blavatsky was naturalized as a U.S. citizen and in December of the same year she and Colonel Olcott left for India via England. They arrived in Bombay in February, 1879, and there established their Theosophical Headquarters. A. P. Sinnett, editor of *The Pioneer*, added importance to their activities by publishing frequent reports. After a tour of northwestern India, they returned to Bombay and started their first Theosophical Journal, *The Theosophist* in October, 1879, with Helena as editor. From then

on the society experienced rapid growth, and the journal is still published today.

In May 1882, the society purchased a large estate in southern India at Adyar, near Madras, and the Theosophical Headquarters was moved there. During this period Colonel Olcott engaged in widespread **mesmeric healings** until February 1884, when he left for London to petition the British Government on behalf of the **Buddhists** of Ceylon (Sri Lanka). Helena, then in very poor health, went to Europe with him. She produced many marvels at **séances** she held over an extended period. So much publicity was generated by her mediumship that it provoked the **Society for Psychical Research** to send an investigator to Adyar. This was **Richard Hodgson** who, after a superficial examination, claimed to find nothing but fraud. He also accused Madame Blavatsky of being a Russian spy. Alex and Emma Coulomb, a couple who had been with Helena since 1880, stated that they had been instruments in perpetrating much of the fakery. Helena wanted to sue the couple but was overruled by a Committee of leading Theosophical Society members. In disgust, she resigned as Corresponding Secretary of the Society and, on March 31, 1885, left for Europe, never again to return to India.

She settled first in Italy and then, in August, 1885, at Wurzburg, Germany, where she worked on *The Secret Doctrine*, much of which was written either by **automatic writing** or by **inspirational writing**. The vicious attack on Helena had a most unfavorable effect on her health. In July 1886, she relocated to Ostend, Belgium, and in May of the following year, at the invitation of English Theosophists, she moved to a small house in London. Immediately after her arrival in England, Theosophical activities began to move rapidly. The Blavatsky Lodge was formed and started publicizing Theosophical ideas. She continued to work on her book, which was finally completed and published in two volumes in October and December, 1888.

The Secret Doctrine was to become the crowning achievement of Blavatsky's literary career. It is an account of the root knowledge of all religion, philosophy, and science. Also in October 1888, she formed the Esoteric Section (or School) of the Theosophical Society, "for the deeper study of the Esoteric Philosophy by dedicated students." In July 1890, she established the European Headquarters of the Theosophical Society in London. Helena Petrovna Blavatsky died on May 8, 1891, in London during a severe epidemic of flu in England. She had been suffering from Bright's disease. Colin Wilson said, "It seems fairly certain that Madame Blavatsky was a genuine medium of unusual powers. It is more certain that, when her somewhat erratic powers were feeble, she helped them out with trickery— a temptation to which dozens of bona fide mediums and magicians have succumbed."

Sources:

Blavatsky, Helena Petrovna: *Isis Unveiled*. New York: J. W. Bouton, 1877

Blavatsky, Helena Petrovna: *The Secret Doctrine*. London: Theosophical Publishing Company, 1888

Blavatsky Study Center: http://www.blavatskyarchives.com

Cranston, Sylvia: *H.P.B.: The Extraordinary Life & Influence of Helena Blavatsky, Founder of the Modern Theosophical Movement*. New York: G. P. Putnam's, 1993

Fodor, Nandor: *An Encyclopedia of Psychic Science*. London: Arthur's Press, 1933

Harrison, Vernon: *H.P. Blavatsky and the SPR: An Examination of the Hodgson Report of 1885*. Pasadena: Theosophical University Press, 1997

Symonds, John: *Madame Blavatsky: Medium and Magician*. London: Odhams, 1959

Williams, Gertrude Marvin: *Priestess of the Occult: Madame Blavatsky*. New York: Alfred A. Knopf, 1946

Wilson, Colin: *The Supernatural: Mysterious Powers*. London: Aldus Books, 1975

Book of Life *see* **Akashic Records**

BOOK OF SPIRITS

Also known as *The Spirits' Book*, this was written by **Allan Kardec** (Léon Dénizarth Hippolyte Rivail) in 1857, and later translated into English from the original French. The book contains, "The principles of **Spiritist** Doctrine on the immortality of the soul; the nature of **spirits** and their relations with men; the moral law; the present life; the future life; and the destiny of the human race—according to the teachings of spirits of high degree, transmitted through various **mediums**."

Sources:

Kardec, Allan: *The Spirits' Book*. (1857) New York: Studium, 1980

BOOK TEST

A book test is an experiment designed to ensure that **telepathy** is not the explanation of particular **Spiritualist** phenomena. The idea of book tests was started by Sir **William Crookes**, when he tried to devise a way of ensuring that a medium working with a **planchette** was not picking up any information through **extrasensory perception**. He asked the spirit if it could see the contents of the room and, on getting an affirmative answer, he reached back to the table behind him and picked up a copy of *The Times* that was lying there. Without looking, he placed a finger haphazardly on the open page. He then asked the spirit to give the word that was covered by his finger. In this instance the spirit spelled out "however." Crookes found it to be the correct word. This result was published in the *Quarterly Journal of Science* for January, 1874.

In some book tests, the spirit communicates through the **medium** to give correct quotes from a book placed in a locked box, a book selected haphazardly by a bookseller and wrapped with others, and from a book sealed and given to a third party. Usually the book selected is one that the **spirit** knew and enjoyed when alive. The spirit is asked to give the passage from a particular randomly selected page and paragraph of the book, found on a particular shelf of a bookcase in the home of the sitter at the **séance**. Mediums through whom the spirits were particularly accurate included **William Stainton Moses** and **William Eglinton**.

One very striking example of a book test is given in *Mysteries of the Unknown: Spirit Summonings* (1989). The medium was **Gladys Leonard** and the sitter Lord Glenconner, whose son Edward—known to the family as "Bim"—had been killed in the battle of the Somme in 1916. The séance took place in December, 1917. The spirit of Bim directed his father to look at "the ninth book on the third shelf, counting from the left to the right, in the bookcase on the right of the door in the drawing room as you enter; take the title and look at page 37." Lord Glenconner had a passion for forestry and a particular concern about wood-destroying beetles. This was such a strong passion that Bim and the rest of the family frequently joked about it. When he went to the designated book he found that it was titled *Trees*. On page 37 he found the sentence, "Sometimes you will see curious marks in the wood; these are caused by a tunneling beetle, very injurious to the trees."

Sources:

Fodor, Nandor: *Encyclopedia of Psychic Science*. London: Arthurs Press, 1933

Foreman, Laura (ed): *Mysteries of the Unknown: Spirit Summonings*. New York: Time-Life Books, 1989

Myers, Frederick W. H.: *Human Personality and Its Survival of Bodily Death*. London: Longmans, 1903

BORLEY RECTORY

B orley Rectory has been described as "the most haunted house in England." Situated not far from Manningtree, Essex, it was the home of the notorious seventeenth century "Witchfinder General" Matthew Hopkins.

Mysterious lights were frequently seen in the windows of Borley Rectory, writing would appear on the walls, stones were thrown about, and strange noises were heard. There was even a phantom coach and horses that drove about the property. The neighboring Borley Church also had its share of **hauntings**, though not as spectacular as those at the rectory. The church had phantom organ music, ghostly chanting, and the **ghost** of a nun moving about the churchyard.

The Reverend Henry Bull built the rectory in 1863. Bull's son Harry took over as rector after his father's death. Harry had a great interest in **Spiritualism**, and it has been suggested that this is a reason for the proliferation of ghostly phenomena there. From small beginnings, the hauntings and **poltergeist** activity grew more and more involved. By the 1930s, several years after the death of the younger Bull, they were spectacular. By that time the poltergeist phenomena were centered around Marianne Foyster, wife of the then-resident rector. Objects were thrown at her, furniture was violently moved, bells rang, and door-knockers banged. Pencil scrawls appeared on walls asking for prayers for the ghosts.

Psychical researcher **Harry Price** (1881–1948) carried out the main investigation of Borley and later authored two books on the subject. Price founded the **National Laboratory of Psychical Research** and he was also a foreign research officer for the **American Society for Psychical Research**. Price's methods of investigating were harshly criticized in some quarters. As much from local legends as from any hard evidence, Price pieced together a story of illicit love in the fourteenth century, with the murder of a nun taking place on the site of the rectory. The ghostly happenings apparently connected to this early tale began to take place shortly after the Reverend Mr. Bull built the house. They slowly grew in intensity when his son Harry succeeded him as rector.

Local residents swore they had seen a phantom coach being driven past the church, and a girl dressed in white at a window of the rectory. There were sounds of dragging footsteps and of bells clanging. A phantom nun was seen in the churchyard.

The Reverend G. E. Smith and his wife moved into the house in 1929 but did not stay long due to the hauntings. They were succeeded by the Reverend Mr. Foyster and his wife Marianne. The Foysters were familiar with the stories connected with the rectory, and it seems Marianne took a special interest in Harry Price and his investigations. It has even been suggested

Investigators digging at Borley Rectory, attempting to locate the grave of the "Phantom Nun", c. 1955. *Thurston Hopkins/Picture Post/Getty Images.*

that she was in cahoots with Price in fabricating some of the phenomena, though this has never been proven. In any case, she did seem to promote the haunting. Much of the poltergeist activity centered around her and took place when no one else was present or when no one was able to control the circumstances in any way. In 1935, the Foysters left the rectory and things quieted down. Two years later Price himself rented the house for a year.

Price called in "observers" to help him in his investigations. There was little for them to observe, for nothing much happened. Not long after Price had vacated, a Captain Gregson took possession. At that time a fire gutted the building. Rather than laying the ghosts, the fire brought about a whole new interest. Tourists

flocked there and swore they saw figures at the windows of the empty building. A photograph was published that shows a brick which, allegedly, flew up from the ground and stayed suspended in space while the photograph was taken.

After Price's death in 1948, the **Society for Psychical Research** appointed a panel to investigate his investigations. They were extremely critical, stopping just short of calling Price a fraud and accusing him of creating all the phenomena himself. They apparently ignored the fact that there had been haunting at the rectory, and on its site, long before Price started looking at the place. A more recent investigation was conducted by the society's R. J. Hastings, whose review was much more restrained and less personal than the previous attack on Price. Acknowledging

Price's apparent need for publicity and the amateurishness of some of his investigations, Hastings did conclude that there was no evidence of outright fraud on the part of Price.

Because Borley Rectory has long since been razed, it is now too late for a proper look into all that might have happened there. But from the many years of stories—true or false—the rectory will forever be remembered as "the most haunted house in England."

Sources:

Buckland, Raymond: *Ray Buckland's Magic Cauldron.* St. Paul: Galde Press, 1995

Price, Harry: *The End of Borley Rectory.* London: Longmans, Green, 1946

Price, Harry: *The Most Haunted House in England.* London: Longmans, Green, 1940

BOSTON SOCIETY FOR PSYCHICAL RESEARCH

The Boston Society for Psychical Research was founded in Boston, Massachusetts, in May 1925 as a result of conflict within the **American Society for Psychical Research** (ASPR). It was founded "in order to conduct psychic research according to strictly scientific principles, thus maintaining the standards set by **(Richard) Hodgson** and **(James Hervey) Hyslop**." Hodgson died in 1905 and Hyslop in 1920. Although the ASPR had been in Boston since its formation in 1885 (patterned on the prestigious British **Society for Psychical Research**), its headquarters was moved to New York on Hodgson's death. Politics entered into the society and many of its academically oriented members became dissatisfied with the organization. Research Officer **Walter Franklin Prince** was prevailed upon by **Gardner Murphy**, **William McDougall**, and Elwood Worcester to leave the ASPR and join them in forming the Boston society.

The Boston Society for Psychical Research remained active until 1941, publishing many important books and bulletins. It did not, however, achieve the renown of the ASPR. Among its publications were Dr. **J. B. Rhine's *Extra Sensory Perception***, published in 1934, and the bulletins with the first exposure of the fraudulent thumbprints of the Boston **medium** "Margery" **(Mina Stinson Crandon)**, also published in 1934. Other publications included Walter F. Prince's *The Case of **Patience Worth*** (1928), John F. Thomas's *Case Studies Bearing on Survival* (1929), and *Beyond Normal Cognition* (1937).

Prince, who was the moving energy of the society, died in 1934. By 1941 the original problems at the ASPR had been resolved and the Boston society disbanded and rejoined the ASPR.

Sources:

Guiley, Rosemary Ellen: *The Encyclopedia of Ghosts and Spirits.* New York: Facts On File, 1992

BOURSNELL, RICHARD (1832–1909)

As a nineteen-year-old photographer in Fleet Street, London, Richard Boursnell was frustrated when unexplained markings began to appear on his photographic plates when the pictures were developed. His partner was unhappy at the expense and accused him of not cleaning the plates properly. This eventually led to the two parting company. Boursnell had no idea how the markings got on the plates, and decided to stop working in photographic processing. He kept to that decision for forty years.

In 1891, Boursnell returned to photography and again had unexplained markings on his photographic plates. This time they were not abstract but distinctive forms. He had no idea where the extra figures were coming from and destroyed so many plates that it almost put an end to his business. Then **William T. Stead**, a well known **Spiritualist** and **automatist**, saw the photographs and persuaded Boursnell to take pictures under conditions that he, Stead, specified. Many **spirit** forms began to appear in the photographs that Stead referred to as "shadow pictures." At first they

Spirit photographs taken by English photographer Richard Boursnell, c. 1891. *Courtesy Fortean Picture Library.*

were not recognizable but later they were. Stead wrote: "I (repeatedly) sent friends to Mr. Boursnell giving him no information as to who they were, nor telling him anything as to the identity of the person's deceased friend or relative whose portrait they wished to secure, and time and again when the negative was developed, the portrait would appear in the background, or sometimes in front of the sitter."

In 1903, the Spiritualists of London presented Boursnell with a testimonial signed by a hundred representative Spiritualists together with a purse of gold, to show their high esteem of him and his work. The walls of the Psychological Society, where the presentation took place, were hung with three hundred chosen photographs of spirit "extras" taken by Boursnell.

Sources:

Awtry-Smith, Marilyn: *"They" Paved the Way*. New York: Spiritualism & More, nd

Doyle, Sir Arthur Conan: *The History of Spiritualism*. New York: Doran, 1926

BRITISH COLLEGE OF PSYCHIC SCIENCE

Founded by **James Hewat McKenzie** in London in 1920, the British College of Psychic Science (BCPS) attempted to emulate the French **Institut Métapsychique International** in Paris. After McKenzie's death in 1929, his wife took over the running of the college. A little over a year later she relinquished control to Mrs. Philip Champion de Crespigny, daughter of the Rt. Hon. Sir Astley Cooper-Key. Mrs. De Crespigny was the author of more than twenty novels and a prolific writer on **metaphysical** subjects. One of her novels, *The Dark Sea*, was about **direct voice** phenomena and another, *The Mark*, was on **reincarnation**.

The BCPS merged with the International Institute for Psychical Research in December,

1938, to form the Institute for Experimental Metaphysics. This organization was later replaced by the **College of Psychic Studies**. A quarterly journal, titled *Psychic Science*, was published until 1945. The aims of the college were to scientifically study **mediums** and **mediumship** and to collect evidence of survival after bodily death.

Sources:

Fodor, Nandor: *Encyclopedia of Psychic Science*. London: Arthurs Press, 1933

Guiley, Rosemary Ellen: *The Encyclopedia of Ghosts and Spirits*. New York: Facts On File, 1992

BRITISH NATIONAL ASSOCIATION OF SPIRITUALISTS

The British National Association of **Spiritualists** (BNAS) was established in 1873, mainly through the efforts of Dawson Rogers. Centered in the London area, the group followed the defunct **Association of Progressive Spiritualists of Great Britain**, which failed as a national association. Its first meeting was held April 16, 1874, under the chairmanship of S. C. Hall. The association's research committee investigated **mediums**, including **William Eglinton**, **Frank Herne**, and **Charles Williams**.

Although BNAS struggled valiantly to be the official national organization, the majority of Spiritualists never accepted it as such. In 1882, the association changed its name to The Central Association of Spiritualists. Then in 1883, it reconstituted as the London Spiritual Alliance, serving the local area. It was not until 1902 that a true national organization came into being, with the **Spiritualists National Union** Ltd.

Sources:

Fodor, Nandor: *Encyclopedia of Psychic Science*. London: Arthurs Press, 1933

Nelson, Geoffery K.: *Man, Myth & Magic: Spiritualism*. London: BPC Publishing, 1970

BRITTEN, EMMA FLOYD HARDINGE (1823–1899)

Known among **Spiritualists** as "The Silver-Tongued Lecturer," Emma Hardinge Britten was a **medium**, writer, and lecturer. She was the daughter of a sailor, Captain Floyd, and as a child she showed gifts of music and elocution. As a young woman she worked under contract by a theatrical company and by the age of thirty-four, she traveled to America to play the part of Mrs. Bracebridge in the Broadway play *The Tragedy Queen*. While in America, Britten experienced **séances** with Ada Hoyt and subsequently converted to Spiritualism. She went on to develop her own mediumistic powers and even sat publicly for the Society for the Diffusion of Spiritual Knowledge of New York.

In **trance**, Britten was the **channel** for Philip Smith, a crew member of the mail steamer *Pacific*. The *Pacific* was the ship on which Britten and her mother had originally traveled to America. They had gotten to know several members of the crew, including Smith. The **spirit** of Smith claimed that the ship had sunk on the high seas, saying, "My dear Emma, I have come to tell you that I am dead. The ship *Pacific* is lost, and all on board have perished; she and her crew will never be heard from more." When Britten disclosed this tragedy the owners of the vessel threatened to prosecute her. But it turned out that the facts presented by the spirit through Emma Britten were true; the *Pacific* had indeed sunk. This was one of the best attested cases of early spirit return.

Britten was adept at **automatic writing, healing, prophecy, psychometry**, and inspirational speaking. She gained an international reputation as a speaker. Her extemporaneous talks were delivered on subjects chosen by a member of the audience. In 1870, she married Dr. William Britten, a passionate Spiritualist, and joined him as a missionary for the religion. They travelled throughout the United States as well as Australia, New Zealand, Canada, and Britain, enthusing about Spiritualism. She was among the founders of the **Theosophical Society** in New

York in 1875. In 1887, she founded the Spiritualist magazine *Two Worlds* (which is still published today) and edited it for five years. According to Stemman she was also the founder, in 1890, of the **Spiritualists' National Union** in Britain. Her books include *Modern American Spiritualism* (1870), *Art Magic* (1876), *Ghost Land* (1876), *Nineteenth Century Miracles* (1884), and *Faith, Fact, and Fraud of Religious History* (1906).

Sources:

Awtry-Smith, Marilyn: *"They" Paved the Way*. New York: Spiritualism & More, nd

Fodor, Nandor: *Encyclopedia of Psychic Science*. London: Arthurs Press, 1933

Stemman, Roy: *The Supernatural: Spirits and Spirit Worlds*. London: Aldus, 1975

BROWN, MARGARET LUMLEY

Margaret Lumley Brown was born toward the end of the nineteenth century, in Northamptonshire, England. Her father was a squire who lost most of his money to a swindling lawyer. He was fascinated, if not obsessed, with pre–George III England and insisted on schooling Margaret and her sister from school books of that period. Her mother had little in common with her father but was completely dominated by him.

Her father died when Margaret was twelve and after debts had been settled she, her elder sister, and her mother moved into a small house. A great-aunt sent Margaret to boarding school but she soon left school to return to her mother's home. There she read voraciously and wrote articles and poems that were mostly rejected as fast as they were submitted for publication. She received three offers of marriage but she rejected all of them.

Her mother died when Margaret was twenty-two. She found herself with nothing but half an annuity from a great-aunt. It was 120 pounds per year, to be shared with her sister. She moved to London where she lived in various boarding houses and obtained and lost a variety of jobs. Eventually, after her sister returned from Europe,

the two settled into an apartment in Maida Vale where they lived for two years. In 1918, she lived for a while in a house near London's Marble Arch that was very **haunted**. From experiences she had there, she developed a strong sensitivity to place memories. In her later years she complained about being kept awake by the marching feet of the **Roman** Legions, outside the house where she was staying. It was built at an old Roman crossroads.

A variety of literary journals published Margaret's poetry and a collection of her poems was favorably reviewed. She developed an interest in the legend of **Atlantis**. She also felt that in a past life she had been a young boy during the 1745 Stuart rebellion, and also had a strong attraction to the Babylonian civilization and to the goddess Ishtar in particular. She tried, unsuccessfully, to make contact with "an **Occult** Community" and corresponded with the explorer Colonel P. H. Fawcett, who hoped to put her in touch with "one of the Great Lodges." Unfortunately Fawcett was lost in the Amazon jungle in 1925, before he could do so. He was searching for evidence of the lost Atlantis continent.

Margaret Lumley Brown continued her interest in the occult throughout her life and, in 1944, she joined the **Society of the Inner Light** and met its founder, **Dion Fortune**. Margaret's sister had recently died and Dion Fortune offered to let Margaret live at the society's headquarters in Queensborough Terrace, London. There Margaret acted as parlor maid and cook while enjoying the lessons, exercises, and rites of the society. It quickly became obvious that she had some natural **psychic** abilities. Dion Fortune was the Arch Pythoness of the Society, **channeling** information while in **trance**. It was, as she later said in spirit through Margaret Lumley Brown, "bringing through these messages from Masters and Entities as well as **inspirational** messages from the inner planes. It is entirely different from what is known as **Spiritualism**."

When Fortune died in 1946, Margaret was encouraged to develop her gifts and take over as

Arch Pythoness. She made contact with Dion Fortune's spirit and was coached by the deceased leader. Margaret's first major trance address was made at the society's Summer Solstice celebrations in June of 1946, in front of the whole Fraternity. From there she went from strength to strength, becoming affectionately known to the Fraternity as "MLB" or "Morgan," after Morgan Le Fay. Charles Fielding and Carr Collins, biographers of Dion Fortune, said of Margaret that she was "probably the finest medium and psychic of this century…She raised the arts of psychism and mediumship to an entirely new level and the high quality of communication that came through her has not been equaled."

In the early 1960s, the society underwent a change of direction with a greater emphasis placed on **Christianity**. By then Margaret Lumley Brown was in her seventies and her role as Pythoness diminished. She did, however, remain a member for the rest of her life. She died at the age of eighty-six.

Sources:

Knight, Gareth: *Dion Fortune & the Inner Light*. Loughborough: Thoth, 2000

Knight, Gareth: *Pythoness: the Life and Work of Margaret Lumley Brown*. Oceanside: Sun Chalice Books, 2000

BROWN, ROSEMARY (B. 1917)

For several decades Rosemary Brown received **spiritual** messages in the form of music from deceased composers. Brown's mother was supposed to have been a **psychic**. Brown claimed that since her childhood she has been in contact with such people as Chopin, Liszt, and Beethoven. Liszt (1811–1886) first came to her when she was seven years old;.she saw him only as a white-haired old man. It wasn't until ten years later that she saw a picture of Liszt and recognized him as that old man. All of these composers dictated new compositions to Brown, who dutifully copied them down.

In 1964, Brown had suffered injuries including broken ribs in an automobile accident. She spent a large part of her recuperation sitting at the piano. She had little formal training and at that time she had not played for at least twelve years, but suddenly she found herself playing. She claims she felt the spirit of Liszt guiding her hands. Liszt went on to introduce to her Bach, Beethoven, Berlioz, Brahms, Chopin, Debussy, Grieg, Monteverdi, Rachmaninov, Schubert, Schumann, and Stravinsky.

On April 14, 1970, CBS television's *Sixty Minutes* carried a segment on Rosemary Brown. The material that Brown produced impressed a number of notable musicians, including André Previn and Virgil Thomson. Previn stated that it would require someone with a great deal of musical knowledge and technique to fake that kind of music, though he added that he felt the quality of the compositions was far below the usual standards of the attributed composers. Others have acknowledged that the works are in the style of the claimed composers, but say they lack the quality of the masters. Some critics said that what they heard from Brown was simply reworkings of the composers' known works, but they admitted that it would take a person of considerable musical knowledge and ability to pull off such a feat. Brown did not have that ability. In fact, she had great difficulty playing the compositions she wrote down.

British composer Richard Rodney commented in *Time* magazine (July 6, 1970), "If she is a fake, she is a brilliant one and must have had years of training … I couldn't have faked the Beethoven."

As word spread about her **mediumship**, Brown started to give public performances. She received more than four hundred compositions from the various dead composers. She issued a recording of some of the works in 1970, under the title *Rosemary Brown's Music*. She also authored three books: *Unfinished Symphonies*, *Immortals By My Side*, and *Look Beyond Today*.

Sources:

Brown, Rosemary: *Unfinished Symphonies: Voices from the Beyond*. New York: William Morrow, 1971

Fishley, Margaret: *The Supernatural*. London: Aldus 1976

Rosemary Brown, an automatic composer, works on a piece inspired by Chopin. *Courtesy Fortean Picture Library.*

Guiley, Rosemary Ellen: *The Encyclopedia of Ghosts and Spirits*. New York: Facts On File, 1992

Litvag, Irving: *Singer In the Shadows: The Strange Story of Patience Worth*. New York: Macmillan, 1972

BROWNE, SYLVIA
(B. 1936)

Born Sylvia Shoemaker in Kansas City in 1936, Browne claims to have exhibited **psychic** ability from the age of three. She was raised a Roman Catholic but was always interested in the religious backgrounds of her extended family, including Episcopalian, Lutheran, and Jewish faiths. She claims that Ada Coil, her maternal grandmother, was a respected **healer** and counselor. Browne taught in Catholic schools for eighteen years.

In 1964, Browne moved to California. Nine years later she began her professional career as a psychic. On May 8, 1973, Browne held a small **séance** in her home, aided by her **spirit guide** Francine. Within a year she had attracted enough followers that she formed an incorporated business under the name The Nirvana Foundation for Psychic Research. In April 1986, the name was changed to Society of Novus Spiritus, based on Christian Gnostic theology.

Browne's philosophy of life is based on a belief in **reincarnation**, which she investigates through **hypnosis**, **past life regression**, and deep **trance channeling**. She diagnoses health problems and communicates with the dead. Her books have included *Journey of the Soul*, *Conversation With the Other Side*, *Astrology Through the Eyes of a Psychic*, and *Past Lives; Future Healing*.

Browne has appeared on many popular television talk shows. On national television, Browne agreed to take the James Randi challenge not once but three times. The challenge awards one million dollars to whoever can show, under observing conditions, evidence of any paranormal, supernatural, or **occult** power or event. She procrastinated time and again, continuing to say she would take the test but not doing so. To date she has still not done so. She continues to have many ardent followers.

Sources:

SpiritSite.com: http://www.spiritsite.com

Sylvia Browne Homepage: http://www.sylvia.org

BUDDHISM

Gautama Siddhartha (ca. 563–483 BCE) was a young prince of northeast India. He was born among the Sakyas, a tribe of the Kshatriya warrior caste in what is now Nepal. His father ruled the Gautama clan and in later years Siddhartha himself became known as Gautama, though it was not his given name. His mother died shortly after his birth, and his father sheltered him from all contact with anything but pleasure and luxury. At age 29, Siddhartha became aware that most people did not share this priveledged life experience, and that pain and suffering were everywhere. On this realization, Siddhartha renounced his home and family and set out to seek the "supreme peace of Nirvana." He had two Brahmin religious teachers, but became dissatisfied and looked elsewhere. He tried many practices, including extreme asceticism, before finally finding **meditation**.

It is said that enlightenment came to him as he sat under a *boddhi* tree, or Tree of Wisdom. This enlightenment was the realization of four basic truths, usually referred to as the "Four Noble Truths:" Life entails dissatisfaction (pain); dissatisfaction is a result of clinging and craving; there is an end to all dissatisfaction; the way to the end of dissatisfaction is the path. In turn "the Path," or "the Eightfold Path," is Wisdom (right

A Buddhist monk receives offerings in the cave-enclosed temple of Wat Suwan Kuha in Phuket, Thailand. *Courtesy Fortean Picture Library.*

view; right thought), Morality (right speech, right action, right livelihood) and Meditation (right effort, right mindfulness, right concentration). Furthermore, he determined that the cause of all the suffering in the world, and of the endless series or birth and rebirth, was due to selfish craving and desire. If this could be extinguished, he reasoned, one could achieve freedom from the Wheel of Life and the never-ending suffering associated with it. In discovering this, Siddhartha became *Buddha*, or "the Enlightened One."

For the next 45 years, Buddha wandered the countryside teaching what he had learned. He organized a community of monks known as the *sangha* to continue his teachings after his death. They preached "The Word," known as the *Dharma*. It was not until sixty years after his death, that Buddha's teachings were set down in writing. These teachings became known as the *Sutras* (from the Sanskrit meaning "thread"). Buddhism's simple formula is: "I take refuge in the Buddha; I take refuge in the Dharma; I take refuge in the Sangha"… the Buddha, the Teaching, and the Order. There is no priesthood and there are no other rites or creeds. All that the teacher can do is set the listener on the path by example and precept.

Buddhism is today the religion of Burma, Thailand, Cambodia, Laos, Sri Lanka, Tibet, half of Japan, much of China, and is found in many other countries around the world. It has a large following in the United States, where there are now more Buddhists than can be found in India.

Sources:

Bechert, H. and R. Gombrich: *The World of Buddhism*. London: Thames & Hudson, 1984

Buckland, Raymond: *Signs, Symbols & Omens*. St. Paul: Llewellyn, 2003

Fields, Rick: *How the Swans Came to the Lake*. Boston: Shambhala, 1981

Gach, Gary: *The Complete Idiot's Guide to Understanding Buddhism*. Indianapolis: Alpha, 2002

Snelling, John: *Elements of Buddhism*. Shaftsbury: Element Books, 1990

BURROUGHS, HUGH GORDON

Author of the **Spiritualist** classic *Becoming a Spiritualist*, which sets forth some of the teachings leading to the advancement of the individual on the path toward realization. It is considered to be one of the best books on the subject. Burroughs was himself a **medium** whose **spirit guide** was named Father Murphy.

Sources:

Burroughs, H. Gordon: *Becoming a Spiritualist*. Lily Dale: NSAC, 1962

C

CABINET

The enclosed space in which a **Spiritualist** medium works is known as the cabinet. This can be anything from a carefully constructed wooden structure (as was used by the **Davenport Brothers**) to a simple curtained-off corner of a room. Most mediums favor the latter. According to **mediums**, the cabinet is necessary in order to condense the psychic energy needed for séance room manifestations. **Hereward Carrington** compared it to a battery cell that could be charged. The medium usually sits outside the cabinet, though some few do sit inside. The curtains may be dark or light in color; it seems to make no difference.

Some mediums, such as **William Stainton Moses**, and **Daniel Dunglas Home**, never used a cabinet. **Eusapia Paladino** was typical of those who, although they had a cabinet, sat outside it; about twelve inches away from the material of the cabinet. **Materializations**—such as a hand—emerged from the cabinet behind her. Sir **Arthur Conan Doyle** described the medium **Eva C.** using a cabinet that was "a small space shut in by curtains at the back and sides and top, but open in front."

When **Harry Houdini** was investigating the medium **Mina Crandon**, he designed a special

cabinet in which she could sit with only her head and hands visible. The second time this cabinet was used, Mina Crandon's spirit guide, Walter, accused Houdini of placing incriminating evidence inside the cabinet, to be discovered after the séance. This was found to be a folding ruler. Houdini denied the charge and in turn accused Mina of planning to use the ruler to manipulate a small box. After Houdini's death in 1926, an assistant of his confessed that he had placed the ruler there, on Houdini's instructions.

The Davenport Brothers had a special cabinet made with three doors at the front and a bench inside, running the full length of the cabinet. The center door had a small diamond-shaped opening covered by a curtain, through which various phenomena could manifest. The Davenport Brothers performed at theaters and would allow audience members to examine the cabinet before the start of their performance. They would then sit astride the bench, facing one another, where they were securely tied so that they could not move. Within seconds of the doors being closed, **rappings**, musical sounds, and a wide variety of phenomena occurred. At the end of the show they were discovered still tightly bound.

Bill Grant, director of the Findhorn Community in 1999. *Courtesy Fortean Picture Library.*

Sources:

Doyle, Sir Arthur Conan: *The History of Spiritualism*. New York: Doran, 1926

Shepard, Leslie A: *Encyclopedia of Occultism & Parapsychology*. New York: Avon Books, 1978

Stemman, Roy: *The Supernatural: Spirits and Spirit Worlds*. London: Aldus, 1975

CADDY, PETER AND EILEEN

Many gardeners claim that they have seen nature **spirits** among their flowers and vegetables. In the 1960s, Peter Caddy founded a community known as Findhorn, on the barren, windswept coast of Inverness, Scotland. When Peter Caddy and his wife Eileen started to work the area it was a truly inhospitable place, with sandy soil and sparse desertlike life. But in a few years the Caddys and some others who joined them were producing huge vegetables (42-pound cabbages and 60-pound broccoli plants), beautiful flowers, 21 types of fruit, 42 herbs, and a total of 65 different vegetables. They said their work prospered through love, and it was always acknowledged that their achievements were due to the help of the spirits of the land: the **fairies** and elves.

Prior to forming Findhorn, Peter and Eileen Caddy and their friend Dorothy Maclean all followed disciplined spiritual paths for many years. They first went to northeast Scotland in 1957 to manage the run-down Cluny Hill Hotel in the town of Forres. This they did with remarkable success. Eileen received guidance in her **meditations** from an inner divine source she called "the still small voice within." Peter ran the hotel according to this guidance, following to the letter

Eileen Caddy, founder of the Findhorn Community in Scotland, which is based on the values of planetary service, co-creation with nature and attunement to the divinity within all beings. *Courtesy Fortean Picture Library.*

the instructions of the "voice" in complete faith. In this unorthodox way, Cluny Hill swiftly became a thriving and successful four-star hotel. However, after several years Peter and Eileen were released from employment. With nowhere to go and little money, they moved with their three young sons and Dorothy to a trailer in the nearby seaside village of Findhorn.

Trying to feed a family of six with small unemployment benefits, Peter decided to start growing vegetables, despite the sandy, dry, and inhospitable soil of the area. Dorothy discovered she was able to intuitively contact the spirits of plants—the *devas*—who gave her instructions on how to make the most of their fledgling garden. Peter translated this guidance into action and drew from the barren sandy soil of the Findhorn

Bay Trailer Park huge plants, herbs, and flowers of dozens of kinds, most famously the now-legendary 40-pound cabbages. Word spread, horticultural experts came and were stunned, and the garden at Findhorn became famous. Other people came to join the Caddys and Dorothy in their work and soon the original group of six grew into a small community.

Dorothy published a book which helped spread word of this strange but wonderful community. New community members came to live in trailers beside Peter's and Eileen's, and in specially built cedarwood bungalows that still house guests and workshop participants today. In the late 1960s, the Park Sanctuary and the Community Centre were built. The community still uses the facilities for meals and meetings.

In 1972, the community was formally registered as a Scottish Charity under the name The Findhorn Foundation. In the 1970s and 1980s, Findhorn grew to approximately 300 members. In 1975, the Foundation purchased Cluny Hill Hotel as a centre for its educational courses and for members' accommodation, renaming it Cluny Hill College. In the late 1970s, the Universal Hall centre for the arts was built by volunteer work. Its impressive stained glass facade housed a modern theatre and concert hall, a holistic café, dance and recording studios, and photographic and computer labs.

Throughout the 1970s and 1980s, the foundation continued to expand and published further volumes of Eileen's and Dorothy's guidance. These were translated into many languages. Dorothy's autobiography, *To Hear the Angels Sing*, was published in 1980. In 1982, the Foundation bought the Findhorn Bay Trailer Park. Neighboring Cullerne House, whose gardens became the centre of organic vegetable production, was also acquired in the 1980s along with Drumduan House in Forres, where community members established the Moray Steiner School. Eileen's autobiography, *Flight Into Freedom*, was published in 1989.

Today the Findhorn Foundation is the central educational and organizational heart of a widely diversified community of several hundred people spanning dozens of holistic businesses and initiatives. Community members are linked by a shared positive vision for humanity and the earth and a commitment to the deep and practical nondoctrinal spirituality established in the Findhorn Community by its founders. Eileen Caddy still lives in the Findhorn Community. Dorothy Maclean now lives in North America and leads workshops around the world. She visits Findhorn almost every year. Peter Caddy left the Community in 1979 to work internationally, but returned regularly until his death in Germany in 1994. Peter's autobiography, *In Perfect Timing*, was published in 1997.

Sources:

Buckland, Raymond: *Wicca For One*. New York: Citadel, 2004

The Findhorn Foundation: http://www.findhorn.org

CAHAGNET, ALPHONSE (1809–1885)

Cahagnet was a cabinet maker who became fascinated with **mesmerism** and Spiritualism. His book *The Celestial Telegraph*, originally titled *Magnétisme Arcanes de la vie future dévoilé* in three parts. The first part appeared in 1848, the second part in 1849, and the third part in 1851. In *Modern Spiritualism*, **Frank Podmore** said of Cahagnet's work, "In the whole literature of **Spiritualism** I know of no records of the kind which reach a higher evidential standard, nor any in which the writer's good faith and intelligence are alike so conspicuous."

The first volume included a summary of his experiments with eight somnambulistic subjects and **spirit** communications from thirty-six entities who claimed to have lived up to 200 years prior to that time. They furnished detailed descriptions of the afterlife and the spirit spheres.

The second volume covered a series of **séances** and included testimonies of sitters, many of whom were extremely skeptical at first. The **medium** at these sittings was France's first Spiritualist medium, **Adèle Maginot**. She gave detailed descriptions of deceased and of still-living people known to the sitters. Cahagnet got the sitters to sign a statement as to what was true and what was not, after the séance. He went on to write *The Sanctuary of Spiritualism* (1850), *Encyclopedia of Magnetic Spiritualism* (1861), and *The Therapeutics of Magnetism and Somnambulism* (1883).

Sources:

Fodor, Nandor: *Encyclopedia of Psychic Science*. London: Arthurs Press, 1933

Podmore, Frank: *Modern Spiritualism*. London: 1902; reprinted as *Mediums of the Nineteenth Century*. New York: University Books, 1963

CAMP CHESTERFIELD

Camp Chesterfield was a **Spiritualist** community run by the Indiana Association of Spiritualists. It was established in 1891 and began offering educational programs in 1933.

In 1843, Dr. John Westerfield began promoting speakers on **clairvoyance**, **healing**, **trance**, **spirit** contact, and phrenology, at his newly built Union Hall, in Anderson, Indiana. In 1855, he and his wife Mary Ellen lost their only child, John, Jr., at the age of 14. Westerfield and his wife turned to Spiritualism to find solace and, working with **mediums**, made contact with their deceased son. In 1883, the Westerfields and some friends visited a new Spiritualist camp named Frazier's Grove, near Vicksburg, Michigan. The visit inspired them to found the Indiana Association of Spiritualists in 1886. They then started looking for a suitable location to have their own Spiritualist camp.

A grove meeting was held on the banks of the White River in 1890, on land owned by Carroll and Emily Bronnenberg. The following year Camp Chesterfield was opened on that site. The Indiana Association of Spiritualists purchased the land from the Bronnenbergs.

Sources:
Camp Chesterfield: http://www.campchesterfield.net

CAMP EDGEWOOD

Organized in 1898 and incorporated in 1899, Camp Edgewood is a **Spiritualist** center located on Surprise Lake, near Tacoma, Washington. The campgrounds were purchased in 1903, and an auditorium was built by 1927. The camp was extensively refurbished in 2004. The old hotel became the new **Healing** Center, with bedrooms on the second floor. The Spirit Center has a **séance** room in addition to a large classroom for various workshops and development classes. There is also a chapel, gazebo, and rose garden. The original bell is still rung to announce services. Cabins and homes cover a ten-acre area.

Sources:
The National Spiritualist Summit. Glendale: NSAC, Number 949; September 2004

CAMP MEETINGS

Early gatherings of **Spiritualists** were often called camp meetings, taking place on the shores of a lake or some other rural place. They later came to be called assemblies. The first camp meetings took place at Lake Pleasant, Massachusetts. Originally a gathering of tents, these meetings later grew to include 500 cottages, a grocery store, hotel, and refreshment stands. Such gatherings would often last throughout the summer with **mediums** and lecturers—many of them prominent—becoming temporary residents on the site. Onset, Massachusetts, was another early camp meeting place as was **Lily Dale**, New York, on the shores of Lake Cassadaga.

Small camp meetings first appeared in the 1850s, with low attendance and lasting only a few days. These gradually grew into the larger gatherings that lasted all summer long and attracted thousands. As they grew and became regular events, cottages were built to replace tents, and other amenities were added. There was generally a festive attitude though great attention was paid to the speakers and mediums.

Although Lake Pleasant was the largest of the early gatherings, the Cassadaga Lake Free Assembly—later renamed Lily Dale—became the most popular. It was established in 1879, in Chautauqua County, New York. By 1893, it had 215 cottages with approximately forty families living there year round. In 1888, the United States Postal Service installed a post office there. It currently covers 160 acres and is the largest and most active of such communities. In 1894, the Southern **Cassadaga Spiritualist Camp** Meeting Association was established in Florida, as a counterpart to the New York assembly. On the west coast, the **Harmony Grove Spiritualist Camp** Meeting Association was formed and incorporated in San Diego in 1896. It still operates today.

Sources:
Buckland, Raymond: *Buckland's Book of Spirit Communications.* St. Paul: Llewellyn, 2004

Guthrie, John J. Jr.; Phillip Charles Lucas; and Gary Monroe (eds): *Cassadaga: the South's Oldest Spiritualist Community*. University Press of Florida, 2000

CAMPBELL BROTHERS: ALLEN B. CAMPBELL (1833–1919) AND CHARLES SHOURDS (D. 1926)

Allen Campbell was born in England in 1833. He emigrated to the United States where he met Charles Shourds. Together they termed themselves the "Campbell Brothers." They were fast friends and were import/export traders and world travelers who ran a business in Atlantic City, New Jersey. By the late 1890s, they had also made their mark as **Spiritualists** and producers of some of the most amazing **spirit** paintings.

The Cassadagan, a monthly newspaper published in Meadeville, Pennsylvania, stated in the July 17, 1894 issue that Allen Campbell was a medium through whom beautiful art productions were obtained, and that he was kept busy with engagements. Charles Shourds was mentioned in the same issue as giving two **materialization** séances per week. The first mention of the two men working together as a team was made seven years later, in 1897.

The Campbell Brothers produced spirit paintings in much the same way that the **Bangs Sisters** did, never working in complete darkness. Another of their phenomena was the production of messages from a typewriter. A Williams typewriter was placed inside a cabinet with **slates**, porcelain, paper, pencils, and cardboard. Both **mediums** and all sitters were outside the **cabinet**, and sat with joined hands. The typed messages came out of the cabinet on folded paper. The messages were read and whoever claimed them, received them. At one sitting more than sixty messages were distributed, with details pertinent to the individual sitters. In addition to the typewritten notes, there was beautifully painted porcelain (such as an exquisite miniature of the actor Edwin Booth), and messages and drawings on slates.

Like the Bangs Sisters, the Campbell Brothers were best known for their precipitated paintings. The examined blank canvas were be placed on a table with oil paints in a receptacle underneath the table, and all was then covered with a black cloth. The mediums and sitters would join hands or place their hands down on the table. When the cover was lifted there would be a finished painting, the like of which would take a professional artist many days to produce. One of the most impressive paintings (which may be seen today in the parlor of the **Maplewood Hotel** at **Lily Dale Assembly**, Lily Dale, New York) is the life-size portrait of Allen Campbell's spirit guide Azur. It was done on June 15, 1898, on a canvas measuring forty inches by sixty inches and was produced in front of a number of witnesses. Each sitter in turn sat with Allen Campbell inside the cabinet while the painting was being produced. Every time the curtain was drawn back to allow a change of sitter, it was observed that a little more of the painting had developed. A group of witnesses stated that when the finished painting was finally brought out (after one hour and thirty minutes) a six-pointed star that was not originally there slowly materialized at the back of Azur's head.

Allen Campbell died in Atlantic City in 1919. Charles Shourds died in Lily Dale, New York, in 1926. The combined ashes of both men were spread in the Atlantic Ocean, off the beaches of Atlantic City.

Sources:

Nagy, Ron: *Precipitated Spirit Paintings: Beyond the Shadow of Doubt*. Lakeville: Galde Press, 2005

Caodaism *see* **Vietnamese Spiritualism**

CARINGTON, WALTER WHATELEY (1884–1947)

Born Walter Whateley Smith, Carington changed his name in 1933 for family reasons. He was the author of a number of books on **Spiritualism** and **telepathy**. He founded and edited the journal ***Psychic*** *Research Quarterly* and in 1920 he became a member of the council of the **Society for Psychical Research**. Along with **E. J. Dingwall**, he investigated the French medium Marthe Beraud. Prior to this, in 1916–17, he had investigated the medium **Gladys Osbourne Leonard** and the Irish medium Kathleen Goligher.

Carington's books included *The Foundations of Spiritualism* (1920) , *A Theory of the Mechanism of Survival* (1920), *The Death of Materialism* (1932), *Telepathy: An Outline of its Facts, Theory and Implications* (1945), and *Matter, Mind and Meaning* (1949; completed by H. H. Price).

Sources:

Shepard, Leslie A: *Encyclopedia of Occultism & Parapsychology*. New York: Avon Books, 1978

CARRINGTON, HEREWARD (1881–1959)

British-born Hereward Carrington's interest in **psychic** matters was aroused at the age of eighteen. His inclination was to disbelieve reported psychic phenomena, until he read *Essays in Psychical Research* by "Miss X" (London, 1899). ("Miss X" was A. Goodrich-Freer, the Marquess of Buze.) In 1900, at the age of nineteen, Carrington became a member of the **Society for Psychical Research** and from then on devoted his life to the study of the paranormal.

Carrington quickly established a reputation for his intellect and common sense. After Dr. **Richard Hodgson** died, and Professor **James Hervey Hyslop** took over the leadership of the Society for Psychical Research, Carrington became Hyslop's assistant, a position he maintained until 1908. He went to Naples to investigate the **medium Eusapia Paladino**, on whom he reported favorably, saying "genuine phenomena do occur and, that being the case, the question of their interpretation naturally looms before me. I think that not only is the **Spiritualist** hypothesis justified as a working theory, but it is, in fact, the only one capable of rationally explaining the facts."

Hereward Carrington, distinguished British psychical investigator and author. *Courtesy Fortean Picture Library.*

In 1921, Carrington was the American delegate at the first International Psychical Congress in Copenhagen. That same year he founded the **American Psychical Institute and Laboratory**. In 1924, he sat on the committee of *The Scientific American* for the investigation of the phenomena of Spiritualism.

In 1929, Carrington wrote *The Projection of the Astral Body* after becoming acquainted with Sylvan Muldoon, who was an expert on **astral projection**. Carrington wrote seventeen books in all.

Sources:

Buckland, Raymond and Hereward Carrington: *Amazing Secrets of the Psychic World*. New York: Parker Publishing, 1975

Fishley, Margaret: *The Supernatural*. London: Aldus, 1976

Shepard, Leslie A: *Encyclopedia of Occultism & Parapsychology*. New York: Avon Books, 1978

CARTER, DR. JEREMIAH F. (1814–1897)

Jeremiah F. Carter was born in Franklin City, New Hampshire, in February 1814. On July 6, 1836, in Laona, New York, he married Joan Bull (1813–1889) and they had four children: Dexter, Ellen, Wesley, and William.

In the 1840s, a **mesmerist** from Vermont, Dr. Moran, was invited by William Johnson to lecture in Laona. Johnson was the son of a minister and the father of Marion Skidmore, who became a leading **Spiritualist**. Carter had been having medical problems and hoped to be treated by Moran, but Moran left the area again before that could be arranged. Johnson suggested that they try Moran's techniques themselves and Carter quickly went into a **trance**. Through him, a spirit guide named Dr. Hedges spoke. Hedges had been well known as a skilled physician in the Chautauqua area before his death. Through Carter, Hedges gave messages to various people and also taught the art of laying-on of hands for **healing**. Carter became a very successful **spirit healer** and diagnostician. However, this activity brought him conspicuously before the public and as a consequence he and his family suffered greatly from persecution and ridicule by the local Orthodox Christian community. Carter remained firm in his beliefs and practices, and he and his wife made their home an asylum for the sick and afflicted.

Carter was one of the founding members of the **camp meetings** held in upper New York State that eventually led to the **Lily Dale Assembly**. He belonged to The **Religious Society of Free Thinkers**, started in 1855. In 1871, the members of the society began gathering for picnics at Alden's Grove on the shore of **Cassadaga** Lake. The grove was owned by **Willard Alden**, also a member of the society.

In the spring of 1877, Carter was sitting at home reading a newspaper when he heard a voice say to him, "Go to Alden's and arrange for a camp meeting." He tried to ignore the voice but it was insistent, repeating its command time and again. Carter went to bed and tried to shut out the spirit voice. He was unsuccessful and spent a sleepless night. The following morning he walked the six miles from his home to the Alden Farm, home of fellow Spiritualist Willard Alden. There they made plans for a big camp meeting to be held in Alden's land. They presented these plans to the membership at the annual meeting in June, 1877, and as a result a committee was formed to organize everything. The committee met at Jeremiah Carter's home and decided to hold a camp meeting that would start on Tuesday, September 11, and close on Sunday, September 16, 1877. This laid the groundwork for what would eventually grow into the Lily Dale Assembly. At that first camp meeting, Jeremiah Carter stood in the roadway and collected a fee of ten cents for each visitor. By the following year the camp season was extended to ten days and Carter and three others arranged for the grounds to be fenced in and saw to the building of the first cottage.

Jeremiah Carter died on August 7, 1897, at the Cassadaga Lake Free Assembly.

Sources:

Vogt, Paula M. and Joyce LaJudice: *Lily Dale Proud Beginnings: A Little Bit of History*. Lily Dale: Lily Dale Museum, 1984

CASSADAGA SPIRITUALIST CAMP

see also Lily Dale Assembly

The first notable meeting of **Spiritualists** in Florida took place in January 1893, at DeLeon Springs, Volusia County. It was organized by the National Spiritual and Liberal Association and a thousand people attended. Harrison D. Barrett, of Lily Dale, New York, called the meeting to order, welcomed everyone, and then introduced the main speaker, **medium** George P. Colby. Mrs. M. C. Thomas of Ohio was another speaker. The meeting was a huge success and the local residents and storekeepers invited the Spiritualists to set up a permanent site there for their winter gatherings. Considering it, a committee appointed by the Spiritualists' association also visited various other locations, such as Daytona, St. Petersburg, St. Augustine, Tampa, and Tarpon Springs. The board finally settled on the DeLeon Springs site—especially when John B. and H. H. Clough donated twenty-five acres of land to the association. However, George P. Colby entered the picture a little later to offer *his* land, which was six miles from DeLeon.

Colby had been living in Wisconsin twenty years earlier, when his **spirit guide** Seneca had advised him to travel to the south and establish a major Spiritualist center there. He went to Florida and in the course of his searching, fell into a **trance** and was led by spirit guides to the place he was to purchase. In 1880, he filed a homestead claim for seventy-five acres and was granted the land four years later. When he offered it to the National Spiritual and Liberal Association for their permanent home, mediums Emma J. Huff and Marion Skidmore went to view it. They played crucial roles in the founding of **Lily Dale Assembly**. On their recommendation, Colby's land was chosen for the site of the new Spiritualist community. A non-profit stock company was formed and named the Southern Cassadaga Spiritualist **Camp Meeting** Association (named for the lake at Lily Dale, New York).

On February 8, 1895, the very first meeting was held in Colby's home, and more than 100 people went to that three-day event. From there the community grew. In March of 1897 an auditorium was added to the collection of buildings that had sprung up. By 1900, the Webster Sanitarium had joined them, along with the Cassadaga Hotel.

According to John J. Guthrie, "By 1910 the Cassadaga Assembly had become much more than a series of tent meetings. Many fine cottages, as well as an auditorium, the pavilion, Harmony Hall, and other structures that accommodated the winter season, all stood as monuments to the efforts of early Cassadagans to fulfill Colby's dream of establishing a 'Spiritualist Mecca' in Florida."

Sources:
Guthrie, John J. Jr.; Phillip Charles Lucas; and Gary Monroe (eds): *Cassadaga: the South's Oldest Spiritualist Community*. University Press of Florida, 2000

CAYCE, EDGAR (1877–1945)

Known as "The Sleeping Prophet" from the fact that he delivered his **predictions** while in **trance**, Edgar Cayce is one of America's most famous **psychics** and seers. He was actually a photographer by profession, though when his psychic abilities developed fully they left him with little time to pursue that career.

Cayce was born on March 18, 1877, near Hopkinsville, Kentucky. With four sisters, he grew up surrounded by uncles, aunts, and other relatives, all of whom lived close by. From the family background and atmosphere, Cayce developed an early interest in the **Bible** which remained with him throughout his life. At the age of six, he told his parents that he was able to see visions and even talk with the **spirits** of dead relatives. His parents didn't believe him. At thirteen he had a vision of being visited by a goddess-type figure who asked him what he most wanted in life. He replied that he wanted to help others, and in particular he wanted to help sick children.

For a short period, Cayce demonstrated a special talent of being able to absorb knowledge by sleeping on books, papers, etc. He would sleep with his head on a book. On waking, he could relate everything about the material in the book, even repeating whole passages word for word.

When the family moved from their farm into the city of Hopkinsville, Cayce found employment in a bookstore. There he met and fell in love with Gertrude Evans. The two became engaged in March, 1897. For a short while he lived in Louisville, but returned to Hopkinsville by the end of 1899. He formed a business partnership with his father, an insurance agent. Cayce started traveling and selling insurance, supplementing this income with the sale of books and stationery. The salesman job ended when Cayce developed a severe case of laryngitis that lasted for months, despite attention from a number of doctors. Having to give up the insurance salesman job, he took a position as assistant to a photographer, where he wouldn't have to speak to anyone.

A traveling entertainer named Hart **hypnotized** Cayce and found that under hypnosis, the young man's voice could be normal. But when out of a trance, Cayce's laryngitis returned. Hart moved on but a local hypnotist named Al Layne took over. Cayce put himself into trance and had Layne give him suggestions. Layne asked Cayce what was wrong with his throat and Cayce responded with a full and detailed diagnosis. He further urged Layne to give the suggestion that the throat return to normal. When Cayce woke up, everyone was amazed to find that he spoke normally for the first time in almost a year. The date was March 31, 1901. This was Cayce's first diagnosis whilst in trance.

Al Layne, the hypnotist, had himself long been bothered with a stomach problem. Inspired by Cayce's recovery, he prevailed upon the young man to go into trance and diagnose for him. Reluctantly Cayce did so, and prescribed a dietary and exercise regimen to solve Layne's problem. Within a week it had worked; again after a number of doctors had been unsuccessful.

Although Cayce wanted to be left alone to be a photographer and raise a family, he reluctantly gave in to pressure from his father and others, and continued to give trance **readings** for people in need. He cured a five-year-old girl named Aime Dietrich who had been seriously ill for three years. Cayce did not understand how his abilities worked. He had no medical knowledge and frequently, on waking, did not remember what he had said while asleep. But the cures continued.

On June 17, 1903, he and Gertrude got married and moved to Bowling Green, Kentucky, where he opened a photographic studio. Later a disastrous fire wiped out everything and he, his wife and his son returned to Hopkinsville. Cayce began an association with Dr. Wesley Ketchum, a homeopath. This led to Dr. Ketchum reading a paper about Cayce's abilities to the American Society of Clinical Research. *The New York Times* picked up on this and featured an article titled, "Illiterate man becomes doctor when hypnotized." Soon Cayce was swamped with readings.

He had earlier found that the person for whom he was reading did not have to be physically present. All that was needed was the name and location of the person and Cayce could perform an accurate reading.

In the late summer of 1911, Gertrude contracted tuberculosis and nearly died. Cayce's diagnosis and recommendation of revolutionary treatment brought about her complete recovery by the end of the year. He was able to perform a similar service for his son Hugh Lynn some time later. By this time, the family had moved to Selma and Cayce had a new photographic studio. Hugh was playing with flash powder when it exploded in his face. Doctors said that he had severely burned his eyes and recommended removing one of them. Cayce thought otherwise and prescribed from trance for his son. Two weeks later Hugh could see again.

As Cayce's reputation grew, so did a problem with treating people. Doctors were reluctant to follow the diagnoses that the "Sleeping Prophet" recommended. Cayce began to dream of having a hospital fully staffed with doctors and nurses working solely on the cases he prescribed. He attempted to use his psychic talents to make the money to establish such a hospital, but very quickly realized that he could not use his gift for making money.

In 1923, he hired Gladys Davis as his secretary. She wrote down all the information he produced in his readings. His wife Gertrude was by this time conducting the readings and asking him the necessary questions. About this time a man who had received successful readings for two of his nieces asked Cayce for a "**horoscope** reading." In the course of it, Cayce made mention of a **past life** that the man had once had. This opened the door to a whole new field of psychic investigation, however Cayce's personal attachment to Christianity (he read the Bible and taught Sunday school) made him uneasy. Re-reading the Bible in its entirety, he finally realized that the concept of **reincarnation** was not incompatible with any religion and actually followed his own ideas of what it meant to be a good Christian. So began what became known as the "Life Readings;" trance readings that looked at a person's past lives and the relationship to the present life. In time this further expanded into mental and spiritual counseling, philosophy, **dream** interpretation, and so on.

Finally, and very reluctantly, Cayce had to give up his photographic career for lack of time. He began to accept donations toward the hospital he still wanted to build. Readings that he gave indicated that it needed to be established at Virginia Beach, Virginia. In September of 1925, the Cayce family moved with Gladys Davis to that location. Two years later, the Association of National Investigators was formed to research the information from Cayce's readings, now rapidly growing in volume.

The Edgar Cayce Hospital opened on November 11, 1928. Patients came from all over the country and were diagnosed and prescribed for by Cayce. They were then treated by the staff of doctors, nurses, and therapists.

The Depression forced the hospital to close in 1931 when financial backing was lost, but later that same year the **Association for Research and Enlightenment** was formed as a research body for all the information in the readings.

Cayce continued to develop psychically, picking up information in the waking state as well as when in trance, seeing **auras** around people and even diagnosing from these. With the onset of World War II, Cayce was inundated with requests for readings and despite warnings about his own health (given from his own readings), he began to grow weak from overwork. His readings continuously told him to rest, but he felt obliged to keep going. He finally collapsed in 1944. His last reading was for himself, in September of that year, when he was told that he must rest until either he got better or he died. Shorty after, he had a stroke and became partially paralyzed. He died on January 3, 1945. Within three months, Gertrude also died.

Copies of more than 14,000 case histories of Cayce's readings, including all follow-up reports received from the individuals concerned, are available for reference at the Association for Research and Enlightenment, Inc. (ARE), in Virginia Beach. This material represents the most massive collection of psychic information ever obtained from a single source. The ARE organization has grown from a few hundred supporters in 1945 to one which today is worldwide.

Countless individuals have been touched by the life work of this man who was raised a simple farm boy and yet became one of the most versatile and credible psychics the world has ever known. He has been called "the father of holistic medicine." In history, the Cayce readings gave insights into Judaism that were verified a decade after his death. In world affairs, he saw the collapse of communism nearly fifty years before it happened. Even in the field of physics, a professor and fellow of the American Physical Society theorized a connection between the elementary particle theory and the way in which Edgar Cayce received his information. Repeatedly, science and history have validated concepts and ideas explored in Edgar Cayce's psychic information.

Sources:
Buckland, Raymond: *The Fortune–Telling Book: The Encyclopedia of Divination and Soothsaying.* Detroit: Visible Ink Press, 2004

Cayce, Hugh Lynn: *Venture Inward.* New York: Paperback Library, 1969

Edgar Cayce Homepage: http://www.edgarcayce.org

Langley, Noel: *Edgar Cayce on Reincarnation.* New York: Paperback Library, 1967

Stearn, Jess: *Edgar Cayce: The Sleeping Prophet.* New York: Doubleday, 1967

Sugrue, Thomas: *There Is a River: The Story of Edgar Cayce.* New York: Dell, 1970

CENTER FOR SPIRITUALIST STUDIES

The Center for Spiritualist Studies is an educational arm of the **National Spiritualist Association of Churches**, along with the **Morris Pratt**

Institute. It is headquartered at **Lily Dale**, New York, in a newly renovated building. The college is accredited and offers a wide variety of courses for members and students. It has recently changed its name to the **College of Spiritualist Studies**.

CHAIR TEST

The chair test was devised by Dutch **parapsychologist** Professor **Wilhelm H.C. Tenhaeff** at the University of Utrecht. Professor Tenhaeff set up an Institute of Parapsychology at the university, similar to the one founded by Dr. **Joseph Banks Rhine** at Duke University, and the famous **psychic Gérard Croiset** of the Netherlands. The chair test required Croiset to describe, in detail, the future occupant of a randomly chosen chair in a lecture hall.

Seats for lectures could not be reserved and sometimes even the actual venue was not determined till close to the date of the lecture. The number of a chair in a lecture hall was chosen at random, days or even weeks ahead of the scheduling of a lecture. Anywhere from a few hours to several days before the lecture, Croiset was asked to describe the person who would occupy the chair on the specified date, including a number of personal details. These descriptions were very specific, often including hair and eye color, height, physique, age, dress, even marks on the body. Croiset's **predictions** were recorded, and the recording was placed in a sealed bag and locked away in a safe. At the lecture, the recording would be played back and the occupant of the chair asked to stand up and comment on Croiset's observations. Croiset showed incredible accuracy with this test and with many others. Occasionally Croiset was unable to get any information. On those occasions it turned out that the seat remained empty for the lecture. Sometimes he got very confusing images, which were later explained by the fact that more than one person used the chair.

The first such test was given in Amsterdam in October 1947, in front of the Dutch Society for **Psychical Research**. By 1951, experts from around the world had been invited to participate and to monitor the conditions, gradually improving the test to make it more severe. In 1961, Professor Tenhaeff published a scholarly collection of records of the tests in a 300-page book titled *De Voorschouw* (**Precognition**).

One of the cases is quoted by Pollack, in his book on Croiset. He calls it "Last Minute Ticket:"

On the afternoon of March 6, 1950, when nosing around for a story, Amsterdam journalist E.K. telephoned Gérard Croiset in Enschede asking for some concrete evidence of his powers, the news of which was then spreading over the Netherlands.

"Well, in two days," replied Croiset, "I am giving a chair test before the Utrecht chapter of the Society for Psychical Research. Please pick a chair number for then. Name any number you want."

"Row 7, third chair from the right," volunteered the Dutch journalist.

"All right," replied Croiset. "Please make a note of these impressions that I am now giving you. I see on this chair will sit a lady with gray hair. She has a slim figure and is a lean type. She likes to help people, but calls everything she does "Christian social work."

When these facts were checked under Dr. Tenhaeff's supervision on the evening of March 8, this particular chair was found to be occupied by a Protestant Sister of Mercy, Sister L.B., who, indeed, did Christian social work. Croiset's description of her was a direct hit. It couldn't possibly have fitted anyone else present.

Sister L.B. acknowledged the paragnost's description of her as being accurate. She said that she had almost stayed at home, and her choice of the seat was unpremeditated ... Investigator Tenhaeff's later checkup revealed:

"Sister L.B. was not a member of the Dutch Society for Psychical Research. It was purely accidental that she received an admission ticket as late as 5:40 pm on March 8. Croiset gave his information to journalist E.K. when the participants of the test had not yet received their invitations. Moreover, the person who gave Sister L.B. her ticket did not know any of the facts furnished by the paragnost."

Sources:

Pollack, Jack Harrison: *Croiset the Clairvoyant*. New York: Doubleday, 1964

Wilson, Colin: *The Supernatural: Mysterious Powers*. London: Aldus Books, 1975

CHAKRA

hakra is the name given to the seven **psychic** centers of the body connecting the physical body to the **etheric**. The chakras are linked with actual physical glands and are positioned at the gonads (the lumbar or base chakra), the adrenals (the second, spine chakra), the lyden (third, solar plexus chakra), the thymus (fourth, heart chakra), the thyroid (fifth, throat chakra), the pineal (sixth, **third eye** chakra), and the pituitary (seventh, crown chakra). The **Theosophists** regard the chakras as the sense organs of the ethereal body.

An energy travels through the body connecting these chakras. This energy is known as the *kundalini* force, sometimes referred to as the Serpent Power, from the fact that ancient Hindu mystics saw it as a coiled serpent at the base of the spine, waiting to uncoil and reach upward. Getting the kundalini power to flow through the chakras sets up a vibration, the increase of which can enhance psychic abilities. As the power flows, the chakras begin to open up, in successive order, and the individual achieves a sense of well-being and peace. The subconscious clears itself of the negative and undesired patterns of feelings and images that have been programmed throughout the lifetime. As the opening continues, the individual's awareness and perception of life flows

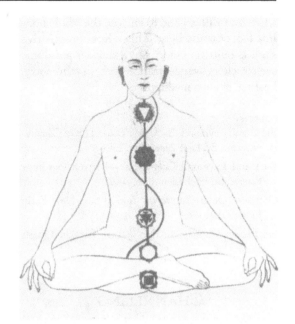

Image depicting the seven chakras, the psychic centers that connect the physical body to the etheric body. *Courtesy Fortean Picture Library.*

continually from within and a new vibrancy permeates the entire being.

Each of the chakras is associated with a color: the base chakra with red, spine with orange, solar plexus with yellow, heart with green, throat with blue, pineal gland with indigo, and the crown with violet. An exercise practiced by many **mediums** and psychics to "awaken the Serpent Power" is to imagine each of the chakras as a flower (traditionally a lotus blossom) and to see it immersed in its particular color. This is one method recommended by the English medium **Ivy Northage**. Starting with the base chakra, imagine a red-colored flower swirling around in a clockwise direction, gathering energy to itself as it swirls. It becomes a spinning ball, going faster and faster. After a while, imagine the swirling light moving upward to the second, or spine, chakra and changing color to orange. It spins there for a while and then continues on up the body, changing color for each of the different chakras. At the crown, the light will change from violet to a pure white and will expand to enclose the whole body in a ball of white light. This is how a protective shell is built up before any exercises are done, such as **clairvoyance**, **trance** work, **psychometry**, **healing**, or even **meditation**.

Sources:

Buckland, Raymond: *Buckland's Book of Spirit Communications*. St. Paul: Llewellyn, 2004

Buckland, Raymond: *Color Magic—Unleash Your Inner Powers*. St. Paul: Llewellyn, 2002

Garrison, Omar: *Tantra the Yoga of Sex*. New York: Julian Press, 1964

Leadbeater, Charles W.: *The Chakras*. London: Quest, 1972

CHANNELING

Although **mediums** are channeling information, they are not "channels" in the nomenclature of the New Age. Similarly, channels are not mediums. The differences are subtle but important.

Mediums are part of the world of **Spiritualism**. They are the intermediaries between the world of the living and the "other" world beyond death. They bridge the gap between those who are still alive and their deceased relatives and loved ones who have "crossed over." Usually, though not always, there is a direct relationship between the two personalities connected through the agencies of the medium. The medium may or may not go into **trance**. He or she may use **clairvoyance**, **clairaudience**, **clairsentience**, **direct voice**, or any one of a number of different ways to bring through the messages from the other side. The messages can, and usually do, come from a wide range of **spirits** of many different people who have lived before. The living receivers are often able to ask questions of the deceased and receive answers, advice, and confirmation of a continued existence.

Channels bring information from "entities" that may or may not have ever lived on this earth and are generally not related in any way to the receivers of the information. Each channel usually produces information from only one particular source, frequently delivered as a lecture. Some of these sources claim to originate from places such as ancient **Atlantis**, other planets, other worlds, or other universes. Information comes through the vocal cords of the channel, who is usually in trance and completely unaware of what is going on. The channel is the direct voice conduit for the entity who preaches to the audience. A medium usually works with a small, intimate group while a channel may speak in a large auditorium.

There are extant examples of some of the paraphernalia used by ancient **Egyptian** priests when claiming to channel messages from the Egyptian gods, for example, the mask worn when representing Anubis, the jackal-headed god. In the Mayan temples the priests played the part of gods, giving and relaying instructions, messages and advice to the people. In **Vodoun**, a possessed worshipper channels the deity, known as a *loa*. In modern Panchmuda, northwest of Calcutta, India, at the Temple of Manasa during the Snake Festival, the Serpent Mother takes possession of a worshipper, much as in Vodoun, and speaks through him or her.

Writers, musicians and artists have long composed through a process of channeling. Wolfgang Mozart heard music in his head and simply wrote down what he heard, verbatim. Many visual artists claim they work the same way, simply putting onto canvas what is processed through them.

"Seth" was an entity channeled by **Jane Roberts** (1929–1984). Seth defined itself as "an energy personality essence no longer focused in physical reality." It claimed various lifetimes on earth, stating that such lifetimes are actually occurring simultaneously; past, present, and future being all in existence at the same time. **Judy "Zebra" Knight**, another channeler, claimed to be the instrument for a character she called "Ramtha." He was supposed to have lived 35,000 years ago on the now lost continent of Lemuria. However, his speech patterns and mannerisms were remarkably like those of Judy Knight herself. **Jessica Lansing** channeled

"Michael," who said he was "of the mid-causal plane" and made up of a thousand fragments of an entity like himself. **Jach Pursel**'s "Lazaris" says that he has never been in human form; he is a "group form" living in another dimension. **Elizabeth Clare Prophet** channeled what she described as "ascended masters" no longer living on the physical plane. **Darryl Anka**'s "Bashar" says he is from the planet Essassani, 500 light years away. Interestingly, regardless of the sex of the channel, the entity that comes through always seems to be masculine.

Many of the channels bring "doom and gloom" **prophesies**, some claiming that the world will end in a certain period of time. Some, such as "Ramtha," appear extremely egotistical and strangely materialistic. Some have urged their followers to give away all their worldly goods or to sell them and donate the proceeds to the organization supporting the channel.

Although there are the charlatans and suspects among the channelers, most of the lectures that come through are positive, leading to a better standard of life. The listener should be prepared to decide for him- or herself what is right, rather than being told what to do.

In the same way, there are many mediums who are charlatans and also those who are self-deceived. From the very beginning of Spiritualism in the middle of the nineteenth century, there have been frauds who found it easy to prey on those who were bereaved. But—again as with channelers—just because there are fakes does not mean that all are fakes. There have been, and still are, excellent mediums who are above reproach. **John Edward** is probably the prime example today, doing a regular television program where he contacts the dead relatives of members of his studio audience.

Sources:

Bentine, Michael: *The Door Marked Summer*. London: Granada, 1981

Bentine, Michael: *Doors of the Mind*. London: Granada, 1984

Buckland, Raymond: *Buckland's Book of Spirit Communications*. St. Paul: Llewellyn, 2004

Cook, Mrs. Cecil: *How I Discovered My Mediumship*. Chicago: Lormar, 1919

Guiley, Rosemary Ellen: *Harper's Encyclopedia of Mystical & Paranormal Experience*. San Francisco: Harper SanFrancisco, 1991

Klimo, Jon: *Channeling: Investigations on Receiving Information from Paranormal Sources*. Los Angeles: Jeremy P. Tarcher, 1987

Roberts, Jane: *The Seth Material*. New Jersey: Prentice-Hall, 1970

Roberts, Jane: *Seth Speaks*. New Jersey: Prentice-Hall, 1972

CHAPMAN, GEORGE (B. 1921)

George Chapman, of Liverpool, England, became interested in **Spiritualism** after the death of his daughter in 1945. He received messages from different **mediums** that proved to him that life continued after death. He went on to study Spiritualism and became a medium and **healer**.

Chapman initially worked with the spirit of a Cree **Native American** healer named "Lone Star" and with "Chang," a Chinese surgeon. Both gave Chapman advice on medical problems. Very quickly, however, these two **spirits** moved back to let another come forward and work with Chapman. This was the spirit of the deceased eminent eye specialist and surgeon Dr. **William Lang** (1852–1937), who took control in 1947.

There are two types of healers: those who are directed by spirit and those who are controlled by a spirit. **Harry Edwards** is a good example of a healer directed by spirit. He works as himself but is directed by discarnate spirit helpers. Chapman is a controlled healer. He goes into **trance** and a spirit speaks through him, manipulating his arms and hands to perform necessary actions. Chapman's uttered words and actions are those of Dr. Lang.

When Lang takes over, Chapman's face becomes wrinkled and looks many years older than Chapman's actual age. Chapman also adopts a stooped stance that was characteristic of Lang when he was alive. The voice is a high-pitched, slightly quavery one, which old associates of Lang's say is his. Also, as he works, Chapman/Lang snaps his fingers when he needs surgical instruments passed to him, again typical of the late Dr. Lang. Yet Chapman and Lang never met. Chapman was only sixteen when Lang died and he had no knowledge of the doctor.

No actual surgical instruments are used. Chapman, as the "doctor," moves his hands over the patient and, in effect, mimes the actions of the surgery. The patient remains fully awake and fully clothed. After the operation Chapman goes through the motions of sewing up the incision. One patient claimed that she could feel every move made and that the stitching was very apparent to her. She said that although it was in no way painful, she could feel the flesh being drawn together. Throughout the operation Chapman's eyes remain tightly closed. Afterward he claims to remember nothing of what took place after Dr. Lang's arrival. Chapman operates a clinic in Aylesbury, Buckinghamshire, where many people have received permanent cures for their ailments.

Sources:

Buckland, Raymond: *Buckland's Book of Spirit Communications*. St. Paul: Llewellyn, 2004

Wilson, Colin: *The Supernatural: Healing Without Medicine*. London: Aldus Books, 1975

Ch'i

Ch'i (pronounced "chee") is the Chinese name for the "vital energy," or **psychic** energy, that flows through everything. All things in the physical world are endowed with Ch'i. Because it is forever flowing, it is often referred to as a "sea of Ch'i."

There are three basic foundations for Ch'i: It animates, it connects, and it moves everything through the cycles of life. Inanimate things also contain Ch'i—buildings are viewed as living bodies in the art of Feng Shui. Terah Kathryn Collins says, "We live in an interconnected web of life, where everything is related to every other thing.

Throw a pebble in a pond and watch the whole pond be affected by the ripples of one small stone. This gives a special importance to your neighborhood and community, because the Ch'i flowing through them is also flowing, relatively undiluted, through your home or workplace."

Viewing Ch'i as flowing not only through the living but also the deceased, there is an obvious connection between the here and the hereafter that must facilitate communication with the world of **spirit**. In that sense, **mediums** are utilizing Ch'i when they communicate with the deceased.

Sources:

Collins, Terah Kathryn: *The Western Guide to Feng Shui*. Carlsbad: Hay House, 1996

CHINA

China has a long history of spiritism. **J. M. Peebles** said, "English officials, American missionaries, mandarins and many of the Chinese literati (Confucians, Taoists and **Buddhist** believers alike) declare that **spiritism** in some form, and under some name, is the almost universal belief of China. It is generally denominated 'ancestral worship'." Dr. John Nevius said, "*Tu Sein* signifies a **spirit** in the body, and there are a class of familiar spirits supposed to dwell in the bodies of certain Chinese who became the **mediums** of communication with the unseen world. Individuals said to be possessed by these spirits are visited by multitudes, particularly those who have lost recently relatives by death, and wish to converse with them."

A large part of the communication is focused on casting out demons, since there is a widespread belief that demons surround the living at all times. There is an equally widespread belief that the living are surrounded by the spirits of the dead.

Meditation plays an important role, with the ancient Chinese method best exemplified in the Taoist teachings. **Divination** is also considered important and is very popular; the *I-Ching* being the most popular method.

Sources:

Nevius, John L.: *The Chinese*. Chicago: Revell, 1893

Peebles, J. M.: *The General Principles and the Standard Teachings of Spiritualism*. Mokelumne: Health Research, 1969

Spence, Lewis: *An Encyclopedia of Occultism*. London: Routledge, 1920

CHURCH OF THE NEW JERUSALEM, THE

The Church of the New Jerusalem was inspired by **Emanuel Swedenborg** (1688–1772). Swedenborg neither preached nor founded a church, but he gave a new interpretation of Scripture. The New Jerusalem Church was founded by a few disciples of his in 1784, including two Anglican clergymen who were especially instrumental in forming the church. They were Thomas Hartley (d. 1784), rector of Winwick, and John Clowes (1743–1831), vicar of St. John's, Manchester, England. Five prominent preachers adopted his teachings and, in spite of disagreements with Hartley and Clowes, this led to the formal organization of the New Jerusalem Church on May 7, 1787. It remains small but even today has branches all over the world.

In 1782, a society was formed in Manchester, for publishing Swedenborg's writings. In 1786, C. F. Nordenskiold formed the Philanthropic Xegetic Society in Sweden, with the purpose of collecting and publishing Swedenborg's writings. In 1875, the society of "Confessors of the New Church" was founded in Stockholm. In 1784, James Glen delivered lectures and circulated Swedenborg's works in Boston, Massachusetts and Philadelphia, Pennsylvania. Over the following decade a number of prominent men gave support to the teachings. The first society for worship was formed in Baltimore, Maryland in 1792. Other churches were established in Boston, Cincinnati, New York, and Philadelphia.

Sir **Arthur Conan Doyle** was very critical of the Church of the New Jerusalem, saying that it tried to separate Swedenborg from **Spiritualism** and thereby showed "a complete misapprehension of his gifts, and their true place in the general scheme of Nature."

Sources:

Doyle, Sir Arthur Conan: *The History of Spiritualism*. New York: Doran, 1926

Encyclopedia Britannica. Chicago: William Benton, 1964

The New Church: http://www.newchurch.org

CHURCHILL, SIR WINSTON LEONARD SPENCER (1874–1965)

Churchill was born on November 30, 1874, at Blenheim Palace, Oxfordshire, England. His father was Lord Randolph Churchill and his mother was Jeanette Jerome, an American. After private tutors, Churchill went on to school at Harrow before entering the Royal Military College at Sandhurst. He graduated in 1894, ranked eighth in a class of 150. He served as both soldier and journalist in various military conflicts, starting with the Spanish-American war in Cuba. His writing brought him some celebrity and in 1898 he wrote his first novel *Savrola*. In 1899, he resigned his commission and entered politics, where he eventually rose to be Prime Minister of Great Britain for the turbulent years of World War II.

Churchill's political career is well known but less known is his interest in **psychic** matters and the many incidents that occurred throughout his life. In 1940, when Churchill had just been selected as the new Prime Minister, he addressed the nation in a radio broadcast where he referred to Britain's "physical energy and psychic strength." In the middle of World War II he said, "Only faith in a life after death, in a brighter world, where dear ones will meet again—only that and the measured tramp of time can give consolation."

In his early years Churchill experienced **automatic writing**. As he described it, he had held a pencil "and written while others had touched my wrist or hand. I acted in exactly the same unconscious manner now." This referred to his escape from being a prisoner of the Boers in Pretoria, during the Boer War. He broke free of his captors and hid aboard a train, and then jumped off in unknown territory. Not knowing whether or not to trust the people in the Kaffir kraal he approached, he relied on his psychic instincts and went straight to one particular house. It turned out to be the only house in the whole area that was sympathetic to the British.

Baroness Asquith revealed that Churchill made a number of **predictions** in the 1920s and 1930s and that they had all come true. In 1925, Churchill saw a future with the H-bomb, radar, and the V1 and V2 German missiles. He said, "May there not be methods of using explosive energy more intense than anything yet discovered? Might not a bomb no bigger than an orange be found to possess a secret power to … concentrate the force of a thousand tons of cordite? Could not explosives … be guided automatically in flying machines by wireless or other rays, without a human pilot?"

Churchill made a habit of visiting anti-aircraft gun sites at night, during the height of the London blitz. Once he was at a site in Richmond, preparing to leave. Normally he sat on the left side of the car in which he traveled. This time, for no apparent reason, he walked around and got in on the right side. On the way back to London a bomb fell near the car. If he had been sitting in his usual seat the vehicle would undoubtedly have turned over, but with his extra weight on the far side it tipped up on two wheels but then righted itself again. He later said, "It appeared to me I was told I was meant to open the door on the other side and get in and sit there—and that's what I did."

One October he was dining at Downing Street when the air raid sirens sounded. He had a flash of inspiration. He later said that in his mind he saw the 25-foot-high plate glass window in the kitchen being blown apart. He summoned the butler and had all the staff taken to the shelter. Within minutes a bomb fell nearby, shattering the window, destroying the kitchen, and sending

Former British Prime Minister Winston Churchill is pictured in London on March 28, 1940. AP/Wide-World Photos.

huge shards of glass about the area. At the end of the war, in 1945, when he had been confident of re-election, he awoke from a deep sleep with the sudden conviction that he would not be continuing as Prime Minister. The next morning the election results confirmed that.

In his retirement, Churchill was working from a photograph and painting a portrait of his deceased father. Suddenly his father appeared, sitting in a nearby leather armchair. Churchill said that they had a good conversation, discussing politics and the changes that had occurred over the years.

Sources:

Churchill, Winston: *The Second World War* (6 vols.). Boston: Houghton Mifflin, 1948–1954

Leonard, Sue (ed): *Quest For the Unknown—Life Beyond Death*. Pleasantville: Reader's Digest, 1992

Ortzen, Tony: *The Psychic Life of Britain's Greatest Premier—Psychic News #3729*, December 2003. Stanstead: Psychic News Press, 2003

CIRCLE

Sitters at a **séance** invariably are seated in a circle, either around a table or with an open area in the center. Hence, séances are often referred to as "circles." A **Spiritualist** circle usually calls for a **medium** to be among the number. There can be any number of people at the sitting, but twelve is usually preferred. This circle is made up, as far as possible, of equal numbers of positive and negative energies. Although most females are sensitive and negative and most males positive and magnetic, there are exceptions, and energies do not necessarily indicate gender. Some circles are arranged with the negative energy on one side of the medium and the positive energy on the other. Circles are also sometimes arranged with the negative and positive energies alternating around the circle.

Janet Cyford (*The Ring of Chairs*) said, "The movement of energy in the **development circle** is clockwise. A ring of closed energy forms when we join with others and sit in a ring of chairs." The circle of people may hold hands or, if there is a table in the center, may rest their hands on the table with each touching his or her neighbor's hands. Usually the medium is included in the circle though sometimes the medium sits apart from the circle, either inside or in front of a **cabinet**.

Sources:

Cyford, Janet: *The Ring of Chairs: A Medium's Story*. Baltimore: Thirteen-O-Seven Press, 2000

Shepard, Leslie A: *Encyclopedia of Occultism & Parapsychology*. New York: Avon Books, 1978

CITY OF LIGHT, THE

The "City of Light" was the name given in 1903 to what later became the **Lily Dale Assembly**. When Theodore Alden demanded rent for the use of grounds that had previously been provided free by his late father **Willard Alden**, the **First Spiritualist Society of Laona** in New York purchased land for themselves alongside Lake **Cassadaga** in 1879. Mrs. Amelia Colby named the camp the Cassadaga Lake Free Assembly. In 1903, this name was changed to the City of Light. That name, however, only lasted three years. In 1906, the name was again changed to the Lily Dale Assembly, because of the profusion of water lilies on the lake there.

Sources:

Buckland, Raymond: *Buckland's Book of Spirit Communications*. St. Paul: Llewellyn, 2004

CLAIRALIENCE

Clairalience is "clear smelling." It is also known as **clairgustance**. Quite often at **séances** the sitters are aware of a strong and particular scent that is associated with the spirit being contacted. This can be the smell of flowers such as roses or lavender, or a particular tobacco. Sometimes it is only the **medium** who is aware of the smell, but more generally everyone senses it. Such odors can be of great importance in providing proof of contact and proof of survival.

Sources:

Buckland, Raymond: *Buckland's Book of Spirit Communications*. St. Paul: Llewellyn, 2004

CLAIRAUDIENCE

Clairaudience is, literally, "clear hearing," or the ability to hear sounds and voices from other dimensions, usually from **spirits** of the dead at **séances**. Most **clairvoyants** seem also to be occasionally clairaudient. A **Spiritualist medium** can receive messages from spirits in various ways. The medium may "hear" inside their head what the spirits are saying, or may see and desribe the actions of spirits almost as is done in the game "charades." The medium may also simply sense what is being passed on. These are the main forms of clairaudient communication, although there are others.

Hearing what is communicated can be just like hearing someone whispering in your ear, though no one else physically present will hear any sound. It can also be similar to sensing, in that you hear the voice and the words themselves, in your head, yet are not aware of the sound originating externally. Clairaudience can also include hearing music, songs, and other sounds.

Clairaudience can sometimes be experienced when in the **hypnagogic** and **hypnapompic** states, just as you are falling asleep and just as you are awakening. It can even occur during **meditation**.

A classic example of clairaudience was the case of **Joan of Arc**. In the fifteenth century, she heard voices that she attributed to God and various angels. In her father's garden, at age thirteen, she first heard a voice she believed came from God. During the next five years she heard voices two or three times per week and was able to distinguish these as being Saints Catherine, Margaret and Michael. Her voices directed her to lead the French army against the English, in an attempt to restore the Dauphin to his throne.

Throughout history, people have been guided by voices they heard either internally or externally. Examples are Samuel, Moses, Solomon, and other characters in the **Bible**, who believed they heard God speaking. In the same way, the ancient **Greeks** heard whispered advice from *daimones* or *genii*, regarded more or less as guardian spirits. Socrates claimed to be advised by a specific daimon. The English poet William Cowper, in the eighteenth century, was advised of upcoming events in his life by voices he heard in his ear. **Wolfgang Mozart** heard music in his head and simply wrote down what he heard, note for note. Aura May Hollen, in the late 1920s, began to write her many books of poetry and song from what was dictated to her in her head.

Clairaudience is sometimes confused with **"direct voice,"** which is actually quite different. Direct voice occurs when the medium speaks with the voice of a deceased spirit or, more accurately, a spirit speaks through the medium, using the medium's vocal cords.

Beginning mediums often use seashells as tools for initiating clairaudience. Holding a seashell to the ear and listening can gradually lead the listener to distinguish human voices, perhaps initially vague and far-off. Over a period of time these voices become louder and clearer, until distinct speech is heard and even individual voices are recognized. A disconnected telephone can also be used as a development tool. Even an imaginary telephone will serve the purpose. The medium takes up the receiver, or imagines holding it, and may hear a voice speaking on the end of the line. Some mediums use this as their way of "turning on" the clairaudience gift. They will imagine a telephone beside them and know that when it rings (in their head), there will be a spirit waiting to speak to them.

Sources:

Buckland, Raymond: *Buckland's Book of Spirit Communications*. St. Paul: Llewellyn, 2004

Cowan, Tom: *The Book of Séance*. Chicago: Contemporary Books, 1994

Hollen, Henry: *Clairaudient Transmissions*. Hollywood: Keats Publications, 1931

Klimo, Jon: *Channeling: Investigations on Receiving Information from Paranormal Sources*. Los Angeles: Jeremy P. Tarcher, 1987

Owens, Elizabeth: *How to Communicate With Spirits*. St. Paul: Llewellyn, 2002

Shepard, Leslie A: *Encyclopedia of Occultism & Parapsychology*. New York: Avon Books, 1978

CLAIRGUSTANCE

Similar in many ways to **clairaudience**, **clairvoyance** and **clairsentience**, clairgustance is the smelling of scents coming from other dimensions. It is frequently grouped under the general heading of clairvoyance, but is actually a separate and distinct form of psychic cognizance. It is also known as **clairaliance**.

Many times at a **séance**, the **medium** and all present will be aware of the perfume of a particular flower of significance to someone at the sitting. Specific pipe tobacco might similarly be smelled. Any odor that is significant to someone at the séance may be smelled by any or all present. Not all smells received are pleasant but all are significant, frequently tied in to some memory of a past event.

Sources:
Owens, Elizabeth: *How to Communicate With Spirits*. St. Paul: Llewellyn, 2002

CLAIRHAMBIENCE

Clairhambience is "clear tasting". It is not as common as other forms of psychic cognizance such as **clairaudience**, **clairvoyance**, and **clairsentience**. Occasionally a **medium** will get a very specific taste in the mouth, such as peppermint or licorice. Perhaps the **spirit** coming through the medium had a habit of sucking on peppermints in life. The medium's speaking of this taste will then be very palpable evidence that there is contact with the deceased.

Sources:
Buckland, Raymond: *Buckland's Book of Spirit Communications*. St. Paul: Llewellyn, 2004

CLAIRSENTIENCE

Clairsentience is the **psychic** perception of sights, sounds, smells, tastes, emotions, and physical sensations. Many **mediums** receive all their information by means of psychically sensing it. They may sense that words are said, rather than actually hearing them. Or they may sense that a deceased person is tall and elderly, for example, rather than actually "seeing" them **clairvoyantly**. They may sense the spirit's previous occupation, likes and dislikes. All of these things, and more, are sensed, or "picked up," by the medium and relayed to the sitter(s).

Many people experience clairsentience without realizing that they do. Many people have had a sense, or sense perception, of something about to happen. They might think they have had a "flash," or fleeting impression of some scene or sound. This

is actually clairsentience. A far more common clairsentient experience often occurs on meeting someone for the first time. For example, you might feel intense dislike for a particular person yet are unable to find any logical reason for it. You just "feel," or "know," that you do not like the person. This sometimes extends to a feeling that the person is in some way evil. Sometimes later investigation brings to light good reasons for the feeling.

Many psychics (as opposed to mediums) use clairsentience. They may get initial impressions directly from the person they are **reading** but then supplement this information with other material they get through clairsentience.

Sources:
Buckland, Raymond: *Doors To Other Worlds*. St. Paul: Llewellyn, 1993

Guiley, Rosemary Ellen: *Harper's Encyclopedia of Mystical & Paranormal Experience*. San Francisco: Harper SanFrancisco, 1991

Owens, Elizabeth: *How to Communicate With Spirits*. St. Paul: Llewellyn, 2002

CLAIRVOYANCE

Clairvoyance is "clear seeing," the ability to see in the mind's eye people and things in another dimension. Many **Spiritualist** mediums are clairvoyants, able to actually see and describe spirits of the deceased. In the **Bible** there is reference to the **Woman of Endor**, visited by Saul (I Samuel 28). She is described as "a woman that hath a familiar **spirit**." In other words, a **spirit guide** or **guardian angel**. She is a Spiritualist **medium** (*not* a witch, as is the common misconception). When Saul meets with her—despite the fact that he tried to get rid of all such mediums—she describes exactly what she sees clairvoyantly: "I *saw* gods ascending out of the earth. An old man cometh up and he is covered with a mantle." This turns out to be Samuel and Saul is able to speak with him, through the agencies of the medium. Similarly, Isaiah had a clairvoyant vision of "the Lord ... high and lifted up" attended by seraphim (Isaiah 6).

William E. Butler differentiates clairvoyance by psychological clairvoyance, spatial clairvoyance, **astral** clairvoyance, and true spiritual clairvoyance, though he tends to combine clairvoyance with **clairsentience** in many instances. Lewis Spence distinguishes the ability to see people and events in the present from the ability to see things in the past. **Nandor Fodor** recognizes **X-ray clairvoyance**, medical clairvoyance, traveling clairvoyance, and **platform** clairvoyance. X-ray clairvoyance is the ability to see inside closed objects such as sealed envelopes and behind brick walls. Medical clairvoyance is seeing illnesses and reading **auras** to diagnose disease. The term is used to also cover medical clairsentience. Traveling clairvoyance is also sometimes called "remote viewing" and is seeing actual people and events at a great distance. Platform clairvoyance is the demonstration of the facility literally on a platform before an audience, or in the **séance** room.

One of the most striking examples of clairvoyantly seeing the past is the case that has become known as the Versailles adventure. On August 10, 1901, two young English women, Annie E. Moberly and Eleanor M. Jourdain, were traveling in France and visited the Petit Trianon at Versailles. Annie Moberly was the daughter of the bishop of Salisbury and her friend was the daughter of a Derbyshire vicar. As Eleanor Jourdain recalled, "We went on in the direction of the Petit Trianon, but just before reaching what we knew afterwards to be the main entrance I saw a gate leading to a path cut deep below the level of the ground above, and as the way was open and had the look of an entrance that was used, I said 'Shall we try this path? It must lead to the house,' and we followed it ... I began to feel as if I were walking in my sleep; the heavy dreaminess was oppressive. At last we came upon a path crossing ours, and saw in front of us a building consisting of some columns roofed in, and set back in the trees. Seated on the steps was a man with a heavy black cloak round his shoulders, and wearing a slouch hat. At that moment the eerie feeling which had begun in the garden culminated in a definite impression of something uncanny and fear inspiring. The man slowly turned his face, which was marked by smallpox, his complexion was very dark. The expression was very evil and though I did not feel he was looking particularly at us, I felt a repugnance to going past him." The two women further described points of architecture and landscape which seemed to pinpoint the date of the building and its surrounds to around 1770, since alterations were later made to parts of the Petit Trianon. The ladies saw men in three-cornered hats, a woman with a large white hat, and others in the dress of the eighteenth century. The Petit Trianon was built by Louis XV for his mistress, the Marquise de Pompadour, who was later succeeded by Madame Dubarry. Later, Louis XVI gave the house to Marie Antoinette. This seems to be a fine case of clairvoyance where the mediums were able to see, and later describe in detail, events in a past century.

There is also the well known case of Captain Youatt who saw, in a dream, a group of emigrants trapped on a mountain in the snow. Especially obvious was a white cliff face and other landmarks. He saw this dream repeatedly and related it to a friend who recognized some of the features and believed it to be the Carson Valley Pass, about 150 miles from where they were. A company of men, with mules, blankets, food, and other supplies, set off and actually found the stranded group just as Youatt had described them. This story was published in the 1875 volume of *Sunday at Home* magazine.

Clairvoyance may manifest in internal or external visions. Most examples of clairvoyance are connected to the here and now. It can be brought about by mechanical means, using drugs, incense, **hypnotism**, **crystal gazing**, drumming, or any one of a number of methods. It can also be a part of ritual dance and song. Bringing about *ekstasis*, or ecstasy—getting out of oneself — has been a part of ritual for thousands of years, frequently leading to clairvoyant visions. Virtually anyone can develop clairvoyance, with suitable training.

Sources:

Buckland, Raymond: *Buckland's Book of Spirit Communications*. St. Paul: Llewellyn, 2004

Butler, William E.: *How to Develop Clairvoyance*. New York: Samuel Weiser, 1971

Cowan, Tom: *The Book of Séance*. Chicago: Contemporary Books, 1994

Holroyd, Stuart: *The Supernatural: Minds Without Boundaries*. London: Aldus Books, 1975

Iremonger, Lucille: *The Ghosts of Versailles*. London: Faber & Faber, 1957

Owens, Elizabeth: *How to Communicate With Spirits*. St. Paul: Llewellyn, 2002

Shepard, Leslie A. (ed.): *Encyclopedia of Occultism & Parapsychology*. New York: Avon Books, 1978

Clar, Lydia *see* Edward, John

COLBURN, NETTIE (MRS. WILLIAM PORTER MAYNARD) (D. 1892)

Nettie Colburn Maynard was an American inspirational speaker held in high esteem by **Abraham Lincoln**. As a teenage girl in the winter of 1862, she visited Washington to see her brother in the Federal Army hospital. While in the capital, she went to a **séance** that was also attended by Lincoln. During the séance, she went into spontaneous **trance** and lectured the President on the necessity for emancipation. She spoke to him for almost an hour. When she came out of her trance she was frightened and embarrassed to see to whom she had been speaking. Lincoln placed his hand on her head and said, "My child, you possess a very singular gift, but that it is of God I have no doubt. I thank you for coming here tonight. It is more important than perhaps anyone present can understand." The same thing happened two days later, when both Nettie Colburn and Lincoln and his wife were at another séance. Once again the young girl went into a spontaneous trance and once again she lectured the president about the necessity of freeing the slaves. She also urged him to visit the camps to boost the morale of the army. Colonel Simon F. Case, a lobbyist for railroad interests, was also present and later reported, "President Lincoln was convinced as to the course he should pursue; the command coming from the all-seeing **Spirit** through the instrumentality of the **angel** world was not to be overlooked ... thus the **prediction** of the **medium** was verified."

Nettie Colburn, in later life, gave many séances for Lincoln and gave messages concerning the welfare of the nation, especially in regard to the Civil War. She wrote a book, *Was Abraham Lincoln a Spiritualist?* published in 1891.

Sources:
Awtry-Smith, Marilyn: *"They" Paved the Way*. New York: Spiritualism & More, nd

Doyle, Sir Arthur Conan: *The History of Spiritualism*. New York: Doran, 1926

COLLEGE OF PSYCHIC STUDIES

The College of Psychic Studies continued the work of the **British College of Psychic Science**, which, in 1938, amalgamated with the International Institute for Psychical Research and became known as the Institute for Experimental Metaphysics. The college had an excellent library of more than 10,000 volumes on all aspects of metaphysics. It published the quarterly journal *Light*.

Sources:
Fodor, Nandor: *Encyclopedia of Psychic Science*. London: Arthurs Press, 1933

COLLEGE OF SPIRITUALIST STUDIES

In 2004, the College of Spiritualist Studies, previously known as the Center for Spiritual Science, received a certificate of incorporation issued by the University of the State of New York Education Department. It is one of the two educational arms of the **National Spiritualist Association of Churches** and is headquartered at **Lily Dale**, New York. It is an accredited institution able to award degrees in Spiritualist Studies.

Sources:
Egby, Robert: *Parapsychic Journal*. E-journal #22, October 14, 2004

COLVILLE, WILBERFORCE JUVENAL (1860–1917)

Wilberforce Juvenal Colville was born on September 5, 1860, on board a transatlantic ship halfway between England and America. Attending an **inspirational lecture** given by Cora L. V. Tappan on May 24, 1874, Colville suddenly became conscious of the presence of **spirits**. He was fourteen years old at the time. He determined to be like Tappan and demonstrate **Spiritualism**, but his guardian made him wait two years until he was sixteen. At that time, Colville traveled and demonstrated his **mediumship**, sitting on platforms and giving detailed lectures and reciting hours of inspired poetry based on any suggested theme from the audience. He toured England from March 1877 until October 1878. Because of his young age he became known as "The Kitten Orator." He usually had no memory of anything he said while in **trance**. On occasion, he would hear what he was saying as if it were being said by someone else.

In addition to being an inspired orator, Colville was also an excellent **physical medium**, causing tables and other furniture to move at **séances**. He was very good at **automatic writing**. Although working tirelessly to further the Spiritualist cause, Colville actually regarded himself as a **Theosophist**, saying, "I must remain the freelance I have ever been, and work wherever I am called to operate, and therefore cannot pose as exclusively a Spiritualist, inclusively I am as thoroughgoing an advocate of Spiritualism as any of its most enthusiastic representatives."

Among the books written by Colville are *Inspirational Discourses* (1886), *Old and New Psychology* (1897), *Life and Power From Within* (1900), *Universal Spiritualism and Modern Revelations* (1910), and *Stepping Stones to Spiritual Health, Spiritual Therapeutics* (1914).

Sources:

Awtry-Smith, Marilyn: *"They" Paved the Way*. New York: Spiritualism & More, nd

Fodor, Nandor: *Encyclopedia of Psychic Science*. London: Arthurs Press, 1933

COMPTON, ELIZABETH J. (B. 1830)

Elizabeth Compton lived in New York and worked as a washerwoman. She married a Mr. Marker and had nine children. She suddenly became a powerful **medium** in 1875, at the age of 45. She was investigated by Colonel Henry Steel Olcott (1832–1907), who founded the **Theosophical Society** with Madame **Helena Blavatsky**.

Elizabeth Compton had pierced ears, so Olcott utilized those in his investigation. He had Compton sit in a **cabinet** and then removed her earrings and passed thread through the holes in her ear lobes. These threads he took to the back of the chair in which she sat and fastened them to the chair with sealing wax impressed with his seal. He also fastened the chair to the floor with thread and wax. In this way he was convinced that any untoward movement of the medium in the chair would break the threads.

In the course of the **séance**, with the medium closed up inside the cabinet, her **spirit guide** Katie Brink appeared outside the cabinet. Olcott had placed a weighing platform beside the cabinet. Compton weighed 121 lbs. The **spirit** stepped onto the scales and was found to weigh only 77 lbs. A little later when she was weighed she weighed only 52 lbs. She gave Olcott permission to go into the cabinet, asking only that he not touch the medium's chair. Olcott did go in and was amazed to find the chair empty. When Olcott exited the cabinet, the spirit went in and a **Native American** person emerged. Olcott again went into the cabinet, this time with a small lantern. In his book, *People From the Other World*, he wrote, "I went inside with a lamp and found the medium just as I left her at the beginning of the séance, with every thread unbroken and every seal undisturbed. She sat there with her head leaning against the wall, her flesh as pale as marble, her eyeballs turned up beneath the lids, her forehead covered with a death-like dampness, no breath coming from her lungs, and no pulse at her wrist. When every person had examined the threads and seals, I cut the flimsy bonds with a pair of scissors and, lifting the chair by its back and seat, carried the cataleptic woman out into the open air of the chamber. She lay thus inanimate for eighteen minutes, life gradually coming back to her body, until respiration and pulse and the temperature of her skin became normal."

Dr. J. B. Newbrough had a similar experience when investigating Compton. He used shoemaker's wax in fastening her to the chair and nailed her dress to the floor, but still she disappeared during the séance and then reappeared when the spirit had departed. The spirits that appeared at these séances bore no resemblance to Elizabeth Compton but were easily recognized by relatives of the deceased. The spirits were sometimes fat, sometimes thin, or taller or shorter than the medium. They also provided details of themselves and their lives that were verified by the sitters.

Sources:

Doyle, Sir Arthur Conan: *The History of Spiritualism*. New York: Doran, 1926

Fodor, Nandor: *Encyclopedia of Psychic Science*. London: Arthurs Press, 1933

COMPUTERS

Spiritualists and others communicating with spirits used to work with slates, but the modern trend today is toward computers. Messages purporting to come from the spirit world have been received on personal computers. The origin is difficult to prove, however, because of the ability of some to "hack" into other's computers.

A common practice since the earliest days of séances was to tie two blank slates together and place them in the circle. At the end of the séance these would be separated and writing would be discovered on one or both of the slates. This writing was often identified as being in the handwriting of the departed spirit and was often a message from that spirit to one of the sitters.

A modern form of slate writing might be experienced using a laptop computer. This could be set to a word processing program, with a new blank file opened. Closing up the computer (which usually turns it off), it could then be left in the center of the séance circle. At the end of the sitting the laptop could be turned on again and the file accessed. It is possible that the file would no longer be empty but would contain a message from spirit.

"**Ghost** writing" has appeared on computer screens in the past. In *The Vertical Plane* (1988), Ken Webster tells of his experience after he had moved into an old cottage in North Wales. His old Acorn desktop computer suddenly started to display messages on its screen when it was left unattended. Over a period of two years close to 300 such messages appeared, attested to by Webster's family and friends. This was before the Internet, so there was no connection with other computers. The messages appeared to come from various sources, including a man named Tomas Harden who claimed to have lived in the cottage in the sixteenth century. The **Society for Psychical Research** has reportedly investigated this case but no results have been forthcoming.

Sources:

Buckland, Raymond: *Buckland's Book of Spirit Communications*. St. Paul: Llewellyn, 2004

Randles, Jenny & Peter Hough: *The Afterlife: An Investigation into the Mysteries of Life after Death*. London: Piatkus, 1993

Webster, Ken: *The Vertical Plane*. London: Grafton, 1988

CONE OF POWER

The "Cone of Power" is the energy generated in a consecrated ritual circle used by Wiccans (modern day Witches). When Witches generate power or energy within the ritual **circle**, it masses in the form of a cone whose base follows the consecrated line of the circle that has been described by the group leader. The energy from this cone can be directed, in ritual, to cause change—in other words to work magic.

Energy is raised by dancing and chanting, and a variety of other methods. It can be done by a group (coven) or by an individual (Solitary). The energy is **psychic**, drawn off from the body and drawn up from the earth. It is of a positive nature. In Wicca, it does not involve the conjuring of any spirits or entities of any sort.

Sources:
Buckland, Raymond: *The Witch Book: The Encyclopedia of Witchcraft, Wicca and Neo-Paganism.* Detroit: Visible Ink Press, 2002

CONTROL

"**C**ontrol" is the term often used to designate the **spirit** operator of a **séance**. A more common name is "guide." This entity regulates what is happening in terms of which spirits are allowed to come through to the **medium**, what form of communication is being used (**clairvoyance**, **direct voice**, etc.), whether or not such physical phenomena as **apports** might be apparent, and so on. Some people have more than one guide and the control is the chief one, or the one who is in control of the proceedings at any particular time.

Nandor Fodor said, "The body of the medium is an instrument which requires considerable practice in efficient handling. The control is a communications expert who watches over the fluency of the proceedings, often steps in if he vacated his place to explain confusion and repeats unintelligible expressions. The easygoing, conversational aspect of the séances is largely due to his presence … [the controls] are patient and ready to produce the phenomena to the sitters' satisfaction. But they do not take orders, expect courteous treatment, appreciation for what they do and have their own caprices." Controls are not all-knowing. Many times a control will admit to ignorance of a subject, or the answer to a question, and will say that he will ask another who knows.

Not all controls are male, although the majority seems to be. It is not known why this is. Controls often have helpers to assist with such things as the presentation of **physical phenomena**. These helpers can also aid in the explanation of incoherent messages.

William Stainton Moses recorded some blunders by controls. Once, perfume was supposed to be produced so that the sitters could smell it. Instead, such a terrible odor filled the room that the sitters had to leave. Another time heavy volumes of phosphoric smoke were produced, making the medium believe he was enveloped in fire. Usually when some untoward event such as these takes place, the control immediately orders the end of the session and the medium comes out of **trance**.

Sources:
Fodor, Nandor: *Encyclopedia of Psychic Science.* London: Arthurs Press, 1933

COOK, FLORENCE (1856–1904)

Florence Cook saw **spirits** and heard their voices as a child, but she was told that it was all her imagination. At a tea party when she was fifteen, someone suggested they try **table turning**. The table responded vigorously and, in addition, Cook was **levitated**. This led to her and her mother sitting at home and trying to contact spirits. Cook became very effective at **automatic writing**. In one message done in "mirror writing," (where the words are written backward, as though seen in a **mirror**) she was told to go to a certain book store and ask about the Dalston Society. She did so and this led to her meeting the editor of *The Spiritualist* magazine. Much later, after she had become a renowned **materialization** medium, Sir **William Crookes**, President of the Royal Society, wrote three letters to *The Spiritualist* championing Cook's abilities and hitting out at her critics.

After attending Dalston Society materialization **séances** given by **Frank Herne** and **Charles Williams**, Cook gave some sittings of her own. This gave her a somewhat sensational debut as a **medium**. While in **trance**, she was levitated above the heads of the sitters and had her clothes stripped off her and then replaced. This proved embarrassing to Florence's mother, and the young girl was thenceforth allowed only to preside in the circle at home, with family members and the maid.

The personality who came through most strongly, and remained with her for three years, was Katie King. King was supposedly the daughter of John King, otherwise known as the buccaneer Henry Owen Morgan. John King was one of the characters that made frequent appearances at the séances of Herne and Williams. Katie King first appeared in April 1872, when Cook was sixteen years old. At first, only a face materialized, but as Cook became more proficient, an entire figure would manifest from the **cabinet**. Eventually the spirit allowed photographs to be taken. Cook and King looked remarkably similar in facial features though it was said that the two were different in stature and personality. Additionally, Cook's ears were pierced for earrings while King's were not. The similarity of looks, however, led many to suppose that Cook was doubling as the supposed spirit. Yet repeatedly it was verified that the medium, dressed in a black velvet gown, was seated in the cabinet—usually tied to the chair—while the spirit was dressed in white and, on occasion, seen at the same time. Eventually Sir William Crookes, physicist and President of the Royal Society, began an intensive investigation of the medium. In 1874, he published a report of a long series of experiments conducted in the Cook home and in his own laboratory. It aroused a storm of ridicule and sarcasm, including charges that Crookes had become enamored of the young medium and that she had become his mistress. The charges were never proven.

Crookes was sometimes able to hold King in his arms, to ascertain that the figure was a fully materialized woman. He was also sometimes allowed into the cabinet to see Cook while the King figure was still outside. In one instance both Cook and King were together in the cabinet with Crookes. In fact he witnessed a highly emotional, tearful farewell between the two when King finally prepared to leave the medium. Her place was later taken by another entity named Marie.

Many others also examined Florence Cook, including the novelist Florence Marryat (Mrs. Ross-Church), who saw both Cook and King

The materialized spirit of Katie King, who appeared at the séances of medium Florence Cook. *Courtesy Fortean Picture Library.*

together at the same time. At one séance Marryat was also tied to Cook with a length of rope, inside the cabinet, so that she could be with the medium while Katie King was appearing outside.

In 1874, Florence Cook married Elgie Corner and gave up public mediumship for some time. She did, however, accept an invitation to sit under test conditions for the Sphinx Society in Berlin in 1899. Marie materialized there and some astounding phenomena were produced.

Sources:

Awtry-Smith, Marilyn: *"They" Paved the Way.* New York: Spiritualism & More, nd

Doyle, Sir Arthur Conan: *The History of Spiritualism.* New York: Doran, 1926

Fodor, Nandor: *Encyclopedia of Psychic Science.* London: Arthurs Press, 1933

COOK, KATIE

Katie Cook was one of **Florence Cook**'s sisters, and was also a **materialization medium**. She gave very few public **séances** and was not examined by as many people as her sister Florence. Dr. Alfred Russel Wallace examined her and gave very favorable reports in his book *My Life* (1875). Cook had two **guides**, Nada and Afid, both of whom might appear outside the medium's **cabinet** at the same time.

Sources:

Awtry-Smith, Marilyn: *"They" Paved the Way*. New York: Spiritualism & More, nd

Fodor, Nandor: *Encyclopedia of Psychic Science*. London: Arthurs Press, 1933

CRANDON, MINA STINSON ("MARGERY") (1888–1941)

Mina Stinson Crandon, daughter of a Canadian farmer, became one of the leading **Spiritualist** mediums of the 1920s. She was also one of the most controversial, with differences of opinion over the genuineness of her phenomena deeply dividing the **American Society for Psychical Research** (ASPR). As a teenager, she moved to Boston to play piano, cello, and cornet with various orchestras and dance bands. She also worked as an actress, ambulance driver, and secretary. In 1910, she married the owner of a grocery store but after eight years divorced him and married Dr. LeRoi Goddard Crandon.

Dr. Crandon was Professor of Surgery at the Harvard Medical School for sixteen years. He read Dr. W. J. Crawford's book *The Psychic Structures in the Goligher Circle* (1921), which detailed the results obtained with the **medium** Kathleen Goligher and others of her family. He then started his own experiments at home with his wife Mina and close friends. The first sitting, a **table tipping** séance, was held in May, 1923. Mina Crandon seemed to have more luck than anyone else at causing the table to move. In further sittings she was able to produce **raps** and later went into

trance. Earlier Mina Crandon had visited a medium and received a message from her deceased older brother Walter. He was to become her **spirit guide** and to lead her **séances**.

The group found that they could dispense with a table and sit in a **circle** with their hands joined in a chain. They made a **cabinet** which Mina—who later took the name "Margery" for public demonstrations—would sit in. She produced **automatic writing**, psychic music, and eventually **direct voice**. At one séance, the **spirits** demonstrated their presence by wrecking the cabinet. Clocks would also be stopped at announced times.

Word quickly spread of the phenomena that Margery was producing. Scientific investigations began, conducted by a Harvard group consisting of Professor **William McDougall**, Dr. Roback, Dr. **Gardner Murphy** and his assistant Harry Helson. Margery's guide Walter produced phenomena all over the house and the investigators had to request him to keep it to one room, for the purposes of better control.

By the end of the year the Crandons visited Europe. In Paris, Margery was investigated by Professor **Charles Richet**, Dr. Geley, and others. Despite strict control, excellent phenomena were produced. In London, the **Society for Psychical Research** (SPR) tested Margery using a special "fraudproof" table designed by **Harry Price**. In full light, the table was twice levitated to a height of six inches. Photographs were taken at séances at the British College of Psychic Science, establishing Margery as a powerful medium.

On her return from Europe, Margery developed as a **materialization** medium. **Nandor Fodor** listed some of the phenomena she produced almost immediately, "Psychic lights signaled the first phase, ghostly fingers lit up the darkness and produced contacts, curious forms, called by Walter his '**psychic** pet animals,' were observed, **independent writing** developed on a phosphorescent background. Materialized hands performed pickpocketing stunts and, as a further evolution in vocal phenomena, whistling and syncopated raps, rendering tunes, followed."

On the recommendation of Sir **Arthur Conan Doyle**, the *Scientific American* committee started its investigation on April 12, 1924. Scientific instruments were used. Fodor reported, "Effects were produced in a sealed glass jar, on scale and electric bells under a lid. A paraffin glove was manufactured by an invisible hand." **Hereward Carrington** pronounced the mediumship as genuine, and **J. Malcolm Bird** agreed with him. **Harry Houdini** did not agree, and Malcolm Bird and William McDougall wanted to see more before committing themselves. Other investigative committees followed. Dr. **Eric J. Dingwall**, who had sittings with Margery in January and February of 1925, stated that "phenomena occurred hitherto unrecorded in mediumistic history … the mediumship remains one of the most remarkable in the history of psychical research." Arthur Conan Doyle summed up the committee's results by saying, "It was difficult to say which was the more annoying: Houdini the conjurer, with his preposterous and ignorant theories of fraud, or such 'scientific' sitters as Professor McDougall, of Harvard, who, after fifty sittings and signing as many papers at the end of each sitting to endorse the wonders recorded, was still unable to give any definite judgement, and contented himself with vague innuendos. The matter was not mended by the interposition of Mr. E. J. Dingwall of the London SPR, who proclaimed the truth of the mediumship in enthusiastic private letters, but denied his conviction at public meetings."

Some results stand out from the many experiments and tests that were developed. The first is the thumb prints produced in wax by Walter; he claimed they were his own prints from the spirit world. These were produced at séances on various occasions. The prints were eventually found to be fraudulent, and actually belonged to Dr. Frederick Caldwell, Margery's dentist. The disclosure of this fraud brought about a major split in the ASPR, with Dr. **Walter F. Prince** breaking away and forming the **Boston Society for Psychical Research**. It also led to the eventual failure of

Mina Stinson Crandon, one of the leading Spiritualist mediums of the 1920s. *Courtesy Fortean Picture Library.*

Margery's mediumship and loss of her followers and admirers.

Another more positive test result was the Chinese writing produced as part of a **cross correspondence** experiment. Two columns of Chinese characters were produced by Margery, in total darkness, on specially marked paper. She had no knowledge of Chinese. In a cross correspondence experiment, Malcolm Bird picked out a sentence which was to be received in Chinese by Dr. Henry Hardwicke, located 450 miles away in Niagra Falls. The sentence was, "A rolling stone gathers no moss." Dr. Hardwicke sent a telegram, followed two days later by his original manuscript, in which he had written a Chinese sentence roughly meaning "A traveling agitator gathers no gold," accompanied by the symbols for bird and hill and the name Kung-fu-tze.

The members of the American Society for Psychical Research were split on whether or not they could accept the various phenomena produced by Margery. Their disputes continued into the 1930s, and researchers and historians still debate the issue. The complete story of Margery's mediumship is covered in *Margery, the Medium* by J. Malcolm Bird (Boston, 1925).

Dr. Crandon died in 1939 as the result of a fall. Margery took to drinking and died on November 1, 1941.

Sources:

Awtry-Smith, Marilyn: *"They" Paved the Way*. New York: Spiritualism & More, nd

Doyle, Sir Arthur Conan: *The History of Spiritualism*. New York: Doran, 1926

Fodor, Nandor: *Encyclopedia of Psychic Science*. London: Arthurs Press, 1933

Gauld, Alan: *Man, Myth & Magic: Psychical Research*. London: BPC Publishing, 1970

Heywood, Rosalind: *Man, Myth & Magic: Mediums*. London: BPC Publishing, 1970

CROISET, GÉRARD
(1909–1980)

Gérard Croiset was born in Laren, the Netherlands, on March 10, 1909. His parents were in show business and often neglected him as a child. His father Hyman was a prominent actor and his mother was a wardrobe mistress. His parents were never officially married, and separated when Gérard was eight, leaving him to move through a series of orphanages and foster homes.

Gérard had visions from the age of six. During his early years, he was frequently punished by his elders when he spoke of them. He dropped out of school when he was thirteen and took a variety of unskilled jobs, none of which he held for very long. He finally got a job at one of the grocery stores in the Albert Heyn chain. He kept this job for several years.

At age twenty-five, Gérard married Gerda ter Morsche, an Enschede carpenter's daughter. The following year he opened a grocery store with money loaned by his in-laws. Unfortunately it didn't last long, and Gérard went bankrupt very quickly. About that time he came into contact with some local **Spiritualists** and was finally able to work on developing his **clairvoyant** talents. These developed quickly and his reputation as a **psychometrist** and **psychic** blossomed. He was instrumental in locating lost children and animals. He found that he also had an inherent **healing** ability. With the start of World War II, he was able to do healings for injured soldiers. There were a number of scenes from the war, which he saw clairvoyantly before the actual outbreak of hostilities. He predicted the war at least four years before it began.

During the war, Gérard spent time in a concentration camp but was released in 1943. He aided the Dutch resistance with his clairvoyant powers but was arrested again by the Gestapo in October of 1943.

After the war, in December 1945, Gérard attended a lecture on **parapsychology** given by Professor **Willem Tenhaeff**. The two men spoke together after the lecture and Tenhaeff went on to run tests on Gérard. Gérard accompanied the professor to the University of Utrecht, where he was subjected to the Rorschach personality test, the Murray Thematic Apperception test, the Pfister-Heisz color pyramid test, the Luscher color selection test, and the Szondi test. The **chair test** produced the most startling results. Professor Tenhaeff reported, "In early 1946 I made many psychoscopic tests with him. I realized fairly soon that he was very gifted. The more I tested him, the more I became persuaded that Croiset was a remarkable subject for parapsychological research." Tenhaeff introduced Gérard to the Dutch Society for Psychical Research. The society's members admired his abilities and looked upon him as a talented artist with rare paranormal gifts. Soon nearly all of Holland adopted this view of Gérard Croiset.

The Croiset cases have been meticulously documented over the years. He worked with the police, with private individuals, and with institutions, tracing lost people and objects, tracking down thieves and murderers, and solving numerous puzzles and problems both in his own country and in many other countries. Parapsychologists all over the world tested him and all reached the same conclusions. Gérard specialized in cases dealing with young children, especially when they were missing. He dealt with many of the cases over the telephone. He accepted no payment for any of the things he did, though he did accept donations to his healing clinic. At the clinic, it was not unusual for him to deal with more than one hundred cases per day. Much like **Edgar Cayce**, Gérard Croiset could sense the condition of a patient, identify what was wrong and how to correct it. Unlike Cayce he did not have to go into trance to do so. Gérard Croiset died on July 20, 1980. His son Gérard Croiset, Jr. took over the clinic.

Gérard Jr., second oldest of five children, seemed to have inherited his father's talents. From Holland, he directed South Carolina police in a search for two missing girls. He drew a detailed map of the area where he saw them to be, at a place called Folly Beach, near Charleston. The bodies of the girls were found there, in shallow graves in the sand.

Sources:

Guiley, Rosemary Ellen: *Harper's Encyclopedia of Mystical & Paranormal Experience*. HarperSanFrancisco, 1991

Pollack, Jack Harrison: *Croiset the Clairvoyant*. New York: Doubleday, 1964

Wilson, Colin: *The Supernatural: Mysterious Powers*. London: Aldus Books, 1975

CROOKALL, DR. ROBERT (1890–1981)

Dr. Robert Crookall was a British geologist who became a well known investigator of out-of-body experiences (**OOBEs** or **astral projection**). He initially lectured on botany at Aberdeen University, Scotland, but went on to become the principal geologist at the governmental Geological Survey, in London, England.

When Crookall retired, in 1952, he started collecting records of people's out-of-body experiences, amassing several thousand such records. He went on to publish nearly twenty books on that and related subjects. Crookall divided the material into six main categories:

1. Testimonies from astral projectors, **clairvoyants, mediums,** deathbed observers, and those who had **near-death experiences.**

2. Cooperation between the living and the dead, as in **Spiritualist** communication.

3. Comparisons and references found in major religious literature.

4. The stages of astral projection.

5. The **silver cord**.

6. Various types of non-physical bodies and non-physical realities.

Crookall believed that it was what he termed the "vital body," or "soul body," that left the physical body in astral projection. He regarded this vital body as the center of thinking. In the first stage of the projection, he said, the vital body is connected to the physical with an infinitely elastic silver cord. This eventually separates at death. He felt that it takes three days for the complete separation to take place. Many observers saw the vital body emerging from the head, at death, as a vaporous substance.

Crookall found that there are four distinct planes or realities. He believed that everyone can move through the four realities, shedding an outer body and proceeding with a less dense body as the progression is made. The densest reality is that of the physical body and here on the physical plane. Next is the **etheric** or vital body. Then the soul body, also known as the emotional or psychical body. Finally there is the spiritual body, the divine, cosmic, or celestial body.

Among Crookall's many books are: *The Study and Practice of Astral Projection* (1960), *The Techniques of Astral Projection* (1964), *During Sleep*

(1964), *Intimations of Immortality* (1965), *The Interpretation of Cosmic and Mystical Experiences* (1969), *Case-Book of Astral Projection* (1972), and *Ecstacy* (1973).

Sources:

Crookall, Robert: *The Study and Practice of Astral Projection*. London: Aquarian, 1960

Crookall, Robert: The Techniques of Astral Projection. *London: Aquarian, 1964*

Fishley, Margaret: *The Supernatural*. London: Aldus, 1976

Spirit Online: http://www.spiritonline.com

CROOKES, SIR WILLIAM (1832–1919)

William Crookes was born in London on June 17, 1832. His father was a tailor. As one of sixteen children, Crookes was largely self-taught. At the age of sixteen he enrolled in the Royal College of Chemistry and graduated in 1854. From there he went to Radcliffe Observatory, Oxford, in the position of Superintendent of the Meteorological Department. In 1855, he became Professor of Chemistry at Chester Training College.

Crookes married Ellen Humphrey in 1856. They had eight children. Five years after marrying, Crookes discovered the element thallium and the correct measurement of atomic weight. He was elected Fellow of the Royal Society at the age of 31.

Keenly interested in **Spiritualism** and **mediums**, William Crookes was president of the **Society for Psychical Research** from 1896 to 1899. As a scientist, Crookes made many important discoveries in addition to thalium. He also invented the radiometer and edited the prestigious *Quarterly Journal of Science*. At different times he was president of the Royal Society, the Chemical Society, the Institute of Electrical Engineers, and the British Association. He was knighted in 1897 and received a number of medals of distinction. Crookes is considered to be one of the greatest physicists of the nineteenth century.

Sir William Crookes, celebrated physicist, chemist, and researcher. *Courtesy Fortean Picture Library.*

Crookes first came into contact with **psychic** phenomena in July, 1869, at a **séance** with Mrs. Marshall. He attended this after the death of his youngest brother, Philip. From there he took an interest in **J. J. Morse**, **Henry Slade**, and others, and announced his intention of starting a thorough investigation of **psychic** phenomena. The newspapers and journals of the time were delighted to hear this, presuming that Crookes would do an exposé of Spiritualism.

They were extremely disappointed. Crookes did intensive investigations of many **mediums** and psychics, only to endorse them and to endorse most psychic phenomena. After intensive examination of the sensational British physical medium **Daniel Dunglas Home**, Crooke stated, "Of all the persons endowed with a powerful development of this Psychic Force, Mr. Daniel Dunglas Home is the most remarkable and it is mainly owing to the many opportunities I have had of carrying on my investigation in his presence that I am enabled to affirm so conclusively the existence of this force."

Many years later, in 1917, Crookes told *The International Psychic Gazette*, "I have never had any occasion to change my mind on the subject. I am perfectly satisfied with what I have said in earlier days. It is quite true that a connection has been set up between this world and the next."

Sources:

Fishley, Margaret: *The Supernatural*. London: Aldus, 1976

Fournier, D'Albe: *The Life of Sir William Crookes*. London: T. Fisher Unwin, 1923

Guiley, Rosemary Ellen: *The Encyclopedia of Ghosts and Spirits*. New York: Facts On File, 1992

CROSS CORRESPONDENCE

A cross correspondence occurs when **spirit** communication received through one **medium** is connected to communication received through another, different, medium or mediums. The two or more mediums are usually located at some considerable distance apart and frequently unaware of the connecting message(s). Discovering that connecting message involves a great deal of research on the part of a facilitator, or coordinator, who has to sift through all of the received information and has to be able to recognize the connections between the messages.

For example, two separate groups ("A" and "B") might use **talking boards** (such as the Ouija® board) to communicate with spirits. There is an unbiased Coordinator. Each group starts by advising its particular spirit contact of what they wish to do. This may be done in the following fashion:

Spokesperson: "We want to do a cross-correspondence with our other group. They are meeting at 115 Main Street, tomorrow night at 9:00 pm. During our sitting here tonight please start a message that you will continue with them."

Somewhere within the material that each group receives will be part of a message, though it may not be obvious. On the face of it there will be nothing unusual; the particular message may blend in with whatever else is received. Each group sends the records of its sitting to the Coordinator. He or she should be an intelligent, fairly learned person. The Coordinator's job is to search through both sets of material and find a total message. Here is an example of such a cross correspondence. Among the many pages of Group A's material the Coordinator finds this:

"What sort of place are you in now?"

IT IS VERY PLEASANT, AS THOUGH THE WINTER IS PAST, THE RAIN IS OVER AND GONE, AND EVERYTHING IS NICE AND FRESH AGAIN. ALMOST A REBIRTH.

Something may strike the Coordinator as sounding vaguely familiar. Very carefully going through Group B's equally lengthy material, this is discovered:

"Was there anything you knew on this level that you miss?"

NO

"Can everything be experienced where you are, then?"

YES

"The different seasons?"

YES. EVEN WHEN THE FLOWERS APPEAR ON THE EARTH, THE TIME OF THE SINGING OF BIRDS, GAMBOLING OF LAMBS—EVERYTHING REALLY.

The Coordinator may then recognize the whole phrase as a quotation from the **Bible**, *The Song of Solomon* (ii. 11,12): "For lo, the winter is past, the rain is over and gone; the flowers appear on the earth; the time of the singing of birds is come, and the voice of the turtle is heard in our land." The first part was received by Group A and the second part by Group B. Such a cross-correspondence could be continued for a number of sessions. The main point is that neither group would see the other's notes and neither know what quotation to expect.

Arthur Conan Doyle explained, "The cross correspondence of the SPR is in the main of a much more complicated character. In this, one script is not a mere reproduction of statements made in another; the scripts seem rather designed to represent different aspects of the same idea, and often the information in one is explanatory and complementary of that in another."

Sometimes when experimenting, the Coordinator will select a quotation beforehand, which will make his or her job that much easier. The Spokespersons would then ask that "the continuing message be the one being thought of by our Coordinator." However, in this case it rather defeats the object for there is always the possibility of unconscious **extrasensory perception** between the Coordinator and someone in each of the groups, rather than it being actual spirit contact. To have no one know what the quotation will be beforehand, although much tougher on the Coordinator, is much more convincing.

Cross correspondence was first discovered in 1876 by Alice Johnson, Research Officer of the **Society for Psychical Research** (SPR). The spirit of then-deceased **Frederick W. H. Myers** suggested that cross correspondence was originated by spirit to demonstrate that there was no human **telepathy** at play. Hundreds of pages of the SPR *Proceedings* were devoted to the subject and aroused great controversy. Cross correspondences were found in groups as far apart as New York, London, and Bombay. After the eminent Greek scholar and psychical researcher Professor A. W. Verrall passed over, an intricate Greek mosaic and literary puzzle called "The Ear of Dionysius" was transmitted as a cross correspondence. It has been considered one of the most striking evidences of survival yet obtained.

Sources:

Buckland, Raymond: *Buckland's Book of Spirit Communications*. St. Paul: Llewellyn, 2004

Doyle, Sir Arthur Conan: *The History of Spiritualism*. New York: Doran, 1926

Fodor, Nandor: *Encyclopedia of Psychic Science*. London: Arthurs Press, 1933

CRYSTAL GAZING

Crystal gazing is one of the oldest forms of **divination**. It falls under the general heading of scrying (or skrying), which covers the use of any and all reflective surfaces. The word scrying means "seeing;" pertaining in particular to seeing the future. There are also a number of specific terms under that heading; for example *crystallomancy* is working with **crystals** in general, be they balls or rough minerals, while *spheromancy* is the use of a crystal ball, specifically.

Crystal gazing is one way of promoting **clairvoyance**. However, a possible problem is that the practitioner may come to rely on the crystal and not be able to make contact without it. This is because of externalizing the visions rather than producing/receiving them inside the head.

For best results, a crystal or glass ball should be of about three to four inches in diameter and as clear as possible (e.g., free of bubbles or other defects). If a ball cannot be obtained then it is possible to proceed using a tumbler of water filled to the brim. This should be a clear, non-patterned glass. Ball or glass, it should stand on a piece of black cloth (velvet is best) so that there is nothing immediately around it in the field of vision that will draw attention and distract. The crystal ball should rest on a table at a comfortable height, though if preferred, the ball may be held it in the palm of the hand. With this form of clairvoyance it is a good idea to start by working in a quiet, semi-darkened room, with any light being behind the practitioner.

The eyes are closed initially and the mind made blank. Then, after a few moments, the eyes are opened to gaze into the crystal, with the mind still kept as blank as possible. The practitioner should try to look into the very center of the ball, rather than at the surface. The eyes should not be kept open and unblinking—just blinking naturally when necessary. One of two things will eventu-

A clairvoyant looks into the future through a crystal ball. *Courtesy Fortean Picture Library.*

ally happen. Someone or something may be immediately seen in the ball or else the ball will seem to start filling with white smoke. If it is the latter, then the smoke will fill the ball before gradually dissipating again and leaving a scene of a person or thing. The smoke filling the ball is known as "clouding." Gray or even black smoke is no call for panic.

Many people get nothing at all the first time they try this. Initially, no more than ten minutes should be spent looking. Much longer than that will merely strain the eyes, so the experiment should be given up and tried again the following day. Some people see images right away but many more have to try for days or even weeks before getting results. The secret—if there is one—is as with so much in psychic development: do not strain to get results; just relax and let it happen.

The scene that does appear is akin to looking at a miniature television screen. It will usually be in color, although a few people do see only in black and white, and may be a still picture but is more likely to be moving. Anything might be seen, probably with no control over what comes at first. As progress is made, what or whom had been mentally asked for will appear. As in all **mediumship** exercises, it's a good plan to try to contact a **spirit guide** before trying any scrying.

Sources:

Besterman, T.: *Crystal-Gazing*. London: Rider, 1924

Buckland, Raymond: *The Fortune-Telling Book: The Encyclopedia of Divination and Soothsaying*. Detroit: Visible Ink Press, 2004

DaEl (Dale Walker): *The Crystal Book*. Sunol: The Crystal Company, 1983

Grand Orient (A.E. Waite): *The Complete Manual of Occult Divination: Volume 1—Manual of Cartomancy*. London: William Rider, 1912

Harold, Edmund: *Focus on Crystals*. New York: Ballantine Books, 1986

Lane, E.W.: *An Account of the Manners & Customs of the Modern Egyptians*. London: C. Knight, 1856

Spence, Lewis: *An Encyclopedia of the Occult*. London: George Routledge & Sons, 1920

CRYSTALS

It has long been held that crystals of all types possess energies that can be beneficial to humankind. This energy is sometimes described as electromagnetic. **Healing** is done with crystals. They are used as synthesizers in **meditation** and **prayer**, for **chakra** purification, programming, treating plants and animals, and a host of other things. Crystals of particular minerals—amethyst, jade, obsidian, tourmaline, etc.—are used for specific purposes (see below) but the quartz crystal is the one most generally used, and seems to be the panacea.

Because crystals appear to stimulate the senses, they can help bring about awareness of the past, present, and even of the future, contributing as a tool for **divination**. There can also be a noticeable improvement in **mediumistic** abilities when working with a crystal. One method is to place four crystals around you, at east, south, west, and north, or simply to hold a crystal in your hands while working. The crystals at the four cardinal points act as amplifiers for the energies at work, and considerably enhance scrying, meditation, and mediumship.

In healing, the different colors of crystals are what principally govern their use. Below are the traditional properties of the various colored precious and semiprecious stones.

AGATE: A banded, or irregular variegated, *chalcedony*, or crystalline quartz. Basically browns. Supposed to be good for vision, for **clairvoyance**, and also for hardening gums.

AMBER: Fossilized resin, known variously as *burmite*, *pimetite*, *puccinite*, and *ruminate*. Good for throat problems, asthma, catarrh, also for aiding kidneys and liver.

AMETHYST: *quartz*. Its color may be due to traces of manganese; can be anything from bluish-violet to deep purple in color. Traditionally sobers the drunk, but is also good for expelling all types of poison and generally toning the body.

BERYL: Can appear white, yellow, green, or blue. Good for liver complaints.

BLOODSTONE (or *heliotrope*): Plasma variety of quartz. It contains small spots of red jasper, though it is basically green (from bright green to dark leaf green). It is excellent for stopping bleeding and hemorrhages; perfect for nosebleeds.

CARNELIAN: *chalcedony*, or *quartz*. Properties similar to bloodstone. A blood purifier.

CHRYSOLITE (or *peridot*): *olivine*. Usually olive green but sometimes yellow, brown, or even red. The greens and yellows will prevent fevers. It is also said to prevent nightmares.

CORAL: *calcium carbonate* (skeletons of marine organisms). Both red and white coral prevent bleeding. Also said to avert the "evil eye." Coral is frequently hung about the necks of children for general good health. Good for scars and ulcers.

CRYSTAL: A colorless quartz or rock crystal. A symbol of purity and a great **spiritual** protector.

DIAMOND: Considered something of a panacea, diamonds are especially good for coughs and mucus problems.

EMERALD: Green variety of *beryl*. An antidote for poisons and very good for any diseases of the eyes.

GARNET: A deep red, good for the heart and as a general stimulant.

JADE: The green is a soothing, healing color. It is good for eye problems, kidney and urinary problems, and helps strengthen muscles.

LAPIS LAZULI: *lazurite*. Ranges in color from rich azure-blue through violet-blue to greenish-blue. Good for eye problems. Very strong; it should be used for short periods only.

LAPIS LINGUIS: *azurite*. Various shades of blue. Good for meditating, and for bringing out your **psychic** abilities.

LAPIS LINGURIUS: *malachite*. Bright green. A protection from the "evil eye." Also good for rheumatism and cholera.

MOONSTONE: *adularia* variety of *orthoclase*. Pearly opalescent, similar to opal. As the Moon rules the water, so does the moonstone govern affections of a watery nature.

OPAL: A non-crystalline form of quartz; a silica gem containing varying amounts of water. There is what is termed *precious* opal, *fire* opal, and *black* opal. The precious opal contains a wide variety of delicate colorings; blue, green, yellow, and pink being especially noticeable. Fire opal, as its name suggests, is predominantly red though it can vary to honey-yellow with glimpses of red. Black opal has a dark green background with black flecks. Pliny described the opal as "made up of the glories of the most precious gems ... among them is the gentler fire of the ruby, the rich purple of the amethyst, the sea-green of the emerald, glittering together in union indescribable." Opals are especially good for use on children, perhaps because of their delicate colors. The opal has been called "the gem of the gods," and is a stone of love ... unless the lovers be false, then beware! It is often used for mental illness.

PEARL: A concretion formed by a mollusk. The Hindus listed the pearl as one of the five precious stones in Vishnu's magical necklace (the other four were diamond, emerald, ruby, and sapphire). It has always been considered a cure for irritability. It is an ideal jewel to use in conjunction with another colored stone; the pearl adding its soothing qualities to the other's healing.

RUBY: *corundum.* A deep red in color, the ruby is especially connected with the blood and with the red end of the spectrum. Good for chills and lack of body warmth, poor circulation, constipation, ulcers, boils, and biliousness.

SARDONYX: *cryptocrystalline quartz.* Different colored layers, mainly clear to brownish red along with white, brown, and black. Good for hemorrhages but mainly used for emotional states.

TOPAZ: *alumino-fluorosilicate.* A mineral of granites and other igneous rocks. Usually brown, yellow, or pink (there is also a *false topaz* that is a brownish quartz). Used for soothing and calming, it is especially good for banishing nightmares and curing insomnia.

TURQUOISE: *copper and aluminum phosphate.* Light to dark blue, blue-green, and green in color. For general healing. Good for lowering fevers and for calming nerves.

A number of Scottish families possess amulets and talismans that have been passed down through their families for generations. The Stone of Ardvorlich is possessed by the Stewarts of that name. It is an egg-shaped rock crystal set in four silver hoops. Legend has it that it was the badge of office of an ancient Arch-Druid. The Stone of the Standard, or *Clach na Bratach*, is also a crystal. It adhered to a clod of earth that stuck to the standard of the Chiefs of Clan Donnachaidh, when it was drawn out of the ground at Bannockburn. Other famous stones include the Glenorchy Charm stone (rock crystal), Keppoch Charm rock (rock crystal), the Auchmeddan Stone (a black ball of flint mounted in silver), the *Clach-Bhuai* of the Campbells of Glenlyon, and the *Leug*, or Charm Stone, of the Macleans. With all of these, it is believed that so long as they remain in the possession of the various clans, the families will survive and prosper.

Sources:

Buckland, Raymond: *Scottish Witchcraft.* St. Paul: Llewellyn, 1992

Buckland, Raymond: *Color Magic—Unleash Your Inner Powers.* St. Paul: Llewellyn, 2002

DaEl (Dale Walker): *The Crystal Book.* Sunol: The Crystal Company, 1983

Harold, Edmund: *Focus on Crystals.* New York: Ballantine Books, 1986

CULL, JEAN (B. 1943)

Jean Cull was a well known English **medium.** Her psychic experiences started at the age of eleven, when she and a friend discovered a neighbor who had committed suicide by putting her head inside the gas oven (a common method in those days). The following night Jean saw the **spirit** of the neighbor, Phyllis, standing at the foot of her bed. Phyllis apologized for frightening the two girls and added that she was now happy.

Jean saw many different spirits of those she knew had died. She became frightened and would hide in a wardrobe, hoping the spirits wouldn't find her. She soon realized that the spirits could not and would not harm her. It was not until many years later that she accepted her ability to so easily contact spirit. She was married on March 24, 1962 and a few years later came to know her two spirit guides, Lucy and Henry. She became adept at **clairvoyance** and **clairaudience**. Later her husband Robert also began to use his own gift of **healing**, working with his **guide** Chi.

Sources:

Cull, Robert: *More to Life Than This: The Story of Jean Cull, the Medium.* London: Macmillan, 1987

CUMMINS, GERALDINE
(1890–1969)

Born in Cork, Ireland, Geraldine Cummins was the daughter of Professor Ashley Cummins. She became a well known **medium** specializing in **automatic writing**. Her mediumship started in December, 1923, when she sat with a Miss E. B. Gibbes. Normally Cummins's writing was done slowly but when acting as an **automatist** she wrote at very high speed while in a light **trance**. On March 16, 1926, she wrote 1,750 words in just over an hour and went on to produce her first book, *The Scripts of Ceophas*, which supplemented the Acts of the Apostles and the Epistles of St. Paul as found in the **Bible**. Her second book, *Paul in Athens*, continued the story of the first. She also wrote a third book, *The Great Days of Ephesus*. The material Cummins produced in these three books was scrutinized by eminent theologians who believed they gave new meaning to several obscure passages in the Acts of the Apostles and that they showed close acquaintance with the apostolic circle and that age.

According to Sir **Arthur Conan Doyle**, Dr. Oesterley—Examining Chaplain of the Bishop of London and one of the foremost authorities on Church history and tradition—declared that the Ceophas books bore "every sign of being from the hand of one who lived in those days, and who was intimately connected with the Apostolic circle." Doyle himself went on to say that the scripts "represent, in the opinion of the author [Doyle], two of the most cogent proofs of **spirit** communi-

cation which have ever been afforded upon the mental side. It would seem to be impossible to explain them away."

Cummins's fourth book was *The Road to Immortality*, claiming to be a series of communications from **Frederick W. H. Myers** dealing with his vision of the progression of the human spirit through eternity. Sir **Oliver Lodge** wrote in his preface to the book, "I believe this to be a genuine attempt to convey approximately true ideas, through an amanuensis of reasonable education, characterized by ready willingness for devoted service, and of transparent honesty."

In 1957, W. H. Slater, honorary secretary of the **Society for Psychical Research**, approached Cummins and asked if she would do an experiment. She agreed and for the next three years received scripts from Winifred Coombe Tenant, who had died the year before. During her life, Mrs. Tennant had been known as "Mrs. Willett" and herself had produced many automatic writings. What came to be known as the Cummins-Willett Scripts gave full details of the Tennant family, with names, dates, and family history. The results were published in Cummins's book *Swan on a Black Sea* (1965). Tennant's son, Major Henry Tennant, was initially a skeptic but later wrote, "The more I study these scripts the more deeply I am impressed by them ... There was no tapping of my mind because much appears that I never knew."

Among Cummins' other books are *Perceptive Healing* (1945), *They Survive: Evidence of Life Beyond the Grave* (1946), *Unseen Adventures: A Biography Covering Thirty-Four Years of Work in Psychical Research* (1951), *Mind in Life and Death* (1956), and *Healing the Mind* (1957).

Sources:

Doyle, Sir Arthur Conan: *The History of Spiritualism.* New York: Doran, 1926

Fodor, Nandor: *Encyclopedia of Psychic Science.* London: Arthurs Press, 1933

Shepard, Leslie A: *Encyclopedia of Occultism & Parapsychology.* New York: Avon Books, 1978

Stemman, Roy: *The Supernatural: Spirits and Spirit Worlds.* London: Aldus, 1975

CURRAN, PEARL (1883–1937)

In the earlier part of the twentieth century, a St. Louis housewife encountered a **spirit** named Patience Worth. Mrs. Pearl Curran was persuaded by her friend Emily Hutchinson to use a **Ouija®** board. Although not particularly interested, Mrs. Curran agreed and worked the board with her friend a number of times. On the evening of July 8, 1913, the **planchette** started spelling out a message that read: "Many moons ago I lived. Again I come; Patience Worth my name."

The spirit identified herself as a seventeenth century Englishwoman who had lived in the county of Dorset. She said that she was a spinster and that she had emigrated to America where she was murdered. Curran and Hutchinson started speaking with Patience Worth on a regular basis. Then they found that Mrs. Curran could contact her by herself, whereas Mrs. Hutchinson had no luck alone.

From the Ouija® board, Pearl Curran went on to **automatic writing** and, through that, produced 2,500 poems, short stories, plays, allegories, and six full-length novels—all authored by Patience Worth! She produced a total of more than four million words within a period of five years. One of the stories she produced—*The Sorry Tale* (350,000 words)—is considered by Dr. Usher, Professor of History at Washington University, to be the greatest story penned of the life and times of Jesus since the Biblical Gospels were written.

What is especially interesting about the Patience Worth case is that Pearl Curran had dropped out of school at the age of fourteen and had virtually no knowledge of life in the mid-sixteen hundreds, either in England or in the American Colonies. Yet experts have examined the writings produced and have not found a single anachronism. The writings reveal an amazing insight into the life and times of that period. The vocabulary of the writings was 90 percent Old English. This is probably one of the best recorded examples ever of spirit contact. The writings continued through from 1913 to the late 1920s. Pearl Curran died in 1937.

Sources:

Awtry-Smith, Marilyn: *"They" Paved the Way*. New York: Spiritualism & More, nd

Buckland, Raymond: *Buckland's Book of Spirit Communications*. St. Paul: Llewellyn, 2004

Prince, Walter Franklin: *The Case of Patience Worth*. Boston: Boston Society for Psychical Research, 1927

Yost, Casper S.: *Patience Worth: A Psychic Mystery*. New York: Henry Holt, 1916

DECEPTION

DAVENPORT BROTHERS: IRA ERASTUS (1839–1911) AND WILLIAM HENRY (1841–1877)

The Davenport Brothers were Ira Erastus Davenport and William Henry Davenport. Ira was born on September 17, 1839, and William on February 1, 1841, both in Buffalo, New York. Their father worked at the police department. Their mother was born in Kent, England, and moved to America as a child. The Davenport Brothers became famous **mediums** who demonstrated their controversial phenomena on theater stages in front of large audiences. Their demonstrations were so sensational that many people spent time testing them.

The phenomena started in 1846, two years before the **Hydesville** rappings with the **Fox family**. The Davenport brothers were still children. The brothers were present when **rappings**, knocks, bumps, and various other assorted sounds were produced by **spirits** at their home in Buffalo. By 1850, the two boys and their younger sister Elizabeth were trying **table tipping** and were very successful at it. Several witnesses saw the three children levitate, together with the table. The children continued their experiments for several nights, producing **levitation** of objects and **direct**

voice communications. The rappings continued and Ira began **automatic writing**. On the fifth night a human figure appeared, giving his name as John King. He remained with the brothers as their **spirit guide** for many years.

Once they got older, the two brothers decided to become professional entertainers. They constructed a large **cabinet** that they used on stage. It had three doors at the front and a long bench running inside the length of the cabinet. In the center door there was a small, diamond-shaped opening covered by a curtain. Various phenomena could manifest through this opening. At the start of each performance, members of the audience thoroughly inspected the cabinet and the Davenport Brothers themselves. The brothers would then seat themselves astride the bench, facing one another, where they would be securely tied to prevent any movement. Over the years the brothers frequently complained about the brutality that was exhibited in the tying of the knots to secure them.

Within moments of their being tied and the doors of the cabinet being closed, raps would be heard along with the sound of musical instruments being played and a wide variety of other phenomena. Public committees were set up to examine the brothers and rope-tying was developed to an art of torture. In one experiment conducted in 1857 and sponsored by the *Boston Courier*, Professor Benjamin Pierce sat inside the cabinet between the two brothers. He reported that a phantom hand shot the bolt to lock the doors, and then was thrust out through the triangular opening. The professor also felt the hand about his face and head. A cacophony of sound erupted almost immediately, including banging drums and various musical instruments playing. One report stated that when the cabinet was finally opened, the Davenport Brothers were free and their ropes were found twisted around the professor's neck, however there is no confirmation of this.

The Davenport Brothers never claimed that their phenomena were produced by spirits. They made no connection to **Spiritualism**, although they did acknowledge John King. They insisted that the phenomena they produced were genuine. In a letter to **Harry Houdini**, Ira Davenport wrote, "We never in public affirmed our belief in Spiritualism. That we regard as no business of the public. Nor did we offer our entertainment as the result of a sleight-of-hand or, on the other hand, as Spiritualism. We let our friends and foes settle that as best they could between themselves, but, unfortunately, we were often the victims of their disagreements."

According to them, it was not a magician's performance. Among the many who investigated them was the stage magician and escapologist Harry Houdini. He wrote, in a private letter to Sir **Arthur Conan Doyle**, "I was an intimate friend of Ira Erastus Davenport. I can make the positive assertion that the Davenport Brothers never were exposed. I know more about the Davenports than anyone living. I know for a fact that it was not necessary for them to remove their bonds in order to obtain manifestations." Doyle himself stated, "In spite of all the interested claims of Maskelyne [a famous illusionist of the time] and other conjurers, [the Davenport Brothers] were never exposed, nor even adequately imitated."

Professor Mapes, part of the *Boston Courier* investigatory committee, had an interesting experience at the Davenports' home in Buffalo. He had a conversation that lasted for half an hour with the voice of John King. During that time his hand was seized by a large, powerful hand. It was released but when seized again the hand was much larger and covered with hair. A large table was suddenly lifted and passed over the heads of the sitters and put down again in the far part of the room.

In 1864, the Davenport Brothers went to England and held **séances** every night for almost two months at the Queen's Court Concert Rooms in Hanover Square, London. Their first séance in London, however, was at the home of the famous actor and author Dion Boucicault. Scientists and members of the press attended. What were termed "light and dark séances" were held; in full light and in darkness. In the former, one of the sitters was allowed to sit between the brothers and observe at close quarters. In the dark séance one of the brothers said that he would discard his coat. A quick turn on of the lights then revealed him sitting in his shirt sleeves, but with his hands still securely tied to the chair. Next he asked for a volunteer to lend him a jacket. The next turn on of the lights showed him wearing that borrowed jacket, though still tied into his chair. *The Times* reported the event without being able to offer any explanations. *The Standard* pointed out that the ropes holding the Davenport Brothers had been tied by "a nautical gentleman who was profound in the matter of knots." The reporter from the *Daily Telegraph* didn't know whether or not to class the feats as "the annihilation of what are called material laws."

Despite being investigated by a number of committees, they were never caught in fraud. Even so, audiences became extremely hostile, apparently believing that there must be some trick to what was presented. A riot broke out in Liverpool and so much hostility was encountered in Huddersfield, Hull, and Leeds that the brothers cancelled all further appearances. They made the statement, "Were we mere jugglers we should

Brothers Ira Erastus and William Henry Davenport, two of the most spectacular and controversial mediums of the 19th century, photographed here in 1864. *Courtesy Fortean Picture Library.*

meet with no violence, or we should find protection. Could we declare that these things done in our presence were deception of the senses, we should no doubt reap a plentiful harvest of money and applause ... But we are not jugglers, and truthfully declare that we are not, and we are mobbed from town to town, our property destroyed and our lives imperiled."

They had better luck in France, where they appeared before Emperor Napoleon III and Empress Eugénie at the Palace of St. Cloud. In Leningrad, the Czar received them in the Winter Palace. In 1876, the Davenport Brothers visited Australia, giving their first demonstration in Melbourne on August 24. William died in Sydney, Australia, in July of the following year. Ira died in America, in July 1911.

Sources:

Doyle, Sir Arthur Conan: *The Edge of the Unknown.* New York: G. P. Putnam's, 1930

Doyle, Sir Arthur Conan: *The History of Spiritualism.* New York: Doran, 1926

Fodor, Nandor: *Encyclopedia of Psychic Science.* London: Arthurs Press, 1933

DAVIS, ANDREW JACKSON (1826–1910)

Andrew Jackson Davis was born in Blooming Grove, New York, on August 11, 1826. He grew up with little schooling. His father Samuel was described as a drunkard who earned a scanty living as a weaver and later as a shoemaker. His mother Elizabeth (Robinson) was an uneducated woman who was very superstitious. In his first sixteen years, Davis read only one book, yet by the time he was twenty he was to write what Sir **Arthur Conan Doyle** has called "one of the most profound and original books of philosophy ever produced."

At the age of twelve, Davis started to hear voices giving him advice. On this advice he convinced his father to leave and move to Poughkeepsie, New York. A year or so after the move, Davis began seeing things. At his mother's death he saw a beautiful house in a wonderful land of brightness, and knew it was where his mother had gone. The younger Davis apprenticed to a shoemaker named Armstrong. He worked at that trade for two years.

In 1843, Dr. J. S. Grimes, Professor of Jurisprudence in the Castleton Medical College, gave a series of lectures on **mesmerism**. Davis volunteered as a subject but was found not to be suitable. A local tailor named William Levingston later tried his hand at mesmerism with Davis and had great success. It was found that while in **trance** the boy had tremendous **clairvoyant** powers. So much so that Levingston quit his profession to work fulltime with Davis, diagnosing disease. Davis said that the human body became transparent to his **spirit** eyes—which actually seemed to work from the position of the **third eye**. Each organ then stood out clearly and with a radiance that was only dimmed by disease. Davis was also able to diagnose at a distance, his **astral body** soaring away over the land to the person whose body he needed to view.

On March 6, 1844, Davis suddenly left Poughkeepsie. In a state of semi-trance, he wandered forty miles into the Catskill Mountains. He later claimed that while there he met and talked with the spirits of Claudius Galen, a second century Greek physician, and **Emanuel Swedenborg**. Swedenborg was a brilliant eighteenth century Swedish seer who was the first to explain that death means no change; that the spirit world is a counterpart of this physical world.

In 1845, Davis felt the need to write a book. He was nineteen years old. He broke his partnership with Levingston and teamed up with a Dr. Lyon, from Bridgeport, as hypnotist for this work. Lyon gave up his practice and took the young man to New York, where a Reverend William Fishbough also gave up his work to act as secretary and take the dictation Davis gave while in trance. In November, 1845, Davis began to dictate his great work *The Principles of Nature, Her Divine Revelations, and a Voice to Mankind*. The dictation lasted for fifteen months, and the book was published in 1847.

Dr. George Bush, Professor of Hebrew at the University of New York, was present at many of the trance utterings. He later said:

I can solemnly affirm that I have heard Davis correctly quote the Hebrew language in his lectures [dictation], and display a knowledge of geology which would have been astonishing in a person of his age, even if he had devoted years to the study. He has discussed, with the most signal ability, the profoundest questions of historical and Biblical archæology, of mythology, of the origin and affinity of language, and the progress of civilization among the different nations of the globe, which would do honor to any scholar of the age, even if in reach-

ing them he had the advantage of access to all the libraries of Christendom. Indeed, if he had acquired all the information he gives forth in these lectures, not in the two years since he left the shoemaker's bench, but in his whole life, with the most assiduous study, no prodigy of intellect of which the world has ever heard would be for a moment compared with him, yet not a single volume or page has he ever read.

By the time he was twenty-one, Davis was able to put himself into trance and no longer needed a **hypnotist**. Later still, his writing was purely inspirational. He attracted the attention of numerous famous personalities, including Edgar Allan Poe, and became a prolific author. His **psychic development** continued. One time he sat beside a dying woman and observed every detail of her spirit's departure from the body, detailing it in his book *The Great Harmonia* (1852).

On December 4, 1847, the first issue of the magazine *Univercælum* appeared, with the Universalist minister Rev. S. B. Brittan as Editor-in-Chief. The stated object of the publication was "the establishment of a universal system of truth, the reform and the reorganization of society." Davis contributed many articles to the publication.

Davis predicted the birth of **Spiritualism** in the **Fox family** home. On March 31, 1848, the man who became known as the "Poughkeepsie Seer" wrote in his journal:

About daylight this morning a warm breathing passed over my face and I heard a voice, tender and strong, saying: 'Brother, the good work has begun—behold a living demonstration is born.' I was left wondering what could be meant by such a message.

This was the exact date of the **Hydesville** rappings.

Much of Davis's work reflected Swedenborg's earlier thoughts but, as Sir Arthur Conan Doyle said,

They went one step farther, having added just that knowledge of spirit power which

Swedenborg may have attained after his death ... Is it not a feasible hypothesis that the power which controlled Davis was actually Swedenborg? ... But whether Davis stood alone, or whether he was the reflection of one greater than himself, the fact remains that he was a miracle man ... [who] left his mark deep upon Spiritualism.

Before 1856, Andrew Jackson Davis **prophesied** the development of the automobile, the typewriter, and the airplane. In his *Principles of Nature* (1847), he prophesied the coming of Spiritualism when he said, "It is a truth that spirits commune with one another while one is in the body and the other in the higher spheres—and this, too, when the person in the body is unconscious of the influx, and hence cannot be convinced of the fact; and the truth will ere long present itself in the form of a living demonstration. And the world will hail with delight the ushering in of that era when the interiors of men will be opened, and the spiritual communion will be established...."

Catherine De Wolf (b. July 16, 1806) was married to Joshua Dodge of Mount Hope, Rhode Island. She became Andrew Jackson Davis's patron and, later, his mistress. She separated from her husband, was granted a divorce in June of 1848, and married Davis—who was twenty years her junior—on July 1, 1848. Catherine was always sickly and she died on November 2, 1853. Davis claimed that he continued to meet with her in spirit after her death. In 1854, Mary Fenn (Robinson) Love (b. July 17, 1824) attended a lecture given by Davis. She subsequently divorced her husband Samuel Gurley Love, and married Davis on May 15, 1855, in Clarendon, New York. Thirty years later, in 1885, Davis announced to Mary that they were not true "affinities" and that his true "affinity" was with someone else. He filed for divorce.

Davis married his third wife, Delphine (Della) Elizabeth Markham (b. January 9, 1839), in Boston on August 11, 1885. They were married by Spiritualist and Justice of the Peace Allen Put-

Andrew Jackson Davis (1826–1910), noted American spiritualist, became a professional clairvoyant known as the "Poughkeepsie Seer," after being mesmerized in 1843. *Courtesy Fortean Picture Library.*

nam. Della Markham had previously been married to John Sprague Youngs, then Dumont Charles Drake. John Youngs had died and she had divorced Dumont Drake.

In 1883, Davis was awarded an M.D. and a Doctor of Anthropology degree from the U.S. Medical College. He went on to run the Progressive Bookstore in Boston. He also dispensed herbal remedies for patients at his medical office on Warren Street. Davis died in Watertown, Massachusetts, on January 13, 1910, at the age of eighty-four.

Sources:

Andrew Jackson Davis Article: http://www.spirithistory.com/ajdavis.html

Buckland, Raymond: *Buckland's Book of Spirit Communications*. St. Paul: Llewellyn, 2004

Doyle, Sir Arthur Conan: *The History of Spiritualism*. New York: Doran, 1926

Fodor, Nandor: *Encyclopedia of Psychic Science*. London: Arthurs Press, 1933

DEANE, ADA EMMA

Ada Emma Deane was a well known English **spirit photographer**. A **spirit** face was discovered on a photograph she took in her studio in June, 1920. This began her **psychic** career. Initially there was much suspicion when she insisted on keeping the photographic plates to herself, for "magnetizing," before developing them. By November, 1924, however, she was no longer handling the plates herself. At a sitting at the **William T. Stead** Borderland Library, she had absolutely no contact with the plates at any time yet the paranormal effects appeared on them just the same.

Dr. Allerton Cushman, Director of the National Laboratories of Washington, had what he described as a "remarkable" sitting with Deane. This was recorded in the *Journal* of the **American Society for Psychical Research** (ASPR). Cushman paid an unexpected visit to the **British College of Psychic Science** in July, 1921. There Deane photographed Cushman and on the finished photograph was a second figure, which Cushman immediately recognized as his daughter Agnes, who had died the previous year.

Perhaps the most famous of Deane's photographs were the ones she took at the Cenotaph in Whitehall, London, during 1922–1924. These photographs were taken on during the two-minute silence observed there on November 11 each year (Armistice Day). In the photographs she took each year during the silence, the faces of a number of prominent deceased soldiers appeared.

Psychic investigator Dr. **Hereward Carrington** wrote in the May, 1925 ASPR *Journal* about his experiences with Deane on September 5, 1921, "Upon six of my plates curious marks appeared. On two plates these marks were mere smudges,

Spirit photograph of medium Ada Emma Deane with her own double taken at the British College of Psychic Science. *Courtesy Fortean Picture Library.*

which are not evidential, though I think curious. On the next plate, however, the result is quite striking. I had silently willed that a shaft of white light should emerge from my right shoulder, and appear on the plate. Sure enough, upon development, a column of white light, surmounted by a sort of psychic cabbage, was distinctly visible. It will be remembered that this was upon my own plate, placed in the camera, and afterwards removed and developed by myself." The following year Carrington obtained even stranger results, with comet-like lights and a woman's face, again on his own photographic plates.

Sources:

Doyle, Sir Arthur Conan: *The History of Spiritualism*. New York: Doran, 1926

Fodor, Nandor: *Encyclopedia of Psychic Science*. London: Arthurs Press, 1933

DE GASPARIN, COUNT AGENOR (1810–1871)

Count Agenor de Gasparin was one of the first investigators of **table tipping** and telekinetic, or **psychokinetic** (PK), phenomena in France. In 1854, he published a book on his experiments in Velleyres, Switzerland, under the title *Des Tables Tournantes, du Surnaturel en général, et des Esprits*. These experiments were conducted under strict test conditions. He established the movement of objects without human contact and the alteration of the weight of objects. However, he did not accept the **spirit** hypothesis. He arrived at the following conclusions:

1. The will, in a certain condition of the human organism, can act, from a distance, upon inert bodies, and by an agent different from that of muscular action.

2. Under the same conditions thought can be communicated directly, though unconsciously, from one individual to another.

In the preface to a later edition of his book in 1888, he stated that the time elapsed since the original publication had not been sufficient to solve the problem, but that "some day an edifice would be erected on the same stone which was laid [in his book] in 1854."

Sources:

Gasparin, Count Agenor: *A Treatise on Turning Tables.* New York: 1857

Shepard, Leslie A: *Encyclopedia of Occultism & Parapsychology.* New York: Avon Books, 1978

DE GULDENSTUBBÉ, BARON L. (1820–1873)

Baron de Guldenstubbé was a Scandinavian nobleman who was the first to introduce **table tipping** to France in 1853. For many months he had difficulty even in getting the French people to accept the idea of **séances**. In 1850, when news of the American **Spiritualist** movement first reached France, the Baron believed he had found what for so many years he had searched for—indisputable demonstration of the immortality of the soul. After months of persistence, he got regular sitters such as the Abbé Châtel, the Comte d'Ourches, and the Comte de Szapary, to sit with his **medium** M. Roustan. They experienced the same **rappings** and other phenomena as demonstrated by the **Fox sisters** in America. From there the French group progressed to table tipping.

The Baron was best known, however, for his experiments with **direct writing**. He would leave writing materials on the pedestals of statues, in niches in churches and public galleries, and even in tombs. Writing would be discovered later, even in boxes that had been sealed with the writing materials inside. He obtained writings that purportedly came from such people as Plato, Cicero, Juvenal, Spencer, and Mary Stewart. They were written in English, French, Latin, German, or Greek. He acquired more than 2,000 specimens in twenty different languages, collected between 1856 and 1872. He gave an account of his experiments in *Practical Experimental Pneumatology: or, the reality of* **spirits** *and the marvelous phenomena of their direct writing* (Paris, 1857). He wrote,

On August 1, 1856, the idea came to the author of trying whether spirits could write directly, that is, apart from the presence of a medium. Remembering the marvelous direct writing of the Decalogue, communicated to Moses, and that other writing, equally direct and mysterious, at the feast of Belshazzar, recorded by Daniel; having further heard about those modern mysteries of **Stratford** (Connecticut) in America, where certain strange and illegible characters were found upon strips of paper, apparently apart from mediumship, the author sought to establish the actuality of such important phenomena, if indeed within the limits of possibility.

The Baron placed a sheet of blank paper and a sharpened pencil in a box which he locked. For twelve days there was nothing, but on August 13,

1856, he unlocked the box to find "mysterious characters" written on the paper. He repeated the experiment ten times more the same day and each time got results. He eventually left the box open and claims that he actually saw the letters forming as he looked at the paper. He then decided to dispense with the pencil. He "placed blank paper sometimes on a table on its own, sometimes on the pedestals of old statues, on sarcophagi, on urns, etc., in the Louvre, at St. Denis, at the Church of Ste. Etienne du Mont, etc." All came to show writing, in various languages. Various people assisted the Baron and witnessed the events. These included Prince Leonide Galitzin, the Swedish painter Kiorboe, and the German Ambassador at the Court of Wurttemberg. As **Frank Podmore** stated, "the publication of Guldenstubbé's book created a profound impression in Spiritualist circles, alike in France and in this country, and his experiments are constantly referred to by the earlier English Spiritualists as striking demonstrations of spiritual agency."

Sources:

Fodor, Nandor: *Encyclopedia of Psychic Science*. London: Arthurs Press, 1933

Podmore, Frank: *Modern Spiritualism*. London: 1902; reprinted as *Mediums of the Nineteenth Century*. New York: University Books, 1963

DÉJÀ VU

The literal meaning of this French phrase is "already seen." **Psychical researchers** apply the phrase to those times when a person feels that a scene or event has happened before. A related term, though not used as much, is *déjà entendu*—"already heard." The term déjà vu was first used by F. L. Arnaud in 1896, though the experience has been recorded as early as 10 BCE by the **Roman** poet Ovid.

There are many instances of people visiting a particular location for the first time but knowing, and describing quite accurately, what lies just around a corner or just over a hill. Their feeling is that they have "been there before," though they know that they have not. Déjà vu is often used in instances when a person has a strong feeling of having experienced something in a previous lifetime. It is, therefore, frequently equated with belief in **reincarnation**. Psychologists try to explain it away with terms such as cryptomnesia, redintegration, paramnesia, false memory, and the like. But they don't explain such cases as the one recorded in Martin Ebon's book *Reincarnation in the Twentieth Century* (1970). Ebon details the experience of Inge Ammann, a twenty-six-year-old German woman who, in 1966, felt a strong sense of déjà vu when driving through the countryside near Germany's border with Czechoslovakia. She was with her husband, and told him of a side road leading to a village. They took the road and then she explained the layout of the village and told him details of the life of a family that had lived there during World War II. She recognized the old innkeeper and he confirmed all that she said about both the village and the family. He told them that the family's youngest daughter had been killed when kicked by a horse. At that moment Inge experienced a vivid recall of the event, even crying out in pain.

Sources:

Ebon, Martin: *Reincarnation in the Twentieth Century*. New York: New American Library, 1979

DENTON, PROFESSOR WILLIAM (1823–1883)

Born in Darlington, England, in January 1823, William Denton was Professor of Geology in Boston, Massachusetts. In 1849, he learned of Dr. J. Rhodes Buchanan's work in **psychometry** and met with Buchanan. Denton began his own experiments using geological samples. He found that his sister, Mrs. Anna Denton Cridge, was an excellent psychometrist, as was his wife Elizabeth. On one occasion he gave his wife a specimen to hold from a carboniferous formation. She closed her eyes and immediately began to describe swamps, trees with tufted heads and scaled trunks, and great frog-like creatures that lived in that age.

He then gave her lava from a Hawaiian volcanic eruption. She held it and described a "boiling ocean; a cataract of golden lava."

Denton's mother was a skeptic with no belief in psychometry. He gave her a meteorite to hold and she said, "I seem to be traveling away; away through nothing—I see what looks like stars and mist." His wife gave a similar description, adding that she saw a revolving tail of sparks.

Denton authored a number of books including *The Soul of Time* (1863) and *Our Planet; Its Past and Future* (1869).

Sources:
Buckland, Raymond: *Buckland's Book of Spirit Communications*. St. Paul: Llewellyn, 2004

D'ESPERANCE, MADAME (ELIZABETH HOPE— 1855–1919)

Elizabeth Hope's earliest friends were **ghosts**. When she was a small child she lived with her family in an ancient house in England and she saw a number of ghostly figures passing to and fro about the building. Some would smile and nod to her and she would smile back. Her mother did not believe her stories of seeing these people and the family doctor warned of future madness if she kept up what he saw as a pretense.

When Elizabeth was twelve she had to write an essay on "Nature" for school. Try as she might, she was unable to think of anything to write. She worked at it for several days but without result. Eventually, the night before the essay was due, she fell asleep crying at her inability to write. The next morning she was amazed to find the blank paper she had left on her desk was now covered with writing—her own—and it was a long essay on the needed subject. Her teacher was most impressed with the quality of the writing, as was the local rector.

At age nineteen Elizabeth married and became Mrs. Reed. She first encountered **Spiritualism** around that time and was unimpressed.

Even so, she had rapid results with **table tipping** and, later, with **automatic writing**. She then became successful at **clairvoyance**. Through her automatic writing, she began to produce detailed scientific material. One of her many **guides**, Humnur Stafford, described very minutely an instrument which later proved to be the telephone. T. P. Barkas, a prominent citizen of Newcastle, England, would write out long lists of questions covering every branch of science. In complete darkness Elizabeth read the questions, which had been sealed in an envelope, and gave the answers immediately, sometimes in English, sometimes in German, and sometimes in Latin.

Time was spent in the south of France, where Elizabeth took the name Madame d'Esperance. Then in Sweden, Elizabeth began **materializations**. Over a period of six weeks she developed the technique with another guide, Walter Tracey. Yolande, a fifteen-year-old Arabic girl, became a frequent materialized visitor. **Nandor Fodor** said, "It took about ten to fifteen minutes to build up her body from a filmy, cloudy patch which was observed on the floor, while the process of melting away usually took place in two to five minutes, the drapery being the last to disappear in one half to two minutes time ... The last and greatest work of Yolande (who often produced **apports**) was achieved on June 28, 1890, when she apported a seven-foot-high Golden Lily with eleven perfect blossoms. The feat was witnessed by Professors Boutlerof, Fiedler, Aksakof, and others." Yolande would materialize when Elizabeth was sitting outside the medium's cabinet, so that both **medium** and materialized spirit were visible to the sitters at the same time.

At one materialization **séance**, a sitter grabbed at the figure and, in doing so, caused tremendous harm to the medium. Elizabeth suffered hæmorrhaging of her lungs and a prolonged illness. This was not to be the only time she so suffered. Three times her life was endangered through the willful actions of sitters thinking to catch her in fraud. An incident in 1893 caused Elizabeth's hair to turn white and indisposed her for two years.

Madame Elizabeth D'Esperance (Elizabeth Hope), a materialization medium who could produce full-body apparitions. *Courtesy Fortean Picture Library.*

In 1893, at a séance in the home of a Professor E., an **Egyptian** woman named Nepenthes materialized. At the request of the professor, the materialized figure dipped her hand into a bucket of paraffin wax and then removed it, leaving behind a perfect imprint. It was mentioned that it would normally be impossible to pull out a hand and leave an undamaged mold, but that is what the figure did. Fodor states,

> "Nepenthes vanished from their presence as she came, lowered her head on which a diadem shone, little by little became a luminous cloud and gradually faded away. Previous to her disappearance she wrote a message in her own hand in ancient Greek in the pocketbook of one of the sitters. All present were ignorant of ancient Greek letters. The translation read: 'I am Nepenthes

thy friend; when thy soul is oppressed by too much pain, call on me, Nepenthes, and I will come at once to relieve thy trouble.'"

The strangest phenomenon was the partial dematerialization of Elizabeth's body, from the waist downward. The well known **psychic researcher** Professor Alexander Aksakof, of St. Petersburg, published a full account of it in his book *A Case of Partial Dematerialization* (Boston, 1898). Elizabeth herself wrote *Shadow Land* (London, 1897) and *Northern Lights* (London, 1900). The former Sir **Arthur Conan Doyle** ranks it alongside **Andrew Jackson Davis**'s book *The Magic Staff*, saying it is "among the most remarkable psychic autobiographies in our literature." Elizabeth was virtually imprisoned in France at the outbreak of World War I, and her manuscripts and all her séance notes were destroyed.

Sources:

Doyle, Sir Arthur Conan: *The History of Spiritualism*. New York: Doran, 1926

Fodor, Nandor: *Encyclopedia of Psychic Science*. London: Arthurs Press, 1933

DEVELOPMENT CIRCLE

As its name suggests, a development circle is a group of people meeting on a regular basis to practice and develop as **mediums**. Also known as "Home Circles"—from the fact that they usually took place in someone's home—they were once the very backbone of the **Spiritualist** movement. **Emma Hardinge Britten** said, "The mediumistic faculty in all its forms can be cultivated by sitting in the spirit circle, which tends to perfect and spiritualize the magnetism of the sitters by their mutual action on each other and by the influence of the spirits."

There is no need for such a group to have an already established medium present. The whole point is to develop the sitters themselves as mediums. In *The Ring of Chairs* (2000), Janet Cyford points out, "There are many folk who will not form or lead a group, without a practicing Medium. This is a self-defeating attitude for it disregards the ability of **Spirit** to guide us by inner inspiration. In the early days of modern Mediumship, people sat together without a fully developed Medium and under Spirit's guidance all types of phenomena occurred."

Sitting once per week is the ideal, though once every two weeks is acceptable if weekly is not feasible. Building energy is important to development. This is initiated by everyone singing upbeat songs at the start of the proceedings. In addition to building the group energy, this also helps balance the individual energies of the sitters into a more harmonious whole. Exercises are performed in a variety of disciplines leading to development of **clairvoyance, clairaudience, clairsentience, psychometry**, etc.

The number of sitters is not important and will probably be governed initially by the size of the meeting place. Sitters may come and go as Spirit finds the right mix, but eventually will settle to a regular group dedicated to their development. It is perfectly safe to include teenagers in such a group, so long as they understand the purpose of the sittings. Many good mediums of today started as teenagers in such development circles in the past.

Sources:

Buckland, Raymond: *Buckland's Book of Spirit Communications.* St. Paul: Llewellyn, 2004

Cyford, Janet: *The Ring of Chairs: A Medium's Story.* Baltimore: Thirteen-O-Seven Press, 2000

DINGWALL, ERIC JOHN (1890–1986)

From 1921 to 1922, Eric John Dingwall was Director of the Department of Physical Phenomena at the **American Society for Psychical Research**. From 1922 to 1927, he was Research Officer for the (London) **Society for Psychical Research** (SPR). He attended the second International Conference for Psychical Research held in Warsaw, Poland. While there he took part in experiments with the Polish sensitive Stephan

Ossowiecki. He also sat with medium **Eusapia Paladino**.

In 1924, in Boston, Massachusetts, Dingwall investigated the **medium** known as Margery (**Mina Stinson Crandon**), as part of the *Scientific American* committee. Sir **Arthur Conan Doyle** complained about Dingwall, saying that he "proclaimed the truth of the mediumship in enthusiastic private letters, but denied his conviction at public meetings." Dingwall had further sittings with Margery in January and February of 1925, and subsequently stated that "phenomena occurred hitherto unrecorded in mediumistic history ... the mediumship remains one of the most remarkable in the history of psychical research." (*Proceedings*, Vol. VI) Speaking about **ectoplasm** produced by Margery, Dingwall said in a letter to a friend, "The materialized hands are connected by an umbilical cord to the medium. They seize upon objects and displace them."

In 1936, Dingwall visited the West Indies, studying social and religious aspects of **mental mediumship** phenomena. He wrote a number of books, including *Some Human Oddities* (1947), *Very Peculiar People* (1950), and *The Unknown; Is It Nearer?* (with J. Langdon-Davies, 1956). He also contributed many articles to the SPR *Proceedings*.

Sources:

Fodor, Nandor: *Encyclopedia of Psychic Science.* London: Arthurs Press, 1933

Foreman, Laura (ed): *Mysteries of the Unknown: Spirit Summonings.* New York: Time-Life Books, 1989

DIRECT VOICE

Just as **direct writing** is produced by **spirit** without using the **medium**'s hand and arm, so direct voice is the voice of spirit produced without using the medium's vocal chords. Direct voice may come from the **trumpet**, from the **cabinet** independent of the medium, or from anywhere in the room. It is also known as Independent Voice. **Nandor Fodor** said, "Physically the phenomenon requires the supposition that some material, more solid than air, is withdrawn from the medium's or from the sitters' bodies to produce the necessary vibrations in the surrounding atmosphere. Indeed, **séance** room communications speak of improvisation of a larynx." **Arthur Findlay**, in his *On the Edge of the Etheric* (1931), gives a description of the building of this artificial larynx.

"From the medium and those present a chemist in the spirit world withdraws certain ingredients which for want of a better name are called **ectoplasm**. To this the chemist adds ingredients of his own making. When they are mixed together a substance is formed which enables the chemist to **materialize** his hands. He then, with his materialized hands, constructs a mask resembling the mouth and tongue. The spirit wishing to speak places his face into this mask and finds it clings to him, it gathers round his mouth, tongue and throat. The etheric organs have once again become clothed in matter resembling physical matter, and by the passage of air through them your atmosphere can be vibrated and you hear his voice."

William Stainton Moses said of a spirit voice box, "I did not observe how the sound was made, but I saw in a distant part of the room near the ceiling something like a box round which blue electric light played, and I associate the sound with that."

Most mediums have no trouble speaking even when the direct voice is also speaking, but some mediums are unable to speak at the same time, indicating a connection of some sort between the two. Fodor reported that the medium Mrs. Thomas Everitt (1825–1915) could diminish the level at which the voice spoke by placing her hand over her mouth. Her **spirit guide**, John Watt, explained it by saying that he used the medium's breath in speaking. Mrs. Everitt could never speak at the same time that John Watt was speaking.

Direct voice communicators have been known to laugh, whistle, and sing; there seems to be no restriction on the vocalizing. Foreign tongues, such as Welsh, Greek, Japanese, and Hindustani,

have been heard and even recorded. The strength of the direct voice can vary considerably. Sir **Arthur Conan Doyle** compared one voice to the sound of a roaring lion. David Duguid (1832–1907), a Scottish medium, on one occasion had the spirit voice so loud that it alarmed and frightened the sitters and they asked him to go away! **Elizabeth Blake's** guide had a voice that could be heard a hundred feet away. Similarly, George Valiantine's guides, Hawk Chief and Kokum, always spoke with tremendously booming voices. Some mediums—a good example is **Leslie Flint**—have the spirits speak quite loudly from various places, without the aid of a trumpet, and the medium is not in trance so is able to listen to what the spirits have to say. In the case of Leslie Flint, the voices have been recorded and on occasion more than one voice is heard speaking at the same time.

Sources:

Brown, Slater: *The Heyday of Spiritualism*. New York: Hawthorn Books, 1970

Doyle, Sir Arthur Conan: *The History of Spiritualism*. New York: Doran, 1926

Findlay, J. Arthur: *On the Edge of the Etheric*. London: 1931

Flint, Leslie: *Voices In the Dark: My Life as a Medium*. New York: Bobbs-Merrill, 1971

Fodor, Nandor: *Encyclopedia of Psychic Science*. London: Arthurs Press, 1933

DIRECT WRITING

While **automatic writing** is produced by spirit using the arm and hand of the **medium**, direct writing (also known as independent writing) is produced purely by spirit. Direct writing can appear anywhere, on any substance. It has often appeared at the sites of **poltergeist** activity, written on walls, floor, or ceiling. An early form of direct writing was **slate writing**, in which two clean slates would be bound together and placed in the **séance** circle. When the slates were opened later, they were found to be covered with writing. A slightly more modern form is when paper and pencil are placed in a sealed box in the séance **circle**. On opening the box at the end of the séance, the paper is found to be covered with writing … and this writing is often in the hand of the deceased who was contacted at the sitting. Many times the sound of chalk on slate, or pen on paper, can be heard during the séance, coming from the slates or box.

The noted **Spiritualist Baron L. de Guldenstubbé** (1820–1873) was a Scandinavian nobleman who was the first to introduce **table tipping** to France. He would leave writing materials on the pedestals of statues, in niches in churches and public galleries, and even in tombs. He obtained writings that purportedly came from such people as Plato, Cicero, Juvenal, Spencer, and Mary Stewart. They were written in English, French, Latin, German, or Greek. He acquired more than 2,000 specimens in twenty different languages, collected between 1856 and 1872.

Henry Slade was a medium noted for the slate writings produced at his séances. **Nandor Fodor** said, "The hands of **Henry Slade** were sometimes feverishly hot and emitted, during the writing, which was nearly always in his own hand, crackling and detonating sounds. These detonations occasionally amounted to veritable explosions and pulverized the slate."

Most of the direct writings obtained by Mrs. Thomas Everitt (1825–1915) were quotations from various sometimes inaccessible books, bearing on the teachings of **Emanuel Swedenborg**. Investigating Mrs. Everitt, Sir **William Crookes** noted that there were never any indentations made on the paper by the writing, no matter the thickness of the paper. Her husband wrote, "The paper and pencil are whisked up into the air, a rapid tick-tick-ticking is heard lasting barely a few seconds, then paper and pencil fall to the table and a call is made to turn on the lights. The writing is finished! The speed production varies from 100 to 150 words a second." (*Light*, July 7, 1894)

Sir William Crookes attended a séance with Kate Fox-Jencken (one of the original **Fox Sisters**) and described the appearance of a phantom hand. He reported, "A luminous hand came down from the upper part of the room, and after hovering near me for a few seconds, took the pencil from my hand, rapidly wrote on a sheet of paper, threw the pencil down, and then rose up over our heads, gradually fading into darkness." Fodor noted that Robert Dale Owen, in a sitting with Henry Slade on February 9, 1874, that took place in low gas light, saw "a white, female, marble-like hand, which was detached and shaded off at the wrist, creep up to his knees, write on the note sheet placed there on the slate, then slip back with the pencil under the table." Fodor comments, "One is reminded of that most dramatic account in Daniel 5:5: 'In the same hour came forth fingers of a man's hand, and wrote over against the candlestick upon the plaster of the wall of the king's palace; and the king saw the part of the hand that wrote.'"

When Henry Slade's slate writing came into question, Sir **William Barrett** (1845–1926), one of the distinguished early psychic researchers, declared that he took a clean slate, placed a crumb of a slate pencil below, and held it firmly down with his elbow and only allowed the tips of Slade's fingers to touch the slates. Barrett said, "While closely watching both of Slade's hands which did not move perceptibly, I was much astonished to hear scratching going on apparently on the under side of the table, and when the slate was lifted up I found the side facing the table covered with writing."

Sources:

Doyle, Sir Arthur Conan: *The History of Spiritualism*. New York: Doran, 1926

Fodor, Nandor: *Encyclopedia of Psychic Science*. London: Arthurs Press, 1933

Spence, Lewis: *An Encyclopedia of the Occult*. London: George Routledge & Sons, 1920

DISTANT HEALING

see also Healing

Psychic healing is done in a wide variety of ways. Sometimes there is a laying-on of hands and sometimes the hands do not come in contact with the body. There may be color healing, **auric** healing, or **crystals** may be used. One common form of healing is distant healing—sometimes called "absent healing"—where the healer and the patient may be separated by distances of up to thousands of miles.

One of the earliest instances of distant healing connected with **Spiritualism** occurred when a Mr. E. W. Capron visited the **Fox Family** at Rochester, New York. He mentioned to an entranced Leah Fox that his wife, Rebecca, was suffering from a severe and persistent cough. While in **trance**, Leah said, "I am going to cure Rebecca of her cough." She went on to give a very accurate description of Capron's wife and then pronounced her cured. On returning home, Capron found that his wife was indeed cured and the cough never returned. Earlier than that, distant healing had been done by the Catholic priest and one-time prince, Alexander Leopold Franz Emmerich von Hohenlohe-Waldenburg-Schillingfürst (b. 1794). He generally cured people by laying on his hands. When the medical profession frowned on that, he would cure by simply **praying** for people. In 1821, he let it be known that at certain times of the day he would be offering up a special Mass for the sick. Those who wrote to him would be included in it. Apparently many were cured this way; though not actually being present.

Edgar Cayce found that the person for whom he was **reading** did not have to be physically present. All that was needed was a name and location of the person and Cayce could focus on that person and the problem, no matter how far away they might be. However, Cayce generally prescribed rather than affected the cure.

Healers generally project their thoughts both toward the sick person and toward the spiritual world, establishing a link between the two. Once the link has been established, the healing energies can start to flow. The famous British spiritual healer **Harry Edwards** would concentrate on the name of the person when doing distant healing. He received 2,000 or more letters per day from people around the world, and had a documented 80 percent recovery rate from diseases such as arthritis, cancer, epilepsy, and tuberculosis.

Distant healing can also be done by working with a photograph of the patient or even from a sample of their handwriting. Bill Finch of St. Louis, Missouri, designed a clear chromo-light unit, with a holder for the photograph and a color filter, and a low watt bulb as the light source. With this setup it is possible to perform distant healing using color (*chromotherapy*). Gem therapy can also be done at a distance by placing colored stones on a photograph.

Sources:

Buckland, Raymond: *Color Magic—Unleash Your Inner Powers*. St. Paul: Llewellyn, 2002

Edwards, Harry: *The Healing Intelligence*. London: Taplinger, 1971

Fodor, Nandor: *Encyclopedia of Psychic Science*. London: Arthurs Press, 1933

Kingston, Jeremy: *The Supernatural: Healing Without Medicine*. London: Aldus, 1975

Turner, Gordon: *An Outline of Spiritual Healing*. London: 1963

DIVINATION

D ivination is so called because it is considered a gift of the divine, or a gift from the gods. It is the art of foretelling the future—of obtaining knowledge of the unknown—using **omens**, portents, visions and divinatory tools. It is an art which many have perfected over the years, in various forms. Most **Gypsies**, for example, are experts at one or more branches of divination such as card reading (*cartomancy*), palm reading (*cheiromancy*), casting runes or dice, **crystal gazing** (*scrying*), and more. They recognize what is important in what they see and present it to the person questioning (known as the Querant). Divination was originally a tool of royalty, used in determining natural and unnatural disasters, wars and plagues, and lines of succession. The Babylonians and the Chaldeans had priests who spent all of their time in divination. The Chinese had court diviners

Early nineteenth century print of Roman vestal virgins performing a divination ritual. *Courtesy Fortean Picture Library.*

who threw the yarrow stalks (*I-Ching*). The ancient **Egyptians** had priests who did nothing but attempt to **dream** the future for the pharaohs.

There are many methods of divining, possibly hundreds of them, ranging from observing dust (*abacomancy*) to observing the behavior of animals (*zoomancy*). *Pyromancy*, or gazing into the flames of a fire and "seeing" pictures, is something which many people have done, probably without realizing that they were indulging in divination. But whatever tools are used, they are only that … tools. They serve as a focal point for the **psychic** senses. It is the interpretation of what is seen that is important. The diviner must see and then interpret the signs, awakening in him- or herself the psychic ability to recognize what is important to the person for whom the reading is being done.

There may be warnings of danger, of illness, even of death. In the case of the latter, it is up to the reader to determine how best to present what is seen so as not to alarm the Querant.

Divination has been a tool of priests, **seers**, **shamans**, astrologers, medicine men, Gypsies, wise men and women for thousands of years. It is frequently referred to in the **Bible**. Even when divination extended beyond strictly royal use, in many civilizations only a special class of people were allowed to do the divining. The ancient **Greeks** had the **oracles** and **sibyls**. The **Romans** had a special priest class called augurers, and the ancient Egyptians also had special priests. The Celts had the Druids. Divination was done both for an individual and for a group, often being used to determine the fate of kingdoms and countries.

In its simplest form, divination can be gauging what the future may hold judging by the flight of a bird or birds. A complex form might be throwing down yarrow stalks to form hexagrams for the ancient Chinese practice of *I-Ching*, or mathematically working through **numerology**. There are enough types of divination, ranging from very basic to very complex that, with practice, most people can achieve some sort of results.

It has been said that divination falls into three categories: interpretation of natural phenomena, interpretation of artificial phenomena (such as the casting of lots), and direct communication with deity through dreams, visions, trance, etc.

Sources:

Anderton, Bill: *Fortune Telling*. North Dighton: JG Press, 1996

Buckland, Raymond: *A Pocket Guide to the Supernatural*. New York: Ace, 1969

Buckland, Raymond: *The Fortune–Telling Book: The Encyclopedia of Divination and Soothsaying*. Detroit: Visible Ink Press, 2004

Foli, Prof. P.R.S.: *Fortune–Telling by Cards*. Philadelphia: David McKay, 1902

Gibson, Walter B. and R. Litzka: *The Complete Illustrated Book of the Psychic Sciences*. New York: Doubleday, 1966

Grand Orient (A.E. Waite): *The Complete Manual of Occult Divination: Volume 1—Manual of Cartomancy*. London: William Rider, 1912

Gray, Magda (ed.): *Fortune Telling*. London: Marshall Cavendish, 1974

Guiley, Rosemary Ellen: *Harper's Encyclopedia of Mystical & Paranormal Experience*. San Francisco: Harper SanFrancisco, 1991

DIVINING ROD

Divining rods were used by the ancient Greeks, Romans, Persians, and Scythians to discover the location of water or of various minerals. Basically a forked or Y-shaped stick, the hazel twig seems to have been the favorite, especially for finding water. For finding metals, popular woods were: hazel for silver, iron and steel for gold, ash for copper, and pitch pine for lead and tin. Other popular general purpose sticks are of ash, rowan, or willow.

The method is for the operator to hold the two ends of the stick in his or her hands and to walk over the area thought to be the probable source for the water or mineral. As the operator crosses the underground source, the twig will twist in the hands, often with such force that any bark may be stripped from the wood. In the **Bible**, Moses dowsed for water in the desert, using his staff as a divining rod (Exodus 17; Numbers 20). Marco Polo found rods in use throughout the orient in the late thirteenth century. Georg Agricola gave the first printed description of a dowsing or divining rod in his book *De re metallica* (Basel, 1556). Agricola's interest was primarily with mining and locating minerals, but the techniques he describes are the same as those used for water divining or water witching. A well known illustration from his book shows a variety of men both digging and walking about with Y-shaped rods in their hands. One man is in the act of cutting a forked branch from a tree.

In Sebastian Münster's *Cosmographia universalis* (Basel, 1544), there is an illustration of a man divining with a forked stick and showing a cross-section of the ground beneath him, where miners are at work. There is a bas relief in the Shantung Province of China showing Yu, a "master of the science of the earth and in those matters concerning water veins and springs." He is shown holding a forked instrument.

Modern dowsers have developed such sensitivity and skill that they are able to measure the actual depth at which the substance will be found and, in the case of water, the rate of flow. According to the British Society of Dowsers, although no thorough scientific explanations for dowsing have yet been found, it is generally acknowledged that there is some correlation between the dowsing reaction and changes in the magnetic flux of the site being dowsed. In 1910, German scientist Baron Karl von Reichenbach

Water diviner John Caleb Wade, shown in 1939 at age nine, locating water under ground using a forked hazel twig. *Harry Shepherd/Fox Photos/Getty Images.*

said that the movement of the rod was due to earth force fields sending out radiations and vibrations which are picked up by the dowser.

As well as branches, many dowsers today use tools as varied as bent wire coat hangers, **pendulums** (with cavities for a "witness"—samples of what is being sought), and commercially produced, swinging rods especially designed for the purpose. Many modern well-drilling companies employ a diviner, or dowser, on their force. Some even guarantee that if they can't find water, there will be no charge.

Dowsers have been widely employed around the world. The Government of India had an official Water Diviner who, between 1925 and 1930, traveled thousands of miles and located numerous wells and bore holes. In more recent years, the British Society of Dowsers had one of their

experts go to southern India, where he sited boreholes for more than 1,800 previously dry villages.

As with any form of **psychic** or **mediumistic** skill, everyone has within them the inherent ability. But as with any other psychic skill, it is by practice and constant use that that skill is developed. As with so much in the field of psychic and mediumistic development, young children seem to be able to draw upon the skill much more easily and naturally than do adults.

Sources:

Buckland, Raymond: *The Fortune–Telling Book: The Encyclopedia of Divination and Soothsaying.* Detroit: Visible Ink Press, 2004

de Givry, Grillot: A *Pictorial Anthology of Witchcraft, Magic & Alchemy.* London: Spottiswoode, Ballantyne, 1931

Guiley, Rosemary Ellen: *Harper's Encyclopedia of Mystical & Paranormal Experience.* HarperSanFrancisco, 1991

Maury, Marguerite: *How to Dowse: Experimental and Practical Radiesthesia.* London: Bell, 1953

Mermet, Abbé: *Principles and Practice of Radiesthesia.* London: Watkins, 1975

Pike, S.N.: *Water-Divining.* London: Research Publications, 1945

DIXON, JEANE (1918–1997)

Jeane (Pinkert) Dixon was one of the best known, albeit controversial, **psychics** of recent times. It was her possible **prediction** of the death of President John F. Kennedy that catapulted her into the national limelight.

Jeane was born to a wealthy lumber family in Medford, Wisconsin on January 3, 1918. At the age of eight, she had her fortune told by a **Gypsy** who said that she would become a famous **seer**. The family moved to California when she was still young. Jeane attended high school in Los Angeles and took acting and singing lessons.

In 1939, at the age of twenty-one, she married James L. Dixon, an automobile dealer. They moved to Detroit, Michigan and started a real estate business. The couple moved to Washington, DC, and continued in real estate. Working with the Home Hospitality Committee, a Washington socialite organization, Dixon entertained servicemen by making predictions. A devout Roman Catholic, Dixon saw no problem with giving predictions, saying, "A revelation is something special. Sometimes two, three, or even four years go by without God granting me a revelation, and then some mornings I wake up and feel inspired and know that something great is going to happen. ... Another but a less certain way through which I receive knowledge of future events is what I call the 'psychic way.' Often when I meet people and shake their hands, I feel vibrations. But sensing and interpreting these vibrations, I can tell many things about that person. I 'see' even more if I have a chance to *touch* their hands with the tip of my right hand. My fingers are supersensitive, and many times a gentle touch enables me to pick up an individual channel of communication with eternity." She claimed she could see the past, present, and future.

Jeane attracted much public attention after she claimed to have predicted the death of President Kennedy. **Ruth Montgomery** was a newspaper political columnist who wrote the book *A Gift of Prophesy: the Phenomenal Jean Dixon* (1965). The book sold more than three million copies and launched Dixon on the lecture circuit. But the basis of the book left many in doubt. Many of Jeane's predictions were called into question and debated in the national press.

A 1956 article in *Parade* magazine stated, "As for the 1960 election, Mrs. Dixon thinks it will be dominated by labor and won by a Democrat. But he will be assassinated or die in office." However, Dixon also said that the occurrence would "not necessarily (be) in his first term." At another time she made the statement that "During the 1960 election, I saw Richard Nixon as the winner." At that time, she went on to add that "John F. Kennedy would fail to win the Presidency." She also predicted that World War III would start in 1958, that there would be a cure for cancer found in 1967, and that the Russians would put the first

Jeane Dixon, one of the best-known American astrologers and psychics of the twentieth century. *Courtesy Fortean Picture Library.*

man on the moon. In 1956, she said that Indian Prime Minister Nehru would be ousted from office, yet he served until his death in 1964. She also said that Fidel Castro would be overthrown. In the July, 1995, issue of the *Star*, Dixon said, "A stunning outcome to the O.J. Simpson trial will be a result no one predicted. I can see that O.J. will walk." She was correct on that—but she could just as easily claim success if Simpson had been found guilty or the jury had failed to reach a decision. "A guilty verdict or hung jury will keep O.J. Simpson in jail through most of this year," she predicted in the January 17, 1995 issue of the *Star*. "I don't see him walking away a free man until an appeal," was her prediction in the April 25, 1995, issue of the tabloid.

However, Dixon did make some very dramatic accurate predictions. She warned Carole Lombard not to travel by air just a few days before the actress died in a plane crash. She similarly predicted the death of Dag Hammarskjöld, also in a plane crash. But most of her predictions were couched in such a way that she could claim to have been right no matter what happened.

Sources:

Bringle, Mary: *Jeane Dixon: Prophet or Fraud?* New York: Tower Books, 1970

Dixon, Jeane: *My Life and Prophesies*. New York: Bantam, 1970

Jeane Dixon Obituary: http://www.cnn.com/SHOW BIZ/9701/26/dixon

Montgomery, Ruth: *A Gift of Prophesy*. New York: Morrow, 1965

Doorkeeper *see* **Control**

DOYLE, SIR ARTHUR CONAN (1859–1930)

Born in Edinburgh, Scotland, on May 22, 1859, Arthur Ignatius Conan Doyle was the third child and eldest son of ten siblings born to Charles Altamont Doyle and Mary (Foley) Doyle. Arthur became best known as a novelist and as the creator of literary detective Sherlock Holmes. He was involved with **Spiritualism** for most of his life, and adopted it as his religion in 1918.

Doyle attended Hodder College, Stonyhurst College, and Feldkirch College (Austria) before going to Edinburgh University to study medicine. From February to September of 1880, Doyle served as a surgeon on the Greenland whaler *Hope*, and in 1881–82 on the steamer *Mayumba* to West Africa. In June of 1882, he moved to Southsea, near Portsmouth in the south of England, where he stayed until 1891. After a number of short stories and non-fictional articles, Doyle published A *Study in Scarlet* in 1887. He moved to Upper Wimpole Street, off Harley Street in London, where he set up business as an eye specialist. The first six Sherlock Holmes stories appeared in *Strand Magazine* in 1891 and *The White Company*, a historical novel, was also published that year.

In 1885, Doyle married Louise Hawkins, the sister of one of his patients. From 1885–88 Doyle participated in **table tipping** experiments at the house of General Drayson, a patient of his and a teacher at the Greenwich Naval Academy. These **séances** prompted Doyle to become a member of the **Society for Psychical Research** (SPR) and to carry out an investigation of the **medium** Mrs. Ball. In 1902, Doyle was knighted for his work in the military field hospitals in South Africa during the Boer War. In 1906, Doyle's wife died of tuberculosis. The death affected Doyle deeply, though a year later he married Jean Leckie.

Although Doyle hadn't arrived at a definite conclusion regarding life after death by the time he met Sir **Oliver Lodge**, he was very much impressed by **Frederick W. H. Myers**'s book *Human Personality and Its Survival After Bodily Death* (1903). It has been suggested that one of the factors contributing to Doyle's conversion to Spiritualism was the death of his son, Captain Alleyne Kingsley Conan Doyle, who died from influenza aggravated by wounds incurred in World War I. Doyle denied this, saying he had proclaimed himself a Spiritualist in April, before his son's death.

In early 1918, Doyle and his wife began traveling and speaking on Spiritualism, visiting Australia, New Zealand, America, and Canada, and speaking on Spiritualism. He toured all the principal cities of Great Britain, and was in America in 1922 and South Africa in 1928. By the end of 1923, he had traveled 50,000 miles and addressed nearly a quarter million people. Doyle became known as the "St. Paul of Spiritualism."

Doyle's wife Jean became a medium and delivered many messages through her **guide** Phineas. Some years after the death of his son Kingsley, Doyle attended a séance with a Welsh medium and his son came through, giving a great deal of information known only to Kingsley and his father. At a different séance, with another medium, Doyle's mother and nephew materialized "as

Sherlock Holmes author Sir Arthur Conan Doyle, who was closely involved with Spiritualism for most of his life. *Courtesy Fortean Picture Library.*

plainly as ever I saw them in life," according to Doyle. In 1925, Doyle's Spiritualist novel *The Land of Mist* featuring Professor Challenger (of *The Lost World*) began serialization in *Strand Magazine*. It was published in book form the following year.

Felicia Scatcherd, a friend of Doyle's, contacted him in 1920 to tell him of photographs that had been taken which seemed to prove the existence of fairies. These had been taken in Yorkshire by two young girls; Elsie Wright (age 16) and her cousin Frances Griffiths (age 10). Doyle's Theosophist friend Edward L. Gardner examined the photos and proclaimed them genuine. Doyle accepted Gardner's word. In the Christmas 1920 issue of *Strand Magazine*, Doyle published an article about the fairies, complete with photographs. Two years later he published the book *The Coming of the Fairies*, which gave a full account of the

girls' encounter with the little people. He then left for Australia. While he was away, it came out that the photos taken by the two girls were of cut-outs from a 1915 picture book (*Princess Mary's Gift Book*). The photographs were fake. Doyle returned from his trip to find himself a laughingstock. Ruefully, he admitted that he may have been taken in. It wasn't until the early 1980s, however, that Elsie and Frances themselves admitted to the hoax.

In 1922, a falling out with the Society for Psychical Research occurred. Doyle eventually resigned from the society, widening the gulf between the SPR and Spiritualists. Other members followed Doyle's lead. In that year also the Doyles had a falling out with **Harry Houdini**, who had been a close friend for years.

In 1924, Doyle wrote and published at his own expense *The History of Spiritualism* (dedicated to Sir Oliver Lodge) and actually opened a Spiritualistic bookstore. He said he wrote the book "to give man the strongest of all reasons to believe in spiritual immortality of the soul, to break down the barrier of death, to found the grand religion of the future." In 1925, he was elected honorary president of the International Spiritualist Congress in Paris and later that year trounced Sir Arthur Keith in a public discussion on Spiritualism held in London.

Doyle was president of the London Spiritualist Alliance when one of its mediums, a Mrs. Cantlon, was charged with fortune-telling. He wrote a stirring letter to *The Times* against what he saw as persecution of Spiritualists and Spiritualism and began a drive to modify the Fortune-Telling Act. Doyle led a deputation to the Home Secretary on July 1, 1930, but six days later he died at his home in Crowborough.

Sources:

Buckland, Raymond: *Buckland's Book of Spirit Communications.* St. Paul: Llewellyn, 2004

Fodor, Nandor: *Encyclopedia of Psychic Science.* London: Arthurs Press, 1933

Guiley, Rosemary Ellen: *The Encyclopedia of Ghosts and Spirits.* New York: Facts On File, 1992

DREAMS

All people dream, though not everyone remembers his or her dreams. Frequently dreams seem ridiculously involved and mixed up. This is because only the *highlights of several dreams* are being remembered. The average person experiences a large number of dreams during the course of a normal night's sleep. These dreams actually may be the remembrance of **astral projections**; journeys undertaken by the unconscious while the conscious mind is at rest. Suppose that in the dream state—more correctly, on the **astral plane**—your astral body takes a trip to Scotland and does some salmon fishing. From there you travel to the Orient and have a pleasant journey in a sampan. Then there may be a visit to the pyramids in Egypt before rounding out the night reenacting a battle of the Civil War. On waking, there may be only a confused recollection of what seemed like one long, very strange, dream. In it, you were drifting down the Nile River in a Chinese junk that suddenly disappeared and left you fighting Confederate soldiers with nothing more than a salmon-fishing pole!

The steps to remembering astral journeys start with remembering dreams. These should be written down in as much detail as possible, *immediately* upon waking. Very little may be remembered to start with, but perseverance will provide more and more details. Slowly the various separate dreams will be remembered until they can all be noted in detail.

Many times in dreams you meet with friends and loved ones who are actually deceased. These dreams usually seem very real. In fact you *are* meeting with these "dead" people. **Nandor Fodor** describes the astral plane as, "The first sphere after bodily death. It is said to be material but of a refined texture. There are many speculations concerning this world of existence. **Theosophy** claims definite knowledge of its conditions and denizens. Many descriptive accounts are to be found in Spiritualistic after-death communications." There are, indeed, many **Spiritualist** writings and records of communications received from **spirits** describing the "Summerland," as that first sphere is often called. The writings of **William Stainton Moses** are a good example. The Summerland is where the dreamtime meetings take place between your astral body and deceased friends and loved ones.

Many people have received evidential messages in their dreams, confirming that there is a continuance of life after death. Many people have also dreamed of something that is going to happen in the future. There are innumerable examples of **prophetic dreams**. Lewis Spence says, "By the ancients sleep was regarded as a second life, in which the soul was freed from the body and therefore much more active than during the waking state."

Sources:

Crookall, Robert: *The Study and Practice of Astral Projection.* London: Aquarian, 1960

Fodor, Nandor: *Encyclopedia of Psychic Science.* London: Arthurs Press, 1933

Fox, Oliver: *Astral Projection: A Record of Out-of-Body Experiences.* London: Rider, 1939

Hart, Hornell: *The Enigma of Survival.* London: Rider, 1959

Spence, Lewis: *An Encyclopedia of the Occult.* London: George Routledge & Sons, 1920

DROP-IN

Sometimes a **spirit** unknown to any of the sitters in attendance will "appear" at a **séance**. Usually the **medium**'s **spirit guide** will ensure that this does not happen, but occasionally a "drop-in" does appear. Occasionally, if the medium is engaged in **direct voice** (the spirit is speaking through the medium), a drop-in will speak in a foreign language. Guiley states that in rare cases, "The appearance of a drop-in is accompanied by physical phenomena such as **table tilting**, **rappings**, mysterious lights, **apports**, scents, and strange whistles, whisperings and breathing."

Uncontrolled séances such as **talking board** sessions or **automatic writing** are prone to entertain drop-ins. Frequently these are spirits who want to make contact with those they have left behind on the physical plane, and are hoping to make use of the sitters to arrange a connection with those particular people. Others are simply lonely spirits wanting to speak with anyone, or to achieve something in particular. An example of the latter was **Patience Worth**, who originally contacted **Pearl Curran** by way of an Ouija® board and used Curran as a means of producing vast amounts if literature; novels and poetry.

One of the positive aspects of drop-ins is that they invariably show proof that the medium is not receiving intelligence by way of **extrasensory perception** from the sitters. Usually information provided by drop-ins is totally unknown to *anyone* present and has to be verified by careful research. In 1971, Nottingham University Professor of Psychology Alan Gauld worked with information received from a drop-in via both a talking board and automatic writing. After careful research, Gauld found that in ten cases out of thirty-seven, the information given by the drop-in about identity and former life was correct. The information included exact names, addresses, and occupations.

Sources:

Gauld, Alan: *Proceedings, #55—A Series of Drop-In Communicators*. London: Society for Psychical Research, July 1971

Guiley, Rosemary Ellen: *The Encyclopedia of Ghosts and Spirits*. New York: Facts On File, 1992

Holroyd, Stuart: *The Supernatural: Psychic Voyages*. London: Aldus, 1976

Stevenson, Ian and John Beloff: *Proceedings, No. 427-447—An Analysis of Some Suspect Drop-In Communicators*. London: Society for Psychical Research, September 1980

DRUMMER OF TEDWORTH

The story of the Drummer of Tedworth is an early account of **poltergeist** phenomena. It was first detailed in Joseph Glanvill's *Saducismus Triumphatus* of 1668, the phantom drummer manifesting in the home of magistrate John Mompesson in April, 1661.

The occurrence took place in the town of Tedworth, Wiltshire, England, and began as a simple case of vagrancy. William Drury—described as an itinerant magician and drummer—was caught in some shady dealings, charged, found guilty, and had his drum confiscated. He was made to leave the district and his drum was not returned to him. Instead, it was placed in the home of the magistrate John Mompesson.

Mompesson had to travel away from home for a few days. On his return, he was greeted with stories of strange disturbances and noises issuing from his house, especially at night. There were the sounds of drums being played, plus banging on the roof and **rapping** on furniture and walls. A drum could be clearly heard playing roundheads, cuckolds, and tattoos at all hours of the night and even in the daytime. Mompesson acted at once. He had William Drury's drum destroyed by breaking it into pieces. But the noises continued.

The Reverend Joseph Glanvill, chaplain to King Charles II, went to investigate. He stated that when he went upstairs in Mompesson's house he found two young girls, aged seven and eleven, sitting up in their bed, very fightened. There were scratching noises coming from the head of the bed and from the wall panels. The girls' hands were in full view on top of the bed covers, so Glanville knew it was not them causing the sounds. Glanville noticed a linen bag, similar to a laundry bag, hanging from the bedpost of another bed in the room. It was swinging back and forth even though no one was anywhere near it. Glanville grabbed the bag and emptied it. There was nothing unusual to be found. He searched thoroughly but could find no satisfactory explanation. It was a situation that was to be repeated more than 200 years later with the **Fox Family** in New York State.

Eventually everything quieted down. Magistrate Mompesson learned that William Drury, the drummer, had been arrested for theft in the city of Gloucester, and had been transported out of the country and to the colonies. With his leaving, things seemed to settle down and quietness returned.

But eventually the noises started up again. Somehow Drury had managed to return to England and, whatever the connection, the drumming was worse than ever. Other poltergeist phenomena now added to the drumming. Shoes **levitated** and flew through the air, chamberpots were emptied onto the beds, windows shook, and terrible sulfurous smells permeated the house. Some of the noises were so loud that they could be heard by the rest of the village.

No explanation could be found for any of the occurrences. They continued unabated for almost a year. Then, suddenly, they stopped. There is no record of what ultimately became of William Drury, and what connection he had with the noises or with their termination, but his drum was heard no more.

Sources:

Buckland, Raymond: *Ray Buckland's Magic Cauldron.* St. Paul: Galde Press, 1995

Glanvill, Joseph: *Saducismus Triumphatus: Or, Full and Plain Evidence concerning Witches and Apparitions.* (1689) Gainesville: Scholars' Facsimiles & Reprints, 1966

DUNCAN, HELEN VICTORIA (1897–1956)

Helen Victoria Duncan was a **materialization** medium who lived in Scotland and earned a very mixed reputation. She was very much a tomboy as a child and consequently earned the nickname "Hellish Nell." As a young woman, her family banished her when she became pregnant but was unwed. She subsequently married Henry Duncan, who lived in Dundee. They eventually had six children.

In 1931, Duncan allowed herself to be examined by the London Psychic Laboratory, the research division of the London Spiritual

Alliance. The results were published in the May 16, 1931, issue of the journal **Light**. Although no conclusions were reached, the journal conveyed a very favorable impression of her. Duncan produced **ectoplasm**, figures appeared at the séances, and objects many feet away from the **medium** were moved. The medium herself had been stripped and placed inside a special sack with arms ending in attached, stiff, buckram mittens. The sack suit was sewn in at the back and fastened with cords and tape to the chair in which she sat. Reportedly, at the end of the sittings she was often found sitting outside of the suit, though its fastenings were still intact.

The **National Laboratory of Psychical Research** also examined Duncan. The *Morning Post* of July 14, 1931, carried an article claiming that Duncan had been exposed as a fraud. Researcher **Harry Price** called her "one of the cleverest frauds in the history of **Spiritualism**." It transpired that the "ectoplasm" was in fact a composition of wood pulp and egg white, which she was able to swallow and then regurgitate. On July 17 the *Light* carried a follow-up article also branding her as a fraud and carrying a confession from her husband. However, subsequent issues of the journal carried numerous testimonies from those who had found Duncan to be genuine. Will Goldston, a well known magician, said that he had witnessed phenomena that were inexplicable by any trickery he knew.

In January, 1932, Duncan was again caught in fraud when Peggy, her supposedly materialized child **control**, was grabbed by a Miss Maule and it was found to be none other than Duncan herself. The exposers took her to the Edinburgh Sheriff Court and there the President of the **Spiritualists' National Union** said that he "had no doubt that the fraud was deliberate, conscious and premeditated." But after a large number of defense witnesses had testified, he modified his views. Duncan was found guilty of fraud and fined ten pounds.

During World War II, Duncan again made news, but in a way that was to establish her as a Spiritualist martyr.

On January 21, 1944, Helen Duncan had been holding a séance in a room above Ernest and Elizabeth Homer's pharmacy shop, in Portsmouth, England, when the sitting was raided by the police. It was a materialization séance and a spirit figure was gliding across the room when the police forced their way in. One of the policemen grabbed the figure. He later claimed that it was made of cheesecloth and was suspended on a string—but no such figure, or any cheesecloth, was ever found in the room despite a careful search. A BBC radio recreation of the event reported that the room "was combed inside and out in every conceivable corner. No one was allowed to leave the building that night." Duncan's **spirit guide** Albert, who regularly materialized, had been there when the police broke in but he also completely disappeared.

The reason the police raided the séance was because of reports they had received of Duncan giving out classified war secrets. She had revealed to a worried couple the fact that their son had drowned on the sinking of the war ship the *HMS Barham*. But at that time there was no public report of the *Barham* having been sunk. No official statement had been made about the fate of the ship. It later transpired that the *Barham* had indeed sunk and the young man drowned. The authorities were horrified that military secrets were being given away by a Spiritualist medium. National security was at stake, they claimed, and this was not an isolated incident. Psychic investigator Alan Crossley said, "During World War II servicemen killed in action were regularly manifesting at her séances. Relatives of these men were startled when their sons told them that they were killed at such and such a place … or sailors named the ship on which they had died … The Admiralty didn't release such information for as long as three months. They were alarmed that through Mrs. Duncan's mediumship, the men were manifesting and telling the world about it within hours of the tragedy. They had to stop her."

The medium was initially charged under the 1824 Vagrancy Act, but by the time the case reached the Old Bailey, Duncan was accused of "conspiring to pretend to exercise a kind of conjuration, to wit that **spirits** of deceased persons appear to be present, and the said spirits communicating with living persons then and there present contrary to the **Witchcraft Act** of 1735."

Helen Duncan was being tried under the eighteenth century Witchcraft Act! When Prime Minister **Winston Churchill** heard of it he was furious. He sent a note to the Home Secretary saying, "Let me have a report on why the Witchcraft Act should be used in a modern court of justice. What was the cost to the state? I observe that witnesses were brought from Portsmouth and maintained here in this crowded London for a fortnight and the recorder [judge] kept busy with all this obsolete tomfoolery to the detriment of necessary work in the courts."

During the trial, her counsel offered to have Duncan demonstrate materialization in the courtroom, but the judge refused. More than 60 witnesses spoke up in Duncan's favor, with another 300 willing to testify. Many gave amazing descriptions of evidential appearances of deceased relatives at Duncan's séances. The trial lasted seven days and Duncan was found guilty. She was given a nine-month prison sentence.

As a result of Helen Duncan's trial, the old Witchcraft Act was finally repealed and replaced in 1951 with the **Fraudulent Mediums Act**.

Sources:

Fodor, Nandor: *Encyclopedia of Psychic Science*. London: Arthurs Press, 1933

International Survivalist Society: http://www.survivalafterdeath.org

Psychic News #3754, June 19, 2004. Stansted, Essex

Leonard, Sue (ed): *Quest For the Unknown—Life Beyond Death*. Pleasantville: Reader's Digest, 1992

ECTOPLASM

The word "ectoplasm" comes from the Greek *ektos* and *plasma*, meaning "exteriorized substance." Professor **Charles Richet** (1850–1935) coined the term in 1894. Ectoplasm has been described as the spiritual counterpart of protoplasm. It is a white substance that appears to stream out of the body of some **mediums** during a **séance**. It can come from any orifice, such as the ears, nose, eyes, mouth, nipples, vagina, or even from the navel. It can form itself into a materialized **spirit**, or part of a spirit (an arm, hand, or face, for example) in a **materialization** séance. It can also extrude from the medium's body and extend to support a **trumpet** or a **levitating** table. It is often accompanied by a slight smell of ozone. **Harry Edwards**'s book *The Mediumship of Jack Webber* (1940) contains a number of excellent photographs, taken in **infrared** light, showing ectoplasm issuing from the British medium **Jack Webber**.

Ectoplasm can be photographed with infrared film but seems to disappear in white light. If exposed to a sudden flash of white light, ectoplasm will immediately snap back into the medium's body, often times causing injury to the medium. As early as 1700, **Emanuel Swedenborg** (1688–1722) spoke of "a kind of vapour streaming from the pores of my body." Gustav Geley (1868–1924), when investigating Eva Carriere (known as **"Eva C"**), spoke of a dimly phosphorescent column which formed beside him. A luminous hand slowly emerged out of this column, perfectly formed and of natural size. This spirit hand then patted him several times on the arm in a friendly way.

Some mediums who do not usually produce materializations often speak of feeling a "cobwebby type of feeling" over the face, which is probably a beginning form of ectoplasm. Elizabeth Hope (1855–1919), who used the name **"Madame d'Esperance,"** described a feeling of being "covered with luminous spider webs." She said, "I feel that the air is filled with substance, and a kind of white and vaporous mass, quasi-luminous, like the steam from a locomotive, is formed in front of the abdomen." At another time she said, "It seemed that I could feel fine threads being drawn out of the pores of my skin."

Guiley states, "In experiments in the early 1900s with her colleague, Juliette Bisson, and later with German physician Baron Albert von **Schrenck-Notzing**, [Marthe] Beraud would produce masses of amorphous white or gray material.

Famous medium Stanislava Tomczyk produces ecto-
plasm during an experiment with Baron von Schrenck-
Notzing in the early twentieth century. *Courtesy
Fortean Picture Library.*

She was thoroughly examined before each sitting,
often wearing tights or a veil. Schrenck-Notzing
even had Bisson examine Beraud's genitalia to verify that she concealed nothing." The ectoplasm
was described as "sticky, gelatinous icicles dripping
from her mouth, ears, nose and eyes and down her
chin onto the front of her body." If touched, the
ectoplasm would immediately withdraw into the
body. It could, however, pass through fabric material without leaving a trace. A Canadian medium,
"Mary M." produced ectoplasm in which miniature human faces appeared. Medium **Florence
Cook** (1856–1904) produced enough ectoplasm to
form the life size figure of her spirit guide Katie.

Unfortunately some fraudulent mediums produce what looks like ectoplasm but is actually
fine cheesecloth, gauze, or similar. **Helen Dun-**

can (1897–1956) was once caught with ectoplasm made from a combination of wood pulp
and egg white, and another time with cheesecloth. One fraudulent medium admitted that he
had drawn a face on gauze rolled in goose fat.

Sources:

Doyle, Sir Arthur Conan: *The History of Spiritualism.*
New York: Doran, 1926

Edwards, Harry: *The Mediumship of Jack Webber.* London: Rider, 1940

Fodor, Nandor: *Encyclopedia of Psychic Science.* London: Arthurs Press, 1933

Guiley, Rosemary Ellen: *The Encyclopedia of Ghosts and
Spirits.* New York: Facts On File, 1992

EDDY BROTHERS:
HORATIO AND WILLIAM

The Eddy Brothers supposedly came from a long
line of family **psychics** and **mediums**. Sir
Arthur Conan Doyle said, "The mediumship of
the Eddy Brothers ... has probably never been
excelled in the matter of **materialization**, or, as we
may now call them, **ectoplasmic** forms." According
to Doyle, an observer had described the brothers as
"sensitive, distant and curt with strangers, looking
more like hard working rough farmers than
prophets or priests of a new dispensation, have
dark complexions, black hair and eyes, stiff joints, a
clumsy carriage, [they] shrink from advances, and
make newcomers ill at ease and unwelcome."

The brothers were born in Chittenden, near
Rutland, Vermont. According to **Nandor Fodor**,
"In 1692, in Salem, their grandmother four times
removed was sentenced to the pyre as a **witch**."
This was not true. Firstly *no one* was "sentenced to
the pyre" in Salem, for New England came under
the same laws as Old England in that the penalty
for witchcraft was hanging, not burning at the
stake. But more importantly, there was no one
named Eddy charged or found guilty of witchcraft,
either in Salem or anywhere in England, Scotland, or Ireland. It is, of course, possible that the
report refers to a "grandmother four times
removed" on the mother's side of the family, with

a name other than Eddy. Fodor's notes come from the original published report of Henry Steele Olcott, who, in 1874, investigated the Eddy Brothers for several months, at the instigation of the New York *Daily Graphic*. Olcott published his report in the newspaper in fifteen installments. These were later published as a book: *People From the Other World* (Hartford, 1875).

Olcott, who approached his task with a somewhat skeptical mind, stayed with the Eddy family in Vermont. He learned that the two boys had exhibited mediumistic powers from an early age. Their father had initially been fanatical in his response to this, viewing their gifts as "diabolical powers." When the boys slipped into **trance,** the father had poured boiling water over them in an attempt to bring them out of it. He had also tipped burning coal on their heads. Doyle records that the boys' mother, "who was herself strongly psychic, knew how unjustly this 'religious' brute was acting." Eventually, however, the father had come to realize that he could make money from the boys, as mediums. Olcott saw the evidence of the brutality that had been used on the Eddy Brothers, not just from their father but also from unprofessional investigators who used handcuffs that were too tight, hot sealing wax, and similar. Doyle observed, "The rumors of strange doings which occurred in the Eddy homestead had got abroad, and raised an excitement ... Folk came from all parts to investigate."

Although most reports concern the Eddy brothers, apparently there were also sisters in the family with similar abilities. According to Doyle, Olcott mentions, "The hands and arms of the sisters as well as the brothers were grooved with the marks of ligatures and scarred with burning sealing wax, while two of the girls had pieces of flesh pinched out by handcuffs." Yet little else is mentioned of these siblings.

In ten weeks with the Eddy Brothers, Olcott witnessed approximately 400 materializations. The spirits were of both sexes and varied in age and appearance, height and weight, also in ethnic origin. There were even small children and babes in arms materialized. The main **spirit guides** were two **Native Americans,** Santum and Honto. Olcott was able to measure the materialized spirits, weigh them, and work freely with them. While the medium was five feet nine in height, Santum was six feet three and Honto five feet three. Olcott said that William Eddy was the main producer of materializations and that he worked inside a **cabinet.** His brother Horatio sat outside a simple cloth screen, rather than a full cabinet, and was always within sight. Musical instruments were played behind the screen and phantom hands showed themselves over the edge. Apparently the phenomena were much stronger when the **séance** was conducted in total darkness. For the majority of the sittings, however, there was "the illumination from a shaded lamp."

Nandor reports, "Mad Indian dances shook the floor and the room resounded with yells and whoops. Olcott's words were, 'As an exhibition of pure brute force, this Indian dance is probably unsurpassed in the annals of such manifestations.'" The colonel also gave a list showing the range of mediumistic abilities, including "**rappings,** movement of objects, painting in oils and water colors under influence, **prophecy,** speaking strange tongues, **healing,** discernment of **spirits, levitation,** writing of messages, **psychometry, clairvoyance,** and finally the production of materialized forms."

Sources:

Burr, George Lincoln: *Narratives of the Witchcraft Cases: 1648–1706.* New York: Barnes & Noble, 1914

Doyle, Sir Arthur Conan: *The History of Spiritualism.* New York: Doran, 1926

Fodor, Nandor: *Encyclopedia of Psychic Science.* London: Arthurs Press, 1933

Hansen, Chadwick: *Witchcraft at Salem.* New York: George Braziller, 1969

EDMONDS, JOHN WORTH (1816–1874)

John Worth Edmonds was born in Hudson, New York, in 1816. It has been said of him that "he is the man who has done the most to make the movement of **Spiritualism** the vital force and power it has become." He was certainly the most influential early American Spiritualist.

When he was eighteen, Edmonds started studying for a legal career. In 1835, at the age of nineteen, he entered the practice of law in the office of former United States President Martin Van Buren. He went on to become a member of both branches of the State Legislature of New York, president of the Senate, and Judge of the Supreme Court of New York.

His attention was first drawn to Spiritualism in January, 1851. He was going through a period of depression at the time, reading a great deal on the subject of death and dying. He felt somewhat after many years of listening to preachers give their versions of what came after death, saying, "I did not know what to believe. I could not, if I would, believe what I did not understand, and was anxiously seeking to know, if, after death, we should again meet with those whom we had loved here, and under what circumstances." A great outcry developed against his Spiritualist beliefs when they became known, to the point that he eventually had to resign his position as Judge of the Supreme Court of New York.

In a letter to the *New York Herald*, published on August 6, 1853, Edmonds said, "I went into the investigation [of Spiritualism] originally thinking it a deception, and intending to make public my exposure of it. Having from my researches come to a different conclusion, I feel that the obligation to make known the result is just as strong." He witnessed both mental and **physical mediumship** and kept careful record of all he encountered. These records included 1,600 pages. He eventually developed mediumship himself and, between 1853 and 1854, with a small circle of friends, received many **spirit** communications. Among the spirits communicating were **Emanuel Swedenborg** and Roger Bacon. Edmonds published their messages in *Spiritualism*.

In addition to his own mediumistic encounters, Edmonds' daughter Laura became a **trance** medium. She developed incredible musical pow-

ers and the gift of tongues (**glossolalia**). Although normally she could speak only English and a smattering of French, while entranced by Spirit she spoke a large number of different languages with great fluency: Spanish, French, Greek, Italian, Portuguese, Latin, Hungarian. Indian dialects were also identified. These phenomena, and many others, were all very meticulously recorded by Edmonds.

John Edmonds never wavered in his beliefs nor in his advocacy of Spiritualism. He was a true champion for the cause, and he suffered dearly for it. Despite his amazing legal and political career and his even more amazing intellect, the press, and therefore the public, condemned him for his support of Spiritualism and, especially, for his support of the **Fox sisters** and the Rochester **rappings**.

Sources:

Awtry-Smith, Marilyn: *"They" Paved the Way*. New York: Spiritualism & More, nd

Fodor, Nandor: *Encyclopedia of Psychic Science*. London: Arthurs Press, 1933

EDWARD, JOHN (B. 1969)

John Edward was born John Edward McGee, on Long Island, New York, in 1969. He was an only child. His father, Jack, was a New York City police officer and his mother, Perinda, was a secretary. John's grandmother read tea leaves and his father admitted to having a number of personal **psychic** experiences in his younger days. John's parents separated when he was eleven.

John's mother was a regular attendee at local psychic fairs and frequently had psychics come to the house. It was at one such home gathering that John encountered Lydia Clar. Clar claimed that the main reason she was at the house was to give John a sense of direction and to encourage him in developing his own psychic abilities. From a very young age, John experienced phenomena such as **astral projection** and displayed psychic talent, speaking knowledgeably of relatives he had never met and who died long before he was born. Despite this, John himself was a great skeptic of all psychic matters. However, as a teenager he bought himself a deck of **tarot cards** and started reading them for others. Very quickly John started to do **readings** at psychic fairs and rapidly developed a following because of the accuracy of his readings. He had **premonitions** of the Challenger disaster, the Oklahoma City bombing, and the crash of Pan Am's flight 103 in Scotland.

At college, John studied Health Care Administration and Public Administration. He worked as a phlebotomist at a hospital for several years. As his psychic and **mediumistic** gifts developed, he realized that he needed to devote himself full time to them. At age twenty-six, John left the security of his hospital employment. When his mother died, on October 5, 1989, he started looking for the signs that the two of them had agreed she would send to confirm her continued existence in the afterlife. Although one of the signs came at the funeral, John had to wait several years before he got the other confirmations.

John became a regular guest on television shows, including *Larry King Live*. In 1998 he published his first book, an autobiography titled *One Last Time*. He also appeared in an HBO television special, *Life After Life*. By the year 2000, John had his own show, *Crossing Over*, which was to become a major success and to make John a star. It was syndicated in the United States and eventually appeared on television in Great Britain and Australia. His second book, *Crossing Over With John Edward* was an instant best seller. In 2001, *Time* magazine published an unfair attack on John, when a journalist named Leon Jaroff wrote a story of half-truths, innuendos, and pure speculation. He wrote it without ever interviewing John, without attending the show, and with talking to only one disgruntled audience member named Michael O'Neill. Despite strong letters to *Time* from network executives, and consideration of a lawsuit, the magazine declined to print a retraction. By contrast, scientific tests were carried out at the University of Arizona in Tucson, using five mediums: John Edward, **George Anderson**, **Anne Gehman**, Suzane Northrop, and Laurie Campbell. The whole session was

Psychic John Edward in New York, late 2004. *Evan Agostini/Getty Images.*

televised and included a feedback from nineteen electrodes attached to the mediums' heads, to measure heart and brain activity readings. The final results showed that while a group of control subjects (non-mediums) scored 36 percent accuracy, the true mediums scored an average of 83 percent accuracy.

Today John lives with his wife Sandra and their two dogs, Jolie and Roxie, on Long Island, New York. His continues his television show, private readings, lectures and workshops. His great success is a testament to what has been repeatedly described as his "down-to-earth approach, and obvious sincerity."

Sources:

Buckland, Raymond: *Buckland's Book of Spirit Communications*. St. Paul: Llewellyn, 2004

Schwartz, Gary E. and William L. Simon: *The Afterlife Experiments*. Pocket Books: New York, 2002

EDWARDS, HARRY
(1893–1976)

Edwards was born Henry James Edwards and became the best known healer in Britain, if not the world. He began **healing** in 1935 and claimed to have cured more than 10,000 people; many of them previously pronounced "incurable." His mail totaled tens of thousands of letters a year; sometimes as many as 5,000 letters in one week. He practiced both direct healing and **absent healing**, with a success rate of between 85 percent and 90 percent.

During World War I, Edwards was working in the Middle East building a railroad. In the course of the work many of the laborers injured themselves and went to Edwards for healing. They referred to him as *hakim*, "healer." Edwards himself didn't think he was doing anything unusual, attributing their fast recovery to them rather than to himself. On returning to England, after the war, he didn't pursue his healing abilities.

Edwards attended a **Spiritualist** church service in 1922 and was very impressed with it. However, it was not until 1935 that he went with a friend to a small Spiritualist service held in a house close to where he lived. He received a number of messages from the **mediums** telling him that he had a tremendous healing potential. At the time he ran a small printing and stationery business. He started going to two different **development circles** and received encouragement regarding the healing gift. His first attempt at a healing involved a man in Brompton Hospital, who had been dying from consumption and pleurisy, but recovered fully and returned to work.

Shortly after this first incident, a woman went into Edwards's shop without really knowing what had impelled her to enter it. She told him that her husband had been in a London hospital, suffering from advanced lung cancer. The doctors had given up and sent him home to die. Edwards told the woman he would seek **spirit** healing for the man. He did so and the very next morning that man was up and making a cup of tea for his wife. When the man next went to the hospital a new doctor refused to believe that the records in front of him applied to the man he was examining, who was obviously doing well. Soon the man was back at work and, to Edwards's knowledge, lived at least another twenty years. Such cures continued. His next patient had tuberculosis and a cavity in her lung, and healed completely after Edwards did a healing. Edwards said, "Later she became a nurse in the same sanatorium where she had been a patient less than a year before. This girl never suffered again. She married, has a family and is fully well today."

Edwards said, "The healer does not heal of himself or by reason of any technique or ritual that he may adopt. The healing directive comes from Spirit." He thought of himself not as the healer but as the channel for healing energy. As Edwards went on to explain, "These three cases proved to me that there was 'something' in healing. Coincidence was ruled out." (*Spirit Healing*, 1960). Before long he opened his house in Shere, Surrey, as a healing sanctuary where the sick came in ever-increasing numbers. The Harry Edwards' Spiritual Healing Sanctuary is still in operation today. At Edwards's death in 1976, Joan and Ray Branch, who had worked with Edwards for many years, took over the running of it. Like Cayce, Edwards found that he was able to heal just as successfully absently, when the patient was hundreds or even thousands of miles away. He had many spectacular successes, including several cancer cures.

Edwards publicly demonstrated his gift of healing in every major city and town in Great Britain and in many countries abroad, performing what the press often termed "miracles of healing." His clients included members of the British royal family, and other royal families, cabinet ministers and politicians, movie stars, sports personalities, and religious leaders. Many doctors and specialists were frequent observers at his healings and would bring their own patients for healing. He had a great respect for the Native Americans' knowledge of herbs and healing and for other similar cultures. He believed that it was

Native Americans who worked through him. Edwards also later came to recognize that he was working with **spirit guides** that included Louis Pasteur and Lord Lister, the nineteenth century English surgeon.

Sources:

Edwards, Harry: A *Guide to the Understanding and Practice of Spiritual Healing*. Guildford: Healer Publishing Company, 1974

Edwards, Harry: *Spirit Healing*. London: Herbert Jenkins, 1960

Fishley, Margaret: *The Supernatural*. London: Aldus, 1976

Miller, Paul: *Born to Heal*. London: Spiritualist Press, 1962

EGLINTON, WILLIAM (B. 1857)

Born in Islington, London, on July 10, 1857, William Eglinton first heard of **Spiritualism** at the age of seventeen when he attended a debate at the London Hall of Science with his father. The debate between Dr. Sexton and Mr. Foote was lively enough to inspire Eglinton's father to go home and start a **development circle**. Eglinton was part of the circle but quickly became disillusioned when nothing seemed to happen. He fixed a sign on the door of the circle room saying "There are lunatics confined here; they will shortly be let loose. Highly dangerous." His father was not amused and told him to either join the circle or leave the house while the **séance** was in progress. Eglinton chose to stay, though was determined to undermine any eventual phenomena.

Instead, Eglinton went into a **trance** and caused the table to move. Later he said, "Something did happen, but I was powerless to prevent it. The table began to show signs of life and vigour; it suddenly rose off the ground and steadily raised itself in the air, until we had to stand to reach it. This was in full gaslight ... The next evening ... after we had read the customary prayer, I seemed to be no longer of this earth. A most ecstatic feeling came over me,

and I presently passed into a trance." He produced **materializations**, through his **guides** Joey Sandy and Ernest. These materializations appeared in full moonlight. News of his successes spread and he was soon so inundated with requests for séances that he gave up his job with a printing firm and became a full time **medium**. Eventually his mediumship developed to rival even that of **Daniel Dunglas Home**. Sir **Arthur Conan Doyle** said, "His work resembles that of D. D. Home. His séances were usually held in the light, and he always agreed willingly to any proposed tests. A further point of similarity was the fact that his results were observed and recorded by many eminent men and by good critical witnesses."

For twelve years Eglinton was subjected to the severest examination by such people and bodies as the Brixton Psychological Society, **British National Association of Spiritualists**, Archdeacon Colley, Scientific Research Committee of the BSA, **Society for Psychical Research**, Upsala University, Alfred Russel Wallace, Professors **Charles Richet**, Tornebom, Edland, Zöllner, Dr. Myers (brother of **Frederick W. H. Myers**), and many others. The well known stage magician Harry Kellar said of Eglinton, "I went as a sceptic, but I must own that I came away utterly unable to explain, by any natural means, the phenomena that I witnessed."

Staying at Malvern as the guest of Dr. and Mrs. Nichols, Eglinton displayed incredible materialization in the open air; out in the Nichols's garden. In *The Scientific Basis of Spiritualism* (Boston, 1882) Epes Sargent wrote, "Mr. Eglinton lay on a garden bench in plain sight. We saw the bodies of four visitors form themselves from a cloud of white vapour and then walk about, robed all in purest white, upon the lawns where no deception was possible." Eglinton was constantly in sight and there was no possibility of an accomplice scaling a wall without being seen.

In the June 2, 1876, issue of *The Spiritualist*, Archdeacon Colley described how Eglinton was "entranced and carried by invisible power over

Medium William Eglinton with a fully materialized spirit, c. 1878. *Courtesy Fortean Picture Library.*

the table several times, the heels of his boots being made to touch the head of our medical friend [Dr. Malcolm]. Then he was taken to the further end of the dining room, and finally, after being tilted about as a thing of no weight whatever, was deposited quietly in his chair." On March 16, 1878, Eglinton held a séance at the home of Mrs. Makdougal Gregory and at it transported himself from the room into another room on the floor above. The account of the séance was published in the March 22, 1878 issue of *The Spiritualist.* Eglinton traveled to various parts of the world, including South Africa, India, Denmark, Germany, France, and Russia.

On October 29, 1884, Eglinton held a séance for the British Prime Minister William Ewart Gladstone, described as "the greatest British statesman of the nineteenth century." (*Encyclopedia Britannica*) Gladstone did not profess to be a Spiritualist, although after this séance he did become a member of the Society for Psychical Research. Gladstone said, "I have always thought that scientific men run too much in a groove. They do noble work in their own special lines of research, but they are too often indisposed to give any attention to matters which seem to conflict with their established modes of thought. Indeed, they not infrequently attempt to deny that into which they have never inquired, not sufficiently realizing the fact that there may possibly be forces in nature of which they known nothing."

Sources:

Doyle, Sir Arthur Conan: *The History of Spiritualism.* New York: Doran, 1926

Fodor, Nandor: *Encyclopedia of Psychic Science.* London: Arthurs Press, 1933

EGYPTIANS

The ancient Egyptian religion was deeply imbued with the cult of the dead and a strong belief in a life after death. The *Ka*, or etheric double, was a copy of the physical body though was not to be confused with the *Ba*, or *Bai*, which was the soul, and the *khu*, or spirit. The conception of the *ka* wandering about after death promoted the ancient Egyptian belief in ghosts. The *ka* generally lived in the tomb with the deceased body, and could be visited there by the *khu*. If the *ka* was not provided with sufficient food and drink, it would wander about beyond the tomb, searching for nourishment.

There were various orders of priests, ranked according to their particular office. The priest who offered sacrifice and libation in the temple was the highest of the priests and was generally called "the Prophet." He dressed in a leopard skin fitted over his linen robes. He was a very eminent personage and sometimes carried a special name. For example, the high Theban pontiff was "First Prophet of Amon in Thebes," while the one in Heliopolis was "He who is able to see the Great God" (later changed to "The great one with visions of the god Re"). The duty of the **prophet** was to be well versed in all religious matters, the laws, the worship of the gods, and the discipline of the whole order of the priesthood. He presided over the temple and the sacred rites.

There were also priests known as *horologues* (priest-timekeepers), and the astrologers. The astrologers had to know the mythological calendar and to be able to explain all the important dates. Each day of the year was labeled as either good, neutral, or bad, according to events of the past that had occurred on those days. Magical papyri contain instructions not to perform certain ceremonies on particular days, because hostile powers would be present to prevent the desired outcome. In the last epochs of the Egyptian civilization, the astrologer-priests tied in the destiny of every person to the cosmic circumstances of his or her birth, drawing a horoscope to show the astral influences.

There were also priests known as *pastophores* who were bearers of sacred objects and slayers of sacrificial beasts. Then there were those the Greeks called the *oneirocrites*. They interpreted **dreams**. For a period there was a custom of spending a night in the temple in order to receive guidance from the gods. This guidance came in dreams which had to be interpreted by the oneirocrites. The Egyptians believed that, even without sleeping in a temple, the gods could make their will known to the people through dreams, and great importance was attached to dreams which included figures of the gods. The skill to interpret dreams was cherished. There are many examples in the Egyptian texts of important dreams that were interpreted by priests.

Sources:

Budge, Sir E.A. Wallis: *Egyptian Magic*. New York: Bell Publishing, 1991

Rawlinson, George: *History of Ancient Egypt*. New York: Dodd, Mead, 1881

Sauneron, Serge: *The Priests of Ancient Egypt*. New York: Grove Press, 1960

Wilkinson, Sir J. Gardner: *The Ancient Egyptians: Their Life and Customs*. New York: Crescent Books, 1988

EISENBUD, JULE (1908–1998)

Born in 1908, Jule Eisenbud became a physician, psychiatrist, **parapsychologist**, and founding member of the Medical Section of the **American Society for Psychical Research**. Eisenbud authored many articles on psychiatry and psychoanalysis and also contributed articles on parapsychology to such journals as *Journal of Parapsychology, Psychoanalytic Quarterly, Journal of the ASPR,* and *Journal of the SPR (London).* Eisenbud practiced psychiatry beginning in 1938, and in 1950 moved his practice to Denver, where he was a clinical professor at the University of Colorado Medical School.

Eisenbud experimented with **extrasensory perception, telepathy,** and the **psi** faculty. In 1963, he published an article arguing that it is impossible, in the field of parapsychology, to devise an experiment that is truly repeatable. His best known book was *The World of* **Ted Serios**: *Thoughtographic Studies of an Extraordinary Mind* (1967). This was based on his experiments with an alcoholic bellhop from Chicago, who could produce photographs using his mind alone. By concentrating his thoughts, Serios could look into the lens of a Polaroid camera and cause the ensuing photograph to be of what he was thinking. Eisenbud tested and examined Serios for some years and found no trickery or fraudulence of any kind. Two reporters, Charles Reynolds and David Eisendrath, claimed that Serios was a fake but they had never had the chance to examine the "gismo" Serios used (a small paper tube he pointed at the camera to aid his concentration), as had Eisenbud.

Sources:

Eisenbud, Jule: *The World of Ted Serios: Thoughtographic Studies of an Extraordinary Mind.* New York: William Morrow, 1967

Shepard, Leslie A: *Encyclopedia of Occultism & Parapsychology.* New York: Avon Books, 1978

Jule Eisenbud (left) published his study on the abilities of Ted Serios (right), who claimed to generate photos on film using only his mind. *Courtesy Fortean Picture Library.*

Wilson, Colin: *The Supernatural: Mysterious Powers.* London: Aldus Books, 1975

ELECTRONIC VOICE PHENOMENA (EVP)

Harold Sherman said, "By use of an ordinary tape recorder and/or a radio set attuned to unused frequencies, **spirit** voices of purported entities are being received" (*You Can Communicate With the Unseen World,* 1974). This is known as Electronic Voice Phenomenon (EVP).

People have experienced amplified and recorded spirit contact since the birth of electronic receiving and recording devices, and spirit voices have been heard over the telephone since its ear-

liest days. From the days of the first radios, spirit voices have come through the radio speakers. But the phenomena grew in frequency near the end of World War II, with the gradual spread of the use of the first wire recorders, which then gave way to tape recorders. Wire recorders had been used by the military during the war and had worked well. It soon became apparent, however, that tape was a better medium for recording, first coated paper tape and later magnetized plastic tape.

In the 1920s, Thomas Alva Edison is reported to have said: "If our personality survives, then it is strictly logical or scientific to assume that it retains memory, intellect, other faculties and knowledge that we acquire on this Earth. Therefore ... if we can evolve an instrument so delicate as to be affected by our personality as it survives in the next life, such an instrument, when made available, ought to record something." In the Jun, 1922 issue of *Popular Radio*, there was a major article titled "Can the Dead Reach Us by Radio?" Other periodicals of the period also touched on the subject. But today spirit communication goes even further than tape recorders and radios. It includes televisions, **computers**, cell phones, and satellite dishes.

The spirit world operates at a different frequency from the physical world. In order to communicate, **mediums** have to speed up their vibrations while the spirits slow down theirs. It's a delicate operation that takes practice for both sides to arrive at the same vibration suitable for communication. With tape recording, since the spirit messages are at a higher frequency, it helps to have more than one speed on the machine, or the ability to vary the speed. Recording can then be done at a fast speed and played back at a slow speed, with the volume as high as possible. Access to an amplifier is also helpful.

Two of the first serious investigators of electronic spirit communication were **Friedrich Juergenson** and Latvian psychologist Dr. **Konstantin Raudive**. In 1967, Juergenson's book *Radio Contact with the Dead* was translated into German. In it he detailed how outdoor recordings of bird songs had also apparently picked up the voice of his deceased mother, calling him by his childhood name. Raudive read the book skeptically, and then visited Juergenson to learn his methodology. Consequently, Raudive decided to experiment on his own. He soon began developing his own experimental techniques. Like Juergenson, Raudive too heard the voice of his own deceased mother, who called him by his boyhood name: "Kostulit, this is your mother." Over a number of years Raudive collected dozens of tapes of recorded spirit messages, totaling 72,000 voices; many recorded under strict laboratory conditions.

At the eleventh annual conference of the **Parapsychological Association**, held at the University of Frieburg, Germany, in September 1968, Dr. Raudive played some of these tapes to Dr. **Jule Eisenbud** (who worked with **Ted Serios** on thought photography), Mrs. K. M. Goldney from the British **Society for Psychical Research**, Dr. Walter Uphoff of the University of Colorado, and others. As Dr. Uphoff described it:

> "All we could do was listen and try to figure out what might explain what we were hearing. Some voices were clearer and more distinct than others; the level of static or background noise was high because the volume had to be turned to maximum level in order to reproduce the otherwise faint voices; and the cadence certainly suggested that these were not likely to be bits of stray radio signals."

Most of the received voices had been inaudible at the time of recording. George W. Meek's book *After We Die, What Then?* (1987) deals with breakthroughs in electronic spirit communication. Meek predicted, "A workable, dependable, repeatable two-way communication with the mental-causal levels of consciousness should be demonstrated in Europe, the United States, or South America well before the end of the century." In 1982, Meek traversed the globe distributing recordings of communications between his associate William O'Neil and a scientist who had been dead for fourteen years. Meek also provided wiring diagrams, guidelines, photographs, and technical data for research in a 100-page technical report he had prepared.

Experiments were conducted using such things as low frequency oscillators, ultraviolet and infrared lights, variable speed tape decks. In the mid-1980s, Ken Webster received messages on his computer that supposedly came from a Thomas Harden of sixteenth century England. Harden seemed to think that Webster was living in his house (an ancient building dating back to that time). The many messages have been examined through research at Oxford Library and confirm the language, dialect, spelling, etc., of the period. Webster later produced a book, *The Vertical Plane*, which details the events.

In the mid 1980s, Klaus Schreiber received on his television pictures of the faces of various deceased people, including Romy Schneider and Albert Einstein. He got the pictures by focusing a video camera onto the screen of the television and feeding the camera's output back into the television, forming a feedback loop. About this time a couple in Luxembourg started getting amazing voice contacts through their radio. The deceased Konstantin Raudive spoke through the apparatus to them in 1994, saying, "It can only work when the vibrations of those present are in complete harmony and when their aims and intentions are pure." Innumerable people have received contact from deceased persons including relatives, friends, and others they didn' know. Sarah Estep started the American Association of Electronic Voice Phenomena in 1982. In the 1990s, the International Network for **Instrumental Transcommunication** (INIT) was started by Mark Macy, though this was later fragmented due to the skepticism and pressure of the scientific community.

Robert Egby's *Parapscyhic Journal* (Issue #22, October 14, 2004) included this report:

> "This month we heard from *Parapsychic Journal* subscriber Maryse Locke who, together with her husband John Locke, lives in a suburb south of Paris, France. Nothing unusual about that except that Maryse and John operate www.Transcommunication. org, an expansive and informative website devoted to Electronic Voice Phenomena and Instrumental Transcommunication. In the auto sales vernacular, this website is 'loaded' with everything you might wish to know in metaphysics, Spiritualism and electronic recording devices—and more important [sic], how to do it … The website is also bilingual—English and French. It also has a very useful index of terms."

Sources:

Buckland, Raymond: *Buckland's Book of Spirit Communications*. St. Paul: Llewellyn, 2004

Instrumental Transcommunication—EVP & ITC: http://transcommunication.org

Meek, George W.: *After We Die, What Then?* Columbus: Ariel Press, 1987

Raudive, Konstantin: *Breakthrough: An Amazing Experiment in Electronic Communication with the Dead*. London: Smythe, 1971

Sherman, Harold: *You Can Communicate With the Unseen World*. New York: Fawcett, 1974

World ITC Organization: http://www.worlditc.org

Emanations *see* **Ectoplasm**

EMPATH

An empath is one who psychically tunes into another person or group of people. This may be done consciously or unconsciously. For example, it may be a case of **precognition**, as in waking in the middle of the night aware of a disaster that has taken place and then finding, the following morning, that there was such a disaster. Or it may be a case of having an uncertain feeling of unease for a period and then, when a national calamity occurs, having the feeling dissipate. It is more specific than simply being a **psychic**.

Sources:

Bletzer, June G.: *The Encyclopedia Psychic Dictionary*. Lithia Springs: New Leaf, 1998

ENDOR, WOMAN OF

In the **Bible** there is reference to the Woman of Endor, visited by Saul (I Samuel 28). She is described as "a woman that hath a familiar **spirit**." In other words, a **spirit guide** or **guardian angel**. The woman is a **Spiritualist** medium (*not* a witch, as is the common misconception). Endor is a small hamlet on the northern slope of a hill, four miles south of Mount Tabor. When Saul meets with her—despite the fact that he tried to get rid of all such **mediums**—the woman describes exactly what she sees **clairvoyantly**. She says, "I *saw* gods ascending out of the earth. An old man cometh up and he is covered with a mantle." This turns out to be Samuel and Saul is able to speak with him, through the agencies of the medium. Saul went to consult this medium on the eve of the battle of Bilboa, because he was afraid of the massed armies of the Philistines. The woman immediately recognized him, despite his disguise, but Saul assured her he would cause her no harm.

In the King James translation of the Bible, James heads the chapter, "Saul, having destroyed all the witches, and now in his fear forsaken of God, seeketh to a witch ..." Yet nowhere in the actual passages is the word "witch" used. The woman is simply described as having a "familiar spirit," and there is no description of her, of her age, or her house. Yet later writers continue to refer to her as a witch and depict her as an old hag living in a hovel. Indeed, Montague Summers, a supposed authority on witchcraft, says, "In a paroxysm of rage and fear the haggard crone turned to him (Saul) and shrieked out: 'Why hast thou deceived me?'" This is pure imagination on the part of Summers.

Reginald Scott, as early as 1584, doubted the existence of witches and suggested that Saul actually saw nothing but "an illusion or cozenage."

Sources:

Buckland, Raymond: *The Witch Book: The Encyclopedia of Witchcraft, Wicca and Neo-Paganism.* Detroit: Visible Ink Press, 2002

Scott, Reginald: *Discoverie of Witchcraft.* London: 1584

Summers, Montague: *The History of Witchcraft and Demonology.* New York: University Books, 1956

Ethereal Body *see* Astral Body

Etheric Double *see* Astral Body

EVA C. (CARRIERE)

Eva Carriere, whose real name was Marthe Béraud, was discovered as a **medium** in Algiers by a General Noel and his wife. "Eva" had been engaged to their son Maurice, before his death in the Congo. Eva was the daughter of a French army officer and became one of the most controversial **physical mediums** of the early twentieth century.

General Noel invited noted physiologist and **psychical researcher** Professor **Charles Richet** to investigate Eva. At the Villa Carmen in Algiers,

Richet saw the materialization of a full-size figure known by Eva as Bien Boa. Bien Boa was supposedly a 300-year-old Brahmin Hindu and the spiritual guide for the Noel family. He had a sister named Bergoglia, who also occasionally manifested. In photographs Bien Boa looks like a large cardboard cutout, as do several of the **materializations** produced by Eva C. Richet noted an artificial quality to Bien Boa's beard but seemed satisfied that the medium had produced him paranormally. The professor published the results of his investigation in the April, 1906, edition of *Annales des Sciences Psychiques.*

Some years later in Paris, Eva C. was examined by psychic researchers Baron A. von **Schrenck-Notzing** and Gustav Geley. (It was the baron who gave the medium her professional name of Eva C.) Geley later published a book, *Clairvoyance and Materialization* (New York, 1927), which contained a number of photographs taken of Eva C producing **ectoplasm** while in **trance**. Fodor reported that during her trances, Eva "suffered much, writhing like a woman in childbirth and her pulse rose from 90 to 120."

Eva C. was also studied by the British Psychical Research Society, though she failed to impress them. In her later séances, she was unable to produce as well-developed forms as earlier and the materializations were much slower and seemed more difficult. Eva was made to wear special dresses or even, on many occasions, to sit in the nude. A battery of eight cameras, two of them stereoscopic, was trained on her and 225 photographs obtained, the sittings being held in good light. Of a séance held on April 15, 1912, Professor Richet said, "The manifestations began at once. White substance appeared on the neck of the medium; then a head was formed which moved from left to right and placed itself on the medium's head. A photograph was taken. After the flashlight the head reappeared by the side of Eva's head, about sixteen inches from it, connected by a long bunch of white substance. It looked like the head of a man ... a woman's head then appeared on the right." The medium was carefully searched both before and immediately after the sitting.

Medium Eva C. (Carriere) produces ectoplasm in the shape of a face in 1912. *Courtesy Fortean Picture Library.*

At a séance on November 26, 1913, conducted by Baron von Schrenck-Notzing, a strong emetic was given to Eva, to answer the charge that the ectoplasm was actually regurgitated material. It satisfied the researchers that she had swallowed nothing. A number of experiments took place at Dr. Gustav Geley's laboratories in 1917 and 1918. Nearly 150 scientists and others witnessed the sittings. Geley said,

"The usual precautions were rigorously observed during the **séances** in my laboratory. On coming into the room where the séances were held and to which I alone had previous access, the medium was completely undressed in my presence and dressed in a tight garment, sewn up the back and at the wrists; the hair, and the cavity of the mouth were examined by me and my collaborators before and after the séances. Eva was walked backwards to the wicker chair in the dark **cabinet**; her hands were always held in full sight outside the curtains and the room was always quite well lit during the whole time. I do not merely say: there was no trickery; I say there was no possibility of trickery. Further, I cannot repeat it too often, nearly always the materializations took place under my own eyes, and I have observed their genesis and their whole development."

Such was the thoroughness of the investigations of Eva C. Yet during the two months that the medium was in London, being examined by the **Society for Psychical Research** (SPR), only twenty of the thirty-eight séances produced phenomena and those were very weak. Professor Charles Richet said, "They (the SPR) admit that the only possible trickery is regurgitation. But what is meant by that? How can masses of mobile substance, organized as hands, faces, and drawings, be made to emerge from the oesophagus or the stomach? … How, when the medium's hands are tied and held, could papers be unfolded, put away and made to pass through a veil?" In the November 1954 issue of the *Journal of the SPR* (Vol. 37, No. 682), Rudolf Lambert published a detailed article on *Dr. Geley's Reports on the Medium Eva C.*

Sources:

Fodor, Nandor: *Encyclopedia of Psychic Science.* London: Arthurs Press, 1933

Holroyd, Stuart: *The Supernatural: Minds Without Boundaries.* London: Aldus, 1975

EVANS, COLIN

Born in Wales, Colin Evans was a British **medium** who had the ability to levitate. He was photographed in the 1930s levitating three feet off the ground. This levitation took place at London's Conway Hall, before a large audience during a public **séance**. His feat seemed to emulate that of **Daniel Dunglas Home** which was described in August, 1852 by F. L. Burr, editor of *Hartford Times,* "Suddenly, without any explanation on the part of the company, Home was taken up into the air … Again and again he was taken from the floor, and the third time he was carried to the ceiling of the apartment."

Colin Evans similarly rose into the air while in trance. His **levitation** took place in the center of the auditorium, where there was no possibility of fraud from hidden wires or similar.

Sources:

Buckland, Raymond: *Buckland's Book of Spirit Communications*. St. Paul: Llewellyn, 2004

Picknett, Lynn: *Mysteries of Mind Space & Time; the Unexplained: Defying the Law of Gravity*. Westport: H. S. Stuttman, 1992

EXORCISM

From the Greek *exousia*, meaning "oath," to exorcise is to ritually expel by means of conjurations and **prayers**. It is, in effect, a magical ceremony. Ancient civilizations of Babylonia, Assyria and Mesopotamia believed 5,000 years ago that various **spirits** or entities existed and could possess a person, causing both physical and mental illness. The ancient **Egyptians** believed in possession and practiced exorcism. The practice is found universally, with exorcism rituals common in many societies. The idea of such possession was especially prominent in the Middle Ages, when the Christian Church was almost totally preoccupied with the Devil and believed all possessions were by demons.

Far more frequent than the possession of people is the possession of houses by spirits. The entity possessing a building is known as a *poltergeist* ("rattling ghost"), which differs from a **ghost**. A ghost is usually the spirit of a person who once lived and is now dead, while a poltergeist is an entity, force, or buildup of **psychic** energy, that has no connection to anyone who was once alive.

Anyone can perform an exorcism. A knowledge of demonology and ceremonial magic can be very useful but is not essential. The main thing is

that the exorcist must be able to speak and act with complete confidence and authority, for the entity must be ordered out of the person or thing it possesses, and is always reluctant to leave.

The Church believes that the subject is possessed either by Satan himself or by one of his minions, a devil. The Church's rites, therefore, command in the name of God, **Jesus**, the Holy Scriptures, etc. The fact that these rites are not always effective seems evidence in favor of the pagan point of view that, rather than a "Satanic demon," it is actually a malignant spirit. Because such spirits existed long before Christianity, there is no reason why they should be swayed by the names and terms of Christianity. It is certainly not unusual for a priest to have to make numerous attempts to exorcise before being successful. However, speaking in general terms, there is no reason why one form of exorcism should not be as effective as another. Much depends upon the exorcist him or herself, and whether or not the right presence and voice of authority is presented.

While Christianity considers exorcism a battle for the possessed one's soul, in Hinduism, **Buddhism**, Islam, Shinto, and many other religions, it is simply a matter of getting rid of an inconvenience and a nuisance.

Sources:

Ebon, Martin (ed): *The Devil's Bride: Exorcism: Past and Present*. New York: Harper & Row, 1974

Guiley, Rosemary Ellen: *Harper's Encyclopedia of Mystical & Paranormal Experience*. San Francisco: Harper SanFrancisco, 1991

Thurston, Rev. Herbert: *Ghosts and Poltergeists*. London: Regnery, 1950

EXTRASENSORY PERCEPTION (ESP)

Extrasensory Perception, *psi*, *Paragnosis*, or ESP as it is more generally known is today commonly accepted as fact. This is mainly due to the work of Dr. **Joseph Banks Rhine**, one of the pioneers of **parapsychology**, and Dr. **Samuel**

George Soal. For many years, Soal conducted parapsychological studies on the various forms of **mediumship** and statistical experiments in **telepathy** in England. In later years, Soal was found guilty of fraud in some of his telepathic experiments. This certainly tarnished his image, yet he had done outstanding work in the field for decades. The term "extrasensory perception" was coined by Dr. Rhine and used by him as the title of a book published in 1934.

Serious investigation of possible "thought transference" dates from the late nineteenth century, when a number of experiments were conducted in England by Mrs. A. Verrall and C. P. Sanger. By the late 1920s, in similar experiments, Miss I. Jephson and R. A. Fisher found that the everyday playing cards previously relied upon were not ideal for testing purposes. This led to the introduction of the Zener deck of cards, developed by Dr. **Karl E. Zener** during the 1930s. They consisted of twenty-five cards, with five each of five different designs. The designs were basic black ink on white backgrounds, showing circle, square, cross, star, and wavy lines. Today these **Zener cards** are used almost exclusively for testing ESP.

The point of ESP testing is to ascertain whether or not a person can know what is in another person's mind a greater number of times than could be explained purely by chance. With one person looking at the twenty-five **Zener cards**, it is known that a second person would guess correctly which card was being looked at five times out of the twenty-five, if it was simply by chance. Going through the deck a number of times, the *average* correct guesses would be five per twenty-five cards. Scores above that are notable. As an example of what has been achieved in such tests, Hubert E. Pearce, Jr. was tested at Duke University in Durham, North Carolina, and guessed correctly 3,746 cards out of 10,300. In London, B. Shackleton guessed correctly 1,101 cards out of 3,789. Shackleton guessed not the actual card being looked at, but the card that was going to be looked at next! Such scores, carried out in laboratory conditions, would seem to prove beyond doubt that extrasensory perception is a fact.

If two people sit down facing one another, at opposite sides of a room, with one holding the cards in front while the other tries to guess which card is being looked at, this would not be "laboratory conditions." No matter how impressive the scores, they would not be seriously considered. Many minor factors could contribute to the Guesser's choices. The cards may have odd marks such as spots, specks, scratches, or other visual clues on their backs. If only unconsciously, these could help the Guesser differentiate one card from another. Another factor might be the face of the Sender. An unconscious facial movement might trigger the Guesser's choices. Many precautions must be taken for the results to be truly under laboratory conditions. The two participants must not be in the same room. Moving on from one card to the next should be signaled by a flashing light or a buzzer. Even the cards should not be picked by the Sender; they should be shuffled by a machine and put into truly random order. Every possible precaution should be taken and even then, if your mind is set against it, you can discount the results. For example, if a person guesses 8,000 correct cards out of 10,000 (astronomical odds against chance), who is to say that if they went on to try another 10,000 they might not be so far off that the overall score would be no more than chance?

In **Spiritualist** mediumship the aim is to show that ESP is not a factor. Mediums contact spirits of the dead and receive from them information of an evidential nature that is unknown to the medium or to the sitter(s). It is only on later investigation that there is confirmation of the accuracy of the messages received, proving that ESP was not a factor. On the other hands, in many **psychic readings** (such as with **tarot cards**, palmistry, etc.) ESP is frequently a factor; the reader merely picking up information from the mind of the sitter. Of course, if this is complex, accurate information, then it is very credible evidence of the psychic's ESP ability.

Sources:
Buckland, Raymond: *A Pocket Guide to the Supernatural*. New York: Ace Books, 1969

Buckland, Raymond: *The Fortune–Telling Book: The Encyclopedia of Divination and Soothsaying.* Detroit: Visible Ink Press, 2004

Ebon, Martin: *True Experiences in Telepathy.* New York: Signet, 1967

Holroyd, Stuart: *The Supernatural: Minds Without Boundaries.* London: Aldus, 1975

Rhine, Joseph Banks: *Extrasensory Perception.* Boston: Bruce Humphries, 1934

Rhine, Joseph Banks: *New Frontiers of the Mind.* New York: Farrar & Rinehart, 1937

Spraggett, Alan: *The Unexplained.* New York: New American Library, 1967

EXTRATERRESTRIALS

In *Mysteries of Mind Space & Time; the Unexplained: Reach for the Stars* (H. S. Stuttman, 1992), Ron Hyams wrote, "Some biologists believe that intelligence confers such advantages that evolutionary pressures will always tend to promote the development of intelligent species—and that an intelligent species is likely to develop a technology that will enable it to reach out and make contact with beings on other planets." But theorists have raised the question: Even if it could be assumed that there is intelligent life on other planets, how long might such civilizations endure? Hyams continues, "It would be reasonable to suppose that each civilization lasts for a very short time only … As intelligence is unlikely to reach an advanced stage on two planets at the same time, it could be argued that we are not likely to encounter another civilization at the brief moment of its full flowering … technologically skilled civilizations from different planets may never meet."

Why, then, is belief in extraterrestrial life so widespread? In 1947, the first sightings were recorded of what became known as "flying saucers," or UFOs (unidentified flying objects). On June 24, 1947, Kenneth Arnold of Boise, Idaho, alerted the world when he observed nine shining disks flying in formation across the peaks of the Cascade Mountains in Washington State.

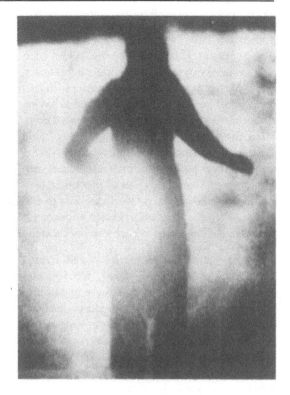

Famous photograph of an extraterrestrial emerging from a UFO, taken by Howard Menger in the 1950s. *Courtesy Fortean Picture Library.*

Arnold was a private pilot, at the time searching for the wreckage of a downed commercial airplane. In talking to reporters, Arnold mentioned that the disks looked "like a saucer skipping across water," and the term "flying saucer" was born.

Yet UFO sightings have been a part of all recorded history. Shortly before discovering the New World, Christopher Columbus sighted a distant glimmering light in the sky that vanished then reappeared a number of times and over several nights. He and his crew witnessed the event. During the reign of Charlemagne (742–814), several people from Earth were said to have been taken away by beings from space, and later returned. They were apparently abducted to be shown how the space people lived. On their return, however, their fellow humans viewed them as sorcerers and put them to death. A sixteenth century woodcut shows a sky filled with strange dark balls over the city of Basel, Switzerland in August 1566. Similar objects had been seen in the sky over Nürnberg four years earlier. The **Bible** mentions Ezekiel's encounter with four "living creatures," which were described as having identical shining wheels that accompanied them when they rose from the ground. They could move in any direction without turning. NASA space engineer Josef F. Blumrich researched various interpretations of this Ezekiel encounter, feeling he would be able to refute them, only to end up a convert. He went on to design a spacecraft such as might have been encountered by Ezekiel.

Sightings and even photographs (well-investigated, not just obviously fake), movies, and videos have been obtained of these apparently extraterrestrial vehicles. No amount of dismissal by "scientists" equating the sightings with weather balloons, the planet Venus, automobile headlights, swamp gas, and other implausible explanations can deter those who actually see them. And they have been seen by people from all walks of life, from around the world.

One theory holds that the UFOs come not from outer space but from "inner space", another dimension. Certainly some of the sightings would seem to support this view, where UFOs have seemingly suddenly **materialized** or dematerialized. There are certain areas of the United States, and indeed of the world, that are termed "door-ways," where such appearances and disappearances have taken place more or less regularly.

Some of the people who **channel** claim that the entity they are channeling is from another planet or far distant galaxy. **Darryl Anka**'s "Bashar" says he is from the planet Essassani, five hundred light years away. **Jessica Lansing** channeled "Michael," who said he was "of the mid-causal plane" and made up of a thousand fragments of an entity like himself. **Jach Pursel**'s "Lazaris" says that he has never been in human form; he is a "group form" living in another dimension.

The Aetherius Society in Britain originated in London in May, 1954, and believes that through its leader, George King, its members are in communication with advanced beings from outer space. These beings, the members claim, visit Earth in huge spaceships and watch over all of Earth's inhabitants, fearful that we will destroy ourselves. These advanced mystics are supposed to live on Venus, Mars, or Neptune. George King declares that the different spacecraft are sent to Earth on the direct orders of the Interplanetary Parliament.

Sources:

Hyams, Ron: *Mysteries of Mind Space & Time; the Unexplained: Reach for the Stars.* Westport: H. S. Stuttman, 1992

Stemman, Roy: *The Supernatural: Visitors From Outer Space.* London: Aldus, 1976

NEW FRIEND

F

FAIRIES

Belief in fairies (or *faeries*—spellings differ) is ancient and widespread. Among the Celts of Scotland, Ireland, the Isle of Man, Wales and Britanny, and the Teutonic races of Scandinavia, Germany and Britain, the fairies are seen as counterparts of humankind. They live in societies, with families and dwellings. The Irish word for fairy is *sheehogue*. The fairies are the "Gods of the Earth," according to the *Book of Armagh*. As the *Tuatha De Danaan*, they were the gods of pagan Ireland. In Highland Scotland, fairies are called *daoine sithe* or "men of peace."

J. G. Campbell said, "I believe there once was a small race of people in these [British] islands who are remembered as fairies, for the fairy belief is not confined to the Highlanders of Scotland. This class of stories is so widely spread, so matter-of-fact, hangs so well together, and is so implicitly believed all over the United Kingdom that I am persuaded of the former existence of a race of men in these islands who were smaller in stature than the Celts; who used stone arrows, lived in conical mounds like the Lapps, knew some mechanical arts, pilfered goods and stole children; and were perhaps contemporary with some species of wild cattle and horses."

The dwarfs of Yesso in Japan were small people who survived till the beginning of the seventeenth century. They were less than four feet in height and lived in semi-subterranean pit dwellings. A belief about them has grown in recent times. The Aino word for "pit-dweller" is not unlike the word for a burdock leaf. It was known that these people were small; it did not take long, therefore, for the belief to spring up that their name meant they were "people who lived under burdock leaves" (rather than "in pits"). So, to many modern natives of Yesso, those historical dwarves were "so small that if caught in a shower of rain they could shelter under a dock leaf!" Similar thinking must have made the European fairy into the diminutive creature generally thought of today. The writings of Shakespeare (despite his probable accuracy in *The Merry Wives of Windsor*) and Spenser romanticized the fairies and made them part of the larger world of sprites and **spirits**; the elves, gnomes, goblins, brownies and similar.

The size of fairies is open to some controversy. Campbell believed they were "smaller in stature than the Celts" yet not diminutive. Evidence from the **witchcraft** trials supports this. It was said of Joan Tyrrye (1555) that "at one time she met with one of the fairies, being a man, in the market of Taunton, having a white rod in his hand, and she came up to him, thinking to make an acquaintance of him, and then her sight was clean taken away for a time." This, apparently, was not unusual. Many times when the fairies did not wish to be seen, the observer lost his or her sight for a period. Joan, apparently, did not even realize he was a fairy but took him to be just another person in the marketplace. In Orkney, in 1615, Jonet Drever was found guilty of "fostering a bairn in the hill of Westray to the fairy folk, called on her our good neighbors." In 1588, Alesoun Peirsoun of Fifeshire said, "a man in green appeared to her, a lusty man, with many men and women with him." She also mentioned the fairies making their medicines, saying, "the good neighbors make their salves with pans and fires, and gathered their herbs before the sun rising." In 1566, Master John Walsh consulted with the fairies in Netherbury, Dorset, and "went among the hills" to do it. He consulted with them at noon and at midnight. In 1662, the Auldearne witch, Issobell Gowdie, said she was "in the Downie-hills, and got meat there from the Queen of Fearrie, more than I could eat. ... The Queen of Faerrie is brawlie clothed in white linens, and in white and brown clothes, and the King of Faerrie is a braw man, well favored, and broad faced." In these and many more instances, the fairies were almost the same size as the humans. Sometimes a human would meet with a fairy and not realize, till later, that it was a fairy. There were even marriages recorded between fairies and humans. Shakespeare admitted their size when, in *The Merry Wives of Windsor*, he had Mistress Page, a full grown woman, not only dress as a fairy but expect to be accepted as one.

In the *Historia de Gentibus Septenrionalibus*, of Swedish bishop Olaus Magnus (1558), there is an illustration of a knight visiting a fairy hill. The fairies are shown as smaller than the knight, but by no means diminutive. Another indicator of the size of fairies is found in the references to *changelings*. It is said that sometimes fairies fancied a human child and would carry it away, leaving their own child in its place. The exchange

might not be discovered for years, since the children were of comparable size.

One theory regarding the identity of the "little people" is that they were the people historically known as the *Picts*. The Picts were of the same race as the Lapps. Lapps, Picts, and fairies were all small-statured races. The fairies were said to live inside hollow hillocks and under the ground. In Scotland and other areas of Britain, there are numerous underground structures and artificial mounds whose interiors show them to have been dwelling places, and these are popularly known as "fairy hills" and, in some areas, as "Picts' houses." A manuscript of the Bishop of Orkney, dated 1443, states that when Harald Haarfagr conquered the Orkneys in the ninth century, the inhabitants were the two nations of the *Papae* and the *Peti*, both of whom were exterminated. The *Peti* were certainly the Picts. The Picts of Orkney "were only a little exceeding pygmies in stature and worked wonderfully in the construction of their cities, evening and morning, but in the midday, being quite destitute of strength, they hid themselves in little houses underground."

Christina Hole speaks of "those primitive tribes who were conquered but not destroyed by the Celtic invaders and who continued for long afterwards to live in scattered communities in the wilder parts of the country. They were people of small stature and quick movements who dwelt in low turf-covered houses resembling green hillocks at first sight and easily overlooked by any casual traveler. ... That they sometimes inter-married with their conquerors seems clear from the many tales of fairy-wives, or of human women carried away to the fairy kingdom."

Although **witches** probably knew very little of the history of this small race, the two had many things in common, not least being their knowledge and use of herbs for medicinal purposes and their use of magic. Both also used the "elf bolts," the small arrowheads shot from the fingers.

Fairies frequented many parts of Durham, in England. There is a hillock, or *tumulus*, near Bishopton, and a large hill near Billingham, both of which used to be "haunted by fairies" according to local legend. Even Ferry-Hill, between Darlington and Durham, is evidently a corruption of "fairy hill."

Many modern day people do believe in spirits of nature, who they frequently see as tiny in size, and include "fairies" in with them. It is possible that, over the years, the labels have become confused.

Sources:

Buckland, Raymond: *The Witch Book: The Encyclopedia of Witchcraft, Wicca and Neo-Paganism*. Detroit: Visible Ink Press, 2002

Buckland, Raymond: *Witchcraft From the Inside*. St. Paul: Llewellyn, 1995

Campbell, John Gregorson: *Popular Tales of the Western Highlands*. Edinburgh, 1890

Campbell, John Gregorson: *Superstitions of the Highlands and Islands of Scotland*. Glasgow, 1900

Davidson, Thomas: *Rowan Tree & Red Thread*. Edinburgh: Oliver & Boyd, 1949

Hole, Christina: *Witchcraft in England*. New York: Charles Scribner's, 1947

Hughes, Pennethorne: *Witchcraft*. London: Longmans, Green, 1952

James, E.O.: *Prehistoric Religion*. New York: Barnes & Noble, 1962

FAITH HEALING

Faith healing is a general term usually applied to nonmedical cures. It implies that the subject has an expectation of being healed; he or she has faith and is imbued with the idea that the acceptance of certain beliefs or doctrines (sometimes religious) will precipitate a cure. The method of healing may be hands-on, **spiritual**, reflexology, Reiki, dietary, herbal, by prayers, **meditation**, **hypnotherapy**, or any of a number of methods.

In many societies, a **shaman** performs healing. In the third century BCE, King Pyrrhus of Epirus cured colic by the laying on of hands (though, to be accurate, he touched with his feet and toes, rather than with his hands). English kings, start-

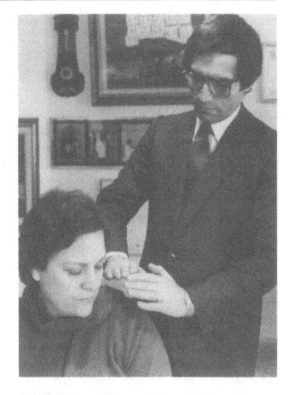

Faith healing being performed by Nicola Cutolo, healer, psychologist and President of the Italian Society for Psychical Research. *Courtesy Fortean Picture Library.*

ing with Edward the Confessor in the eleventh century CE, cured the tubercular affliction of the glands of the neck, known as scrofula, by the laying on of hands. This cure for what became known as "the King's Evil," continued through the line of English monarchs until Queen Anne. In France, King Robert the Pius did similar curing of the sick in the eleventh century and it continued in that country for many years. The recipients of these healings all believed beyond any doubt that the monarch's touch would cure them. It was, therefore, pure faith healing.

Sources:

Barbanell, Maurice: *This Is Spiritualism*. Oxshott: The Spiritual Truth Press, 1959

Bletzer, June G.: *The Encyclopedia Psychic Dictionary*. Lithia Springs: New Leaf, 1998

Kingston, Jeremy: *The Supernatural: Healing Without Medicine*. London: Aldus Books, 1975

Fate Magazine *see* Fuller, Curtis

FAY, ANNIE EVA

Annie Eva Fay was a controversial American **medium**. She seemed to pass every test to which she was subjected, but later it was alleged that she offered to sell the secrets of her mediumship to a stage magician.

The phenomena produced by Fay were similar to those produced by the **Davenport Brothers**. On a visit to England in 1874, Fay did a demonstration at the Crystal Palace in London. The psychic researcher Sir **William Crookes** was so impressed that he invited her to sit at his house. There she was enclosed in an electric circuit with electrodes held in her hands. A galvanometer recorded any variation of pressure or movement of her hands. During the **séance** various objects were moved, a locked bureau was opened, and a bell was rung. Crookes was impressed but **Frank Podmore** suggested that she knew about the test ahead of time, from records of a similar trial conducted by Crookes, and employed resistant coils to bypass the electrodes.

Fay had a falling out with her manager, who subsequently offered explanations on how Fay operated. These were not taken seriously until the stage magician J. N. Maskelyne claimed to have in his possession a letter from Fay offering to sell him her secrets. It is not known, however, whether Maskelyne actually had such a letter.

Sources:
Fodor, Nandor: *Encyclopedia of Psychic Science*. London: Arthurs Press, 1933

FAY, MRS. H. B.

Mrs. H. B. Fay was an American materialization **medium**. As many as fifty different forms would appear at her **séances**, varying in age from very young to elderly. At one séance, one of the sitters was unable to recognize a **materialization** claiming to be her brother, who had died when quite young. The materialized form obligingly changed, in full view of the sitters, to a young boy whom the lady then recognized. Alfred Russel Wallace (1823–1913), the famous British naturalist, was one of the many sitters who attested to the mediumship of Mrs. Fay. E. A. Bracket recorded the events of many of her séances in his book *Materialised Apparitions*.

Sources:
Fodor, Nandor: *Encyclopedia of Psychic Science*. London: Arthurs Press, 1933

FIELDING, FRANCIS HENRY EVERARD (1867–1936)

Fielding was a barrister by profession, and also a psychical researcher and one of the early members of the **Society for Psychical Research** (SPR) in London. From 1903 until 1920, he was secretary of the SPR. He investigated famous **mediums** such as **Florence Cook** and **Eusapia Paladino**. In 1919, Fielding married Stanislawa Tomczyk, a **physical medium**.

Sources:
Fodor, Nandor: *Encyclopedia of Psychic Science*. London: Arthurs Press, 1933

Findhorn *see* **Caddy, Peter**

FINDLAY, JAMES ARTHUR (1883–1966)

Findlay was one of the most respected modern leaders of British **Spiritualism**. He was born on May 16, 1883, in Glasgow, Scotland. In his autobiography, Findlay wrote, "[My birth] happened without my being aware of the fact and, moreover, my consent was not asked beforehand. It occurred without any desire on my part." His father, Robert Downie Findlay, was a stockbroker and then an officer in the First Lanark Volunteers army reservists. His mother was Margaret (Galloway) Findlay.

As a child, Findlay traveled extensively with his parents. He had a private tutor and later attended the Albany Academy for a year. In 1895, he went to Ardvreck School at Crieff in Perthshire. At fourteen, Findlay went to Fettes College in Edinburgh, and two years later completed his education at Abbotsholme in Derbyshire.

Findlay became involved in a wide variety of enterprises including agriculture, finance, the British Red Cross, and **psychical research**. In 1913, he married Gertrude Walker and received the Order of the British Empire in 1919 for his organizational work with the Red Cross during World War I.

In 1918, Findlay found a Spiritualist church in Glasgow and attended a service. He attended a **séance** being given by **direct voice** medium John Campbell Sloan soon after. Findlay received evidential messages from his deceased father and another man. The messages were of a very personal nature and contained information known only to Findlay. During the next five years, Findlay attended thirty-nine séances with Sloan, sometimes at the **medium**'s home and sometimes at places of Findlay's choosing. Over the course of these séances eighty-three separate and distinct voices spoke. Findlay gave full details of these sittings in his book *On the Edge of the **Etheric*** (1931).

Findlay retired from business life at age 40 to devote himself to psychical research. In 1920, he founded and was Vice President of the Glasgow Society for Psychical Research. He also founded the Quest Club and The International Institute for Psychical Research, of which he was Chairman, and held office in a number of other institutions. In February of 1925, Findlay moved from Scotland to Stansted Hall in Essex, England, a stately home dating from the late sixteenth century. During World War II, Findlay was displaced from Stansted Hall when it was commandeered by the Red Cross for use as a hospital for American troops. It was not until October 1945 that he was able to return to his home. When Findlay died in 1966, he left Stansted Hall to the **Spiritualists' National Union**. It is now the home of the Arthur J. Findlay College.

Findlay wrote a number of books on psychic research, including *An Investigation of Psychic Phenomena* (1924), *On the Edge of the Etheric* (1931), *The Rock of Truth* (1933), *The Unfolding Universe* (1935), *The Psychic Stream* (1939), *The Way of Life* (1956), and *The Curse of Ignorance* (1956). He also wrote on finance and economics.

Sources:

Findlay, Arthur: *Looking Back.* Stansted: Spiritualists' National Union, 1955

Fodor, Nandor: *Encyclopedia of Psychic Science.* London: Arthurs Press, 1933

First World War *see* World Wars

Firth, Violet Mary *see* Fortune, Dion

Fish, Leah *see* Fox Family

FLAMMARION, CAMILLE (1842–1925)

Flammarion's introduction to **Spiritualism** came through Allan Kardec's book *Le Livre des Esprits (The Spirits' Book)* (1856). After reading the book and visiting the author, Flammarion became a member of Kardec's Society for Psychologic Studies. The society's weekly **séances** focused on **inspirational writing**. Activities with the society then brought Flammarion entrance to various French **Spiritist** groups, though he did not himself become a Spiritist.

Flammarion experimented with various techniques including **automatic writing**, **rapping**, use of the **planchette**, but after two years deduced that there was no evidence to suggest actual **spirit** communication. In 1865, he published *Unknown Natural Forces*, which offered a critical study of the phenomena produced by such **mediums** as the **Davenport Brothers**. He coined the word "**psychic**" in this book. He stated, "these forces are as real as the attraction of gravitation and as invisible as that." In 1907, he published an enlarged version of the book under the title *Mysterious Psychic Forces*. When Kardec died on March 30, 1869, Flammarion gave the funeral oration.

Flammarion attended séances given by many mediums; some of whom became famous. He sat with Mme. De Girardin at the home of Victor Hugo, and also with Mlle. Huet. He experienced **levitations** in full daylight, with drumbeats, the sound of wood-sawing, rushing water, and similar sounds that a medium would not be able to produce. He underwent a series of experiments with the medium **Eusapia Paladino**. In 1898, she gave eight séances in Flammarion's home. A number of scientists were present and it is reported that "surprising manifestations were witnessed". A later investigative series was conducted with Paladino in 1905 and 1906. Flammarion reported, "Mediumistic phenomena have for me the stamp of absolute certainty and incontestability, and amply suffice to prove that unknown physical forces exist outside the ordinary and established domain of natural philosophy."

In October 1923, in a Presidential address before the **Society for Psychical Research**, Flammarion said, "There are unknown faculties in man belonging to the spirit, there is such a thing as the double, thought can leave an image behind, psychical currents traverse the atmosphere, we live in the midst of an invisible world, the faculties of the soul survive the disaggregation of the corporeal organism, there are **haunted** houses, exceptionally and rarely the dead do manifest, there can be no doubt that such manifestations occur, **telepathy** exists just as much between the dead and the living as between the living."

Sources:

Flammarion, Camille: *Mysterious Psychic Forces*. London: Unwin, 1907

Fodor, Nandor: *Encyclopedia of Psychic Science*. London: Arthurs Press, 1933

FLETCHER, JOHN WILLIAM (1852–1913)

John William Fletcher's mother had the gift of "second sight" and as a boy Fletcher puzzled his school teachers by reciting something that had been presented to him in a vision instead of writing what was prescribed. By the time he was seventeen he was already being sought after as a **trance** speaker. His **spirit guide** was a **Native American** girl named Winona.

Fetcher married Susie Willis, who had been a **clairvoyant** and public lecturer from the age of fifteen. They set up as professional **mediums** at the **Lake Pleasant** Camp Meeting in Massachusetts in 1873. Four years later, Fletcher went to England but was badly received and heavily criticized by *The Spiritualist* magazine. He gave test **séances** at the home of Mrs. **Guppy-Volckman**, at the Dalston Association, and at the **British National Association of Spiritualists**.

In England in 1881, Fletcher's wife was sentenced to twelve months hard labor for unduly influencing Mrs. Hart Davies to give up her home and possessions to the Fletchers. At the time Fletcher himself was in Boston, lecturing to an audience of 3,000. Fletcher was a palmist in New York in later years. In June, 1913, the police raided his rooms with a warrant for his arrest. Fetcher collapsed and died of a heart attack.

Sources:

Shepard, Leslie A: *Encyclopedia of Occultism & Parapsychology*. New York: Avon Books, 1978

FLINT, LESLIE (1911–1994)

Leslie Flint was possibly the best independent **direct voice** medium of all times. He was born in a Salvation Army home in Hackney, London, in 1911. His mother was a vivacious unmarried woman, living with her own mother. When she brought home the baby Leslie, his father offered to marry her and make the baby legitimate. However, after three years of discord, Flint's father joined the army to serve in World War I, and his mother went to work in a munitions factory. Because his mother loved to go out and have a good time, Flint would be dropped off at the local cinema most evenings. There he developed a great love for films, but the arrangement didn't last long for his mother ran off with one of her admirers and Flint never saw her or his father again. He went to live with his grand-mother.

When he was seven, Flint had his first **psychic** experience. His aunt received the news that her husband had been killed in the war and when she went to see her mother—Flint's grandmother—Flint saw the **spirit** of the dead man with her, there in the family kitchen. No one believed him when he told them. At another time he saw a neighbor who had died some weeks before.

Flint grew up to take a variety of menial jobs including gravedigger, cemetery gardener, semi-professional dancer, cinema usher, barman, and coal miner. When he was eighteen or nineteen he started going to a wide variety of churches, look-ing for "some clue, some grain of truth in which I could believe. … After many weeks of earnest seeking in the various denominations of the Christian church I had found neither conviction nor any hope of it and I was beginning to despair." Then he learned of a meeting of **Spiritualists** and decided to attend. At that meeting, **trance** medi-um Annie Johnson singled out Flint for a reading. She told him that he had a **spirit guide** who liked to dress in an Arabian manner, and that he him-self would one day be a great **medium**. After attending several meetings and getting the same message from different mediums, Flint accepted an invitation to a **development circle**. He also received a letter from a stranger in Germany claiming that Rudolph Valentino was trying to contact him. On demanding proof, the heavy din-ing table at the development circle lifted itself up onto two legs. Much later in his development, Valentino came and spoke through him.

Flint continued to sit for seven years with a dedicated **circle**, after his first group broke up. This second group was led by Edith Mundin, who later became Flint's wife. Flint found himself slip-ping into trance and not knowing what took place but, upon waking, discovered that he had been the instrument to bring comfort to many others. Flint had a spirit guide who was a Cock-ney boy named Mickey, who had been killed in a street accident in Camden Town in 1910, and a Native American named White Wing. Rudolph Valentino also became one of his guides.

When at the cinema, Flint would hear whis-perings of voices. Other members of the audience also heard them and blamed Flint for creating a disturbance. He would eventually have to leave the movie house. As the voices grew in strength, Flint no longer went into trance and was able to hear all that was said by the spirit voices. Edith learned of a Spiritualist church whose medium had run off with a member of the congregation. Flint went there and did his first public presenta-tion, falling into trance again and delivering many valid messages. From there he was invited to many of the surrounding churches.

Flint and Edith very much wanted to present to a wider audience the direct voices that Flint produced for their more intimate circle. This, however, required complete darkness, as does all **physical mediumship** (an artificial voice box is built up from **ectoplasm** taken from the medium, and darkness is necessary for this). Flint met Noah Zerdin, one of the founders of The Link Association of Home Circles, at a **séance**. Through Zerdin's circles, Flint's direct voice mediumship advanced to the point where Zerdin thought it should be tested on the general pub-lic. To do so, they built a lightproof **cabinet** in which Flint would sit, with the cabinet standing on the stage of the auditorium. He demonstrated in this way at the Scala Theater, the Kingsway Hall, and in Birmingham, Leeds, and Manches-ter. No microphones were allowed in the cabi-net; the Tannoy Company overseeing that and assuring the audience there were no hidden microphones anywhere, only the ones visible out on the stage. As Flint later said, "The extraordi-nary thing was that the voices were clear even though the microphones were up to two feet away from the cabinet."

Flint himself never received a fee for his demonstrations, being solely interested in bring-ing comfort to others. The voices of Thomas Alva Edison, Sir **Arthur Conan Doyle**, Sir **Oliv-er Lodge**, Lord Birkinhead, Charlotte Bronte,

Maurice Chevalier, Sir **Winston Churchill**, Mahatma Ghandi, Ellen Terry, Oscar Wilde, Rudolph Valentino, former Archbishop of Canterbury Dr. Cosmo Lang have all come through Leslie Flint and have all been recorded. These tapes still available.

Flint worked tirelessly for many years. He allowed all sorts of tests to be made on him by the **Society for Psychical Research** and others. He was photographed by **infrared** to detect any movement. He allowed his mouth to be taped shut and he was tightly bound into a chair. He was made to hold a specific amount of colored water in his mouth for a long period of time and then had it measured afterward. He had a throat microphone attached to his throat. Through all of this, the voices still came, and sometimes more than one voice would speak at the same time. Leslie Flint finally retired to Brighton and died there on April 16, 1994, at the age of eighty-three. Aubrey Rose said, "Leslie Flint displayed a rare dedication to his calling as a significant avenue linking two worlds. We salute him as one of the outstanding mediums and dedicated servants of this disappearing twentieth century."

Sources:

Cull, Robert: *More to Life Than This: The Story of Jean Cull, the Medium.* London: Macmillan, 1987

Flint, Leslie: *Voices In the Dark: My Life as a Medium.* New York: Bobbs-Merrill, 1971

Leslie Flint Homepage: http://www.leslieflint.com

Meek, George W.: *After We Die, What Then?* Columbus: Ariel Press, 1987

FLOWER READINGS

Some **mediums** do flower **readings**. The sitters each bring a flower and place it in the center of the **circle**. It can be any sort of flower, though if there happen to be more than one of a type (two roses, for example) then one will be tied with thread about its stem to help tell the one from the other. The medium does not know who has brought what flower.

The medium takes up the flowers one at a time and concentrates on them. He or she is able to say who brought which flower and, through it, reach that person's **spirit** contact.

Sources:

Buckland, Raymond: *Buckland's Book of Spirit Communications.* St. Paul: Llewellyn, 2004

FODOR, NANDOR (1895–1964)

Nandor Fodor was born in Beregszasz, Hungary, on May 13, 1895. He studied law at the Royal Hungarian University of Science in Budapest, where he received his doctorate in 1917. Four years later he went to New York and worked as a journalist. After reading **Hereward Carrington**'s book *Modern Psychic Phenomena* (1919), Fodor contacted Carrington and the two quickly became friends. Carrington introduced him to Sir **Arthur Conan Doyle**. Some years later, Fodor and Carrington co-authored *Haunted People* (in Britain titled *Story of the Poltergeist Down the Ages*). While in New York, Fodor interviewed Sandor Ferenczi, an associate of Sigmund Freud's. Fodor believed that psychoanalysis could provide insight on psychic phenomena. Freud later came to support Fodor and his work.

Fodor moved to England in 1929, and worked for newspaper tycoon Lord Rothermere. Five years later he became an editor of *Light*, the oldest British journal of **Spiritualism**. Fodor was interested in Spiritualism while in New York, and attended a **séance** given by **direct voice medium** William Cartheuser. In England, Fodor started to seriously investigate all forms of **psychic** phenomena, visiting sites of **hauntings**, **poltergeist** activity, **levitations**, and **materializations**. In 1934, he authored his most important book, the *Encyclopedia of Psychic Science*. **Sir Oliver Lodge** was sufficiently impressed with Fodor's work that he contributed a preface to the book. In 1935, Fodor became London correspondent for the **American Society for Psychical Research**. He resigned that position in 1939, and returned to live in New York.

Fodor was on the teaching staff of the Training Institute of the National Psychological Association for Psychoanalysis for many years. He was an editor of *The Psychoanalytic Review*. He was a member of the New York Academy of Science and an honorary member of the Danish Society for Psychical Research and the Hungarian Metaphysical Society. His books include *Haunted People* (1951), *On the Trail of the Poltergeist* (1958), *The Haunted Mind* (1959), *Mind Over Space* (1962), and *Between Two Worlds* (1964).

Sources:

Fishley, Margaret: *The Supernatural.* London: Aldus, 1976

Guiley, Rosemary Ellen: *The Encyclopedia of Ghosts and Spirits.* New York: Facts On File, 1992

Shepard, Leslie A.: *encyclopedia of Occultism & Parapsychology.* New York: Avon Books, 1978

FORD, ARTHUR AUGUSTUS (1897–1971)

Arthur Augustus Ford was born on January 8, 1897, in Titusville, Florida. At that time it was a tiny town with a population of about three hundred. He had three siblings. His father, a steamboat captain, was an Episcopalian who seldom attended church; his mother was an ardent southern Baptist. As a child, Arthur Ford was increasingly skeptical of church teachings—especially on Heaven and Hell—his independent thinking fired by meetings and discussions with a number of Unitarians. At age sixteen he was excommunicated from the Baptist church. Despite this, he decided he wanted to become a minister and studied for that at Transylvania College in Lexington, Kentucky. Ford's chosen affiliation was with the Disciples of Christ, but his studies were interrupted by World War I. In 1917, he was stationed at Camp Grant in Sheridan, Illinois.

In 1918, a great flu epidemic raged across the country and struck the Camp Grant area especially hard. Every night soldiers died of influenza. One night Ford dreamed that he had been handed a sheet of paper on which were written the names of those who were to die that night. The names were written in large, clear letters. The following morning the daily camp bulletin list of dead matched Ford's **dream** list. This continued for several days to the point where his buddies shunned him as a harbinger of death. He quickly learned to keep his knowledge to himself.

After the war, Ford returned to his studies and was able to review these dreams with a friendly professor, Dr. Elmer Snoddy. Snoddy told Ford of many current studies in America and England, by such people as **Henry Sidgwick**, Sir **Oliver Lodge**, Dr. **William James**, and **Frederick Myers**. The professor assured Ford that he was a rare and gifted **medium**. He encouraged Ford to develop his gifts and use them to help others. This helped Ford adjust and he actively sought out people whom he felt might be able to help him. He went to New York in 1921 and spoke with Gertrude Tubby, the secretary of the **American Society for Psychical Research**. She arranged for him to meet with Dr. Franklin Pierce and with other more practiced mediums.

In 1922, at twenty-five years of age, Ford became an ordained minister and was appointed to a church in Barbourville, Kentucky. That year he also married Sallie Stewart. Shortly after, Dr. Paul Pearson persuaded Ford to give a series of lectures in New England in 1924. This was the start of his career as a platform medium. The lectures were a great success and Ford traveled on the lecture circuit. Sallie did not go with him; they became estranged and divorced.

In 1924, Ford's **spirit guide** Fletcher made himself known. Ford was advised by swami **Paramahansa Yogananda**, who had great influence on him. Gradually Ford increased his public **readings** and was soon traveling the globe. During a visit to England, Ford impressed Sir Arthur Conan Doyle with his abilities.

Ford is perhaps best known for his breaking of the "Houdini code." When **Harry Houdini** (Ehrich Weiss) died he left a message with his wife Beatrice. Houdini spent many years unmasking **fraudulent mediums** and told Beatrice that only a true medium would be able to give her his message. Many tried but it wasn't until Arthur Ford who succeeded. Ford gave Beatrice the message "Rosabelle, believe," which was done in the long, complicated code which the two Houdinis had used in a vaudeville act they had done many years before. This made Ford world famous.

In 1930, Ford was involved in an auto accident which killed his sister and a friend. Ford was hospitalized with slim chance of recovery. The attending physician gave injudicious amounts of morphine to him, so much so that when he finally recovered from the accident, many months later, he found he was addicted. Going "cold turkey," Ford managed to break the habit only to become addicted to alcohol instead. In 1938, Ford married his second wife, Valerie McKeown, an English widow. They settled in Hollywood, California.

With alcoholism, Ford began to miss lecture appointments and even his guide, Fletcher, disappeared. His health deteriorated and finally Valerie divorced him. In 1949, Ford had a breakdown, but was finally able to recover through Alcoholics Anonymous. Despite this he never fully gave up drinking. In 1950, Fletcher returned and Ford was able to resume his mediumship. Ford founded several organizations, among them **Spiritual Frontiers Fellowship** which he started in 1956. In 1967, he held a televised **séance** with **Bishop James A. Pike**, whose twenty-year-old son had committed suicide the previous year. Ford provided what seemed to be evidence of contact with the son.

During the last twenty years of his life, Ford suffered several heart attacks. Each time, until the last, it seemed that there was someone on hand—or inexplicably drawn to the scene—who was able to summon the necessary help. Ford died on January 4, 1971.

Sources:

Buckland, Raymond: *Buckland's Book of Spirit Communications*. St. Paul: Llewellyn, 2004

Shepard, Leslie A: *Encyclopedia of Occultism & Parapsychology*. New York: Avon Books, 1978

FORTUNE, DION (1891–1946)

Dion Fortune was the pseudonym of Violet Mary Firth. Born in Wales in 1891, she grew up in a Christian Science family. Firth demonstrated mediumistic talents when in her teen years and claimed to have memories of a **past life** as a priestess in Atlantis. She studied Freud and Jung and worked for the Medico-Psychological Clinic in London. She had plans to practice as an analyst and to that end took classes at the University of London. She even undertook clinical work under the auspices of the London School of Medicine for Women (Royal Free Hospital). After some years, however, Firth came to the conclusion that neither Freud nor Jung had all the answers and that the truth lay in the **occult**.

Although fascinated by the works of **Helena Blavatsky**, Firth was not enthused about occultism presented in an Eastern setting and therefore was not drawn to the **Theosophical Society**, though she was a member of it for a brief period. At the age of twenty-eight, Firth joined the Alpha and Omega Lodge of the Stella Matutina, an outer division of the Hermetic Order of the Golden Dawn led by J.W. Brodie-Innes. On initiation, she took the magical name *Deo Non Fortuna* ("By God, not chance"). She later shortened this to Dion Fortune and used it as her pen name. Five years later she left the Order after a disagreement with Moina Mathers, the widow of MacGregor Mathers who then led the group. She founded the Community and Fraternity of the Inner Light based on contacts she claimed to have made with "Inner Planes" of wisdom. Today this is known as the Society of the Inner Light.

Fortune learned Ceremonial Magic from Brodie-Innes and quickly became an adept. In 1927, she married Dr. Thomas Penry Evans. In 1936, she wrote one of her best known books, *The Mystical Qabbalah*, dealing with the use of the Qabbalah by modern occultists. She had previously written *Sane Occultism* (1929) and *Psychic Self-Defense* (1930), the latter resulting from a **psychic** attack she received from an employer in 1911. She had, at that time, been working in a school where the principal took a dislike to her. It was this attack that had led to her study of Jung and Freud.

Fortune wrote a number of fiction and nonfiction books teaching the Western Esoteric Tradition. Her two novels, *The Sea Priestess* (1938) and *Moon Magic* (published posthumously in 1956), contain much practical occult knowledge, telling the story of a priestess of Isis who comes to restore paganism to a world that has lost touch with nature. *The Goat-Foot God* (1936) is another novel enjoyed by modern day **pagans**, dealing as it does with the powers of Pan.

In *Spiritualism in the Light of Occult Science* (1931), Fortune says,

> What have **Spiritualists** to do with the ancient wisdom? More than most of them realize, for occultism is traditional Spiritualism. Whether we study the Delphic Oracles or the Witch trials of the Middle Ages, we encounter authentic psychic phenomena. Spiritualists would find themselves on familiar ground if they penetrated to the caves of Tibet or the temples of Ancient Egypt, for the Secret Tradition has been built up by generations of psychics and spirit controlled mediums.

It's a little known fact that Dion Fortune was herself an accomplished **medium**. She had been taught by **Margaret Lumley Brown,** who took over many of Fortune's functions at the Society of Inner Light after Fotrune's death from leukemia in 1946. Margaret Lumley Brown has been called by some the finest medium and psychic of the twentieth century. Gareth Knight—a student of Fortune's and literary executor of Margaret Lumley Brown—stated, "The mediumship of Dion Fortune has been a well-kept secret within the Inner Group of the Fraternity, but it has recently been decided to make a secret of it no longer in order that certain of the teachings thus received may be made available for all who follow the Path."

In the early 1920s, Fortune acted as a medium when working with Frederick Bligh Bond, at Glastonbury. Bond was absorbed in psychic archaeology at the site of Glastonbury Cathedral. The July, 1922 issue of the journal **Psychic Science**—published by the College of Psychic Science—carried an article by Fortune, using her name Violet M. Firth, titled "Psychology and Occultism." She wrote in the article, "In entering the trance condition one sees the medium become abstracted, and then, closing down the avenues of the five physical senses, enter a subjective state. In some mediums one can observe this condition very well, especially when it is the intention to get trance speech, the contact is maintained with the vocal organs."

Sources:

Fortune, Dion: *Through the Gates of Death*. York Beach: Weiser Books, 2000

Knight, Gareth: *Dion Fortune & the Inner Light*. Loughborough: Thoth, 2000

FORTUNE–TELLING BOOK, THE

Encyclopedia of divination, soothsaying, and all methods of fortune-telling, written by Raymond Buckland and published by Visible Ink Press. The book provides detailed explanations of more than 400 of the various methods, discussing everything from Aeromancy (seeing by observing atmospheric phenomena) to Zoomancy (divination by the appearance or behavior of animals). Included are many of the phenomena of **Spiritualism**, such as **clairvoyance, clairaudience, psychometry**, and more.

Sources:

Buckland, Raymond: *The Fortune–Telling Book: The Encyclopedia of Divination and Soothsaying*. Detroit: Visible Ink Press, 2004

FOUNDATION FOR RESEARCH ON THE NATURE OF MAN, THE

A nonprofit research facility founded in 1962 by Dr. **Joseph Banks Rhine** and his wife Louisa E. Rhine. It was an outgrowth of the former

Parapsychology Laboratory at Duke University in Durham, North Carolina, and is intended to act as a clearinghouse for research information and a training base for those studying **psi**. The Foundation publishes the quarterly *Journal of Parapsychology*. Dr. Rhine started his research at Duke University in 1935, but moved his studies to the Foundation in 1962, believing that an independent, privately funded organization would give more freedom to his work. In 1995, to honor the 100th anniversary of Rhine's birth, the Foundation was renamed the Rhine Research Center.

Sources:

Shepard, Leslie A: *Encyclopedia of Occultism & Parapsychology*. New York: Avon Books, 1978

FOWLER, LOTTIE (1836–1899)

Lottie Fowler was the name used by Charlotte Connolly when working as a **medium**. She diagnosed disease by **clairvoyance**. In 1870, during the dangerous illness of Prince Albert Edward (Prince of Wales; later King Edward VII) she was much consulted by Court officials. From the outset she **predicted** that the prince would recover, which he did.

Fowler was an American by birth, though she lived for many years in England and earned a good reputation there as a medium. It was Lottie Fowler's **séances** in 1872 which first attracted Rev. **William Stainton Moses** to **Spiritualism**. In that same year Fowler herself was transported as an apport at one of the **séances** given by **Frank Herne** and **Charles Williams**, in much the same way that Mrs. Guppy was relocated in that famous incident (*see* **Guppy-Volckman**).

Fowler followed the trend in giving **materialization** sittings, though her specialty was clairvoyance. Her guide was a German woman named Annie. Fowler located the stolen body of Lord Lindsay of Balcarres, an acquaintance of Daniel Dunglas Home. The body had been stolen from the family vault. She also predicted the Tay Bridge disaster and a London riot.

Sources:

Doyle, Sir Arthur Conan: *The History of Spiritualism*. New York: Doran, 1926

Fodor, Nandor: *Encyclopedia of Psychic Science*. London: Arthurs Press, 1933

Podmore, Frank: *Modern Spiritualism*. London: 1902; reprinted as *Mediums of the Nineteenth Century*. New York: University Books, 1963

FOX FAMILY

The modern **Spiritualist** movement began in New York in 1848 as a result of publicity surrounding happenings at the Fox homestead in Hydesville. The house was a small weatherboard one with two parlors, a pantry, and bedroom. There was a stairway leading to the second floor and there was a cellar.

Ever since moving into the house on December 11, 1847, the Fox family—who were Methodists—had been plagued with strange sounds echoing through the wooden cottage. There were knockings and **rappings** that neither John Fox nor his wife Margaret were able to trace. They tried all the obvious possibilities such as loose shutters and window sashes, frequently getting up in the middle of the night to go searching through the house with candle in hand. On the night of Friday, March 31, they and their two daughters had just retired to bed when the noises once again started up—in particular what sounded like someone or something rapping sharply on wood. Mrs. Margaret Fox later stated,

It was very early when we went to bed on this night—hardly dark. I had been so broken of rest I was almost sick … I had just lain down. It commenced as usual. I knew it from all the other noises I had ever heard before. The children, who slept in the other bed in the room, heard the rapping, and tried to make similar sounds by snapping their fingers.

My youngest child, Cathie, said "**Mr. Splitfoot**, do as I do," clapping her hands. The sound instantly followed her with the same number of raps. When she stopped the sound ceased for a short time. Then Margaretta said, in sport: "No, do just as I do. Count one, two, three, four," striking one hand against the other at the same time; and the raps came as before. She was afraid to repeat them....

I then thought I could put a test that no one in the place could answer. I asked the "noise" to rap my different children's ages successively. Instantly, each one of my children's ages was given correctly, pausing between them sufficiently long to individualise them until the seventh, at which a longer pause was made, and then three more emphatic raps were given, corresponding to the age of the little one that died, which was my youngest child.

I then asked: "Is this a human being that answers my questions so correctly?" There was no rap. I asked: "Is it a **spirit**? If it is, make two raps." Two sounds were given as soon as the request was made.

The Foxes went on with their questions and slowly learned that the spirit was a thirty-one year old man, a peddler who had been murdered in the house. Mrs. Fox called, "Will you continue to rap if I call in my neighbors, that they may hear it too?" The raps were affirmative. She called in her neighbor, Mrs. Redfield. The testimony continues,

Mrs. Redfield is a very candid woman. The girls were sitting up in bed clinging to each other and trembling in terror ... Mrs. Redfield came immediately (this was about half past seven), thinking she would have a laugh at the children. But when she saw them pale with fright and nearly speechless, she was amazed and believed there was something more serious than she had supposed. I asked a few questions for her and she was answered as before. He told her age exactly. She then called her husband, and the same questions were asked and answered.

The Foxes went on to call in the Dueslers, the Hydes, the Jewells, and several others.

Catherine (Kate) Fox, noted medium whose family's famous 1848 spirit communication in Hydesville, New York, is credited with starting the Spiritualist movement in the United States. *Courtesy Fortean Picture Library.*

On first looking at the phenomenon it would seem to be typical of **poltergeist** activity. There were young children in the house: Margaretta was seven and Cathie (Kate) was ten years of age. With children of that age it's not uncommon for there to be spontaneous physical activity brought about by raw energy, for want of a better word, thrown off by the children. But the Fox episode differs from "normal" poltergeist activity in that the noises responded intelligently to questions. Indeed, they acknowledged being a "spirit." Poltergeist activity is completely unpredictable and uncontrollable, so here was a very real difference.

With the crowd of neighbors in the house that Friday night, the spirit was thoroughly tested with questions of all sorts. All were answered to the satisfaction of the questioners. The spirit also gave all the details of his murder, which was done with a butcher knife and in order to steal his money. Margaret Fox and the two girls left for the night, leaving the house overflowing with people, and still the rapping continued.

The next evening, Saturday, it was said that as many as 300 people gathered to witness the rapping. The spirit claimed that its body had been buried ten feet below the surface of the ground. Immediate excavations turned up hair and bones, pronounced by medical experts to be human. But it wasn't until fifty-six years later that the whole skeleton was discovered. According to a report in the November 23, 1904 *Boston Journal*, parts of a basement wall collapsed and revealed an entire human skeleton together with a peddler's tin box! The peddler's name was Charles B. Rosna, and the tin box is now on view in the Lily Dale Museum in Lily Dale, New York.

It is a little known fact that the house had a prior history of strange noises. The tenants previous to the Foxes were a Michael and Hannah Weekman, who vacated the premises because of the noises. Before the Weekmans was a couple named Bell. A maid named Lucretia Pulver, who had worked for the Bells when they lived in the house, testified that she remembered a peddler once stopping there. Lucretia was sent off for the night and when she returned the next morning she was told the peddler had left. In her statement Lucretia said that both she and a friend, Aurelia Losey, had subsequently heard strange noises in the house during the night. The Bells were never charged with the murder.

The Fox family was greatly affected by the events at the house. Margaret Fox's hair turned white within a week of the affair. The two children were sent away; Kate to stay with her brother David, in Auburn, and Margaretta to stay with her sister Leah (married name Fish), in Rochester. But the raps continued in the house even after they had left.

Not only did the raps continue at the house, but they also followed the girls to their new abodes. In Rochester, Leah, a staid music teacher, was suddenly exposed to violent disturbances. The phenomena reverted to poltergeist-like outbursts, with Margaretta and Leah the targets of pinpricks and of flying blocks of wood. Leah said, "Pins would be stuck into various parts of our persons. Mother's cap would be removed from her head, her comb jerked out of her hair and every conceivable thing done to annoy us." It took a while for them to remember that they had been able to converse with the spirit in the Hydesville house, through asking for raps in answer to questions. They started again to ask questions, and once again they got answers. Then they got the most important message of all:

Dear friends, you must proclaim this truth to the world. This is the dawning of a new era. You must not try to conceal it any longer. When you do your duty, God will protect you and the good spirits will watch over you.

From that moment the messages started to pour forth.

On November 14, 1849, a group of people met at Corinthian Hall in Rochester and a panel was formed to investigate the girls. This panel determined that there was no fraud involved in what was produced. However, many present were not satisfied with this report and demanded that a second committee be formed. This was done and the second group reached a similar conclusion. They stated that when the girls were "standing on pillows, with a handkerchief tied round the bottom of their dresses tight to the ankles, we all heard rapping on the wall and floor distinctly."

As interest in the phenomena spread, it was found that other people were able to act as **channels** or "**mediums**" for the spirits. Leah's ability developed and she found herself so much in demand that she had to give up her music teaching and became the first professional medium. The sisters started a tour, going to Albany in May, 1850 and then to Troy. In June they were in New York. There **Horace Greeley**, editor of the *New York Tribune*, investigated them. He was joined by Fenimore Cooper, George Bancroft, the poets Willis and Bryant, and others. Greeley reported in his newspaper,

> We devoted what time we could spare from our duties out of three days to this subject, and it would be the basest cowardice not to say that we are convinced beyond a doubt of their perfect integrity and good faith in the premises. Whatever may be the origin or cause of the "rappings," the ladies in whose presence they occur do not make them. We tested this thoroughly and to our entire satisfaction.

The early rappings gave way to other phenomena; **table tipping**, **automatic writing**, **materialization**, and even **levitation**. In 1853, it was reported that Governor Talmadge was levitated while sitting on a table. The governor also claimed that he had received direct writing from the spirit of John C. Calhoun.

Mediums started springing up all over the place. Not surprisingly many of them were exposed as frauds. The phenomena were of the sort that *could* be produced fraudulently and therefore many charlatans tried to "jump on the bandwagon." Exposures became almost commonplace and finally even reached out toward the Fox sisters themselves. They were accused of producing the raps by "cracking" their knee joints and toe joints. An alleged "confession" was presented by a relative, Mrs. Norman Culver, who claimed that Catherine had told her that this was how they worked. In trying to explain how the raps could continue at an investigation where the committee held the ankles of the sisters, Mrs. Culver said that they had their servant rap on the floorboards from down in the cellar. There were several problems with this accusation. The investigations in question had been held in the different homes of various members of the committee plus in a public hall, and at the time the Fox sisters didn't have a servant. Not only that, but a Mr. Capron was able to show that at the time of the so-called "confession," Kate Fox was actually residing at *his* home, seventy miles distant.

Margaretta Fox, who became one of the first Spiritualist mediums after her family's dramatic communication with spirit in her childhood. *Courtesy Fortean Picture Library.*

Unfortunately the accusations did damage the reputation of the Fox sisters and for a time they found themselves with few defenders other than Horace Greeley. There was tremendous pressure put upon the sisters at this time to "perform." Precautions for mediumship were then unknown. In her *Autobiography*, Mrs. **Emma Hardinge Britten** wrote of a conversation with Kate Fox at a Spiritualist gathering, saying, "Poor patient Kate, in the midst of a captious, grumbling crowd of investigators, repeating hour after hour the letters of the alphabet, while the no less poor, patient spirits rapped out names, ages, and dates to suit all comers."

Interestingly, although the method of producing the sounds was frequently questioned, and many and marvelous explanations were forthcoming, seldom did anyone question the incredible amount of information that was produced. This information was unobtainable elsewhere and was absolutely correct. For example, from 1861 to 1866, Kate worked exclusively for the New York banker **Charles F. Livermore**, bringing him endless messages and information from his late wife, Estelle. During all that time Estelle actually materialized and also wrote notes in her own handwriting. This was all information that would have been unknown to Kate but which Livermore was able to accept.

In 1852, Margaretta married the famous Arctic explorer Dr. Elisha Kane. In November 1858, Leah married her third husband David Underhill, a wealthy insurance man. In 1871, Kate visited England where the first Spiritualist church had been established in Keighley, Yorkshire, in 1853. Her trip was financed by Livermore, in gratitude for the years of consolation that she had brought him. He wrote,

> Miss Fox, taken all in all, is no doubt the most wonderful living medium. Her character is irreproachable and pure. I have received so much through her powers of mediumship during the past ten years which is solacing, instructive and astounding, that I feel greatly indebted to her.

In England Kate sat for the well known psychic investigator and physicist Professor **William Crookes**, among others. At one of the **séances** a *London Times* correspondent was present. In light of earlier accusations made against the Fox sisters, claiming that they made the rapping noises with their joints, it is interesting to read the *Times'* correspondent's report. He said that he was taken to the door of the séance room and invited to stand by the medium and hold her hands. This he did "when loud thumps seemed to come from the panels, as if done with the fist. These were repeated at our request any number of times." He went on to give every test he could think of, while Kate gave every opportunity for examination and had both her feet and hands held securely.

Of one séance Crookes wrote,

> I was holding the medium's two hands in one of mine, while her feet rested on my feet. Paper was on the table before us, and my disengaged hand was holding a pencil. A luminous hand came down from the upper part of the room, and after hovering near me for a few seconds, took the pencil from my hand, rapidly wrote on a sheet of paper, threw the pencil down, and then rose above our heads, gradually fading into darkness.

In December 1872, Kate married H. D. Jancken, a London barrister and one of England's early Spiritualists. They had two sons, both of whom were extremely psychic, before Jancken died in 1881. In 1876, Margaretta traveled across the Atlantic to visit her sister.

A quarrel developed between the three sisters, with Kate and Margaretta eventually siding together against the older Leah. Hearing of a growing problem of alcoholism in her sisters—especially Margaretta—Leah tried to have Kate separated from her two children. It has been suggested by such people as Sir Arthur Conan Doyle that this may have prompted an attack by Margaretta, who had been through some severe financial problems. Additionally, she had come under strong Roman Catholic influence, pressuring her to acknowledge that her gift came from the devil. Margaretta swore to avenge herself and her sister against Leah.

Thinking to hurt Leah by harming the entire Spiritualist movement, Margaretta wrote a letter to the *New York Herald* in which she denounced the movement and promised a full exposure of it. This she tried to do before a panel in August, 1888. The following month Kate came over from England to join her. Although Kate didn't promise any exposé, she did seem to back her sister in the fight against Leah. In the Hall of Music on October 21, 1888, Margaretta made her repudiation, claiming that all had been faked. She even managed to produce some minor raps to back up what she was saying. Kate kept silent, though by doing so she seemed to endorse here sister's statements.

Suddenly, on November 17, less than a month later, Kate wrote to a Mrs. Cottell,

"I would have written to you before this but my surprise was so great on my arrival to hear of Maggie's exposure of Spiritualism that I had no heart to write to anyone. The manager of the affair engaged the Academy of Music, the very largest place of entertainment in New York City; it was filled to overflowing. They made fifteen hundred dollars clear. I think now I could make money in proving that the knockings are not made with the toes. So many people come to me to ask me about this exposure of Maggie's that I have to deny myself to them. They are hard at work to expose the whole thing if they can; but they certainly cannot."

On November 20, 1889, about a year after the "exposé," Margaretta gave an interview to the New York press, saying,

"Would to God that I could undo the injustice I did the cause of Spiritualism when, under the strong psychological influence of persons inimical to it, I gave expression to utterances that had no foundation in fact. This retraction and denial has not come about so much from my own sense of what is right as from the silent impulse of the spirits using my organism at the expense of the hostility of the treacherous horde who held out promises of wealth and happiness in return for an attack on Spiritualism, and whose hopeful assurances were deceitful."

She was asked, "Was there any truth in the charges you made against Spiritualism?" to which she replied, "Those charges were false in every particular. I have no hesitation in saying that … When I made those dreadful statements I was not responsible for my words. Its genuineness is an incontrovertible fact." Asked what her sister Catherine thought of her present course, she said, "She is in complete sympathy with me. She did not approve my course in the past."

The three Fox sisters died within a year or two of each other; Leah in 1890, Catherine in 1892, and Margaretta in 1893. The final word on them comes from a doctor—not a Spiritualist—who attended on Margaretta at her death. At a meeting of the Medico Legal Society of New York, in 1905, Dr. Mellen stated that Margaretta was lying in a bed in a tenement house on Ninth Street. According to the doctor she was unable, at that time, to move hand or foot. Yet knockings came from the wall, the floor, and from the ceiling, in answer to Margaretta's faint questions. "She was as incapable of cracking her toe-joints at this time, as I was," the doctor said.

Sources:

Britten, Emma Hardinge: *Modern American Spiritualism.* New York: (1870) University Books, 1970

Buckland, Raymond: *Buckland's Book of Spirit Communications.* St. Paul: Llewellyn, 2004

Cadwallader, M. E.: *Hydesville in History.* Stansted: Psychic Press, 1995

Doyle, Sir Arthur Conan: *The History of Spiritualism.* New York: Doran, 1926

FOX, OLIVER (1885–1949)

"Oliver Fox" was a pseudonym of Hugh G. Callaway, a British pioneer exponent of **astral projection**. He was born in Southampton on November 30, 1885. He studied science and electrical engineering at Harley Institute, in Southampton. He experienced his first astral projection at the age of seventeen.

In 1907, Callaway/Fox married Bertha Knight. He briefly joined a theatrical touring company and then invested in two unsuccessful businesses. In 1910, Fox inherited a small legacy and wrote poetry and short stories with some success. In 1919, the couple moved to London and his writing took an **occult** emphasis. After publishing a number of articles in the *Occult Review*, he published *Astral Projection: a Record of Out-of-Body Experiences.* It was the first major British publication on the subject. He died on April 28, 1949.

Sources:

Fox, Oliver: *Astral Projection: a Record of Out-of-Body Experiences.* London: Rider, 1939

Shepard, Leslie A: *Encyclopedia of Occultism & Parapsychology.* New York: Avon Books, 1978

Fox Sisters *see* **Fox Family**

FRAUDULENT MEDIUMS ACT

In Great Britain prior to 1951, if anyone was caught cheating using **Spiritualism**, fortune-telling, or the like, the only way they could be prosecuted was under the old **Witchcraft Act**. This seemed rather silly in the middle of the twentieth century, so the Witchcraft Act was repealed and it was replaced by the Fraudulent Mediums Act.

The Fraudulent Mediums Act, 22nd June, 1951

An Act to repeal the Witchcraft Act, 1735, and to make, in substitution for certain provisions of section four of the Vagrancy Act, 1824, express provision for the punishment of persons who fraudulently purport to act as spiritualistic **mediums** *or to exercise powers of* **telepathy**, **clairvoyance** *or similar powers.*

Be it enacted by the King's most Excellent Majesty, by and with the advice and consent of the Lords Spiritual and Temporal, and Commons, in this present Parliament assembled, and by the authority of the same, as follows:

I. (1) Subject to the provisions of this section, any person who:

(a) with intent to deceive purports to act as a spiritualistic medium or to exercise any powers of telepathy, clairvoyance or other similar powers, or,

(b) in purporting to act as spiritualistic medium or to exercise such powers as aforesaid, uses any fraudulent device, shall be guilty of an offence.

(2) A person shall not be convicted of an offence under the foregoing subsection unless it is proved that he acted for reward; and for the purpose of this section a person shall be deemed to act for reward if any money is paid, or other valuable item given, in respect of what he does, whether to him or to any other person.

(3) A person guilty of an offence under this section shall be liable on summary conviction to a fine not exceeding fifty pounds or to imprisonment for a term not exceeding four months or to both such fine and such imprisonment, or on conviction on indictment to a fine not exceeding five hundred pounds or to imprisonment for a term not exceeding two years or to both such fine and such imprisonment.

(4) No proceedings for an offence under this section shall be brought in England or Wales except by or with the consent of the Director of Public Prosecutions.

Nothing in subsection (1) of this section shall apply to anything done solely for the purpose of entertainment.

II. The following enactments are hereby repealed, that is to say:

(a) the Witchcraft Act, 1735, so far as still in force, and

(b) section four of the Vagrancy Act, 1824, so far as it extends to persons purporting to act as spiritualistic mediums or to exercise any powers of telepathy, clairvoyance or other similar powers, or to persons who, purporting so to act or to exercise such powers, use fraudulent devices.

III. (1) This Act may be cited as the Fraudulent Mediums Act, 1951.

(2) This Act shall not extend to Northern Ireland.

The Constitution of the United States of America doesn't contain anything similar to the British Fraudulent Mediums Act. However, there are various state and local laws that do cover the legality of so-called fortune-telling and mediumship. The present day legal position of mediums varies from state to state, and many mediums go under the protective shell of ordination, adopting the religious title of "Reverend." The **National Spiritualist Association of Churches** is one legal protective organization, offering valid legal ordination of mediums.

Sources:
Buckland, Raymond: *Buckland's Book of Spirit Communications*. St. Paul: Llewellyn, 2004

Friends, Society of *see* **Quakers**

FRY, COLIN

Colin Fry is a British psychic **medium** who hosts the television show *6th Sense With Colin Fry*. This first aired in 2002 and was an immediate success.

Like so many mediums and **psychics,** Fry was aware of his abilities at a very early age. He says, "When you're a little child, people think it's endearing. Then you grow into your teens and you tell the people you go to school with, they are either totally fascinated by it or totally freaked out by it." He became a professional medium at seventeen, originally appearing under the name "Lincoln" and presenting physical phenomena. However, at one **séance** in the 1990s, a light was inadvertently turned on that seemed to show Fry standing holding up a **trumpet** when he was supposedly bound in a chair. There has been much controversy over this incident, with Fry's explanation accepted by some but rejected by others.

Fry was a member of the Noah's Ark Society—dedicated to investigating and promoting **physical mediumship**—until it was dissolved in 2004. In recent years he has become a Director of the **Leslie Flint** Trust. In 2000, Fry became a principle tutor at the **International College of Spiritual Science & Healing** in Ramsbergsgarden, Sweden, and in February 2003, he bought the college. Today he promotes courses offered there by himself and other mediums, psychics, and **healers.** The stated purpose of the college is, "To promote and advance spiritual gifts in the students, being **clairvoyance, clairaudience, clairsentience,** healing, psychic art, physical mediumship, psychic abilities." The foundation of the college is based on the principles of Spiri-

tualism and certification is offered in many fields, after examinations and proven demonstrations.

Sources:
International College of Spiritual Science and Healing: http://www.colinscollege.com

FULD, WILLIAM

William Fuld was an American businessman who popularized the **talking board** in the form of the Ouija® Board. He first marketed it as a game in 1892. Fuld purchased the rights to the board from its inventor, Elijah J. Bond, who obtained the original patent in 1891. On obtaining the rights, Fuld formed The Southern Novelty Company of Baltimore, Maryland, and began producing what he called the "Oriole Talking Boards." Later the name of the company was changed to the Baltimore Talking Board Company.

The name of the board comes from the French *oui* and the German *ja*, both meaning "yes." During World War I, the board sold by the thousands when families wanted to contact those who had been killed in the war. Fuld made a fortune from the board though he appears to have used the board only briefly himself. He is quoted as saying, "I'm no **Spiritualist!** I'm a Presbyterian. I built this factory on Ouija's® advice, but I haven't consulted the board since. Things have been moving along so well I didn't want to start anything." Things moved along well for Fuld throughout his life. In 1966, the major toy and game manufacturer Parker Brothers purchased the rights to the board and moved the factory to Salem, Massachusetts.

Sources:
Covina, Gina: *The Ouija® Book*. New York: Simon and Schuster, 1979

Hunt, Stoker: *Ouija®: The Most Dangerous Game*. New York: Harper & Row, 1985

FULLER, CURTIS

For many years Curtis Fuller was the publisher and editor of the popular *Fate* magazine. His wife Mary assisted him. The magazine originally had been founded by Fuller and Ray Palmer, who had been editor of *Amazing Stories*. Fuller bought the magazine outright from Palmer in 1955 and under his editorship, *Fate* expanded its range and coverage extensively, with a regular distribution of 100,000 copies.

Fate hit the newsstands in the spring of 1948 with a cover story by Kenneth Arnold, describing his UFO sighting in 1947. This story set the tone of *Fate*, which focused on unusual events and experiences. The story drew world attention to the fledgling magazine. In 1988, the Fuller family sold the magazine to Llewellyn Publications. In his farewell editorial Fuller wrote, "Our purpose throughout this long time has been to explore and to report honestly the strangest facts of this strange world—the ones that don't fit into the general beliefs of the ways things are. All of us see the world distorted by our upbringing and our training. We hope that our perspectives have helped to expand your horizons and, more importantly, to help you understand that there are many realities that may be as valid as the ones that are familiar to us."

In 1994, the familiar digest size of *Fate* was changed by Llewellyn to a full size, and full color was employed throughout. In 2001, Phyllis Galde took over the magazine, two years later returning it to its original digest size. In 2004, Galde Press bought *Fate* outright from Llewellyn and continues its publication.

Sources:

Llewellyn Worldwide: http://www.llewellyn.com

Shepard, Leslie A: *Encyclopedia of Occultism & Parapsychology*. New York: Avon Books, 1978

GALLUP POLL

A 1980 Gallup Poll revealed that 71 percent of Americans believe in an afterlife. A 2001 Gallup Poll showed that 38 percent believe it is possible to make contact with the dead; 54 percent believe in the effectiveness of spiritual healing; 42 percent believe in ghosts and hauntings.

GARRETT, EILEEN JEANETTE VANCHO LYTTLE (1893–1970)

In his introduction to Eileen Garrett's autobiography, Allan Angoff wrote, "Eileen Garrett holds no professional degrees and has no license to practice any of the **healing** arts, but she has helped and apparently cured hundreds of physicians, scientists, writers, editors, secretaries, psychiatrists, psychologists, bereaved parents and children, and the prime minister of a very large country."

Born on March 17, 1893, at Beau Park in County Meath, Ireland, Eileen Jeanette Vancho Lyttle showed **psychic** abilities from a very early age. Suffering from tuberculosis and bronchial asthma, she spent many long weeks confined to her bed. As a young child, she claimed that she was able to speak with the dead. Her **mediumship** started in earnest following the end of World War II. She came to be considered one of the greatest **mediums** the world has ever known.

During the war, and after a failed marriage to a young architect named Clive Barry, Eileen ran a hostel for wounded soldiers. She had **precognitive visions** of many of the men with whom she came into contact, often seeing them killed on returning to action. One of the soldiers she saw die in this way was a man who, as she nursed him, she agreed to marry. At the end of the war in 1918, she married James William Garrett, another wounded soldier. Like her two previous marriages, this one did not last long. It ended in divorce and Garrett did not marry again.

One day Garrett joined a group of women who were doing **table tipping**. In the middle of the session Garrett went into a **trance** and started speaking of seeing dead relatives of the women around the table. The women were so surprised and startled that they shook her awake. Garret was persuaded to consult with a man who would help her understand this aspect of herself. When the man put her into a light **hypnotic** trance, a **spirit guide** named Uvani came through and stated that Garrett would be active as a trance medium for the next several years. This turned out to

Trance medium Eileen Garrett, regarded as one of the greatest trance mediums in the world. *Courtesy Fortean Picture Library.*

be true. It took a while for her to come to terms with this new role, but eventually—through the agencies of people such as **James Hewat McKenzie** and the **British College of Psychic Science**—she accepted her gift.

Garrett came to work with people such as **Hereward Carrington**, **Nandor Fodor**, Sir **Arthur Conan Doyle**, and Sir **Oliver Lodge**. In 1931, she was invited to visit the **American Society for Psychical Research**, which she did. While in America she also worked with other notable mediums, Dr. **Joseph Banks Rhine**, **William McDougall**, and Dr. Anita Mühl. In 1938, she wrote a book titled *My Life as a Search for the Meaning of Mediumship* (Rider, London 1939), which was quite successful. Shortly after its appearance, she traveled to Juan-les-Pins, France. At the beginning of World War II, she

tried to remain in France to help orphaned children, but eventually had to leave.

On March 8, 1941, back in New York, Garrett was inspired by the name of the Life Extension Building to start a publishing company at its location on East Forty-Fourth Street. On impulse she rented two rooms on the eighteenth floor and planned to launch a magazine to be called *Tomorrow*, which would deal with serious investigation of the paranormal. The proceeds, she decided, would go to the starving children of France. She actually started by publishing two books, one on **Nostradamus**, by Lee McCann, and one of her own called *Telepathy*. These were under the banner of her publishing company, Creative Age Press, though this name was later changed to Helix Press. The first issue of her magazine *Tomorrow* appeared on September 1, 1941. Garrett became a U.S. citizen in 1947.

In 1951, Garrett founded the **Parapsychology Foundation** to promote organized scientific research into **parapsychology**. The Foundation published the *International Journal of Parapsychology*. Garrett was always somewhat uncertain about psychism generally, and her own in particular, and allowed herself to be subjected to numerous tests at such institutions as Johns Hopkins University and the New York Psychiatric Institute. In the 1960s she worked with psychologist **Lawrence LeShan** in his studies of alternate realities, assisting him in describing "**clairvoyant** reality."

Guiley said, "While many other mediums believed in the literal existence of spirits of the dead and of their spirit controls, Garrett retained an objectivity and even skepticism about them." Eileen Garrett died on September 15, 1970 in Nice, France, after a long illness. She has been acclaimed as one of the world's greatest mediums.

Sources:

Angoff, Allan: *Eileen Garrett and the World Beyond the Senses*. New York: William Morrow, 1974

Fishley, Margaret: *The Supernatural*. London: Aldus, 1976

Garrett, Eileen: *Many Voices: The Autobiography of a Medium*. New York: G. P. Putnam's, 1968

Guiley, Rosemary Ellen: *The Encyclopedia of Ghosts and Spirits*. New York: Facts On File, 1992

GATEKEEPER

A term used for a **medium**'s personal **spirit guide**, who oversees the coming and going of **spirits** trying to make contact at a séance. Used interchangeably with "Door Keeper," this guide organizes the spirits who want to make contact with the sitter(s). He or she will ensure that the spirits are there and will help them, if necessary, to make the contact. The Gatekeeper will also keep away unwanted spirits who may want to contact this physical world but are not directly connected to the sitter. **Estelle Roberts**'s Gatekeeper and personal guide was "Red Cloud." **Ena Twigg**'s was "Philip." **Arthur Ford** had "Fletcher," William Rainen had "Dr. Peebles," and **Ivy Northage** had "Chan." Many times these Gatekeepers and spirit guides are in the form of **Native Americans.**

Sources:

Barbanell, Maurice: *This Is Spiritualism*. Oxshott: The Spiritual Truth Press, 1959

Buckland, Raymond: *Buckland's Book of Spirit Communications*. St. Paul: Llewellyn, 2004

GEHMAN, REV. BEATRICE ANNE

B eatrice Anne Gehman was born into a family of Amish Mennonites in Petoskey, Michigan. She was the seventh child in the family. She described her parents as religious people who were very spiritual and of a "**psychic** temperament." Gehman was the youngest **medium** ever certified by the **National Spiritualist Association of Churches**, having begun her platform work at the age of fifteen. At seventeen she was demonstrating at **Lily Dale Assembly**, New York. Speaking of her gifts, she said, "I came by it naturally ... but I don't think [my parents] understood much about it until late in their lives ... I can't remember a time when I didn't hear voices or have visions and see auras. It was just something that was very natural to me."

Gehman exhibited **physical mediumship** at the age of eleven. She said, "I do remember at times I had a lot of physical phenomena that occurred around me. We would sit down to the dinner table, and the end of the table would lift up and the silverware would move around. I remember my father praying for me, his huge hands pouncing down on top of my head and his prayer to remove this horrible affliction that I had." Some years later—after her sister died—she experienced a full **materialization** of her sister in the center of her sitting room. From high school, Gehman had gone to nursing school and, after graduating, continued further studies in X-ray and laboratory work. But as she said, "I never used any of it and never wanted to."

At fifteen, at a time of depression after leaving home, she attempted to end her life by taking an overdose of sleeping pills, but was saved by **spirit** and guided to a meeting with medium Wilbur Hull. She was led there by the spirit of a medium named Rose, who had originally been Hull's teacher. Hull guided her and taught her the fundamentals of Spiritualism. She met him at **Cassadaga**, the Spiritualist community in Florida.

For some years Gehman lived in Orlando, Florida. She had her own church there and headed the Spiritual Research Society, where she taught classes and workshops and conducted four or five public services a week. At that time she was the wife of investment banker Robert Robeson. They had a daughter, Rhonda.

In 1980, Gehman moved to Springfield, Virginia, just outside of Washington, D.C. There she and her present husband, Wayne Knoll, founded the Center for Spiritual Enlightenment (CSE), of which she is pastor. The charter from the National Spiritualist Association of Churches was issued in 1988. In 2003, CSE purchased a historic building that formerly housed the First Congregational Church. Today the CSE is a thriving organization with members throughout North America. It offers weekly services and a wide variety of workshops and other programs.

Gehman is a **trance** medium and also occasionally does red-light **transfiguration**. She spends her summer months at Lily Dale, where she teaches workshops on Spiritualism and mediumship. She characterizes her work as being about "love … and service. I think it has to be based on love."

Sources:

Sherman, Harold: *You Can Communicate With the Unseen World*. New York: Fawcett, 1974

Zolar: *Zolar's Book of the Spirits: All the Most Famous and Fabulous Lore about Contacting the Spirit World*. New York, Prentice Hall, 1987

GELLER, URI (B. 1946)

Uri Geller was born in Tel Aviv on December 20, 1946. He was the son of Hungarian Jewish immigrants. Geller discovered his paranormal powers when still a child. As young as age three, he found that he could bend and even break metal by gently rubbing it and concentrating on it, and he could stop watches by concentrating on them. It wasn't until he was much older—after serving in the Israeli army in the Six Day War—that he started giving public demonstrations of his skills. He appeared numerous times on television in Europe and the United States, and was subjected to intensive investigations by scientists and **psychical** researchers. At Stanford Research Institute in California in 1972, Geller demonstrated metal bending and correctly guessed the contents of metal cans and the numbers on dice shaken in enclosed boxes. In the laboratory of Professor John Taylor of London University in 1974, Geller deflected the needle of a Geiger counter and even bent a number of metal rods that were enclosed inside plastic tubes, with metal mesh screens around them so that they could not be physically touched.

Stage magician James Randi tried to reproduce what became known as "the Geller effect" but his simple stage-style sleight of hand was a far cry from the numerous effects produced by Geller under strict scientific conditions. Geller stopped an escalator in a Munich department store simply by concentrating on it. He similarly stopped a cable car. He bent metal that was a distance from him and was not touched by anyone; he caused a piece of metal resting on a scale to bend upward, rather than downward (and with no more than half an ounce of pressure ever measured), and also resulted in the needle of the scale being bent. He told others, including young children, how to concentrate, and they bent metal. He has stopped clocks and caused long-broken clocks to start working again, all with his mind power. He has even involved television viewers in starting and stopping clocks and bending metal. After a visit by Geller to Tokyo, Japan, in 1973, thousands of Japanese children apparently manifested similar powers of mind over matter. The following year eight of these children were singled out for investigation by Dr. Shigemi Sasaki, professor of psychology at the Denki Tsushin University. One twelve-year-old, Jun Sekiguchi, showed an amazing ability to bend spoons and to recharge dead electric batteries by simply holding them. Dr. **Joseph Banks Rhine** of Duke University in Durham, North Carolina, said, "The tests in Tokyo have shown that PK power exists among many of their children. The research is of great significance."

During experiments at Birbeck College in England, he caused a Geiger counter to click loudly when he concentrated on it and bent a crystal molybdenum disk without touching it. In another experiment at Kent State University in Ohio, Geller deflected a magnetometer and also scored exceptionally high in experiments involving a die and film cans. In front of television cameras in Toronto, Ontario he was tested by scientist Dr. A. R. G. Owen under conditions Owen said were a rigorous as any in a laboratory. Both Owen and the television audience were totally convinced by the demonstrations.

There have been plenty of detractors for Geller but none have been able to explain all of his effects nor to duplicate them. In the house of

Uri Geller demonstrates his ability to bend metal using only his psychic forces. *Courtesy Fortean Picture Library.*

American doctor and parapsychologist **Andrija Puharich**, Geller produced rappings of the type heard in the home of the **Fox family** in 1848. When visiting the pianist Byron Janis, a death mask of Chopin standing on the piano shed tears.

In the home of Hollywood screen writer Jesse Lasky, he produced **apports**. Many explanations have been offered—including, of course, outright fraud—but none has explained all of the phenomena produced by Geller.

Sources:

Geller, Uri: *My Story*. New York: Praeger Publishers, 1975

Shepard, Leslie A: *Encyclopedia of Occultism & Parapsychology*. New York: Avon Books, 1978

Taylor, John Gerald: *Superminds: An Investigation into the Paranormal*. London: Granada, 1975

Wilson, Colin: *The Supernatural: The Geller Phenomenon*. London: Aldus Books, 1976

GHOST

A ghost is an apparition or vision of a **spirit** of the dead; "apparition" is the term preferred by **parapsychologists**. Ghosts are found in the folklore, art, and literature of all nations. Throughout England, there are haunted sites galore where numerous witnesses have seen a ghost or ghosts ... single individuals to whole armies from the past. Houses, castles, gardens, woods, and crossroads are sites for these **hauntings. Frederick W. H. Myers**, founder of the **Society for Psychical Research**, defined a ghost as, "A manifestation of persistent personal energy, or as an indication that some kind of force is being exercised after death which is in some way connected with a person previously known on earth."

It is not always the ghost of a deceased person which is witnessed. There are records of ghosts of animals and even of inanimate objects such as coaches, trains, and airplanes. It is said that a belief in ghosts grows out of the universal human need for some assurance of survival of death. Ancestor worship is one form of religious awareness that ties in with a belief in ghosts. In some areas, these ancestral ghosts take on the power of minor gods and it is felt that unless steps are taken to propitiate them, they can be harmful to the living. Generally speaking, however, ghosts are not able to harm the living. Their appearance may be frightening, especially in its unexpectedness, but there are virtually no records of actual physical hurt coming from an apparition.

Ghosts are seldom, if ever, floating sheeted figures of the cartoon variety. Some early forms were of the dead as they had been buried in their winding sheets, but the majority seem to appear much as they had in life, fully and appropriately clothed. Ghosts are occasionally harbingers of death. It is said that Josephine's ghost appeared to Napoleon some days before he died, to signal his coming death, and a Black Friar supposedly appeared to members of Lord Byron's family for the same reason. A phantom drummer—the once-young lover of the Lady Airlie—drums to signal an approaching death in the family of the Ogilvys, Earls of Airlie, Scotland.

Many ghosts seem to haunt particular places because of some tragedy or traumatic event that occurred to them either at death or just prior to it, while others are there because of extreme happiness known in those places. This signals the fact that the ghost is actually a spirit that either is unaware of its own death or is unwilling to admit to it. Many **Spiritualist** groups form what are called **Rescue Circles**, designed specifically to contact such spirits and to persuade them to move on, as they need to do.

Many ghosts and apparitions have been photographed. As with much in the general field of parapsychology and Spiritualism, it is easy to fake such photographs. However, there are a very large number of photographs that have been examined and verified by photographic experts. One example is the photograph taken by the vicar of Newby Church in Yorkshire, England, that shows a cowled figure standing to the right of the altar. The "Brown Lady of Raynham Hall" in England has been photographed descending the main staircase. A photograph taken of Isabella Houg of Newark, New Jersey, in 1922, showed an accompanying figure of her long dead uncle when the picture was developed. Mr. and Mrs. Chinnery of Ipswich, England, had been to visit the grave of Mrs. Chinnery's deceased mother and, as they were preparing to leave, Mrs. Mabel Chinnery—on impulse—turned and took a photograph of her husband sitting in their family car. When the photograph was developed it showed the figure of her deceased mother sitting in the back seat of the car. All of these photographs have been proven not to have been faked. Rarely, however, is the ghost actually seen by the photographer. It is only on development of the picture that the apparition is discovered.

The psychical researcher **Harry Price** referred to **Borley Rectory** in Suffolk, as "the most haunted house in England." For forty years Price investigated ghosts and hauntings. He founded the **National Laboratory of Psychical Research,** now part of the University of London. He claimed that the large nineteenth century house built by the Reverend Henry Bull in the 1860s was the scene of more ghostly activity than anywhere else. It certainly did have the ghost of a nun, a phantom coach, writing that appeared on walls, poltergeist activity, and more. At **séances** held by Price at the house, there were rappings, apparitions, and pebbles flying through the air, keys pushed out of locks, and a whole host of similar phenomena. Although the vast majority of reported ghost sightings can be explained away, a small percentage cannot.

Sources:

Guiley, Rosemary Ellen: *The Encyclopedia of Ghosts and Spirits.* New York: Facts On File, 1992

Myers, Frederick W. H.: *Human Personality and Its Survival After Bodily Death.* London: Longmans, 1903

Price, Harry: *The Most Haunted House in England.* London: Longmans, Green, 1940

Smyth, Frank: *The Supernatural: Ghosts and Poltergeists.* London: Aldus, 1975

Steiger, Brad: Real Ghosts, Restless Spirits, and Haunted Places. *Detroit: Visible Ink Press, 2003*

Stemman, Roy: *The Supernatural: Spirits and Spirit Worlds.* London: Aldus, 1975

Thurston, Rev. Herbert: *Ghosts and Poltergeists.* London: Regnery, 1950

Gladstone, William Ewart (1809–1898)
see Eglinton, William

GLOSSOLALIA

From the Greek *glossa*, "tongue", and *lalia*, "chatter," glossolalia is the term used for "speaking in tongues." Sometimes at religious gatherings or in **séances**, someone will go into a **trance** and start speaking in an unknown language. Many times witnesses to such an event will make extravagant claims, such as that the person was "Speaking in ancient Egyptian" or that they were "speaking Greek." It is not known exactly what ancient **Egyptians** sounded like, and unless there was someone present who could actually verify that language, there can be no evidence for such utterances. Far more frequently the speech is utter gibberish. In fact, one definition of glossolalia is "speaking in *pseudo*-tongues". Professor **Charles Richet** (1850–1935) preferred the term Xenoglossis, which covered both speaking and writing in unknown languages, whether real or pseudo.

Nandor Fodor reports that in the pamphlet *Drei Tage in Gros Almerode* written by a theological student of Leipzig, J. Busching, there is information on ten cases of xenoglossis at a religious revival at Almerode, Hesse, in 1907. He said, "The phenomena began with a hissing or peculiar gnashing sound. These sounds were caused by the subject, not wishing to disturb the order of service by interrupting a **prayer** already commenced, exerting himself to repress the inward impulse acting on his organs of speech. But all that had to come came, and the momentarily repressed glossolalies only burst forth with increased vigor."

The **Spiritualist** medium Laura Edmonds, daughter of Judge **John Worth Edmonds** (1816–1874), claimed the gift of tongues. Although normally she could speak only English and a smattering of French, while entranced by **Spirit** she spoke a large number of different languages with great fluency, including Spanish, French, Greek, Italian, Portuguese, Latin, and Hungarian. Indian dialects were also identified. These phenomena and many others were all very meticulously recorded by her father. She was possibly the first Spiritualist **medium** to exhibit glossolalia. According to **Emma Hardinge Britten**, medium Jenny Keyes sang in Italian and Spanish, languages with which she was not familiar.

Sources:

Britten, Emma Hardinge: *Modern American Spiritualism.* (1870) New York: University Books, 1970

Fodor, Nandor: *Encyclopedia of Psychic Science.* London: Arthurs Press, 1933

Shepard, Leslie A: *Encyclopedia of Occultism & Parapsychology.* New York: Avon Books, 1978

GOLIGHER GIRLS

A Goligher family of Belfast were **mediums** who produced physical phenomena. Of Mr. Goligher and his four daughters, son, and son-in-law, the main medium was the oldest daughter, Kathleen Goligher (b. 1898). **Spiritualism** was the family religion. They were investigated by **psychic researcher** William Jackson Crawford, a mechanical engineer and Extra-Mural Lecturer at Belfast's Queen's University. His investigations lasted from 1914 until his death in 1920. Throughout the investigation, the family refused to accept any payment.

Séances were held either at the Goligher home or at Crawford's home. They took place in dim red light, since it was physical phenomena that were produced. Six members of the family formed the **circle** while Crawford was left free to roam the room at will, for better observation. Kathleen would sometimes go into **trance** and speak to Crawford, but much of the time communication was by way of **rappings**.

Levitation of a table was achieved with **ectoplasm** formed into what Crawford described as "rods." These emanated from Kathleen's body, emerging from between her legs. The rods were capable of lifting heavy weights. Crawford used scales to record differences in weight that occurred during a sitting; sometimes the medium gaining weight and sometimes losing it.

Sources:

Crawford, W. J.: *Experiments in Psychical Science.* New York: E. P. Dutton, 1919

Crawford, W. J.: *The Psychic Structures at the Goligher Circle.* London: John M. Watkins, 1921

Crawford, W. J.: *The Reality of Psychic Phenomena: Raps, Levitations, etc.* New York: E. P. Dutton, 1918

Doyle, Sir Arthur Conan: *The History of Spiritualism.* New York: Doran, 1926

Fodor, Nandor: *Encyclopedia of Psychic Science.* London: Arthurs Press, 1933

GRANT, JOAN (B. 1907)

Joan Grant was born in England on April 12, 1907. She grew up firmly believing that she was **reincarnated**, having lived previous lives in ancient **Egypt**, the Holy Land, and pre-Columbian America. In later years she wrote a number of best-selling books based on her memories of these past lives, including *Winged Pharoah* (1937), *Eyes of Horus* (1969), *The Lord of the Horizon* (1974), *So Moses Was Born* (1974), *Scarlet Feather* (1975), and *Return to Elysium* (1976). In her memoir *Far Memory*, Grant explained that after a short visit to Egypt she returned to London where she was shown a collection of scarabs. When she took the oldest in her hand, she said that she saw vivid scenes of the time and place from which the scarab had come—an example of **psychometry**.

Sources:

White Eagle Lodge: http://www.whiteagle.org

GREECE

The **Oracles** of Greece were of great antiquity. They featured **divination** and prophesy inspired by various means. The Oracles of Delphi, Dodona, Epidaurus, and Trophonius were most famous, though there were many others.

At Epidaurus the temple was dedicated to Æsculapius the Healer and Dream-sender. There people would go to sleep in the temple and have **dreams** that would tell them how to **heal** their sickness. At Trophonius there were a great many caverns. It was reported that in the caverns the sounds of underground waters could be heard, while vapors rose up from them. Seekers would sleep in these caverns for several days and nights. When they were awakened by the priests, they would be questioned. Most of them woke feeling terrible sorrow and melancholy.

The Oracle at Dodona was dedicated to Pelasgic Zeus and was the oldest of the Oracles, lasting for 2,000 years. Divination was done there by interpreting the rustling of leaves in the sacred groves, the sound of wind blowing chimes, and the sound of water rushing and falling over rocks. The three priestesses there were known as *Peliades*, meaning "doves." They had titles that signified "Diviner of the Future," "Friend of Man," and "Virgin Ruler of Man."

Delphi is probably the best known of all the Oracles. It was located in Phocis, on the southern slope of Mount Parnassus. Although dedicated to Apollo, it seems certain that the shrine was not originally Apollo's. The site was formerly known as Crisa. It has been said that the Oracle was built above a volcanic chasm and that the Pythia gave her answers to questions in a state of **trance** induced by intoxicating fumes. According to Justinian (Flavius Anicus Iustinianus, 483–565 CE), "In a dark and narrow recess of a cliff at Delphi there was a little open glade and in this a hole, or cleft in the earth, out of which blew a strong draft of air straight up and as if impelled by a wind, which filled the minds of poets with madness." However, both geologically and architecturally this is impossible. There is no crack or cleft, and the local strata have never been capable of producing any kind of gas.

Apart from the **seers** and **sibyls** of the Oracles and the various temples, there was a class of diviners known as interpreters who would divine by the flights of birds, inspecting entrails, thunder, lightning, dreams, and the various other methods common to the area. They would accompany armed forces, if necessary, so that they could advise the commanders before battle. They also advised the government, to prevent uprisings or revolts of any kind. Æschylus (ca. 525–456 BCE), the earliest and perhaps greatest Greek tragic poet, in a passage in his work *Prometheus Vinctus*, has Prometheus tell of the subjects in which he first instructed humankind.

He lists dreams and their interpretation, chance words overheard, chance meetings on the road, auspices, observation of the flight of birds, augury from entrails and from **visions** seen in the fire. In ancient Greece, divination from hearing chance words (cledonomancy) was very popular and well established as a religious form of divination. Lawson relates how an enquirer at the temple of Hermes Agoræus would burn incense before the statue of the god, fill bronze lamps with oil and light them, place a certain bronze coin on the altar, then whisper his question in the ear of the statue. The petitioner would then immediately put his hands over his ears and leave the temple. Once outside he would remove his hands and the first words he heard spoken he would accept as the god's answer to his question. At Thebes, Apollo Spodios gave his answers in the same way.

Sources:

Buckland, Raymond: *The Fortune–Telling Book: The Encyclopedia of Divination and Soothsaying*. Detroit: Visible Ink Press, 2004

Halliday, W.R.: *Greek Divination*. London: William Rider, 1913

Lawson, John Cuthbert: *Modern Greek Folklore and Ancient Greek Religion*. New York: University Books, 1964

Lissner, Ivar: *The Living Past*. New York: Capricorn Books, 1961

Spence, Lewis: *An Encyclopedia of the Occult*. London: George Routledge & Sons, 1920

GREELEY, HORACE (1811–1872)

Horace Greeley was a political leader and newspaper editor. He was born near Amherst, New Hampshire, on February 3, 1811, the eldest of the five children of Zaccheus Greeley, a poor farmer. He had irregular schooling but om 1826 he apprenticed to the publication *Northern Spectator* in East Poultney, Vermont. By 1834, he had become senior editor of the then-new literary magazine called the *New Yorker*. In 1836. he married Mary Youngs Cheney, a schoolteacher.

April 10, 1841, Greeley started the *New York Tribune*, a Whig newspaper dedicated to reform, economic progress, and the elevation of the masses. He was still editing this paper—by then of high standard—when the **Fox sisters** first visited New York in June, 1850. Greeley was the first to call upon the Fox sisters and publicly admitted that he was puzzled by the phenomena they produced. He did, however, emphasize that the good faith of the sisters should not be questioned. Giving his opinion of the sisters, in the *New York Tribune*, Greeley said,

> Mrs. Fox and her three daughters left our city yesterday on their return to Rochester, after a stay here of some weeks, during which they have subjected the mysterious influence, by which they seem to be accompanied, to every reasonable test, and to the keen and critical scrutiny of hundreds who have chosen to visit them, or whom they have been invited to visit. The rooms which they occupied at the hotel have been repeatedly searched and scrutinized; they have been taken without an hour's notice into houses they had never before entered; they have been all unconsciously placed on a glass surface concealed under the carpet in order to interrupt electrical vibrations; they have been disrobed by a committee of ladies appointed without notice, and insisting that neither of them should leave the room until the investigation has been made, etc., etc., yet we believe no one, to this moment, pretends that he has detected either of them in producing or causing the "**rappings**," nor do we think any of their contemners has invented a plausible theory to account for the production of these sounds, nor the singular intelligence which (certainly at times) has seemed to be manifest through them.

Greeley later stated in *Recollections of a Busy Life* (1868) that "the jugglery hypothesis utterly fails to account for occurrences which I have personally witnessed…certain developments strongly indicate that they do proceed from departed **spirits**."

Greeley has been described as quick-tempered, with frequently faulty judgement. He had a desire for public office that amounted to being an obsession. At one time he was a candidate for the United States presidency. However, he was very warm-hearted and had great patience with his extremely eccentric wife. He was also one of the early supporters of the Fox sisters, championing them for several years. For this he has become known as "The **Abraham Lincoln** of **Spiritualism**." He is said to have provided funds for Margaret Fox's education and offered his home to the whole Fox family.

Sources:

Doyle, Sir Arthur Conan: *The History of Spiritualism*. New York: Doran, 1926

Encyclopedia Britannica. Chicago: William Benton, 1964

Fodor, Nandor: *Encyclopedia of Psychic Science*. London: Arthurs Press, 1933

GUARDIAN ANGELS

Some people believe that a "Guardian Angel" is present with every individual from the moment of birth. Others believe that they are there only when needed in moments of crisis. The chief function of a guardian angel is to protect the individual, helping him or her to make the best decisions and to lead a positive and productive life. In **Spiritualism**, the guardian angel may be equated with the **Gatekeeper**, the chief **spirit guide**.

In some societies the term used is guardian **spirit**, tutelary spirit, protective spirit, or guardian genius. "Genius" is the Latin term for each man's protector; "Juno" is the feminine form. The genius was honored in **Roman** birthday celebrations. There was also a *genius loci* which guarded a particular place. In ancient **Greece**, the equivalent was the personal dæmon, which accompanied a man throughout his life. Some societies equate the guardian spirit with a deceased ancestor. In many **Native American** traditions, the "vision quest" involves finding

A protective guardian angel watches over a child.
Hulton Archive/Getty Images.

one's guardian spirit, though legend has it that the guardian spirit might appear spontaneously in a dream, often in animal form.

In the Old Testament there is mention in Daniel chapters 10 and 12 of angels who watch over different kingdoms and different people. In Mohammedan belief every person is guarded by two angels during the day and another two at night.

Sources:

Cavendish, Richard (ed.): *Man, Myth & Magic: An Illustrated Encyclopedia of the Supernatural.* London: BPC, 1970

Gluckman, M.: *The Allocation of Responsibility.* Manchester: Manchester University Press, 1970

GUIDE

The majority of **Spiritualist** mediums have a guide. Many have more than one. The guide is a **spirit** who can serve as a "Master of Ceremonies" at a **séance**, introducing spirits who wish to communicate through the **medium**, regulating which spirits are allowed to come through and what form of communication is being used (**clairvoyance**, **direct voice**, etc.), and whether or not such **physical phenomena** as **apports** might be apparent, and so on. Some mediums have specific guides for specific purposes. For example, if they do **healing** they may have an exclusive guide who makes him- or herself known only for that purpose. This is often the spirit of someone who was a doctor or healer of some sort when on the earth plane.

"**Control**" is a term sometimes used to designate the guide. Descriptively, "Guide" is the better term. **Nandor Fodor** said, "The body of the medium is an instrument which requires considerable practice in efficient handling. The control is a communications expert who watches over the fluency of the proceedings … The easygoing, conversational aspect of the séances is largely due to his presence … They are patient and ready to produce the phenomena to the sitters' satisfaction. But they do not take orders. [They] expect courteous treatment and appreciation for what they do and have their own caprices." They are not all-knowing. Many times a guide will admit to ignorance of a subject, or the answer to a question, and will say that he will ask another who knows.

Not all guides are male, though the majority seem to be. It is not known why this is. Guides often have helpers for certain tasks, for example to prepare for the presentation of physical phenomena. These helpers can also assist in the explanation of incoherent messages.

Sources:

Fodor, Nandor: *Encyclopedia of Psychic Science.* London: Arthurs Press, 1933

GUIDED MEDITATION

As its name suggests, this is **meditation** where a leader quietly speaks the words that suggest a mental journey. These words are imagery in story form, together with suggestions for relaxation and well-being. It is meditation with a specific purpose. For example, to take a person on a mental journey in order to find their personal **spirit guide**. A guided meditation also can be used in many ways to help in **mediumistic** development. The guided meditation can be directed by a person who is present, or by a recording.

Sources:

Bodian, Stephan: *Meditation for Dummies*. New York: Wiley Publishing, 1999

Goleman, Daniel: *The Meditative Mind: The Varieties of Meditative Experience*. New York: Tarcher/Putnam, 1988

GUPPY-VOLCKMAN, AGNES NICHOL (D. 1917)

Born in England, Agnes Nichol began exhibiting signs of psychism and **mediumship** whilst still a small child. She saw **apparitions** and caused **rappings** to occur. Her abilities developed as she grew, and by the time she was in her twenties she had become a notable **physical medium**. She was able to demonstrate **levitation**, apports, independent music, **table tipping** and movement, **psychokinesis**, and more.

She was "discovered" by Dr. Alfred Russel Wallace (the famous naturalist and, with Darwin, co-discoverer of the principles of evolution) in November 1866, about a year after Wallace started his serious investigation of **Spiritualism**. Wallace encountered Agnes Nichol at the house of his sister, Mrs. Sims. At that sitting the **medium**—who even at that age was large and stout—was lifted and placed on the **séance**-room table, while still sitting in her chair. At another sitting with Wallace, the room was filled with anemones, tulips, chrysanthemums, Chinese primroses, and several ferns. Wallace said, "All were absolutely fresh as if just gathered from a conservatory. They were covered with a fine cold dew. Not a petal was crumpled or broken, not the most delicate point or pinnule of the ferns was out of place."

In 1867, Agnes Nichol married Samuel Guppy, a very rich widower, and they lived in various parts of Europe before returning to England in 1870. When Samuel Guppy died, she remarried and became Agnes Guppy-Volkman. At one notable séance one of the sitters requested of Mrs. Guppy that a sunflower be apported. It arrived over six feet tall and with a huge clump of earth still clinging to it. At another séance, the Duchess d'Arpino asked for some sand from the sea. Instantly sand, sea water, and a star fish were deposited on the séance table! The Princess Marguerite at Naples just *thought* about a prickly cactus and more than twenty dropped onto the table and had to be removed with tongs. One time dozens of butterflies descended from the ceiling, another time it was a shower of feathers. Live eels, lobsters, stinging nettles, foul-smelling flowers all were apported on various occasions.

Frank Podmore, who assumed that most mediums were frauds hoping to make money, said, "Mrs. Guppy, even during the few months in which, as Miss Nichol, she practiced as a professional Mesmerist, can scarcely have found her main incentive in the hope of gain. On the assumption of fraud, the mere cost of the flowers lavished on her sitters must have swallowed up any probable profit from her increased mesmeric clientele. And even such a motive would have ceased with her marriage." Later séances were conducted by Mrs. Guppy in full light but the earlier ones were in darkness. Sir **Arthur Conan Doyle** said she "showed powers which in some directions have never been surpassed."

On one occasion Mrs. Guppy herself became an apport. The two mediums, **Charles Williams** and **Frank Herne**, specialized in apport séances. At one of their sittings someone jokingly suggested that they should apport Mrs. Guppy, who lived only a short distance from their séance room in High Holborn, London. This suggestion was greeted with laughter since Mrs. Guppy was a very large woman. But within a matter of minutes, a very large figure suddenly appeared, with a thump, on the top of the table. It was Mrs. Guppy, wearing a dressing gown, holding a pen wet with ink, and looking very startled. (*see* **Apports**)

Sources:

Doyle, Sir Arthur Conan: *The History of Spiritualism*. New York: Doran, 1926

Fodor, Nandor: *Encyclopedia of Psychic Science*. London: Arthurs Press, 1933

GURNEY, EDMUND (1847–1888)

Edmund Gurney was the son of an English clergyman. As a young man he studied classics, music, and medicine. He became a Fellow of Trinity College in Cambridge and was a founder and Secretary of the **Society for Psychical Research** (SPR). He was editor of the SPR journal *Proceedings*, to which he contributed many important papers.

Gurney attended a number of **Spiritualist séances** between 1874 and 1878 though he did not make public what he learned from these. He became especially interested in **telepathy** and studied **hallucinations** and the psychological side of **hypnotism**. Between 1885 and 1888, he devised a large number of experiments which, according to **Nandor Fodor**, "proved that there is sometimes, in the induction of hypnotic phenomena, some agency at work which is neither ordinary nervous stimulation, nor suggestion conveyed by any ordinary channel to the subject's mind." With **Frederick W. H. Myers** and **Frank Podmore**, Gurney authored the classical work *Phantasms of the Living* (1886).

After Gurney's death, several mediums including Mrs. A. W. Verrall, Mrs. Forbes, and Mrs. Holland, claimed to have received communications from him through automatic writing. When Sir **Oliver Lodge** sat with the medium Leonore Piper in 1889–1890, messages were received regarding matters known only to Lodge and Gurney.

Sources:

Fishley, Margaret: *The Supernatural*. London: Aldus, 1976

Fodor, Nandor: *Encyclopedia of Psychic Science*. London: Arthurs Press, 1933

GYPSIES

The Gypsies are a nomadic population who originated in northern India. A mass exodus from that area began about the middle of the ninth century and large groups of people departed their homeland and moved westward. They were driven out of their homeland by successive armies of invaders: **Greeks**, Scythians, Kushites, Huns, and Mohammedans. The Gypsies passed through Pakistan, Afghanistan and Persia, eventually reaching the Caspian Sea, north of the Persian Gulf. There they split into two distinct groups, one going northward through Turkey and into Bulgaria by way of Byzantium; the other, smaller band, going southward, sweeping down through Jordan into Egypt. By 1348, the nomads were in Serbia with others heading north through Walachia and into Moldavia. By the turn of that century they were to be found as widely spread as in Peloponnesus and Corfu; Bosnia, Transylvania, Hungary, Bohemia; and, in the early 1400s, in Central Europe. They were in Germany by 1417 and England and Wales by 1430.

As they spread across Europe and other areas, the local populations wondered where these travelers had come from. With their dark, swarthy skin and colorful dress, many people believed that they were descendants of the ancient **Egyptians**. The idea caught on and they were referred to as "Egyptians." This was sometimes shortened to "'Gyptians," and eventually to "Gypsies." The Gypsies themselves played up to this idea, claiming to have originated in "Little Egypt."

Gypsies—more correctly Romanies, or Roma—were in many places equated with **witches** and sorcerers. They were wrongly accused of engaging in black magic and dealing with the devil. In many countries they were banished, but they managed to hang on tenaciously. They did whatever they could in order to survive. Along with making metal and wooden objects, weaving baskets, and

Two modern-day gypsy women and a young girl walk through town in Sibiu, Romania. *AP/WideWorld Photos.*

mending pots and pans, they trained animals to dance and to do tricks. They also told fortunes. Everybody was interested in trying to learn what the future held, so fortune-telling was a big attraction. Not being great mathematicians, the Gypsies seldom got into astrology or **numerology**, but they did do a great deal of palmistry, tea leaf **reading**,

and various forms of card reading. People treated them as mystics and **mediums** and the Gypsies filled that role. They carried **tarot cards** and they worked magic, did spells, held **séances**, and performed **divination**. The Gypsies were probably most responsible for the spread of tarot cards across Europe, because they traveled and took the cards with them wherever they went.

Charles Godfrey Leland (1824–1903), the scholar and litterateur who was founder and first president of the Gypsy Lore Society, wrote, "Next to the **Bible** and the Almanac there is no *one* book which is so much disseminated among the millions, as the fortune-teller in some form or other ... Gypsies have done more than any other race or class on the face of the earth to disseminate among the multitude a belief in fortune-telling, magical or sympathetic cures, amulets and such small sorceries as now find a place in Folklore ... By the exercise of their wits they have actually acquired a certain art of reading character or even thought, which, however it be allied to deceit, is in a way true in itself, and well worth careful examination."

Sources:

Buckland, Raymond: *The Buckland Romani Tarot: The Gypsy Book of Wisdom.* St. Paul: Llewellyn, 2001

Buckland, Raymond: *Gypsy Witchcraft and Magic.* St. Paul: Llewellyn, 1998

Clébert, Jean-Paul: *The Gypsies.* New York: Penguin, 1967

Fraser, Angus: *The Gypsies.* Oxford: Blackwell, 1992

Leland, Charles Godfrey: *Gypsy Sorcery & Fortune Telling.* London: Fisher-Unwin, 1891

HALLUCINATION

Lewis Spence defined hallucination as, "A false perception of sensory vividness arising without the stimulus of a corresponding sense-impression." He went on to say that it differed from illusion, which is merely the misinterpretation of an actual sense-perception. Visual hallucinations are the most common, with auditory ones a close second. **Nandor Fodor** observed, "In the years following the foundation of the SPR [**Society for Psychical Research**] the hallucination theory of **psychic** phenomena was in great vogue. If no other explanation were available the man who had a supernormal experience was told that he was hallucinated, and if several people testified to the same occurrence, that the hallucination of one was communicated to the other." Unfortunately this is often still the case today. Rather than accept the possibility of a supernormal happening, many will dismiss the witnessing of phenomena as "hallucination."

Sir **William Crookes** made a wonderful comment on the subject, saying, "The supposition that there is a sort of mania or delusion which suddenly attacks a whole roomful of intelligent persons who are quite sane elsewhere, and that they all concur, to the minutest particulars, in the details of the occurrences of which they suppose themselves to be witnesses, seems to my mind more incredible than even the facts which they attest." (*Researches In the Phenomena of* **Spiritualism** London, 1874)

Fodor gives the example of Sir John Heschel, who had been watching the demolition of an ancient building. The day after its demolition, in the evening, Sir John was passing the site and saw, in its entirety, the building standing as before. "Great was my amazement," he said, "to see it as if still standing, projected against the dull sky. I walked on and the perspective of the form and disposition of the parts appeared to change as they would have done as real." In other words, as he walked past, the building appeared as it would have done if viewed from various angles.

Fodor concludes by saying much the same as Spence, "The difference between hallucination and illusion is that there is an objective basis for the illusion, which is falsely interpreted. In hallucination, though more than one sense may be affected, there is no external basis for the perception."

Sources:

Fodor, Nandor: *Encyclopedia of Psychic Science.* London: Arthurs Press, 1933

Spence, Lewis: *An Encyclopedia of the Occult*. London: George Routledge & Sons, 1920

Halo *see* **Aura**

HAMILTON-PARKER, CRAIG (B. 1954) AND JANE (B. 1950)

Craig Hamilton-Parker was born on January 24, 1954, in England. As a child Craig could see lights around people's heads (**auras**), and was very much aware of people's moods. He began a career as a painter but took time out to live for a while in a Kibbutz in Israel. On returning to England, he continued painting and had a show at Southampton Art Gallery. After marrying and becoming a father, Craig had to give up full-time painting and took a job as a graphic designer. He later developed his own advertising agency. The marriage didn't last and Craig found himself as a single parent, raising his daughter Celeste.

At the time of the breakup of his marriage in 1982, Craig came into contact with British **medium Doris Stokes**, who urged him to develop his gifts. He then encountered medium Peter Close, whose **spirit guide** had intimated that Craig should join their **development circle**. Craig did join it and went weekly to Hammersmith, London, to develop his mediumship. He became a full-time medium in 1990, going to local **Spiritualist** churches and demonstrating his mediumship.

It was on March 6, 1988 that Craig first met Jane Willis—the date and the woman's name predicted by Doris Stokes. The meeting was arranged by **spirits**: Jane's deceased grandmother told her to go to a demonstration to be given by Craig at Eastleigh (Hampshire) Spiritualist Church. She was to wear a blue dress. On stage, Craig had Jane's grandmother come through and urge him to speak to "the lady in blue." He was told that she, too, was a medium and that he should have a sitting with her. He asked her for one right there and then. As it happened, Jane was also divorced. Within three months the two were married, driven by a strong feeling that they had been together in past lives. Jane had two children, Justin and Chantal, but she and Craig soon had a daughter named Danielle. She, too, is extremely **psychic**, as was Jane when a child.

Both Craig and Jane appear on television in Britain and in America. They have held séances in churches, theaters, and on cruise ships, and did a **séance** on American television to contact the late Princess Diana. Craig has authored a number of books and they produce an Internet web site that is visited by people from around the world.

Sources:

Craig Hamilton-Parker Biography: http://www.psychics.co.uk/television/television_biog_craig.html

Hamilton-Parker, Craig: *Circle of Light*. New York: Sterling, 2005

Hamilton-Parker, Craig: *What To Do When You Are Dead*. New York: Sterling, 2001

HARDY, MARY M.

Mary M. Hardy was a **medium** who lived in Boston, Massachusetts. In 1875, paraffin casts of **spirit** hands were obtained for the first time through her **mediumship. William Denton** (1823–1893), Professor of Geology, investigated Hardy's mediumship under rigid test conditions over a number of years. In a public demonstration given by Hardy in Paine Hall, with Denton present, a cast of a spirit face was produced.

Hardy's **séances** were usually held in public halls, with large numbers of witnesses; sometimes several hundred. On the platform, she would have a table with two containers of liquid underneath it. One of the containers held paraffin wax and the other cold water. The table was draped with a cloth that extended to the ground, to give some darkness for the development of the phenomena. Sitting beside the table, Hardy would wait—sometimes as long as fifteen minutes or more—until, a **rapping** was heard. Then the cloth would be lifted and a wax mold would be found floating in the vessel of water.

Other mediums later demonstrated similar paraffin wax molds of spirit hands. Among them were Annie Fairlamb Mellon and **William Eglin-**

ton. In England, William Oxley described how a beautiful mold of a woman's hand was obtained on February 5, 1876, with the medium Mrs. Firman. A mold was then taken of Mrs. Firman's hand and was found to be quite different.

Sources:

Doyle, Sir Arthur Conan: *The History of Spiritualism*. New York: Doran, 1926

Shepard, Leslie A: *Encyclopedia of Occultism & Parapsychology*. New York: Avon Books, 1978

HARMONY GROVE SPIRITUALIST COMMUNITY

I n the late nineteenth century, Mary Nulton held **development circles** in her home in southern California. She was told by **spirit** to organize a **Camp Meeting**. As a result, Harmony Grove Spiritualist Camp Meeting Association was formed and incorporated in 1896. Its purpose was "to further the teachings of **Spiritualism** as a religion, philosophy, and science." The first meeting was held on July 4, 1896.

The following year S. D. Nulton leased a three-acre portion of his ranch to the Association. The only access to the site was by a road from Escondido. This road followed the southeast bank of Escondido Creek. Water for the site was obtained from a well, with a windmill and storage tank at the creek's edge. In 1916–1917, heavy rains washed back the creek bank causing the windmill and storage tank to topple over.

Prior to 1916, a platform was laid down for the Old Chapel. This was composed of movable sections that could be stood on edge for winter storage, and was covered by a canvas roof. Around 1920, a country road was built on the northwest side of the creek and a wooden bridge put in to connect to the camp site. Two years later, an adjoining ten- acre tract was granted to the Association, with the provision that the land be used only for the dissemination of Spiritualism. This land was divided into lots by the Camp Meeting Association, and made available for lease. A dining build-

ing and a three-apartment stucco building were erected, as was a Fellowship Hall. The Chapel was given a permanent floor and roof at this time. Bus loads of people flocked to the Grove with as many as 300 arriving for breakfast. Musicians would play for Saturday night social dances and a **Lyceum** was started. In 1942, the name was changed to Harmony Grove Spiritualist Association. In 1945, before the original 50-year lease was to expire, the Association purchased the original three acres.

In January, 1937, Jeannie Quisquis, daughter of Eloise Quisquis, was the first child born to a resident of the Grove. **Physical mediumship** became a feature of Harmony Grove, with demonstrations by such famous mediums as the **Bangs Sisters**, Maude Kline, and others. Today there are approximately thirty homes on the site although the dining hall and original stucco buildings are no longer standing.

Sources:

Harmony Grove Spiritualist Association: *2004 Summer Program*. Escondido: HGSA 2004

HAUNTING

A haunting is the appearance of a **ghost** or disturbances of a supernormal character attributed to a deceased person or persons. It is also the site for such an occurrence. Although the majority of hauntings are associated with the **spirits** of deceased persons, there are records of supposed ghosts turning out to be the astral bodies of someone who is alive and well. It is unusual for an **astral body** of one person to become visible to another but it is not unknown. Even with ghosts, not everyone can see them. A place may be haunted, and ghosts may be seen by a wide variety of people, but there is no guarantee that everyone visiting that site will see a ghost.

Hauntings are usually associated with old houses but this is not always the case. A modern building can be as haunted as an ancient one. There are instances of a house being built on the site of an old **Native American** burial ground, for example, resulting in appearances of Native

Americans in the modern building. However, the majority of hauntings do seem to be related to older buildings. The Tower of London, Sandringham, Hampton Court Palace in England, the Octagon in Washington D.C., Rocky Hill Castle in Alabama, the Whaley House in San Diego, the Myrtles Plantation in Louisiana … these and many hundreds if not thousands more old homes are haunted, some by a large number of ghosts.

Haunting can consist of spectral appearances by a ghost or ghosts but can also consist of auditory effects. The original **rappings** heard in the Fox cottage at Hydesville, New York, in 1848, were of this type. Through the questioning of the **Fox sisters** and their mother, a dialogue was established between them and the deceased peddler, **Charles B. Rosna**. Many times, however, when there is no attempt to establish such a discourse, the noises are accepted as simply phantom noises.

Many times, when a haunting can be traced to the spirit of a recently deceased person who has not accepted their own death, or who does not want to leave their long familiar surroundings, the spirit can be persuaded to acknowledge that death and move on. This can be done by **Spiritualist Rescue Circles**, which sit for just that purpose.

Sources:
Steiger, Brad: *Real Ghosts, Restless Spirits, and Haunted Places*. Detroit: Visible Ink Press, 2003

HEALING

see also Distant Healing; Spiritual Healing

There are a number of methods of healing apart from the standard medical approach. Laying-on of hands, Reiki, spiritual, herbal, magnetic, **faith**, auric, distant, color, and **crystal** are some of the types and terms used. Healing is making well someone who is ill. The method used to bring about the positive change is what varies.

A **psychic** healer is one who has a basic desire to help those in need and who will dedicate him- or herself to that task. Bletzer suggests that "all methods of orthodox and unorthodox medicine

and therapies are designed to help change the body chemistry in their particular way, making the cells normalize to make it easier for the body to heal itself." In other words, it is the body that is healing itself; it is not a person, specific therapy, or outside power that is doing it.

Invariably the healer has no knowledge of the process of healing, and does not know what actually takes place within the body. With the laying-on of hands, for example, there may be the general supposition that when the hands come into contact with the patient's body there is a magnetic current that passes from healer to *healee* (a term often applied to the one receiving unorthodox healing). The healer may imagine that current coming from deity, from the **Infinite Intelligence**, from the earth, or from any number of origins. Seldom does a healer believe that it originates in him- or herself. **Nandor Fodor** said, "[The problem of psychic healing] bristles with interesting and stubborn facts which refuse to be fitted into pigeonholes. Suggestion is entirely ruled out when healers cure animals. The process is interwoven with psychical manifestations, the success of healing often serving as evidence of the supernormal, and the supernormal serving as evidence of extraneous intervention."

Fodor said of early healers, "In England the first spiritual healer, a lecturer on mesmerism, named Hardinge, became convinced through spirit communications that epilepsy was demoniac possession and undertook to cure such cases by spirit instruction. J. D. Dixon, a homeopathic doctor was the next English healer who, being converted to **Spiritualism** in 1857, treated his patients with prescriptions obtained by **raps**." A nineteen-year-old English boy named Daniel Offord wrote prescriptions in Latin, a language of which he had no knowledge. Two months before it happened, he predicted the cholera epidemic of 1853. As an antidote he prescribed a daily dose of a half teaspoonful of carbon.

In **spiritual healing** it is frequently the **spirit** of a deceased doctor or surgeon who comes through the **medium** to give or suggest the necessary healing.

Healing demonstrations at the 1997 Festival of Mind, Body and Spirit in London. *Courtesy Fortean Picture Library.*

Munich-born Dr. Adolf Fritz, who died in 1918, worked through Brazilian psychic healer **José Arigó**. Sometimes it is the **spirit guide** of the medium. **Gladys Osborne Leonard**'s **Native American** guide, North Star, would work through her.

Sources:

Bletzer, June G.: *The Encyclopedia Psychic Dictionary.* Lithia Springs: New Leaf, 1998

Fodor, Nandor: *Encyclopedia of Psychic Science.* London: Arthurs Press, 1933

Leonard, Gladys Osborne: *My Life in Two Worlds.* London: Two Worlds, 1931

HEALTH

Health is something that is frequently neglected by a developing medium, yet is most important. It is especially so if that person wishes to do any spiritual healing. From *Buckland's Book of Spirit Communications* (Llewellyn, 2004):

The first requirement for you, as a spiritual healer, is good health for yourself. You cannot hope to heal others if you are the one in need of health. To this end you need to follow a good diet, cutting out junk food and things like sugar (the "white death") and bleached flour. Eat plenty of fruit and vegetables. Acidic fruits, such as the pear, peach, plum, orange and lemon, are especially good for you, since they act upon the liver and tend to cleanse the blood.

I don't for one moment suggest you become a vegetarian (I personally believe that can actually be unhealthy for all but a few people). However, don't overindulge in red meats. Try to keep a balanced diet—though what is balanced for one may not be for another. Avoid becoming grossly overweight or underweight. Drink only decaffeinated tea and coffee—and make sure they are naturally decaffeinated, not chemically. The teas I drink are actually caffeine free, rather than decaffeinated. One is Celestial Seasonings' "Caffeine-Free Tea," which is fairly easy to find. Another is called "Kaffree" tea (distributed by Worthington Foods, Inc.) and is made from the leaves of the Rooibus shrub (*Aspalathus linearis*); an African herb. There are also the "Rooibos Leaf Caffeine Free Tea Bags" put out by Alvita and available in health food stores. All of these taste very much like a pekoe tea, yet are caffeine free.

Try to develop a mind that is sympathetic and receptive, in an attitude of kind helpfulness. If you feel at all selfish it sets up an immediate barrier to helping others.

Sources:
Buckland, Raymond: *Buckland's Book of Spirit Communications*. St. Paul: Llewellyn, 2004

HERNE, FRANK

In 1871, Frank Herne joined forces with **Charles Williams**, another **medium** and together they presented some notable **séances**, including the famous teleportation of Mrs. Guppy (*see* **Apports**). Both mediums were English.

Herne's **mediumship** started in January, 1869. Initially—according to *The Spiritualist* of November 19, 1869—he gave **clairvoyant readings** and described and interpreted the sitter's **aura**. Quickly, however, **physical mediumship** developed and in 1870, at the house of Dr. Jacob Dixon, his body was seen to elongate. Dr. Dixon was a homeopathic doctor and **Mesmerist** who contributed to the *Spiritual Messenger* and other similar publications. Herne produced **direct voice**, psychic music, levi-

tations, and apports. Herne also coached **Florence Cook** in her early mediumship.

It was during the partnership with Williams that Herne really established himself. The two of them began demonstrating at 61 Lamb's Conduit Street, London, and worked with a **spirit guide** who claimed to be a deceased buccaneer named John King. In later years their protégée Florence Cook worked with King's daughter, Katie King. Initially the pair produced **rappings** and **table tipping** but when the lights were lowered their repertoire increased to include spirit voices, the touches of spirit hands, spirit lights, flowers and musical instruments floating in the air, and movement of furniture. Their early séances were sponsored by **Agnes Nichol Guppy**, the very lady they were later to apport.

Frank Podmore seemed unimpressed by the performances of Herne and Williams. He stated, "The sittings were nearly always held in the dark, or under illumination so faint as to preclude any possibility of accurate observation; active investigation on the part of any too curious sitters was discouraged by the linking of hands; suspicious sounds were drowned by the noise of the musical box or by the request on the part of the 'spirits' that all present should join in singing, so as to promote the harmony of the circle. ... Finally, the phenomena presented under such conditions were as a rule palpably within the capacity of any fairly active and intelligent mortal who had acquired with practice some manual dexterity." However, in 1875 Mr. St. George Stock attempted to expose Herne. Later in 1877, he wrote to *The Spiritualist* and apologized for the part he played in the attempted exposure.

Sources:
Podmore, Frank: *Modern Spiritualism*. London: 1902; reprinted as *Mediums of the Nineteenth Century*. New York: University Books, 1963
Shepard, Leslie A: *Encyclopedia of Occultism & Parapsychology*. New York: Avon Books, 1978

HISTORY OF SPIRITUALISM, THE

The *History of Spiritualism* was written by Sir Arthur Conan Doyle and first published in

1926 by George H. Doran Company, London, in two volumes. Doyle dedicated it "To Sir **Oliver Lodge**, F.R.S., a great leader both in physical and in **psychic** science, in token of respect this work is dedicated."

Doyle said, "This work has grown from small disconnected chapters into a narrative which covers in a way the whole history of the **Spiritualistic** movement ... It is curious that this movement, which many of us regard as the most important in the history of the world since the Christ episode, has never had a historian from those who were within it, and who had large personal experience of its development."

Doyle produced *The History of Spiritualism* to "give man the strongest of all reasons to believe in spiritual immortality of the soul, to break down the barrier of death, to found the grand religion of the future."

Sources:

Doyle, Sir Arthur Conan: *The History of Spiritualism.* New York: Doran, 1926

HODGSON, DR. RICHARD (1855–1905)

In **Nandor Fodor**'s estimation, Dr. Richard Hodgson was "one of the main pillars of the SPR [**Society for Psychical Research**] in its early years, the keenest, most critical investigator, a man of brilliant intellect and scholarly education."

Hodgson was born in Melbourne, Australia, on September 24, 1885. He attended the University of Melbourne and received a doctor of law degree in 1878. He arrived in England that same year and in 1881, attended St. John's College in Cambridge, where he studied poetry. He was active in the undergraduate **Ghost** Society, which was intent on investigating all forms of psychical phenomena. One of Hodgson's professors at Cambridge was **Henry Sidgwick**, who became the first president of the Society for Psychical Research. Hodgson himself became a member of the society and, in November 1884,

was part of a committee set up to investigate **Helena Blavatsky**. Traveling to India, he spent three months there investigating and finally exposing a huge network of fraud in the **Theosophical Society**, and with Blavatsky in particular. Hodgson became especially skeptical of **physical mediumship** and phenomena, believing that "nearly all professional **mediums** form a gang of vulgar tricksters, who are more or less in league with one another." The president of the London Spiritualist Alliance, E. Dawson Rogers, commented that Hodgson was "a very Saul persecuting the Christians." In 1895, Hodgson investigated **Eusapia Paladino** and found nothing to change his opinion. In fact the change which did eventually come about did so very slowly and gradually, as Hodgson tried to resist what he began to recognize as true phenomena.

The **American Society for Psychical Research**, founded in 1885 and led by **William James**, was suffering from lack of members and, more importantly, lack of funds. Hodgson was asked if he would go to America and attempt to get the ASPR back on its feet. He agreed to do so and in 1887 traveled to Boston and became Secretary for the society. He also became Manager of Research and began an exhaustive investigation of the trance medium **Leonora E. Piper**. Hodgson was eventually so impressed by her performances and the evidence she produced that he became converted to **Spiritualism** himself. He reported in *Proceedings* (Vol. XIII, 1897), "I cannot profess to have any doubt but that the 'chief communicators' ... are veritably the personalities that they claim to be; that they have survived the change we call death, and that they have directly communicated with us whom we call living through Mrs. Piper's entranced organism. Having tried the hypothesis of **telepathy** from the living for several years, and the 'spirit' hypothesis also for several years, I have no hesitation in affirming with the most absolute assurance that the 'spirit' hypothesis is justified by its fruits and the other hypothesis is not." Hodgson had been stunned with the personal information that Mrs. Piper provided about his family. Her details about deceased persons were so accurate that Hodgson hired private detectives to carry out surveillance to see if she actually obtained the information fraudulently.

In 1897, Hodgson returned to England to become an SPR Council member and editor of the *Journal* and *Proceedings*. A year later, however, he returned to Boston and continued working with Mrs. Piper. On December 20, 1905, Hodgson was playing handball when he had a heart attack and died. He was fifty.

Sources:

Buckland, Raymond: *Buckland's Book of Spirit Communications*. St. Paul: Llewellyn, 2004

Fodor, Nandor: *Encyclopedia of Psychic Science*. London: Arthurs Press, 1933

Guiley, Rosemary Ellen: *The Encyclopedia of Ghosts and Spirits*. New York: Facts On File, 1992

HOLLIS-BILLING, MARY J.

Mary Hollis-Billing was an American **medium**. She had two spirit guides: Ski, a **Native American**, and James Nolan. She twice visited England, in 1874 and again in 1880. Sir **Arthur Conan Doyle** described her as "a lady of refinement."

Hollis was initially known as a **slate** writer. Frequently the writing on the slate would be produced by a **spirit** hand in full view. Hollis did not go into **trance** but sat in front of a **cabinet**. Many times spirit hands would appear from out of the cabinet. These hands would appear very quickly. Once, as a test, Hollis's hand was blackened with burnt cork but the spirit hands, when they appeared, were clean and white. On another occasion six spirit heads appeared at the same time. Sometimes the spirit visitors were people who had been famous when alive. Napoleon appeared, as did Empress Josephine.

From 1871 through 1873 Dr. N. B. Wolfe of Chicago investigated her and was very impressed, writing of his experiences in *Startling Facts in Modern Spiritualism*. At most of the **séances** there was **direct voice**, with as many as thirty-

four different voices speaking during one séance. Sometimes more than one voice would be speaking at once.

Sources:

Doyle, Sir Arthur Conan: *The History of Spiritualism*. New York: Doran, 1926

Fodor, Nandor: *Encyclopedia of Psychic Science*. London: Arthurs Press, 1933

HOME, DANIEL DUNGLAS (1833–1886)

Sir **William Crookes** (1832–1919) said of Home, "Of all the persons endowed with a powerful development of this Psychic Force, Mr. Daniel Dunglas Home is the most remarkable and it is mainly owing to the many opportunities I have had of carrying on my investigation in his presence that I am enabled to affirm so conclusively the existence of this force." Home has come to be regarded as the greatest physical phenomena **medium** in the history of modern **Spiritualism**.

Daniel Dunglas Home was born in the village of Currie, near Edinburgh, Scotland, on March 20, 1833. He was the third child of William Humes and Elizabeth (Betsey) McNeal. His mother had the "second sight" and his father, an engineer, had a connection to the noble Border house, the Homes of Dunglass. (The spelling of the names had been changed after a furious quarrel between two brothers.) According to Daniel, his father was the illegitimate son of the tenth Earl, and this was not disputed by the family concerned. At the age of four, Daniel started exhibiting the second sight himself. He would spontaneously describe far-off happenings as though he were right there witnessing them.

Because of Daniel Home's delicate health, he was sent to live with a childless aunt named Mary McNeal Cook and her husband. At the age of nine, Home was taken to America by the Cooks and settled in Connecticut at Greenville, Norwich. The rest of his family had already moved there two years earlier, in 1840. His **clairvoyance** developed and when his sister Mary Betsey died at the age of twelve, her **spirit** would visit the family so frequently that it came to be accepted as a casual occurrence. At the age of thirteen, Home saw the **vision** of a close boyhood friend who had recently died. His appearance was in keeping with a promise the two had made to each other that the first to die would visit the other. Four years later, Home had a vision of his mother, the sighting announcing her death to him.

By 1850—just two years after the **Fox Sisters** had introduced modern Spiritualism to the world—Home started experiencing moving furniture (**psychokinesis**) and **rappings**. These last were so loud that it sounded as though the furniture was being pounded with a hammer. Local ministers were called in to pray over the boy but to no avail. As Jean Burton wrote in *Heyday of a Wizard* (London, 1948), "Soon the neighbors, who had got wind of these developments, laid siege to the house ... everyone knew that questions could be answered through the raps. And within a week after Daniel's gift was officially established they were told where to find so many long-lost relatives, title-deeds, and misplaced brooches, and so many striking proofs of spirit identity were obtained, as would be tedious to enumerate." By the time Home was in his early teens, the Cooks turned him out of the house because they could not cope with the many phenomena constantly taking place.

Home had no trouble finding lodgings. He stayed with various families, all intrigued by his spiritualistic abilities. George Bush, Professor of Oriental Languages in New York University and a distinguished theologian, was the first scientist to investigate him, in the summer of 1851. Bush had been an Episcopalian clergyman but had resigned his living to become a **Swedenborgian**. The following year Home stayed for some time in the home of Rufus Elmer of Springfield, Massachusetts, and became acquainted with a delegation from Harvard. Among them was the poet William Cullen Bryant. At the end of one of Home's séances, Bryant, B. K. Bliss, William Edwards, and Professor David A. Wells all signed

Representation of medium Daniel Dunglas Home levitating out of a window. *Courtesy Fortean Picture Library.*

a manifesto titled "The Modern Wonder," testifying that the **séance** table turned around and moved with such force that it pushed against each of them in turn, moving the sitter and his chair across the floor. The table was also seen to rise into the air "and to float in the atmosphere for several seconds, as if sustained by some denser medium than air." The Elmers offered to adopt Home and make him their heir, but Home declined. In fact throughout his life Home refused to accept any money for his abilities.

Home's first **levitation** occurred in the South Manchester, Connecticut, house of Ward Cheney. F.L. Burr, editor of the *Hartford Times*, described the occurrence of August 8, 1852, saying, "Suddenly, and without any expectation on the part of the company, Home began his ascent ... I had hold of his hand at the time, and I felt his feet—they were lifted a foot from the floor! … Again and again, he was taken from the floor; and the third time he was carried to the lofty ceiling of the apartment, with which his hand and head came in gentle contact." Later Burr added that he felt a "wave of cold air, which felt, in that close, sultry August night, almost like a sudden bath of ice water."

Home's time was called upon constantly and his health declined. It was discovered that his left lung was badly infected. He had intended to start medical studies but these plans had to be abandoned. A trip to Europe was suggested and Home landed in England in April, 1855. He first stayed at Cox's Hotel, London, but soon became the guest of J. S. Rymer, a solicitor residing in Ealing. Some of the first to attend Home's séances were Lord Brougham—a hardened skeptic and one time Lord Chancellor of England—and Sir David Brewster, well known Victorian scientist. The poet Robert Browning and his wife, Elizabeth Barrett Browning, attended some séances. She was a Spiritualist and became an ardent admirer of Home. For some reason her husband did not share her enthusiasm and Robert went on to write the poem *Mr. Sludge the Medium*, loosely based on Home. Yet Browning had never caught Home in trickery at any of the séances he and his wife attended.

In the fall of 1855, Home traveled on to Florence, Italy. There his fame spread but the local peasants believed him to be a sorcerer and necromancer. Such was the feeling that on December 5, 1855, a man attempted to kill Home. The medium was stabbed three times with a dagger and was lucky to escape with his life. The would-be assassin was never charged and Home soon afterward left the country and went on to Paris.

On the evening of February 10, 1856, the spirits had told Home that his power was going to leave him for a period of one year. No reason was given for this but it was as they said; for a whole year Home was unable to produce any phenomena. When he was in Paris, the whole city seemed aware of when his powers were due to return and waited with baited breath for that moment. On the evening of February 10, 1857, as Home described it, a spirit hand appeared and touched his brow at midnight and he heard spirit voices say, "Be of good cheer, Daniel; you will soon be well." The following morning the Marquis de Belmont called, sent by the Emperor, to enquire if all was well. Immediately loud rappings were heard. The Marquis then told Home that Napoleon III summoned him to Tuilleries. At the Royal Court, Home gave séances for the Emperor and Empress, his first taking place on Friday, February 13. At this sitting the Empress felt the hand of her deceased father grasp her own. She recognized it by a characteristic defect in one of the fingers. Napoleon had questions answered which he had only been thinking and had not spoken out loud; questions to which only he and the Empress Eugénie knew the answers. Despite the Emperor calling in various professors from the Sorbonne, and even the great stage magician Robert Houdin, no one could explain how the phenomena were produced. Houdin said that it could not have been produced by any sleight of hand. Subsequent séances were even more effective, with heavy tables lifted and moved and a luminous vapor appearing a few inches off the surface of the séance table. This vapor slowly formed into a child's hand. After disappearing, the haze returned and formed into a man's hand which grasped a pencil and wrote "Napoleon." The Emperor examined it and declared that it was the signature of Napoleon I.

Home left France for America on March 20, 1857. He spent only a short time in the United States, visiting many of his old friends, before collecting his sister Christine and returning with her to France and to the Royal Court. There the Empress took Christine as her protégée and placed her in the exclusive Convent of the Sacred Heart in the rue de Varennes. Christine stayed there for seven years. Home continued with his sittings with the Emperor and Empress.

Home went on to visit with and hold sittings for many of the leading figures of Europe, including the King of Naples, the German Emperor, Queen Sophia of Holland, and the Tsar of Russia.

When in Russia Home met and eventually married Alexandrina (Sacha) de Kroll, sister-in-law to the count Koucheleff-Besborodka and god-daughter of the late Tsar Nicholas. Count Alexis Tolstoy, the poet, was a groomsman at the wedding held in St. Petersburg, with Alexander Dumas as best man. Later the couple had a son and shortly after that the Homes returned to England. Alexandrina died in July, 1862, of tuberculosis.

Perhaps the most famous of Home's feats was his levitation out of one window and in at another, seventy feet above the ground. It occurred at Ashley House, Victoria Street, London. Present were **Lord Adare** the sporting young Irish peer, his cousin Captain Charles Wynne, and the Honorable Master of Lindsay (later Earl of Crawford and Balcarres). In 1869, Lord Adare and Home were sharing an apartment in London. In such close contact with the medium, Adare was in a position to ascertain that there was no trickery involved in Home's performances. Both Adare and Lindsay wrote separate accounts of what happened that evening.

After a normal beginning to the séance—normal for Home's séances, that is, with telekinetic phenomena and the appearance of an apparition—Home began to pace the floor. He was in a trance state, as he had been all evening. He walked through to the next room and a window was heard to be raised. Lindsay states that he heard a voice whisper in his ear, telling him that Home would pass out of one window and in at another. The next moment they all saw Home floating in the air outside their window.

There was no ledge of any sort between the windows, which were nearly eight feet apart and seventy feet above the ground. Although there was no light on in the room, the moon provided sufficient illumination for all to distinguish each other and to see quite clearly the furniture in the room.

After remaining in position for a few seconds outside the window, with his feet about six inches above the sill, Home opened the window and "glided into the room feet foremost." Adare went to close the window in the adjacent room and found that it had only been opened twelve to fifteen inches. Home was asked how he had managed to pass through so small a space, and replied by showing them. Adare said, "He then went through the open space, head first, quite rapidly, his body being nearly horizontal and apparently rigid. He came in again, feet foremost; and we returned to the other room." (*Experiences of Spiritualism with Mr. D. D. Home*, London, 1870) Later, when Home came out of his trance, he was "much agitated; he said he felt as if he had gone through some fearful peril, and that he had a most horrible desire to throw himself out of the window."

In other demonstrations Home would elongate. On one occasion—with Home lying on the floor, Lord Lindsay holding his feet and Lord Adaire at his head—he was measured, by Samuel Carter Hall, and found to be seven feet tall! Home's natural height was five feet ten inches. On another occasion the medium elongated to six feet six inches whilst standing against a wall and having his feet held, with one observer watching his waist and another at his head. Another phenomenon was Home's fire handling. He would reach into a fire, stir the embers to a flame, and bring out a live coal. Carrying it around the circle of sitters, it would be found to be so hot that no one else could stand to have it closer than six inches from them.

Other mediums had arrived in England from America, amongst them Mrs. **Emma Hardinge Britten**, the **Davenport Brothers**, Lottie Fowler and **Henry Slade**. By that time the focus was on spirits actually speaking through the medium, rather than conversing by way of raps. **Slate writing** was also introduced, as was **billet reading**, **spirit photography**, **apports,** and telekinetic demonstrations. Home occasionally worked with other mediums, among them Kate Fox and **William Stainton Moses** (1839–1892). Moses, the medium and religious teacher, described a **trance** of Home's which he witnessed.

By degrees Mr. Home's hands and arms began to twitch and move involuntarily. I should say that he has been partly paralyzed, drags one of his legs, moves with difficultly, stoops and can endure very little physical exertion. As he passed into the trance state he drew power from the circle by extending his arms to them and mesmerizing himself. All these acts are involuntary. He gradually passed into the trance state, and rose from the table, erect and a different man from what he was. He walked firmly, dashed out his arms and legs with great power ....

Home had no one particular **spirit guide** but a number of them. They usually referred to him as either Daniel or Dan. The guides did have a few idiosyncrasies, according to Jean Burton. For example, they objected to dogs being present in the séance room, they did not like tobacco smoke, and for some reason they disliked Home sitting on a silk cushion. When Home came out of trance his hand and arm were sometimes rigid and his jaw temporarily locked. He was often reluctant to come out of trance, saying that he wished "to remain among the bright and beautiful." When he did come out of it and was told all the things that had transpired, he would invariably say that he didn't believe a word of it! Homes always preferred to work in natural or bright light to darkness, and encouraged his sitters to chat normally and even stand up and move about. He never insisted they all sit and hold hands and concentrate. Home was responsible for the acceptance of Spiritualism by such figures as William Makepeace Thackeray, Anthony Trollope, Robert Bell, Lord Lytton, Lord Adare, The Earl of Dunraven, The Master of Lindsay, and Lord Brougham.

Home authored two books: *Incidents in My Life* (1863, with a second edition of it appearing in 1872) and *Lights and Shadows of Spiritualism* (1873). Daniel Dunglas Home died on June 21, 1886, at the age of fifty-three, after a period of declining health. He was buried at St. Germain, Paris. On his tombstone it says, "To another discerning of Spirits" (I Cor. xii.10). With the exception of **direct voice** and **apports,** Homes

produced every known phenomena of **physical mediumship. Frank Podmore,** an outspoken critic of fraudulent mediums, said "Home was never publicly exposed as an imposter; there is no evidence of any weight that he was even privately detected in trickery."

Sources:

Buckland, Raymond: *Buckland's Book of Spirit Communications.* St. Paul: Llewellyn, 2004

Burton, Jean: *Heyday of a Wizard: Daniel Home the Medium.* London: George G. Harrap, 1948

Doyle, Sir Arthur Conan: *The History of Spiritualism.* New York: Doran, 1926

Fodor, Nandor: *Encyclopedia of Psychic Science.* London: Arthurs Press, 1933

Home, Daniel Dunglas: *Incidents in My Life.* London: Longmans, Green, 1871

Podmore, Frank: *Modern Spiritualism.* London: 1902; reprinted as *Mediums of the Nineteenth Century.* New York: University Books, 1963

Hope, Elizabeth *see* d'Esperance, Madame

HOPE, WILLIAM (1863–1933)

William Hope was a controversial **spirit photographer.** He was accused of fraud several times, but there seems to have been circumstances beyond his control that lent others the opportunity to make it appear that Hope was at fault. **Nandor Fodor** states, "The great number of signed testimonies, with a detailed account of the precautions taken, speaks in an impressive manner for the genuine powers of Hope."

A carpenter by trade, in 1905 William Hope took a photograph of a workmate. The incident took place at the factory where both men worked, in Crewe, Cheshire, England. When the picture was developed, the plate showed a young woman standing beside his friend. She was transparent, with the brick wall behind her showing through. Hope's friend immediately recognized the figure as his deceased sister. Hope said, "I knew nothing at all about **Spiritualism** then. We took the photograph to the works on Monday, and a Spiritualist there said it was what was called a Spirit photograph. He suggested that we should try again on the following Saturday at the same place with the same camera, which we did, and not only the same lady came on the plate again, but a little child with her. I thought this very strange, and it made me more interested, and I went on with my experiments."

On the basis of these photographs, the two friends formed a **development circle** of six, helped by a Mrs. Buxton, organist of the Crewe Spiritualist Hall. Fearing that Roman Catholics might hear of their experiments and accuse them of being in league with the devil, they destroyed all the plates they developed immediately after use. It wasn't until 1908 that Archdeacon Colley found out about the group, questioned Hope, and told him not to destroy any more. The Archdeacon sat with the Crewe Circle for the first time on March 16, 1908. He brought his own camera, diamond-marked plates and dark slides, and development plates with his own chemicals. Hope had only to press the bulb for the exposure. This he did. On one of the resultant plates there appeared two spirit figures.

The Archdeacon recognized one of the spirit extras as his deceased mother, who had never actually been photographed. But Hope thought it looked like a woman in a photograph he had copied two years earlier. He took the picture to Mrs. Spencer, of Nantwich, who thought she recognized the figure as her grandmother. But the Archdeacon was equally certain it was his mother and advertised in the Leamington newspaper inviting all who remembered his mother to meet with him at the rectory. Eighteen people chose the photograph from several others and said the figure was definitely the Archdeacon's mother.

Hope willingly allowed himself to be investigated over a number of years. Sir **William Crookes**, the physicist and great psychical researcher, in the *Christian Commonwealth* of December 4, 1918, described his sitting with Hope, where Crookes used his own marked plates, under his own conditions, and obtained a

Controversial spirit photographer William Hope c. 1925. *Courtesy Fortean Picture Library.*

picture of his deceased wife. Sir **William Fletcher Barrett**, Professor of Physics at the Royal College of Science for Dublin, and one of the most distinguished of psychical researchers, claimed to have received from Hope "indubitable evidence of supernormal photography."

In 1922, there was a controversy when **Harry Price**, the well known researcher, published a report in the *Journal* of the **Society for Psychical Research** (SPR) charging Hope with fraud. Price sat with Hope on February 24, 1922, at the **British College of Psychic Science** where the photographer produced a spirit photograph. Price claimed that plates had been switched from a marked set that had been provided. It turned out that the package had been interfered with by someone unknown while it was in the offices of the SPR for a period of four or more weeks. Nothing was proven either way, but Harry Price subsequently said that the test "does not rule out the possibility that Hope has other than normal means."

Hope continued to make himself available for any and all tests. He ignored any criticisms and for the photographs never charged more than his hourly rate as a carpenter. He became a very devout Spiritualist, relying on the advice of his **spirit guides** for everything he did. He died on March 7, 1933, at age seventy.

Sources:

Doyle, Sir Arthur Conan: *The History of Spiritualism.* New York: Doran, 1926

Fodor, Nandor: *Encyclopedia of Psychic Science.* London: Arthurs Press, 1933

HOUDINI, HARRY (EHRICH WEISS) (1874–1926)

Ehrich Weiss was born in Appleton, Wisconsin, on April 6, 1874. His father, a rabbi, was Dr. Mayer Samuel Weiss and his mother Cecilia Weiss. His parents had come to America from Hungary. One Internet web site suggests that Ehrich was actually born in Budapest and came to the United States with his parents when he was four years old, but the majority of references state that he was born in Wisconsin. He had four brothers—Theodore, Leopold, Nathan and William—and a sister, Carrie.

From a very early age, Ehrich showed skill at conjuring and at picking locks; he once picked the lock to his mother's pie cabinet in order to steal a piece of pie. When a circus came to town, he amazed the manager with rope tricks he had taught himself. The manager offered him a job and he did perform while the circus was in town, but his father forbade him from traveling with the show.

By the time he was eleven, Ehrich could pick any lock, having worked—as one of many odd jobs—with a local locksmith. He dreamed of becoming a stage magician, avidly reading a book on the French conjurer and illusionist Jean-Eugene Robert-Houdin (1805–1871). With a

friend named Jack Hayman, Ehrich worked up an act using some of the tricks and mind-reading codes from the Houdin book. The two boys called themselves the Houdini Brothers in honor of their inspiration. Later Hayman dropped out and Ehrich's brother Theodore (later known as Hardeen) joined him. They performed at local clubs, dime museums, and side shows. While performing at a girls' school in 1893, Ehrich—now calling himself Harry Houdini—accidentally spilled some acid on a girl's dress. His mother made the girl a new dress and Houdini delivered it to her. The girl was Wilhelmina Beatrice (Bess) Rahner, a Roman Catholic, and she later became Houdini's wife. She also later joined him in his act, assisting in mind-reading tricks. In an effort to make money when times were hard, Houdini and Bess resorted to holding fake **séances**, working with information obtained through local tipsters. Houdini was amazed at how easily the "**mediumship**" was accepted.

By 1900, Houdini had perfected his lock-picking skills to the point that he could challenge any audience member to lock him up in their own handcuffs and he would get out of them. He made headlines escaping from a Chicago prison and also from handcuffs applied at England's Scotland Yard. He dreamed up spectacular feats, such as escaping from straight-jackets, coffins, locked boxes submerged in water, and ropes suspended from high buildings. His name became synonymous with escapology.

In 1920, a friendship between the Houdinis and the Doyles began, lasting four years. On a tour of England, Houdini and Bess met Sir **Arthur Conan Doyle** and his wife Jean. They became friends, corresponding regularly on the Houdini's return to America. In 1922, it was the Doyle's turn to cross the Atlantic and they met with Houdini and Beatrice in Atlantic City in June of that year. Lady Jean Doyle had developed her mediumship, being especially good at **automatic writing**, and offered to try to contact Houdini's mother for him. Houdini had a very close bond with his mother and was devastated when she died. For years afterward, he visited various

mediums in the hopes of getting a **message** from her. When he did not, he blamed the medium. Certainly, many of them were fraudulent—but no match for the master conjurer. When Lady Doyle offered to try to make contact, Houdini accepted. Bess—using a code from one of their mind-reading acts—advised her husband that the previous evening she had given Lady Doyle a lot of information about his mother. Bess left the room and the séance began. Lady Doyle received a message that referred to Mrs. Weiss's "darling boy" and described her happiness in the **Summerland** (the Spiritualist afterlife). She spoke a lot of her love for her son, and then asked God's blessing before she left. Six months later Houdini denounced the material produced, pointing out that his mother was Jewish and would not have drawn a cross at the start of the message. Also, she spoke little English and would not have been able to write so fluently. Sir Arthur explained that Lady Doyle *always* started her writings by drawing a cross, as a protective measure. Also, it is not uncommon for **spirits** to come through in the language most easily understood by the medium, regardless of the spirit's actual original language. The two families disagreed and the friendship was broken, never to be mended. By 1924, there was open hostility between them.

Matters came to a head when in January, 1923, when *Scientific American* magazine offered a prize of $2,500 to the first person who could produce a **spirit photograph** under test conditions and $2,500 to anyone who could produce physical paranormal phenomena and have it recorded by scientific instruments. The committee was made up of top psychical researchers, including **William McDougall** of Harvard, Daniel F. Comstock of the Massachusetts Institute of Technology, Malcolm Bird of *Scientific American*, Walter Franklin Pierce of the **American Society for Psychical Research, psychic** investigator **Hereward Carrington**, and Houdini. **Mina Stinson Crandon**, known professionally as Margery, was the medium to be tested for **physical mediumship**. The investigation started in November, 1923, while Houdini was out of the country, tour-

Legendary escape artist Harry Houdini, c. 1900. *Hulton Archive/Getty Images.*

ing. He returned in July of the following year, furious that the others had not waited for him. Despite the glowing reports that the rest of the committee had given Margery, Houdini insisted on investigating himself. He claimed to have caught the medium in various little tricks, though could not actually prove that she was cheating. The press proclaimed that Margery had stumped Houdini. In August, he provided a box he had designed especially for the next séance. Margery had to sit in it and have a lid closed which effectively left only her head free. Margery's **spirit guide**, Walter, accused Houdini of leaving articles in the box so that it would look as though the medium had put them there to aid her in deception. Many years later an assistant of Houdini's admitted that he was responsible for putting the item (a folding ruler that could have been used for reaching out to move things) in the box at Houdini's suggestion. Doyle and other

Spiritualists attacked Houdini for his actions though, in fact, many Spiritualists had previously applauded Houdini for exposing the frauds. They did not, however, appreciate him making true mediums appear to be fraudulent.

Although Houdini continued harassing mediums, exposing fraudulent ones, and claiming many secrets without actually revealing any, he was still anxious to find the one medium who would connect him with his mother. Looking toward his own eventual death, he and Bess worked out a code from their mind-reading act, to be used to tell her if he had made contact from the other world. The test was not far off. On October 22, 1926, in Montreal, Houdini—who boasted of the immense strength of his stomach muscles—was unexpectedly punched in the stomach by a student, backstage at a magic show he was giving. In extreme pain, he went on with the act and refused medical help. Nine days later Houdini died of peritonitis.

After Houdini's death, numbers of mediums claimed to have heard from him and gave Beatrice the messages they had received. She found none of them relevant, until more than a year after her husband's death. Then a medium named **Arthur Ford**, pastor of the First Spiritualist Church of New York, gave her a message which contained a word that Houdini had long sought from his mother. It came in a **séance** held February 8, 1928. The word was "Forgive." Beatrice Houdini was amazed. She made a public statement that this was "the sole communication received among thousands up to this time that contained the one secret keyword known only to Houdini, his mother, and myself." In a personal letter to Ford she said that "Houdini waited in vain all his life" for that one word. "It is indeed the message for which he always secretly hoped, and if it had been given him while he was still alive, it would I know, have changed the entire course of his life."

It was at a sitting in November, 1928, that the first word of Houdini's own message was obtained. Over the next two and a half months the entire message came through, word by word, at different sittings with different people. The first word announced by Fletcher, Ford's spirit guide, was "Rosabelle," which was Houdini's pet name for his wife. The message, in total, was "Rosabelle; answer; tell; pray; answer; look; tell; answer; answer; tell." Decoded, it meant: "Rosabelle, believe."

A group of the Spiritualists from Ford's church visited Bess Houdini and gave her the message. She had suffered a fall and was lying on a couch. She said, "It is right! My God! What else did he say?" Following the suggestions given by Houdini to Fletcher, a séance was arranged and the following day Ford went to Beatrice's house. At that sitting Houdini came through and, after greeting his wife, repeated the words.

Bess signed a statement to the effect that Ford had broken the Houdini code and given his message from the afterlife. She said, "Regardless of any statements made to the contrary, I wish to declare that the message, in its entirety, and in the agreed upon sequence, given to me by Arthur Ford, is the correct message prearranged by Mr. Houdini and myself."

In his autobiography *Nothing So Strange* (1958), Arthur Ford tries to put into perspective Houdini's attacks on Spiritualists.

In the early twenties Houdini turned his fabulous tenacity to exposing the whole Spiritualist movement. There were probably then about a million people in the country who called themselves Spiritualists. In these days when university research in the field of **parapsychology** has made psychic interests respectable, when **extrasensory perception** is seriously considered in psychology courses, when the physical scientists are far less dogmatic about the non-physical world than was formerly the case, it is difficult to recover the violent reaction of the orthodox against Spiritualism in Houdini's day. In the orthodox mind all Spiritualists were equated with the lunatic fringe and all mediums were tools of the devil, even if there were no devil. Here Houdini took his stand with the orthodox and lined up his targets ... There is no doubt that Houdini informed himself in the field of psychic phenomena, but always from the point of view of looking for the catch. When he read a report based on the testimony of top scientists, he merely averred that they were not as clever as he in seeing through a ruse.

Very quickly after the breaking of the Houdini code, the mentalist Joseph Dunninger claimed that the code word had been given in a 1927 biography of Houdini. This seems unlikely, because Houdini and Beatrice had made such a point of using it to prove survival. But Dunninger did bring pressure to bear on the widow and she eventually issued a retraction of her statement. Bess kept a full-time publicist on her payroll for sixteen years after her husband's death, just to keep the Houdini legend alive.

Sources:

Doyle, Sir Arthur Conan: *The Edge of the Unknown.* New York: G. P. Putnam's, 1930

Fishley, Margaret: *The Supernatural.* London: Aldus, 1976

Fodor, Nandor: *Encyclopedia of Psychic Science.* London: Arthurs Press, 1933

Ford, Arthur with Margueritte Harmon Bro: *Nothing So Strange.* New York: Harper & Row, 1958

Guiley, Rosemary Ellen: *The Encyclopedia of Ghosts and Spirits.* New York: Facts On File, 1992

HOWE, LYMAN C. (1832–1910)

Lyman C. Howe was born in a log cabin in Butternuts, New York, on February 11, 1832. He was one of ten children. His father couldn't afford a good education for his children but he taught them to fear God, religiously educating them "line upon line, and precept upon precept." He was a strict Calvinist who tried to live by the Bible. He very much believed in "spare the rod and spoil the child."

Lyman's mother died in 1842, when Howe was ten, and the family broke up. At thirteen Howe went to live with Perry Aylsworth, a man described as having great love for his fellow beings, who did not fill the young boy's mind with the terrible dogmas of his religion. Howe stayed there for nearly three years; in 1847, he moved in with his brother in Hornell, Steuben County, New York. From age ten until he was eighteen, Howe attended public school for at least a part of each year. In 1851, he started teaching school. He planned an academic career but his health did not allow it.

In the years 1853–4 Howe developed as a Spiritualist **medium**, though his forte lay in **inspirational speaking**. By 1858, he was speaking in public in Laona, New Albion, and Smith's Mills. In 1862, he married Sarah E. North of New Albion. They had one child, Maude (who later became Mrs. Maude E. Cobb), born July 5, 1867, the same year they moved to Laona. In 1868, they relocated to Liberty Street, Fredonia.

Howe's inspirational speaking was in great demand, resulting in him traveling the country. A. W. McCoy (**Cassadaga**—*Its History and Teaching*) said, "His services have been required in all of the largest cities as well as in the smaller towns and villages, at all of which he has drawn large and intelligent audiences. His inspiration is of the highest and purest order." Howes was the first speaker invited to speak at **Alden**'s Grove for the very first meeting of **Spiritualists** in what was to become the **Lily Dale Assembly**. This took place on Sunday, June 15, 1873. He went on to serve twenty-five years at Lily Dale without missing a season. Lyman C. Howes died on December 23, 1910, at age seventy-seven.

Sources:

McCoy, A. W.: *Cassadaga—Its History and Teaching.* New York: nd

HUDSON, FREDERICK A. (B. CA. 1812)

Frederick A. Hudson was the first English **spirit photographer**. According to **Nandor**

Fodor, the **physical medium Agnes Guppy** and her husband had been trying to obtain spirit photographs but without success. On a whim, they went to Hudson's studio and had him take a picture. When developed, it showed a white patch that looked vaguely like a draped figure. Encouraged, Hudson took another photograph and this time it again showed the white, draped figure standing behind Mr. Guppy. In Sir **Arthur Conan Doyle**'s *The History of Spiritualism*, however, he says that the first sitter for Hudson's spirit photographs was a Miss Georgiana Houghton, who described the incident in her *Chronicles of the Photographs of Spiritual Beings* (1882).

William Howitt (1792–1879), a pioneer English **Spiritualist** and constant contributor to the *Spiritual Magazine*, had a photograph taken by Hudson that showed very clearly the likeness of his two deceased sons. A friend who was with Howitt at the time did not even know of the existence of one of the sons. Howitt called the images "perfect and unmistakable." A Dr. Thompson, of Clifton, had a **spirit** show up on his photograph that was later identified as Dr. Thompson's mother, even though no photograph of her had ever been taken before. Dr. Alfred Russel Wallace (1823–1913), the famous British naturalist, obtained two different portraits of his mother. They were quite unlike any other photograph of her taken when she was alive and were from different periods of her life. He said of the pictures, "I sat three times, always choosing my own position. Each time a second figure appeared in the negative with me … the moment I got the proofs, the first glance showed me that the third plate contained an unmistakable portrait of my mother—like her both in features and expression; not such a likeness as a portrait taken during life … yet still, to me, an unmistakable likeness."

Hudson's photographs were examined by J. Traill Taylor, the editor of the *British Journal of Photography*, who then had more pictures taken, but using his own collodion and plates. There were spirit figures in all the pictures. Taylor observed "Collusion or trickery was altogether out of the question." However, from time to time it seems that Hudson deliberately cheated and made double exposures. It seems he was afraid of losing his power to produce the pictures and so tried to satisfy the constant demand from clients. He was not above dressing up in costumes and photographing himself so that he could later use the picture as half of a double exposure with a standard portrait. He produced a number of spirit photographs to agree with Rev. **William Stainton Moses**'s visions, but Moses exposed them as fake. Over the years, however, Hudson did re-establish his credibility.

Sources:

Fodor, Nandor: *Encyclopedia of Psychic Science*. London: Arthurs Press, 1933

HUGHES, IRENE

Irene Finger was born in a log cabin in Tennessee, near the Mississippi River. She was part Cherokee and part Scots-Irish. Like so many other **psychics** and **mediums**, she first exhibited her abilities when still a child, seeing **apparitions** and knowing things ahead of time (**precognition**). In 1945, she married William Hughes and worked in a hospital in New Orleans. After the war—when her husband served at Pearl Harbor and in the Pacific—the couple moved to Chicago, Illinois. They had four children. They paid for the trip to Chicago out of the winnings they received from Irene's forecasting of horse race winners.

In 1961, Hughes had a major operation and after it discovered that she had a Japanese **spirit guide**. She went on to establish herself as a professional medium and psychic, lecturing and writing newspaper articles. She also edited *The International Journal of Neuropsychiatry*, a medical publication.

It has been stated that Irene Hughes has received commendations from the police for helping solve more than fifteen murder cases. In 1963, she had her psychic abilities tested at the Parapsychology Laboratory in Durham, North Carolina, by parapsychologist W. B. Roll, and found to be above average. But not all of Irene

Hughes's **predictions** have been accurate. She said that the Ayatollah Khomeini would be assassinated in 1983, and that Jacqueline Onassis would wed a prominent publisher in Paris. She also predicted that television performer Vanna White and her husband would purchase a "haunted" mansion in Beverly Hills, from which they would flee in terror a week later, and that singer Madonna's career would be interrupted by a "mystery illness" but she would recover after having a religious vision and would become a gospel singer.

Sources:

Shepard, Leslie A: *Encyclopedia of Occultism & Parapsychology.* New York: Avon Books, 1978

Steiger, Brad: *Irene Hughes on Psychic Safari.* New York: Warner, 1972

HULL, MOSES (1835–1907)

Moses Hull was born January 16, 1835, near Norton, Ohio. He was a second-born twin, his brother Aaron being born ten minutes before he was. According to his mother, Aaron lived only "two years, two months, two weeks, and two days." Moses was the seventh child of a seventh son. His father was James Hull; his mother Mary Brundage. The Hulls had sixteen children.

Hull was very sickly as a child, suffering a wide variety of diseases including two attacks of typhoid-pneumonia. When he was four years old the family moved to the **Native American** Reservation in the wilds of Wabash County. There were no schools there so Hull was educated, as he later put it, "at the hoe handle." His entire formal education consisted of less than eighteen months schooling. Before leaving school at fourteen, he "got religion," as he put it, and joined a "mongrel" church made up mainly of Methodists.

Hull had a thirst for knowledge. He became an Adventist and attended regular prayer meetings. From the circuit preacher, Rev. John Todd, he received a paper allowing him to "improve his talent" as en exhorter. He said in *The Greatest Debate* (1904), "I became an Adventist during a bitter fight between everybody else and the

Adventists. I immediately felt the 'call' to go and preach, which I did. I was ordained before I was eighteen years old." He worked six days per week and preached on Sundays and occasional weekday evenings, becoming known as "the boy preacher."

Feeling the need for education, Hull studied English, Latin, and even Greek Grammars. This planted the seed for what was to come in Hull's future. He said, "Measuring myself by my lost opportunities, or, rather by the opportunities I never had, has made me a crank on the subject of education. I hope to leave behind me, as a monument, a school where honest young men and women, whether they have money or not, can go and get such an education as I shall never have until I shall have graduated from some of the colleges on the other side of life."

He continued studying everywhere he could, asking help from anyone who would give it. He never in his life took a vacation; never took off a single day. He developed a flair for discussion and the Adventists pushed him to participate in any and all that came along. He became their champion speaker. Unfortunately, Hull became so adept at picking to pieces the arguments of others that he picked to pieces the arguments of the Adventists as well. He said, "I began to see the weakness of their arguments, and gradually to overthrow even my own arguments, which had at one time seemed to me invulnerable." Finally, in a discussion with a Methodist preacher, Rev. Joseph Jones, in June, 1862, he began to hear voices **clairaudiently** which questioned the points he was trying to make. The voices stated points that Hull could neither answer nor forget. Later, when alone, he responded to the voices with, "Get behind me, Satan; I will not tolerate you." Back came the reply, "You pray for light, and when it comes, you call it Satan and ask it to go to the rear … You are a coward; when a thought comes to you for your good, you order it to the rear." His preaching brethren assured Hull that he was indeed pursued by the devil. He asked them some of the questions that the voices had put to him, and they were unable to answer them. They preached to him and prayed for him.

Hull was scheduled to debate with Professor William F. Jamieson, an Adventist preacher and Secretary of the National Liberal Party of Cincinnati, Ohio; the debate to be held in Paw Paw, Michigan, in October 1862. The debate was on **Spiritualism**. Hull eagerly looked forward to it, feeling that in some way it would resolve his inner conflicts. He found Jamieson to be a worthy opponent and, in fact, the two became fast friends, the friendship lasting more than forty years. The two debated six sessions and turned out to be the factor that brought Hull to Spiritualism. He said, "When I returned home from that debate with the word that both the phenomena and philosophy of Spiritualism looked more like the truth to me than ever before, my good Adventist brethren cried and prayed over me; they pleaded hard for me to remain with them." Hull did, in fact, stay several more months but finally said, "I could stand it no longer; I must have my freedom; I turned my back upon every prospect in life and proclaimed myself a Spiritualist. Though starvation seemed to stare me, my wife, and my four little daughters in the face, I was a free and happy man."

From then on Hull would speak whenever and wherever he could, invariably with no remuneration. He gradually lost money till he "was stripped of all except wife and babies." Yet he gradually became very popular as a lecturer and debater. Then came the episode with Victoria C. Woodhill, the Spiritualist **medium** who ran for President of the United States and who inspired **Susan B. Anthony**. Woodhill was jailed and Hull, a good friend of hers, took it upon himself to, as he put it, "draw the enemy's fire." This he did so well that he spent the next several years fighting his own battles but relieving the problems of Victoria Woodhill.

Moses Hull wrote a number of books including *The Encyclopedia of Biblical Spiritualism, Joan the Medium*, and *The Spiritual Birth or Death and Its Tomorrow*. He pressed for education in Spiritualist teachers, saying, "Every one who aspires to be a teacher in Spiritualism, before he appears before the public, should have character, education and devotion to the cause sufficient to

enable him to build up societies and keep them alive." Hull felt so strongly that he founded a small school at Maple Dell Park in Mantua, Ohio. Soon Rev. A. J. Weaver, a lifelong educator, joined him and they moved the school to Lily Dale, New York. Hull's second wife, Mattie, formed the nucleus of the teachers with Mrs. Alfarata Jahnke and Rev. Weaver. By 1901, **Morris Pratt** of Whitewater, Wisconsin, became interested enough to give them a fine college building and the Morris Pratt College was opened with Moses Hull as its President. Hull also became pastor of the first Spiritual Church of Buffalo, and president of the New York State Association of Spiritualists. He died on January 14, 1907, at age seventy-one.

Sources:

Awtry-Smith, Marilyn: *"They" Paved the Way*. New York: Spiritualism & More, nd

Hull, Rev. Moses and Prof. W. F. Jamieson: *The Greatest Debate Within a Half Century Upon Modern Spiritualism*. Chicago: Progressive Thinker, 1904

Victoria Woodhull Biography: http://www.victoria-woodhull.com/tiltonbio.htm

HURKOS, PETER (1911–1988)

Peter Hurkos was born Pieter Cornelis van der Hurk. He was born in Dordrecht, the Netherlands, on May 21, 1911. He was a sickly child and a poor student at school. He ran away from home at fourteen and—since he was nearly six feet tall and looked eighteen—managed to sign on as a cook's assistant on a ship. On one of his home leaves he met a Ducth girl named Bea van der Berg, fell in love and they married. They had a son, Benny, and a daughter, named Bea after her mother.

On July 10, 1941, when he was thirty, Hurkos was working with his father as a house painter, painting a four-story building on The Hague, when he fell nearly forty feet from a ladder. He landed on his head and shoulders, breaking his shoulder and fracturing his skull. He was unconscious for four days in the Zuidwal Hospital. When he recovered he found that he had **psychic** abilities. He knew things about people simply by touching something they had handled (**psychometry**).

During World War II, Hurkos worked for the Dutch Resistance movement. That was when he changed his name to Peter Hurkos, which was a Hungarian name. He was caught with forged papers by the Germans, and sent to Vught concentration camp, which was comparable to the notorious Buchenwald camp. When the war ended he was decorated by Queen Juliana of The Netherlands. Hurkos began demonstrating his psychic abilities, giving performances in theaters in order to get money to live. He and his family drifted apart and eventually he and Bea divorced. Hurkos left Holland for Belgium and then Paris, France. He also spent time in Spain, where he did **readings** for Generalissimo Franco. By this time Hurkos had remarried, though the marriage did not last long. He was later married, for a third time, to Stephany Courtney.

In 1956, **psychical researcher Andrija Puharich** took him to the United States, where he was tested for two and a half years by the Round Table Foundation, in Glen Cove, Maine. It was Henry Belk, a chain store magnate, who put up the money to bring him to America. Hurkos did amazingly well and Puharich continued his research over a period of seven years. Using his psychometric powers, Hurkos was able to help police in many states to reconstruct crimes. Cases in which his expertise was called for included the Boston Strangler case, Sharon Tate murders, Ann Arbor Coed murders, the missing Thai Silk King Jim Thompson, and the stolen Stone of Scone in England. He is said to have worked with the FBI, CIA, INTERPOL, and INTERTEL. He was decorated by Pope Pius XII.

In later years, he worked in Hollywood with many movie actors and actresses. He made numerous radio and television appearances and had more than fifteen hours in prime time television specials. He also appeared in a number of motion pictures as himself. He died on June 1, 1988, in Los Angeles.

Sources:

Browning, Norma Lee: *The Psychic World of Peter Hurkos*. New York: Doubleday, 1970

Wilson, Colin: *The Supernatural: Mysterious Powers*. London: Aldus Books, 1975

HUSK, CECIL (1847–1920)

From early childhood, in England, Cecil Husk was aware of his potential **mediumship**, frequently experiencing **clairvoyance** and **psychokinesis**. His father was a professional singer but also a **Spiritualist**, which made it easier for Cecil to understand and accept his gifts. Of his teen years, Husk said, "On several occasions persons that I did not recognize would open the door, walk into the room where I happened to be sitting, and without a word would just walk out again." Although nothing was said on either side, he understood what the **spirit** was trying to convey to him.

Husk sat two or three times per week to develop his mediumship, and quickly developed the ability to do **table tipping**. As he grew older he followed his father into the music profession and became a member of the Carl Rosa Opera Company. While traveling on tour, he would give **séances**. By 1875, he was able to produce materializations. At his sittings, musical "fairy bells" would be heard and often seen flying about the room, like **orbs**.

Husk had five **spirit guides**, the main one being the ubiquitous John King, who seemed to have been a guide for many different **mediums**. Many times the sitters would hear the guides speaking among themselves before beginning phenomena. On one occasion King described the process of **materialization** and that it was a concerted effort which frequently encountered difficulties in exactly replicating a person's physical body.

Husk often produced the phenomenon of matter through matter; one example being when Dr. George Wyld held a ring that was too small to slide over Husk's hand onto his wrist, yet while Wyld held the medium's hand, the ring was suddenly found to be on Husk's wrist. Husk was examined by Sir **William Crookes** and three other **psychical researchers** on April 17, 1885. Careful measurements were taken of the internal circumference of the ring, which was 182.5mm while the widest part of Husk's hand was 194mm. However, they declined to definitely attribute anything to spirit intervention. Another investigator was Sir **William Barrett**, who recognized Husk's materializations as the only valid ones he had witnessed.

There were many witnesses to Husk's séances over the years. One such—Admiral Moore, sitting in 1904—testified to the movement of objects about the séance room and to the materialization of fifteen different persons. In 1908, the Maharaja of Nepal visited England and had sittings with Husk and with **spirit photographer Richard Boursnell**. Materialized forms in the photographs were recognized by the Maharaja.

By 1917, Husk was virtually blind, paralyzed, and bed-ridden, but was given financial support by other Spiritualists and admirers. A Husk Fund was set up for him. He remained cheerful and spoke of continuing his communication with John King. Husk died in 1920.

Sources:

Boddington, Harry: *The University of Spiritualism*. London: Spiritualist Press, 1947

Cecil Husk Biography: http://homepage.ntlworld.com/ annetts/mediums/cecil_husk_physical_medium.htm

Doyle, Sir Arthur Conan: *The History of Spiritualism*. New York: Doran, 1926

Marryat, Florence: *The Spirit World*. London: F. V. White, 1894

HYDESVILLE

Hydesville was a community in Wayne County, New York, made famous by being the home of the **Fox family**, who heralded Modern **Spiritualism** to the world. The village was founded by Dr. Henry Hyde. On some old maps it is spelled Hydeville but is more generally referred to as Hydesville.

Dr. Henry Hyde settled the hamlet in 1815, though there had been scattered buildings there from 1790, when pioneers traveled from New England and Long Island, New York. The fertile land in the area had enticed them to settle and farm. The building of the Erie Canal opened a free route of navigation by water, bringing trade to the area. Dr. Hyde was one of the early settlers and one of the buildings he erected was a framed one-and-a-half story cabin built at a crossroads, to be rented by the Fox family in December, 1847. Other cabins quickly followed, along with a small school and a Methodist church with a graveyard.

Sources:

Pond, Mariam Buckner: *The Unwilling Martyrs—the Story of the Fox Family*. London: Spiritualist Press, 1947

HYPNAGOGIC STATE; HYPNOPOMPIC STATE

The *hypnagogic* state is that level of light **trance** which is entered at the time just prior to falling asleep at night. It is also the state entered when daydreaming; a state between being fully awake and being asleep. It has been described as "an artificially induced **dream** state with a resemblance to hypnosis." (**Hypnotism Comes Of Age**, 1948) It can be characterized by illusions of vision or sound. The hypnagogic state was first noted about 1845, by J. G. F. Baillarger (1809–1890) in France and W. Griesinger (1817–1868) in Germany. The *hypnapompic* state is the light trance when just emerging from sleep. Both are at the alpha level, when the brainwave activity is between 8 and 13 cycles per second.

Sources:

Shepard, Leslie A: *Encyclopedia of Occultism & Parapsychology*. New York: Avon Books, 1978

Wolfe, Bernard and Raymond Rosenthal: *Hypnotism Comes Of Age*. New York: Bobbs-Merrill, 1948

HYPNOTISM

Hypnotism, or hypnosis—from the Greek *hypnos*, meaning "sleep"—may occur spon-

The Fox Family cottage in Hydesville, New York where sisters Margaretta and Kate lived when they began to communicate with spirit in 1848. The cottage was bought and moved to Lily Dale, New York by Benjamin Bartlett in 1916. *Courtesy Fortean Picture Library.*

taneously or may be induced by a trained hypnotist. A very large percentage of people are capable of being hypnotized. Shepard defines hypnotism as, "A peculiar state of cerebral dissociation distinguished by certain marked symptoms, the most prominent and invariable of which is a highly increased suggestibility in the subject." The *Encyclopedia Britannica* says it is "applied to a unique, complex form of unusual but normal behavior which can probably be induced in all normal persons under suitable conditions ... functioning at this special level of awareness is characterized by a state of receptiveness and responsiveness in which inner experiential learnings and understandings can be accorded values comparable with or even the same as those ordinarily given only by external reality stimuli."

Edmunds (*Hypnotism and **Psychic** Phenomena*, 1961) makes the point that, "Despite the vast amount of enquiry and research that has been made and the numerous works on the subject that have been published, the true nature of hypnosis is still very much a mystery." Yet hypnosis is almost as old as civilization itself. It was known to the **shamans** of primitive tribes, to priests and magicians of ancient civilizations such as Chaldea, **Egypt**, **Greece**, India, Persia, and **Rome**. It was used for both religious and therapeutic purposes. The Egyptian Ebers papyrus, dating from ca. 1500 BCE, describes the "laying-on of hands" treatment for disease and a bas relief from an ancient tomb at Thebes shows a priest seemingly in the act of hypnotizing a subject.

A hypnotist at work, using a watch to lull his subject into a hypnotic state. *Orlando/Hulton Archive/ Getty Images.*

Modern hypnotism is a development of the early *Mesmerism*, introduced in 1772 by Count Friedrich (**Franz**) **Anton Mesmer** (1734–1815), a Viennese physician. Mesmer expounded the principles of "Animal Magnetism," which then became known as Mesmerism. It was a system of **healing** based on the belief that a disturbance of equilibrium of a "universal fluid" causes disease in human beings. A magnetic readjustment of this invisible fluid would cure disease. In carrying out his therapies, Mesmer induced a hypnotic state without even being aware that he had done so. It was his pupil the Marquis Armand de Puysegur, who actually discovered the hypnotic **trance**. He termed it "artificial somnambulism." It was not until 1841 that a Manchester, England, physician named Dr. James Braid became interested in the subject and in 1843, coined the terms "hypnotism" and "hypnosis." In 1892, a British Medical

Association committee unanimously accepted hypnotism as a genuine, valuable, therapeutic tool. After that not much progress was made until World War I when there was recognition of the re-educative possibilities of hypnotism, especially with the treating of shell shock. Further advances came with World War II, helping free the subject from many of the misconceptions, fears, and superstitions that had hampered its scientific investigation and acceptance.

In 1882, the **Society for Psychical Research** was established with the purpose of scientifically investigating "that large group of debatable phenomena designated by such terms as mesmeric, psychical, and spiritualistic." Among the founding members were such people as Sir **William Barrett**, **Edmund Gurney**, **William James**, Professor **Henry Sidwick**, **Frederick W. H. Myers**, and **Frank Podmore**. Several of these, along with many of the early Spiritualists, had a great interest in Mesmerism. Another scientist with such an interest was Sigmund Freud, though he later abandoned hypnosis and concentrated on his own method of psychoanalysis.

Hypnotism has come to be used as a tool toward the development of **clairvoyance** and other **mediumship** phenomena. By using self-hypnosis, it is possible to bring about a suitable trance condition that will aid in bringing out latent mediumistic abilities. From working with self-hypnosis, a fledgling **medium** can then move on to spontaneous trance induction.

Sources:

Arons, Harry: *New Master Course in Hypnotism, The.* Irvington: Power Publishers, 1961

Arons, Harry & M. F. H. Bubeck: *Handbook of Professional Hypnosis.* Irvington: Power Publishers, 1971

Edmunds, Simeon: *Hypnotism and Psychic Phenomena.* North Hollywood: Wilshire, 1961

Encyclopedia Britannica. Chicago: William Benton, 1964

Estabrooks, G. H.: *Hypnotism.* New York: E. P. Dutton, 1934, rev. ed. 1957

Kuhn, Lesley and Salvatore Russo: *Modern Hypnosis.* New York: Psychological Library, 1947

Shepard, Leslie A: *Encyclopedia of Occultism & Parapsychology.* New York: Avon Books, 1978

HYSLOP, JAMES HERVEY
(1854–1920)

James Hervey Hyslop was Professor of Logic and Ethics at Columbia University, New York, from 1889 until 1902. He was one of the most distinguished **psychical researchers** of his day, though some thought him too ready to believe in life after death. He formed his conclusions after long and careful investigation. Hyslop was Secretary-Treasurer of the **American Society for Psychical Research** from 1906 until his death in 1920.

James Hyslop was born August 18, 1854, near Xenia, Ohio. His parents were devout Presbyterians. A twin sister of Hyslop's died at birth and an older sister died a few years later. A younger brother and a sister both died of scarlet fever when Hyslop was ten. It has been suggested that these sibling deaths may well have affected his thinking and his views on death.

Hyslop intended to follow his parents' expectations and to enter the ministry, but as Rosemary Guiley (*The Encyclopedia of Ghosts and Spirits*, 1992) reports, "While at the College of Wooster [Ohio], from which he graduated with a bachelor of arts degree in 1877, he suffered a crisis of faith that over the next five years led him to reject the divinity of Christ and embrace a materialistic philosophy instead." He received a Ph.D. in psychology from Johns Hopkins University in 1887. Four years later he married Mary Fry Hall, whom he had met in Germany. Hyslop went to study philosophy at the University of Leipzig, under Wilhelm Wundt, founder of the first formal psychology laboratory in 1879.

In 1886, Hyslop's attention was caught by an article on **telepathy** in *Nation* magazine. Contacting the author, he was persuaded that the **apparition** phenomenon described in the article was genuine. Then in 1889, he heard **Richard Hodgson** lecture and quickly became involved in psychical research. He joined both the British **Society for Psychical Research** (SPR) and the Boston-based American Society for Psychical Research (ASPR). He also helped organize a New York chapter of the ASPR.

Hyslop's wife died unexpectedly in 1900 and the following year Hyslop had a nervous breakdown. In 1902, medical reasons forced him to resign from Columbia University. Within a year, however, he had made a full recovery and determined to spend his full time on psychical research. When Richard Hodgson died in 1905, Hyslop took his place as Chief Investigator of the **medium Leonore E. Piper.** After an astounding amount of verified evidence had been produced in his sittings with Piper, in 1888 Hyslop said, "I have been talking with my father, my brother, my uncles. Whatever supernormal powers we may be pleased to attribute to Mrs. Piper's secondary personalities, it would be difficult to make me believe that these secondary personalities could have thus completely reconstituted the mental personality of my dead relatives. To admit this would involve me in too many improbabilities. I prefer to believe that I have been talking to my dead relatives in person; it is simpler."

Hyslop devoted himself to reorganizing the new American Society for Psychical Research and became the mainstay of that organization. In January, 1907, the first *Journal* was published by the society. Hyslop was initially assisted by Dr. **Hereward Carrington** and later by Dr. **Walter Franklin Prince.**

Hyslop suffered a stroke and died June 17, 1920. He was a prolific writer. His books included *Problems of Philosophy* (1905), *Science and a Future Life* (1905), *Borderland of Psychical Research* (1906), *Enigmas of Psychical Research* (1906), *Psychical Research and the Resurrection* (1908), *Psychical Research and Survival* (1914), *Life After Death: Problems of a Future Life and Its Nature* (1918), and *Contact With the Other World* (1919). In *Life After Death*, he said, "I regard the existence of discarnate spirits as scientifically proved and I no longer refer to the sceptic as having any right to speak on the subject."

Sources:

Fodor, Nandor: *Encyclopedia of Psychic Science*. London: Arthurs Press, 1933

Guiley, Rosemary Ellen: *The Encyclopedia of Ghosts and Spirits*. New York: Facts On File, 1992

Hyslop, James Hervey: *Life After Death: Problems of a Future Life and Its Nature*. New York: 1918

ILLNESS

Imagery *see* Guided Meditation

IMPERATOR

Imperator was the **spirit guide** of **William Stainton Moses** (1839–1892), one of the greatest physical mediums after **Daniel Dunglas Home**. Beginning in March, 1872, Moses started a series of **automatic writings** that continued for ten years without interruption. They were produced through Moses by various **spirit** guides, the major one calling himself Imperator. This guide also officiated at Moses's **physical mediumship séances**. Selections from the twenty-four notebooks Moses filled with the writings were eventually published as *Spirit Teachings* (London, 1883)

Imperator first announced his presence on September 19, 1872, signing his name to the automatic writing Moses had just completed. The signature was "Imperator S. D." (*Servus Dei*). At other times he would sign simply I.S.D. preceded by a cross or a crown. On July 6, 1873, he revealed himself as the **prophet** Malachias, though he advised Moses not to disclose this identity to others without his permission. Moses did eventually see Imperator **clairvoyantly**, and described him in Book VI of *Spirit Teachings*.

An extract from a June, 1873 discourse from Imperator speaking of the afterlife reads, "Of punishment we know indeed, but it is not the vindictive lash of an angry God, but the natural outcome of conscious sin, remediable by repentance and atonement and reparation personally wrought out in pain and shame, not by coward cries for mercy and by feigned assent to statements which ought to create a shudder."

On January 18, 1874, speaking for himself and the other guides who worked with him, Imperator wrote about Moses, "We are real in power over you; real in the production of objective manifestations; real in the tests and proofs of knowledge which we adduce. We are truthful and accurate in all things. We are the preachers of a Divine Gospel. It is for you to accept the individual responsibility from which none may relieve you, or deciding whether, being such as we are, we are deceivers in matters of vital and eternal import. Such a conclusion, in the face of all evidence and fair inference, is one which none could accept save a perverted and unhinged mind; least of all one who knows us as you do now."

Souces:

Doyle, Sir Arthur Conan: *The History of Spiritualism*. New York: Doran, 1926

Fodor, Nandor: *Encyclopedia of Psychic Science*. London: Arthurs Press, 1933

Podmore, Frank: *Modern Spiritualism*. London: 1902; reprinted as *Mediums of the Nineteenth Century*. New York: University Books, 1963

Trethely, A. W.: *The 'Controls' of Stainton Moses*. London: 1923

INDEPENDENT SPIRITUALIST ASSOCIATION OF AMERICA

The Independent **Spiritualist** Association of America (ISA) was founded in 1924 by Amanda Flower, who was also its first President. The ISA "advocates the use of the Holy **Bible** as a textbook, teaching the Fatherhood of God and the Brotherhood of man … The ISA strives for harmony by tempering every thought or situation with its Declaration of Principles." The Declaration of Principles is the same as that adopted by the **National Spiritualist Association of Churches**. The ISA is represented by members in twenty-three states.

Sources:
ISA Annual Convention Program, 1996

Independent Voice *see* Direct Voice

Independent Writing *see* Direct Writing

INFINITE INTELLIGENCE

"Infinite Intelligence" is the term used by **Spiritualists** for a "supreme impersonal power, everywhere present, manifesting as life, through all forms of organized matter, called by some, God, by others, **Spirit** and by Spiritualists, Infinite Intelligence." In the philosophy of Spiritualism, Infinite Intelligence pervades and controls the universe, is without shape or form, and is impersonal, omnipresent, and omnipotent.

Sources:
National Spiritualist Association of Churches: *Spiritualist Manual*. Lily Dale: NSAC, 1911; 2002

INFRARED

Infrared is the electromagnetic radiation outside the color spectrum range of visibility, at the lower end and next to the red. Infrared film has been sensitized to this radiation. Infrared film is commonly used at séances where there is total darkness, or where the light is too dim to allow regular photography. In this way it is possible to photograph things which cannot be seen under many **séance** conditions (e.g. ectoplasm, spirit forms).

Sources:
Bletzer, June G.: *The Encyclopedia Psychic Dictionary*. Lithia Springs: New Leaf, 1998

INSPIRATIONAL SPEAKING, WRITING, ART

There is a **psychic** state in which a **medium** becomes susceptible to creative influences from **spirit** and lends him- or herself as an instrument for free flowing thoughts and ideas. **Wolfgang Mozart** said, "When all goes well with me, when I am in a carriage, or walking, or when I cannot sleep at night, the thoughts come streaming in upon me most fluently; whence or how is more than I can tell." Most musicians, writers, and artists of all sorts have experienced this. This is what leads to inspirational writing, speaking, or art of various types. It is more than just putting down ideas on paper; it is as though spirit dictates what is to be recorded.

There was what became known as a "preaching sickness" that swept across Sweden in the middle of the nineteenth century. A great many people, including some children, spoke out eloquently and passionately as if possessed. In Finland, a number of "sleeping preachers" were reported from the 1770s to the 1930s. These were people who suddenly dropped into a deep **trance** and began to preach.

Emma Hardinge Britten, known as "The Silver-Tongued Lecturer," was a speaker who gained an international reputation. Her extemporaneous talks were on subjects chosen by a member of the audience. They were spirit-inspired inspirational speeches. There were many other **Spiritualist** speakers who worked the same way. There are many today who do likewise.

Inspirational writing differs from **automatic writing** in that in the latter the operator focuses his or her attention elsewhere and spirit force takes over and directs the hand and arm, moving them to produce the writing. In inspirational writing, the attention is on what is being written and the operator is in full control of hand and arm. It is almost as though in inspirational writing the medium is taking dictation from spirit.

Sources:

Fodor, Nandor: *Encyclopedia of Psychic Science.* London: Arthurs Press, 1933

Mühl, Anita M.: *Automatic Writing.* Dresden: Steinkopff, 1930

Wilson, Bryan R.: *Man, Myth and Magic: Enthusiasm.* London: BPC Publishing, 1970

INSTITUT MÉTAPSYCHIQUE INTERNATIONAL

Founded in 1918 by **Jean Meyer**, the French industrialist and enthusiastic follower of the teachings of **Allen Kardec**, the institute was located at 89 avenue Niel, Paris, France. (Meyer also founded the **International Spiritualist Federation**.) The Institute's first director was Professor Gustave Geley (1868–1924), physician and psychical researcher who gave up his medical practice to become director of the institute. Members included Professor **Charles Richet**, **Camille Flammarion**, and Sir **Oliver Lodge**. The institute invited men of science to witness the investigations they conducted with various **mediums**. When working with **Eva C.**, for example, invitations were extended to a hundred notable psychical investigators.

The institute was most proud of its testing apparatus, including expensive **infrared** cameras able to take 1,000 pictures per second. However,

the apparatus was so noisy that it turned out not to be practical. The institute was recognized by the French government as being "of public utility." It had an excellent laboratory, reading room, lecture hall, and reception room. Reports on its activities were carried in *La Revue Métapsychique*.

Sources:

Doyle, Sir Arthur Conan: *The History of Spiritualism.* New York: Doran, 1926

Fodor, Nandor: *Encyclopedia of Psychic Science.* London: Arthurs Press, 1933

INSTITUTE OF NOETIC SCIENCES

Founded by astronaut **Edgar D. Mitchell** in 1973, the Institute of Noetic Sciences (INS) is a 200-acre center in Palo Alto, California. It was formed to encourage and conduct basic research on mind-body relations, in order to gain new understanding of human consciousness. The institute explores phenomena that do not necessarily fit conventional scientific models, while maintaining a commitment to scientific rigor. In 1971, when Mitchell was an astronaut on Apollo 14, he looked out at planet Earth and felt a profound sense of universal connectedness. In his own words, "The presence of divinity became almost palpable, and I knew that life in the universe was not just an accident based on random processes." Yet the Noetic Institute is not a spiritual association, nor a political action group or single-cause institute. It honors open-minded approaches and multiple ways of knowing.

The term "noetic" (from the Greek *nous*, meaning "mind") means pertaining to, or originating in, intellectual or rational activity; mental functions; highest character of the mind principle consciousness. Noetic science is the study of altered states of consciousness and the reaction of the mind-body to those altered states. The subjects of programs at INS include **psychical research**, **healing**, personal awareness, and control of interior states.

Sources:

Bletzer, June G.: *The Encyclopedia Psychic Dictionary*. Lithia Springs: New Leaf, 1998

Institute of Noetic Sciences: http://www.noetic.org

Shepard, Leslie A: *Encyclopedia of Occultism & Parapsychology*. New York: Avon Books, 1978

INSTRUMENTAL TRANSCOMMUNICATION (ITC)

ITC includes two-way communication between the physical plane and the spiritual plane of the afterlife. This communication may be by telephone, radio, computer, fax, or any other special device. The interaction may be stored by use of technical means and can include images and text as well as voices. Instrumental Transcommunication is similar to **Electronic Voice Phenomena (EVP)**, both being different aspects of the electronic work. EVP is capturing **spirit** voices—however faint—on tape, or hearing them on the telephone or radio, while ITC is a two-way communication.

In the 1990s, the International Network for Instrumental Transcommunication (INIT) was started by Mark Macy, though this was later fragmented due to the skepticism and pressure of the scientific community.

Sources:

Buckland, Raymond: *Buckland's Book of Spirit Communications*. St. Paul: Llewellyn, 2004

Meek, George W.: *After We Die, What Then?* Columbus: Ariel Press, 1987

Raudive, Konstantin: *Breakthrough: An Amazing Experiment in Electronic Communication with the Dead*. New York: Taplinger, 1971

Sherman, Harold: *You Can Communicate with the Unseen World*. New York: Fawcett, 1974

World ITC Organization: http://www.worlditc.org

INTERNATIONAL COLLEGE OF SPIRITUAL SCIENCE AND HEALING

This college is located at Ramsbergsgarden, Sweden. In 2000, British **medium Colin Fry** became the principal tutor at the college and in February 2003 he purchased the college. Today he promotes courses offered there by himself and other mediums, **psychics**, and **healers**. The stated purpose of the college is "to promote and advance spiritual gifts in the students, being **clairvoyance, clairaudience, clairsentience,** healing, psychic art, **physical mediumship,** psychic abilities." The foundation of the college is based on the principles of **Spiritualism** and certification is offered in many fields, after examinations and proven demonstrations.

Sources:

International College of Spiritual Science and Healing: http://www.colinscollege.com

INTERNATIONAL FEDERATION OF SPIRITUALISTS

Headquartered at Maison des Spirites, 8 rue Copernic, Paris, France, the International Federation of Spiritualists (ISF, also known as International Spiritualist Federation) was founded by **Jean Meyer**. Meyer was a French industrialist and enthusiastic follower of the teachings of **Allen Kardec**. He also founded the **Institut Métapsychique International**. E. W. Oaten, former editor of *Two Worlds* magazine, was the first President of the ISF. Honorary Presidents have included Sir **Arthur Conan Doyle** (1925–1930) and Lady Doyle (1931–1940). The Federation grew rapidly with affiliated associations in Belgium, England, France, Germany, Holland, Mexico, South Africa, Spain, Switzerland, and the United States. Today there are both individual and group members of the Federation in thirty-five countries.

According to Kay Rumens, Members' Secretary in London, England, "We are the Spearhead uniting Organizations and Individuals in many lands all seeking Spiritual knowledge." One of the members is the **National Spiritualist Association of Churches** in America, which has been a member for more than fifty years. The basic principles of International **Spiritualism** are defined in the Constitution of the ISF as, "Spiritualism is founded on the facts of (a) personal survival of bodily death, and (b) communion between this world and the **Spirit** world."

World Spiritualist Conferences were held in Barcelona (1888), Paris (1889) and Liverpool (1901). Several attempts to form an international federation were made and almost succeeded when they were interrupted by the 1914–1918 war. The war led to the rapid development of Spiritualism in many parts of the world and this in turn provided further incentive to concentrate forces under a single banner, which was finally successful in 1923 at Liège, Belgium. Subsequent Congresses were held in Paris, London, The Hague, Barcelona and Glasgow until World War II stopped all international work. In 1947, a new start was made and in July of that year a special conference was held in Bournemouth, England, when a small number of delegates from Great Britain, France, South Africa, Canada and Sweden attended at the invitation of the Spiritualists' National Union of Great Britain. All the records of the original organization had been lost from the Paris headquarters of the ISF due to the war, and a complete reorganization was necessary. The enthusiasm for international unity was demonstrated by the fact that no fewer than forty-two nations were represented at the first post-war Congress, held in London the following year. Congresses have been held in many countries since 1948 including Sweden, France, Denmark, Scotland, England, Holland, Spain, and the United States.

Sources:

A Brief History of International Spiritualism: http:// www.spiritualist.freeuk.com/History.htm

INTERNATIONAL GENERAL ASSEMBLY OF SPIRITUALISTS

The International General Assembly of Spiritualists (IGAS) was incorporated in Buffalo, New York, in 1936. It was founded by **Arthur Ford**, Fred Constantine, and eight other **Spiritualist** ministers. Ford was the first President. Fred Jordan, a retired navy commander, was ordained by Ford in 1937 and became President of IGAS in 1938. He held that position until 1947, when he was succeeded by Jerry Higgins.

In 1946, the Declaration of Principles as given by the **National Spiritualist Association of Churches** was adopted. Emphasis was placed on **healing**, prayer, spiritual unfoldment, and **psychic/ mediumistic** development.

Sources:

Melton, J. Gordon: *The Encyclopedia of American Religions.* Wilmington: McGrath, 1978

INTERNATIONAL PSYCHIC GAZETTE

A monthly magazine founded in 1912 as the official organ of the International Club for Psychical Research. After only a few months this connection ceased.

Sources:

Shepard, Leslie A: *Encyclopedia of Occultism & Parapsychology.* New York: Avon Books, 1978

INTUITION

Intuition has been defined as "a non-thought which bypasses the process of thinking and brings through a whole body sensation of 'this information is important;' information that one did not know before through education of past experiences, did not logically think out or reason with." It is an inner knowing and usually happens spontaneously. It can be linked with **clairsentience**, the **mediumistic** ability to sense information. With clairsentience, the information sensed is from **spirit**, while with intuition it is not necessarily so. **Psychic** ability which does not connect with spirit can be largely due to intuition.

Sources:

Bletzer, June G.: *The Encyclopedia Psychic Dictionary.* Lithia Springs: New Leaf, 1998

ITALY

Sir **Arthur Conan Doyle** felt that Italy showed itself superior to all other European states in its treatment of **Spiritualism**, "in spite of the constant opposition of the Roman Catholic Church, which has illogically stigmatized as diabolism in others that which it has claimed as a special mark of sanctity in itself."

The Italian publication *Civitta Catholica* presented an article on Spiritualism at the turn of the last century, summing up with the three notes, "i: Some of the phenomena [of Spiritualism] may be attributed to imposture, **hallucinations**, and exaggerations in the reports of those who describe it, but there is a foundation of reality in the general sum of the reports which cannot have originated in pure invention or be wholly discredited without ignoring the value of universal testimony. ii: The bulk of the theories offered in explanation of the proven facts, only cover a certain percentage of those facts, but utterly fail to account for the balance. iii: Allowing for all that can be filtered away on mere human hypotheses, there is still a large class of phenomena appealing to every sense which cannot be accounted for by any known natural laws, and which seem to manifest the action of intelligent beings."

This report may have been due to the visits of **Daniel Dunglas Home**, who toured the major cities of Italy, ending in Florence in 1855. Such was the success of his demonstrations that numerous Spiritualist **development circles** were formed, though numerous disputes arose, with controversies in many journals throughout the country. By 1863, articles lauding Spiritualism began to appear in the respected journal *Annali dello Spiritismo* ("Annals of Spiritualism"), published by Niceforo Filalete of Turin. In Florence, about this time "The Magnetic Society of Florence" was formed with members of literary and scientific skills together with those of Italian high society. Seymour Kirkup, of Florence, began to send records of Italy's Spiritualistic development to the *London Spiritual Magazine*.

In the fall of 1864, lectures on Spiritualistic subjects began to be presented. They started in Messina and Leghorn. In 1868, the renowned physical medium Mrs. **Agnes Nichol Guppy** visited Italy with her husband. They took up residence in Naples and stayed for nearly three years. By 1870, more than a hundred different societies had been formed across the country. In 1872, the psychical researcher Signor Damiani discovered the medium **Eusapia Paladino**. Paladino was also investigated by Professors Morselli and Porro, together with "the dean of Italian psychical researchers and Spiritualists" Ernesto Bozzano. Bozzano (1862–1943) had been incensed by **Frank Podmore**'s slighting references to **William Stainton Moses** and published the notable *A Defence of William Stainton Moses*.

Sources:

Doyle, Sir Arthur Conan: *The History of Spiritualism*. New York: Doran, 1926

Fodor, Nandor: *Encyclopedia of Psychic Science*. London: Arthurs Press, 1933

J

JAMES, WILLIAM (1842–1910)

William James was Professor of Psychology at Harvard University. He was one of the founders of the **American Society for Psychical Research**. He was its Vice President from 1890 to 1910 and President for 1894 and 1895.

William James was born in New York City on January 11, 1842. He was the eldest of five children born to Henry and Lucy (Walsh) James. The next eldest was Henry James, who became the distinguished author. The James family was descended from "farmers, traders and merchants, prosperous and Presbyterian." William's father attended Union college in Schenectady, and then the Princeton theological seminary. While there, he developed a violent "antipathy to all ecclesiasticisms," which he expressed with scorn and irony throughout his later years. When William was two, someone introduced his father to the works of **Emanuel Swedenborg**. His father built a system of his own from these teachings and William preserved the best of them in *The Literary Remains of Henry James* (1886).

James' own schooling was erratic as the family moved around. He was educated in New York, Boulogne, France, Geneva, Switzerland, and elsewhere. At the age of eighteen and living in New-

port, Rhode Island, James tried his hand at art but rapidly tired of it. In 1861, he went to the Lawrence scientific school of Harvard university. With breaks over the years—to go with Louis Aggasiz up the Amazon, for example—he finally received his medical degree at Harvard, in June, 1869. Due to constant ill health, however, he was unable to practice medicine. From 1872 until 1876, he was an appointed instructor in physiology at Harvard. But he wanted to take the step from teaching physiology to teaching psychology.

In 1878, James married Alice H. Gibbens, of Cambridge, Massachusetts; a union that seemed to give new vigor to his life. He wrote an innovative textbook on psychology, *The Principles of Psychology*, which appeared in 1890. With its publication—after ten years of writing it—he seemed to lose interest in the subject. He went on to become the world leader in the movement known as pragmatism and to be regarded as one of the most renowned thinkers in the United States.

In 1885, James's mother-in-law, Mrs. Gibbens, visited the **Spiritualist** medium **Leonora E. Piper**. This led to James and his wife Alice visiting her also, though incognito. James later commented, "My impression after this first visit was that Mrs. P. was either possessed of supernormal powers or knew the members of my wife's family by sight and had by some lucky coincidence become acquainted with such a multitude of their domestic circumstances as to produce the startling impression which she did. My later knowledge of her sittings and personal acquaintance with her has led me to absolutely reject the latter explanation, and to believe that she has supernormal powers."

For the next eighteen months James investigated Leonora E. Piper, before asking the **Society for Psychical Research** to do the same. In a lecture James gave in 1890, he said, "To upset the conclusion that all crows are black, there is no need to seek demonstration that no crow is black; it is sufficient to produce one white crow; a single one is sufficient." In his view the **medium** Leonora E. Piper was that one white crow. In a lecture at Oxford in 1909, he announced his firm conviction that "most of the phenomena of **psychical research** are rooted in reality."

James published several papers in the SPR journal *Proceedings*. In London in 1902, he published an important essay on psychical research, *The Will to Believe*, and *Varieties of Religious Experience*. Of the forty-five lectures that he gave at Harvard, one third of them were on psychical research and Spiritualism. He died in 1910.

Sources:
Encyclopedia Britannica. Chicago: William Benton, 1964

Fodor, Nandor: *Encyclopedia of Psychic Science*. London: Arthurs Press, 1933

Gauld, Alan: *Man, Myth & Magic: Psychical Research*. London: BPC Publishing, 1970

Podmore, Frank: *Modern Spiritualism*. London: 1902; reprinted as *Mediums of the Nineteenth Century*. New York: University Books, 1963

Shepard, Leslie A: *Encyclopedia of Occultism & Parapsychology*. New York: Avon Books, 1978

JESUS

The **Biblical** figure Jesus is not regarded by **Spiritualists** as being the son of God, other than in the context that we are *all* sons and daughters of God. As Harry Boddington points out in *The University of Spiritualism* (1947), "**Spiritualism** defines God for no man. Definitions imply limitations and we refuse to limit the illimitable or define the indefinable." Jesus is simply looked upon as being a great **medium** and **healer**; his healing of the leper, and of the blind man at Bethsaida, for example, being similar to healings done by such people as **Harry Edwards**. Jesus *and* the disciples performed many healings, showing it was not just Jesus who had the ability.

A. R. G. Owens suggests in *Man, Myth & Magic: Miracles* (1970), "Bearing in mind that a condensed oral tradition is not a set of doctor's case notes, it appears that [the miracles] are all capable of being interpreted as psychological cures: exorcisms, cures of paralyses, hemorrhage, or skin disease (the term 'leper' was not a specific medical description) or catalepsy (the affliction of Jairus's daughter). Even the '**absent healing**' fits into the picture … Studies of the miracles at Lourdes show that where sufficient data are available, the cures appear to fall into the regular pattern of healings by suggestion." Phenomena termed "miracles," such as the turning of water into wine at the marriage at Cana, for example, are no more than **physical mediumship**. Spiritualists do not believe in "miracles," since everything *must* follow Natural Law.

There is almost no direct historical evidence to corroborate the existence of Jesus. One view is that he was purely mythical, however certain peculiarities of the gospels do suggest that there was such a historical figure. The chief error lies in confusing "Jesus of Nazareth" with "Jesus Christ," the latter representing a theological interpretation of the former. It should also be remembered that Jesus the Christ did not mean Jesus the God, or even Son of God, but meant Jesus the *anointed*; anointing being a common practice when priests were ordained.

To again quote Boddington,

"Love and hatred cannot co-exist side-by-side—the one destroys the other.

Spiritualism repudiates all such imperfections as vice, hatred, partiality, or injustices as attributes of God. God never made mistakes. He did not create Adam and Eve or place them where he knew they must 'fall' and curse humanity for ever. Nor would He need to drown the consequences of His errors in a flood or sacrifice one third of Himself to atone for the mistakes of the other two thirds. These are the mazes from which Christianity cannot disentangle itself so long as it uses words with obsolete meanings."

Spiritualists do not believe that anyone can "die for your sins." They believe in self-responsibility. And to accept personal responsibility is to do away with any and all concepts of a "Savior." It is better to ask forgiveness of the person wronged, than to pray to a God to remove your "sin" and yet leave the person suffering.

Sources:

Boddington, Harry: *The University of Spiritualism*. London: Spiritualist Press, 1947

Owens, A. R. G.: *Man, Myth & Magic: Miracles*. London: BPC Publishing, 1970

JOAN OF ARC (1412–1431)

In the countryside of Domremy, France, she was known as Jeanette, with the surname of Arc or Romée. She is also mentioned in contemporary documents as Jeanne, commonly called *la Poucelle*, the Maid. She was born on January 6, 1412, to Jacques d'Arc and Isabelle de Vouthon, two devout Catholics. Her two brothers were Pierre and Jean du Lys. Her father owned horses and cattle and was the head man of his village of Domremy. Joan was very pious; while the other girls her age were dancing, she chose to attend church.

When Joan was thirteen, she was in her father's garden when she **clairaudiently** heard a voice she believed came from God. During the next five years she continued to exhibit this **mediumistic** ability, hearing **spirit** voices two or three times per week, and claimed to be able to

distinguish between Saints Catherine, Margaret and Michael. They even appeared to her **clairvoyantly**, wearing crowns. She determined to remain a virgin and lead a godly life.

The Hundred Years War between France and England, over who should rule France, was in full swing. The dauphin Charles, son of Charles VI, battled the English who had control of large portions of the country. Joan's spirit voices told her to help the dauphin and get him crowned King of France. In May 1428, Robert de Baudricourt, commandant at Vaucouleurs, about twelve miles from Domremy, was approached by Joan. She was accompanied by Durand Lassois, a relative on her mother's side. Joan told Baudricourt that she had been sent by God to place the dauphin on the throne, and she would like to speak with him. The commandant sent her home again.

In July 1428, the village of Domremy was threatened by the English and the inhabitants retreated to Neufchâteau. It was October before they were able to return, only to find the village burned to the ground. The English, meanwhile, had laid siege to Orléans. When news of this reached Domremy, Joan again set out to see the dauphin. Again, at Vaucouleurs, she encountered Robert de Baudricourt. She also met a young squire, Jean de Metz, in whom she confided. De Metz lent her men's clothes. Baudricourt finally authorized her departure for Chinon, where Charles had his court. The people of Vaucouleurs bought her a horse and she was given a sword.

Louis de Bourbon, count of Vendôme, presented Joan to the dauphin, who talked with her for two hours. According to Jean Pasquerel, her confessor, she told him, "I am God's messenger, sent to tell you that you are the true heir to France and the king's son." Charles had her interrogated by a commission presided over by the Archbishop of Riems, who found her honest and ruled in her favor. Joan then assured Charles that she would raise the siege of Orléans and have him crowned.

In a suit of "white armor," Joan, accompanied by Gilles de Rais, led 4,000 men and on the night

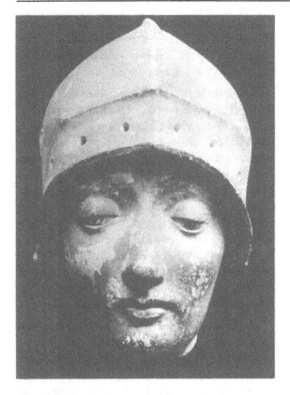

Joan of Arc. When Joan was about 12 years old, she begin hearing voices that she believed were sent by God. She was later burned at the stake by the British after being ruled a heretic. *Courtesy Fortean Picture Library.*

of April 28 entered Orléans. On May 5, they stormed the Bastille and captured the Tourelles. On May 8 the first thanksgiving procession was held, the origin of what has become the great Festival of Orléans. Joan went on to Troy and then Reims by July 14. Two days later Charles was crowned King Charles VII of France, with Joan standing beside him. On December 29, 1429, Joan was ennobled and her village exempt from taxation.

The following May, Joan attempted to raise the siege of Compiègne. She and her forces made a sortie against the Burgundian camp. Joan got cut off and was taken prisoner by the Duke of Burgundy, an English ally. He handed her over to the Bishop of Beauvais, also an English ally. On

January 3, 1431, Joan was passed on to Pierre Cauchon, bishop of Beauvais, an ambitious man who hoped to obtain the vacant see of Rouen. She was to be tried by tribunal, which had been selected by Cauchon and consisted of 10 Burgundian theologians, 22 canons of Rouen (all in the hands of the English), and some monks of different orders. Interrogation began on February 21. Judgement was to be based on seventy different points, including charges that she indulged in **divination**, had **prophetic dreams**, was a sorceress, **witch**, and conjurer of evil spirits. Eventually these charges were dropped to twelve. Her judges were of the opinion that her visions were worthless and denied her the gift of **prophecy**. They censured her for dressing in masculine clothing and for "sinful pride" and believing that she was responsible only to God and not to the church which the judges represented. This last was the charge that most incensed her accusers.

On May 23, Joan was taken to the cemetery of Saint-Ouen and sentenced to be burned at the pyre unless she submitted. Tired and worn out, Joan signed what was presented to her and was returned to her cell to serve life imprisonment. A woman's dress was given to her but she either did not put it on or else she returned to her men's clothing, for on May 27, Cauchon found her so dressed and declared her to have relapsed. He handed her over to the English secular arm. On May 30 she was made to appear in the Old Market Square of Rouen, though she had again been dressed as a woman. There she was burned for being a relapsed heretic.

It has been said that throughout Joan of Arc's capture and imprisonment, Charles made no attempt to assist her or obtain her release. In fact on December 15, 1430, hearing the news that Joan had fallen into the hands of the Duke of Burgundy, Charles sent an embassy to Philippe le Bon saying that if there was nothing that could be offered to set Joan free, then Charles would exact vengeance for her upon Philippe's men that he held captive. There is correspondence that states, "The English wished to burn her [Joan] as a heretic, in spite of the Dauphin of France who tried to bring threatening forces against the English." But Charles's attempts seemed half-hearted. Finally in 1450, he instituted a preliminary inquiry into her trial and execution, but it was not fully followed through. It wasn't till June 16, 1456 that the judgement was annulled by Pope Calixtus III. Joan was eventually beatified in 1909 and then canonized by Pope Benedict XV, in 1920.

Sources:

Barrett, W. P. (trans.): *The Trial of Jeanne d'Arc*. New York: Gotham House, 1932

Encyclopedia Britannica. Chicago: William Benton, 1964

Murray, Margaret Alice: *The Witch Cult in Western Europe*. London: Clarendon Press, 1921

JUERGENSON, FRIEDRICH (1903–1987)

Friedrich Juergenson was born in Odessa in 1903 and later naturalized in Sweden. He became a well known film director and portrait painter. One of Juergenson's hobbies was making tape recordings of bird songs. One day in June, 1959, he was amazed to discover the sound of a man's voice on his recording of a bird. The voice commented on "bird voices in the night." He listened carefully a number of times and was then further surprised to make out the sound of his deceased Mother's voice saying, in German, "Friedrich, you are being watched. Friedel, my little Friedel, can you hear me?" On hearing this, Juergenson felt he had made an important dis-covery. He spent the next twenty-eight years taping hundreds of paranormal voices.

In 1964, Juergenson published a book in Swedish, *Voices From the Universe*. Three years later this was translated into German, which gave it a much wider circulation and thereby made Juergenson better known in this field. Dr. **Konstantin Raudive** read the books and although he was initially very skeptical, met with Juergenson and was quickly caught up in the **Electronic Voice Phenomena**. Raudive eventually catalogued tens of thousands of such voices, using Juegenson's methods.

Other of Juegenson's books are *Radio-Link With the Beyond*, and *Voice Transmissions with the Deceased*. He died on October 15, 1987. It is said that he appeared to a Swedish couple, Claude and Ellen Thorlin, on their television set a few days later. Ellen is a **psychic**. Claude took a Polaroid photograph of the dead Juegenson on the screen. The television set was tuned to a channel that does not carry any programming.

Sources:

Buckland, Raymond: *Buckland's Book of Spirit Communications*. St. Paul: Llewellyn, 2004

Butler, Tom and Lisa: *There Is No Death and There Are No Dead*. Reno: AA-EVP, 2003

Fredrich Jurgenson Biography: http://www.paravoice.dk/friedrich%20jurgenson.htm

Voices from Space Article: http://www.fiu.edu/~mizrachs/voices-from-cspace.html

World ITC Organization: http://www.worlditc.org

Kardec, Allan (1804–1869)

Allan Kardec was born Léon-Dénizard-Hippolyte Rivail, in Lyons, France, in 1804. His was an old family of Bourg-en-Bresse, distinguished for many generations in the legal profession. Both his father and his grandfather were barristers. His mother—described by many as a very beautiful woman—was adored by both her husband and her son.

Rivail attended the Institution of Pestalozzi at Yverdun (Canton de Vaud), and developed an inquisitiveness and desire for investigation that lasted his whole life. He enjoyed teaching and even at the age of fourteen directed the studies of his fellow students, often tutoring others. His main interest was in botany and he would often walk as many as twenty miles or more in a day, searching for specimens. Despite his young age, he spent a lot of time **meditating** on a means to bring about a unity of the Catholic and Protestant elements in his country.

Rivail returned to Lyons in 1824, intending to devote himself to law. However, after witnessing various acts of religious intolerance, he moved to Paris. He translated French books into German for younger readers. In 1828, he purchased a large and flourishing school for boys and devoted himself to teaching, for which he was very well suited. Two years later he also rented a large hall in the rue de Sèvres and offered free lectures on chemistry, physics, astronomy, and comparative anatomy. These free lectures continued for ten years. He invented an ingenious method of computation and constructed a mnemotechnic table of French history that could help students remember important events and dates. He published a number of works, including *A Plan for the Improvement of Public Instruction* (1828), *A Course of Practical and Theoretical Arithmetic* (1829), *A Classical Grammar of the French Tongue* (1831), and many more. He was also a member of several learned societies, including the Royal Society of Arras, the Phrenological Society of Paris, and the Society of Magnetism. This latter led to his investigation of somnambulism, **trance**, **clairvoyance**, and similar phenomena.

The phenomenon of **table tipping** came to France in 1850. Rivail saw it as an important step in the communication between the worlds of the living and the dead. The two daughters of a friend and neighbor became **mediums**, though much of the information they produced seemed of a frivolous nature. But when Rivail sat with them the messages became much more serious. The spirits told Rivail—when he asked—that it was because "spirits of a much higher order than those who habitually communicated through the two young mediums came expressly for him." Rivail tested this by drawing up a list of questions on life and the universe, and worked with the two sisters for over two years. In 1856, Victorien Sardou introduced Rivail to the séances of Celina (Bequet) Japhet, where further research was conducted.

Ravail was not himself a medium and so had to rely on others for all of his information. During the course of his work, he collected a lot of information and was encouraged by the **spirits** to publish his findings and to do so using the name Allan Kardec. Allan was a name he'd had in a previous life, as was the name Kardec. The two names were combined for his *nom de plume*. On the advice of the spirits, his first book of spirit teachings was titled *Le Livre des Esprits* or *The Spirits' Book* (1857). The book sold extremely well throughout France and across Europe. Allan Kardec quickly became a household name. Shortly after publication of the book, Kardec founded the The Parisian Society of Psychologic Studies and published a monthly magazine, *La Revue Spirite*.

Kardec received many teachings, including one that acknowledged **reincarnation** as a fact. This was—as it still is with **Spiritualists**—a controversial subject. Kardec made a point of publishing only views that agreed with his acceptance of reincarnation. He also dismissed such things as **physical mediumship** in Spiritualism, totally ignoring famous physical mediums such as **Daniel Dunglas Home**, for example, because Home did not believe in reincarnation.

The other great Spiritualist pioneer in France was M. Pierart, who disbelieved in reincarnation. Pierart published the rival magazine *La Revue Spiritualiste*, and for years there was intense rivalry between the two camps. Kardec later published *The Mediums' Book* (1861), which came to rank right alongside its precursor.

Over the years Kardec's influence faded in his native France, but flourished in South America—especially Brazil—and, to a lesser extent, in the Philippines. Kardec had adopted the terms

"**Spiritism**" and "Spiritist" for his version of Spiritualism. These terms were used in South America along with the term "Kardecism" (*Kardecismo*). Today in Brazil there are Kardecist psychiatric hospitals in operation and fully accepted. The Instituto Brasileiro de Pesquisas Psicobiofisic, or the Brazilian Institute of Psycho-Biophysical Research, collects and studies Spiritist works. It was founded in 1963 by Hernani Andrade.

Allan Kardec died on March 31, 1869. Shortly before his death he organized "The Joint Stock Company for the Continuation of the Works of Allan Kardec." It was also designed to continue the publication of *La Revue Spirite*. He is buried in the cemetery of Père Lachaise, Paris. The tomb features a large dolmen, to indicate Kardec's believed past life as a Druid.

Sources:

Doyle, Sir Arthur Conan: *The History of Spiritualism*. New York: Doran, 1926

Fodor, Nandor: *Encyclopedia of Psychic Science*. London: Arthurs Press, 1933

Guiley, Rosemary Ellen: *The Encyclopedia of Ghosts and Spirits*. New York: Facts On File, 1992

Kardec, Allan: *The Spirits' Book*. (1857) New York: Studium,1980

Playfair, Guy Lion: *The Flying Cow: research into paranormal phenomena in the world's most psychic country*. London: Souvenir Press, 1975

Kardecism *see* **Spiritism**

KARMA

A doctrine found in **Buddhism**, Hinduism, Brahmanism, and **Theosophy**, and also in many neo-pagan religions. The word *karma* comes from a Sanskrit root and means "action," and is the law of cosmic requital for one's good and bad deeds. Karma represents the sum total of the causes set in motion in **past lives**, which make a pattern for present and future lives. Every person born, therefore, carries the seeds of what he or she was formerly. If a soul brings with it into life an accumulation of bad karma from a previous life, it will have to spend that new life expiating it in order to advance in the growth process. This belief accounts for the apparent injustices and inequalities of life, and explains differences of personalities, circumstances, intelligence, and special gifts. It can also be an incentive to live life as worthily as possible so as to avoid negative karma in the next life.

The Hindu often believe that bad karma will bring punishment in the form of having to live the next life as a lower caste person or even a despised animal, while good karma will ensure the next life as a Brahmin or a sacred cow. In some branches of Wicca, there is a variation on such karma belief. It is felt that everything must be experienced over a number of lives. Although there will be both "good" and "bad" incarnations, one is not dependent upon another. So a life of crime, for example, will not mean that the next life must be spent atoning for that. Yet at some time, in some future life, there will be the opposite experience as the victim of crimes.

Where there is no belief in **reincarnation**, there can still be a belief in karma. Without reincarnation, the quality of the life lived dictates any rewards and punishments in the afterlife—whatever its form. This follows the **Spiritualist** law of cause and effect and the **Greek** concept of *heimarmene* or destiny.

Sources:

Bletzer, June G.: *The Encyclopedia Psychic Dictionary.* Lithia Springs: New Leaf, 1998

Holroyd, Stuart: *The Supernatural: Psychic Voyages.* London: Aldus, 1976

Stemman, Roy: *The Supernatural: Spirits and Spirit Worlds.* London: Aldus, 1975

Walker, Benjamin: *Man, Myth & Magic: Karma.* London: BPC Publishing, 1970

KELLY, REV. THOMAS JOHN (JACK) (1899–1964)

Thomas John Kelly—known as "Jack" Kelly—was born in Wales, Great Britain, on August 3, 1899. In his teens he enlisted as an artilleryman in the British Army. He was discharged at the end of World War I in 1919. Like many Welshmen, Kelly worked as a coal miner and developed black lung disease. He was described as a gentle, analytical, accepting man. He would play checkers for hours, enjoying the mental stimulation without allowing the game to become a bitter duel.

Kelly emigrated from Britain to America. He became a **Spiritualist** years before leaving Wales and developed into an excellent **medium**. He settled in Buffalo, New York, and would demonstrate his **clairvoyance** by driving an automobile down Buffalo's Main Street while wearing a blindfold. He placed coins placed over his eyes and then three separate blindfolds were wrapped around his head. He finally stopped this publicity stunt when police requested him to do so; they said he was a distraction for other drivers. Kelly also helped police with murder cases. He became **Mae West**'s favorite medium when she visited **Lily Dale Assembly**. He was the chief medium there for many years and principal medium at state and national conventions for a large number of years.

On November 22, 1950, Kelly married Estelle Zagora at The Spiritualist Church of Life in Buffalo, New York. This was a second marriage for both of them. Kelly had one son and Estelle had three sons by previous marriages. The sons were all ushers at the wedding. Kelly was the founder and pastor of The Spiritualist Church of Life.

Kelly became an excellent **spiritual healer** and is best known for healing a woman's blindness. As reported in the August 3, 1952, issue of *The Dunkirk Observer,*

> Mrs. Donna Ball, of Gulf Avenue, Pittsford, NY, who has been attending the Lily Dale Assembly at Lily Dale, has reported that she has regained the sight of both eyes, which were injured in an auto accident March 14, at Pittsford, and that her right hand, which was paralyzed, has also become strengthened. Mrs. Ball attributes this healing entirely to the spiritual powers of Rev. Thomas J. Kelly of Buffalo ... on

July 13 she reports that Rev. Kelly gave her a "healing by laying on of hands" in the Lily Dale Auditorium, which was witnessed by approx. 40 persons and that she immediately regained sight in both eyes.

Jack Kelly died in Estaboga, Alabama, on November 18, 1964. His obituary said that he was survived by his "wife and one son, one daughter, three step sons, three sisters, seven grandchildren."

KILNER, WALTER JOHN (1847–1920)

Walter John Kilner was born on May 23, 1847, at Bury St. Edmunds in Suffolk, England. He was educated at the local Grammar School and then St. John's College at Cambridge University. He studied medicine at St. Thomas's Hospital in London, receiving his B.A. in 1870, M.R.C.S. and L.S.A. in 1871, and M.B. in 1872. Kilner was appointed in charge of electro-therapy at St. Thomas's in June, 1879. Four years later he became a member of the Royal College of Physicians and at that time opened a private practice at Ladbrooke Grove, London.

Kilner became interested in the human **aura**, a luminous area surrounding all living things and visible to sensitives. Baron Georg von Reichenbach (1772–1826), a German astronomical instrument maker, claimed to be able to see auras around the poles of magnets and around human hands. This intrigued Kilner and in 1908, he began experimenting to see if he could produce a screen which, if looked through, would make the aura visible to the non-sensitive eye. By 1911, he had devised a system using a dilute solution of a dye called *dicyanin*, a product of coal tar. Another method he tried initially was looking first at a bright light through a strong alcoholic solution and then looking at the subject. This, however, proved to be very dangerous, causing damage to the eyes. Kilner eventually perfected his dicyanin method and produced what became known as the Kilner Screen. He published his findings in *The Human Atmosphere* (1911). In his method, researchers looked at a subject through the screen, in daylight, with the dicyanin contained in two pieces of hermetically sealed glass. The subject was a naked person standing against a dark background. In this way, three distinct radiations could be seen. The first was dark and colorless and extended from the body no more than a fraction of an inch. The second extended beyond the first about three inches. The last was at least a foot in length. The first aura Kilner termed the **etheric double**; the second, the inner aura; and the last, the outer aura. Illness was seen to affect the color and size of the aura, with mental deterioration causing reduction in size and impending death shrinking the aura to almost nothing.

Kilner's book was the first to study the human aura as a scientific fact, rather than as a questionable **psychic** phenomenon. His book was reprinted in 1920 and re-issued under the title *The Human Aura* in 1965. **Nandor Fodor** mentions that psychical researcher **Hereward Carrington** referenced a forgotten book, *Ten Years With Spiritual Mediums* (1874), published by Francis Gerry Fairfield, which claimed that all organic structures have a special nerve-aura.

Kilner died on June 23, 1920. Since then a method has been developed to photograph the aura. This is known as **Kirlian photography.**

Sources:

Buckland, Raymond: *Color Magic—Unleash Your Inner Powers*. St. Paul: Llewellyn, 2002

Fodor, Nandor: *Encyclopedia of Psychic Science*. London: Arthurs Press, 1933

Kilner, Walter J.: *The Human Aura*. New York, University Books, 1965

King, Katie *see* Cook, Florence

KIRLIAN PHOTOGRAPHY

Kirlian photography was developed by Semyon and Valentina Kirlian, a Russian husband and wife who used high frequency electrical

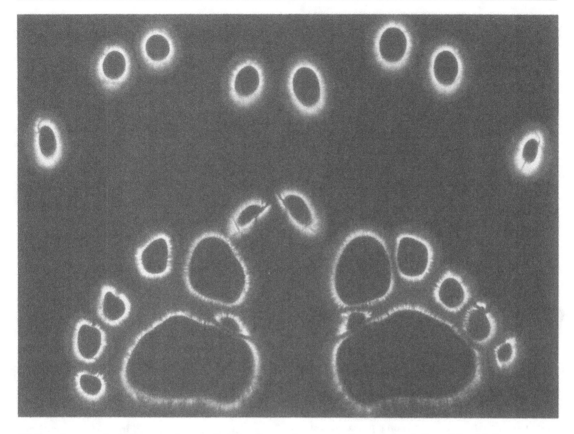

Kirlian photograph of fingers and toes taken for diagnostic purposes by naturopath Pater Mandel. *Courtesy Fortean Picture Library.*

currents to make visible the colored **auras** around all living things.

About fifty years ago, Semyon Kirlian, an electrical engineer, saw a demonstration of a high frequency electro-therapy machine at a southern Russian research institute. He noticed tiny flashes of light between the machine's electrodes and the patient's skin and wondered what would happen if he placed a photographic plate there. He experimented using himself as a guinea pig. From a crude and painful first experiment, he and his wife progressed to a technique that gave astonishing results. The object to be photographed is placed on sensitive photographic paper which then goes underneath a specially constructed, high frequency, spark generator. This produces 75,000 to 200,000 oscillations per second. When

the generator is switched on, the radiation from the object is transferred to the paper.

The Kirlians referred to the aura as a "bioplasmic body." Early photographs of this type have shown that in plants, the onset of a disease can be seen before the disease is actually visible by normal means. In one experiment, a leaf was photographed and produced a good Kirlian image. Then part of the leaf was cut away and it was photographed a second time. In this second picture, there was again an image of the complete leaf. This gave rise to the conjecture that the "bioplasma" of a living thing remains even after the physical body has gone. This may be the scientific proof of the existence of **spirit** after death, as believed in by **Spiritualists** and others for many years.

Changes in the human aura can be indicators of problems to come, as has been discovered at the Kazakh State University in Alma-Ata, Russia. Kirlian photography has shown that there are emissions from the hands and fingers of a **healer**, and that they are of exceptional length and intensity at the time of doing a healing. Kirlian photography has also revealed that there are correspondences, in the color and intensity of light, between the points of the body where an acupuncturist sticks the needles.

Sources:

Holroyd, Stuart: *The Supernatural: Magic, Words, and Numbers*. London: Aldus, 1975

Krippner, Stanley (ed.), et al: *Galaxies of Life: The Human Aura in Acupuncture and Kirlian Photography*. New York: Gordon & Breach, 1974

Stemman, Roy: *The Supernatural: Spirits and Spirit Worlds*. London: Aldus, 1975

KLUSKY, FRANEK (B. 1874)

Franek Klusky was the pseudonym of a distinguished Polish poet and writer who possessed great **psychic** gifts. He had **visions, premonitions**, and saw **spirits** when he was a child. He thought this quite natural and conversed with the spirit forms he saw. His ability was not recognized until his early forties, when he attended a **séance** of the materialization **medium** Jan Guzik (1875–1928). Klusky reluctantly agreed to be examined by **psychical researchers**.

Klusky demonstrated all aspects of physical **mediumship**, including **materializations**. During these he retained consciousness. He happily agreed to make himself available to the Polish Society for Psychical Research and also sat at the **Institut Métapsychique** of Paris in 1920, with Professor **Charles Richet**, Count de Grammont, and Gustave Geley. He allowed paraffin casts of materialized limbs to be taken and it is said that these were the finest and best objective evidences of **Spiritualistic** power ever produced. An unusual aspect of his séances was that he sometimes produced materialization of animals. In 1926,

Col. Norbert Ocholowicz published *Wspomnienie Z. Seansow Z*, a book on Klusky's mediumship.

Sources:

Fodor, Nandor: *Encyclopedia of Psychic Science*. London: Arthurs Press, 1933

KNIGHT, GARETH (B. 1930)

Gareth Knight was born in Colchester, England, in 1930. He was interested in **psychic** matters from a young age. By the time he was twenty-three, he enrolled in the **Society of Inner Light** study course. **Dion Fortune** (1891–1946), the author, **medium**, and magician, founded the society as the Fraternity of the Inner Light in 1924. By 1959, Knight had worked through the magical grades and achieved initiation into the Greater Mysteries of the society. He also became the society's librarian. In 1963, Knight became a contributor to the **occult** magazine *New Dimensions*, produced by Llewellyn Publications under the editorship of Basil Wilby. Knight started a series of articles on **tarot cards** in the April/May, 1963 issue. By that time, he was becoming unhappy with the direction of the Society of Inner Light—Fortune died in 1946, and without her influence the fraternity took a new direction and was renamed the Society of the Inner Light. In 1965, he published *A Practical Guide to Qabalistic Symbolism*, drawing largely from unpublished material in the library's archives.

He relocated to Gloucestershire and founded Helios Books, a small publishing venture that took over publication of *New Dimensions* in 1973. Knight also started a correspondence course on the **Qabbalah** with William E. Butler. In 1973, this was reworked and offered as "The Servants of Light." That same year he founded a new school, drawing on the regular attendees at the lectures he gave at Hawkwood College. When *New Dimensions* ran its course, he replaced it with *Quadriga* in 1976. Original distribution was to the members of Knight's correspondence course. In 1999, Knight reorganized his various groups into two main ones, The Avalon Group and The Companions of the Inner Abbey.

In 1976, Knight received an honorary Humanities Doctorate from the Sangreal Foundation, Dallas, Texas, "in recognition of distinguished attainments," and the award of Outstanding Humanitarian for 1976. At the same time, he was appointed Consultant in Archetypal Symbolism to the C.G.Jung Institute, Dallas. Knight began to expand his field of influence with lectures in France, **Greece**, and the United States. In 1987, he offered a new correspondence course in tarot. This was later published in book form as *The Magical World of Tarot*.

In 1997, the Society of the Inner Light invited Knight to edit, for publication, Dion Fortune's letters from the war years. Also in 1997, more of her unpublished work was released, with Knight writing companion chapters for each of Fortune's chapters. This was published as *An Introduction to Ritual Magic*. In 1998, Knight was invited to rejoin the society to assist in the inner restructuring of it. Since that time he has produced a series of books based on Dion Fortune's material.

Sources:

Knight, Gareth: *Dion Fortune & the Inner Light*. Loughborough: Thoth, 2000

Knight, Gareth: *Pythoness: the Life and Work of Margaret Lumley Brown*. Oceanside: Sun Chalice Books, 2000

Voices from Space Article: http://www.fiu.edu/ ~miz rachs/voices-from-cspace.html

KNIGHT, JUDY "ZEBRA" (B. 1946)

Judith Darlene Hampton was born in Roswell, New Mexico, on March 16, 1946. Living in Roswell, she grew up with a belief in flying saucers. She was also interested in pyramidology, wearing a pyramid on her head for spiritual enhancement and enlightenment. As a young girl, she was abandoned by her alcoholic father and claims to have been molested by her uncle. Her mother tried to give her a Christian upbringing in the midst of all this. She had an older sister who drowned in an accident.

In 1977, Knight was a thirty-one-year-old housewife living in Tacoma, Washington. She was standing in her kitchen with a miniature pyramid on her head when she was visited by a **spirit** calling itself "Ramtha." This entity claimed to have lived as a warrior 35,000 years ago, on the lost continents of Lemuria and **Atlantis**. According to Knight—who saw him **clairvoyantly**—he said to her, "Beloved woman, I am Ramtha the Enlightened One, and I have come to help you over the ditch. It is called the ditch of limitation, and I am here, and we are going to do a grand work together." Knight's husband was with her in the kitchen but did not see the **apparition**.

From then on, Knight acted as a **channel** for Ramtha, relaying his messages to the world. Her nickname as a child had been "Zebra," so she took the initials of Judith and Zebra to form her professional name "J. Z. Knight". She appeared on national television and gave hundreds of performances on stage and by way of private seminars at a reputed $1,000 per person. Today she is the founder and Director of The Ramtha School of Enlightenment, also known as The American Gnostic School, is President of JZK, Inc., and Chairman of the J. Z. Knight Humanities Foundation. Knight has copyrighted the name Ramtha and claims that no one else can channel him.

Ramtha's messages started out as the usual benign words of love and hope common among channeled entities. Gradually, however, his words changed to those of doom and gloom, predicting a dire future for both California and Florida, the former falling into the ocean and the latter becoming a vast sinkhole. He also spoke of "getting rid of" homosexuals. Knight, meanwhile, built up a multimillion dollar mansion, with Arabian horses kept in a barn lit with chandeliers. She drove a Rolls Royce while exhorting her followers to dispense with earthly comforts. Laura Foreman reports that one of Knight's staff resigned after hearing Knight practicing Ramtha's voice. Another left when she saw Knight suddenly assuming the Ramtha mantle without first going into trance, as was the usual procedure.

Ramtha's messages are even more vague than many channeled messages. When asked about his true nature, he replied, "I am Ramtha, the Enlightened One, indeed, that which is termed servant unto that which is termed Source, to that which is termed the Principal Cause, indeed, unto that which is termed Life, unto that which is termed Christos—God experiencing that which is termed Man, Man experiencing that which is termed God—am I servant also."

Sources:

Foreman, Laura (ed): *Mysteries of the Unknown: Spirit Summonings.* New York: Time-Life Books, 1989

Leonard, Sue (ed): *Quest For the Unknown—Life Beyond Death.* Pleasantville: Reader's Digest, 1992

KOENIG, HANS-OTTO

Hans-Otto Koenig was an electronics engineer and acoustics expert. He invented the "Koenig Generator," which caused a sensation on Radio Luxembourg in 1982. It was named by the radio station presenter.

Koenig followed the work of **George W. Meek**. Meek studied **Electronic Voice Phenomena** and felt certain that a device could be designed that would promote two-way conversation between the living and the dead. Meek was instructed by a discarnate **spirit** during a **séance** to build such a machine. He eventually assembled the machine as instructed and produced some fascinating results. Meek called the apparatus the "Spiricom." Despite its success, the media did not respond as Meek had hoped, and the Spiricom fell into disuse. But Hans-Otto Koenig did not want the idea to die, and he approached the same objective in his own way. He used extremely low-beat frequency oscillators with ultraviolet and infrared lights.

On January 15, 1982, the Koenig Generator was set up for a live broadcast in the studios of Radio Luxembourg. To preclude any fraudulent phenomena, station engineers supervised the set up and did not allow Koenig to touch anything. The machine was turned on, and someone asked Koenig if the voices of the spirits would come on

request. Immediately, from the device, came the words, "Otto Koenig makes wireless with the dead." The station presenter, Rainer Holbe, assured his listeners, "I tell you, dear listeners of Radio Luxembourg, and I swear by the life of my children, that nothing has been manipulated. There are no tricks. It is a voice and we do not know from where it comes."

A statement was later issued by the station's engineers to the effect that they had no natural explanation for the voices broadcast during the program. The *VTF Post* newsletter of the German EVP association *Vereins Für Tonbandstimmenforschung* said, "Now there are microphone-recorded voices of unexpected strength, precision, clear and noise-free. People can no longer say that one is hearing something in the background noise that isn't there."

Koenig demonstrated his equipment at a VTF conference in Frankfurt, Germany, in 1984, claiming that the dead oscillate on a width frequency of 5 Khz. Someone commented, "One can hear the answers from the other side at once, so this is really like a call with a telephone." One of the voices that came through was that of **Konstantin Raudive**, who died in 1974. After this, George Meek was persuaded to fly to Germany. After he saw a demonstration of the Koenig Generator, Meek flew back to America determined to raise funds for further development.

Despite the seemingly amazing results of both the Spiricom and the Koenig Generator, no more seems to have been heard of them, though there are rumors that in 1994, Koenig began manufacturing his generator.

Sources:

Butler, Tom and Lisa: *There Is No Death and There Are No Dead.* Reno: AA-EVP, 2003

KOONS, JONATHAN

Jonathan Koons is best remembered as the inventor of the **trumpet** used in many Spiritualist séances. He was an early American medium who lived in Millfield Township, Ohio. In 1852, he became interested in **Spiritualism** and was told by **spirit** that he was "the greatest **medium** on earth." Koons had eight children and was also told that each of them, even the seven-month-old baby, had special **psychic** gifts.

Koons built a log cabin for the spirits. It was one large room, sixteen feet by twelve, and was equipped with every possible noisemaking device. These were all used during the course of a sitting, which was frequently presided over by oldest son Nahum, aged eighteen. Nahum would sit at the "spirit table" with rows of benches in front of him for the sitters. When the lights were extinguished there would be a cacophony of sound, with the banging of drums, shrieking of whistles, and even the firing of pistols. Materialized hands and faces were seen in the light of phosphorized paper. These hands carried objects around. Cone-shaped megaphone trumpets floated overhead, with the voices of the spirits coming from them. The voices would call out the names of the sitters, even if they had tried to hide their identity, and give pertinent messages proving survival after death. Although seventy miles from the closest town, the Koons' spirit house was always full, with people coming from states all around Ohio.

As many as 165 spirits were usually in attendance. According to **Nandor Fodor**, these spiritis claimed to belong "to a race of men known under the generic title Adam (red clay), antedating the theological Adam by thousands of years." Fodor said they were most ancient **angels**. One of them was named Oress and instructed the **circle**. They signed themselves in any written communications (**automatic writing**) as "King No. 1", "King No. 2", "King No. 3", etc, and sometimes as "Servant of God" or "Scholar of God." The main "King" claimed to be the pirate Henry Morgan. Sir **Arthur Conan Doyle** mentions John King speaking at a Koons **séance** in 1855. The spirit John King seems to have spoken to or through a large number of different mediums at different times.

The messages of these spirits were collected by investigator Dr. J. Everett and published under the title *Communications From Angels*. He also published a chart of the **spheres**, drawn by Nahum Koots while in **trance**, and affidavits testifying to the phenomena. In 1852, Charles Partridge visited the spirit house and wrote a report for the *Spiritual Telegraph*. In it he said,

The spirit room holds from twenty to thirty people. After the Circle is formed and the lights extinguished, a tremendous blow is struck by the drumstick, when immediately the bass and tenor drums are beaten with preternatural power, like calling the roll on a muster field, making a thousand echoes. The rapid and tremendous blows on these drums are really frightful to many persons; it is continued for five minutes or more and when ended, 'King' usually takes up the trumpet, salutes us with 'Good evening, friends,' and asks what particular manifestations are desired. After the introductory piece on the instruments, the spirits sang to us. They first requested us to remain perfectly silent; then we heard human voices singing, apparently in the distance, so as to be scarcely distinguishable; the sounds gradually increased, each part relatively, until it appeared as if a full choir of voices were singing in our room most exquisitely. I think I never heard such perfect harmony. Spirit hands and arms were formed in our presence several times, and by aid of a solution of phosphorous, prepared at their request by Mr. Koons, they were seen as distinctly as in a light room.

The tremendous din of the drums and other instruments could be heard a mile away from the spirit house. Perhaps not surprisingly, Koons's neighbors did not take well to this. The house was often attacked by unruly mobs; barns, outbuildings, and crops were set on fire, and the Koons children were frequently beaten. Eventually the family left the area and wandered the country as Spiritualist missionaries for many years.

Interestingly, a neighboring family named Tippie were very similar. They, too, had a spirit house that they constructed to the same pattern as that of the Koons family. The John Tippie family had ten children and every one of them was supposedly a medium. Manifestations took place in the Tippie house, which were almost identical to those in the Koons house.

Sources:

Doyle, Sir Arthur Conan: *The History of Spiritualism.* New York: Doran, 1926

Fodor, Nandor: *Encyclopedia of Psychic Science.* London: Arthurs Press, 1933

Kosmon Church *see* Newbrough, Dr. John Ballou

KÜBLER-ROSS, ELISABETH (1926–2004)

Elisabeth Kübler was born one of triplet sisters in Zurich, Switzerland, on July 8, 1926. Early in her childhood, and against the wishes of her father, she decided on a medical career. She graduated from the medical school at the University of Zurich. It was there she met her husband-to-be, fellow student Emanuel Robert Ross.

After World War II, working with former Nazi concentration camp survivors, she became convinced that something unexpected occurred at the moment of death. This was the first time anyone had seriously considered the process of death. Ross was a member of the International Voluntary Service for Peace, a post-war group that helped in ravaged communities. At the concentration camp Maidanek, she saw butterflies carved into the walls by the prisoners spending their final hours there. Ross adopted the butterfly as her symbol for the transformation that takes place at death.

In 1958, Ross and her husband came to the United States. She worked at hospitals in Chicago, Colorado, and New York. There she found that patients who were dying were treated very poorly, with no one being really honest with them. Many were shunned, and some were even abused. Ross made it part of her job to sit with terminal patients and listen to them. She began

giving lectures, at which she would feature dying patients speaking about their thoughts and feelings. Ross said, "My goal was to break through the layer of professional denial that prohibited patients from airing their innermost concerns."

In 1969, she published her bestselling book *On Death and Dying.* It made her name known internationally. It is still required reading in most major medical, nursing, and psychology programs. Throughout the 1970s, Ross led hundreds of workshops and helped bring the hospice movement into the mainstream. She was also responsible for the introduction of such things as living wills and home health care. Her "five psychological stages of dying" (denial, anger, bargaining, depression, acceptance) became accepted as common knowledge throughout the world. She founded the Elisabeth Kübler-Ross Center and the Shanti Nilaya Growth and Healing Center and from these she gave "Life, Death, and Transition" workshops. She also continued an ongoing personal interest in mysticism, the afterlife, and unconventional forms of **healing**.

In the 1980s, she purchased 300 acres in Head Waters, Virginia, and named it Healing Waters. It was to serve as a healing and workshop center. In 1995, at the age of sixty-nine, she retired to Arizona after suffering a series of strokes. A fire had also destroyed her home and all of her belongings. But even in retirement, Ross continued to get visits from people from all around the world, including many celebrities. The March 29, 1999, issue of *Time* magazine named her one of "The Century's Greatest Minds." She settled to anticipating her own death, seeing it as a "transition." With **Spiritualists**, she shared a strong belief that "Life doesn't end when you die. It starts." After a prolonged illness, Ross died on August 24, 2004, in Scottsdale, Arizona, at the age of seventy-eight. She had published more than 20 books, many of which had been translated into nearly thirty foreign languages. Her books included *To Live Until We Say Good-Bye, On Children and Death, AIDS: The Ultimate Challenge,* and her autobiography, *The Wheel of Life.* Her most recent book, *Real Taste of Life,* was a photographic journal produced

Swiss-born psychiatrist Elizabeth Kübler-Ross revolutionized the way the world looks at the terminally ill with her groundbreaking book, *On Death and Dying. AP/WideWorld Photos.*

in collaboration with her son, Kenneth. She had recently finished drafting her final book, *On Grief and Grieving*, with longtime collaborator and friend, David Kessler.

Sources:

Elisabeth Kübler Ross Homepage: http://www.elisabethkublerross.com

Kübler-Ross, Eliabeth: *On Death and Dying.* London: Tavistock, 1970

KUHLMAN, KATHRYN
(1907–1976)

Kathryn Kuhlman was born in Concordia, Missouri, on May 9, 1907. Her German father, Joseph Adolph Kuhlman, was a Baptist and her mother, Emma Walkenhorst Kuhlman, a Methodist. Kathryn went to a Baptist seminary. At the age of thirteen, she had "a religious experience" and felt drawn to the ministry. Two years later she dropped out of school and started preaching as an itinerant evangelist. She traveled throughout the Midwest states with her sister Myrtle and brother-in-law Everett Parrott. After a year of this, Kuhlman attended the Simpson **Bible** School in Seattle for two years. At twenty-one, she went out on her own to preach. She became well known in Idaho, Utah, and Colorado.

In 1933, Kuhlman settled in Colorado and opened her own church in an old Montgomery Ward warehouse. She named it the Denver Revival Tabernacle. She had made a name for herself by then and many well known evangelists, including Burroughs Waltrip Sr., came to visit and preach at her church. Waltrip became enamored of Kuhlman and subsequently deserted his wife and two young sons in order to pursue her. They married in 1938 and she left him in 1944.

In 1946, she moved to Franklin, Pennsylvania, to try to escape the gossip about her failed marriage. While preaching in Franklin in 1946, she did her first **healing**, curing a woman of a tumor. The healing came as a surprise to Kuhlman. From then on, she decided to focus her ministry on **psychic** healing. From 1947 on, Kuhlman held regular healing services in the Carnegie Auditorium in Pittsburgh. A large number of cases of spontaneous healing were reported there over the next twenty years. At her services, after an organ prelude she would appear on stage in a long white or blue robe and would begin to speak. She spoke sincerely but very emotionally until she became transformed by what was termed the "Holy **Spirit**." At this point she would become **clairvoyant** and see who in the congregation was suffering from disease. She would then describe the disease being cured and ask the person to come to the stage. When they did so, she would pass her hands over them and they would fall backward (caught by assistants) to lie seemingly unconscious for several minutes.

On standing up they would claim to feel wonderful. People from all over the world came to her services; the hall was always full. In 1967, Kuhlman transferred to the First Presbyterian Church in downtown Pittsburgh.

Kuhlman appeared regularly on radio and television, being a guest on talk shows such as Merv Griffin, Dinah Shore, Johnny Carson, and Mike Douglas. On the latter show she was confronted by Dr. William Nolen who had been studying her healings. He claimed she was "medically ignorant," and although he claimed he believed her to be a "good person," he felt that her powers did not come from God. On the same show, Dr. H. Richard Casdorph refuted Nolen's charges. Kuhlman continued to heal for vast crowds of believers and supporters.

Kathryn Kuhlman died in Tulsa, Oklahoma, on February 20, 1976, following open heart surgery. She was buried in Forest Lawn Memorial Park, Glendale, California, where her tombstone says: "I believe in miracles, because I believe in God."

Sources:

Fodor, Nandor: *Encyclopedia of Psychic Science*. London: Arthurs Press, 1933

Kathryn Kuhlman Biography and Links: http://nyny. essortment.com/kathrynkuhlman_rfbt.htm

Kuhlman, Kathryn: *I Believe in Miracles*. New York: Prentice-Hall, 1962

Spraggett, Allen: *Kathryn Kuhlman: The Woman Who Believes in Miracles*. New York: Thomas Y. Crowell, 1970

Kundalini *see* Chakras

LEGAL

Lake Cassadaga *see* Cassadaga

LAKE PLEASANT

Lake Pleasant, Massachusetts, is one of five villages in the town of Montague in Franklin County, approximately ninety miles west of Boston. It claims to be the oldest continually existing **Spiritualist** community in the United States, older even that **Lily Dale Assembly** in New York. Lake Pleasant was founded in 1870 (Lily Dale has been a community since 1879) as a summertime recreational community in the woods of the Upper Pioneer Valley. Within a couple of years Spiritualists had begun to gather there, making it a "tent city." By 1874, the New England Spiritualist Camp-meeting Association had been organized and was attracting Spiritualists from around the world. From a bustling town of 3,000, today Lake Pleasant comprises approximately 300 residents.

According to David James (*Spirit and Spa*, 2003), "The **National Spiritual Alliance** was formed after members of the New England Spiritualist Campmeeting Association were unable to resolve philosophical differences (primarily regarding **reincarnation**) and decided to follow separate Spiritualist paths. Members of the New England Spiritualist Campmeeting Association who did not believe in reincarnation—contending that reincarnation is retrogressive—continued affiliation with the National Association of Spiritualist Churches, while members who believed that reincarnation was a learning vehicle which assisted the soul's progression toward perfection split from the New England Spiritualist Campmeeting Association and formed the independent TNSA. Lake Pleasant was thus the home of rival Spiritualist organizations, each with its own temple and followers, until the New England Spiritualist Campmeeting Association temple burned in 1955 and was not rebuilt. The New England Spiritualist Campmeeting Association continued operations until 1976, before donating its remaining property to the Town of Montague and disbanding."

Sources:

Egby, Robert: *Parapsychic Journal.* #19, July 16, 2004

Shattuck, Louise and David James: *Spirit and Spa: A Portrait of the Body, Mind, and Soul of a 133-Year-Old Spiritualist Community in Lake Pleasant, Massachusetts.* Greenfield: Delta House, 2003

LANG, DR. WILLIAM (1852–1937)

Dr. William Lang was an eminent eye specialist and skilled surgeon who, after death, became the **spirit guide** of George Chapman. Lang was born in England in 1852, and became a highly regarded ophthalmologist and a Fellow of the Royal College of Surgeons. He published several works concerning diseases of the eye. Lang died in 1937.

Ten years after his death, twenty-six-year-old **medium** and psychic **healer** George Chapman started speaking with Lang's voice while in **trance**. Eventually Lang took full control of Chapman's body and performed **psychic surgery** on patients. When Lang took over, Chapman's eyes would be tightly closed and he assumed a slightly stooped stance. He spoke in a high pitched, quavery voice recognized as Lang's by the doctor's associates and other people who knew him when alive. Lang normally had a warm, friendly manner but in the operating room his commands were short and crisp and he would peremptorily snap his fingers to indicate which instrument he needed. Chapman worked in exactly the same manner, though without any physical instruments.

The **spirit** of Lang examined the body of a patient, diagnosed the problem, and performed the operation through the body of George Chapman. Chapman's hands would move about an inch away from the body before him. The patient remained fully clothed and no actual surgical instruments were used. A witness said, "I had seen Dr. Lang make about sixty stitches after operating, but without touching the patient. When I told [the patient] this she could not believe it. She said she felt every move that was made. The stitching was very apparent to her, though not painfully so, as she had felt the flesh drawing together."

Lang's son Basil assisted with the "operations". In conversation with Robert W. Laidlaw of the **American Society for Psychical Research**, Lang explained that Basil was being trained, from the spirit world, to take over after Chapman dies.

Sources:

Holroyd, Stuart: *The Supernatural: Psychic Voyages.* London: Aldus, 1976

Kingston, Jeremy: *The Supernatural: Healing Without Medicine.* London: Aldus Books, 1975

LANSING, JESSICA

Jessica Lansing is the pseudonym of a **channeler** who lives in the San Francisco Bay area. For more than thirty years, she has channeled an entity named Michael, who claims that every person is the essence of Tao, the ancient Chinese principle of cosmic unity. Michael first appeared in 1970, by way of the Ouija® **talking board**. He claims that humans are fragments of an entity slowly evolving back to Tao. But in order to achieve this cosmic oneness, this state of perfection, the fragments must come together as a single entity and transcend seven planes of existence.

Michael validates the seven planes or spheres which were the suggested existences put forward by **Emanuel Swedenborg** (1688–1772), **Helena Blavatsky** (1831–1891), Rudolf Steiner (1861–1925), and many **Spiritualists**. He keeps returning to the number seven, with seven basic stages of the soul, seven incarnations, and seven roles to be experienced. Michael represents himself as being made up of a thousand "old soul fragments," and as being a "recombined entity." Writer Chelsea Quinn Yarbro has written two books on Lansing's entity, *Messages from Michael* (1979) and *More Messages from Michael* (1986).

In recent years more than a dozen other people—mostly in the same San Francisco Bay area—have claimed to be channeling this same entity, Michael. He is coming through by means of **trance** utterings, **automatic writing**, and **clairaudience**.

Sources:

Foreman, Laura (ed): *Mysteries of the Unknown: Spirit Summonings.* New York: Time-Life Books, 1989

Klimo, Jon: *Channeling: Investigations on Receiving Information from Paranormal Sources.* Los Angeles: Jeremy P. Tarcher, 1987

LAONA FREE ASSOCIATION

In Laona, New York, an organization called "The Religious Society of Free Thinkers" was flourishing in 1855. Records state that the society "did assemble on the third day of December, 1855, and did elect seven discreet persons ... as trustees." At that same meeting, it was decided to rename the organization "The Laona Free Association." It was to eventually grow into the **Lily Dale Assembly** that still operates in that location today.

Many well known people attended the Laona Free Association meetings. In 1871, the **Spiritualists** began holding picnics and then **camp meetings** at Middle Lake in the **Cassadaga** Lakes. The well known orator **Lyman C. Howe** spoke at the first gathering. On August 23, 1879, following a disagreement with the original owners of the land where the camp meetings usually took place, a meeting was held at which it was decided to "organize a corporate body under the New York laws." A board of trustees was named and Mrs. Amelia H. Colby was invited to name the new organization. She suggested calling it "The Cassadaga Lake Free Association." This was adopted and the necessary papers were signed.

The grounds were dedicated in 1880 and became one of the most important spiritualist camps in the United States. Summer cottages, hotels, and some permanent homes were built to house the adherents of Spiritualism. Later speakers included such people as **Susan B. Anthony**, Rev. Anna Shaw, and Robert G. Ingersoll. When Ingersoll lectured in 1896, 20,000 persons thronged the grounds to hear him. The colony grew to become a self-contained community with its own post office, fire house, electric plant, and numerous stores.

Sources:

Vogt, Paula M. and Joyce LaJudice: *Lily Dale Proud Beginnings: A Little Bit of History*. Lily Dale: Lily Dale Museum, 1984

LAYNE, AL

Al Layne was the **hypnotist** who originally hypnotized **Edgar Cayce** (1877–1945). Cayce had been suffering from a sever throat infection that seemed incurable. Layne put Cayce into a **trance** and asked him to diagnose himself. Cayce did so, stating that he was suffering from a partial paralysis of the vocal cords. He went on to

prescribe an increase in blood circulation in that area for a short time. Layne then asked the entranced Cayce to prescribe for his (Layne's) illness. Cayce again diagnosed and then prescribed. In his diagnosis, Cayce used medical terms that neither man had ever encountered and did not understand. This was the start of Cayce's many years of medical diagnosis and prescription.

Sources:

Wilson, Colin: *The Supernatural: Healing Without Medicine*. London: Aldus Books, 1975

LEADBEATER, CHARLES WEBSTER (1847–1934)

Charles Webster Leadbeater was born on February 17, 1847, in Hampshire, England. Early in his life he was a curate in the Church of England. At the age of thirty-seven, he went to Adyar, Madras, India, to visit the headquarters of the **Theosophical Society** and to meet its cofounders, **Helena Blavatsky** and Henry Steel Olcott. He quickly became enamored of the Society and devoted himself to the cause of Theosophy. This cause was dedicated to the foundation of a universal brotherhood without distinction of race or creed, the study of comparative religion, and the investigation of **metaphysics**—the unexplained faculties in humans.

Leadbeater spent some time traveling through India and Ceylon with Olcott, and publicly professed himself a **Buddhist**. He developed various **psychic** abilities and began to gain a reputation as a **seer** and as an expert at **crystal gazing**. Leadbeater became a leading member of the Theosophical Society. He returned to England in 1890, where he became a private tutor. The following year, on the death of Madame Blavatsky, Leadbeater started working closely with Annie Besant, who grew to fill Blavatsky's place as leader of the Society. She eventually became its President in 1907.

In 1906, while Leadbeater was in the United States, a number of mothers brought charges against him for sexual misconduct with their sons. Leadbeater was a homosexual and had unusual views on the tutoring of young men. Annie Besant couldn't accept these charges, and the charges were brought to Olcott. A judicial committee of the Society summoned Leadbeater to appear before them. In the face of clear evidence, he was asked to resign.

On Olcott's death in 1907, Dr. Weller van Hook, General Secretary of the Society, sent an open letter championing Leadbeater's theories on the sexual upbringing of young boys, even claiming that the defense was dictated to him by one of the Mahatmas. The following year the British Convention of the Society requested of the General Council that Leadbeater and his practices be repudiated. The Council members disagreed among themselves, but Leadbeater was restored to membership. As a result of the controversy, 700 members resigned. Leadbeater went on to exert a powerful influence with his **clairvoyant** teachings and theories on **reincarnation**. He was especially influential in India.

In 1908, Leadbeater and Annie Besant jointly sponsored a young Brahmin boy named Jiddu Krishnamurti, whom they believed to be a Messiah. They founded the Order of the Star of the East to propagate his mission, but in 1929 the young man renounced his role and dissolved the Order. He did, however, go on to become a notable spiritual teacher.

Late in life Leadbeater moved to Australia and became a bishop of the Liberal Catholic Church there. He died in 1934. During his lifetime he had written a number of books which have since become minor classics in their field. They include *Man: Visible and Invisible* (1902), *The Astral Plane* (1905), *A Textbook of Theosophy* (1912), *The Hidden Side of Things* (1913), *Clairvoyance* (1918), and *Man: Whence, How and Whither* (1913). This last was in two volumes and written with Annie Besant. In *Man: Visible and Invisible* Leadbeater included illustrations of **auras**, which he claimed to see clearly. He said that auras and halos were emanations of **astral bodies**.

Sources:

Blavatsky, Helena: *Collected Writings, Vol. xii*. Madras: Theosophical Publishing House, 1991

Shepard, Leslie A: *Encyclopedia of Occultism & Parapsychology*. New York: Avon Books, 1978

LEES, ROBERT JAMES (1849–1931)

Robert James Lees was born in Hinckley, Leicestershire, England, in August 1849. He was one of six children and came from a Calvinistic background. At a very early age he exhibited mediumistic abilities, being able to go into a deep **trance**. His daughter's later description of him said, "Before he was twelve years of age he was a deep trance **medium**, and in that state manifested a high degree of culture, a perfect use of the English language, and a range of philosophic knowledge that astounded his listeners." It was no wonder, then, that his name came to the attention of **Queen Victoria**, who was interested in **Spiritualism**.

Prince Albert died in 1861. Within days of his death, Lees received a message for the Queen from him. A local newspaper editor who happened to be at the **séance** where Lees received the message, and he published it. Upon seeing the report, Queen Victoria sent two representatives to visit the boy medium. The two used false names. Lees again **channeled** information from the Prince, who recognized the two visitors from the Court and called them by their true names. The Prince went on to write a letter to the Queen through the entranced Lees. In the letter, he called Her Majesty by a pet name known only by the two of them. When the Queen received the letter she immediately summoned Lees to the palace.

Lees was invited to give a séance at Windsor Castle and there gave evidence that the deceased Prince Albert was still in attendance upon his wife. A number of séances followed and Lees was offered a permanent position at court. On the advice of his **spirit guide**, Lees declined. The

Queen's personal manservant, John Brown, was named as a substitute, although Lees continued to visit the Queen on a few rare occasions.

Lees went on to distinguish himself in a number of fields. In 1872, at the age of twenty-three, he joined the staff of *The Manchester Guardian* newspaper. There he met the publisher George Newnes, and together they produced the weekly periodical *Titbits*. Lees also became associated with General Booth and the Salvation Army.

In 1886, Lees toured America lecturing. He met Thomas Edison and began a friendship with him. Edison was very much interested in the possibility of life after death. Lees became one of the first people to have his voice recorded by Edison. On his return to England, Lees founded the People's League and spoke before crowds of several thousand. He assisted Scotland Yard on some difficult cases, including one which led to the arrest of Dr. Gallacher and his confederates known as the American-Irish Fenians. They were convicted and imprisoned for plotting to blow up the Houses of Parliament. Lees was also called in on the case of Jack the Ripper.

One Internet web site says, "Perhaps the most remarkable phase of this unique mediumship was the production of the series of volumes of which Robert Lees only claimed to be the amanuensis. One Christmas Eve a stranger suddenly appeared before him, though the door was locked … The stranger proceeded to dictate the remarkable volume *Through the Mists* (London, 1898), outlining the nature of the **spirit world**." This book created tremendous interest and went through more than twenty editions. There followed *The Life Elysian* (1905), *The Heretic* (1901), *An **Astral** Bridegroom* (1909), and *The Gate of Heaven* (1910).

Sources:

Fodor, Nandor: *Encyclopedia of Psychic Science*. London: Arthurs Press, 1933

Lees, Robert James: *Through the Mists*. London: William Rider, 1920

Robert James Lees Biography & Links: http://www.rjlees.co.uk

LEONARD, GLADYS OSBORNE (1882–1968)

Gladys Osborne was born in Lythom, Lancashire, England, on May 28, 1882. As a young girl she saw many visions. In her autobiography, *My Life In Two Worlds* (London, 1931), she wrote,

> In whatever direction I happened to be looking, the physical view of the wall, door, ceiling, or whatever it was, would disappear, and in its place would gradually come valleys, gentle slopes, lovely trees and banks covered with flowers, of every shape and hue. The scene seemed to extend for many miles, and I was conscious that I could see much farther than was possible with the ordinary physical scenery around me.

As a young singer, Gladys experimented with **table tipping**, working with two fellow entertainers in her dressing room. As a result of this she became greatly interested in **Spiritualism**. She developed her **clairvoyance**, clearly seeing **spirits** that came by way of the table. She said that she saw them "like clearly cut shadows, which showed up perfectly against the light background." She also had a little **clairaudience**, though it was not as frequent, nor as developed, as the clairvoyance.

In 1914, at the age of thirty-two—and then married to Frederick Leonard—she was directed to become a professional **medium** by her **spirit guide**. This guide was a young Hindu girl named Feda, who claimed to be her great-great-grandmother. Leonard did become a professional medium, of such quality that she was called "The Queen of English Mediums," "The British Mrs. Piper," (a reference to the great American medium Mrs. **Leonore E. Piper**) and "Greatest Trance Medium." Sir **Arthur Conan Doyle** said that she was "the greatest **trance** medium with whom the author is acquainted" (*The History of Spiritualism* London, 1926). She worked with Sir **Oliver Lodge**, bringing him communications from his son Raymond who had been killed in 1915, dur-

Famous British medium, Gladys Osbourne Leonard (1882–1968). *Courtesy Fortean Picture Library.*

where the spirit would say, for example, "In tomorrow's *Times*, on page 8, column 5, about six inches from the bottom, you will find a name which will recall intimate associations of your youth between the ages of 16-18." Thomas wrote two books on his experiments with the medium, *Some New Evidence for Human Survival* (1922) and *Life Beyond Death With Evidence* (1928).

Gladys Osborne Leonard's contribution to Spiritualism is summed up in the words of Sir Arthur Conan Doyle, "If the truth of Spiritualism depended upon Mrs. Leonard's powers alone, the case would be an overwhelming one, since she has seen many hundreds of clients and seldom failed to give complete satisfaction." Gladys Leonard died on March 19, 1968.

Sources:

Awtry-Smith, Marilyn: *"They" Paved the Way*. New York: Spiritualism & More, nd

Doyle, Sir Arthur Conan: *The History of Spiritualism*. New York: Doran, 1926

Fodor, Nandor: *Encyclopedia of Psychic Science*. London: Arthurs Press, 1933

LE SHAN, DR. LAWRENCE (B. 1920)

Dr. LeShan was head of the Department of Psychology at New York's Trafalgar Hospital and Institute of Applied Biology for ten years. He is one of the pioneers of **parapsychological** research in the United States. He served as a psychologist in the U.S. Army for six years before joining the Trafalgar Hospital. He holds a M.S. in Psychology from the University of Nebraska and a Ph.D. in Human Development from the University of Chicago. He has taught at Roosevelt University, Pace College, and the New School for Social Research, among others.

LeShan began exploring psychic **healing** in hopes of expanding the parameters of orthodox psychotherapy. He taught himself to be a healer mainly through techniques of meditation. This led him to further explore relationships between

ing World War I. In 1916, Sir Oliver Lodge published a book *Raymond, or Life and Death*. It was the founder of the **British College of Psychic Science, James Hewat McKenzie**, who introduced Leonard to Sir Oliver.

Occasionally when doing healings, Feda would defer to North Star, a **Native American** who did not speak but who brought about numerous **healings**. At the end of World War I in 1918, Leonard was engaged by the **Society for Psychical Research**. Out of seventy-three sittings, all of those involved agreed that "good evidence of surviving personality had been obtained and the complete trustworthiness of the medium could not be questioned."

The **psychical researcher** Rev. C. Drayton Thomas continued with experiments with Leonard for many years. Some of the evidential messages that came through were of the type mysticism, modern physics, and **psychic** phenomena. LeShan worked with the famous **medium Eileen Garrett**, spending more than 500 hours with her, and was extremely impressed with her powers of **psychometry**.

From 1970, LeShan was teaching psychic healing in New York. In 1974, he published his book *The Medium, the Mystic and the Physicist* (New York). He felt that there are different types of reality, such as "**clairvoyant** reality," "sensory reality," and "transpsychic reality." He has authored a number of books, which have been translated into eleven languages. They include *The Psychology of War*, *The Dilemma of Psychology*, and *How to Meditate*. LeShan has lectured extensively in the United States, Europe, and Israel.

Sources:

Fishley, Margaret: *The Supernatural*. London: Aldus, 1976

Holroyd, Stuart: *The Supernatural: Minds Without Boundaries*. London: Aldus, 1975

Shepard, Leslie A: *Encyclopedia of Occultism & Parapsychology*. New York: Avon Books, 1978

LEVITATION

Levitation is the raising into the air of physical objects such as tables, pianos, and even human beings, without visible means and contrary to the law of gravity. In **Spiritualism**, this is presumably accomplished through the agencies of the **spirits**. It happens during the **séances** of a **physical medium**. **Nandor Fodor** observes that levitation was well known in ancient times, being recorded in both the Old and the New Testaments of the **Bible**. Many Christian saints are supposed to have levitated (e.g. Saints Dunstan, Dominic, Thomas Aquinas, Edmund, and Ignatius Loyola). In recent times it is a feat claimed by advanced practitioners of **Transcendental Meditation**, after special training under the supervision of the Maharishi Mahesh Yogi at his headquarters in Switzerland. The British Spiritualist medium **Colin Evans** levitated before large audiences on several occasions in the 1930s and 1940s, and was photographed doing so.

The first Spiritualist **medium** to levitate was Henry C. Gordon, in February 1851. The Reverend **Stainton Moses** levitated, as did the famous physical medium **Daniel Dunglas Home**, traveling out of one window and in another, seventy feet above the ground and in front of witnesses. Mrs. **Agnes Nichol Guppy** was also supposed to have levitated. The levitating of séance room tables has been almost commonplace, with photographs often taken of such events (e.g. the sittings of **Eusapia Paladino**). Stainton Moses wrote, "As I was seated in the corner of the inner room my chair was drawn back into the corner and then raised off the floor about a foot, as I judged, and then allowed to drop to the floor whilst I was carried up in the corner." Sir William Crookes said of the phenomenon, "The evidence in favour of it is stronger than the evidence in favour of almost any natural phenomenon the British Association could investigate."

Levitating tables, **trumpets**, and other objects in séances is usually accomplished with the aid of **ectoplasm**, which exudes from the body of the medium. It is impaired by light, hence the fact that most levitations take place in the dark. Not all demand darkness however, including levitations of Daniel Dunglas Home and Colin Evans. Sir **William Crookes** described an occasion with Home:

> On one occasion I witnessed a chair, with a lady sitting on it, rise several inches from the ground. On another occasion, to avoid the suspicion of this being in some way performed by herself, the lady knelt on the chair in such a manner that its four feet were visible to us. It then rose about three inches, remained suspended for about ten seconds and then slowly descended. At another time two children, on separate occasions, rose from the floor with their chairs, in full daylight under (to me) most satisfactory conditions; for I was kneeling and keeping close watch upon the feet of the chair, observing distinctly that no one touched them ... There are at least a hundred instances of Mr. Home's rising from the ground, in the presence of as many persons.

Joe Nuzum demonstrates his ability to levitate.
Courtesy Fortean Picture Library.

Harry Boddington said, "Levitation in various forms is a frequent precursor or concomitant of materialization. ... When a solid sixteen-stone man is levitated, how are the forces of terrestrial gravitation overcome? Do spirit people make him lighter by extracting ponderous matter from his body, or do they fill him with a compound lighter than air which enables him silently, and without the least disturbance of the atmosphere, to float over one's head?" However it is accomplished, it seems that it *is* done.

An interesting case of levitation was demonstrated and photographed in India in 1936. An Englishman, P. Y. Plunkett, described the scene,

"The time was about 12:30 pm and the sun directly above us so that shadows played no part in the performance ... Standing quietly by was Subbayah Pullavah, the performer, with long hair, a drooping mous-

tache and a wild look in his eye. He salaamed to us and stood chatting for a while. He had been practicing this particular branch of yoga for nearly twenty years (as had past generations of his family)."

About 150 people gathered to watch. The performer went into a small tent arrangement and water was poured on the ground all around it. Anyone wearing leather-soled shoes was asked to remove them. After a few minutes helpers moved forward and took down the tent, revealing the yogi lying on his side, in a trance, but suspended in the air about three feet above the ground. He had a cloth-covered stick which stood beside him and his hand rested lightly on it but, according to Plunkett, there was no special connection between the stick and the yogi. Plunkett and friends examined all around, and underneath, the suspended figure but found nothing to explain the levitation. The tent was re-erected around him and Plunkett peeped through a crack to watch what happened. He said,

After a minute he appeared to sway and then very slowly began to descend, still in a horizontal position. He took about five minutes to move from the top of the stick to the ground, a distance of about three feet ... When Subbayah was back on the ground his assistants carried him over to where we were sitting and asked if we would try to bend his limbs. Even with assistance we were unable to do so.

The yogi was rubbed and splashed with cold water for five minutes or more before he came out of his trance. Plunkett's photographs of this event appeared in the *Illustrated London News* for June 6, 1936.

Sources:

Boddington, Harry: *The University of Spiritualism*. London: Spiritualist Press, 1947

Buckland, Raymond: *Buckland's Book of Spirit Communications*. St. Paul: Llewellyn, 2004

Doyle, Sir Arthur Conan: *The History of Spiritualism*. New York: Doran, 1926

Fodor, Nandor: *Encyclopedia of Psychic Science*. London: Arthurs Press, 1933

Illustrated London News. London: June 6, 1936

Spence, Lewis: *An Encyclopedia of the Occult.* London: George Routledge & Sons, 1920

LEY LINES

L eys (pronounced "lays") is the term used to indicate ancient straight lines that connect natural points of power in the earth. In his book *The Old Straight Track* (1925), Alfred Watkins (1855–1935), an early photographer and inventor of the pinhole camera, showed that there was a vast network of straight lines crisscrossing Britain, aligning large numbers of ancient sites, earthworks, standing stones, burial mounds and the like. He also suggested there were such ley lines in other parts of the world.

Many believe that the leys indicate the course of subtle earth energies. Where two or more leys cross is a power point that has, in the past, naturally drawn people to assemble or build structures such as standing stones, barrows, temples and churches. Today many people use dowsing rods and **pendulums** to map out the ley lines. Janet and Colin Bord give several examples of leys, such as the Montgomery ley on the Welsh border. In just six miles it includes six sites: Offa's Dyke; Montgomery Church; Montgomery Castle; Hendomen, the motte and bailey castle predating the Norman castle; Forden Gaer, a Roman camp; and a half mile of straight road exactly along the ley. All are in an exact straight line. One major ley runs from Glastonbury Abbey through Stonehenge and on to Canterbury Cathedral, over one hundred fifty miles from Somerset to Kent.

Sources:

Bord, Janet and Colin: *Ancient Mysteries of Britain.* London: Guild Publishing, 1986

Watkins, Alfred: *The Old Straight Track.* London: Methuen, 1925

LIGHT

L ight is the oldest British **Spiritualist** journal, founded in 1881 by **William Stainton Moses**

and Dawson Rogers. It was issued weekly. In recent years it was issued as the official journal of the **College of Psychic Studies**, London, England.

Sources:

Fodor, Nandor: *Encyclopedia of Psychic Science.* London: Arthurs Press, 1933

LILY DALE ASSEMBLY

O n December 3, 1855, the **Laona Free Association** was formed in Laona, New York. It was a reorganization of the older Religious Society of Free Thinkers and from it developed what is today known as the Lily Dale Assembly.

Lily Dale Assembly, beside Lake **Cassadaga**, is the world's oldest and largest **Spiritualist** community. It presently covers in excess of 160 acres, and has its own fire department and post office. The community was founded in 1879, though it had its beginnings earlier than that, in 1855, a few miles from where Lily Dale is now located.

In 1871, Spiritualists started holding regular picnic meetings on the land of **Willard Alden**, beside Lake Cassadaga. These began simply as excursions for fun and recreation, but quickly led to the dedication of Alden's Grove to the special care of the Spiritualists, with a series of one-day meetings featuring discussions and prominent lecturers. In 1877, **Jeremiah Carter**, one of the foremost members of the group, heard a voice telling him to "Go to Alden's and arrange for a **camp meeting**." The following morning he walked the six miles to the Alden Farm and sat down with Willard Alden to arrange the meeting. Extended camp seasons followed, the first such occurring on Tuesday September 11, 1877, and running till Sunday September 16, 1877. The following year the camp season was extended by ten days, the grounds were fenced in, and a cottage was built. Despite terrible rain storms, the crowd was bigger than before and an even longer meeting was planned for the next year.

Problems developed following Willard Alden's death. His son Theodore Alden demanded rent for use of the grounds. This led to the board deciding

The Forest Temple at Lily Dale Assembly in New York. Lily Dale is the world's oldest and largest Spiritualist community. *Courtesy Fortean Picture Library.*

to purchase their own property in 1879. Twenty acres were purchased on what is the present Lily Dale Assembly site. Mrs. Amelia Colby named the camp The Cassadaga Lake Free Assembly. In 1903, the name was changed to The City of Light, and three years later to The Lily Dale Assembly, because of the large number of water lilies on the lake. Albert Cobb was elected the first president of the association. Whole families toiled to clear trees and brush for camp sites, to build a horse stable, and to erect what became known as the Bough House. This was a building made of entwined boughs, with rough hewn logs for seats, that would be used for services. The first speaker was suffragette Elizabeth Lowe Watson.

The grounds were laid out for lots that could be rented for future cottages; the land was not to be sold. The rental fees for these lots were kept low with regard to the fact that the assembly was for everyone, regardless of wealth or social standing. On August 7, 1880, a hotel was opened. Originally the barn; it is known as a "hung suspension building." When additional floors were needed, each floor was raised and the new additions placed underneath. It was originally known as The Grand Hotel but today is the **Maplewood Hotel**. The first cottage was built by a Mr. Sage on what is today the site of the Marion Skidmore Library building. By 1893, there were 215 cottages with approximately forty families living there year round.

The **Lyceum** (Spiritualist's Sunday School) was started in a tent in 1881. By 1928, this had grown into the building currently there. In

August 1883, a large and impressive auditorium was built, with a floor measuring fifty feet by fifty feet with eleven rows of raised chairs. A tent originally housed the library, though this was later moved into the Assembly Hall. In 1924, the present impressive library building was built.

In 1887, an additional eighteen acres of land were purchased and the following year the United States Postal Service officially recognized the community by installing a post office. In 1888, the Assembly Hall was built and became famous for its "Thought Exchange." In 1892, construction started on the Octagon Building which today houses the **Medium's League**. It is one of only seven such buildings in the state of New York. There was a dance school in Lily Dale and for a short while, there was even a Ferris Wheel there. This had to be removed, however, because the excessive noise of its steam engine disturbed the various programs.

Many celebrities regularly visited Lily Dale, including **Susan B. Anthony**, Sir **Arthur Conan Doyle**, **Mae West**, and the Russian Countess Alexandra Tolstoy (Leo Tolstoy's daughter). It is said that Franklin and Eleanor Roosevelt also visited Lily Dale, but there seems no confirmation of that.

In 1895, the Alden House was purchased by Mrs. Abby Pettengill and renamed the Leolyn, after her granddaughter. Mrs. Pettengill then sold the building to the Assembly. The auditorium was remodeled in 1916, with seating increased to 1,200. Even so, many times during the history of Lily Dale people have stood three deep outside the auditorium in order to hear the lecture. A beautiful **healing** Temple was added by Louis Vosburg in 1955, under the direction of **Thomas John (Jack) Kelly**'s spirit guide.

The original **Fox Family** cottage was moved from **Hydesville** to the Lily Dale site in 1916, a gift from Benjamin Bartlett of Cambridge Springs, Pennsylvania. Tragically it was destroyed by a suspected arson fire in 1955, though some relics were saved, including the original peddler's tin box and the Fox Family **Bible**. Both are now on display in

the excellent **Lily Dale Museum**, run by an enthusiastic **Ron Nagy** and Joyce LaJudice.

As many as 30,000 people flock to Lily Dale each year. Today it is recognized internationally as a community that should be visited by every Spiritualist and everyone seeking comfort and proof of survival after death.

Sources:

Buckland, Raymond: *Buckland's Book of Spirit Communications*. St. Paul: Llewellyn, 2004

Putnam, Betty L: *History of Lily Dale*. Lily Dale: Lily Dale Historical Society, nd

Vogt, Paula M. and Joyce LaJudice: *Lily Dale Proud Beginnings: A Little Bit of History*. Lily Dale: Lily Dale Museum, 1984

LILY DALE MUSEUM

Located at the **Lily Dale Assembly** in New York, the Lily Dale Museum has developed into one of the finest **Spiritualist** museums in America, despite its small size.

Artifacts accumulated and were stored away until 1985, when Joyce LaJudice received permission to use the basement of the Marion Skidmore Library for a museum. However, because of the unsuitability of the basement in the winter months, the museum had to be relocated every year to the second floor of the Assembly offices. In 1995, the museum moved to its present home in the old schoolhouse. This was built in 1890 and used as a schoolhouse until 1938, when the government consolidated all one-room schools. The Community Club then utilized the building until 1995.

LaJudice organized the museum and ran it singlehandedly as Lily Dale's Historian and Museum Curator, until she was joined in 2002 by **Ron Nagy**. Nagy became a second Historian and quickly became a major figure in the organization and running of the museum. He was instrumental in discovering a wide variety of forgotten artifacts in the Assembly offices, including many priceless spirit paintings by both the **Bangs Sisters** and the

Campbell Brothers. Nagy is now considered the authority on such precipitated paintings.

An inventory of more than 3,000 items at the museum includes the **Fox Family** Bible, the peddler's chest that had belonged to the murdered **Charles Rosna**, spirit **slates** and **trumpets**, women's suffrage memorabilia, **medium**'s advertising signs, books by **Andrew Jackson Davis**, historical photographs, newspaper and magazine articles, and much more. It is a one-of-a-kind collection that is sought out by writers and researchers from around the world.

LINCOLN, ABRAHAM (1809–1865)

Abraham Lincoln attended many **séances**, even having some at his own home. He was as much a **Spiritualist** as anything else. He was not of any particular Christian faith, although he certainly did seem to believe in an **Infinite Intelligence**. In the days before the Civil War, only 25 to 35 percent of the population actually belonged to a Christian denomination. The vast majority did not belong to any church, though most seemed to have believed in an afterlife. Spiritualism competed with Christianity and, in the latter part of the nineteenth century, became the fastest growing religion in America.

The Lincolns had lost three of their four sons to childhood diseases so it was natural that Mary Todd Lincoln, the President's wife, wanted to attend séances. Colonel Simon F. Kase told of a notable one in the home of Mrs. Laurie, which both he and the President attended. The Laurie's daughter, Mrs. Miller, was the **medium** and she played the piano while in **trance**. As she played, two legs of the instrument **levitated** several inches off the floor then repeatedly banged back to the floor to beat time to the music. As it kept rising up, Kase and two soldiers who were present climbed on the piano together but were unable to make it settle down again until the medium stopped playing. It was reported that the legs rose as high as four inches off the floor.

Abraham Lincoln had many **prophetic dreams**, including one of his own death. In early April 1865, he dreamed he was lying in bed when he heard the sound of sobbing. Getting up and leaving his bedroom, he went into the East Room of the White House where he saw a line of people filing past a catafalque. They were all paying their respects to the figure lying in state, guarded by four soldiers. The face of the figure was covered so, in the dream, Lincoln asked one of the soldiers who had died. The soldier replied, "The President. He was killed by an assassin." Lincoln later told his wife, Mary, and several friends about the **dream**. It was later that same month that he was shot and killed by John Wilkes Booth. Another of Lincoln's prophetic dreams was of a damaged ship sailing away with a Union ship in hot pursuit. Lincoln had this dream on a number of occasions, each time just before an important Union victory.

At one séance which the Lincolns attended, a teenage girl approached the President. It was **Nettie Colburn** Maynard, a young medium. In trance, she began to lecture Lincoln on the necessity for emancipation. She spoke to him for almost an hour, stating that the Civil War could not come to an end until all men were free. When Nettie came out of her trance and saw to whom she had been speaking, she ran from the room in fright and embarrassment. But two days later, when Lincoln and his wife were at another séance, Nettie appeared again and did the same thing, lecturing the President about freeing the slaves. Kase reported, "President Lincoln was convinced as to the course he should pursue; the command coming from that all-seeing **spirit** through the instrumentality of the **angel** world was not to be overlooked ... thus the **prediction** of the medium was verified."

In 1854, ten years before the end of the Civil War, 15,000 Americans had petitioned Congress for a scientific study of Spiritualism, but the request was denied. The tremendous death toll of the war led to even more of an interest in Spiritualism.

Abraham Lincoln (1809–1865), President of the United States during the Civil War. *Alexander Gardner/Getty Images.*

Sources:

Headon, Deirdre (ed.): *Quest for the Unknown—Charting the Future*. Pleasantville: Reader's Digest, 1992

Shepard, Leslie A: *Encyclopedia of Occultism & Parapsychology*. New York: Avon Books, 1978

Stemman, Roy: *The Supernatural: Spirits and Spirit Worlds*. London: Aldus, 1975

LIVERMORE, CHARLES F.

Charles F. Livermore was a successful New York banker whose wife Estelle died in 1860. As a **Spiritualist**, Livermore believed that it was possible to contact Estelle. He asked Kate Fox, one of the **Fox Sisters**, if she would be the **medium** to make contact for him. In 1861, Kate agreed to do this. By that time Margaret Fox had married and Leah had remarried; both retiring from professional **mediumship**. Kate was the only one of the three Fox Sisters to continue mediumship at that time.

Kate Fox was engaged to hold **séances** exclusively for Livermore. She worked for him for five years, holding nearly 400 séances, mostly at Livermore's home. A number of prominent people attended these sittings. Precautions were taken, such as the locking of all doors and windows, and careful records were kept. Kate, for the first time, began to produce **materializations**. However, it was not until the forty-third séance that Estelle materialized. As a materialized form, she was not able to speak more than a few words. Communication took place mainly by **rappings** and **automatic writing**. Both Estelle and another **spirit** form claiming to be Ben Franklin wrote on special cards provided by Livermore. While Estelle wrote, Kate's hands were held securely by one of the sitters. Livermore claimed that the handwriting on the card was the same as his wife's.

At the 388th séance in 1866, Estelle announced that she would not be returning. Livermore showed his gratitude to Kate for all her years of service by giving her a trip to England, which she undertook in 1871. According to Sir **Arthur Conan Doyle**, "He [Livermore] provided for all her needs, and thus removed any necessity for her to give professional sittings. He also arranged for her to be accompanied by a congenial woman companion."

Livermore himself said, in a letter to Spiritualist Benjamin Coleman, "Miss Fox, taken all in all, is no doubt the most wonderful living medium. Her character is irreproachable and pure. I have received so much through her powers of mediumship during the past ten years which is solacing, instructive and astounding, that I feel greatly indebted to her, and desire to have her taken good care of while absent from her home and friends."

Sources:

Doyle, Sir Arthur Conan: *The History of Spiritualism*. New York: Doran, 1926

Stemman, Roy: *The Supernatural: Spirits and Spirit Worlds*. London: Aldus, 1975

LODGE, SIR OLIVER JOSEPH (1851–1940)

Oliver Joseph Lodge was born at Penkhull, Staffordshire, England, on June 12, 1851. He was destined to become a world famous physicist and psychical researcher. At twenty-one, Lodge entered University College, London, and obtained his doctorate in 1877. Two years later he became assistant professor of applied mathematics at the college. In 1881, he became the Chair of Physics in University College, Liverpool, where he remained until 1900. At that time Lodge became the first principal of Birmingham University. He was knighted in 1902 and retired in 1919.

Although Lodge had dabbled in **psychical research** since 1883, it was from 1910 onward that he became especially prominent in the field. He sat with such **mediums** as **Eusapia Paladino** and **Leonore Piper**. He witnessed Paladino **séances** in the house of Professor **Charles Richet**, on the Île Rouchard. In his report for the *Journal* of the **Society for Psychical Research**, he wrote, "There is no further room in my mind for doubt. Any person without invincible prejudice who had had the same experience would come to the same broad conclusion, *viz.*, that things hitherto held impossible do actually occur." His sessions with Leonore Piper, a **mental medium**, were very thorough, the first sitting taking place in 1889 in England. His first report was published the following year.

In 1908, that Lodge publicly stated that he believed it was quite possible to make the connection and to speak with those who had passed on. In 1913, speaking as President of the British Association, he said he had become convinced that "memory and affection are not limited to that association with matter by which alone they can manifest themselves here and now, and that personality persists beyond bodily death."

On August 8, 1915, Leonore Piper gave Lodge a message from the spirit of **Richard Hodgson**, who had died ten years before. The message was an obscure reference to the Roman poet Horace's

Sir Oliver Lodge, noted physicist, mathematician, and psychical researcher. *Courtesy Fortean Picture Library.*

account of his own narrow escape from a falling tree, due to the intervention of Faunus, the ancient Roman deity of wild nature. The message indicated that Lodge would have such a near-devastating experience but would survive it. Shortly after, Lodge received news that his son, **Raymond**, had been killed in World War I action on September 14, which was a tremendous blow to Lodge.

Lodge was a spokesman for **Spiritualism** who strongly believed in the ability to communicate with the dead. His many books include *Man and the Universe* (1908), *The Survival of Man* (1909), *Life and Matter* (1912), *Science and Religion* (1914), *Raymond, or Life and Death* (1916), *Raymond, Revised* (1922), *Why I Believe in Personal Immortality* (1928), *The Reality of the Spiritual World* (1930), and his autobiography *Past Years* (1931). He died at Lake, near Salisbury, England, on August 22, 1940.

Sources:

Doyle, Sir Arthur Conan: *The History of Spiritualism*. New York: Doran, 1926

Encyclopedia Britannica. Chicago: William Benton, 1964

Fodor, Nandor: *Encyclopedia of Psychic Science*. London: Arthurs Press, 1933

LYCEUM

The **National Spiritualist Association of Churches** defines the Lyceum as "The school of a liberal and harmonious education" whose object is "the unfoldment of the faculties in their due order and degree." The word Lyceum comes from the **Greek** *Lukeios*. The Greek Lyceum was in a grove near Athens and it was there that Aristotle and other philosophers taught. The students made their own rules and, every ten days, elected one of their number to supervise the school.

The first Spiritualist Lyceum in America was started by **Andrew Jackson Davis** on January 25, 1863. It was located at Dodsworth Hall, 806 Broadway, New York. Davis intended to bring lessons pertaining to Nature to children. He had a vision of children grouped together, studying lessons about the natural sciences and the laws of Nature. He saw these lessons freeing the children from fears and superstitions. Davis said that the teachings of the Lyceum would include "healthful development of the body, the exercise of the reasoning faculties, the unfolding of the social and spiritual affections by harmonious and happy methods."

In 1864, The Progressive Lyceum was organized in Philadelphia, Pennsylvania. In 1866, the Chelsea Lyceum was organized in Masachusetts. In 1897, at the Fifth Annual National Convention, the first National Spiritualist Lyceum Association was organized. 1898 saw Lyceums come into being in Boston, East Boston, Charlestown, and the following year at Cambridgeport, Washington, D.C., Philadelphia, Providence, New York, Baltimore, Cincinnati, St. Louis, Memphis, New Orleans, Milwaukee, Chicago, Springfield, and Rockford.

The Lyceums have an official publication called the *Spotlight*, which was started by Rev. Elsie Bunts and ran as *The Spot Light* from 1945 to 1947. There is also an official *Spiritualist Lyceum Manual*.

The first Lyceum in England began in 1866 in Nottingham. Others followed in 1870, 1871, and 1876. The British Spiritualists' Lyceum Union formed in 1890, and published the *British Lyceum Manual*, *The Spiritual Songster*, and *Spiritualism for the Young*. The official periodical was *The Spiritualists' Lyceum Magazine* starting in January 1890, and then the magazine *The Lyceum Banner* appeared in November 1890.

Sources:

Spiritualist Lyceum Manual. Lily Dale: National Spiritualist Association of Churches, 1993

MacLaine, Shirley (b. 1934)

Shirley MacLean Beaty was born in Richmond, Virginia, on April 24, 1934. Her father, a professor at Johns Hopkins and amateur violinst, was Ira Owens Beaty. Her mother, a drama teacher, was Kathlyn MacLean Beaty. Her brother is the actor Warren Beatty.

Having weak ankles, MacLaine was enrolled in ballet classes, which increased her improved strength and love of dancing. After her junior year in Washington-Lee High School, she moved to New York with dreams of becoming a Broadway actress. Her first part was in the chorus of *Oklahoma*. She eventually became an understudy to Carol Haney in *The Pajama Game*. When Haney became indisposed, MacLaine took over, was noticed by Hollywood director/producer Hal. B. Wallis, and went to work for Paramount Pictures.

In 1954, MacLaine married aspiring producer Steve Parker. They had a daughter, Sachi, and lived an estranged marriage for many years, finally divorcing in 1987. During the 1960s, she traveled to **Egypt**, Africa, Calcutta, Indonesia, and the Himalayas, meeting with various leaders and **healers** in her search for truth. Today she lives what she describes as "a rich spiritual life," every morning performing an hour's *xigong* ("cultiva-

tion of the life force"), and arranging house and garden by way of *feng shui*.

From early in her life MacLaine believed that we create our own reality. He father expanded her horizons with his knowledge of psychology and philosophy, instilling in her a strong work ethic. But she felt that her father never really took her seriously until she began writing books in the 1970s. He shared her interest in **metaphysics**. She explored **reincarnation** and **channeling**, even giving seminars in these at one time. She said that she stopped this because "I don't want to be anybody's guru." She added, "I'm still trying to find out who I am. I don't know if I ever will, but the journey is the discovery." She once said that "acting is an extremely metaphysical experience because you're creating your own reality every day."

In her bestselling books *Dancing In the Light* and *Out on a Limb*, MacLaine describes how her life has been changed through contact with **mediums** and channelers. She writes, "I found myself gently but firmly exposed to dimensions of time and space that heretofore, for me, belonged in science fiction or what I would describe as the **occult**. But it happened to me ... What I learned as a result has enabled me to get on with my life

Famed actress Shirley MacLaine risked public ridicule by describing her experiences and theories concerning out-of-body travel and reincarnation in her book, *Out on a Limb. AP/WideWorld Photos.*

as an almost transformed human being." She refers to channeler **Kevin Ryerson** as "one of the (human) telephones in my life."

Sources:

Leonard, Sue (ed): *Quest For the Unknown—Life Beyond Death.* Pleasantville: Reader's Digest, 1992

Shirley MacLaine Homepage: http://www.shirleymac laine.com

Shirley MacLaine Interview: http://www.grandtimes. com/ maclaine.html

MAETERLINCK, MAURICE (1862–1949)

Maurice Maeterlinck was born in Ghent, Belgium, on August 29, 1862. He was edu-cated at the Collège Sainte-Barbe and then at the university of Ghent. In 1887 he settled in Paris, France, but on the death of his father he returned to Ghent permanently.

In 1889, Maeterlinck published a volume of verse and also a play. Two more plays followed the next year and in 1891, he published *Les Sept Princesses.* He developed a strong leaning to mysti-cism which showed in many of his works. In 1898, he issued a monograph on the ethics of mysticism, titled *La Sagesse et la destine.* A number of his works demonstrate his fascination with **psychical** phenomena. He once commented, "The question of fraud and imposture are naturally the first that suggest themselves when we begin the study of these phenomena. But the slightest acquaintance with the life, habits and proceedings of the three or four leading **mediums** is enough to remove even the faintest shadow of suspicion."

Maurice Maeterlinck wrote many essays and plays, and received the Nobel Prize for literature in 1911. He died near Nice, France, on May 6, 1949. Two of his books dealing with the paranor-mal are *The Great Secret* (1920) and *The Unknown Guest* (1914).

Sources:

Fodor, Nandor: *Encyclopedia of Psychic Science.* Lon-don: Arthurs Press, 1933

MAGINOT, ADÈLE

Adèle Maginot was the first French **medium** to have her phenomena recorded and strict-ly tested. She had been **psychic** from childhood and met **Alphonse Cahagnet** (1809–1885), who published the first book on **spirit** communica-tions in 1848 (*Magnétisme Arcanes de la vie future dévoilé*—translated as *The Celestial Telegraph*). Maginot served as a **channel** for spirit communi-cations for Cahagnet, and from the summer of 1848, she put many people in contact with their departed loved ones. She was apparently a fine **clairvoyant.** She was also able to locate missing persons who were still alive on this plane. **Nan-dor Fodor** said, "Adèle was put into **trance.** She saw the spirits of the departed, described them and gave an intimate knowledge of their family circumstances."

Sources:

Fodor, Nandor: *Encyclopedia of Psychic Science*. London: Arthurs Press, 1933

MAK, ARIE (B. 1914)

Arie Mak was born on November 23, 1914, in Alkmaar, the Netherlands. Mak was an instructor and director at Sneek technical School in the Netherlands from 1939 on. He was a member of the Amsterdam Parapsychologische Kring and prior to that, he was Research Officer for the Dutch Society for **psychical research**. He studied **clairvoyance**, **telepathy**, and **psychokinesis**, testing clairvoyance quantitatively. He also made a study of evidence suggesting **reincarnation**.

Sources:

Fodor, Nandor: *Encyclopedia of Psychic Science*. London: Arthurs Press, 1933

MANA

Mana is a general term for the mysterious spiritual power that is found throughout the universe in humans, animals, and even inanimate objects. In general ethnological usage, the term is applied to the concept of spiritual power found in sacred things, places, people and objects. Originally it was specifically a Melanesian and Polynesian term, where it was thought to be a power derived from divine ancestors. Mana is not supernatural. It is a natural force by which shamans, **witches**, magicians, and healers are able to cure sickness, control forces, bless, and even curse.

Mircea Eliade says that anyone possessing large quantities of mana in the Solomon Islands is regarded as *saka*, or "burning." The idea of mystical heat belongs to magic generally and **shamanism** in particular. Many primitive tribes have a word meaning heat or burning to describe

the energy of mana. When hands-on **healing** is done, the patient invariably feels great heat coming from the hands, to the point where sometimes there are red marks left on the body despite the fact that there was no actual physical contact made.

The power of a male or female virgin in magic (and especially as a sacrifice, in novels and movies) comes from the belief that by sexual intercourse the mana is lost to the powers of the earth; this through both the emission of semen and by virtue of the heart generated in the union. A virgin, therefore, possesses far greater mana than a non-virgin. The ancient Chibcha of Colombia would take a young boy at puberty for sacrifice to the sun god. But he would be released if he managed to have intercourse with a woman, for he would have lost his mana. The power generated in witchcraft rituals is referred to as mana, as is the power found in anything from **crystals** to trees. Another term used interchangeably with mana is *prana*, a Sanskrit word with the same meaning as mana. Also used are the Chinese *Ch'i*, or *Q'i*, and the Japanese *Ki*.

Sources:

Buckland, Raymond: *The Witch Book: The Encyclopedia of Witchcraft, Wicca and Neo-Paganism*. Detroit: Visible Ink Press, 2002

Buckland, Raymond: *Witchcraft From the Inside*. St. Paul: Llewellyn, 1995

Eliade, Mircea: *Shamanism: Archaic Techniques of Ecstasy*. Princeton University Press/Bollingen Series LXXVI, 1974

Leach, Maria (ed): Funk & Wagnalls Standard Dictionary of Folklore, Mythology and Legend. New York: Harper & Row, 1984

Manifestation *see* Materialization

MANNING, MATTHEW (B. 1955)

Matthew Manning was born in Devon and grew up in Shelford, Cambridge, England. While still a boy, at the age of puberty Manning caused **poltergeist**-like phenomena to occur in his home. Objects would move around, untouched by

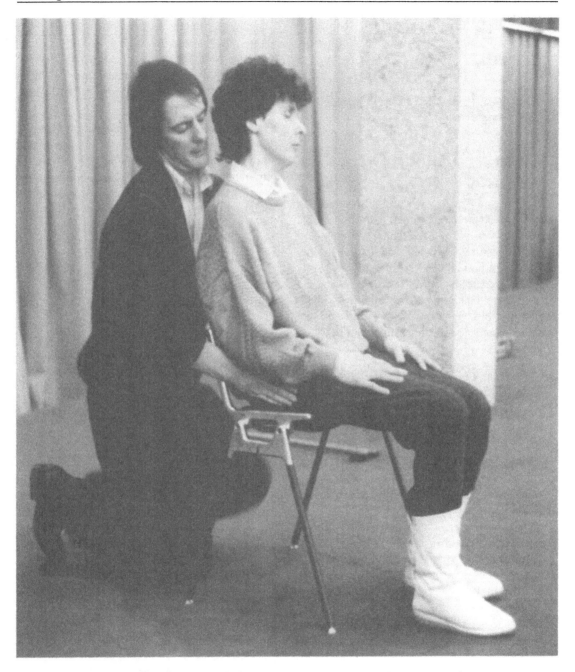

British apport medium and automatic artist Matthew Manning perfoms a healing. Manning began experiencing psychic phenomena and communicating with spirits at the age of 11. *Courtesy Fortean Picture Library.*

human hands, there were **rappings**, and writing would appear on the walls and ceilings. Dr. George Owen, a Cambridge **psychical researcher** and investigator, felt that it was the twelve-year-old boy's unconscious mind that was causing the phenomena.

Manning was sent off to boarding school and his powers went with him. Heavy iron beds were moved about in the dormitory; bricks, pebbles, knives and glass would appear mysteriously as **apports**, together with mysterious pools of water. Manning also found that he was able to do **automatic writing**, which seemed to bring to an end the poltergeist phenomena. The writing would be in English, German, Greek, Italian, Latin, Arabic, and Russian. While still a teenager, he wrote *The Link*, a book in which he described how he made contact with the **spirits** of dead poets and painters. He said that he merely sat quietly with pen and paper ready, and concentrated on the artist's work. He didn't go into a **trance**; the pen would start to move and he produced work in the same style as that of the deceased artist. The pen usually started in the center of the page, and eventually filled the paper with what seemed like carefully planned art. The style was invariably and immediately recognizable as that of a particular deceased artist. Usually it was signed by that artist with what appeared to be an authentic signature. Some of the works produced were copies of existing works by the artists, but there were also some new pictures obviously in the style of the artists claiming to be producing them. All of these works were produced in one or two hours, while living artists would take six or more hours to produce such work.

Producing art from dead artists left Manning feeling extremely tired. He said, "No other communicator tires me as much as Picasso does. After only a few minutes, the time it takes him to do one drawing, I feel worn out and cannot continue for at least twenty-four hours." Pablo Picasso was the first artist who came through Manning starting in 1973, three months after the artist's death in April of that year. Manning said his hand moved with "excessive force" as he worked. Later artists to use the **mediumship** of Manning included Paul Klee, Arthur Rackham, Henri Matisse, Leonardo da Vinci, Albrecht Dürer, Monet, Beatrix Potter, and Aubrey Beardsley. Manning said that Picasso was the only communicator who was not confused about using color. According to

Lynn Picknet, "he directed Matthew Manning's hand to pick out certain felt-tipped pens from a box of mixed colors." Most of his other communicators utilized pen and ink.

Manning's **spirit guide** was named Thomas Penn. Through him, many apports were produced including such unusual items as a loaf of bread thought to be seventy years old, fossils, and an old beeswax candle. After watching **Uri Geller** on television, Manning found he was able to bend spoons and other metal objects, cause alarms to go off, and stop clocks and other machinery. He also developed strong healing abilities and rather than try to "cash in on" his artistic mediumship, has spent many years as a relatively anonymous **healer**.

Sources:

Fishley, Margaret: *The Supernatural*. London: Aldus, 1976

Foreman, Laura (ed): *Mysteries of the Unknown: Spirit Summonings*. New York: Time-Life Books, 1989

Manning, Matthew: *The Link*. London: Holt Rinehart, 1974

Picknett, Lynn: *Mysteries of Mind Space & Time; the Unexplained: A Gallery of Psychic Art*. Westport: H. S. Stuttman, 1992

Randles, Jenny and Peter Hough: *The Afterlife: An Investigation into the Mysteries of Life after Death*. London: Piatkus, 1993

MANSFIELD, DR. J. V.

Dr. J. V. Mansfield has been called the "Spiritual Postmaster" because of the way in which he dealt with sealed letters addressed to the **spirit world**. In the 1870s, Mansfield ran advertisements in the *Banner of Light* **Spiritualist** magazine, asking people to send him sealed letters. This they did; some going to extraordinary lengths to guarantee that the contents were inaccessible. For example, one person sewed up the letter all the way around, on a sewing machine. Mansfield would lay out the letters on a table and then pass his left hand over them. In his right hand he would hold a pen poised over paper. He would suddenly stop at one of the letters, apparently read it **clairvoyantly**, and then start writing an answer from the **spirit** to whom it was addressed. Sometimes the letters, and Mansfield's **channeled** reply, would be in a foreign language. He wrote some in Latin, Greek, Spanish, German, Arabic, Sanskrit, and Chinese.

Mansfield's **séances** were witnessed by many people and his **mediumship** was fully described in Dr. N. B. Wolfe's book *Startling Facts in Modern Spiritualism*.

Sources:

Fodor, Nandor: *Encyclopedia of Psychic Science*. London: Arthurs Press, 1933

Podmore, Frank: *Modern Spiritualism*. London: 1902; reprinted as *Mediums of the Nineteenth Century*. New York: University Books, 1963

MANTRA

A Sanskrit word meaning a significant sound that is known to psychically affect human beings. When repeated over and over, the mantra can be used as the point of focus for **meditation**; the repetition usually being done mentally or silently. The mantra may be a single syllable, a word, or a short series of sounds or words. The sound is usually one designed to bring about a higher state of consciousness in the individual, evoking **psychic** energy throughout the body. The mantra word/sound does not usually have any specific meaning.

Sources:

Bletzer, June G.: *The Encyclopedia Psychic Dictionary*. Lithia Springs: New Leaf, 1998

MAPLEWOOD HOTEL

The Maplewood Hotel is the main accommodation at **Lily Dale Assembly** in New York. The building was originally a stable. Instead of constructing a new hotel, the stable was converted and expanded in 1879. Benjamin Baldwin was hired by Albert Cobb, President of The Cassadaga Lake Free Association, to be responsible for the building of the hotel. Named the Grand Hotel, it was ready for opening on August 7, 1880. The first registered guests were **Wilberforce J. Colville**, well known **Spiritualist** author and lecturer, O. P. Kellogg, W. D. Bugbee, and A. Kendall.

During inclement weather, lectures and classes were held in the Grand Hotel until the auditorium was built in 1883. The hotel building is what is known as a "hung building" in that when a new floor was added, the existing floor(s) was raised and the new one added underneath. This was done in 1883 for the addition of the second floor, and again in 1886 for the third floor. In 1903, the name was changed to the Maplewood Hotel.

Originally the hotel had its own 250-person dining room. In May, 1983, the Leolyn hotel at Lily Dale suffered a fire and consequently the Maplewood dining room was converted into more hotel rooms. There was a full renovation in 1967: The second floor balcony was removed and the building was given aluminum siding. A new roof was put on and the original dormers were removed.

Sources:

Vogt, Paula M.: *Historical Maplewood Hotel: Continuous Use since 1880*. Lily Dale: Lily Dale Museum, nd

Vogt, Paula M. and Joyce LaJudice: *Lily Dale Proud Beginnings: A Little Bit of History*. Lily Dale: Lily Dale Museum, 1984

Margery *see* **Crandon, Mina Stinson**

MARSHALL, MARY (1842–1884)

Mary Marshall was the first professional English **medium**. She introduced both Sir **William Crookes** and Dr. Alfred Russel Wallace to **Spiritualism**. Dr. Wallace began his experiments in the summer of 1865, and was especially impressed by **spirit** messages received through Marshall, who operated in full daylight. Although a stranger to Wallace, Marshal was able to tell him his brother's name, where he died, and the name of the last person who saw him alive. Marshall produced **rappings**, caused a table to move and to **levitate**, and produced writing on glass—a forerunner of **slate writing**.

Thomas P. Barkas was the first to write about Mary Marshall in his book *Outlines of Ten Years' Investigations into the Phenomena of Modern Spiritualism* (London, 1862). Marshall produced some **direct voice** from 1867 onward. At these, the spirit John King manifested.

Sources:

Fodor, Nandor: *Encyclopedia of Psychic Science*. London: Arthurs Press, 1933

MARYLEBONE SPIRITUALIST ASSOCIATION

Marylebone Spiritualist Association is one of the oldest **Spiritualist** organizations in the world and also one of the largest. The headquarters is located in London's Belgrave Square. Founded in 1872, its purpose is to study **psychic** phenomena and disseminate information and evidence obtained through its **mediums**. By 1960, the association changed its name to the Spiritualist Association of Great Britain. It has more than 200,000 visitors per year. Today it holds **séances** and does **spiritual healing**, and its headquarters contains a chapel, library, meeting hall, prayer rooms, and **meditation** rooms.

The association organizes what is billed as "the world's largest séance" at the Royal Albert Hall in London. Held on November 11—Armistice Day in Great Britain—it enables thousands of people to hear the top mediums convey messages from those who died in the two World Wars.

Sources:

Guiley, Rosemary Ellen: *The Encyclopedia of Ghosts and Spirits*. New York: Facts On File, 1992

Stemman, Roy: *The Supernatural: Spirits and Spirit Worlds*. London: Aldus, 1975

MASSEY, GERALD (1828–1907)

Gerald Massey was a popular poet and writer who lost much of his popularity when he endorsed **Spiritualism**. In his volume of poetry *A Tale of Eternity*, he dealt at length with his experiences in a **haunted** house. He said, "For the truth's sake I ought to explain that the spiritualism to be found in my poetry is no delusive idealism, derived from hereditary belief in a resurrection of the dead. My faith in the future life is founded upon facts in nature and realities of my own personal experience ... they have given me proof palpable that our very own human identity and intelligence do persist after the blind of darkness has been drawn down in death."

When **Emma Hardinge Britten** left England for Australia, there was a large gathering at which Gerald Massey presided. His speech, with some later additions, was published under the title *Concerning Spiritualism*.

Sources:

Fodor, Nandor: *Encyclopedia of Psychic Science*. London: Arthurs Press, 1933

MATERIALIZATION

A materialization or manifestation is something that has been brought into form and made evident to the senses. One of the best known examples of materialization is given in the **Bible**, in Matthew 17, when two long-deceased men, Moses and Elijah, appear in solid form before **Jesus** and three Apostles. In **Spiritualist** séances it is the appearance of a **spirit**, frequently through the use of **ectoplasm** exuding from the **medium**. This may be a seemingly solid spirit face, a hand, or a full figure. It is a part of **physical mediumship** and was prevalent in the latter part of the nineteenth century and early part of the twentieth century.

Many mediums were caught producing materializations fraudulently. One such medium, Rosina Showers—a friend of **Florence Cook**—even wrote a confession in which she described a method of working. It involved wearing an easily removable dress with many shifts underneath it, and hiding a filmy muslin veil in her underwear. Florence Cook herself was never caught in fraud.

South American medium Carlo Mirabelli (left, in trance) with Dr. Carlos de Castro (right) and the materialized spirit of deceased poet Giuseppe Parini. *Courtesy Fortean Picture Library.*

She was a very successful materialization medium who was thoroughly investigated by Sir **William Crookes**. Crookes stated that the materialized form of Katie King produced by Florence Cook was actually taller than the medium, had a larger face and longer fingers. Whereas Cook had black hair and a dark complexion, her **spirit guide** King had a fair complexion and light auburn hair. Crookes also saw both medium and spirit side by side at one time. Katie King often allowed the sitters at the séance to touch her drapery. Sometimes she cut as many as a dozen pieces from the lower part of her skirt and made presents of them to different observers. The holes were immediately filled in. Crookes examined the skirt inch by inch, and found no holes or any marks to indicate that anything had been cut out.

Eva C., another materialization medium, was studied by the **British Psychical Research Society**, though she failed to impress them. In her later **séances**, she was unable to produce as well-developed forms as earlier and the materializations were much slower and, seemingly, more difficult. Eva was made to wear special dresses or even, on many occasions, to sit in the nude. Of a séance held on April 15, 1912, Professor **Charles Richet** said, "The manifestations began at once. White substance appeared on the neck of the medium, and then a head was formed which moved from left to right and placed itself on the medium's head. A photograph was taken. After the flashlight the head reappeared by the side of Eva's head, about sixteen inches from it, connected by a long bunch of white substance. It looked like the head of a man … a woman's head then appeared on the right." The medium was carefully searched both before and immediately after the sitting. However, many of the photographs obtained of ectoplasmic heads look remarkably as though they are two-dimensional pictures cut from a magazine.

Guiley reports, "In his work for the Seybert Commission, Dr. H. H. Furness attended more than twenty materialization séances. He found some mediums more practiced than others, but applauded the charming work of most as they gracefully appeared as spirits, lightly appearing and disappearing through the **cabinet** curtains. Throughout it all, he never ceased to be amazed at the faith of the sitters, who recognized their husbands, fathers, mothers, wives and children in the costumed persona of the medium." On the other hand, Professor Richet said in *Thirty Years of Psychical Research* (1923), "I shall not waste time in stating the absurdities, almost the impossibilities, from a psycho-physiological point of view, of this phenomena. A living being or living matter, formed under our eyes, which has its proper warmth, apparently a circulation of blood, and a physiological respiration which has also a kind of psychic personality having a will distinct from the will of the medium, in a word, a new human being! This is surely the climax of marvels. Nevertheless, it is a fact."

Leah Underhill, one of the **Fox Sisters**, was the first to produce a materialized spirit form. This she did at a séance for Robert Dale Owen in 1860. Owen stated that a luminous, veiled figure appeared and walked about the séance room before disappearing. Shortly after this, Leah's sister Kate produced a materialization of **Charles Livermore**'s deceased wife Estelle. This then became a regular part of the sittings Kate gave for the banker. She also produced the figure of Benjamin Franklin. The first English medium to produce materializations was **Agnes Guppy**. Some of the materialized figures that appear at séances walk freely about the room, touching the sitters and allowing the sitters to touch them. It has been said that the figures feel warm to the touch, like living flesh.

Sources:

Fodor, Nandor: *Encyclopedia of Psychic Science.* London: Arthurs Press, 1933

Guiley, Rosemary Ellen: *The Encyclopedia of Ghosts and Spirits.* New York: Facts On File, 1992

Leonard, Sue (ed): *Quest For the Unknown—Life Beyond Death.* Pleasantville: Reader's Digest, 1992

Melton, J. Gordon: *The Encyclopedia of American Religions.* Wilmington: McGrath, 1978

Spence, Lewis: *An Encyclopedia of the Occult.* London: George Routledge & Sons, 1920

Maynard, Mrs. *see* Colburn, Nettie

McCONNELL, R. A. (B. 1914)

Born in Pennsylvania, R. A. McConnell studied at the Carnegie Institute of Technology, where he obtained a B.S. in physics in 1935. In 1947, he received a Ph.D. in physics from the University of Pittsburgh. A member of the American Physical Society, Biophysical Society, Institute of Radio Engineers, and the **Parapsychological Association,** he was very active in **psychical research** and was the President of the Parapsychological Association in 1958.

McConnell wrote widely on the subject of parapsycholoy and co-wrote, with Dr. Gertrude Schmeidler, *E.S.P. and Personality Patterns* (1958). He contributed chapters to a Ciba Foundation symposium on *Extrasensory Perception* in 1956, and a symposium edited by **Eileen J. Garrett,** *Does Man Survive Death?* In 1971, he published *E.S.P. Curriculum Guide,* which was aimed at teachers wishing to teach **extrasensory perception** and related subjects. He wrote many articles for a variety of publications, including *Scientific Monthly, Journal of Experimental Psychology,* and *Journal of Psychology.*

Sources:

McConnell, R. A.: *E.S.P. Curriculum Guide.* New York: Simon & Schuster, 1971

McDOUGALL, DR. WILLIAM (1871–1938)

William McDougall was born June 22, 1871, in Lancashire, England. He was educated at Owens College, Manchester; St. Thomas Hospital, London; and at Oxford University and Göttingen University. McDougall was a professor at Harvard and one of the leading psychologists of his time. In 1900, he married Anne Amelia Hickmore.

McDougall developed an interest in **psychical research** and was a major influence in the development of **parapsychology**. He was President of the **Society for Psychical Research** in 1920 and President of the **American Society for Psychical Research** in 1921. He was also a member of the *Scientific American* committee that investigated **Mina Stinson Crandon**'s (Margery) **mediumship** from 1923 to 1925. Sir **Arthur Conan Doyle** said of that investigation, "Dr. McDougall was in a position where his whole academic career would obviously be endangered by the acceptance of an unpopular explanation." The general consensus of the committee was that Margery was a fraud, but as Doyle pointed out, the results were strongly slanted by the perceived effects of a positive outcome on the careers of the investigators. Doyle summed up the committee's findings with the comments, "It was difficult to say which was the more annoying: **Houdini** the conjurer, with his preposterous and ignorant theories of fraud, or such 'scientific' sitters as Professor McDougall, of Harvard, who, after fifty sittings and signing as many papers at the end of each sitting to endorse the wonders recorded, was still unable to give any definite judgment, and contented himself with vague innuendoes."

From 1927 to 1938, McDougall was head of the Psychology Department at Duke University in North Carolina. Under his aegis, Dr. **Joseph Banks Rhine** developed his program and founded the Parapsychology Laboratory. McDougall's books include *Group Mind* (1920), *Janus* (1927), *Character and Conduct of Life* (1927), and *Energies of Men* (1933). He also contributed important articles to the *Proceedings of the Society for Psychical Research*, the *Harvard Graduate Magazine*, *Psyche*, and the *Encyclopedia Britannica*. McDougall died November 28, 1938.

Sources:

Doyle, Sir Arthur Conan: *The History of Spiritualism*. New York: Doran, 1926

Fodor, Nandor: *Encyclopedia of Psychic Science*. London: Arthurs Press, 1933

Stemmen, Roy: *Mysteries of Mind Space & Time; the Unexplained: In Search of the Sixth Sense*. Westport: H. S. Stuttman, 1992

McINDOE, JOHN B.

John B. McIndoe was a prominent Scottish **Spiritualist**. He was President of the National Spiritualists' Union in Britain and a trustee and advisory committee member of Edinburgh Psychic College and Library. McIndoe was an authority on **spirit photography** and he also reported on the **mediumship** of Helen Duncan.

Sources:

Fodor, Nandor: *Encyclopedia of Psychic Science*. London: Arthurs Press, 1933

McKENZIE, JAMES HEWAT (1870–1929)

At the age of thirty, James Hewat McKenzie started the study of **psychic** and paranormal phenomena. This study was inspired by his dissatisfaction with science and theology in throwing any light on humankind's destiny. He studied and investigated for many years and presented a series of lectures in London, Edinburgh and Glasgow in 1915. The following year he published *Spirit Intercourse: Its Theory and Practice* and the pamphlet *If a Soldier Dies*, which received very wide circulation.

McKenzie toured America in 1917 and again in 1920, searching for good **mediums**. In 1920, he founded the **British College of Psychic Science**, funding it himself. Sir **Arthur Conan Doyle** commented, "the Psychic College, an institution founded by the self-sacrificing work of Mr. and Mrs. Hewat McKenzie, has amply shown that a stern regard for truth and for the necessary evidential requirements are not incompatible with a

James Hewat McKenzie (1870–1929), psychic researcher and founder of the British College of Psychic Science, began the study of psychic facts in 1900. *Courtesy Fortean Picture Library.*

human treatment of mediums, and a generally sympathetic attitude towards the **Spiritualistic** point of view." Psychic Science, the college quarterly magazine, began in 1922. That same year McKenzie and his wife Barbara visited Germany, Poland, and Austria, investigating mediums and psychics along the way.

McKenzie was especially interested in **physical mediumship** and also did detailed investigating of **Gladys Osborne Leonard** and **Eileen Garrett**. His work greatly advanced the knowledge of psychical matters. On his death in 1929, his wife took over the presidency of the college, and was then succeeded in 1930 by Mrs. Champion de Crespigny.

Sources:
Doyle, Sir Arthur Conan: *The History of Spiritualism.* New York: Doran, 1926

Fodor, Nandor: *Encyclopedia of Psychic Science.* London: Arthurs Press, 1933

McMahan, Elizabeth Anne (b. 1924)

Elizabeth Anne McMahan was born on May 5, 1924, in Mocksville, North Carolina. She studied at Duke University and also at the University of Hawaii, where she received her Ph.D. in 1960.

From 1943 to 1948, McMahan was a research assistant at Duke University and from 1948 to 1954, she was a research fellow at the **Parapsychology** Laboratory there. She held various posts in zoology at Duke, the University of Honolulu, and the University of Chicago. She was a charter member of the **Parapsychological Association** and a member of the American Association for the Advancement of Science and the Entomological Society of America.

McMahan published many papers on parapsychology based on her own investigations into **telepathy**, **precognition**, and **psychokinesis**. Her writings have appeared in volumes of the *Journal of Parapsychology.*

Sources:
Shepard, Leslie A: *Encyclopedia of Occultism & Parapsychology.* New York: Avon Books, 1978

Meditation

Meditation is seen as a means to union with deity or with the absolute. Today it is an established practice, not only among various cults but among ordinary, everyday people. It was common to Hinduism and **Buddhism** but has spread to be incorporated into many Western religions and practices. Meditation is described as "a stilling of the mind," "a listening," "a step to psychism and **mediumship**." It is not an escape from reality nor does it involve a loss of consciousness. These days it is seen especially as a remedy for stress and anxiety.

Buddhists meditate in the Shrine room of Vajraloka Buddhist Meditation Center in North Wales. *Courtesy Fortean Picture Library.*

The Hesychast monks in **Greece** in the Middle Ages followed a system similar to yoga, which emphasized breathing and concentration on the solar plexus. Many of the Roman Catholic saints developed their own meditation techniques. Benjamin Walker mentions St. Francis of Assisi and St. Teresa evolving their own disciplines, and St. Ignatius of Loyola outlining "a stringent procedure in a contemplative process that has led many to spiritual exaltation." There are a number of different techniques for meditating. In the 1960s and 1970s, Transcendental Meditation (TM) was popular, as taught by Maharishi Mahesh Yogi. **Edgar Cayce** put forward a method, as did others. Buddhist meditation has always had its followers.

Some people can meditate anywhere—on a bus or train, in a crowded waiting room, or an air-port lounge. At the other extreme, some Eastern mystics go to a mountain top while others have a special, secluded room especially for the purpose of meditating. Basically, especially for a beginner, it is best to have a place that is quiet and private. It is also a good plan to meditate at the same time each day.

The best position is the one that is most comfortable for the meditator. The general rule is to sit with the back straight. Some sit in a straight-backed chair or a cushion or small stool; some meditate while slowly walking. It is not recommended to lie down while meditating since it is easy to fall asleep that way. It is best to then relax the whole body, loosening all the muscles and letting go of all tension. Deep, rhythmic breathing is an aid, and some even accompany it with soft humming. The **hypnotism** technique of mentally addressing each and every part of the body is useful: starting with the feet and toes, then moving slowly up the legs to the knees and on up to the thighs and hips. Each area is concentrated upon to bring about total relaxation. The hands and fingers, wrists, arms, elbows, upper arms and shoulders, are similarly worked. Then the lower body, waist, and upper body. Finally the concentration moves on to the neck, face, scalp and all of the head. Eventually the full body has been completely relaxed. The next step is to empty the mind, slowly eliminating from the conscious all thoughts of a practical nature, such as domestic and business worries and problems.

In Transcendental Meditation, the practitioner is then instructed to concentrate on a **mantra**, a word/sound that is repeated over and over again to prevent other thoughts from intruding. Mantras are used in some forms of Buddhist meditation, though not all. Rather than repetition of a word or phrase, there may be concentration on a candle flame, a mandala, or other symbol. Since it is the nature of the mind to have constant thought, when extraneous thoughts come into the mind, they are acknowledged but are not dwelt upon. Some meditators do concentrate on an objective, such as some form of self improvement, or on getting rid of a bad habit. Other meditators may use that state to make contact with their **spirit guide** and/or with the **spirits** of deceased loved ones.

It has been proven that regular meditation is extremely beneficial, helping lower blood pressure, relieve stress, and eliminate anxiety. The mind *and* the body benefit from meditation. Twenty minutes per day is a recommended time to spend in the practice. Many spend far longer, or do two or even three sessions every day.

Sources:

Bodian, Stephan: *Meditation for Dummies*. New York: Wiley Publishing, 1999

Goleman, Daniel: *The Meditative Mind: The Varieties of Meditative Experience*. New York: Tarcher/Putnam, 1988

Smith, B.: *Meditation: The Inward Act*. London: McClelland, 1963

Walker, Benjamin: *Man, Myth & Magic: Meditation*. London: BPC Publishing, 1970

MEDIUM; MEDIUMSHIP

A Spiritualist medium is one who is able to act as a connection between this physical world and the world of the afterlife, to facilitate messages between the living and the dead. Although all mediums are **psychic**, not all psychics are mediums. Hence, the terms "medium" and "psychic" are not interchangeable. A medium is acting between this physical world and the world of the deceased; a psychic is dealing only on this level, with no connection to **spirit**. Most professional psychics act in that capacity with no form of certification or anything other than previously satisfied clients to give them veracity. Mediums, on the other hand, have to submit to rigorous examination and are certified by the **National Spiritualist Association of Churches**, the (British) **Spiritualists' National Union**, or similar established professional organizations.

Maurice Barbanell, the British medium through whom the **Native American spirit guide** Silver Birch spoke, said:

Mediumship is sensitiveness, the ability to register vibrations, radiations, or frequencies which cannot be captured by any of the five senses. Man has constructed a variety of instruments which enable him to be aware of sights and sounds that are otherwise lost to his senses. The telescope reveals the majesty of the heavens that the eye cannot see. The microscope enables us to be familiar with minute forms of life which are beyond our vision. Radar, X-ray, radio, and television capture for us vibrations that are beyond the range of our visual and auditory organs. The medium, as the name implies, is a go-between, an intermediary—is in effect a human radio or television set. He or she— it is usually a she because women are more sensitive than men—is able to tune in to a world of activity that for the rest of mankind is invisible and inaudible. Just like the radio or television set, every medium is limited in her range of reception. Unlike their mechanical counterparts, however, mediums can, by development, increase their capacity for reception.

French psychical investigator Dr. Joseph Maxwell said that a medium is "a person in the presence of whom psychical phenomena can be observed." The famous English psychical researcher **Frederick W. H. Myers** (1843–1901) said that the word medium was "a barbarous and question-begging term" because many mediumistic communications are nothing but subconscious revelation such as found with a psychic. **Nandor Fodor** points out that Myers refers to the confusion that is noticeable on the point and is the result of the observation that supernormal phenomena use the same channels for manifestation as do abnormal phenomena. Fodor said, "The abnormal phenomena are degenerative, the phenomena of mediumship are developmental, they show the promise of powers as yet unknown whereas the abnormal phenomena, like hysteria or epilepsy, show the degeneration of powers already acquired."

Lewis Spence suggests that the essential qualification of a medium is an abnormal sensitiveness "which enables him to be readily 'controlled' by disembodied spirits." He added that for this reason mediums are also known as sensitives. Yet most mediums do not look upon their connections with spirit as being "controlled" from the other side. The medium **Hudson Tuttle** (1836–1910) stated, "A medium cannot be controlled to do anything against his determined will, and the plea that he is compelled by spirits is no excuse for wrongdoing. The medium, like anyone else, knows right from wrong, and if the controlling spirit urges towards the wrong, yielding is as reprehensible as it would be to the promptings of passion or the appetite." The National Spiritualist Association of Churches says in *NSAC Spiritualist Manual* that "there is no uniformity of tempera-

ment or personality among **trance**-mediums. They come from among all conditions and grades of social and intellectual life. Many people have erroneously supposed that trance-mediumship causes a loss of individuality or that it is followed by detrimental results to the mentality; but, as a matter of fact, the best trance, as well as inspirational, speakers and mediums, are also the best unfolded otherwise."

The abilities of a medium are not necessarily there for all time. Many well known mediums in the past gradually lost their ability to produce certain phenomena. Some of them were unable to accept the loss of their gift and resorted to deception in order to maintain the illusion of still holding mediumship. The **apport** medium **Heinrich Melzer** was caught with small stones—a regular apport in his sittings—taped behind his ears with flesh-colored plaster tape. Melzer admitted that his power was waning. The mediumship of **Emanuel Swedenborg** did not develop until the age of fifty-five but lasted until his death. **Stainton Moses** maintained his powers for only eleven years. At the age of twelve, the daughter of Dr. Segard, a close friend of Professor **Charles Richet**, showed remarkable **psychokinetic** ability only for three days.

It is within the capabilities of most people to develop mediumship. With careful training, almost anyone can cultivate one of more forms of it, in either the mental or physical branch of the practice. In the mental category, a Spiritualist medium can receive messages from the spirits through **clairvoyance**, **clairaudience**, **clairsentience**, **clairhambience**, **clairalience** or **clairgustance**. He or she may mentally "hear" what the spirits are saying or may see them and describe what is seen, interpreting actions almost as is done in the game "charades," or may simply sense what is being passed on. In physical mediumship, there are such forms as **materialization**, etherialization, transfiguration, apports, **trumpets**, slates, **rappings**, **levitation**, and the production of **ectoplasm**. Mediumship is also expressed in **automatic writing** and drawing, **table tipping**, **direct voice**, and other phenomena.

Sources:

Barbanell, Maurice: *This Is Spiritualism*. Oxshott: The Spiritual Truth Press, 1959

Berkowitz, Rita S. and Deborah S. Romaine: *The Complete Idiot's Guide to Communicating eith Spirits*. New York: Penguin/Alpha, 2003

Boddington, Harry: *The University of Spiritualism*. London: Spiritualist Press, 1947

Fodor, Nandor: *Encyclopedia of Psychic Science*. London: Arthurs Press, 1933

National Spiritualist Association of Churches: *NSAC Spiritualist Manual*. Lily Dale: NSAC, 1911; 2002

Spence, Lewis: *An Encyclopedia of the Occult*. London: George Routledge & Sons, 1920

MEDIUM'S LEAGUE

The **Medium**'s League is an association formed to uphold and fulfill the vision of the workers who founded the camp of Lily Dale in 1879, for the religion of **Spiritualism**. It is headquartered located at 12 Library Street in Lily Dale, New York, as part of the **Lily Dale Assembly**.

The Medium's League meets in a building that is one of only seven octagonal-shaped buildings found in New York. Throughout the summer season, the building is open for regular **Message** Services and for the very popular Thought Exchange. The Medium's League also presents the Monday Night Circles held in the Lily Dale Auditorium throughout the summer.

MEEK, GEORGE W.

George Meek is an American who in 1971, with William O'Neil, opened a small laboratory to conduct research into **Electronic Voice Phenomena** (EVP). At a **séance** attended by Meek, a **spirit** describing himself as "a discarnate scientist" gave Meek the idea of building a mechanical device that could be used to communicate with the dead. Meek was a retired engineer and very interested in the subject of survival after death. He became obsessed with the idea of achieving two-way conversation with spirits through such a device.

Six years later, in 1977, Meek met with a **medium** named Bill O'Neil, who was also an electronics engineer. O'Neil had a **spirit guide** named Doc Nick, who said he used to be a ham radio operator. Doc Nick suggested the use of certain audio frequencies, instead of the "white noise" used by most researchers when trying for such contact. The spirit guide gave the two men technical information for building the communications device, and a list of sensitive frequencies that might be used. George Meek started building the instruments. Another spirit then joined the team: Dr. George Jeffries Müller, who materialized in O'Neil's living room at one of their sittings.

In October, 1977, the first device was built and Dr. Müller spoke through it. Among other things, he gave the listeners his social security number, told them where to find his death certificate, and said that he had been a college professor who died in 1967. Meek and O'Brien subsequently checked out the information and all of it was found to be correct.

Meek named the communication device the "Spiricom." At a press conference given on April 6, 1982, at the National Press Club in Washington, D.C., Meek told reporters that "an elementary start has been made toward the eventual perfection of an electromagnetic-etheric communications system, which will someday permit those living on earth to have telephone-like conversations with persons very much alive in higher levels of consciousness." Tapes of conversations between O'Neil and Dr. Müller were made available at the conference. These ranged in subject matter from mundane discussions about food to technical advice on how to build experimental video equipment.

Meek planned to present the Spiricom itself at the press conference but did not do so when he found only a small number of people attended. He had hoped for a large turnout to really launch his invention. In the end, the resulting media coverage made little impact on the general public. Dr. Müller later informed O'Neil that he needed to "move on" and the conversations came to an end. Others tried using the Spiricom, among them Sarah Estep, founder of the AA-EVP, but no one seemed to have as much success as Bill O'Neil. Meek traversed the globe distributing recordings of the communications between O'Neil and Müller. Meek also provided wiring diagrams, guidelines, photographs, and technical data for research in a 100-page technical report he had prepared.

Two years after the press conference Erland Babcock, a senior electronic technician at the Massachusetts Institute of Technology, came across reference to the Spiricom and wrote to George Meek on university letterhead paper. Eventually a grant was obtained to work on Electronic Voice Phenomena and **Instrumental Transcommunication** (ITC), utilizing both magnetic influences and lasers. In 1985, **Klaus Schreiber** studied Meek's design and subsequently invented what he called the "Vidicom", a device that helped record faces of the deceased by way of a television screen.

George W. Meek's book *After We Die, What Then?* (1987) deals with the 1980s breakthroughs of electronic spirit communication. In this book, Meek predicted, "A workable, dependable, repeatable two-way communication with the mental-causal levels of consciousness should be demonstrated in Europe, the United States, or South America well before the end of the century."

Sources:

Butler, Tom and Lisa: *There Is No Death and There Are No Dead*. Reno: AA-EVP, 2003

Meek, George W.: *After We Die, What Then?* Columbus: Ariel Press, 1987

MELLON, ANNIE FAIRLAMB

Annie Fairlamb Mellon was a nineteenth century English **materialization** medium. At the age of nine, she had her first supernormal experience when she **clairvoyantly** saw her brother at sea in danger of drowning. In her fami-

ly home **circle**, she developed **automatic writing**, which started with a violent trembling in her arm and hand followed by writing at tremendous speed. In a **trance** or with her eyes bandaged, she would produce pages of writing that described things taking place many miles away. She would also receive this information clairvoyantly or **clairaudiently**.

In 1873, Mellon was the official **medium** of the Newcastle Spiritual Evidence Society. Two years later she was examined by Professor **Henry Sidgwick** and **Frederick W. H. Myers**, of the **Society for Psychical Research**. The sittings were held in Cambridge under strict test conditions, and the results were described as excellent. In 1877, T. P. Barkus, a Newcastle Alderman, held tests to obtain **spirit** molds. Unknown to Mellon, he mixed magenta dye with the paraffin. The molds were found to be tinted with magenta, proving that they had not been smuggled into the **séance** room ahead of time. During a Continental tour, German investigators found that Mellon lost almost half of her body weight during materializations.

In Australia after her tour, Annie Fairlamb met and married J. B. Mellon of Sydney. On October 12, 1894, there was a spectacular exposure of the medium. At one of the sittings that took place in her home, another medium named T. Shekleton Henry suddenly grabbed hold of the materialized spirit known as "Cissie." It turned out to be Mellon herself, half undressed. The rest of her garments were found in the **cabinet**. Mellon's explanation was that she felt herself "shoot into the spirit form and become absorbed." It was claimed that she suffered injury of some sort due to being grabbed while in trance. She resolved from then on to always sit out in front of the cabinet, not inside it, in full view of everyone.

As late as 1931, Mellon was still active as a medium, convincing many notable people that she was genuine. Retired magistrate H. L. Williams wrote to **Harry Price**, the well known psychical investigator, "Dr. Haworth, a well known doctor of Port Darwin, has testified before me that at Melbourne, in the presence of leading and professional men, he saw many times a spot of mist on the carpet which rose into a column out of which stepped a completely embodied human being ..." Among others, Sir William Windeyer, Chief Judge, and Alfred Deaking, Prime Minister of Australia, were convinced that Mellon was genuine.

Sources:

Doyle, Sir Arthur Conan: *The History of Spiritualism.* New York: Doran, 1926

Fodor, Nandor: *Encyclopedia of Psychic Science.* London: Arthurs Press, 1933

MELZER, HEINRICH (B. 1873)

Heinrich Melzer was born in Dresden. He became known as an **apport** medium, the first reports of his **mediumship** appearing in *Die Uebersinnliche Welt* (*The Transcendent World*) in November, 1905. He would go into **trance** at the start of his **séances**. He was fastened inside a sack to prevent fraud, and still large quantities of stones and flowers would be apported into the séance room.

Melzer's **spirit guides** were Curadiasamy, a Hindu, Lissipan, an Indian **Buddhist**, and Amakai, a Chinese **spirit**. On occasion two others would make themselves known, Quirinus, a Roman Christian of the time of Diocletian, and Abraham Hirschkron, a Jewish merchant from Mahren.

In 1923, and again in 1926, Melzer visited the **British College of Psychic Science**. Originally he had to sit in complete darkness, but for the College he had developed sufficiently that he was able to operate in red light or even sometimes in full white light. According to **Nandor Fodor**, "Sometimes the **medium** seized upon the (apported) flowers and ate them voraciously, with stalks and soil, often wounding his mouth by thorns on rose stalks."

When his powers seemed to be waning, Melzer resorted to cheating. At one séance in 1926,

the doctor in charge discovered small stones of the type Melzer would "apport" taped behind the medium's ears with flesh-colored tape. Melzer claimed that one of his guides had suggested he do it. But as **James Hewart McKenzie** pointed out, in a report in **Psychic Science** (April, 1926), "there is a difference between stones of a quarter to half an inch in size, and flowers of eighteen inches stalk length, with leaves and thorns. Twenty-five anemones, or a dozen roots of lilies of the valley, with soil attached, pure bells and delicate leaves, or violets appearing fresh and fragrant, after two and a half hours sitting have all been received, when the medium's hands have been seen empty a second before, when no friends of his were in the sittings, and when no opportunity could have presented itself to conceal them that would not have resulted in broken stems and blossoms."

Sources:

Fodor, Nandor: *Encyclopedia of Psychic Science.* London: Arthurs Press, 1933

MENTAL MEDIUMSHIP

Mental mediumship covers such phenomena as **clairvoyance**, **clairaudience**, **clairsentience**, **clairalience/clairgustance**, **clairhambience**, **psychometry**, **glossolalia**, **inspirational speaking** and writing, **precognition** and **retrocognition**. Such phenomena may or may not be produced while the **medium** is in **trance**.

It is not always easy to categorize whether a particular phenomenon falls under the heading of mental or **physical mediumship**. For example, **automatism** may be regarded as mental mediumship because even though the hand of the medium is utilized in producing the material, what is produced seems to come through a mental process. But it is **spirit** that controls the hand and therefore it might well be classed as physical mediumship. Similarly, **table tipping** and **direct voice** are difficult to categorize.

Bletzer defines mental mediumship as the use of "etheric world intelligences when performing mental psychic skills; intelligences use their energy and only the medium perceives (as opposed to physical mediumship in which the intelligences use the medium's energy)."

Sources:

Bletzer, June G.: *The Encyclopedia Psychic Dictionary*. Lithia Springs: New Leaf, 1998

Boddington, Harry: *The University of Spiritualism*. London: Spiritualist Press, 1947

MENTOR

A mentor is classed as "etheric world intelligence," a soul-mind living in the next world/another dimension, higher on the evolutionary scale than the human. In Greek legend, Mentor was the son of Alcimus and a friend to Odysseus, who made him guardian of his household. In the play *Télémaque*, by French writer and mystical theologian François Fénelon (1651–1715), Mentor plays a prominent part, giving the hero good advice. The modern use of the word mentor means adviser or wise counselor.

Mentor was also the name of a **spirit guide** of Rev. **William Stainton Moses**. Mentor was said to be Algazzali, or Ghazali, eleventh century Professor of Theology in Baghdad and representative of the Arabian Philosophical School. Mentor's main duty was to manage the phenomena at the **séances** of Stainton Moses.

Sources:

Bletzer, June G.: *The Encyclopedia Psychic Dictionary*. Lithia Springs: New Leaf, 1998

Encyclopedia Britannica. Chicago: William Benton, 1964

Fodor, Nandor: *Encyclopedia of Psychic Science*. London: Arthurs Press, 1933

MEREDITH, REV. CHRIS

Christopher Meredith was born in a small cotton town in the Northwest of England. He had his first contact with **spirits** at the age of seven. He said, "I would go to bed at night and people would start to appear. They looked so real but they had this habit of just melting into thin air." At the age of thirteen, he came into contact with a **Spiritualist** church. There he developed his **mediumship**. Meredith worked at a variety of Spiritualist churches around England and at the age of nineteen, became the youngest church president in Great Britain. He was an active member of the **Spiritualists' National Union**.

Meredith emigrated to the United States and ran a Spiritualist church in San Diego for several years. He lived at the **Harmony Grove Spiritualist Community** in Escondido, California. He is especially known for his **flower readings**.

MESMER, FRANZ ANTON (1734–1815)

Franz Anton Mesmer was born in the village of Iznang near Lake Constance, Austria, in 1734. He studied theology and medicine. At the age of thirty-two he obtained a degree in medicine from Vienna University, the subject of his thesis being the magnetic influence of the planets on the human body (*De planetarum Influxu*— "The Influence of the Stars and Planets as Creative Powers"). This interest was inspired by the teachings of Paracelsus. Mesmer became convinced that there was a **healing** magnetic power in his own hands. He termed this force "animal magnetism," first using the term in 1775. The idea that a magnet had curative powers had been quite common in the Middle Ages, with people believing that a magnet or magnetic lodestone could literally draw out illness from the human body.

Mesmer believed that the cures which he brought about, especially on hysterical patients, were the result of entirely natural phenomena. News of his "magnetic **séances**" spread rapidly and people flocked to his home from all over Europe. However, the conventional medical fraternity accused him of practicing magic, and in 1778 he was ordered to leave Austria. He went to Paris.

The historian Deleuze describes Mesmer's methods, saying, "In the middle of a large room stood an oak tub—the famous *baquet*, four or five feet in diameter and one foot deep; it was closed by a lid made in two pieces, and encased in another tub or bucket. At the bottom of the tub a number of bottles were laid in convergent rows, so that the neck of each bottle turned towards the center. Other bottles filled with magnetized water tightly corked down were laid in divergent rows were laid with their necks turned outwards. Several rows were thus piled up and the apparatus was then pronounced to be at high *pressure*. The tub was filled with water, to which was sometimes added powdered glass and iron filings. There were also some dry tubs, that is, prepared in the same manner but without any additional water. The lid was perforated to admit the passage of movable bent iron rods, which could be applied to different parts of the patients' bodies. A long rope was also fastened to a ring in the lid, and this the patients placed loosely around their limbs … The patients drew near to one another, touching hands, arms, knees, or feet. The handsomest, youngest and most robust magnetizers held also an iron rod with which they touched the dilatory or stubborn patients … In the midst of the panting, quivering throng, Mesmer, dressed in a lilac coat, moved about extending a magic wand towards the least suffering, halting in front of the most violently excited and gazing steadfastly into their eyes, while he held their hands in his, bringing the middle fingers in immediate contact, to establish the communication." This communication became known as "Mesmerism" and was the forerunner of hypnotism.

Mesmer and his cures became immensely popular but many considered him a charlatan. By 1784, the French government appointed a special commission of scientists and physicians to investigate his work, though he himself refused to submit to them. The commission therefore investigated one of his disciples, Dr. Delson. Among the investigators were the American Ambassador to France Benjamin Franklin, the chemist Lavoisier, and Guillotin, inventor of the guillotine. The

Franz Anton Mesmer, pioneer in magnetic energy healing. His technique became known as Mesmerism, and was the forerunner of hypnotism. *Courtesy Fortean Picture Library.*

commission reported that Mesmer did indeed affect cures but attributed them not to animal magnetism but to some unknown physiological cause. As a result of this, Mesmer was lumped together with other quacks and his popularity waned. He finally retired to private life in Versailles. He moved to Switzerland in 1814 and took up residence in a village near his native Iznang. He died there in 1815.

Sources:

Encyclopedia Britannica. Chicago: William Benton, 1964

Shepard, Leslie A: *Encyclopedia of Occultism & Parapsychology.* New York: Avon Books, 1978

Wolfe, Bernard and Raymond Rosenthal: *Hypnotism Comes Of Age.* New York: Bobbs-Merrill, 1948

Mesmerism *see* **Mesmer, Franz Anton**

MESSAGES

Messages are the communications received from the **spirit world** through the agencies of **mediums**. Messages can be received in various ways: through a medium's **clairvoyance, clairaudience, clairsentience**, etc.; through **rappings, automatic writing, slate writing, independent writing/ voice, table tipping, talking boards**, and so on.

The test of a message is its veracity. Many times the information received is not previously known by the sitter and must be investigated. Finding that it is accurate is authentication that the message comes from **spirit**. There is occasionally criticism by those not familiar with **Spiritualism** that the messages received are invariably trivial. Yet it is the triviality that provides the greatest proof of life after death, for minor personal details are provided by spirit that could never be known except to the individuals concerned.

Much depends upon the ability of the medium, for many messages are symbolic. A medium may try to interpret the **symbolism** and do so incorrectly. It is therefore best if a medium simply relays what is seen, heard, or sensed, without trying to interpret it. Professor **James Hervey Hyslop** (1854–1920) believed that the nature of the medium's mind might also present a difficulty in clear communication. He gave the example of a spirit being a good visualizer and the medium not being so. Any pictorial message then given might come through very imperfectly.

Psychical investigator Dr. **Richard Hodgson** (1855–1905) examined the medium **Leonore Piper** and described three kinds of possible confusion, "(i) the confusion in the spirit; whether he is communicating or not, due primarily to his mental or bodily conditions when living, (ii) the confusion in the spirit produced by the conditions into which he comes when in the act of communicating, (iii) the confusion in the result due to the failure of complete control over the (automatic) writing, or other mechanism of the medium."

There have been cases of messages that apparently originated from living people, though they were unaware of the transmissions at the time. In most cases this occurred when the living person was asleep. **John Worth Edmonds** (1816–1874) was the first in America to suggest the living origins of some messages, in his *Spiritual Tracts* (October 24, 1857). **Allan Kardec**, the **spiritist**, was the first to propose the same idea in France.

Sources:

Shepard, Leslie A: *Encyclopedia of Occultism & Parapsychology*. New York: Avon Books, 1978

METAGRAPHOLOGY

Metagraphology is **psychometry** that uses handwriting as the object. Without even looking at what is written, a **medium** who is a good metagraphologist can hold a piece of writing and provide information about the person who produced it. Otto Reimann, a Prague bank clerk born in 1903, was an accomplished metagraphologist who was studied by the Dutch **psychic researcher** Professor Henri Theodore Fischer (1901–1987).

Sources:

Fodor, Nandor: *Encyclopedia of Psychic Science*. London: Arthurs Press, 1933

METAPHYSICS

Metaphysics is the term proposed by Professor **Charles Richet** for the phenomena and experiments of **psychical research**. Richet suggested the term in 1905, when he was elected President of the **Society for Psychical Research**. *Meta* means "higher" or "beyond." In his inaugural address, Richet said that metaphysics was "a science dealing with mechanical or psychological phenomena due to forces which seem to be intelligent, or to unknown powers, latent in human intelligence." He divided it into objective and subjective metaphysics, the former dealing with external, material phenomena and the latter with internal, **psychic**, nonmaterial facts.

The term actually derives from a title posthumously given to a treatise written by Aristotle after he wrote *Physics*. According to the *Encyclopedia Britannica*, "the word metaphysics then came to be used as a label for the sorts of topics dealt with in Aristotle's *Metaphysics*, or rather, as these topics are very heterogeneous, for the topics in it which have seemed most important." Whatever the historical origin of the term, metaphysics has come to have the connotation of some sort of antithesis between physical and nonphysical exploration.

Although metaphysics is a generally accepted term, in Germany the word "parapsychic" is used more often, with metaphysics applied to those phenomena proved supernormal in character. The term parapsychic was suggested by Emil Boirac, rector of Dijon Academy and noted French psychical researcher.

Bletzer says that metaphysics is "a philosophical doctrine that all things are a part of one main source (intelligence and energy), and that each thing, animate or inanimate, should be respected for its particular form of this one main source."

Sources:

Bletzer, June G.: *The Encyclopedia Psychic Dictionary*. Lithia Springs: New Leaf, 1998

Encyclopedia Britannica. Chicago: William Benton, 1964

Fodor, Nandor: *Encyclopedia of Psychic Science*. London: Arthurs Press, 1933

MEYER, JEAN (D. 1931)

Jean Meyer was an enthusiastic supporter of **Allan Kardec** in France. Meyer founded the Maison des Spirites in Paris to disseminate **spiritist** knowledge. Meyer also founded the **Institut Métapsychique International** in Paris to pursue **psychical research**. In 1919, this organization was recognized by the French government as a public utility.

Meyer was a French industrialist who became quite wealthy. He was able to endow his institute with a large part of his fortune and just before his

death on April 13, 1931, he presented it with a very expensive **infrared** installation.

Sources:

Fodor, Nandor: *Encyclopedia of Psychic Science*. London: Arthurs Press, 1933

MIKHAILOVA, NELYA (B. 1927)

Nelya Mikhailova—a pseudonym of Madame Ninel Sergeyevna Kulagina—first came to the attention of the western world through the book *Psychic Discoveries Behind the Iron Curtain* (1970). A Leningrad housewife who was married to an engineer, Mikhailova was tested by forty top scientists, including two Nobel Prize winners, and found to have exceptional powers of **psychokinesis** (PK), the ability to move objects without physically touching them. She stopped and started a pendulum on a wall clock and moved an assortment of dishes, a pitcher of water weighing a pound, various cups, glasses, and boxes all with the power of her mind alone.

Experiments were conducted with objects enclosed in a clear plastic box, so that they could be observed but could not be physically touched. Movie film was taken of Mikhailova concentrating on this box and of the contents—several cigarettes—rolling about inside it. Other film showed her concentrating on a compass attached to a wristband and causing the needle to spin rapidly. First the needle spun counterclockwise, and then the whole wristband began to spin. She also tilted a pair of scales that had been equally balanced with weights of 30 grams and held down one side of the scales, with her mind, even when 10 extra grams were added to the other side.

Mikhailova was tested by physicists from the Soviet Union's Joint Nuclear Research Institute at Dubna, from the Institute of Physics of the Academy of Sciences of the USSR, and from the Mendeleyev Institute of Metrology. The Mendeleyev Institute of Metrology reported to *Pravda* that the housewife moved aluminum pipes and matches under the strictest test conditions, including observation by closed circuit television cameras. Ostrander and Schroeder said, "Not since the end of the nineteenth century in England and France had so many outstanding scientists looked into a subject as seemingly far out as psychokinesis." Mikhailova lost weight during the process of doing PK, sometimes as much as three pounds at one sitting. The experiments always left her completely exhausted, sometimes taking several days to fully recover.

Born in 1927, Nelya Mikhailova served as a radio operator in the Red Army's Tank Regiment in Tank T-34, fighting the Germans in World War II when she was only 14 years old. She became a senior sergeant of the 226th Tank Regiment. Recovering from injuries in a hospital at the end of the war, she discovered that she had developed psychokinetic powers. She was able to make objects move without physically touching them. The first time it happened was when she was angry about something and a small pitcher moved off a shelf and smashed on the floor. She later found that she could control this energy.

A number of scientists at Moscow State University tested Mikhailova's powers and confirmed them. At the Utomski Institute in Leningrad, Dr. Gerady Sergeyev set up tests and found there was a magnetic field surrounding her body that was only ten times less than that of the earth itself. Mikhailova's brain waves could generate fifty times more voltage from the back of her head than from the front, while the average person generates only four times as much. During PK, her pulse rate climbed to 240 per minute.

An Associated Press release from Moscow stated, "Nelya has astounded Soviet scientists with her ability to move such things as match sticks or wine glasses without touching them." One of the PK demonstrations Mikhailova was able to do was to separate the yolk from the white of an egg by mind power alone. In the 1960s, she was in a hospital for a period of time and discovered that she could "see" the colors of her embroidery threads through the tips of her fingers. This **psychic** sight was later tested and confirmed by Dr. Leonid Vasilier, a notable pioneer in Russian psychic research.

Another Russian woman, Alla Vinogradova, exhibited similar ability, moving her hands over a scattered pile of matches and causing them to move about.

Sources:

Fishley, Margaret: *The Supernatural*. London: Aldus, 1976

Ostrander, Sheila and Lynn Schroeder: *Psychic Discoveries Behind the Iron Curtain*. Englewood Cliffs: Prentice-Hall, 1970

MILLER, C. V.

C. V. Miller was a **materialization** medium born in Nancy, France. He was living in San Francisco when Willie Reichel investigated him and described the results in a book titled *Occult Experiences* (London, c.1908). Miller's **séances** usually followed the same pattern: Miller himself would stand outside a **cabinet**, fully conscious (not in **trance**) and speaking throughout the proceedings. A variety of materialized figures would come out of the cabinet, frequently several at one time. As Reichel described it, "They came out one by one, spoke to the sitters and usually dematerialized in front of the cabinet. They sank through the floor." On one occasion Reichel's deceased nephew floated upward and disappeared through the ceiling. The most spirits Reichel saw at one time was twelve.

Miller visited Europe on two separate occasions. In 1906, he seemed to avoid contact with Lt.-Col. **Eugene Rochas**, the prominent French **psychical researcher** who had arranged for Miller to visit France. Instead, Miller held séances with Gabriel Delanne and Gaston Méry, Chief Editor of *Libre Parole* and Director of the *Echo du Merveilleux*. Méry said that he thought it probable that the phenomena produced by Miller were genuine, but "until there is fuller information we must be satisfied with not comprehending." The sitting was held in Méry's home, where Miller was stripped naked, examined by three doctors, and then dressed in some of Méry's own clothes. Miller was not allowed in the séance room prior to the sitting. Dr. Gérard Encausse (better known as the occultist "Papus"), stated in *L'Initiation* that his expectation was fully satisfied and that he believed Miller displayed mediumistic faculties more extraordinary than any he had encountered previously.

Miller went to Germany and gave well-received séances in Munich. Nandor Fodor stated, "The materialized form was often seen to develop from luminous globes and clouds which at first appeared near the ceiling. If several forms were materialized at the same time they were transparent." Although Miller stopped in France again on his way home to America, Professor **Charles Richet** reported that Miller would not subject himself to intensive investigation under the proposed conditions.

Two years later, Miller returned to Paris. On June 25, 1908, he appeared before forty people and gave a very successful séance under test conditions. The **medium** was stripped, examined, and dressed in black garments provided by the investigating committee, which again included Gaston Méry. The clothing had neither pockets nor lining. As usual, a number of **spirits** materialized and then later dissolved. Cesar de Vesme was unconvinced of the genuineness, though was unable to offer any explanations. Several others of the committee seemed doubtful. No more was heard of C. V. Miller after his return from France.

Sources:

Fodor, Nandor: *Encyclopedia of Psychic Science.* London: Arthurs Press, 1933

MIRABELLI, CARLOS CARMINE (1889–1951)

Carlos (originally Carmine) Mirabelli was born to Italian parents in Botucatu, Sao Paolo, in 1889. His father was a Protestant pastor. Mirabelli first drew attention to himself as a teenager, when he was the center of **poltergeist** activity. When working as a shoe clerk, a large number of shoe boxes flew off the store shelves and chased him into the street. Similar things kept happening and Mirabelli was placed in an asylum for nineteen days for observation. The doctors found nothing physically wrong with him. They said that although he wasn't sick, he wasn't normal either. It was not until August 1929 that Mirabelli's extraordinary mediumistic abilities came to world attention through an article published in Germany in *Zeitschrift für Parapsychologie.* This article was actually based on a little-circulated Brazilian work, *O Medium Mirabelli,* by Amador Bueno.

Nandor Fodor listed phenomena witnessed by many, saying, "The newspapers ... wrote of **telekinetic** movements; of **apports**; of a miraculous transportation of the **medium** from the railroad station of Da Luz to Sao Vincenti, 90 kilometres distance, in two minutes; of his **levitation** in the street two metres high for three minutes; of how he caused a skull to float towards an apothecary; of making an invisible hand turn the leaves of a book in the home of Dr. Alberto Seabra in the presence of many scientists; of making glasses and bottles at a banquet play a military march without human touch; of causing the hat of Antonio Canterello to fly off and float ten metres along a public square; of making and quelling fire by will in the home of Prof. Dr. Alves Lima; of making the cue play billiards without touching it, and finally of having the picture of Christ impressed on plaster in the presence of Dr. Caluby, Director of Police." There are photographs of Mirabelli levitating at a **séance** attended by his son Luiz. A board of enquiry established that the majority of these phenomena occurred spontaneously in daylight in public places, that the phenomena could not be based on trickery, and that the statements of personalities whose reputation was above reproach could not be denied.

In 1919, the Academia de Estudos Psychicos Cesare Lombroso was founded. Mirabelli submitted himself for investigation of his **trance** speaking, **automatic writing**, and the **physical mediumship**. In 1926, the Academy published a report that mentioned 392 sittings in broad daylight, or in a room illuminated by powerful electric light; 349 cases took place in the rooms of the Academy and were attended by 555 people. During the investigations, Mirabelli spoke in twenty-six languages, including seven dialects, and wrote in twenty-eight languages including three dead ones: Latin, Chaldaic, and Egyptian hieroglyphics. The automatic writing included such examples as a treatise of nine pages on the independence of Czechoslovakia, written in twenty minutes, and five pages on the Russo-Japanese war, written in Japanese in twelve minutes. He was able to converse in one language while writing in another. There were incredible phenomena of **materializations**, with medical doctors examining the **spirits** and obtaining pulses, heart beats, testing saliva, eyes, etc. At one sitting the recently dead daughter of Dr. de Souza materialized and he was able to hug her and speak with her for more than half an hour. At another sitting a bishop, who had recently drowned in a ship wreck, appeared and was scrutinized by a medical doctor.

Fodor said, "if they (the phenomena) could be proved to the satisfaction of English and American **psychical researcher**s he (Mirabelli) would have to be ranked as the greatest medium of all time." Psychical researcher **Eric Dingwall** examined the original Portuguese documents and stated in the July, 1930 *Psychic Research*, "I find myself totally at a loss to come to any decision whatever on the case. It would be easy to condemn the man as a monstrous fraud and the sitters as equally monstrous fools. But I do not think that such a supposition will help even him who makes it." He commented on the fact that Mirabelli worked in full light and not in the "feeble glimmer of ruby light" preferred by most British and American physical mediums, and to point out that Mirabelli "submitted himself to the severest tests of … investigators, passively suffering being tied and stripped, until doubt was excluded."

Before publishing their article, editors of *Zeitschrift für Parapsychologie* contacted the Brazilian consul, who assured them that he could personally vouch for the integrity of the majority of the people who had testified on Mirabelli's behalf. Unfortunately there were no funds to send Mirabelli to Europe to be tested and investigated, and the **Society for Psychical Research** dismissed the reports they heard of his mediumship as "too fantastical." They also felt that the Brazilian researchers lacked the necessary expertise to test Mirabelli properly. In the *Journal* of the **American Society for Psychical Research** (#24, 1930) Dingwall reported, *An Amazing Case: the Mediumship of Carlos Mirabelli*. He said, "The chaos in which psychical research finds itself at present prevents any really valuable systematic work being done."

In the November, 1930 issue of *Psychic Research*, Professor Hans Driesch reported that he sat with Mirabelli in Sao Paolo two years previously and that, although there had been some surprising examples of **psychokinesis**, which he could not explain, there had been no materializations nor speaking in languages other than Italian and Esthonian. Yet at one séance Mirabelli was in trance when a bell on the table levitated and started to ring. It woke Mirabelli who then described a man he had seen **clairvoyantly**. As he spoke, that same man began to materialize and two sitters recognized him as the deceased Dr. de Menezes. A physician present tried to examine the form but it floated away. As Fodor said, "the figure began to dissolve from the feet upwards, the bust and arms floating in the air." Mary S. Walker, of the American Society for Psychical Research, did sit with Mirabelli and was most impressed by what she saw, even though his powers were somewhat diminished by that time.

In 1933, Mirabelli was bound and handcuffed yet flowers floated into the room through a locked window, followed by a statue. Mirabelli spoke in Arabic to one of the sitters, who recognized the voice of his mother who had died thirty years before. The sitter became a **Spiritist** on the spot! During a séance in 1934, flowers and bottles materialized, a chair and keys moved about the room, and a picture lifted from the wall and floated across the room, striking one of the sitters on the head in passing. It is claimed that there was an instance of Mirabelli himself dematerializing from a sealed séance room and reappearing in another room, where he was found with his bonds and their seals still intact.

When Mirabelli's biographer Eurico de Goes went to visit the medium on one occasion, Goes realized he had left his umbrella at home. As he entered Mirabelli's house, the umbrella fell from the ceiling—an apport. A similar example of an apport was seen when the British diplomat Sir Douglas Ainslie visited the medium. As Sir Douglas entered the house he suddenly found his traveling alarm clock on the hall table. He had last seen it in his hotel room. Mirabelli's three sons reported to Guy Lion Playfair in 1973 that their father's powers were evident on a daily basis. They could happen "almost every day, any time and any place." Their mother, they said, was resigned to such things as having a newly set dinner table suddenly wiped clear of table cloth, dishes, glasses, and cutlery. None of the sons had inherited the father's abilities.

Since Mirabelli was practicing his mediumship in a Roman Catholic country, he was taken to court fifteen times over the years. Despite this persecution, he continued to demonstrate the reality of survival of the spirit after physical death, bringing happiness to a great many people. Mirabelli died in 1951. Playfair said, "His son Cesar Augusto has movingly described how, while they were on their way to the local cinema, the medium dashed across the road to buy his son an ice cream. He was hit by a car, and died without regaining consciousness."

Sources:

Carlos Mirabelli Biography: http://www.fortunecity.com/roswell/seance/78/mirab.htm

Fodor, Nandor: *Encyclopedia of Psychic Science.* London: Arthurs Press, 1933

Foreman, Laura (ed): *Mysteries of the Unknown: Spirit Summonings.* New York: Time-Life Books, 1989

Playfair, Guy Lion: *The Flying Cow: Research into Paranormal Phenomena in the World's Most Psychic Country.* London: Souvenir Press, 1975

Playfair, Guy Lion: *Mysteries of Mind Space & Time; the Unexplained: "This Perilous Medium."* Westport: H. S. Stuttman, 1992

MIRROR

The mirror can be a useful tool for developing **clairvoyance**. It also features in much ancient folklore. In American lore, if an unmarried woman looks into a mirror by the light of a candle at midnight on Hallowe'en night, she will see the reflection of her future husband looking at her over her left shoulder. An older legend from Europe has it that by gazing into a reflection of the **moon** in a hand mirror, a young woman can tell how many years will pass before she marries, based on the length of time before either a cloud passes before the moon or a bird flies across it.

In earliest times, **Chinese** sages, together with wise men and women of ancient **Greece** and **Rome**, believed that to **dream** of seeing your own reflection—be it in water, polished brass or copper, or wherever—was an omen of death. The death was not necessarily yours but was of a person close to you. Seeing your reflection at various times of the day also had meaning. This was all brought together in what was known as *catoptromancy*, or *enoptromancy*, divination by mirror. Hydromancy, **divination** by water, was but a small part of it.

Catoptromancy, as an aspect of mirror-gazing, is referred to by Sir Thomas Urquhart in *The Third Book of the Works of Mr. Francis Rabelais* (London, 1693), which reads, "Catoptromancy is held in such account by the emperor Didius Julianus," implying that it was practiced in ancient Rome. *The (London) Annual Register* of 1758 says, "He understands all the mysteries of catoptromancy, he having a magical glass to be consulted upon some extraordinary occasions." Pausanius, the fifth century BCE Spartan regent of the Greek forces and admiral of the Greek fleet, described how this form of divination was performed, "Before the Temple of Ceres, at Patras, there was a fountain, separated from the temple by a wall, and there was an **oracle**, very truthful, but not for all events—for the sick only. The sick person let down a mirror (of bronze or silver), suspended by a thread, till its base touched the surface of the water, having first prayed to the goddess and offered incense. Then looking in the mirror, he saw the presage of death or recovery, according as the face appeared fresh and healthy or of a ghastly aspect." The Romans and the Egyptians also used this form of divination.

Mirror gazing is one of the many forms of **scrying**, of divining by looking into a reflective surface. The mirror is used much like a crystal ball in **crystal gazing**, being gazed into with the diviner or **medium** seeing scenes from the past, present, or future. The Roman god Vulcan had a magic mirror in which he was able to see all things. England's Merlin had one that warned him of treason. In Chaucer's *Canterbury Tales*, the mirror of Cambuscan told of misfortunes to come. In Goldsmith's *Citizen of the World*, Lao's mirror reflected pure thought. In the *Arabian Nights*, there is the all-seeing mirror of Al-Asnam, and in *Snow White and the Seven Dwarfs* there is the magic mirror of the wicked Queen, in which she can see Snow White. A drawing by Leonardo da Vinci now in the Library of Christ Church, Oxford, England, shows a woman holding up a mirror to a **seeress** as part of a ritual. In the mirror can be seen the face of an old man.

In Étienne Pasquier's *Recherches de la France* (1560), he speaks of a magic mirror owned and used by Catherine de Médicis (1519–1589). She supposedly could clairvoyantly see the future of France, especially as it pertained to the de Médicis family. According to Grillot de Givry, Père Cotton used that same mirror to show Henri IV all the plots that were being hatched against him.

All types of mirrors have been used over the ages, with polished metal faces, glass, crystal, and obsidian. The mirror may or may not be enclosed in a frame. If it is, the frame is usually engraved or marked in some way with sigils to help generate and amplify the images seen. In Francis Barrett's book *The Magus* (1801), there is shown a mirror set in a frame of "pure gold" with the sacred names MICHAEL, GABRIEL, URIEL, and RAPHAEL inscribed around it, inside a double circle. These are the **angels** ruling over the Sun, Moon, Venus, and Mercury. Above the name Michael is drawn a six-pointed star. On the other side of the frame there is also a circle engraved, inside which (next to the glass) is a six-pointed star together with a five-pointed star and a Maltese-style cross. These are followed by the word TETRAGRAMMATON. The glass, Barrett says, should be "of a lapidary good clear pellucid crystal ... about one inch and a half in diameter." There are also instructions for the preparation and inscribing of the table on which the glass should stand. Other authorities give other instructions and suggestions as to what would be appropriate to mark around the frame, though some leave the frame unmarked.

Many diviners say that a black mirror is far superior to any other. Similarly, a concave mirror is an advantage. One way to make a mirror that follows both these suggestions is to obtain one of the old framed pictures, from around the turn of the previous century, which has an oval, convex glass. Reversing the glass and painting what then becomes the back of it with black paint produces a convex black mirror that is perfect for mirror gazing. Old books of magic state that the glass should be painted three times with asphaltum. To make the asphaltum stick to the glass, it first needs to be cleaned with turpentine. The asphalt should be laid on with a camel-hair brush. However, using modern black enamel from a spray can seems to work just as well. As with all magical practices, while making the object you should be concentrating on its purpose, on it being good for projecting scenes from past, present, and future.

The *Revue Archéologique* of 1846 contains an illustration and description of a magic mirror that belonged to a Spanish family at Saragossa in the seventeenth century. It was a metal, convex mirror decorated with figures and with the words MUERTE, ETAM, TETECEME, and ZAPS. It was said that images appeared on the surface of any liquid reflected in the mirror's surface.

Some people training to become **Spiritualist** mediums will begin their exercises with scrying, using either a crystal ball or a mirror. It can be an effective way to get started so long as the medium does not come to rely solely on the object but merely uses it as a tool for further development.

Sources:

Barrett, Francis: *The Magus, or Celestial Intelligencer; Being a Complete System of Occult Philosophy.* London: Lackington, Allen & Co., 1802

Buckland, Raymond: *Buckland's Book of Spirit Communications.* St. Paul: Llewellyn, 2004

Buckland, Raymond: *The Fortune–Telling Book: The Encyclopedia of Divination and Soothsaying.* Detroit: Visible Ink Press, 2004

Encyclopedia Britannica. Chicago: William Benton, 1964

de Givry, Grillot: *A Pictorial Anthology of Witchcraft, Magic & Alchemy.* London: Spottiswoode, Ballantyne, 1931

Hall, Angus: *The Supernatural: Signs of Things to Come.* London: Aldus, 1975

Leach, Maria (ed): Funk & Wagnalls Standard Dictionary of Folklore, Mythology and Legend. New York: Harper & Row, 1984

Oxford English Dictionary, The. Oxford: Clarendon Press, 1989

MITCHELL, EDGAR D. (B. 1930)

Edgar D. Mitchell was born on September 17, 1930, in Hereford, Texas; however he considers Artesia, New Mexico, his hometown. He started his education in primary school in Roswell, New Mexico, and went to Artesia High School in Artesia. He later received a Bachelor of Science degree in Industrial Management from the Carnegie Institute of Technology and entered the U.S. Navy in 1952. After flight training he was assigned to Patrol Squadron 29 in Okinawa, flying aircraft on carrier duty and Heavy Attack Squadron. He flew A3 aircraft. He obtained a Bachelor of Science degree in Aeronautical Engineering from the U.S. Naval Postgraduate School in 1961 and studied for his doctorate in aeronautics and astronautics at Massa-chusetts Institute of Technology. Mitchell received his doctorate in 1964 and that same year became Chief, Project Management Division, Navy Field Office for Manned Orbiting Laboratory. In April of 1966, Mitchell was selected as an astronaut and became Lunar Module Pilot of Apollo 14, which landed men on the moon February 5, 1971.

Soon after Mitchell's arrival at the NASA Manned Spacecraft Center in Huston, he became interested in **parapsychology**, having become dissatisfied with orthodox theology. He began to investigate areas of mysticism and **psychic** phenomena. In December 1969, he became acquainted with the **medium Arthur Ford**. It was Ford who suggested that it would be interesting to conduct an **ESP** experiment between a man in a rocket orbiting the earth and a man on the ground.

NASA had rejected the idea of parapsychological experiments from space in 1970, so Mitchell's experiment had to be conducted during any free time he might have on a lunar flight. Arthur Ford died before Mitchell's flight but Dr. **Joseph Banks Rhine** agreed to coordinate the tests and evaluate the data. Karlis Osis, the distinguished parapsychologist of the **American Society for Psychical Research**, joined Rhine in this. The experiment was carried out aboard the Apollo 14 mission, but the test results were inconclusive.

Mitchell retired from NASA and from the Navy in 1972. The following year, after a divorce, he married Anita K. Rettig of Medina, Ohio. Anita shared his interest in parapsychology and together they founded the **Institute of Noetic Sciences,** for the study of human consciousness and mind-body relationships. Mitchell supported **Andrija Puharich** in his testing of **Uri Geller**, and himself supervised experiments with Geller at Stanford Research Institute.

Sources:

Edgar Dean Mitchell Biography: http://www.jsc.nasa. gov/Bios/htmlbios/mitchell-ed.html

Institute of Noetic Sciences: http://www.noetic.org

Shepard, Leslie A: *Encyclopedia of Occultism & Parapsychology.* New York: Avon Books, 1978

MONCK, REV. FRANCIS WARD

Rev. Francis Ward Monck gave up his career as a minister of the Baptist Chapel at Earls Barton, England, in order to become a professional **medium** and had a checkered career in **Spiritualism**. He was lauded by well known figures in **psychical research** but also was exposed as fraudulent and spent three months in prison. He recovered from the experience and went on to give many **séances** witnessed by prominent people. He also performed many **healings**, becoming known as "Dr." Monck, although he had no medical credentials. This caused some protests from those in the medical profession.

Monck claimed to have had psychic experiences as a child, which increased in intensity as he grew. He started his Spiritualist career in 1873, announcing himself to be a medium. Two years later he toured Britain to demonstrate his powers. He healed the sick in Ireland, and in London convinced **William Stainton Moses**, Hensleigh Wedgwood (Darwin's brother-in-law), and Dr. **Alfred Russel Wallace** of his gifts. He gave **materialization** séances in broad daylight and also produced many **slate writings**, drawing a great deal of attention to himself. Monck rarely used a **cabinet** in his séances, instead standing in full view. Sometimes he would go into **trance** but not always.

On November 3, 1876, in the town of Huddersfield, a stage magician named Lodge suddenly stopped the séance by demanding that Monck be searched. Monck apparently panicked, ran from the room and locked himself in another room, from which he escaped by way of the window. A pair of stuffed gloves was found in his room. Sir **William Barrett** wrote of "a piece of white muslin on a wire frame with a thread attached being used by the medium to simulate a partially materialized spirit." Monck was taken to trial. Wallace spoke up on his behalf, describing a materialization he had witnessed that he said "could not be produced by any trick." However, the court found Monck guilty and sentenced him to three months imprisonment.

Almost a year later, on September 25, 1877, Monck gave a séance at which his two **spirit guides**, Samuel and Mahedi, produced materializations witnessed by Archdeacon Colley, who had been abroad at the time of Monck's trial and subsequent imprisonment. Colley published an account of the sitting, stating that he had been less than a yard away from the medium throughout the proceedings and had initially seen various faces form about Monck's body and then had witnessed "a full formed figure, in a nebulous condition at first, but growing more solid as it issued from the medium, left Dr. Monck and stood a separate individuality, two or three feet off, bound to him by a slender attachment as of gossamer, which at my request Samuel, the control, severed with the medium's left hand, and there stood embodied a **spirit** form of unutterable loveliness, robed in attire spirit-spun—a meshy web-work from no mortal loom, of a fleeciness inimitable, and of transfiguration whiteness truly glistening." The archdeacon was so sure of his facts that he offered a prize of 1,000 pounds to the great stage magician J. N. Maskelyne if he could reproduce the same effects. Maskelyne tried, but according to the archdeacon, fell far short of the Monck exhibition. Maskelyne sued for the money but lost the case in court, thereby also losing much prestige.

In 1905, Archdeacon Colley published detailed accounts of his many examinations of Monck, stating, "I publish these things for the first time, having meditated over them in silence for twenty-eight years, giving my word as a clergyman for things which imperil my ecclesiastical position and my future advancement."

Sir **Arthur Conan Doyle** said of Monck, "Of all mediums none is more difficult to appraise, for on the one hand many of his results are beyond all dispute, while in a few there seems to be an absolute certainty of dishonesty." The latter part of his life Monck concentrated on healing, spending much time in New York.

Sources:
Doyle, Sir Arthur Conan: *The History of Spiritualism*. New York: Doran, 1926

Fodor, Nandor: *Encyclopedia of Psychic Science.* London: Arthurs Press, 1933

MONROE, ROBERT ALLAN (1915–1995)

R obert Monroe was born in Indiana in 1915. From 1937 to 1949 he worked for an Ohio radio station, writing and producing programs. He rose to become the president of several radio and electronic corporations.

As a child, Monroe experienced what he later came to realize were out of body experiences (OOBEs) or **astral projections**. These became more and more frequent as he got older. In 1956, Monroe started a small research and development program in his New York based company, RAM Enterprises. This was designed to determine the feasibility of learning during sleep. He registered three patents for methods and techniques for inducing and controlling various states of awareness.

From 1965 to 1966, Monroe took part in experiments at the Brain Wave Laboratory of the University of Virginia Medical School. There it was noted that while astrally projecting, his blood pressure fell although there was no change in his heart rate. His brain wave pattern was normal for dreaming sleep.

In 1971, Monroe opened the Mind Research Institute at his farm at the base of the Blue Ridge Mountains in Virginia. That same year he authored the book *Journeys Out of the Body.* Three years later the MRI became the Monroe Institute, which is still functioning today. More than 8,000 people have attended its programs, with an estimated two million worldwide who have used its Hemi-Sync® learning exercises in audio cassettes and CDs.

On one of his projections, Monroe went to an unknown destination and saw a young woman he knew talking to two young girls. He pinched the woman and she reacted as though she felt it. Later, when he saw the woman, he asked her what she was doing at the time he projected and she said she had been talking with the girls. He asked her if she had felt a pinch. Surprised, she said she had and had attributed it to her young brother. She was even able to show Monroe the still-red mark on her body where he had pinched her. This is most unusual, because normally an **astral body** cannot affect the physical plane.

An interesting feature of Monroe's astral projections was that many times he felt that he was someone else, while projecting. Robert Monroe died at the age of 79, on March 17, 1995, of complications of pneumonia.

Sources:

Ellison, A. J.: *Mysteries of Mind, Space & Time; the Unexplained: Points of View.* Westport: H.S. Stuttman, 1992

Fishley, Margaret: *The Supernatural.* London: Aldus, 1976

The Monroe Institute: http://www.monroeinstitute.org

Monroe, Robert A.: *Journeys Out of the Body.* New York: Doubleday, 1971

MONTGOMERY, RUTH (1912–2001)

B orn Ruth Schick on June 11, 1912, in Princeton, Indiana, she attended both Baylor and Purdue Universities though she never obtained a degree. Ruth went into journalism, despite an early desire to be a missionary, and eventually got a job with the International News Service in Washington D.C. She married Robert H. Montgomery, a management consultant whom she met in Detroit. In St. Petersburg, Florida, in 1956, Montgomery attended her first **Spiritualist** séance with **direct voice medium** Malcolm Pantin. She later attended other **séances** in Washington, including those given by **Hugh Gordon Burroughs**. She wrote a newspaper series about séances and started using a **Ouija® board**. Through it, Montgomery believed that she contacted her dead father and also Burroughs's control, Father Murphy.

Montgomery said in an interview, "That initial story led to an assignment to go to a **Spiritu-**

alist camp in Silver Bell, Michigan, to produce an eight-part series. In it, I pointed out the obviously phony things, such as **materialization** séances, but I honestly reported what I couldn't understand that did seem authentic. I did a straight reporting job that was carried in just about every city in America." After meeting medium **Arthur Ford**, and being encouraged by him, Montgomery started doing **automatic writing** and producing material which she published.

From automatic writing she moved on to do automatic typing. In 1965, she wrote a book about medium **Jeane Dixon**, titled *A Gift of Prophesy*. It became a national bestseller. The following year she wrote *A Search for the Truth*, which dealt with her personal spiritual explorations. In 1970, she gave up her syndicated column and moved to Mexico with her husband. By the late 1970s, Montgomery was writing about aliens and UFOs, in *Strangers Among Us* (1979) and *Aliens Among Us* (1985). Her last book, *The Worlds To Come: The Guide's Long-Awaited **Predictions** for a Dawning Age*, was released in 1999 by Harmony Books, New York. In it, Montgomery gave her predictions for the future of planet Earth. These included the view that the planet would shift on its axis and that "in a lot of areas the waters will be where the land is, and vice versa. Lands will rise from the sea."

Sources:

Guiley, Rosemary Ellen: *Harper's Encyclopedia of Mystical & Paranormal Experience*. San Francisco: Harper SanFrancisco, 1991

Montgomery, Ruth: *A Search for the Truth*. New York: Bantam Books, 1968

MOODY, DR. RAYMOND (B. 1944)

Dr. Raymond Moody coined the term "**near death experience**," or NDE, in his 1975 book *Life after Life*. His book gave respectability to what previously had been nothing but anecdotes. He identified such main components of NDE as a sense of being dead, peace and painlessness, an out of body experience (**OBE**), a journey down a tunnel toward a light, meeting deceased loved ones, meeting an ultimate being of light, going through a life review, and not wanting to return from the dead but doing so. Moody observed that in Plato's work there is a scene called "The Myth of Urr," which is the story of a soldier who returns from the dead with stories remarkably similar to those told by people who have undergone the near death experience.

Moody was a young philosophy student when he heard from Dr. George Ritchie the story of Ritchie's apparent death and then return to life. Ritchie had been pronounced dead in Abilene, Texas, in 1943, but had returned to consciousness and was able to relate a variety of experiences while in the "death" state. Moody was so struck by Ritchie's story that he decided to seek out other such stories. Talking with a wide variety of people he found that all the stories were consistent in certain areas. Moody wrote his book working from 150 such cases. Two years later, he supplemented it with a second book titled *Reflection on Life after Death*, including hundreds more cases. These books prompted other doctors and scientists to look more closely at such episodes.

Moody came from a Presbyterian family, though his parents never tried to impose their religious beliefs on their children. In fact, Moody became a Methodist. He was born in 1944, in Porterdale, Georgia, on the day that his father disembarked for World War II. Moody attended graduate school in philosophy at the University of Virginia and received his Ph.D. in 1969. After teaching philosophy for three years at East Carolina University, he decided to go to medical school; he thought of becoming a psychiatrist. He received his M.D. from the Medical College of Georgia in 1976, and served his residency at the University of Virginia Medical School. In 1988, he received the World Humanitarian Award in Denmark. He won a bronze medal in the Human Relations category at the New York Film Festival for the movie version of *Life After Life*. He has appeared on a large number of television talk shows.

Dr. Raymond Moody pioneered the investigation and research near death experiences. *Courtesy Fortean Picture Library.*

The John Dee Memorial Theater of the Mind is located at a farm owned by Moody in Alabama. The theater was named in honor of the Elizabethan scholar, Dr. John Dee, who made frequent use of a **crystal** ball for **scrying**. In Moody's theater is a mirrored room where people could go to **mirror**-gaze and contact **spirits** of deceased loved ones. The mirror is in a soundproof room lined with black velvet. There is a single chair and a stained glass lamp that is hidden from direct view. The large mirror is attached to one wall in such a way that the viewer cannot see him or herself. In his book *Reunions*, Moody said, "I have directly observed more than three hundred individuals as they were mirror-gazing, and afterward interviewed them about the experience." Most of these people spent two to three hours alone in the room and a large percentage claimed to have seen and even talked with the spirit(s) of the deceased.

Moody and his first wife Louise had two sons. They divorced and Moody had a brief second marriage. He and his current wife Cheryl have an adopted son. Now living in Las Vegas, Moody still owns the Alabama farm, though the Theater of the Mind is temporarily closed.

Sources:

Leonard, Sue (ed): *Quest For the Unknown—Life Beyond Death*. Pleasantville: Reader's Digest, 1992

Moody, Raymond: *Life after Life*. New York: Mockingbird Books, 1975

Moody, Raymond: *Reflections on Life after Life*. New York: Bantam, 1977

Moody, Raymond and Paul Perry: *Coming Back: A Psychiatrist Explores Past-Life Journeys*. New York: Bantam, 1990

Moody, Raymond and Paul Perry: *Reunions: Visionary Encounters with Departed Loved Ones*. New York: Villard, 1993

Randles, Jenny & Peter Hough: *The Afterlife: An Investigation into the Mysteries of Life after Death*. London: Piatkus, 1993

MOON

Many **seers**, diviners, **witches**, Wiccans, magicians, **shamans**, and others believe that it is important to work according to the phases of the moon. Basically, constructive magical work is done during the waxing phase and eliminating work during the waning phase, which is an extension of sympathetic magic. Working to bring about something constructive, to bring increase, the person works as the moon is growing and increasing. Working to get rid of bad habits, for example, they work as the moon is decreasing.

Some **divination** is done specifically at the full moon. It is seldom that any is done especially at the new moon. For best results, it is said that **scrying**, for example, should be undertaken at the full moon, though it actually can be done at any time. Some scryers "renew" the energy of their crystal balls by placing them out in the light of the full moon every month.

A guide to the phases of the moon can be found in the times of its rising. The new moon always rises at sunrise. The first quarter always rises at noon. The full moon always rises at sunset. The last quarter always rises at midnight. For each day following the above, the moon will rise about fifty minutes later than the previous day.

Sources:

Buckland, Raymond: *Wicca for Life*. New York: Citadel, 2002

MORRIS, MRS. L. A. MEURIG (B. 1899)

Mrs. L. A. Meurig Morris was a simple West-country woman with limited education. She was born on November 17, 1899, in London, England. The name Meurig is a Welsh name, frequently Anglicized to Morris. The case of Mrs. Meurig Morris is interesting in that it shows a changeover from **mediumship** to pure **channeling**. After attending her first **séance** in Newton Abbot, England, in 1922, she began to develop rapidly as a medium. Within six weeks a **spirit guide** was speaking through her. The guide was a child calling herself Sunshine. There was also a secondary guide named Sister Magdalene, who said she had been a French nun. They predicted that Mrs. Morris would be trained by spirit to be the channel for an entity known only as "Power." This did happen. Within a year, Mrs. Morris began going into **trance**; her voice would change from her own high-pitched feminine one to a deep baritone male voice. Her mannerisms and gestures were described as being "very masculine and priestly." The entity provided no details of its origins, only that it wished to be known as Power. Through Mrs. Morris, Power delivered long lectures which **Nandor Fodor** described as teachings disclosing "an erudition and deep philosophy which was far above the intellectual capacities of the medium."

Well known author and playwright Laurence Cowan met Mrs. Morris in 1929. He was a lifelong agnostic, but after listening to Power's teachings, converted to **Spiritualism**. He was so impressed by Mrs. Morris' mediumship that he wanted to make it available to a wider audience. He arranged a long series of Sunday meetings, first at the Fortune Theater and then at the Aeolian Hall in London. These meetings garnered much publicity and press coverage. Cowen also arranged for Mrs. Morris to tour the country at his expense. A recording of Power's teachings was made, as was a short film. During both of these events, interesting occurrences took place.

The Columbia Gramophone Company made the first recording. Ernest Oaten, President of the **International Federation of Spiritualists**, was to make the introduction. He did this, but did not see the red light signifying that recording was in progress. He leaned across to Mrs. Morris and said, "Wait for the signal." This was picked up by the microphone and heard distinctly by the engineers in the sound booth. Powers went ahead and started the lecture, so there was no way to stop what was in progress, as this was in the days before recordings could be easily edited. Later, when the second side of the record was being cut, other interruptions were heard and recorded. At one point, Mrs. Morris turned away from the microphone and walked several paces around the room before continuing.

A week before the record was ready for reproduction, Power, speaking through Mrs. Morris, assured Columbia executives that everything would be fine, and that there would be no problems at all on the recording. Some thought this so unlikely that they wrote down what was said, sealed it in an envelope, and gave it to Ernest Oaten in Manchester, telling him not to open it until after the record was ready. The record was first played in public at the Fortune Theater on April 25, 1931. It ran perfectly, with no sign of Oaten's original comment, no change in Mrs. Morris' voice when she turned away from the microphone, and none of the other interruptions and apparent problems in evidence. The letter was opened and read, showing that Power's prediction was correct.

The second strange incident occurred in the British Movietone Company studios, where a short film was to be made of Mrs. Morris channeling Power. Seventy people were in the audience and the microphones were strung up out of the line of sight of the movie camera. They were held up by rope that was half an inch thick. Partway through the oration the rope snapped (it was later examined and it looked as though it had been cleanly cut with a sharp knife) and the heavy microphone swung down toward the stage. The cameraman kept filming. The microphone swung across less than an inch from Mrs. Morris' face, but she did not blink, pause in her talk, or register any awareness of the near miss. A newspaper previously suggested that Mrs. Morris was not really in a trance during her Power orations, but this incident seemed to quash that idea. A technician grabbed the rope and pulled it out of sight of the camera, which never stopped rolling. Mrs. Morris/Power never stopped speaking. After an incident such as this, the sound quality should have been severely compromised, but the finished film was perfect. There was no sign of the swinging microphone nor of the change of audio input.

In his book *Past Years* (1931), Sir **Oliver Lodge** wrote, "When the medium's [Mrs. Morris's] own vocal organs are obviously being used, as in most cases of trance utterances, the proof of supernormality rests mainly on the substance of what is being said; but occasionally the manner is surprising. I have spoken of a characteristically cultured mode of expression, when a scholar is speaking, not easily imitated by an uncultured person; but, in addition to that a loud male voice may emanate from a female larynx and may occasionally attain oratorical proportions. Moreover, the orator may deal with great themes in a style which we cannot associate with the fragile little woman who has gone into trance and is now under control. This is a phenomenon which undoubtedly calls attention to the existence of something supernormal, and can be appealed to as testifying to the reality and activity of a spiritual world."

Sources:

Astrotheme (French): http://www.astrotheme.fr/portraits

Fodor, Nandor: *Encyclopedia of Psychic Science*. London: Arthurs Press, 1933

Lodge, Sir Oliver: *Past Years: An Autobiography*. London: Hodder & Stoughton, 1931

The Spirit which made a "Talkie" Article: http://www.survivalafterdeath.org/books/fodor/chapter25.htm

Morris Pratt Institute *see* **Pratt, Morris**

MORSE, JAMES JOHNSON (1848–1919)

Known as "the Bishop of **Spiritualism**," J. J. Morse was a great **trance** speaker. He was born on October 1, 1848, in England. Orphaned at the age of ten, Morse had very little education and worked in a pub. E. W. Cox, Serjeant-at-Law, early **psychical researcher** and author of *What Am I? A Popular Introduction to Mental Physiology and Psychology* (London, 1874), wrote of Morse, "I have heard an uneducated barman, when in a state of trance, maintain a dialogue with a party of philosophers on Reason and Foreknowledge, Will and Fate, and hold his own against them. I have put to him the most difficult questions in psychology, and received answers always thoughtful, often full of wisdom, and invariably conveyed in choice and eloquent language. Nevertheless, in a quarter of an hour afterwards, when released from the trance, he was unable to answer the simplest query on a philosophical subject, and was at a loss for sufficient language in which to express a commonplace idea."

In 1869, Morse started speaking in trance as the ancient Chinese philosopher Tien Sien Tie, who lived during the reign of the Emperor Kea-Tsing. Other **spirits** also spoke through Morse, including one humorous one known as "The Strolling Player." Morse was also a **physical medium**. He demonstrated the fire test and also elongation—making himself taller than he normally was (*see also* **Home, Daniel Dunglas**).

Morse traveled to Australia and New Zealand. From 1901 to 1902 he published *The Spiritual Review*. He edited *The Banner of Light* in 1904, and beginning in 1906, he edited the British ***Two***

Worlds. Over the years, Morse gave more than 6,000 addresses on a wide variety of subjects. He helped form the **British National Association of Spiritualists** in Liverpool, which later became the London Spiritualist Alliance.

Morse's daughter Florence was clairvoyant from childhood. She later became an inspirational speaker and traveled extensively, visiting America, Australia, New Zealand, and South Africa. Unlike her father, she was always fully conscious—never in trance—when speaking.

Sources:

Awtry-Smith, Marilyn: *"They" Paved the Way*. New York: Spiritualism & More, nd

Shepard, Leslie A: *Encyclopedia of Occultism & Parapsychology*. New York: Avon Books, 1978

MOSES, WILLIAM STAINTON (1839–1892)

William Stainton Moses was born at Donnington, Lincolnshire, England, in 1839. His father was headmaster of Donnington Grammar School. The family moved to Bedford in 1852, and Moses attended Bedford Grammar School. He went to Exeter College in Oxford on a scholarship. At Exeter, his health broke down before his final exams and he went abroad, but later returned and received his Master of Arts degree. In 1863, he was ordained as a Minister of the Church of England and spent time as a curate on the Isle of Man and in Dorsetshire. But his health did not hold up to the rigors of the church. He became seriously ill in 1869, convalescing with Dr. and Mrs. Stanhope Templeton Speers and in 1870, becoming a tutor to the Speers' son. He kept that position for seven years.

In 1872, Moses read R. Dale Owen's book *The Debatable Land*. He initially distrusted **Spiritualism**, but at Mrs. Speers' suggestion, went to a number of **séances** given by such **mediums** as **Daniel Dunglas Home** and **Lottie Fowler**. He soon found himself developing his own mediumistic powers. He gave private séances for the Speers and their friends. Dr. Speers kept impeccable records of these sittings, which started with **rappings** and quickly advanced to include **levitations** and **apports**. **Spirit lights** appeared and Moses himself was levitated. He soon became one of the greatest **physical medium** of all, after D. D. Home and **Carlos Mirabelli**. In *What Am I? A Popular Introduction to Mental Physiology and Psychology* (London, 1874) E. W. Cox, Serjeant-at-Law and early **psychical researcher**, described the swaying and rocking of a mahogany table measuring nine by six feet, which would normally require two strong men to move it even a few inches. This took place in daylight. When Cox and Moses stood over it, holding out their hands, the table lifted first on one end and then on the other. The physical phenomena continued until 1881.

Moses' séances frequently featured various scents. The most common were musk, verbena, new mown hay, and an unfamiliar odor referred to as "spirit scent." Without musical instruments in evidence, a variety of musical sounds was heard. **Nandor Fodor** reports, "The character and integrity of William Stainton Moses was so high that Andrew Lang was forced to warn the advocates of fraud that 'the choice is between a moral and physical miracle.'"

Moses was probably best known for the large number of **automatic writings** from various **spirits** that he produced and that were published under the title *Spirit Teachings* (London, 1883). Describing the automatic writing procedure, Moses said,

> It is an interesting subject for speculation whether my own thoughts entered into the subject matter of the communications. I took extraordinary pains to prevent any such admixture. At first the writing was slow and it was necessary for me to follow it with my eye, but even then the thoughts were not my thoughts. Very soon the messages assumed a character of which I had no doubt whatever that the thought was opposed to my own. But I cultivated the power of occupying my mind with other

William Stainton Moses (1839–1892), British medium and theologian, experienced an array of psychic phenomena, including apports, levitation and automatic writing. *Courtesy Fortean Picture Library.*

things during the time that the writing was going on, and was able to read an abstruse book and follow out a line of close reasoning, while the message was written with unbroken regularity. Messages so written extended over many pages and in their course there is no correction, no fault in composition, and often a sustained vigour and beauty of style.

The writings came from forty-nine spirits, including those who were called Imperator, Preceptor, and Rector. The writings lasted from 1872 to 1883, and started to gradually die away in 1877. They filled twenty-four notebooks. They were written while Moses was in the waking state, not in **trance**, and were written in the form of a dialogue. Imperator first spoke directly on

December 19, 1892, but had appeared to Moses **clairvoyantly** earlier than that.

Moses later assisted in the founding of the **British National Association of Spiritualists** and served on the councils of the Psychological Society and the Society for Psychical Research. He was president of the London Spiritual Alliance from 1884 until his death in 1892, and left a deep impression on Spiritualism. His books included *Spirit Identity* (1879), *Psychography* (1882), *Spirit Teachings* (1883), and *Higher Aspects of Spiritualism* (1880).

Sources:

Buckland, Raymond: *The Fortune-Telling Book: The Encyclopedia of Divination and Soothsaying*. Detroit: Visible Ink Press, 2004

Ebon, Martin: *True Experiences in Communicating With the Dead*. New York: New American Library, 1968

Fodor, Nandor: *Encyclopedia of Psychic Science*. London: Arthurs Press, 1933

Moses, William Stainton: *Direct Spirit Writing*. London: L. N. Fowler, 1878

Moses, William Stainton: *More Spirit Teachings*. London: L. N. Fowler, nd

Mühl, Anita M.: *Automatic Writing*. Dresden: Steinkopff, 1930

Spence, Lewis: *An Encyclopedia of the Occult*. London: George Routledge & Sons, 1920

MOZART, WOLFGANG AMADEUS (1756–1791)

The Austrian composer Wolfgang Amadeus Mozart was a child prodigy who began composing at the age of four. He said that his compositions came to him as a whole and all he had to do was write them down. In his own mind, he was a "receptor;" an instrument through which some unknown power **channeled** glorious music.

Mozart was born in Salzburg, Austria on January 27, 1756. He was the youngest of seven children, five of whom died in infancy. His father was the teacher and composer Leopold Mozart and was employed as a violinist in the establishment of the Prince-Archbishop of Salzburg. Mozart's mother was Anna Maria Pertl. At age six, Mozart played the harpsichord so well that his father took him to perform at the Munich court. His sister Maria Anna was equally talented. Later in the same year they both played before the Austrian Emperor and Empress in Vienna.

Some believe that **spirit** performed through Mozart, others that he channeled some unknown entity, and still others that this was a case proving **reincarnation**—that Mozart had been a talented musician in a previous life and that the ability was "carried over."

Sources:

Encyclopedia Britannica. Chicago: William Benton, 1964

Roy, Archie: *Mysteries of Mind Space & Time; the Unexplained: The Genius Within.* Westport: H. S. Stuttman, 1992

MULDOON, SYLVAN JOSEPH

Sylvan Joseph Muldoon was a pioneer researcher of **astral projection** and out of body experiences (OBE). At the age of twelve, he went with his mother to a **Spiritualist** camp at Clinton, Iowa. He was so moved and stimulated by his environment that he experienced spontaneous astral projection, suddenly finding himself floating above his body and looking down on it. His first thought was that he had died in his sleep. He moved through the house, trying to wake members of his family, but without success. Eventually he was drawn back into his body by the **silver cord** that connected the **ethereal double** to the physical body. This was the first of many hundreds of projections he experienced over the years.

In 1927, he read **Hereward Carrington**'s books and found reference to Charles Lancelin. Based on Lancelin's book *Le Fantôme des Vivants*, Carrington considered him the expert on astral projection. Muldoon told Carrington that he knew far more than Lancelin and could write a book himself on the subject. This led to Muldoon and Carrington collaborating on the book *Projection of the Astral Body* (1929), *The Case for Astral Projection* (1936),

and *The Phenomena of Astral Projection* (1951). Muldoon also wrote *Sensational Psychic Experiences* (1941) and *Famous Psychic Stories* (1942).

Sources:

Fodor, Nandor: *Encyclopedia of Psychic Science.* London: Arthurs Press, 1933

Muldoon, Sylvan J. and Hereward Carrington: *The Case for Astral Projection.* Chicago: Aries Press, 1936

Muldoon, Sylvan J. and Hereward Carrington: *The Projection of the Astral Body.* London: Rider, 1929

Tabori, Paul: *Pioneers of the Unseen.* New York: Taplinger, 1973

MÜLLER, AUGUSTE

Auguste Müller of Karlsruhe was the first German somnambulist to claim that she had made contact with **spirits** of the dead. Her **spirit guide** was her deceased mother. Müller gave many exhibitions of her **clairvoyance**. Her case was written up in detail by Dr. Meier in *Höchst Merkwürdige Geschichte der Magnetisch Hellsehenden Auguste Müller* (Stuttgart: Metzler, 1818). According to **Frank Podmore**,

> The young woman in the **trance** was able to diagnose and prescribe for the ailments of herself and other persons in the usual fashion. She said in the trance that she could discern not only the bodies of men, but also their thoughts and characters; but no proofs are offered of this power. She claimed to converse with the spirit of her dead mother. She also said that she could visit her brother in Vienna, and make her presence known to him; but she rejected Dr. Meier's suggestion that she should speak aloud, for fear that she should frighten him. It is recorded that with her eyes closed she could read theatre tickets and songs out of a music book. But no details are given. The nearest approach to a test is as follows: Meier asked her one evening whether she could tell him anything noteworthy which had recently happened in his own family, and the clairvoyant in reply

was able to tell him of the death of his father-in-law at a town fifteen miles off Meier had received the news of this event on the morning of that day, but was confident— a confidence which he does not enable us to share—that the somnambule knew nothing about it. One other case may be cited. A friend of Auguste, one Catharine, happened to be suffering from toothache, and told the somnambule that she would probably be unable to pay her usual visit on the following day. Auguste replied, "I will visit you, then, tonight." That night Catharine is reported to have seen Auguste enter her room clothed in a night dress. The form, which hovered above the floor, came up to Catharine and lay beside her in bed. In the morning Catharine awoke to find her toothache gone, and was much astonished to learn that Auguste had never left her own bed all the night through. The incident is regarded by Meier as a manifest proof of the existence of a **psychic** body. Kieser, as already mentioned, reviewing the case in the Archiv, adduces it as a striking instance of action at a distance, conditioned by the rapport between the young women.

Sources:

The German Somnambules Article: http://www.survivalafterdeath.org/articles/podmore/german.htm

Podmore, Frank: *Modern Spiritualism*. London: 1902; reprinted as *Mediums of the Nineteenth Century*. New York: University Books, 1963

Shepard, Leslie A: *Encyclopedia of Occultism & Parapsychology*. New York: Avon Books, 1978

Mumler, William H. (D. 1884)

According to Sir **Arthur Conan Doyle**, the first **spirit photographs** were probably taken by the English photographer Richard Boursnell, in 1851. Unfortunately none of these photographs were preserved, so William H. Mumler of Boston, Massachusetts, is generally regarded as the first **spirit** photographer.

Mumler was an engraver with Boston jewelers Bigelow, Kennard & Co. He was not a **Spiritualist** or even a professional photographer. One day in 1861, he was at the studio of a photographer friend, amusing himself with the equipment. He tried to take a photograph of himself; the resulting picture showed another figure beside him. His technique was to set up the camera and focus it on a chair. He would then uncap the lens and jump into position, standing beside the chair and holding still while the camera mechanism tripped and took the photograph. On the back of that first photograph, he wrote,

> "This photograph was taken of myself, by myself, on Sunday, when there was not a living soul in the room beside me—so to speak. The form on my right I recognize as my cousin, who passed away about twelve years since."

The photograph shows a young girl sitting in the chair, with the chair itself visible through her body. A contemporary account said that the form faded away into a dim mist that clouds over the lower part of the picture.

News of this phantom photograph spread quickly. Many people approached Mumler and asked him to take their photograph, in the hopes that a ghost would appear in them. So many asked, in fact, that Mumler was obliged to give up his job as an engraver and become a professional photographer. Bookings were made weeks ahead by doctors, ministers, lawyers, judges, professors, mayors, and all types of business men. *The Spiritual Magazine* of 1862 contains detailed accounts of many of the sittings.

Many appointments were made by people who believed that it was some sort of trick. Consequently, they asked Mumler to take photographs with marked plates, with other people's equipment, and with other people handling the whole procedure from loading the camera to developing the picture. But still the spirit forms appeared.

Herald of Progress editor **Andrew Jackson Davis** sent William Guay, a professional photographer, to check out Mumler. Guay reported that he controlled the whole procedure himself on several separate occasions, and always the result was the same—spirit photographs. He was convinced of the genuineness of the affair.

One of Mumler's best known photographs was of Mary Todd Lincoln, widow of the assassinated President **Abraham Lincoln**. Under the pseudonym of "Mrs. Tyndall," she went to Mumler's studio. She was still dressed in mourning black and heavily veiled prior to the taking of the photograph. When the picture was developed another woman present saw an image standing behind Mrs. Lincoln. She said, "Why, that looks like President Lincoln." Mrs. Lincoln replied, "Yes it does. I am his widow."

Not all people believed the results were genuine, however. Even some of Mumler's friends thought that he had to be faking them. In a letter to the *Banner of Light* on February 20, 1863, Dr. Gardner said, "While I am fully of the belief that genuine spirit likenesses have been produced through his **mediumship**, evidence of deception in two cases, at least, has been furnished me, which is perfectly conclusive ... Mr. Mumler, or some person connected with Mrs. Stuart's rooms, has been guilty of deception in palming off as genuine spirit likenesses pictures of a person who is now living in the city." This did happen on occasion—and not only to Mumler—and no one has been able to explain how or why. The "evidence of deception" was the image of someone who was still living appearing in one of the photographs, in the same way that the dead spirits did. Whether or not the charge of fraud was true, this turned pubic opinion against Mumler and he left Boston for New York. However, other people endorsed Mumler, including many professional photographers who were not Spiritualists. Jeremiah Gurney said, "I have been a photographer for twenty-eight years; I have witnessed Mumler's process, and although I went prepared to scrutinize everything, I could find nothing which savoured of fraud or trickery." William Mumler

wrote his own account of this time in *Personal Experiences of William H. Mumler in Spirit Photography* (Boston, 1875). He died penniless in 1884.

The spirit world had predicted the advent of spirit photographs. Thomas Slater, an optician, was holding a **séance** with Lord Brougham and Robert Owen, in 1856, when the received **rappings** spelled out that Slater would one day take spirit photographs. Owen commented that if he was dead by the time such photographs were possible, then he would make a point of appearing in one himself. According to *The Spiritualist* of November 1, 1873, that is exactly what happened.

Sources:

Doyle, Sir Arthur Conan: *The History of Spiritualism*. New York: Doran, 1926

Fodor, Nandor: *Mind Over Space*. New York: Citadel, 1962

MURPHY, DR. EDGAR GARDNER (1895–1979)

Edgar Gardner Murphy was born at Chillicothe, Ohio—site of the famous Indian Serpent Mound—on July 8, 1895. He received a B.A. in 1916 from Yale University and an M.A. in 1917 from Harvard. He received a Ph.D. in 1923 from Columbia University. While at Columbia, he initiated the first telepathic experiments through wireless communication in Chicago and Newark. He reviewed this work at the Clark University's Symposium under the title *Telepathy as an Experimental Problem*.

In 1926, Murphy married Lois Barclay of Lisbon, Iowa. She was the daughter of Wade Crawford and Mary Barclay. Gardner taught psychology, first as an instructor (1921–1925), then an assistant professor (1925–1929), and then as a full professor. He was Chairman of the Department of Psychology, City College of New York, from 1940 to 1952, and Director of Research at Menninger Foundation, Topeka, Kansas, from 1952 onwards. Murphy became a member of the American Psychological Association and was its President in

1944. He was also a member of the American Association for the Advancement of Science. In 1972, he received the Gold Medal Award of the American Psychological Association.

As early as 1917, Gardner Murphy was a member of the **American Society for Psychical Research** (ASPR). **Psychical research** was the focus of his graduate work at Harvard. From 1940 to 1962, he served as Vice President of the ASPR, and then became President. It has been said that his "study of psychology began as a preparation for work in psychical research, but he became one of the most beloved and revered psychologists of the mid-twentieth century, as well as an inspiring leader in psychical research." He wrote many books on both subjects, including *Historical Introduction to Modern Psychology* (1925), *In the Minds of Men* (1953), **William James** *and Psychical Research* (1960), and *The Challenge of Psychical Research* (1961). He contributed a large number of important papers to the *ASPR Journal*.

In 1927, Murphy suffered from persistent influenza and near blindness. Dr. Frank Marlow and Dr. William H. Hay worked with him, using diet, exercise, and natural medicine to overcome his semi-invalid condition. This contributed to his open-mindedness about paranormal phenomena. He commented, "One of the main questions of psychic research is whether we can give up our precious folklore and intuition about vast regions of the unknown without throwing out useful data."

Sources:

Lois Barclay Murphy Biography: http://www.webster. edu/~woolflm/murphy.html

Pesquisa Psi (Italian): http://www.pesquisapsi.com/ News/pesquisadorespsi/41/9/9

Shepard, Leslie A: *Encyclopedia of Occultism & Parapsychology*. New York: Avon Books, 1978

MYERS, DR. ARTHUR THOMAS (1851–1894)

Arthur Thomas Myers was the younger brother of **Frederick W. H. Myers**. Arthur was born in England in 1851. He was a founding member of the **Society for Psychical Research** (SPR) and served on its council from 1888 to 1894. He was especially interested in cases of paranormal **healing** and made a special study of **hypnotism**.

Myers joined with French neurologist Pierre Janet in experimenting with **telepathic** hypnosis. He also participated in some of the SPR sittings with American medium **Leonore Piper**. He contributed articles to medical journals, the *SPR Proceedings: Report on an Alleged Physical Phenomenon*, and *Mind-Cure, Faith Cure, and the Miracles of Lourdes*. He died in London on January 10, 1894.

Sources:

Fodor, Nandor: *Encyclopedia of Psychic Science*. London: Arthurs Press, 1933

MYERS, FREDERICK WILLIAM HENRY (1843–1901)

Frederick William Henry Myers was born in Keswick, Cumberland, England, on February 6, 1843. His parents were Rev. Frederick Myers and Susan Harriet Marshall. Frederick had two younger brothers. When his father died in 1851, the family moved to Cheltenham and Myers was sent to school at Cheltenham College. There he showed outstanding classical and literary ability and in 1860, he went to Trinity College, Cambridge.

Myers graduated from Trinity College in October, 1864. Early the next year, he traveled in Europe, spending time in **Greece** and Italy. Later that same year he visited the United States and Canada. He accepted a Fellowship in Classics at Trinity College, and remained there for four years before resigning and turning to the higher education of women. In 1873, he became an inspector of schools in Cambridge, a position he retained for nearly thirty years until his death in 1901.

While a Fellow at Trinity College during the 1870s, Myers became close friends with **Henry Sidgwick** and **Edmund Gurney**. Sidgwick became a mentor of Myers's and Gurney became Myers's pupil. In 1874, after a sitting with the

Frederick William Henry Myers (1843–1901), psychic researcher, scholar, and psychologist, co-founded the Society for Psychical Research in 1882. *Courtesy Fortean Picture Library.*

medium **William Stainton Moses**, the three formed a loose group to study **mediumship**. In 1882, at the urging of Sir **William Barrett**, the three men formed the **Society for Psychical Research** (SPR), with Sidgwick as President and Gurney as Secretary. In 1888, after Gurney's unexpected death, Myers became Secretary and in 1900, he became President.

Myers was one of the co-authors, with Gurney and **Frank Podmore**, of *Phantasms of the Living*, published by the Society for Psychical Research in 1886. In 1903, Myers's classic two-volume work *Human Personality and Its Survival of Bodily Death* was published posthumously. The first vol-ume of this work deals with various phenomena such as **dreams** and dissociation of the personality, while the second volume examines and reports on the communications of **Spiritualist** mediums, **apparitions** of the dead, and other phenomena of the paranormal.

One of the major contributions made by Myers to the field of **psychical research** was the introduction of **cross-correspondences** as proof that **mediums** are not transmitting anything from their own unconscious nor indulging in **telepathy** (a word coined by Myers) from the sitter. Cross-correspondences are a series of messages that come through a number of different mediums, often spread around the world. Each message is incomplete in itself, but fits together with the others to give a whole. The received messages are sent to a central control—in the early experiments this was the Society for Psychical Research—where they are examined and correlated. The early experiments revolved around obscure classical subjects that made no sense at all to the mediums **channeling** them, but indicated that they came from the then recently deceased Myers, Sidgwick, and Gurney.

Myers's personal life was checkered. As a young man, he was homosexual. He later fell in love with Annie Eliza, the wife of his cousin Walter James Marshall. She returned the love, though it was never consummated. Annie committed suicide in September 1876, but both she and Myers believed they would be together in the afterlife. On March 13, 1880, Myers married Eveleen Tennant and they had three children. By 1900, Myers was seriously ill and traveled to Rome for unorthodox medical treatment. He died in Rome on January 17, 1901.

Sources:

Broad, C.D.: *Man, Myth & Magic: F.W.H. Myers*. London: BPC Publishing,1970

Myers, F. W. H.: *Human Personality and Its Survival After Bodily Death*. London: Longmans, 1903

NAGY, RONALD MICHAEL (B. 1949)

R on Nagy was born on November 2, 1949, in Phoenixville, Pennsylvania. His father was Michael J. Nagy and his mother Margaret E. Gatlos. He has one sister, Carol Ann. Nagy grew up in Royersford, Pennsylvaina, and attended Spring-Ford schools. He graduated high school in 1967 and went on to Western Kentucky University. Nagy enlisted in the U.S. Air Force in October, 1969, and took part in NATO exercises in England, Germany, Spain, and Greece. He left the Air Force in 1971 and served in the Pennsylvania National Guard until 1977. In 1973, he married Virgina Verish of Phoenixville, and they had three children: Sarah, Michael, and Mark. The couple divorced in 1990.

Nagy worked at various heavy industry jobs until 1985. He was a correctional officer from 1985 to 2001. Throughout this last employment, Nagy took an interest in and gradually expanded his knowledge of **psychical research** and **metaphysics**. He had a lifelong interest in the **Association for Research and Enlightenment**, the **Edgar Cayce** Foundation headquartered at Virginia Beach, Virginia. Believing that "nothing happens by chance," Nagy discovered **Spiritual-**

ism and felt a sense of "coming home." The teachings seemed to answer many questions arising from experiences that he had previously considered "coincidental."

Nagy started the **Morris Pratt** Course on Modern Spiritualism, and completed it in record time. He moved to **Lily Dale**, New York, the oldest and largest Spiritualist community in the world. There he met Joyce LaJudice, Historian of the **Lily Dale Museum**, who recognized his potential and engaged him as an assistant. LaJudice shared with him with her intimate knowledge of the 125 years of Lily Dale history and the general history of Spiritualism. Nagy considers her the person who has had the greatest impact on his life.

Nagy gives lecture tours of Lily Dale during the summer tourist season. His talks have been very well received based on his blending of basic facts with the "moods and events of this country during the formative days of Spiritualism." He has helped redesign the Lily Dale Museum and to better present the many artifacts it contains. He has made himself the foremost expert on precipitated **spirit** paintings of the type produced by the **Bangs Sisters** and the **Campbell Brothers**. His book *Precipitated Spirit Paintings: Beyond the Shad-*

ow of Doubt (2005) is the first major work on the subject. He has also contributed many articles to **The National Spiritualist Summit**, the monthly journal of the **National Spiritualist Association of Churches**.

Sources:

Nagy, Ron: *Precipitated Spirit Paintings: Beyond the Shadow of Doubt*. Lakeville: Galde Press, 2005

NATIONAL LABORATORY OF PSYCHICAL RESEARCH

The National Laboratory of Psychical Research was founded in 1925 in London by **psychical researcher Harry Price**. It was established, with Price as Director, "to investigate in a dispassionate manner and by purely scientific means every phase of psychic or alleged **psychic** phenomena." It was located at 13 Roland Gardens, London, SW 7, England, but had ceased to function by 1950. During its lifetime it published a bimonthly, *The British Journal of Psychical Research* which ran from 1925 until 1929. It also published a number of bulletins including *Regurgitation and the Duncan Mediumship* (1932), *Fraudulent **Mediums*** (1932), *The Identification of the "Walter" Prints* (1933), and *An Account of Some Further Experiments with **Rudi Schneider*** (1933).

Sources:

Fodor, Nandor: *Encyclopedia of Psychic Science*. London: Arthurs Press, 1933

NATIONAL SPIRITUAL ALLIANCE OF THE UNITED STATES OF AMERICA

The National Spiritual Alliance was formed after members of the New England Spiritual **Campmeeting** Association were unable to resolve philosophical differences on reincarnation and decided to split into two groups, following separate paths. The group that formed the National Spiritual Alliance firmly believed in **reincarnation** as a learning vehicle that assisted the soul's

progression toward perfection, and that "intercommunication between the denizens of different worlds is scientifically established." The Alliance was incorporated on September 12, 1913, in Lake Pleasant, Massachusetts. Its Constitution was adopted that year and was revised at the organization's annual meeting in July 2000.

Lake Pleasant was also the home of rival **Spiritualist** organizations, each with its own followers and temple. In 1955, the temple of the New England Spiritual Campmeeting Association burned down and was not rebuilt. Its followers continued to meet until 1976. At that time they donated their remaining property to the town of Montague and disbanded. This left The National Spiritual Alliance as the only organization in that location. It continues to be active, with several thousand visitors per year. Sunday services, **psychic fairs**, development classes, and other programs are organized annually. Its official emblem is the pond lily, adopted because "Though it strikes its roots into mud, sends its shoots up through putrid waters and spreads its leaves over the green scum of the pond, yet it evolves purity, beauty, and fragrance, and but dies to live again."

Sources:

The National Spiritual Alliance: http://www.thenationalspiritualallianceinc.org

Shepard, Leslie A: *Encyclopedia of Occultism & Parapsychology*. New York: Avon Books, 1978

NATIONAL SPIRITUALIST ASSOCIATION OF CHURCHES

The National Delegate Convention of **Spiritualists** of the United States of America was organized in Chicago, Illinois, in 1893. The first Convention of the Association was held at 77 Thirty-First Street, Chicago, on September 27-29 of that year. Harrison D. Barrett was elected President by unanimous ballot of the convention. He remained in that position through 1906, when Dr. George B. Warne took over.

The National Spiritualist Association of Churches of the United States of America (NSAC) is a religious body whose Declaration of Principles was first adopted in Chicago in 1899, as the National Spiritualist Association. It declares, "Spiritualism is the Science, Philosophy and Religion of a continuous life, based upon the demonstrable fact of communication, by means of **mediumship**, with those who live in the **spirit world** ... "The Phenomena of Spiritualism consist of **Prophecy, Clairvoyance, Clairaudience, Gift of Tongues, Laying-on of Hands, Healing, visions, Trance, Apports, Levitation, Raps, Automatic** and **Independent Writings** and **Paintings**, Voice, **Materialization, (Spirit) Photography, Psychometry** and many other manifestations proving the continuity of life as demonstrated through the Physical and Spiritual senses and faculties of man."

Today the NSAC is headquartered in Lily Dale, New York and Washington, D.C. It offers church charters for Spiritualist groups of four auxiliary types: state association, church, camp, and educational auxiliary. It also ordains of Ministers, certifies Mediums, Teachers, and **Spiritual Healers**, and commissions Missionaries. Through the **Morris Pratt** Institute and the **College of Spiritualist Studies**, various courses and diploma programs are offered. The Association has several departments and bureaus: **Lyceums**, Phenomenal Evidence, Endowments, Public Relations, Education, Publications, and Missionaries.

The National Spiritualist Summit is the official journal of the NSAC, published monthly. The *Lyceum Spotlight Magazine* is published ten times a year. There is a free monthly e-mail newsletter available from newsletter@nsac.org.

Sources:

National Spiritualist Association of Churches: *NSAC Spiritualist Manual.* Lily Dale: NSAC, 1911; 2002

Morris Pratt Institute: *Educational Course on Modern Spiritualism.* Milwaukee: M.P.I., 1981

NATIONAL SPIRITUALIST SUMMIT, THE

The journal of the **National Spiritualist Association of Churches**. *The National Spiritualist*

Summit was established in 1919 and is published monthly. Its current editor is the Rev. Sandy Pfortmiller.

NATIVE AMERICANS

Many **spirit guides** who work with **mediums** appear as Native Americans. For example, **Estelle Roberts'** Red Cloud, Stephen O'Brien's White Owl, **Maurice Barbanell's** Silver Birch, Kathleen Barkel's White Hawk, and Ronald Hearn's Running Water. **Nandor Fodor** lists many others: North Star (**Gladys Leonard**), White Feather (John Sloan), Greyfeather (J. B. Jonson), Grey Wolf (Hazel Ridley), Bright Eyes (**May Pepper**), Red Crow (Frederick Foster Craddock), Black Hawk (**Evan Powell**), Black Foot (John Myers), Moonstone (Vout Peters), Tecumseh (W. H. Powell), and many more.

In *This Is Spiritualism* (1959), Maurice Barbanell discusses the number of Native American spirit guides, saying, "North American Indians were masters of **psychic** laws, with a profound knowledge of supernormal forces and how they operated. This qualifies them, after their passing, to act as tutors and guides to their mediums." Certainly most Spiritualists acknowledge that by their very lifestyle, being close to nature and working with the earth, Native Americans were probably much more in tune with the forces of nature and so were able to accept communication with **spirits**.

Whether or not it is because modern **Spiritualism** was born in North America, the tie with Native Americans seems firmly established to the point where many mediums—both in America and around the world—enjoy such a figure as their spirit guide. In *Spiritualism Explained*), E. W. Wallis wrote, "Many [American] Indian spirits become true and faithful friends. They act as protectors—'doorkeepers' so to speak—to their mediums. They do the hard work of development in the **circle** and prevent the intrusion of undesirable spirits. Sometimes they are boisterous and exuberant in their operations and manifestations ... we think it is wise to exercise a restraining influence over their

Pueblo Indian near Gallup, New Mexico, in 1937. Spirits and communication with the dead have long been an integral part of Native American culture. *AP/WideWorld Photos.*

demonstrations. They generally possess strong **healing** power and frequently put their mediums through a course of calisthenic exercises."

Scottish medium **Gordon Smith** has a list of popular myths about mediums that he likes to dispel. One is as follows: "*Myth #4: Mediums always have Native American spirit guides.* There are lots of Native American guides, but they're probably only there to try to sort out some of the cowboys who call themselves mediums!"

Sources:

Barbanell, Maurice: *This Is Spiritualism.* Oxshott: The Spiritual Truth Press, 1959

Fodor, Nandor: *Encyclopedia of Psychic Science.* London: Arthurs Press, 1933

Smith, Gordon: *The Unbelievable Truth: A Medium's Guide to the Spirit World.* London: Hay House, 2004

NATURE SPIRITS

According to Carl Jung, nature spirits were an early stage of human evolution. They have been termed deva, **fairies**, **angels**, undines (water spirits), sylvans (woodland spirits), pixies, and gnomes (earth spirits). Many gardeners believe that on occasion they see nature **spirits** among the flowers and vegetables. In the 1960s, **Peter Caddy** founded a community known as Findhorn on the barren, windswept coast of Inverness, Scotland, and watched it blossom into a rich, fertile paradise worked by nature spirits. When Peter Caddy and his wife Eileen started to work the area it was a truly inhospitable place, with sandy soil and sparse, desertlike life. But in a few short years the Caddys and some few others who joined them were producing huge vegetables (42-pound cabbages and 60-pound broccoli plants), beautiful flowers, 21 types of fruit, 42 herbs, and a total of 65 different vegetables. They said the focus of their work was love, and it was always acknowledged that everything was done with the help of the spirits of the land.

There is plenty of evidence for such spirits. Penny Kelly had a similar experience to Caddy's at Lily Hill Farm, though she makes a point of not saying where the farm is located. She claims that the spirits, or elves as she calls them, brought about an annual harvest of one hundred tons of grapes from just thirteen acres of vineyards.

Sources:

Bletzer, June G.: *The Encyclopedia Psychic Dictionary.* Lithia Springs: New Leaf, 1998

Briggs, Katharine: *Abbey Lubbers, Banshees & Boggarts: An Illustrated Encyclopedia of Fairies.* New York: Pantheon Books, 1979

Kelly, Penny: *The Elves of Lily Hill Farm.* St. Paul: Llewellyn, 1997

McCoy, Edain: *A Witch's Guide to Faery Folk.* St. Paul, Llewellyn, 2000

Spence, Lewis: *The Fairy Tradition in Britain.* London: Rider, 1948

NEAR DEATH EXPERIENCES (NDE)

The introduction to *Quest For the Unknown: Life Beyond Death* reads, "The possibility of

Specter of the Broken is a rare atmospheric phenomenon that produces a halo around the shadow of an object and is often mistaken for an apparition. This image was taken at Saddle Mountain, Oregon at sunset. *Dan Sherwood/Photographer's Choice/Getty Images.*

an existence after death fascinates us all. For **psychics, channelers, mediums,** and **reincarnationists** the continuation of life is a certainty. In recent years many ordinary people without mystical connections have also become convinced, having had what they believe to be an inspirational glimpse beyond the grave." That "inspirational glimpse" is referred to as a Near Death Experience (NDE).

In 1976, Dr. Michael B. Sabom of the University of Florida conducted NDE research with psychiatric social worker Sarah Kreutziger. Inspired by the pioneering work of **Raymond Moody,** they interviewed 100 patients who had undergone surgery and had suffered a near fatal crisis.

Dr. Saborn reported, "Near death experiences were reported by 61 (out of 100). The details of these were surprisingly consistent and of three types: self-visualization from a position of height; passage into a foreign region or dimension; or a combination of both." The self-visualization from a height was **astral projection,** after the **spirit** body had separated from the physical body. This usually took place at the point where clinical death was registered. Frequently the patient was later able to correctly repeat conversations that took place between doctors and surgery staff. Some have described, in detail, the surgical procedures that occurred.

Most of the patients spoke of a tremendous feeling of peace that came over them, and of going into total darkness. Some got the sensation of moving through the darkness at great speed, traveling through a long, dark tunnel. To add to the illusion, they would see a light at the far end, sometimes with a figure standing in it. Sometimes this "being of light" turned out to be a religious figure with which they were familiar, and sometimes it was a deceased relative. Many experienced the sound of wonderful music and found themselves in a beautiful garden. Most had the impression of scenes from their whole life flashing by. Many heard a voice saying they must return, or that it was not their time. Many begged to stay. British psychologist Dr. Margot Grey had a near death experience in India in 1976, and distinctly remembers hearing a stern male voice say to her, "Get back. Get back in there." She immediately found herself back in her body.

After a near death experience, the person returns to his or her physical body and to any pain that might be there. All state that their view of life is changed from that moment on, often with a new or renewed interest in spiritual matters. It is believed that many thousands, if not millions, of people have had a near death experience but have not spoken to anyone about it.

Sources:

Leonard, Sue (ed): *Quest For the Unknown—Life Beyond Death.* Pleasantville: Reader's Digest, 1992

Moody, Raymond: *Life After Life*. New York: Mockingbird Books, 1975

NEWBROUGH, DR. JOHN BALLOU (1828–1891)

Dr. John Ballou Newbrough was a New York dentist. As a child he was **clairvoyant** and **clairaudient**. When he grew older, he found that he was also an **automatic writer** and painter. He could paint in total darkness, using both hands at the same time. It is said that he could also read printed materials with his eyes closed. He could lift tremendous weights, as much as a ton, and had memory of **astral projections**.

In 1882, at the age of fifty-four, Newbrough published *OAHSPE: A Kosmon Bible in the words of Jehovah and his Angel Ambassadors*, the book for which he is best known. This new **Bible** was written on a typewriter, a new invention at that time. The book was written in the style of the King James version of the Bible. Newbrough described the composing of the book, saying,

> I was crying for the light of Heaven. I did not desire communication from friends or relatives or information about earthly things; I wished to learn something about the **spirit world**; what the **angels** did, how they traveled, and the general plan of the universe … I was directed to get a typewriter which writes by keys, like a piano. This I did and I applied myself industriously to learn it, but with only indifferent success. For two years more the angels propounded to me questions relative to heaven and earth, which no mortal could answer very intelligently … One morning the light struck both my hands on the back, and they went for the typewriter for some fifteen minutes very vigorously. I was told not to read what was printed, and I have worked myself into such a religious fear of losing this new power that I obeyed reverently. The next morning, also before sunrise, the same power came and wrote (or printed rather) again. Again I laid the matter away very religiously, saying little about it to anybody. One morning I accidentally (seemed accidental to me) looked out of the window and beheld the line of light that rested on my hands extended heavenward like a telegraph line towards the sky. Over my head were three pairs of hands, fully **materialized**; behind me stood another angel with her hands on my shoulders. My looking did not disturb the scene, my hands kept right on printing … printing. For fifty weeks this continued, every morning, half an hour or so before sunrise, and then it ceased, and I was told to read and publish the book *Oahspe*. The peculiar drawings in *Oahspe* were made with pencil in the same way.

The Kosmon Church was founded to practice the teachings of *Oahspe*. It has since become known as the Confraternity of Faithists or the Universal Brotherhood of Faithists. According to Melton, "In 1883, a convention was held in New York City to work toward founding a communal group to care for orphans and foundlings, as directed in *Oahspe*." A settlement was started in New Mexico but only lasted a couple of years.

There are several hundred Faithists in the United States, according to Melton. There are also groups in Britain and in Canada. They issue a quarterly publication, *The Faithist Journal*, and *The Kosmon Church Service Book*, which contains "the Kosmon ritual including liturgy for various masses, **healing**, marriage and dedication of children."

Sources:

Fodor, Nandor: *Encyclopedia of Psychic Science*. London: Arthurs Press, 1933

Melton, J. Gordon: *The Encyclopedia of American Religions*. Wilmington: McGrath, 1978

Newbrough, John B.: *Oahspe*. Los Angeles: 1935; London: Kosmon Press, 1960

New England Spiritual Campmeeting Association *see* **National Spiritual Alliance of the United States of America**

NEWSPAPER TESTS

These were experiments set up initially for testing the **medium Gladys Osborne Leonard**. They were recorded by the Reverend C. Drayton Thomas in his book *Some Recent Evidence for Survival* (London, 1948). The purpose was to rule out **telepathy** as the explanation for apparent **spirit** communications. Many other **psychic researchers** have subsequently used similar tests.

The method required the medium to ascertain, from spirit communication, the details of certain columns that would be published in *The Times* on the following day. The messages were received at a time of day before the newspaper had assembled its pages, therefore no one would know what words, or even which column, would appear on specific pages. The **predictions** were given to the **Society for Psychical Research** by 6:00 pm on the same day the messages were received. In tests conducted on February 13, 1920, at 3:00 pm, of the twelve items that were given, only two were completely incorrect. Enquiries at *The Times* revealed that at the time of the **séance**, in some cases the particular columns and wording referred to might have been set in type but the position in the paper, with regard to page and column placement, had not been decided. In other cases, the type had not even been set.

Sources:

Fodor, Nandor: *Encyclopedia of Psychic Science*. London: Arthurs Press, 1933

NORTHAGE, IVY

Despite one or two isolated instances of **clairvoyance** as a child, Ivy Northage had no idea she would grow up to be one of England's most respected **Spiritualist mediums**. Her serious involvement began with attempts at **table tipping**. She explained, "[I] received amazing evidence from my father whom I never knew since he was killed when I was only three months old. Intimate details of the three short years of my parents' marriage, which I could not possibly have known, were given, and later confirmed by my mother. This left no doubt whatsoever it was indeed my father communicating. The accuracy was astounding...."

With her husband, Northage started attending Spiritualist services. Her husband read many books on the subject, but a medium with whom they sat told him not to bother any more with **table tipping**, because his wife, Ivy, had the making of an excellent medium.

After a few months, Northage began to get the feeling of becoming two people, a "peculiar overshadowing of someone else, although still aware" of herself. This was her introduction to Chan, an Oriental who became her **spirit guide**. Chan led her through development, which included visits to many different Spiritualist churches to critique the techniques of different mediums. Northage made her first public appearance after eight years of development, at a Spiritualist church in Walthamstow, East London. This eventually led to her teaching development classes. From there Ivy Northage became one of the best known teaching mediums in Britain.

Sources:

Northage, Ivy: *Mechanics of Mediumship*. London: College of Psychic Studies, 1973

Northage, Ivy: *Mediumship Made Simple*. London: College of Psychic Studies, 1986

NOSTRADAMUS (MICHEL DE NOSTREDAME, 1503–1566)

Nostradamus was a French astrologer of Jewish descent, though his family converted to Christianity. His real name was Michel de Notre Dame, or Nostredame. He was born at St. Rémy, in Provence, on December 14, 1503. His father was a notary and ancestors on both his father's and his mother's sides were mathematicians and men of medicine. Nostradamus studied philosophy at Avignon and then medicine at the University of Montpellier, graduating from there in 1529. He

Portrait of Nostradamus by Lleonard Gaultier, c. 1618. The famed prophet was a physician by trade and also studied herbalism and astrology. *Courtesy Fortean Picture Library.*

first practiced at Agen. He married; his wife and two small children later died. On their deaths he retired to Provence. From there he was invited to Aix by the Parliament of Provence. He established himself at Salon, near Aix, in 1544, and became famous for his medical work during the plagues at Aix and Lyons. The town of Aix voted him a pension for his services during the contagion.

Nostradamus moved to Salon de Craux, between Avignon and Marseilles. There he married Anne Ponce Gemelle, and the couple had three sons and a daughter (some records say three sons and three daughters). He could read Hebrew, Greek, and Latin, and spoke several languages. In 1540, he published an almanac of weather **predictions** based on his astrological research. In 1547, Nostradamus started giving his major **prophesies**. He collected these and published them at Lyons, in a book titled *Centuries*, in 1555. He dedicated the first edition to his oldest son, Cæsar. An enlarged second edition, dedicated to the king, was published three years later. The book consisted of quatrains (four-line verses) grouped in hundreds. Each group was called a century. Nostradamus claimed that he derived his gift of prophecy from the tribe of Issachar, one of the ten lost tribes of Israel.

Astrology was at a peak at this time and many of Nostradamus's prophesies were fulfilled. Consequently he was appointed Physician-in-Ordinary by Charles IX, and given the title of Counselor. He received the Duke of Savoy at his salon and was invited to visit Queen Catherine de Médicis.

It is said that Nostradamus slept only three or four hours per night. He denied that he was a prophet, though he did feel that he had a gift of divine origin, "an infusion of supernatural light … inspired revelation … participation in divine eternity." He suffered from severe gout and other ailments. Nostradamus died at dawn on July 2, 1566, having foretold the exact day and even hour of his death. His widow set up a marble stone with a Latin inscription, which read,

"Here lie the bones of the illustrious Michel Nostradamus, whose almost divine pen alone, in the judgement of all mortals, was worthy to record, under the influx of stars, the future events of the whole world. He lived 62 years, 6 months, 17 days. He died at Salon in the year 1566. Posterity, disturb not his sweet rest! Anne Ponce Gemelle hopes for her husband true felicity."

For almost 500 years, people around the world have read Nostradamus' prophesies and tried to see how they might apply to the immediate future. They have been hailed as genuine prophetic messages, no matter how obscure the contents of the quatrains. Many have seemed to prove exceptionally accurate in the past, yet the possible meanings of most are perpetually disputed. All are written in such a convoluted manner that they could be applied to any one of a large number of possible historic events. It is possible, of course, that Nostradamus composed them all with his tongue firmly in his cheek. Apparently they were written in this veiled manner so as not to offend the Church of the time.

Enthusiasts claim that Nostradamus foretold the death of Charles I, the rise of Napoleon, the rise of Hitler, the atomic bombing of Japan, the abdication of Edward VIII, and the deaths of John and Robert Kennedy.

Sources:

MacHovec, Frank J.: *Nostradamus: His Prophecies for the Future*. Mount Vernon: Peter Pauper Press, 1972

Ward, Charles A.: *Oracles of Nostradamus*. New York: Charles Scribner's Sons, 1940

NUMEROLOGY

Numerology is **divination** through the **occult** significance of numbers. Pythagoras said, "The world is built upon the power of numbers." He was the one who reduced all to the power of the nine primaries. The numerals 1 through 9 are therefore the basis of all numbers and calculations in numerology. This is done by adding anything above 9. For example, 26 = 2+6 = 8. No matter the size of the number, it can be reduced in the same way. For example: 7,548,327 would become 7+5+4+8+3+2+7 = 36 = 3+6 = 9.

Working in Numerology, the same reduction can take place with words and letters, based on the following:

1	2	3	4	5	6	7	8	9
A	B	C	D	E	F	G	H	I
J	K	L	M	N	O	P	Q	R
S	T	U	V	W	X	Y	Z	

The word CASTLE, for example, would have the values C=3, A=1, S=1, T=2, L=3, E=5; 3+1+1+2+3+5 = 15 = 1+5 = 6. So the numerological value for the word "Castle" is 6.

In Numerology, dates and names are reduced to their primary numbers and then interpreted according to the values attributed to those numbers. Working with this, you can determine everything from where would be best to live, what job would be best for you, what sort of person to marry, and so on. To do this, it is first necessary to find your Birth Number and your Name Number.

For someone born on August 27, 1986, their birth number would be that date reduced to a single digit: 8+2+7+1+9+8+6 = 41 = 4+1 = 5. That person's Birth Number is 5. This number represents the influences at the time of birth and is the number to consider for all important events—such as signing contracts, or getting married. Since it is the number of your birth, it cannot be altered; unlike a Name Number which *can* be altered.

The Name Number is taken from the above chart. For example, Elvis Presley had a name number that was 5+3+4+9+1+7+9+5+1+3+5+7 = 59 = 14 = 5. Notice the 5s that occur. 5 people are physically and mentally active, make friends easily, and get along well with almost any other number. They are usually leaders of one sort or another. Another even more striking example of 5 was John F. Kennedy: 1685 6 2555547 = 59 = 14 = 5. Here there is a tremendous preponderance of 5s, ending with the Name Number itself being 5. Any recurring numeral, such as this, is considered to affect the personality.

The name you reduce in this way should be the name most generally used. Hence, "John F Kennedy" rather than just "John Kennedy" or "John Fitzgerald Kennedy." Based on this, Elvis's stronger Name Number would be simply ELVIS = 5+3+4+9+1 = 24 = 6; the 5 would be a secondary Name Number, contributing some qualities but not the major ones. Marriage compatibility can be seen by comparing birth numbers and considering name numbers.

There are certain values that are traditionally attached to the nine primary numbers. For example, 1 (Letters A, J, S) is associated with the Sun, and with the element of Fire. It is also associated with a leader and driving force who automatically assumes control. Each of the numbers has such associations.

There are also other systems of Numerology. All seem workable, but it is not wise to mix different systems. The above system is the most commonly used, and is referred to as the "modern" system or the "Pythagorean" system. The Hebrew system does not use the number 9, and does not follow the normal arrangement of letters. The Hebrew equivalents of English letters have been used, except where there is no exact parallel:

1	2	3	4	5	6	7	8
A	B	C	D	E	U	O	F
I	K	G	M	H	V	Z	P
Q	R	L	T	N	W		
J		S			X		
Y							

Another system is the one devised and used by Samuel Liddell MacGregor Mathers, of the nineteenth century Order of the Golden Dawn:

1	2	3	4	5	6	7	8
A	B	G	D	E	U	O	F
I	C	L	M	H	V	Z	P
J	K	S	T	N	W		
Q	R			X			
Y							

Sources:

Buckland, Raymond: *The Fortune–Telling Book: The Encyclopedia of Divination and Soothsaying*. Detroit: Visible Ink Press, 2004

Cavendish, Marshall: *The Book of Fate & Fortune*. London: Cavendish House, 1981

Cheasley, Clifford W.: *Numerology*. Boston: Triangle, 1916

Cheiro (Louis Hamon): *Cheiro's Book of Numbers*. New York: Arc, 1964

Leek, Sybil: *Numerology: The Magic of Numbers*. New York: Collier, 1969

Lopez, Vincent: *Numerology*. New York: Citadel, 1961

OBSTACLE

O

Oahspe *see* Newbrough, Dr. John Ballou

OBE or OOBE (Out of Body Experience)
see Astral Projection

OCCULT; OCCULTISM

"**O**ccult" is from the Latin *occulere*, "to conceal." It is that which is concealed or hidden, in the sense of keeping secret. It is something which is hidden behind external appearances and must be studied in order to be revealed. It is usually associated with the mystical and the magical and therefore is a part of Initiation. To some the word occult has a sinister inference, probably stemming from fear of the unknown.

According to Shepard, "Occultism is a philosophical system of theories and practices on, and for the attainment of, the higher powers of mind and **spirit**. Its practical side connects with **psychical** phenomena."

Sources:

Bletzer, June G.: *The Encyclopedia Psychic Dictionary.* Lithia Springs: New Leaf, 1998

Shepard, Leslie A: *Encyclopedia of Occultism & Parapsychology.* New York: Avon Books, 1978

ODIC FORCE

The term "odic force" was first used by Baron Karl von Reichenbach in 1858, and applied to the subtle emanations that he believed come from all matter, ranging from the stars to the human body. Only those who are truly sensitive would be aware of it, he believed, but that did not deny its existence. The Baron found that sensitive people saw luminous emanations coming from magnets and **crystals** observed in a darkened room. The north pole of a magnet gave off a blue color and the south pole gave an orange color. There was some confirmation of this when Professor D. Endlicher of Vienna saw what he described as "flames" coming off the poles of an electromagnet. These flames extended for as much as forty inches and were a mixture of rich colors. He also saw a luminous smoke. This took place in England during experiments conducted by Dr. Ashburner and Dr. William Gregory, Professor of Chemistry at Edinburgh University.

Reichenbach felt that in the human body, the odic force varied dependant upon the health of the person, the time of the day, whether or not the person had eaten or was hungry, and similar variables. The force can most easily be seen coming off the tips of the fingers, especially when the two hands are held with the finger tips pointing at each other in close proximity. The human body showed blue, and felt cool, on the left side and orange, and warm, on the right side. There is a similarity between what Reichenbach believed and what has more recently been demonstrated by Dr. **Walter J. Kilner**, as the **aura**, and by Dr. Wilhelm Reich (with his concept of *Orgone* energy), and the photographs of **Kirlian photography** developed by Semyon and Valentina Kirlian.

In the early days of Modern **Spiritualism** a number of people attributed **rappings, table tipping**, and **poltergeist** phenomena to the actions of the odylic force. It certainly seemed to make more sense when applied to **table tipping** than did Faraday's theory of unconscious muscular action. Lewis Spence said that Samuel Guppy, husband of well known medium **Agnes Guppy**, "regarded the so-called 'spirit' intelligences producing the manifestations as being compounded of odylic vapours emanating from the **medium**, and probably connected with an all-pervading thought-atmosphere."

Sources:

Bagnall, O.: *The Origin and Properties of the Human Aura*. London: Routledge and Kegan Paul, 1957

Crow, W. B.: *Man, Myth & Magic: Double*. London: BPC Publishing, 1970

Fodor, Nandor: *Encyclopedia of Psychic Science*. London: Arthurs Press, 1933

Reich, Wilhelm: *The Discovery of the Orgone*. New York: Orgone Institute Press, 1942

Spence, Lewis: *An Encyclopedia of the Occult*. London: George Routledge & Sons, 1920

OMEN

Omens are presages or prognostications, indications of something that is likely to happen in the future. They developed in a variety of ways, most of them through some unusual occurrence that was closely followed by a remarkable happening, good or bad. If there was a repetition of that combination, then the omen became established. Omens vary from the sighting of a particular bird in flight to the observation of a comet. The movement of cats, behavior of horses, the way a person laughs, the howling of a dog; these can all be taken as omens and, from them, the possible trend of future events may be gauged.

Thomas Carlyle, in *Mrs. C's Letter* (1871), mentions, "… good or ill luck for the whole year being omened by your liking or otherwise of the first person that accosts you on New Year's morning." Also Sir Walter Scott, in *Peveril of the Peak* (1822), says, "These evil omenings do but point out conclusions … most unlikely to come to pass." Yet many people do feel that the things omened *will* come to pass. One definition of the word is "an event or phenomenon believed to be a sign or warning of a future occurrence" (*The Merriam-Webster Dictionary*).

The sightings of comets and the experience of eclipses have been taken as signs that the world is coming to an end. At the trial of King Charles I in England in 1649, the head of his staff fell off. Many saw this as an ill omen. Charles was executed on January 30, 1649. **William Shakespeare** referred to many omens throughout his plays. In *Julius Caesar*, for example, a **Soothsayer** warns Caesar about the Ides of March, presumably based on omens he had observed. There is also a scene (Act 1, Sc. ii) where Casca meets with Cicero in a street, late at night, with a storm raging. Casca comments on the many strange omens that are occurring, "Against the Capitol I met a lion, who glared upon me and went surly by, without annoying me. And there were drawn upon a heap a hundred ghastly women, transformed with their fear; who swore they saw men, all in fire, walk up and down the streets. And yesterday the bird of night [owl] did sit, even at noon day, upon the market place, hooting and shrieking. When these prodigies do so conjointly meet, let not men say, 'These are their reasons; they are natural.' For I believe they are portentous things unto the climate that they point upon." There were many more omens and portents, including **dreams** and the examination of the entrails of sacrificed animals, before Caesar was assassinated. As Calpurnia says in the play, "When beggars die there are no comets seen; the heavens themselves blaze forth the death of princes."

In **Greece**, there are many traditional portents of good and evil. For a potential bride to see a weasel is the worst omen. The weasel, it is said, was once a young girl about to be married (the name means "little bride"). In some way she was robbed of her happiness and transformed into an animal. To see a snake, however, is a very good omen. The spilling of oil is an evil omen but the spilling of wine is good. The upsetting of water is also good, especially if it happens while on a journey. If the logs of the fire crackle it means that good news is coming. But if sparks should fly, then trouble may be expected. The spluttering of a candle flame or lamp flame is also unlucky.

Sources:

Buckland, Raymond: *The Fortune–Telling Book: The Encyclopedia of Divination and Soothsaying*. Detroit: Visible Ink Press, 2004

Lawson, John Cuthbert: *Modern Greek Folklore and Ancient Greek Religion*. New York: University Books, 1964

Oxford English Dictionary, The. Oxford: Clarendon Press, 1989

Shakespeare, William: *The Complete Works*. London: Odhams Press, 1938

OPEN CHANNELING

Open channeling is the reception of **channeled** information from a source that is unidentifiable. The information is from a dimension or level of reality other than the unconscious mind, the physical world, or one's own psychological being. This is separate and distinct from receiving information by **telepathic** means, or **clairvoyantly, clairaudiently,** or similar.

Sources:

Klimo, Jon: *Channeling: Investigations on Receiving Information from Paranormal Sources*. Los Angeles: Jeremy P. Tarcher, 1987

ORACLE

An Oracle is a shrine to a deity, at which questions may be asked. It is also the term

for the answers to those questions. Sometimes the "channel" giving those answers is also referred to as the oracle. The word comes from the Latin *oraculum*, meaning "to speak." Oracles were numerous in antiquity. Among the most celebrated were the Oracle of Delphi, the Oracle of Dodona, of Amphiaraus in Bæotia, and of Trophonius at Lebadea. In Italy, the best known oracle was that of Fortuna at Præneste.

Various methods of presenting the oracles—the answers to questions—were employed, differing from one site to another. The most common method was "incubation." This required the enquirer to sleep in the sacred area until he or she received an answer in a **dream**. Also common was **direct voice** from the priestess, who acted much like a **medium**. Here, however, she was acting as an intermediate between human and deity, rather than between human and **spirit** of the deceased. Sometimes oracles were received by the petitioner **clairvoyantly** or **clairaudiently**.

The expression "to work the oracle" meant to influence the **message** given; to bring pressure to bear to obtain an utterance in your favor.

Sources:

Buckland, Raymond: *The Fortune–Telling Book: The Encyclopedia of Divination and Soothsaying*. Detroit: Visible Ink Press, 2004

Encyclopedia Britannica. Chicago: William Benton, 1964

Parke, H. W.: *Sibyls and Sibylline Prophecy in Classical Antiquity*. New York: Routledge, 1988

Potter, D.: *Sibyls in the Greek and Roman World*. Rhode Island: Journal of Roman Archæology 3, 1990

Rose, H.J.: *Religion in Greece and Rome*. New York: Harper & Row, 1959

ORBS

When materialization **medium C. V. Miller** went to Europe in 1906, he visited Germany and gave a number of test **séances** at private residences in Munich. His **materialization** would often begin as luminous globes, orbs, or clouds appearing near the ceiling. Professor **Charles Richet** witnessed some of the sittings in Paris, France. C. deVesme reported in *Annals of Psychic Science* (#21, 1906), "A white ball, as of gas, about a quarter of a yard in diameter appeared in the air at the upper extremity of the curtains. Finally it came down, rested on the floor, and in less than a minute changed into a long shape, was transformed into a draped human form, which subsequently spoke." In *Looking Back* (1955), British medium **Arthur Findlay** writes of a séance with the medium **John Campbell Sloan**, "Lights the size of half a crown floated about the room, but I could not catch them, however hard I tried."

Sir **William Crookes** wrote in *Researches In the Phenomena of Spiritualism* (1874), "I have seen a solid luminous body, the size and nearly the shape of a turkey's egg, float noiselessly about the room, at one time higher than anyone could reach on tiptoe, and then gently descending to the floor. It was visible for more than ten minutes, and before it faded away it struck the table three times with a sound like that of a hard solid body. During this time the medium was lying back, apparently insensible, in an easy chair." Similar orbs were seen with the mediumship of **William Stainton Moses**.

Sometimes when photographs are taken, a small "orb" is seen on the print when developed. This is indicating **psychic** energy present, or is an indicator that **spirit** is with the person/people in the photograph. The orbs that are seen on many photographs may or may not have the potential for forming into materialized spirits. It probably depends upon the person in the photograph, and whether or not they have the potential to be a **physical medium**. It seems, however, that more and more photographs are showing these orbs.

Examination by experts have brought no explanations for the photographic orbs. They are not generally visible on negatives and they even show up on digital (negativeless) images, when there is no apparent fault with the camera or film used.

Sources:

Findlay, Arthur: *Looking Back*. Stansted: SNU, (1955) 1988

Fodor, Nandor: *Encyclopedia of Psychic Science*. London: Arthurs Press, 1933

Shepard, Leslie A: *Encyclopedia of Occultism & Parapsychology*. New York: Avon Books, 1978

Ouija® *see* Talking Boards

OWEN, REVEREND GEORGE VALE (1869–1931)

George Vale Owen was born in Birmingham, England, in 1869. He was educated at the Midland Institute and at Queen's College, Birmingham. He was ordained and held curacies at Seaforth, Fairfield, and the Scotland Road division of Liverpool. He then became vicar of Orford, near Warrington, where he worked for twenty years, helping build a new church there.

Owen had some **psychic** experiences and developed an ability to do **automatic writing** and **inspirational writing**. This first came through as from his mother, but was continued by higher **spirits** or **angels**. From this writing, Owen received details of what life was like after the transition known as death. Sir **Arthur Conan Doyle** described the information obtained by Owen as "a body of philosophy and advice from unseen sources, which seems to the author to bear every internal sign of a high origin." Owen's findings were published by Lord Northcliffe in the *Weekly Dispatch*. It was said that as a result, the Sunday newspaper's circulation increased tremendously. But another direct result of the publication of his work was persecution by Church authorities, which eventually lead to Owen's resignation.

Owen went on a short lecture tour of England and America, and then settled as pastor of a **Spiritualist** church in London. He continued to write, his best known book being the five-volume *Life Beyond the Veil*, published in 1921–22. Sir Arthur Conan Doyle said that Owen's "great script ... may be as permanent an influence as that of **Swedenborg**." Owen's other books included *Facts and the Future Life* (1922), *The Kingdom of God* (1925), *Body, Soul and Spirit* (1928), *The*

Highlands of Heaven (1929), *The Lowlands of Heaven* (nd), *The Ministry of Heaven* (1928), *The Outlands of Heaven* (nd), and *What Happens After Death* (nd).

Sources:

Doyle, Sir Arthur Conan: *The History of Spiritualism.* New York: Doran, 1926

Fodor, Nandor: *Encyclopedia of Psychic Science.* London: Arthurs Press, 1933

OWENS, ELIZABETH (B. 1948)

Elizabeth Jane Henderson was born in Washington, D.C., on March 6, 1948. Her father served in the army during World War II, and was later a salesman; her mother was a government secretary. Elizabeth grew up in Alexandria and Springfield, Virginia. She was a sensitive child from the time she was three. She drew faces based on **visions** and had aspirations to become an artist. By the time she was seven she also had a great desire to write, but her parents wanted her to pursue secretarial work. After graduating high school, she went to work for the CIA at Langley, Virginia. She married a musician and lived for a while in Columbus, Ohio, but the marriage did not last. She moved to Florida and they divorced.

In Florida, Elizabeth discovered **meditation** and began to investigate astrology, which had interested her for many years. She also began studies in the Spiritualist community at **Cassada-** ga to develop her **mediumship**. There she received **clairvoyant** messages and recognized feelings she had experienced in childhood. She married again—this time a deputy sheriff—but once more the marriage did not work. After seven years, she divorced.

In 1984, Elizabeth was certified as a **Spiritualist** medium. The following year she was ordained. Also in 1985, she began drawing spirit guides in pastel for clients. These were from the sightings she received clairvoyantly. She also began painting abstracts of spiritual beings. In 1990, she met Vincent Owens and they married five years later.

For twenty years, Owens has spoken in churches and presented seminars in Florida, Georgia, Virginia, and Maine. She is a former President and Pastor of the Cassadaga Spiritualist Camp, and served on its board. She has appeared on a variety of television programs as a medium, in the United States as well as Japan, Germany, Australia, France, and England.

In 2000, she published *Women Celebrating Life: A Guide to Growth and Transformation*, followed in 2001 by *How to Communicate With Spirits*, which won the Best Biographical/Personal award from the Coalition of Visionary Resources. In 2004, she published *Discover Your Spiritual Life*.

Sources:

Owens, Elizabeth: *How to Communicate with Spirits*. St. Paul: Llewellyn, 2001

PALADINO, EUSAPIA (1854–1918)

Sir **Arthur Conan Doyle** starts Chapter One of *The History of Spiritualism* (1921) with the words, "The mediumship of Eusapia Palladino marks an important stage in the history of **psychical research**, because she was the first **medium** for physical phenomena to be examined by a large number of eminent men of science. The chief manifestations that occurred with her were the movement of objects without contact, the **levitation** of a table and other objects, the levitation of the medium, the appearance of materialized hands and faces, lights, and the playing of musical instruments without human contact."

Eusapia Paladino (sometimes spelled "Palladino") was possibly the most famous of Italian mediums. She was certainly the most spectacular. In later years, she was caught as a fraud on several occasions, but these few instances could not eclipse the vast majority of her **séances** that were undertaken in the most rigid of investigative circumstances, totally precluding falsity. As a **physical medium**, she was thoroughly investigated for more than twenty years in many different areas of Europe and America. Among those who investigated her were Sir **Oliver Lodge**, Professor

Charles Richet, Richard Hodgson, and Frederick W. H. Myers.

Paladino was born at Minervo-Murge, near Bari, Italy, on January 21, 1854. Her mother died in the childbirth. As a child, Paladino heard **rappings** on walls and furniture. She also saw eyes looking at her through the darkness in her bedroom at night, where invisible hands often stripped off her bedclothes. When she was twelve, her father was killed by brigands. She then went to work as a nursemaid for an upper class family in Naples. It was psychical investigator Signor Damiana who discovered her amazing **psychic** abilities in 1872. He was led to Paladino by **spirit**.

Damiana's wife had attended a séance in Naples and been told by the **spirit guide** there—John King—that she should seek out a woman named Eusapia who would be found at a specific address in Naples (the house number and street were given). King said that the woman had been his daughter in a previous lifetime. When the Damianas went to the house, they met Eusapia Paladino.

According to Doyle, Paladino's mediumship started shortly after she went to live with the family in Naples. The family would sit in a **circle** and would ask Paladino to join them. As Doyle says, "At the end of ten minutes the table was levitated, the chairs began to dance, the curtains in the room to swell, and glasses and bottles to move about. Each sitter was tested in turn to discover who was responsible for the movements, and in the end it was decided that Eusapia was the medium. She took no interest in the proceedings and only consented to have further sittings to please her hosts and prevent herself from being sent to a convent."

Paladino's powers increased at a rapid rate. Initially she seemed to concentrate on **psychokinesis**, moving objects without touching them. **Nandor Fodor** says, "Her control … communicated through raps and in **trance** spoke in Italian alone. Eusapia Paladino was always informed about the phenomenon about to take place, so that she could warn the sitters. She suffered extremely during the process and exhibited a very remarkable synchronism between her gestures and the movement without contact. If she glared defiantly at a table it began to move towards her, if she warned it off it backed away. A forcible motion of her head was accompanied by raps and upward movements of her hand would cause the table to lift in the air." Then **materializations** began to take place. Phantom limbs would spring from her body and gradually build into almost full, but somewhat incomplete, figures. Professor Galeotti, at one séance, stated, "Look! I see two left arms, identical in appearance! One is on the little table, and it is that which M. Bottazzi touches, and the other seems to come out of her shoulder—to approach her, and touch her, and then return and melt into her body again. This is not an hallucination!"

On August 9, 1888, the psychical researcher Professor Ercole Chiaia, of Naples, published an open letter to Professor Cesar Lombroso, the Italian psychiatrist and criminal anthropologist, who had written an article stating that he laughed at **Spiritualism**. Chiaia challenged Lombroso to investigate Paladino, saying, "be it by day or by night she can divert a curious group for an hour or so with the most surprising phenomena. Either

bound to a seat, or firmly held by the hands of the curious, she attracts to her the articles of furniture which surround her, lifts them up, holds them suspended in the air like Mahomet's coffin, and makes them come down again with undulatory movements as if they were obeying her will. She increases her height or lessens it according to her pleasure. She raps or taps upon the walls, the ceiling, the floor, with fine rhythm and cadence." He went on to list other marvels he had witnessed at Paladino séances. It was two years before Lombroso was able to respond and himself have a sitting, but he ended up a fully converted Spiritualist, as did such other original skeptics as Professor Theodor Flournoy, Professor Porro, and Colonel Eugene D'Aiglun Rochas.

All the major psychical researchers investigated Paladino. It was quickly determined that, if given the chance, she would cheat and she was many times exposed. An explanation once given for this was that she obviously experienced pain during some of the phenomena and was frequently completely exhausted for two or three days after a sitting. She cheated rather than subject herself to that pain and exhaustion. But for the few times that she was caught cheating, there were innumerable sittings given where there was no such possibility yet amazing results were obtained. On March 1, 1902, a séance was held in Genoa. Present were Professor Morselli (who recorded and published the results in *Psicologia e Spiritismo* Vol. II, pp 214-237), Ernesto Bozzano, Dr. Venzano, and six other people. The cabinet was carefully examined. A camp bed was placed in it and Paladino lay down on it. Morselli tied her to the bed "in a manner defying attempts at liberation." In fairly good light, six spirits materialized, presenting themselves one by one in front of the cabinet. The last of these was a woman with a baby in her arms. Each time after the spirit returned into the cabinet, Morselli "rushed into the cabinet and found the medium tied as he had left her." There was no doubt in the minds of any of the sitters that the materializations were genuine.

In *The Story of Psychic Science* (1931), psychical researcher **Hereward Carrington** wrote, "To sum up the effects of these séances upon my own mind, I may say that, after seeing nearly forty of her séances, there remains not a shadow of doubt in my mind as to the reality of the vast majority of this phenomena occurring in Eusapia Paladino's presence ... I can but record the fact that further study of this medium has convinced me more than ever that our Naples experiments and deductions were correct, that we were not deceived, but that we did, in very truth, see praeternormal manifestations of a remarkable character. I am as assured of the reality of Eusapia Paladino's phenomena as I am of any other fact of life; and they are, to my mind, just as well established." The great stage magician Howard Thurston added, "I witnessed in person the table levitations of Madame Eusapia Paladino ... and I am thoroughly convinced that the phenomena I saw were not due to fraud and were not performed by the aid of her feet, knees, of hands." He offered to give a thousand dollars to charity if it could be proved that Eusapia could not levitate a table without trickery.

Sir Arthur Conan Doyle recorded, "Eusapia had a peculiar depression of her parietal bone, due, it is said, to some accident in her childhood. Such physical defects are very often associated with strong mediumship. It is as if the bodily weakness caused what may be described as a dislocation of the soul, so that it is more detached and capable of independent action. Thus Mrs. **(Leonore) Piper's** mediumship followed upon two internal operations. **(Daniel Dunglas) Home's** went with the tubercular diathesis, and many other cases might be quoted."

Eusapia married a merchant named Raphael Delgaiz, who lived in Naples. Although illiterate, she managed a shop for her husband. She died in 1918.

Sources:

Buckland, Raymond: *Buckland's Book of Spirit Communications*. St. Paul: Llewellyn, 2004

Doyle, Sir Arthur Conan: *The History of Spiritualism*. New York: Doran, 1926

Flammarion, Camille: *Mysterious Psychic Forces*. London: Unwin, 1907

Fodor, Nandor: *Encyclopedia of Psychic Science*. London: Arthurs Press, 1933

Podmore, Frank: *Modern Spiritualism*. London: 1902; reprinted as *Mediums of the Nineteenth Century*. New York: University Books, 1963

PANCHADASI, SWAMI

Swami Panchadasi is one of the many pseudonyms of William Walker Atkinson, author of *Reincarnation and the Law of Karma* (1908). Others of his *noms de plume* include Ramacharaka, Theron Q. Dumont, Magus Incognito, The Three Initiates, and Theodore Sheldon. As Swami Panchadasi, he wrote *The Human Aura* (1912), *The Astral World: Its Scenes, Dwellers, and Phenomena* (1915), and *A Course of Advanced Lessons in Clairvoyance and Occult Powers* (1916). Most were published by the Yoga Publication Society.

Sources:

Abacci Books: http://www.abacci.com/books

Circulo de Estudos Ramacharaca: http://www.ramacharaca.com.br

PARAKINESIS

While **psychokinesis** is the movement of objects without physical contact, parakinesis is the similar movement of objects but with physical contact which is insufficient to explain the movement. For example, when a large, heavy table is moved by a **medium** placing her hands on an edge of it, although it could never normally be moved by that medium no matter how hard she might try. This is often seen in **table tipping**, when an especially large and heavy table is used.

In Warsaw, psychical researcher and University of Lember psychology lecturer Julien Ochorowicz (1850–1917) used a dynamometer to measure forces exerted by the medium **Eusapia Paladino**. The instrument measured a force three times greater than the medium's normal ability and far in excess of the strongest man present at the séance. At another séance in Breslau at the home of Professor Friese, with the medium

Madame d'Esperance (Elizabeth Hope), the strongest man in Silesia—described as "a veritable Hercules"—was unable to prevent the movements of a table touched by the medium.

Sources:
Shepard, Leslie A: *Encyclopedia of Occultism & Parapsychology*. New York: Avon Books, 1978

PARAPSYCHOLOGICAL ASSOCIATION

The Parapsychological Association was formed in 1957 "to advance **parapsychology** as a science, to disseminate knowledge of the field, and to integrate the findings with those of other branches of science." In 1969, the Association was affiliated with the American Association for the Advancement of Science. The work of the Association is reported in the *Journal of Parapsychology* and the *Journal of the American Society for Psychical Research*.

Sources:
Shepard, Leslie A: *Encyclopedia of Occultism & Parapsychology*. New York: Avon Books, 1978

PARAPSYCHOLOGY

According to Professor **Charles Richet** (1850–1935), parapsychology is "a science dealing with the mechanical or psychological phenomena due to forces that seem to be intelligent or to unknown powers latent in human intelligence." Laurence T. Heron defined parapsychology as "a branch of psychology that deals with phenomena not explainable through data gained by the five senses." Dr. **Joseph Banks Rhine** (1895–1980) said it is "the branch of science that deals with **psi** communications, e.g. behavioral or personal exchanges with the environment which are extrasensorimotor, not dependent upon the senses and muscles." By "extrasensorimotor," Rhine meant a **telepathic** communication between an individual and the earth, as when there is a strong feeling of an impending natural disaster.

The *Encyclopedia Britannica* states that the addition of the **Greek** prefix *para* to the word psychology produces a term meaning something derivative of psychology but with special reference "to those allegedly supernormal capacities of the human organism such as telepathy, **clairvoyance, precognition** and other not generally agreed upon functions." The use of the word "supernormal" is unfortunate because all such "powers" are entirely normal, just uncommon. However, *Encycopedia Britannica* makes the point that the "negative attitude [of many U.S. psychologists] is less characteristic of British and continental psychologists. The net evidence for the reality of **ESP** is approximately as weighty as that for numerous other concepts widely held by psychologists."

The term "parapsychic" was coined by Emile Boirac (1851–1917), the psychical researcher and dean of Dijon Academy. He said it was "all phenomena produced in living beings or as a result of their actions, which do not seem capable of being entirely explained by already known natural laws and forces." He felt that the prefix *para* denoted a relationship to exceptional, abnormal paradoxical phenomena. In the course of his study of human emanations, Boirac rediscovered animal magnetism. According to **Nandor Fodor**, "His observations on the obscure phenomena of exteriorization of sensitivity carried the researches of (Dr. Paul) Joire and (Col. Eugene) Rochas a step farther." His book *La Psychologie Inconnue* (1915), translated as *Our Hidden Forces* (New York, 1917) and also with the title *Psychic Science* (London, 1918), was awarded the Emden Prize by the French Academy of Sciences.

Shepard reports, "During the 1950s and 1960s the scope of parapsychology expanded to include the range of subjects formerly covered under the term 'psychical research,' including **Spiritualism**, evidence for survival after death, clairvoyance, **hauntings, poltergeists**, out-of-the-body traveling (**OBE**), **reincarnation**, psychic **healing** and magical practices amongst primitive peoples."

Eileen Coly, right, president of the Parapsychology Foundation, and her daughter, Lisette Coly, with a photograph of the late Eileen Garrett, founder of the foundation and mother of Eileen Coly. *AP/WideWorld Photos.*

The field of parapsychology is now almost limitless, with parapsychological institutions and societies in most countries around the world. Such relatively modern phenomena as altered states of consciousness, **dreams, biofeedback, Instrumental Transcommunication** and **Electronic Voice Phenomena** have now come under the general umbrella of the word.

Sources:

Bletzer, June G.: *The Encyclopedia Psychic Dictionary.* Lithia Springs: New Leaf, 1998

Encyclopedia Britannica. Chicago: William Benton, 1964

Fodor, Nandor: *Encyclopedia of Psychic Science.* London: Arthurs Press, 1933

Heron, Laurence T.: *ESP in the Bible.* New York: Doubleday, 1974

Shepard, Leslie A: *Encyclopedia of Occultism & Parapsychology.* New York: Avon Books, 1978

PARAPSYCHOLOGY FOUNDATION

Eileen J. Garrett established the **Parapsychology** Foundation in New York in 1951, as a nonprofit educational organization to support "impartial scientific inquiry into the total nature and working of the mind and to make available the results of such inquiry." The Foundation gives grants and publishes pamphlets, monographs, and conference proceedings. From 1953 onward, the Foundation published a bimonthly newsletter, the *Newsletter of the Parapsychology Foundation,* which in 1970 became the bimonthly *Parapsychology Review.* The highly esteemed *International*

Journal of Parapsychology was also published from 1959 to 1968, and the Foundation also publishes paperback books under the Helix imprint. The 10,000 volume Eileen J. Garrett Library provides invaluable research information and facilities to researchers and students.

The Foundation holds an annual International Conference, covering such topics as "The Study of **Mediumship**: Interdisciplinary Perspectives," discussing mediumship from different points of view and from the perspective of different disciplines.

Sources:

Psychic Frontiers Article: http://www.mindreader.com/fate/articles/Fate1294.doc

Shepard, Leslie A: *Encyclopedia of Occultism & Parapsychology*. New York: Avon Books, 1978

Parapsychology Laboratory *see* **Joseph Banks Rhine**

PARISIAN SOCIETY OF PSYCHOLOGIC STUDIES

The title given to **Allan Kardec**'s (Hypolyte Leon Denizard Rivail; 1804–1869) first book of **spirit** teachings was *Le Livre des Esprits* or *The Spirits' Book* (1857). The book sold extremely well throughout France and across Europe. The name Allan Kardec quickly became a household name. Shortly after publication of this book, Kardec founded the The Parisian Society of Psychologic Studies and put out a monthly magazine called *La Revue Spirite*. The Society met weekly at Kardec's home, for the purpose of getting communications from **mediums** doing **automatic writing**. Shortly before his death in 1869, Kardec drew up plans for an organization called "The Joint Stock Company for the Continuation of the Works of Allan Kardec." It had the power to buy and sell, receive donations and bequests, and to continue the publication of *La Revue Spirite*.

Sources:

Doyle, Sir Arthur Conan: *The History of Spiritualism*. New York: Doran, 1926

PARKER BROTHERS

George Parker was born in Salem, Massachusetts, in 1867. He was the youngest of three sons of Mr. and Mrs. George Parker. He wanted to become a journalist, but as an avid game player, he invented a game called *Banking*, and—at sixteen years of age—published it, made a profit, and founded his own game publishing company. His older brother Charles encouraged George and, some years later, Charles and the third brother Edward joined together with their young sibling. By the late 1880s, the Parker Brothers' catalog featured twenty-nine games, most of which had been invented by George. With the introduction of *Monopoly®* in 1935, Parker Brothers' place as a game giant was assured. By the time he died in 1953, George had invented more than 100 games.

The first commercially produced **talking board** was manufactured by Elijah J. Bond, in the 1800s. Bond sold the patent to **William Fuld** in 1892 and Fuld founded the Southern Novelty Company in Maryland, which later changed its name to the Baltimore Talking Board Company. They produced the "Oriole Talking Board" which later was renamed "Ouija®, the Mystifying Oracle." In 1966, Parker Brothers bought the rights to the Ouija® board.

Under Parker Brothers, the Ouija® board sold millions of copies, even outselling the game of Monopoly®, which up until then had been the biggest selling board game ever. In its first year with Parker, more than two million Ouija® boards were sold.

The marketing of the talking board by a toy and game manufacturer—with outlets at such places as Toys-R-Us—did a great disservice to **Spiritualism** in that it presented what was an excellent tool for communication with **spirits** as nothing more than a toy for idle amusement. As a consequence of the Ouija's® connection with frivolous usage, organizations such as the **National Spiritualist Association of Churches** stopped endorsing its use, despite an excellent history of such use by people like **Pearl Curran** (channeling Patience Worth), **Jane Roberts** (channeling Seth), and many others. Sir **Arthur Conan Doyle** was one who had reported favorably on its use, speaking of Sir **William Barrett**'s report on messages received through a Ouija® board in what he called "The Pearl Tie-pin Case."

In 1968, Parker Brothers was bought by General Mills. In 1985, General Mills combined it with Kenner Products to form Kenner-Parker Toys. Two years later this company was acquired by the Tonka Corporation which, in 1991, became a division of Hasbro. Despite all the recent changes of name and association, the Ouija® talking board is still generally associated with Parker Brothers.

Sources:

Covina, Gina: *The Ouija® Book.* New York: Simon & Schuster, 1979

Doyle, Sir Arthur Conan: *The History of Spiritualism.* New York: Doran, 1926

PARKES, F. M.

In 1872, the year in which **Frederick Hudson** obtained the first English **spirit photographs**, F. M. Parkes and M. Reeves also produced photographs of **spirit** images. Parkes and Reeves were in England; Parkes lived at Grove Road, Bow, in the East End of London.

Parkes was described by Sir **Arthur Conan Doyle** as "a natural **psychic**." He had verified **visions** as a child. He learned of **Spiritualism** in 1871. Parkes was a photographer and, with his friend Reeves—the proprietor of a dining room near King's Cross railroad station—he started experimenting to see if he could get spirit pictures like the ones obtained by Frederick Hudson.

Initially only odd streaks, as of light, appeared on Parkes's photographic plates. After three months of trying, however, he did get a spirit inage when photographing Dr. Sexton and Dr. Clarke of Edinburgh. According to Doyle, "Dr. Sexton invited Mr. Bowman, of Glasgow, an experienced photographer, to make a thorough examination of the camera, the dark room and all the appliances in use. This he did, and declared imposition on the part of Parkes to be impossible." Sexton subsequently wrote enthusiastically about Parkes in the *Christian Spiritualist* magazine.

Nandor Fodor says that Parkes was unable to obtain full spirit pictures unless his wife and his partner Reeves were present, somehow lending psychic energy. Spirit directed Parkes to have the photographic plates in his possession, in the darkroom, previous to their being placed in the camera. Since this would tend to raise suspicions of tampering, he had a hole cut in the wall of the studio so that observers could monitor the plates throughout the whole process.

According to Doyle, the most striking thing about Reeves's photographs was the great variety of the designs. Doyle said, "Out of 110 that lie before me now, commencing from April, 1872, and with some intermissions extending down to present date, there are not two that are alike— scarcely two that bear any similarity to each other. Each design is peculiar to itself, and bears upon the face of it marks of individuality." The Rev. **William Stainton Moses** commented further in *Human Nature*, "A considerable number of the earlier pictures … were allegorical. One of the earliest, taken in April, 1872, shows Mr. Reeves' father holding up a cross above his head and displaying an open book on which is written 'Holy Bible.' Another shows a cloud of light covering two thirds of the picture, and made up of the strongest medley of heads and arms, and flashes of light, with a distinct cross in the center." There were also **angels**, giant hands, floating figures, multiple faces, and a large eye, among other things.

Sources:

Doyle, Sir Arthur Conan: *The History of Spiritualism.* New York: Doran, 1926

Fodor, Nandor: *Encyclopedia of Psychic Science.* London: Arthurs Press, 1933

Past Life Recall *see* **Reincarnation**
Peck, Shelley *see* **Edward, John**

PEEBLES, DR. JAMES MARTIN (1822–1922)

Known as "The World Missionary of **Spiritualism**," James Martin Peebles was born in Whittingham, Vermont, on March 13, 1822. His mother was English and his father's side of the family were Scottish Calvinists. James was one of seven children.

Peebles graduated from Oxford Academy, New York, in 1841. Three years later he began preaching Universalism. He was ordained in 1846. He earned further degrees from the University of Pennsylvania, became a medical doctor, and began practicing medicine.

In 1852, at the age of thirty, Peebles became interested in **trance** and then Spiritualism. With a friend, he went to a **séance** in Auburn, New York, and shortly after decided to dedicate himself to Spiritualism. He traveled the world promoting the religion. Marilyn Awtry-Smith said, "Not only did he help bring Spiritualism to the world, he also helped to bring Spiritualism to the Spiritualists. He constantly urged them to 'Spiritualize your life.'"

Peebles became Editor-in-Chief of the journal *The Spiritual Universe* and later of *The American Spiritualist*. He was a prolific author, his books including *Seers of the Ages, Three Journeys Around the World, Five Voyages Around the World, Eight Voyages Around the World, Immortality and Our Future Homes, Obsession or the Reign of Evil **Spirits***, *Immortality and Our Employments Hereafter, The Christ Question Settled, **Seers** of the Ages, Discussion on **Reincarnation**, Death Defeated, Spiritualism vs. Materialism, What Is This Spiritualism?, The Spirit's Path Traced*, and *The General Principles and the Standard Teachings of Spiritualism*. For several of his books, he wavered until a spirit voice came to him and said, strongly and sternly, "Write! Write—the time has come!" He was a friend of Emerson and of Walt Whitman. He died on February 18, 1922, at the age of ninety-nine.

Sources:

Awtry-Smith, Marilyn: *"They" Paved the Way*. New York: Spiritualism & More, nd

Peebles, J. M.: *The General Principles and the Standard Teachings of Spiritualism*. Mokelumne: Health Research, 1969

Peebles, J. M.: *The Spirit's Pathway Traced: Did It Pre-exist and Does It Reincarnate Again into Mortal Life?* Battle Creek: Peebles Institute, 1906

PELHAM, GEORGE (1860–1892)

"George Pelham" was the pseudonym of George Pellew, a lawyer and writer and a friend of Dr. **Richard Hodgson**, the **psychical researcher**. Pelham and Hodgson had many arguments on the possibility of **spirit** survival after bodily death. Pelham said it was "improbable if not inconceivable." Hodgson countered by saying that if not probable it was at least conceivable. In February 1892, Pelham fell from his horse and died. He had promised Hodgson that if he should die first he would return to "make things lively" for his friend.

On March 22, 1892, at one of **Leonore Piper**'s **automatic writing séances**, Pelham returned. Mrs. Piper had a number of different **spirit guides** at various stages of her lengthy mediumistic career. The original was Dr. Phinuit. According to Sir **Arthur Conan Doyle**, "Dr. Hodgson, who had been among the most severe critics of all transcendental explanations (of mediumship), was gradually forced to accept the spiritual hypothesis as the only one that covered the facts. He found that **telepathy** from sitter to **medium** would not do so." The spirit of George Pelham came and took over from Dr. Phinuit as Leonore Piper's main guide. Doyle said, "It was no unusual thing for Phinuit to be talking and Pelham to be writing at the same moment."

Pelham's identity was established by the fact that, over a period of time, he spoke to thirty different old friends of his of whom Piper had no knowledge, and they fully recognized his tone and manner. In turn, the spirit knew them and all about them. Doyle reported, "Never once did he mistake a stranger for a friend. It is difficult to imagine how continuity of individuality and power of communication—the two essentials of

Spiritualism—could be more clearly established than by such a record."

Pelham came through Mrs. Piper from 1892 until 1898. He then began to communicate more rarely. His explanation was that he was advancing and thereby moving farther away. He finally stopped communicating altogether.

Sources:

Doyle, Sir Arthur Conan: *The History of Spiritualism*. New York: Doran, 1926

Fodor, Nandor: *Encyclopedia of Psychic Science*. London: Arthurs Press, 1933

PENDULUM

A pendulum is an instrument used in dowsing or radiesthesia. It is basically a weight on the end of a length of cord or fine chain. Radiesthesia may be defined as **divination** utilizing human sensitivity to radiations emanating from any source, living or inert. It is a refinement of the art of rhabdomancy, or water witching, and its history can be traced back more than 5,000 years to the ancient Orient. The principle instrument used is the pendulum, though rods of various types may also be used. The practice came to the fore during the Middle Ages and remained popular through to the early nineteenth century. It then came to be regarded as a superstition without value, though radiesthesia saw a great resurgence of interest in the twentieth century. The term radiesthesia was coined in France (as *radiesthésie*) by the Abbé Bouly, in 1930. That same year *L'Association des Amis de la Radiesthésie* was founded and three years later, in England, the British Society of Dowsers.

A radiesthetist is a dowser sensitive to hidden information who uses an indicator, such as a pendulum or rod, to amplify that sensitivity. The pendulum is a weight of some sort suspended on a fine chain or length of thread. Some radiesthetists hold a short stick with the pendulum hanging off the end of it, but most modern day diviners hold the end of the chain directly between their fingers. Virtually any small weight will work; some

use a pendant necklace or a ring on the end of a length of silk ribbon. In the Middle Ages a key on the end of a chain was popular. Today there are commercially produced pendula made out of wood, brass, silver, gold, and plastic. A serviceable one can be fashioned from a fishing weight or plumb bob. Some of the commercially produced ones are hollow, and unscrew to give access to an inside cavity. In this can be placed what is known as a "witness;" a sample of what is being sought. For example, if the radiesthetist is looking for gold, then a small piece of gold would be placed inside the pendulum, to help make the connection. The pendulum is often used to diagnose and prescribe for disease. It can also be used to answer questions, in the manner of a **talking board**.

Most radiesthesia is done seated at a table, working with charts, maps, or other simple accessories. The end of the chain, or thread, is held between thumb and first finger—right hand if right handed; left hand if left-handed—allowing the pendulum weight to be suspended about an inch off the surface of the table. A square of paper, placed under the pendulum, is marked with a large cross and the words YES and NO. Resting the elbow on the table, the weight of the pendulum hangs over the center of the cross and questions are asked that can be answered Yes or No. Although held steadily, the pendulum starts to swing along one of the lines of the cross, giving either a Yes or No answer. An alternate method that does not employ any card or paper is simply for the pendulum to be allowed to swing in a clockwise circle for Yes and counterclockwise for No.

The pendulum should swing of its own accord, much as the **planchette** of a Ouija® board moves about without being directed. Although it is not *consciously* made to swing, it is almost certainly the operator's muscles which are bringing it about. But as with the talking board, the question is, who or what is *directing* it to give the answers received? To get more than Yes and No answers, the letters of the alphabet may be placed in a semicircle on a table. With the weight of the pendulum hanging in the center, questions can be asked and answers

A man uses a pendulum to map energies along ley lines. *Courtesy Fortean Picture Library.*

obtained by observing to which letters the pendulum swings. A variation is to hold the pendulum so that it hangs down in the center of a water glass. It can then swing and "chink" against the side of the glass; one hit for A, two for B, three for C, and so on. Again, similar to the message reception obtained from **table tipping**.

A Swedish **medium**, Anna Rasmussen—whose powers first became obvious when she was twelve years of age—has affected pendulums by **psychokinesis**. Professor Winther of Copenhagen studied her intensively between 1922 and 1928. He designed a sealed glass case inside which hung a variety of pendulums. They were of different weights and supported on silk threads. Anna could concentrate on them and cause any one of them, as chosen by the professor, to swing in any direction requested. Anna had a **spirit guide** named Dr. Lasaruz, whom she claimed brought about the movements.

Sources:

Buckland, Raymond: *Color Magic—Unleash Your Inner Powers.* St. Paul: Llewellyn, 2002

Holroyd, Stuart: *The Supernatural: Minds Without Boundaries.* London: Aldus, 1975

Lakhovsky, Georges (tr. Mark Clement): *The Secret of Life: Cosmic Rays and Radiations of Living Beings.* London: True Health, 1963

Maury, Marguerite: *How to Dowse, Experimental and Practical Radiesthesia.* London: Bell, 1953

Mermet, Abbé: *Principles and Practice of Radiesthesia.* London: Watkins, 1975

Wethered, Vernon D.: *The Practice of Medical Radiesthesia.* London: C.W. Daniel, 1967

PEPPER, MAY S.

For many years Mrs. May S. Pepper was the pastor of the First **Spiritualist** Church of Brooklyn. She was earlier a member of the **New England Spiritual Campmeeting Association** at Lake Pleasant, Massachusetts and is listed in their 1879 list of members. Mrs. Pepper spoke at the National Convention of the **National Spiritualists Association** at Masonic Temple in Washington, D.C., in 1897, along with such notables as **Cora L. Richmond**, **Moses Hull**, Mrs. Cadwallader, and Dr. **J. M. Peebles**.

In an interview given October 15, 1973, Mrs. Dorothy Evelyn Begg, an octogenarian lifelong resident of the New England Spiritual Campmeeting Association, spoke of "our great May Pepper Vanderbilt, the very finest **medium** that ever came here and was probably ever anywhere." Presumably this is the same May Pepper, though nowhere else can reference be found to Pepper being a Vanderbilt. However, Mrs. Begg went on to say,

May Pepper Vanderbilt was very well to do, but she had this gift and this is Bright Eyes, her **control**, the little Indian girl. When she was traveling with her husband she went through the reservations out west before she became a public medium and she saw the starvation and privation and everything else there and it upset her awfully and she adopted this little Indian girl and took her home with her and she only lived a few months. We never knew, May never knew, whether it was because she was in a house and was accustomed to running free and so she couldn't take or whatever, but she died. But she was very grateful to May. She said if it was possible to come back she would be her **guide** and she did come back. Every meeting opened with Bright Eyes, her young voice and her cute little broken English, and she was the guide that what we call controlled May Pepper's meetings and certain **circles** on the **platform** work.

When asked if May Pepper was a **trance** medium, Mrs. Begg replied,

Yes. Yes, May Pepper was a trance medium and she was absolutely astounding from the time she got up from her chair back of the podium until 11 o'clock at night. She never stopped. She never rested. She went back and forth on that platform from one end to the other and she had names, dates, figures. Names of relatives way back, full three names never just Mary, you know, but it'd be the whole three names. I was there one night and I saw … she called a man in the front of the audience and she said, to the best of my recollection, she said, "Sir are you so and so and so and so?" He said, "Yes." And she said, "Do you have the gall to come here tonight when you haven't spoken to your own brother for 30 years?" His face was a sight flushed, you know, angry. And she said, "You're not leaving this hall until you've shaken hands with your brother. He's in the back of the hall. Did you know it?" You could see he was stunned. He didn't know his brother was there. So, she said, "Come on, I don't want any back talk. Back you go …" went to the back of the hall and shook hands with a man. She'd never seen either one of them before in her life. "Now," she said, "you can come back

and sit down and I'll give you your **message**." Oh, she did things like that. There was a young Italian at a meeting one night and she called his full name and she said, "Sir, you are very anxious, aren't you?" He said, "Yes." She said, "You want to know how your brother died, don't you?" He said, "I do," and he stood up. She said, "Well, I'm glad to tell you it was not a suicide. He was murdered." This young Italian, he shot up in the air, you know, and he ran right to the platform and people didn't do that. He ran right to the platform, put both hands up on it, and he said, "Tell me. Tell me. Tell me." And she told him the date, the man that did it, how it was done, the whole thing and he kept blessing her and blessing her and weeping and, oh, the whole place was in an uproar. He said, "I've been so afraid it was suicide. So afraid for his soul." Oh, she was a wonderful woman. She suffered extremely from nervous headaches and her chauffeur would drive her around all night long. It was the only way she could get any sleep in the back seat. She'd be lying up. She had to get the oxygen, especially in the summer. Of course, we didn't have oxygen tents then. This, of course, is just a plain dress, but I wish you could have seen her big, you know, and her favorite dress was a deep purple at the top and at the bottom of the skirt and from the bottom of the skirt to the waist were shafts of lavender. Pale pink over the entire dress was a silver mesh, and a great bunch of grapes caught the skirt in swirls. Oh, what a beautiful gown. Then she had a garnet ruby gown with black sequins. Of course, in those days most of our mediums wore sequined gowns in the evening. It was the thing to do and they did it.

Yet, whether a Vanderbilt or not, May Pepper became the pastor of the First Spiritualist Church of Brooklyn, New York. **Nandor Fodor** reports that she caused lively discussion in the press because of her clairvoyant work. The congregation would write letters to deceased friends and loved ones, seal them in envelopes, and place the envelopes on a small table at the front of the church. After a prayer and short sermon, Pepper would randomly pick up a letter and answer the question written and sealed inside. She also asked the spirit she saw **clairvoyantly** to look for its own letter. The pile of letters would move and then one would separate itself and fly out, to fall to the floor, as though an invisible hand had pulled it out. Such well known psychical investigators as **William James** and Professor **James Hyslop** witnessed this and were unable to explain it.

On January 20, 1905, the *Brooklyn Daily Standard Union* newspaper carried an unusual report:

> The Rev. May S. Pepper, the pastor of the First Spiritualist Church, has evidently been sustained by the members of her own church, according to a notice sent out today. Mrs. Pepper was last week the subject of an attack on her character by a man named Pepper, who claimed to be her husband. The attack on Mrs. Pepper's character caused a furor among the Spiritualists of the First Church, who were slow to believe them. Mrs. Pepper arranged to meet the members of the church and its officials and explain her conduct and past history. This was scheduled for last night, but its place of meeting was kept secret.

> The notice sent to The Standard Union contains theses words: "The regular religious services next Sunday will be held at 8 P.M., at which a fine inspirational sermon will be delivered by the pastor, the Rev. May S. Pepper, following which will be given a demonstration of the immortality of the human soul through her psychic gift."

There was no subsequent report so it is unknown what the exchange was about.

Sources:

Dorothy Evelyn Begg Interview: http://www.ghostflowers.com/book2/interview.html

Fodor, Nandor: *Encyclopedia of Psychic Science.* London: Arthurs Press, 1933

RootsWeb.com: http://archiver.rootsweb.com/th/read/NYBROOKLYN/2001-06/0991594736

PERISPIRIT

A term for the **spirit** body, used by **Allan Kardec**. He defined "spirits" as "the intelligent beings of the creation. They constitute the population of the universe, in contradistinction to the forms of the material world." Of the perispirit he said, "As the germ of a fruit is surrounded by the perisperm, so the spirit, properly so called, is surrounded by an envelope which by analogy may be designated as the perispirit."

Sources:

Kardec, Allan: *The Spirits' Book.* (1857) New York: Studium, 1980

Phelps, Rev. Dr. Eliakim *see* **Stratford, CT**

PHINUIT, DR.

Dr. Phinuit is best known as being the first **spirit guide** of **Leonore Piper** (1859–1950), herself known as the foremost **trance medium** in the history of **psychical research**. Phinuit claimed that he was French and that he had been a physician in Metz. However, no convincing proof of his identity was ever forthcoming. His statements about himself were obscure and frequently contradictory, hence they were not trusted. Some researchers went to the trouble of going through the archives at Metz, but could find no trace of such a person ever having lived there.

Phinuit, despite claiming to be French, could not speak the language. When he was questioned as to why this was, he replied that he had so many English-speaking patients at Metz that he had finally forgotten his own language! Later, on closer questioning, he confessed that he wasn't sure whether he was from Metz or from Marseilles. He also looked at the possibility that his name was not Phinuit but Jean Alaen Scliville. The final conclusion of many researchers was that he was nothing more than a secondary personality of Mrs. Piper's, perhaps induced through suggestion at an early séance. However, Phinuit repeatedly, over several years, provided detailed evidence of spirit life, with evidential **messages** to many sitters.

Imperator and a group of **spirits** that originally worked with **William Stainton Moses** went to work with Mrs. Piper in 1897. According to Imperator, Dr. Phinuit was an earthbound spirit who had become confused and bewildered in his first attempts at communication and had lost his consciousness of personal identity. Phinuit was the main control for Mrs. Piper from 1884 to 1892. Then he shared control with **George Pelham** until, in 1897, the Imperator group took over and Phinuit disappeared.

Sources:

Doyle, Sir Arthur Conan: *The History of Spiritualism.* New York: Doran, 1926

Shepard, Leslie A: *Encyclopedia of Occultism & Parapsychology.* New York: Avon Books, 1978

PHYSICAL MEDIUMSHIP

There are two main types of mediumship: **mental** and physical. Mental mediumship is subjective while physical mediumship is objective. Basically, physical mediumship covers that which is done without physical contact. **Levitation, apports, materializations, etherializations, trumpets, slates, ectoplasm, rappings,** and **independent voice** would all come under the heading of physical phenomena.

It is not always easy to categorize whether a particular phenomenon falls under the heading of mental or physical mediumship. For example, **automatism** may be regarded as mental mediumship because although the hand of the medium is utilized in producing the material, what is produced seems to come through a mental process. Yet it is a physical action which produces the results; it is **spirit** that controls the hand and therefore it might well be classed as physical mediumship. Similarly, **table tipping** and **direct voice** are difficult to categorize. Physical mediumship is usually accompanied by

mental, but not necessarily so the other way around.

PICKFORD, MARY (1892–1979)

Born Gladys Marie Smith, silent movie actress Mary Pickford was the oldest of three children born within four years of each other. Her mother was Charlotte; her sister was Lottie and the youngest brother was Jack. Gladys was born April 8, 1892. She was five when her father was killed in an accident at work. To help bring in money, Charlotte rented out a room in their house. The couple who rented it were producing a play and thought that Gladys would be ideal for a part in it. Eventually the whole family became actors.

When Gladys was thirteen she was cast in a play, *The Warrens of Virginia,* by Broadway producer David Bedalsco, who changed her name to Mary Pickford. She was taken on a tour of the dressing rooms at the theatre and at the leading lady's—Frances Starr—she had a **premonition** that one day she would have that same dressing room, complete with the star on the door. In fact she did; when she headlined in Bedalsco's *A Good Little Devil.*

Pickford had a similar premonition one day when standing with her cousin, waiting in the rain for a trolley car. A passing limousine splashed both of them and Pickford had a premonition that one day she would be riding in an even grander vehicle. Six years later she gave the same cousin a ride in her new cream and gray Cadillac.

Once when shooting a picture at sea (*Pride of the Clan*), the fishing boat in which a scene was being filmed started to sink. There was a lifeboat nearby and everyone was told to evacuate to it. Pickford decided to run below decks and get her makeup kit but just as she started to do so, she heard a **clairaudient** voice tell her "Don't you go there!" She turned and immediately got into the lifeboat. It is probable that if she had continued below deck she might well have gone down with the fishing boat.

Mary Pickford rose to fame as an actress in silent films. She is pictured shortly before her death in 1979. *Central Press/Getty Images.*

After her mother died, Mary Pickford regularly saw her in her **dreams**. She was tempted to try to make contact through a **medium** but felt that her deeply religious mother might object to that. In her memoirs, Pickford wrote, "It wasn't long after her passing that I began meeting mother in my dreams … To this day I still see [her] in my dreams … It gives me infinite peace to know that as long as I dream I shall have my mother with me."

When only fourteen, Pickford was touring New Haven, Connecticut, with a play, and went to a park near Yale University. As she walked along, she had a strong feeling that she might see the face of the man she would eventually marry. She said, "Always in my heart I carried a picture of what he would look like. I knew everything about him, his complexion, his eyes, his voice." Many years later, after two marriages (one long and happy one to

Douglas Fairbanks), she finally met the man. It was Charles Edward Rogers, better known as Buddy Rogers. Rogers, who was eleven years younger than Pickford, had been in love with her for many years. They met in 1927. She finally divorced Fairbanks in 1936, and she and Rogers married the following year. She remained married to Rogers for the rest of her life. She died of cerebral hemorrhage on May 29, 1979.

Sources:

Accurso, Lina: *Mary Pickford: Superstitious Superstar.* Lakeville: *Fate* Magazine, October, 2004

Pickford, Mary: *Sunshine and Shadows.* New York: Doubleday, 1955

PIDDINGTON, JOHN GEORGE (1869–1952)

John George Smith was born in 1869. In 1890, he became a member of the **Society for Psychical Research** (SPR). To avoid confusion with other members named Smith, he changed his name to Piddington, his mother's maiden name. He was Secretary of the SPR in London from 1899 to 1907, Ttreasurer from 1917 to 1921, and President from 1924 to 1925. He devoted his life to the cause of **psychical research**. He was a member of the SPR Council from 1899 to 1932.

In 1902, Piddington helped to create the SPR Research Endowment Fund, which enabled the society to have a full time, paid research officer. He visited the United States in 1905 and helped the organization of the **American Society for Psychical Research** as an independent society.

One of the most important roles played by Piddington was in interpreting the scripts of the "SPR Group" of **automatic writers**, who were involved in **cross-correspondences**. This also involved Sir **Oliver Lodge**, Mrs. **Henry Sidgwick**, Gerald W. Balfour (who became Earl after his brother's death), and Alice Johnson. There were more than 3,000 scripts studied in depth. These have since been cited as evidence of survival. Piddington contributed a large number of articles to the *SPR Proceedings*. He died in April 1952.

Sources:

Doyle, Sir Arthur Conan: *The History of Spiritualism.* New York: Doran, 1926

Fodor, Nandor: *Encyclopedia of Psychic Science.* London: Arthurs Press, 1933

PIKE, BISHOP JAMES ALBERT (1913–1969)

James Albert Pike was born on February 14, 1913, in Oklahoma City, Oklahoma. He was the only child of James Albert and Pearl Agatha Pike. He attended the University of California, Los Angeles (1932–1933), University of Southern California (A.B. 1934; LL.B. 1936), and Yale University (J.S.D. 1938). He also studied at Virginia Theological Seminary 1945–1946, General Theological Seminary 1936–1947, Union Theological Seminary (B.D. magna cum laude, 1951).

Pike was raised as a Roman Catholic and lectured at the Catholic University of America Law School in Washington, D.C., from 1939 to 1942. He left the Roman Catholic Church because he disagreed with the Pope's encyclical on birth control. He married Esther Yanovsky in 1942. In 1944, he was ordained as an Episcopal Church priest. He rose from Chaplain to Bishop, and in 1958 became Bishop in the diocese of California. In 1966, he resigned as Bishop to become theologian in residence at the Center for Democratic Institutions, Santa Barbara, California.

Pike was a member of the bar of U.S. Supreme Court and California State. He had a weekly television program from 1957–1960, and wrote a number of books, including *The Faith of the Church* (1951), *Roadblocks to Faith* (1954), *Doing the Truth* (1958), *A New Look at Preaching* (1961), *Teenagers and Sex* (1965), and *You and the New Morality* (1967).

Pike, like some of his relatives and ancestors, had **psychic** powers. He heard **ghosts** shuffling footsteps on the floor and stairs of the library when he was dean of the Cathedral of St. John the Divine in New York City. He also experienced **poltergeist** activity in two of the homes in which he lived. A **medium**—Ethel Myers—was called in to investigate one in Poughkeepsie, New York.

On Friday February 4, 1966, Pike's elder son Jim took his own life in a New York hotel. Jim was twenty-two. He had long experimented with drugs, including marijuana, hashish, LSD, peyote, mescaline, and others. For a few months before his death, Jim spent time with his father and the two became close, sharing an apartment in Cambridge, England, for four and a half months. Pike was especially devastated at the death. Pike had his son's body cremated and the ashes spread over the Pacific Ocean, west of the Golden Gate Bridge.

Within little more than two weeks, still in Cambridge, Pike began to experience **hauntings** suggesting that his son's **spirit** might be behind them. There was a recurrence of a 140 degree angle, from two postcards that mysteriously appeared, to books placed on a shelf, to open safety pins, to the hands of a clock (which, after being stopped for many months, suddenly started working). Pike attempted communication with his son through **automatic writing**, but was unsuccessful. At the suggestion of Canon John Pearce-Higgins, who was an expert on **Spiritualism**, a **séance** was arranged with the medium **Ena Twigg**.

On March 2, 1966, Pike, his secretary Maren Bergrud, and Pearce-Higgins called on Twigg. Using Jim's passport as a **psychometric** link, the medium said that Jim had been trying to contact his father and was asking for forgiveness for the suicide, which he said was an accident (an overdose of pills). She then relayed that Jim was pleased about his ashes being scattered at the Golden Gate Bridge. He urged his father to continue fighting the church officials who opposed Pike's controversial beliefs.

Ena Twigg went on to say that Jim was accompanied by a German intellectual to whom Pike had dedicated his new book. The book was still at the printer. It was called *What Is This Treasure?* and was indeed dedicated to Paul Tillich, a liberal theologian and godfather to Jim. Tillich also urged Pike to fight those church officials who wanted to charge him with heresy.

Twelve days later, just before leaving England to return to the United States, Pike again sat with Twigg. This time she went into **trance** and Jim spoke through her. He **prophesied** Pike's movements in the near future (which came true) and also told his father to contact the **Spiritual Frontiers Fellowship**, and a Father William V. Rauscher, an Episcopal priest, when he got back to America. Twigg apaparently herself knew nothing of either Father Rauscher or of the Spiritual Frontiers Fellowship. In the fall of 1967, Pike was again shaken when his secretary Maren Bergrud committed suicide. He tried to contact her through mediums but without success.

Pike agreed to sit for a televised séance on CTV in Toronto, with medium Rev. **Arthur Ford**. This took place on Sunday, September 3. Allen Spraggett, religion editor of the Toronto *Star*, had arranged the program and acted as moderator. He first talked with Ford about **mediumship** and then with Pike, asking if the Bishop had any personal experience of communicating through a trance medium. Ford then put himself into a trance and his **spirit guide**, Fletcher, came through. Soon Jim, Pike's son, came through and gave evidential details.

On December 20, 1968, Pike married Diane Kennedy, who had taken over Maren Bergrud's position as director of the New Focus Foundation (started by Pike the previous year). Pike left the Church and formed the Foundation for Religious Transition in April 1969. A few months later, Pike and his new wife took a trip to the Holy Land. On September 1, they became lost in the desert. Diane had to leave her husband to go for help and could not locate him again afterward. When Ena Twigg heard of Pike being missing, she had a sitting with her husband Harry and Canon Peace-Higgins. They received a communication from Pike himself, giving directions to

where his body could be found. It was found there, on a cliff in the Judaean desert near the Dead Sea, on September 7. Other mediums, including Ford, had tried to reach Pike but only Twigg managed to do so.

Sources:

Guiley, Rosemary Ellen: *The Encyclopedia of Ghosts and Spirits.* New York: Facts On File, 1992

Pike, Diane Kennedy: *Search: The Personal Story of a Wilderness Journey.* New York: Doubleday, 1970

Pike, James A. and Diane Kennedy: *The Other Side: An Account of My Experiences with Psychic Phenomena.* New York: Doubleday, 1968

Twigg, Ena with Ruth Hagy Bro: *Ena Twigg: Medium.* London: W. H. Allen, 1973

PIPER, LEONORA E. (1857–1950)

L eonora E. Piper was born in Boston, Massachusetts, in 1857. When she was eight years old, she was playing in the garden and felt a blow to the side of her head, on the right ear, which she said was accompanied by "a prolonged sibilant sound." This sound gradually became the letter S, which then was followed by the words, "Aunt Sara, not dead but with you still." Leonora was terrified. When she told her mother, her mother noted the time of day. A few days later they learned that Aunt Sara had in fact died at that very moment. Other childhood experiences for Leonora included bright lights seen in her bedroom at night and an unexplained rocking of the bed.

In 1881, Leonora married William Piper of Boston. In 1884, she discovered her **psychic** and mediumistic abilities. This came about when she visited Dr. J. R. Cocke, a blind **healer** and **clairvoyant**, seeking treatment for a tumor. Cocke went into **trance** but Piper also went into trance. While in that state she wrote down a message to a Judge Frost of Cambridge (another of Cocke's clients), from his dead son. Shortly after that a number of **spirit guides** made themselves known, and as word of her message to Judge Frost spread, she was talked into conducting her own **séances**.

In trance she would undergo spasms and grind her teeth ferociously, though in later years this passed and she went smoothly into trance. She would speak with various voices, many of them deep men's voices. Her guides included a purportedly French "**Dr. Phinuit**," who knew little French and less about medicine. There was also a **Native American** girl named Chlorine. Piper wasn't happy with this development and initially would only sit with relatives and close friends. But when Mrs. Gibbins—who happened to be Professor **William James'** mother-in-law—asked for a sitting, for some reason Leonora accepted her. The results were so amazing that Mrs. Gibbins reported them to her son-in-law. In turn Professor James, a founder of the **American Society for Psychical Research**, was so impressed by Piper's séances that he devoted the next eighteen months to carefully controlling everything she did, making all arrangements, and reporting (in *Proceedings*, Vol. VI, "I repeat again what I said before, that, taking everything that I know of Mrs. Piper into account, the result is to make me feel as absolutely certain as I am of any personal fact in the world that she knows things in her trances which she cannot possibly have heard in her waking state, and that the definite philosophy of her trances is yet to be found." Between 1885 and 1915, Leonora Piper became one of the most investigated **mediums** of all time.

William James examined her and after attending many séances (some with his wife) became convinced that Piper was "in possession of a power as yet unexplained." She was never found cheating. She was examined by James, by Dr. **Richard Hodgson**, Professor Newbold, Dr. William Leaf, and Sir **Oliver Lodge**. James introduced her to Richard Hodgson, who had exposed a number of other mediums. Hodgson was stunned with the personal information that Piper provided about his own family. He tested her with other subjects only to get similar results. Her details about deceased persons were so accurate Hodgson hired private detectives to carry out surveillance to see if she actually obtained the information fraudulently. Then Hodgson decided to remove her from her surroundings. He sent her to England in November, 1889, where she was met by Sir Oliver Lodge. Lodge gave a glowing report on her mediumship after she had eighty-eight sittings between her arrival and February, 1890. All sitters were introduced anonymously to Piper. Servants were changed in houses where she stayed. She wasn't even allowed to go shopping alone and couldn't see a newspaper for three days prior to a sitting.

In the end, on Leonora Piper's return to America and after further testing by Dr. Hodgson, Hodgson reported (*Proceedings*, Vol. XIII, in 1897), "I cannot profess to have any doubt but that the 'chief communicators' ... are veritably the personalities that they claim to be; that they have survived the change we call death, and that they have directly communicated with us whom we call living through Mrs. Piper's entranced organism. Having tried the hypothesis of telepathy from the living for several years, and the 'spirit' hypothesis also for several years, I have no hesitation in affirming with the most absolute assurance that the 'spirit' hypothesis is justified by its fruits and the other hypothesis is not."

On Hodgson's unexpected death in 1905, Professor **James Hyslop** took over. The following year Piper went back to England, and with the later deaths of **Frederick W. H. Myers**, **Edmund Gurney**, and others, started producing **cross-correspondences** from their various **spirits**. Seventy-four sittings were held with her and other sittings with mediums Mrs. Verral and Mrs. Holland. The cross-correspondences were produced by the three mediums.

Because Leonora Piper never had any remembrance of what came through her in the trance state, she always remained unconvinced herself that she was a channel for spirits. But, as Sir Oliver Lodge pointed out, "Little value would be attached to her opinion ... Mrs. Piper in fact is not in a more favorable, but even in a less favorable position for forming an opinion than those who sit with her, since she does not afterwards remember what passes while she is in trance."

Frank Podmore commented, "Mrs. Piper is a typical medium. By a fortunate combination of circumstances she has been saved from the temptation to which nearly every other clairvoyant medium of note has at one time or another succumbed, to advertise her gifts by resorting to **physical phenomena**. So far as I am aware, no other clairvoyant medium of note since 1848 has failed at one time or another to exhibit physical phenomena, if only to the extent of table **rapping**, as part of her mediumistic gifts."

In later years Leonora Piper's abilities faded, especially when she had to devote time to her ailing mother. Various controls took over at different times. The French doctor was pushed out by the spirit of **George Pelham**, a deceased friend of Dr. Hodgson. Then the **Imperator** group took over, producing what was described as a "higher caliber" of spirits making contact. Piper's trance mediumship ended in 1911 and she then did mainly automatic writing. In October, 1924, Dr. **Gardner Murphy** conducted a series of sittings and from 1926 to 1927 the **Boston Society for Psychical Research** took over. Leonora Piper died in 1950, at age 93.

Sources:

Doyle, Sir Arthur Conan: *The History of Spiritualism*. New York: Doran, 1926

Fodor, Nandor: *Encyclopedia of Psychic Science*. London: Arthurs Press, 1933

Piper, Alta L.: *The Life and Work of Mrs. Piper*. London: Kegan Paul, Trench, Trubner, 1929

Spence, Lewis: *An Encyclopedia of the Occult*. London: George Routledge & Sons, 1920

P.K. *see* **Psychokinesis**

PLANCHETTE;
PENCIL PLANCHETTE

The word *planchette* means "plank; small board, or platform." It is, in fact, a small platform used in **Spiritualism** as a tool to communicate with **spirits**. It is usually about three inches wide and four inches long, resting on three small legs. There are many different designs but an early, popular, design was heart shaped; the point of the heart working as a pointer. On a **Ouija®** Board, or similar **talking board**, the planchette slides about the surface of the board, pointing at letters to spell out messages. One, two, or more people lightly rest their finger tips on the top edges of the device, to channel into it the power to make it move.

The three legs are either tipped with felt so that they will slide easily on a polished surface, or have small castor wheels on them. Sometimes, if **automatic writing** is to be done, one of the legs is replaced by a pencil, the point of which traces letters onto a sheet of paper over which the planchette moves. This is known as a "pencil planchette."

The moving platform was invented in 1853 by a well known French Spiritualist named M. Planchette. Fifteen years after its original appearance, it became widely used, thanks to an American toy manufacturer who started producing them in quantity. It is said that a similar form of communicating board was in use in **Greece** at the time of Pythagoras, about 540 BCE. According to a French writer this was a "mystic table on wheels," that moved about indicating signs engraved on a stone slab.

There have been a wide variety of designs for planchettes, some of them connecting the platform to a clock-like dial with the letters of the alphabet on it, some allowing the platform to slide sideways in a track, to do its pointing. The board produced commercially by **William Fuld**, and then later by **Parker Brothers**, has a planchette on three legs whose shape comes to a point under the single leg. In the center area of the device there is a plastic window with a pin in its center, pointing down. The instructions that come with the set say "The mysterious message indicator will commence to move ... as it passes over Ouija® talking board each letter of a message is received as it appears through the transparent window covered by the message indicator." This is not strictly true. Sometimes a string of letters is received that make no sense whatsoever ...

A man and woman attempt to communicate with spirits, using an upturned wine glass planchette and a talking board, c. 1950. *Orlando/Three Lions/Getty Images.*

until it is realized that the planchette is no longer showing the relevant letters through its plastic "window" on the one line, but is pointing to the letters on the line above with its tapered point.

A very simple, yet very effective, **talking board** can be made by writing the letters of the alphabet on pieces of paper and laying them down in a circle, around the edge of a table. A wine glass can then be upturned and used as a planchette, the participants resting their fingers on the now-top edge of the glass. The glass will slide over the table surface to stop in front of appropriate letters.

Sources:

Buckland, Raymond: *Buckland's Book of Spirit Communications*. St. Paul: Llewellyn, 2004

Covina, Gina: *The Ouija® Book*. New York: Simon & Schuster, 1979

Hunt, Stoker: *Ouija®: The Most Dangerous Game*. New York: Harper & Row, 1985

Shepard, Leslie A: *Encyclopedia of Occultism & Parapsychology*. New York: Avon Books, 1978

PLATFORM

"The Platform" is where **mediums** address the public and relay messages received from **spirit**. The **Morris Pratt** Institute Educational Course in Modern **Spiritualism** states,

> Platform decorum is of the utmost importance. The moment you step into view, you are Spiritualism. You may be the main reason many of the people came. To meet the various needs of those attending, to leave a permanent message in their mind, and to be an asset to the movement of Spiritualism, you must know and practice good platform decorum. Our services are religious services, and those serving should act accordingly.

Whether or not there is an actual platform is immaterial. For example, at **Lily Dale Assembly** there are regular daily message services given throughout the summer season at Forest Temple and at Inspiration Stump. A variety of different mediums speak at each service. There is no actual platform from which they speak—they stand in front of the seated people—yet the traditional "platform decorum" still is strictly followed.

Speaking from a platform offers advantages to the medium in that she can see the whole of the audience and can thereby more easily distinguish

the different people who are being contacted by spirit.

Sources:

Morris Pratt Institute: *Educational Course on Modern Spiritualism*. Milwaukee: M.P.I., 1981

PODMORE, FRANK (1856–1910)

Frank Podmore was born on February 5, 1856, in Elstree, Hertfordshire, England. He attended Elstree High School and then Haileybury College. He subsequently obtained a scholarship to Pembroke College, Oxford. Very early as an undergraduate, Podmore took an interest in **psychical research** and especially in **Spiritualism**. He even contributed some articles to Spiritualist journals. He was very impressed by what he read of the American medium **Henry Slade**, who specialized in obtaining **slate writing**.

Slade visited Britain in July 1876, en route to Russia. He stayed for six weeks, but his visit was brought to an abrupt end. At one of his **séances**, Professor Lankester snatched the slate from the **medium**'s hands and found that a message was already written on it. Slade gave an explanation for this but Lankester pressed charges. Slade was tried, found guilty, and sentenced to three months imprisonment with hard labor. The conviction was overturned due to a technicality, and before a fresh summons could be issued the following day, Slade fled the country.

It is not know whether or not Podmore witnessed any of Slade's sittings, or any of the trial, but the revelation of fraud had an effect on him. He became an aggressive skeptic of all psychical phenomena and of mediumship in particular. He joined the **Society for Psychical Research** and served on its first council. After **Edmund Gurney**'s death in 1888, Podmore became joint Secretary with **Frederick W. H. Myers**.

In 1892, Podmore published *Apparitions and Thought Transference*. He had previously contributed to *Phantasms of the Living*, with Gurney and Myers, and was involved in investigating 753 cases of **telepathy** and crisis **apparitions** for it. His conclusions in virtually all cases were that telepathy and **hallucinations** were more likely than contact with the deceased.

Podmore is best known for his two-volume *Modern Spiritualism*, published in 1902. It was severely critical of nineteenth century mediumship, though of them all he could find little, if anything, negative to say about **Leonora Piper**. He was also unable to explain **Daniel Dunglas Home**'s phenomena, other than to state that "to say that because we cannot understand some of the feats, therefore they must have been due to **spirits** or psychic force, is merely an opiate for the uneasiness of suspended judgement, a refuge from the trouble of thinking." His other books include *Studies in Psychical Research* (1897), *The Naturalisation of the Supernatural* (1908), **Mesmerism** *and Christian Science* (1909), *Telepathic Hallucination: the New View of Ghosts* (1909), and *The Newer Spiritualism* (1910). Podmore died on August 14, 1910, a suspected suicide (having been found face down in the New Pool at Malvern, Worcester).

Sources:

Fodor, Nandor: *Encyclopedia of Psychic Science.* London: Arthurs Press, 1933

Guiley, Rosemary Ellen: *The Encyclopedia of Ghosts and Spirits.* New York: Facts On File, 1992

Podmore, Frank: *Modern Spiritualism.* London: 1902; reprinted as *Mediums of the Nineteenth Century.* New York: University Books, 1963

Podmore, Frank: *The Newer Spiritualism.* London: T. Fisher Unwin, 1910

POLTERGEIST

The literal meaning of *poltergeist* is "noisy ghost," from the German *polte*—noise and *geist*—spirit. It seems not to be a **spirit** in the sense of being the **ethereal body** of one who is deceased, but seems instead to be a discarnate entity or raw energy field. Poltergeist activity often takes place around an adolescent going through puberty, or someone in a highly emo-

tional state. The person is usually unaware of the pent-up energy being randomly released in his or her vicinity until the poltergeist activity explodes. Objects will defy gravity and fly through the air, be moved around tables and other surfaces, lights will turn on and off, **apports**—often large in size—will appear, doors will open and close of their own volition, glass and china will be **levitated** and then smashed. Seldom is anyone hurt by such activity, but there is a risk of being hit by flying objects.

It is probably incorrect to speak of poltergeist energy as malevolent energy, because it is impersonal and although usually emanating from an individual is not directed by that individual, either consciously or even unconsciously. It is pure energy running wild. Poltergeist activity has been reported since ancient times, and around the world. **Psychical researchers** have studied the phenomenon since the late 1800s. Rosemary Guiley reports, "In the late 1970s, English researchers Alan Gauld and A. D. Cornell made a computer analysis of 500 poltergeist cases collected from around the world since later than 1800. They found 63 general characteristics, such as: 24 percent of poltergeist incidents lasted longer than a year; 58 percent were most active at night; 48 percent included rapping sounds; 64 percent involved the movement of small objects, by far and away the most common phenomenon; 36 percent involved the movement of large pieces of furniture; and 12 percent were characterized by the opening and shutting of doors and windows."

Early cases of poltergeist activity were blamed on the machinations of the devil. By the beginning of the nineteenth century, the blame was shifted to **Spiritualist mediums**. More recently there is the connection with unconscious and involuntary **psychokinesis**. In the 1960s, William G. Roll of the Psychical Research Foundation in Durham, North Carolina, studied 116 cases from more than four centuries. He felt that cases where a particular person was present during the activity indicated that they were expressions of unconscious psychokinesis.

Borley Rectory, on the Essex-Suffolk border of England, has been described as "the most haunted house in England." It was extensively investigated by psychical researcher **Harry Price,** founder of the **National Laboratory for Psychical Research.** There is a frequently reproduced photograph of the ruins of Borley, when it was being torn down, which shows a single brick that flew up and stayed in mid-air just as the camera shutter was tripped. There were many examples of poltergeist activity at the site, including writing and scribbling that appeared on walls there. Bells rang, stones and other objects flew through the air, a variety of bumps, bangs, **rappings,** and other sounds were heard.

Sources:

Bletzer, June G.: *The Encyclopedia Psychic Dictionary.* Lithia Springs: New Leaf, 1998

Guiley, Rosemary Ellen: *The Encyclopedia of Ghosts and Spirits.* New York: Facts On File, 1992

Owen, A. R. G.: *Man, Myth & Magic: Poltergeists.* London: BPC Publishing, 1970

POSEIDIA INSTITUTE

A nonprofit **parapsychology** research organization located at Virginia Beach, Virginia. Jean Campbell was its Director from 1973 to 1986. Raymond Buckland was the Education Director and also editor of the Institute's journal. The Institute did similar work to that done by the **Association for Research and Enlightenment** (ARE), but worked with living **psychics** while the ARE worked only with the **Edgar Cayce** material. The principle psychic at Poseidia was Ellen Andrews.

POSSESSION

P ossession means to hold occupancy with or without rights of ownership. This exactly describes possession in the **psychic** sense. It is the possession of the physical body with—though frequently without—the permission of the owner. An entranced **medium** is possessed by a **spirit** but can curtail that possession when desired. One who is possessed by a negative spirit cannot get rid of it without external pressure in the shape of an **exorcism.**

Leslie Shepard makes an excellent point,

If no new knowledge is shown in the **trance** state there is no reason to ascribe the communication to an external intelligence. The character of the communicator alone does not furnish convincing proof. Secondary personalities are often hostile and antagonistic to the primary one, the cleavage might not be intellectual alone but also moral, therefore the difference between the normal self of the medium and the communicator does not necessarily clinch the case for possession. Supernormal knowledge which the medium could not have acquired, is an indispensable condition to prove the presence of an external spirit.

True negative possession is rare. There are, however, many cases that might be termed psychological possession, where the person believes him- or herself to be possessed and acts accordingly. Believing in that condition, the individual naturally believes also in exorcism so the performance of a Rite of Exorcism can then seem effective. The official exorcist for the city of Rome claims that he receives many long distance telephone calls from all over the world, from people believing themselves to be possessed. However, he says that he actually performs exorcisms "as rarely as possible."

Sources:

Bletzer, June G.: *The Encyclopedia Psychic Dictionary.* Lithia Springs: New Leaf, 1998

Fortune, Dion: *Psychic Self Defence.* London: Aquarian Press, 1988

Lhermitte, J.: *True and False Possession.* New York: Hawthorne Books, 1986

Shepard, Leslie A: *Encyclopedia of Occultism & Parapsychology.* New York: Avon Books, 1978

Spence, Lewis: *An Encyclopedia of the Occult.* London: George Routledge & Sons, 1920

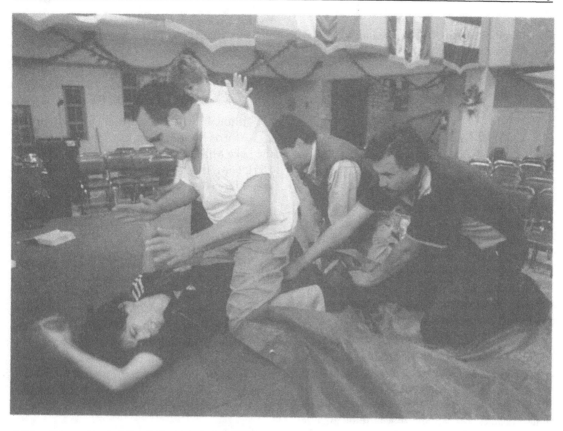

A Protestant priest in Mexico City prays over a man who believed he was possessed by a demon that caused him fits of anger and to spit blood and speak in tongues. *AP/WideWorld Photos.*

POST, DR. ISAAC (1798–1872) AND AMY (1802–1889)

Isaac and Amy Post were Hicksite **Quakers**, followers of Elias Hicks. They came to embrace **Spiritualism** when it was still in its infancy. They may have been present on the night of March 31, 1848, when the **rappings** first occurred at the **Fox Family** Cottage. Certainly four months later, Isaac Post was responsible for connecting messages that were received laboriously by raps. As Sir **Arthur Conan Doyle** said, "Isaac Post had instituted a method of spelling by raps, and messages were pouring through." Later on, when the Fox Sisters were suffering from various charges and attacks, the Posts remained staunch friends and protectors. Isaac called together the very first meeting of Spiritualists.

Amy—who became known as "The Mother of Modern Spiritualism"—was active in the Women's Rights Movement and was a personal friend of **Susan B. Anthony**. The two women worked together in the Abolition and Anti-Slavery Movement. It was due to these activities that the Posts were forced to leave the Quaker movement, since their activities were contrary to the Hicksite Quaker rules.

Isaac developed as a **medium** producing **automatic writing**. He claimed that his hand was guided by such luminaries as George Washington, Thomas Jefferson, **Emanuel Swedenborg**, and John Caldwell Calhoun. In 1852, he wrote *Voices From the Spirit World*. He became very active in the Abolition movement and in politics generally.

Sources:

Awtry-Smith, Marilyn: *"They" Paved the Way.* New York: Spiritualism & More, nd

Postcognition *see* Retrocognition

Poughkeepsie Seer *see* Davis, Andrew Jackson

POWELL, EVAN (B. 1881)

Evan Powell was born in Merthyr Tydvyl, Wales, in 1881, where he grew up to become a coal miner. He moved to Paignton, Devon, England, where he was a small tradesman. He developed mediumistic abilities and had a **spirit guide** named Black Hawk. As a **medium**, Powell would sit inside a **cabinet** securely tied to a chair. He produced physical phenomena such as psychic lights, movement of objects (**psychokinesis**), and **direct voice**. He gave many **séances** for the **British College of Psychic Science**.

At one sitting, Black Hawk insisted that a book had been written about him. No one knew of it, so a friend of Powell commissioned a book agent to find it. It turned out to be a book titled *Life of Ma-Ka-Tai-Me-She-Kia-Kiak or Black Hawk, dictated by himself*. It was published in Boston in 1834. A copy of the book was obtained and presented to Powell. Black Hawk also insisted that there was a memorial to him in Illinois.

Sir **Arthur Conan Doyle** compared Evan to another medium, saying, "Powell's luminous phenomena are equally good. His voice production is better. The author [Doyle] has heard the **spirit** voices as loud as those of ordinary human talk, and recalls one occasion when three of them were talking simultaneously ... Movements of objects are common in the Powell séances, and on one occasion a stand weighing sixty pounds was suspended for some time over the author's head. Evan Powell always insists upon being securely tied during his séances, which is done, he claims, for his own protection, since he cannot be responsible for his own movements when he is in **trance**."

Sources:

Doyle, Sir Arthur Conan: *The History of Spiritualism.* New York: Doran, 1926

Fodor, Nandor: *Encyclopedia of Psychic Science.* London: Arthurs Press, 1933

PRATT, MORRIS

Although little is known of the early life of Morris Pratt, it is on record that he visited the Lake Mills, Wisconsin, **Spiritualist** Center in 1851 (just three years after the **Fox Family's** groundbreaking experiences with **spirits**). As a result of this visit, he became deeply interested in **psychic** phenomena and in what had become the religion of Spiritualism.

Pratt was well educated to the point where he frequently got into arguments with Christian ministers who criticized Spiritualism. On a number of occasions he was even evicted from churches because of his outspokenness. At one time, he was fined for his controversial actions. But, dedicated as he was to the promotion of this new religion, he recognized the need for a large number of educated proponents to spread the word and to address the opponents.

Pratt had recognized his own **spirit guide** in the person of a **Native American**. This guide told Pratt of various mineral deposits unknown to anyone. Pratt promised, "If I am made rich, I will give part of it to Spiritualism." On the information, he invested in a company which was later to become the very profitable Ashland Mine of Ironwood, Michigan. In just a few months, he made more than $200,000. Morris Pratt didn't forget his promise, and he used part of his profits to advance Spiritualism. In 1889, he built and dedicated a temple in Whitewater, Wisconsin. It consisted of a number of lecture rooms, an office, chapel, and dormitories. It was deeded as the Morris Pratt Institute, though it quickly became known locally as "The Spooks' Temple." However, over the years the Pratt Institute earned the respect of the local citizens and even gained national fame, becoming the "Mecca of Modern Spiritualism." In 1946, the original building was sold and a new one built. It maintains an extensive lending library, home to many rare and spiritually historical books.

The Morris Pratt Institute Association became one of the educational arms of the **National Spiritualist Association of Churches**, offering various courses in Modern Spiritualism. The correspondence course provides the required educational information for certification in the Ministry of Spiritualism, as Ordained Minister, Spiritualist Teacher, Licentiate Minister, Commissioned Spiritualist **Healer**, or Certified **Medium**. The Institute is headquartered in Milwaukee, Wisconsin.

Sources:

Morris Pratt Institute: http://www.morrispratt.org/

PRAYER

P rayer has been defined as the act of addressing deity in petition, or a specific order of words used in praying. Bletzer said it is "a continuous string of words either spoken or silent, shouted or sung, that sends power into the ethers in accordance with the emotion and faith behind the words."

Prayer is usually addressed to deity, asking for help, guidance, or the granting of a desire, or expressing devotion, giving thanks, or asking forgiveness. Prayers are frequently rendered in a set formula, though it would seem that words coming straight from the heart would be most appropriate and most effective. They may be delivered standing, kneeling, or even prostrate, depending upon tradition.

Historically there have been many different approaches to prayer, from the pleading to the threatening. It was said that the ancient **Egyptians** had a bullying manner toward their gods. In Morocco, there are many instances of ʿâr the "conditional curse" applied to saints to make them attend to requests if they seem at all reluctant. In Africa, the Zulus will say to the ancestral spirit, "Help me or you will feed on nettles."

Silent prayers probably came about from the use of "words of power" used magically. Rather

than reveal these supposedly powerful words used to command the gods or the **spirits**, the magicians would mumble them or say them silently so that others could not overhear and also use them. At a later stage, when there was more of a distinction between magic and religion, it became common to repeat prayers loudly if only to show that no magical words were being included. Yet prayer seems to have gone full cycle with modern thought that to pray silently is to show communion and silent adoration, bringing a person closer to deity.

In Modern **Spiritualism**, the belief is not focused on a distinctly male anthropomorphic deity. There is an acknowledgement of the duality of the sexes found throughout nature with prayers addressed to "Mother/Father God" or simply to "**Infinite Intelligence**."

Sources:

Bletzer, June G.: *The Encyclopedia Psychic Dictionary*. Lithia Springs: New Leaf, 1998

Encyclopedia Britannica. Chicago: William Benton, 1964

PRECOGNITION

P recognition literally means "to know beforehand." Precognition is paranormal knowledge of future events, an impression that something specific is going to happen. There are many examples, such as **Jeane Dixon's** precognition of the assassination of John F. Kennedy. Another example, though without knowing all the details, was when Colin Macdonald, a 34-year old marine engineer, refused three times to sign on as the second engineer on the *Titanic*, because of precognition that there would be a terrible disaster connected with the ship. Laboratory examples of precognition are seen in the results of **extrasensory perception** tests, where a person knows beforehand what card will be drawn by the Sender.

There is a very fine line between precognition and **premonition**. Precognition implies a more certain knowledge of coming events, while premonitions are vague feelings without the specifics.

Precognition happens most frequently in **dreams**, where the dreamer "sees" an event in the future that later turns out to be true. Such scenes are also experienced in **trance**, visions, **hallucinations**, and even in the waking state. Precognition can be brought about through various forms of **divination**, such as **scrying**, and by **mediumship**.

The vast majority of precognitive experiences deal with death, dying, and other negative events. During the two World Wars and in other wars, there have been innumerable examples of mothers, fathers, spouses, and others knowing when someone was about to be killed, even though that person was hundreds or even thousands of miles away. These impressions came strongly and, usually, within a matter of hours or even minutes of the actual event.

In the Welsh village of Aberfan, on the night of October 20, 1966, a nine-year-old girl named Eryl Jones had a dream that there was no school the following day. She didn't just dream that there would be no classes, but that there would be no school in existence. The next morning she told her mother that "something black came down all over it." But she went to school anyway. Shortly after nine o'clock that morning a half-million-ton mountain of coal waste, saturated by days of unrelenting rain, slid down over the village, burying houses and the entire school. Nearly 150 people, most of them school children and including Eryl Jones, were buried and died. Many other people all over Great Britain had similar dreams before the tragedy. Some saw an actual mountain of coal slag pour down the mountainside onto the village.

In his book *Foreknowledge* (1938), H. F. Saltmarsh suggested that different kinds of time are accessible to different states of consciousness. At the level of general awareness our experience of time is not constant, since time can seem to fly or it can seem to drag. He concluded that we are living in what he termed the "specious present," where the time we perceive is of short duration. For our subconscious, however, the "present" is stretched out so that it actually includes part of the future. In his book he talks about a case published in the *Journal* of the **Society for Psychical Research** which gave details of precognition exhibited by John H. Williams, an eighty-year-old **Quaker**. On May 31, 1933, Williams woke up at 8:55 a.m. with vivid memory of a dream in which he had heard the radio commentary on the Derby horse race, to be run at 2:00 p.m. that afternoon. In the dream he heard the names of four horses, including *King Solomon* and *Hyperion*, and certain details of the race. Williams told both a neighbor and a business acquaintance about this. Although personally uninterested in horse racing and betting, Williams made a point of listening to the commentary when the race was run later that day. He heard the identical commentary, with mention of the same horses, which he had heard in his dream. The other two people he had confided in later confirmed all he had told them.

Stuart Holroyd, in *The Supernatural: Dreamworlds* (1976), gives the details of a scientific experiment that seems to prove very conclusively that effects can precede causes, thus upsetting one of the basic laws of science and of common sense. Drs. Montague Ullman and Stanley Krippner ran a series of closely controlled and very complex tests on British **psychic** Malcolm Bessent, at the Maimonides Medical Center. The idea was to keep track of what Bessent dreamed and to see if it was the same as an incident that was *going to happen* to him. They did this by first using EEG to monitor his brain rhythms and REM (Rapid Eye Movement; the indicator that a subject is having a dream) and then immediately waking him to record the dream. This was carried out by one team, who woke him after four separate dreams then filed away the details of those dreams. The following morning, a second team sat down and decided on a target word. In this case it was "corridor," one out of 1,200 possible words. Around this word they were to construct an elaborate multisensory "happening" for Bessent. Krippner selected Vincent Van Gogh's painting *Hospital Corridor at St. Remy* as the target picture. The "happening" was started when two men, dressed in white hospital uniforms, burst into Bessent's room and forced him into a straight jacket. They took him out and led him down a darkened corridor, while eerie music from the movie *Spellbound* was playing in the background. There was also the sound of distant hysterical laughter. The men took Bessent to an office where Krippner, seated at a desk and laughing wildly, forced him to swallow a pill and swabbed his face to "disinfect" him. Obvious, on the wall of the office, was the Van Gogh painting. Krippner then turned off the lights and showed Bessent slides of weird drawings done by mental patients.

When the dream records were opened and studied, they showed that Bessent had had recurring visions of a mental hospital, a large concrete building, doctors and psychologists in white coats, and the theme of a female patient disguised as a doctor trying to escape down a corridor toward an archway. The dreams were all characterized by a feeling of hostility. This was an amazingly accurate series of dreams, dreamed before the events took place and all done under strict laboratory conditions. It would seem to be conclusive proof of precognition in dreams.

Sources:

Buckland, Raymond: *Buckland's Book of Spirit Communications*. St. Paul: Llewellyn, 2004

Buckland, Raymond: *The Fortune–Telling Book: The Encyclopedia of Divination and Soothsaying*. Detroit: Visible Ink Press, 2004

Guiley, Rosemary Ellen: *Harper's Encyclopedia of Mystical & Paranormal Experience*. San Francisco: HarperSanFrancisco, 1991

Holroyd, Stuart: *The Supernatural: Dream Worlds*. London: Aldus, 1976

Saltmarsh, H.F.: *Foreknowledge*. London: G. Bell & Sons, 1938

PREDICTION

A prediction is the action of foretelling future events, or **prophecy**. In his masterful *An Encyclopedia of the Occult* (1920), Lewis Spence refers to **Andrew Jackson Davis**'s amazing predic-

tions of the automobile and the typewriter, both of which were given in 1856. The first practical automobile was the Benz of 1885 and the first practical typewriter was placed on the market by Remington in 1874. Davis said, "Look out about these days for carriages and traveling saloons on country roads—without horses, without steam, without any visible motive power—moving with greater speed and far more safety than at present. Carriages will be moved by a strange and beautiful and simple admixture of aqueous and atmospheric gases—so easily condensed, so simply ignited, and so imparted by a machine somewhat resembling fire engines as to be entirely concealed and manageable between the forward wheels. These vehicles will prevent many embarrassments now experienced by persons living in thinly populated territories. The first requisite for these land-locomotives will be good roads, upon which, with your engine, without your horses, you may travel with great rapidity. These carriages seem to be of uncomplicated construction." About the typewriter, he said, "I am almost moved to invent an automatic psychographer—that is, an artificial soul-writer. It may be constructed something like a piano, one brace or scale of keys to represent the elementary sounds; another and lower tier to represent a combination, and still another for a rapid recombination so that a person, instead of playing a piece of music may touch off a sermon or a poem."

In February, 1914, Australian **Spiritualist medium** Mrs. Foster Turner told Sir **Arthur Conan Doyle**, before an audience of nearly 1000 people, "Although there is not at present a whisper of a great European war at hand, yet I want to warn you that before this year, 1914, has run its course, Europe will be deluged in blood. Great Britain, our beloved nation, will be drawn into the most awful war the world has ever known. Germany will be the great antagonist, and will draw other nations to her train. Austria will totter to its ruin. Kings and kingdoms will fall. Millions of precious lives will be slaughtered, but Britain will finally triumph and emerge victorious."

There have been many tens of thousands of predictions made that have turned out to be accurate. Some are made as statements, some by mediums while in **trance**, some have been seen in **dreams**. Predictions are given based on astrological charts, on the layout of **tarot** and other cards, based on **omens** such as the sighting of animals or birds, based on the actions of people or animals, and so on. Predictions are the utterances of those who divine the future.

Sources:

Buckland, Raymond: *The Fortune–Telling Book: The Encyclopedia of Divination and Soothsaying.* Detroit: Visible Ink Press, 2004

Spence, Lewis: *An Encyclopedia of the Occult.* London: George Routledge & Sons, 1920

PREMONITION; PRESENTIMENT

A premonition, or presentiment, is a warning of a future event. Premonitions range from vague feelings to **visions** and auditory warnings. **Dreams** also may bring premonitions which may be presented in a straightforward manner or purely symbolically. Premonitions differ from **predictions** in that the latter states that a certain thing will definitely come about, and may include minute details, while the former is simply a strong feeling that something is *likely* to happen.

Nandor Fodor (1895–1964) says that a premonition should have two fundamental conditions: (i) "The fact announced must be absolutely independent of the person to whom the premonition has come," and (ii) "The announcement must be such that it cannot be ascribed to chance or sagacity."

The **Society for Psychical Research**, in its early days, collected 668 cases of premonitions of death; 252 more were added in 1922 alone. **Camille Flammarion** (1842–1925) collected 1,824 cases.

Sources:

Fodor, Nandor: *Encyclopedia of Psychic Science.* London: Arthurs Press, 1933

PRICE, HARRY (1881–1948)

Harry Price was a **psychical researcher** who founded the **National Laboratory of Psychical Research** in England. He was its Director and also the Foreign Research Officer of the **American Society for Psychical Research**. Price was an amateur stage magician and Honorary Vice President of the Magician's Club in London. He also had some early training as an engineer. As an accomplished conjurer, he was well suited to examine **mediums** and **psychics** who might have been fraudulent. He investigated **Rudi Schneider** and **Stella C.** (Mrs. Leslie Deacon), among others.

In his examination of Rudi Schneider, Price devised a test where the medium and all the sitters (six, including Price) wore metallic gloves and shoes. Each touched the hands and feet of his or her neighbor. In front of each person was a red light bulb that remained lit as long as no one broke the circuit. If anyone were to remove a hand or foot, the light bulb would go out. Despite these precautions, Schneider produced **materializations** of arms and hands. Price wrote, "Never, in the recorded history of any psychic, have phenomena been witnessed under such a merciless triple control of medium and before sitters of such repute." Stemman said, "Price's extensive notes on this series of **séances** constitute one of the most impressive documents on physical mediumship in the history of psychical research" (*The Supernatural: Spirits and Spirit Worlds*, 1975). Yet despite all the precautions, in one séance Price neglected to make the electrical connections and a photograph, triggered to be taken automatically, showed Schneider with an arm free. Schneider was accused of fraud and, despite Price's defense of him for many years, a personal quarrel developed.

Once, on a train journey, Price got into conversation with a Mrs. Leslie Deacon (who later became known as the medium Stella C.). From what she mentioned to Price, in talking—the sensation of cold breezes in closed rooms, for example—he realized that she had tremendous psychic and mediumistic potential. She agreed to be examined at Price's National Laboratory of Psy-

Image of Harry Price, from his book *Search for Truth* (1942). Price was a British psychical researcher who conducted an investigation of Borley Rectory, the "most haunted house in England." *Courtesy Fortean Picture Library.*

chical Research. Price developed various tools for examining psychics and mediums. One of these was a fraudproof table that he used with Stella C. It could have various musical instruments and the like placed inside a compartment which then became inaccessible by normal means. Despite this and other precautions, the musical instruments played and a bell rang during the séance. Price also used an automatic thermograph, which recorded a significant fall in temperature during sittings. It was common for him to sprinkle starch powder on the floor, to detect any foot movements if there should be any. He would also seal windows with masking tape and initial the tape.

Price conducted what has been described as the most famous ghost hunt of modern times—

the investigation of **Borley Rectory**, on the Essex-Suffolk border of England. The Rectory is known as "the most **haunted** house in England." There is a frequently reproduced photograph of the ruins of Borley, when it was being torn down, which shows a single brick that flew up and stayed in mid-air just as the camera shutter was tripped. There were many examples of **poltergeist** activity at the site, including writing and scribbling that appeared on walls there. Bells rang, stones and other objects flew through the air, a variety of bumps, bangs, **rappings**, and other sounds were heard. After Price's death, the Society for Psychical Research (SPR) investigated Price's investigations. They were extremely critical and all but called Price a fraud and accused him of creating some of the phenomena himself.

This was probably due to bad blood between Price and the SPR, which had existed and grown after Price founded his National Laboratory. Apparently the SPR completely ignored the fact that Borley Rectory had been haunted—and exhibiting a wide variety of phenomena—from long before the time Price began investigating it. A later review by the society's R. J. Hastings was much more balanced and admitted that there was no evidence to show fraud on Price's part.

Many felt that Price was too much of a publicity seeker, loving the limelight and knowing how to appeal to the media but, as Holroyd points out (*The Supernatural: Minds Without Boundaries*, 1975), personal profit was not his motive. He funded most of his research work himself and eventually donated the National Laboratory to the University of London, along with his personal library of 17,000 volumes.

Price wrote many books himself, including *Cold Light on Spiritualistic Phenomena* (1922), *Revelations of a Spirit Medium* (1922), *Stella C.* (1925), *Catalogue of Works on Psychical Research* (1929), *Rudi Schneider: a Scientific Examination of His Mediumship* (1930), **Regurgitation** and the **Duncan** Mediumship (1931), *An Account of Some Further Experiments With Rudi Schneider* (1933), *Leaves from a Psychist's Case-book* (1933), *Confessions of a* **Ghost** *Hunter* (1936), *Fifty Years of Psychical Research* (1939), *The Haunting of Cahshen's Gap* (1936), and *The End of Borley Rectory* (1946).

Sources:

Buckland, Raymond: *Ray Buckland's Magic Cauldron*. St. Paul: Galde Press, 1995

Holroyd, Stuart: *The Supernatural: Minds Without Boundaries*. London: Aldus, 1975

Shepard, Leslie A: *Encyclopedia of Occultism & Parapsychology*. New York: Avon Books, 1978

Stemman, Roy: *The Supernatural: Spirits and Spirit Worlds*. London: Aldus, 1975

PRINCE, DR. WALTER FRANKLIN (1863–1934)

Walter Franklin Prince was an ex-minister of the Episcopal Church. He was Research Officer for the **American Society for Psychical Research** (ASPR) from 1920 to 1924, founder and Research Officer for the **Boston Society for Psychical Research**, and President of the (British) **Society for Psychical Research** (SPR) from 1931 to 1932. Over a period of eighteen years, Prince investigated many different types of paranormal phenomena in hundreds of cases, for both the SPR and the ASPR.

Walter Franklin Prince was born on April 22, 1863, in Detroit, Maine. He graduated from Maine Wesleyan Seminary in 1881 and received a B.D. from Drew Theological Seminary in 1886. He received a Ph.D. from Yale in 1899. In 1885, at the age of twenty-two, he married Lelia Madora Colman. They had no children, but in 1908 adopted a young woman whom they named Theodosia, who had been a psychological patient of Prince's.

The Princes moved to New York City in 1916 and he became director of therapeutics at St. Mark's Church. Prince had been corresponding with **James Hervey Hyslop** of the American Society for Psychical Research on split personalities exhibited by Theodosia, and in little over a year resigned his position to join the staff of the ASPR. There he established himself as a painstaking researcher. When Hyslop died in 1920, Prince became the ASPR's Research Officer and Editor of the *Journal* and *Proceedings*. With **Harry Houdini**, he assisted in the investigation of Margery (**Mina Stinson Crandon**).

Initially Prince had doubts about certain phenomena but eventually came to the conclusion that **telepathy** and **clairvoyance** had been "absolutely and scientifically proved." He was also inclined to believe in survival of personality after bodily death. He wrote many articles for the ASPR *Journal* and publications for the SPR. He authored a number of books including *The Psychic in the House* (1926), *The Case of* **Patience Worth** (1928), *Noted Witness for Psychic Occurrences* (1928), *The Enchanted Boundary* (1930), and (with Mrs. Allison) *Leonard and Soule Experiments*. In January 1925, after some disagreements,

Prince left the ASPR and went on to found the Boston Society for Psychical Research, moving to Boston at that time. That same year, Prince's wife died, which affected him considerably.

He continued to do a lot of worthwhile **psychical research**, and eventually became President of the Society for Psychical Research in London, England, holding that position in 1931 and 1932. He was the first American after **William James** to hold that position. Prince died on August 7, 1934, at his home in Hingham, Massachusetts.

Sources:

Fodor, Nandor: *Encyclopedia of Psychic Science*. London: Arthurs Press, 1933

Guiley, Rosemary Ellen: *The Encyclopedia of Ghosts and Spirits*. New York: Facts On File, 1992

PROPHET, ELIZABETH CLARE (B. 1939)

E lizabeth Clare Wulf was born in Red Bank, New Jersey, on April 8, 1939 (another source says she was born in Long Branch, New Jersey). Her father was a World War I German U-Boat captain; her mother came from Switzerland. She claims that as a teenager she "had a supernatural experience with the Master Saint Germain" which compelled her to devote her life to spreading these teachings. Her first of four marriages was in 1960 to Dag Ytreburg, a Norwegian lawyer. This marriage ended in 1961, when she met Mark Prophet (1918–1973). Prophet was a traveling salesman, also married at the time they met. Elizabeth believed that she and Mark had met in a previous lifetime, in Camelot, when she was Guinevere and he was Lancelot. Two years later, Mark got a divorce, leaving behind a wife and five children, and married Elizabeth. They had four children, Sean, Erin, Moira and Tatiana.

Mark founded The Summit Lighthouse in 1958. When he was seventeen years old, Mark felt he was "supernaturally" contacted by El Morya, an "Ascended Master;" one of the Great White Brotherhood favored by **Helena Blavatsky** and the **Theosophical Society**. Mark taught his new wife to "take dictation" from dozens of Ascended Masters ranging from **Buddha** to **Jesus** to K17 (head of the "cosmic secret service"). According to Prophet, these masters spoke only through Elizabeth, and have done so more than 2,000 times. She often closed her eyes when delivering this **inspirational speaking**, placing her fingertips on her temples. She once told an interviewer that "the energy is stupendous. It is exhilarating."

The Prophets lived in Washington D.C. for several years and then moved to Colorado Springs. In 1973, Mark died of a stroke and the church claimed that he had become another Ascended Master named Lanello (a combination of names from two previous lives: Lancelot and Longfellow). Elizabeth Clare Prophet took over leadership of The Summit Lighthouse, marrying an aide, Randall Kosp, a few months after Mark's death. She renamed the group The Church Universal and Triumphant. The church grew rapidly and moved first to Santa Barbara and then to Malibu. Elizabeth's marriage to Kosp ended in 1980. The following year Elizabeth married Ed Francis and, in 1994, at fifty-five years of age, she gave birth to their son Seth Thomas Francis. In 1998, she and Francis divorced, although their marriage had been hailed as being divinely inspired.

Prophet's followers call her Vicar of Christ, Messenger, Mother of the Flame, Mother, and Ma Guru. The church purchased a 32,000 acre ranch in Montana. From its headquarters there, Prophet spreads the word of the masters through regular publications and multiple weekly television programs. She predicted that there would be a Soviet missile strike on the United States on April 23, 1990. The many church followers who live at the ranch (estimates have been as high as 3,000) built underground bunkers and the church sold space in them for $12,000 per person. (The state of Montana has since banned use of the shelters.) When the attack did not take place, Prophet claimed that she did not mean an actual nuclear holocaust but rather the beginning of a "twelve year cycle of negative **karma**."

Federal officials ordered the evacuation of thirty-five underground fuel tanks at the ranch, when it was found that more than 20,000 gallons of fuel had leaked from the tanks. Eventually 650,000 gallons of fuel were removed. The church's tax exempt status was challenged—with $2.6 million owing in back taxes—when it was found that they were stockpiling weapons. Prophet's husband, also the Vice President of the church, was arrested and served prison time for assumed identity and purchase of military-style equipment for the church.

One ex-member of the church received a $1.8 million judgement against the church on the grounds that he was made a slave there. Four of Prophet's adult children have turned their backs on the church, with three of them publicly criticizing her and one of them calling it a "dangerous cult" and her "a hypocrite." Despite legal challenges and a variety of problems, the church claims that its membership is increasing. Prophet herself is said to be suffering from the onset of Alzheimer's disease, though some claim this to be a stunt designed to keep her from testifying in potential lawsuits filed by ex-members. Others say the disease is real.

Sources:

Church Universal and Triumphant: http://religious movements.lib.virginia.edu/nrms/cut.html

Elizabeth Clare Prophet Article: http://www.hcn.org/servlets/hcn.Article?article_id=4852

Klimo, Jon: *Channeling: Investigations on Receiving Information from Paranormal Sources.* Los Angeles: Jeremy P. Tarcher, 1987

PROPHET; PROPHECY

A prophet is one who speaks the will of a deity, quite often revealing future events. The ancient Hebrews called a prophet *nabhi*. In the early period (c.1050–1015 BCE), a nabhi appeared to be little more than a fortune-teller. Rather than claiming to use any special techniques that would draw such information, the nabhi simply made him or herself *receptive* to whatever messages or prophecies might come from deity. David Christie-Murray said, "The prophets aimed not so much at foretelling the future as at describing what they saw as the will of God in the circumstances of their time. But in doing so, their prophesies *were* fulfilled, often in ways more profound and long lasting than they ever imagined."

The **Bible**'s Old Testament used the term prophet very loosely, applying it to all those who were "friends" of God. For example, Abraham, Moses, Aaron, and Miriam were all named as prophets though Moses was the only true prophet of the four, as "the appointed mouthpiece of divine laws," according to Geoffrey Ashe. There were those who became known as the "Fanatical Prophets." In I Samuel, 10, there are bands of prophets who existed c.1000 BCE, in Gibeah and Ramah. They were devotees of the national deity Jehovah (Yahweh). They were stimulated by rhythmic music, dancing and chanting, building up into *ekstasis* (ecstasy) when their frenzied behavior exercised a **hypnotic** effect on the onlookers.

In ancient **Greece** the prophets were generally attached to the **oracles**, and in **Rome** they were represented by the **augurs**. In ancient **Egypt** the priests of Ra at Memphis acted as prophets. The Druids were frequently prophets to the Celtic people.

Sources:

Ashe, Geoffrey: *Man, Myth & Magic: Prophecy.* London: BPC Publishing, 1970

Christie-Murray, David: *Mysteries of Mind Space & Time: The Unexplained.* Westport: H.S. Stuttman, 1992

Spence, Lewis: *An Encyclopedia of the Occult.* London: George Routledge & Sons, 1920

PROPHETIC DREAMS

Premonitions frequently come in **dreams**. People dream that something is going to happen and hours, days, weeks, months, or even years later it does happen. When it does, there is frequently doubt that the event actually was dreamt about earlier. It is only when such a prophetic dream is recorded at the time it happens that there can be validation.

An excellent example of prophetic dreams is found in the case of the Aberfan tragedy that took place in Wales on October 20, 1966. On that day a half-million-ton mountain of coal waste, saturated from days of unrelenting rain, slid down and buried most of the little Welsh village of Aberfan. Dozens of houses and the village school were buried. Sixteen adults and 128 children died. There are records of a number of people dreaming of this tragedy before it actually happened. One such person was nine-year-old Eryl Jones, who lived in the village. On the morning of October 20, she told her mother that she had dreamed the night before that there was no school that day. Not that school was cancelled, but that there was literally no school. She went to school herself, but at 9:15 am her prophetic dream was fulfilled; she died along with her fellow pupils. Sybil Brown of Brighton, England, had a dream of a child screaming with fear, trapped in a telephone booth as a "black, billowing mass" descended on her. There were many people who dreamed of this particular disaster. So many, in fact, that it led to the founding, in 1967, of the British Premonitions Bureau.

Nandor Fodor gives the details of what he says is "one of the best authenticated cases of prophetic dreams." A man living in Cornwall, England, dreamed that he was in the lobby of the House of Commons, in London, and saw a small man enter, dressed in a blue coat with a white vest. Then, immediately after that, he saw a man dressed in a brown coat, with brass buttons, draw a pistol from under his coat and shoot the first man. The man fell, shot a little below the left breast. The dreamer saw the murderer seized by some men who were nearby, and got a good view of his face. He asked who had been shot and received the answer that it was the Prime Minister. The dreamer then woke up, woke his wife and told her of the dream, but she made light of it. He went back to sleep and dreamed the same scenario twice more. Each time the details were

exactly the same. The next morning he felt so strongly about it that he wanted to contact the Prime Minister, Spencer Perceval (1762–1812), but his friends dissuaded him, telling him he'd be taken for a fool. Eight days later, on May 11, 1812, Perceval was assassinated by an insane man named Bellingham. He was shot in the lobby of the House of Commons. The prime minister was wearing a blue coat with a white vest; the gunman wore a brown coat with brass buttons. He was shot a little below the left breast.

Prophetic dreams have been recorded since ancient times, when **oracles** were consulted for advice and glimpses of the future. Various methods of obtaining answers to questions about the future were employed, differing from one site to another. The commonest method was known as "incubation." This meant that the enquirer would sleep in a sacred area until he or she received the answer in a dream. The main oracle for this was at the temple of Asclepius at Epidaurus, though many other oracles also provided it. In ancient Babylonia, wise men would divine the future from visions seen in dreams. The ancient Hebrews would try to dream of the future by sleeping in cemeteries.

In 1970, the Soviet psychiatrist Dr. Vasily Kasatkin reported on a twenty-eight year study of eight thousand dreams, concluding that dreams could warn of the onset of a serious illness several months in advance.

Sources:

Buckland, Raymond: *The Fortune–Telling Book: The Encyclopedia of Divination and Soothsaying.* Detroit: Visible Ink Press, 2004

Encyclopedia Britannica. Chicago: William Benton, 1964

Fodor, Nandor: *Encyclopedia of Psychic Science.* London: Arthurs Press, 1933

Muldoon, Sylvan J. and Hereward Carrington: *The Projection of the Astral Body.* London: Rider, 1929

Spence, Lewis: *An Encyclopedia of the Occult.* London: George Routledge & Sons, 1920

PSI

P si, the twenty-third letter of the Greek alphabet, was coined by Dr. **Joseph Banks Rhine** as a term for **extrasensory perception**. It later came to include **psychokinesis** and other paranormal phenomena. It is sometimes used as a short form of "**psychic**," as in "psi ability" meaning "psychic ability."

Sources:

Bletzer, June G.: *The Encyclopedia Psychic Dictionary*. Lithia Springs: New Leaf, 1998

Holroyd, Stuart: *The Supernatural: Minds Without Boundaries*. London: Aldus, 1975

PSYCHIC

From the Greek *psychiokos* meaning "soul," psychic, as an adjective, means an attunement of mind and body with subtle vibrations. The word as a noun is also applied to a person who is a sensitive; susceptible to spiritual influences. **Camille Flammarion** (1842–1925) was the first to use the word in France. E. W. Cox (d. 1879) was the first to use it in England.

A psychic picks up knowledge **clairvoyantly**, **clairaudiently**, **clairsentiently**, while fully conscious or, occasionally, in **trance**. He or she differs from a **Spiritualist medium** in that the latter receives information from the **spirit world** while the psychic gets the information purely through his or her own sensitivity. In other words, a psychic operates solely on the earth plane while a medium connects between the earth plane and the higher **ethereal** plane.

Much of the information received by a psychic may be obtained through **extrasensory perception**. The psychic may attune to another person to the point where they are able to "read" that person's thoughts and get the information directly from them. However, many times the psychic will pick up information which is totally unknown to the person they are reading.

Psychics are also able to receive information from inanimate objects, such as handwriting, letters, and jewelry. This is termed **psychometry**. Many people claim to be psychic because they have occasional flashes of paranormal knowl-

edge. Although no psychics seem to have a 100 percent success rate, many do have a very high percentage of success.

Often a psychic will need a "trigger" to spark the psychic knowledge. This may be in the form of **tarot** cards, a **pendulum**, or a **crystal** ball, for example. Others need no more than a few moments of concentration. Most people have the latent ability, which can be brought out through a strict regimen of exercises and constant practice. Some people seem to be born with the psychic facility, and from childhood demonstrate their abilities. A few, such as **Peter Hurkos**, seem to acquire an amazing degree of psychic ability after an illness or an accident of some sort, or a physical trauma often involving a blow to the head.

Sources:

Buckland, Raymond: *The Fortune–Telling Book: The Encyclopedia of Divination and Soothsaying*. Detroit: Visible Ink Press, 2004

Guiley, Rosemary Ellen: *Harper's Encyclopedia of Mystical & Paranormal Experience*. San Francisco: HarperSanFrancisco, 1991

Shepard, Leslie A: *Encyclopedia of Occultism & Parapsychology*. New York: Avon Books, 1978

PSYCHIC DEVELOPMENT

Everyone is born with psychic abilities. In some people, the abilities come out quite naturally; in others they suddenly emerge after an accident or traumatic event (*see* **Peter Hurkos**). In still others they must be brought out through a series of exercises over a period of time. Such things as **meditation, affirmations**, and **psychometry** can all help in the development. As with most things, practice makes perfect. Children usually have better developed psychic abilities than do adults, who have had most of their natural ability drilled out of them by the mundane world and by the intolerance of most established religions.

Sources:

Boddington, Harry: *The University of Spiritualism*. London: Spiritualist Press, 1947

Buckland, Raymond and Hereward Carrington: *Amazing Secrets of the Psychic World*. New York: Parker Publishing, 1975

PSYCHIC FAIRS

So-called Psychic Fairs are popular in many areas. They usually consist of a variety of people offering psychic services to the public, such as **tarot card** readings, astrology, **healing** of various disciplines, sale of **crystals**, incense, and **psychic** tools of all types. The fairs range in size from small one-room affairs to large expos filling convention centers. The larger fairs and expos usually also feature lectures and workshops by figures well known in their respective fields.

Psychic Photography *see* **Spirit Photography**

PSYCHIC NEWS

The *Psychic News* is Britain's premier newspaper covering **psychic** and **Spiritualist** subjects. It was established in 1932 and is the world's oldest weekly newspaper of its kind. The first issue was published May 28, 1932. Today it has worldwide distribution.

The newspaper was founded by **medium** and psychic researcher **Maurice Barbanell**, who was its editor for many years. He was inspired by spirit guides to call it Psychic News. **Hannen Swaffer**, the well known journalist and Spiritualist, was closely involved in the startup, as was medium **Arthur Findlay**.

Sources:
Psychic News Bookshop Online: http://www.psychic-newsbookshop.co.uk

PSYCHIC SCIENCE

Psychic Science was the quarterly journal of the **British College of Psychic Science** (BCPS). It was originally called *Quarterly Transactions* and was edited by Stanley de Brath. It was published from 1939 to 1945. In 1945, *Psychic Science* changed its name briefly to *Experimental* **Metaphysics** and then, in December 1948, was superceded by *Light*, as the journal of the **College of Psychic Studies**.

PSYCHIC SURGERY

A psychic surgeon usually goes into **trance** and then cuts into the patient with any sharp object, such as scissors, a knife (a kitchen knife, or even one with a rusty blade), a razor blade, or a letter opener. Something is usually removed from the patient and the wound is closed up simply by pressing the two sides of the cut together, causing all signs of any incision to disappear. The removed object is frequently referred to as a tumor. A number of alleged "**psychic** surgeons" have been found to be fraudulent, not actually cutting into the patient's body but "palming" such objects as chicken livers or other animal tissue to produce as the "removed" tumor. However, a number of untrained, unskilled peasants have been carefully observed by actual surgeons and found to have done what they claimed to do, with x-rays taken before and after the event to prove it.

José Pedro Arigó lived in a small town in Brazil. He was probably one of the best known of the "psychic surgeons." Born in the town of Congonhas do Campo in 1918, he performed surgery on many patients while in trance, with a deceased German surgeon named Dr. Fritz working through him. Francis King said, "(Arigó's) psychic surgery was subjected to intense examination by physicians, surgeons, and psychic investigators. They never detected any sign of fraud or sleight-of-hand. Films were also taken of Arigó in action. They seemed to show him conducting major operations without shedding more than a few drops of blood." David St. Clair, a former Brazilian correspondent for *Time* magazine and author of a number of books, claims that he witnessed Arigó remove the eye from the socket of a blind boy, scrape the back of it, and then replace it, giving the boy back his sight. King said, "The fact that some of Brazil's psychic sur-

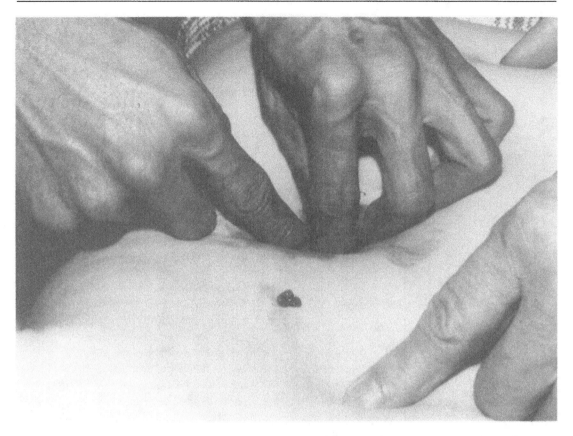

Psychic surgeon Feliciano Omilles working in Mexico in the early 1970s. *Courtesy Fortean Picture Library.*

geons have been detected in fraud does not invalidate the achievements of others ... A substantial number of the patients these surgeons have treated—often people whose lives were despaired of—have recovered their health." Arigó was killed in a car crash in 1971.

Lourival de Freitas is another Brazilian healer. He has three **spirit guides** to help him with his surgery. They are the **Roman** emperor Nero, a woman of Nero's court, and a Japanese man names Sheka. Sheka specializes in lung and bronchial problems. English journalist and **psychical researcher** Anne Dooley had de Freitas work on her. She had a bronchial condition which her own doctors had pronounced incurable. After a brief operation where the surgeon made a small cut in her back and from which he withdrew a large clot of blood, Dooley returned

to England. She was x-rayed and found to be cured. Another Brazilian psychic surgeon of note is Edivaldo Siva, a schoolteacher whose spirit guides include doctors from various countries, including Arigó's Dr. Fritz. Silva works in a trance.

The Philippines is also home to a number of psychic surgeons. One of the most notable is Tony Agpaoa. He makes his incisions with his bare hands, in a matter of seconds. Any malignant growth is pulled out, alcohol is poured over the wound, and the incision is pressed closed. There is invariably no sign of a scar afterward. Another well known Filipino healer is Angelo, of Manila, which has become a thriving center of psychic surgery and **Spiritualist** healing. Today more than four hundred **healing** centers allied with Spiritualists exist through the Philippine islands. Josephine Sison is another respected Filipina healer. She has been studied and filmed by British scientist Dr. Lyall Watson. Watson witnessed more than two hundred operations performed by Sison and concluded that "about 85 percent of them involved **materialization** phenomena." He believes that such healers possess a form of materialization **mediumship**. Watson wrote of his experiences in a book, *The Romeo Error* (1975).

Sources:

King, Francis: *The Supernatural: Wisdom From Afar.* London: Aldus, 1975

Playfair, Guy Lion: *The Flying Cow: Research into Paranormal Phenomena in the World's Most Psychic Country.* London: Souvenir Press, 1975

St. Clair, David: *Psychic Healers.* New York: Doubleday, 1974

Stemman, Roy: *The Supernatural: Spirits and Spirit Worlds.* London: Aldus, 1975

Watson, Lyall: *The Romeo Error.* New York: Anchor Press, 1975

Wilson, Colin: *The Supernatural: Healing Without Medicine.* London: Aldus Books, 1975

PSYCHIC TELEPHONE

The Psychic Telephone was an instrument invented by F. R. Melton of Nottingham, England. It consisted of a wooden box containing a rubber bag connected to a pair of earphones. Melton's idea was that if a **medium** blew into the bag, inflating it and sealing it, the bag would then act as a substitute for the medium. Earphones connected to it would then pick up the sounds of the **spirits** normally heard **clairaudiently** by the medium. **Direct voice** would also come through the earphones. **Harry Price** thoroughly tested the Psychic Telephone at the **National Laboratory for Psychical Research**, and found that it did not work.

Sources:

Fodor, Nandor: *Encyclopedia of Psychic Science.* London: Arthurs Press, 1933

PSYCHICAL RESEARCH

Psychical Research is the scientific investigation of **psychic** and **mediumistic** phenomena. The term is used interchangeably with "**parapsychology**"—the study of such psi abilities as **extrasensory perception, clairvoyance, clairaudience, psychokinesis, precognition**, and similar. Psychical research also covers investigation of such things as **ghosts** and **hauntings, poltergeist** activity, **levitation, rappings, apparitions, Instrumental Transcommunication, Electronic Voice Phenomena, spirit photography, Electronic Voice Phenomena**, and more.

In 1882, the **Society for Psychical Research** (SPR) was founded. Its original prospectus stated, "It has been widely felt that the present is an opportune time for making an organized and systematic attempt to investigate that large group of debatable phenomena designated by such terms as mesmeric, psychical, and spiritualistic. From the recorded testimony of many competent witnesses, past and present, including observations recently made by scientific men of eminence in various countries, there appears to be, amid much delusion and deception, an important body of remarkable phenomena, which are *prima facie* inexplicable on any generally recognized hypothesis, and which, if incontestably established, would be of the highest possible value." One of the "scientific men of eminence" who did much early research was the world famous physicist Sir **William Crookes**. He first came into contact with **Spiritualism** in July, 1869, and the following year announced his intention of entering into an intense and thorough investigation of the phenomena.

The SPR originally grouped phenomena into five separate sections, each covered by a committee. The first of these examined "the nature and extent of any influence which may be exerted by one mind upon another." The second looked at "**hypnotism** and the forms of so-called mesmeric **trance**." The third did a "critical revision of (Baron **Karl von**) **Reichenbach's** researches with certain organizations called 'sensitive,' and an enquiry whether such organizations possess any power of perception beyond a highly exalted sensibility of the recognized sensory organs." The fourth section carried out "a careful investigation of any reports, resting on strong testimony, regarding apparitions at the moment of death." The fifth held "an enquiry into the various **physical phenomena** commonly called spiritualistic; with an attempt to discover their causes and general laws." The **American Society for Psychical Research** was founded in 1885 and, since then, many other similar professional groups have come into being.

Psychical Research has been going on for centuries. As early as 1323, Pope John XXII called on the services of Brother John Goby, Prior of the Benedictine Abbey near Avignon, to investigate the ghost of Alais, in southern France. Goby submitted a full report of his investigation which was later printed in the official *Annales ecclesiastici*.

Nandor Fodor points out that the first concern of psychical research is to establish the occurrence of the claimed facts. He said, "If they are not due to fraud, observational error, the laws of chance, i.e., if they are found to occur, the next stage of the inquiry is to establish the reason of their occurrence, whether the known natural laws are sufficient to explain them or whether there is reason to suppose the action of unknown forces."

In *An Assessent of the Evidence for Psychic Functioning*, Professor Jessica Utts studied psychic functioning research conducted over a twenty year period to determine whether or not the phenomenon had been scientifically established. She stated, "Using the standards applied to any other areas of science, it is concluded that psychic functioning has been well established. The statistical results of the studies examined are far beyond what is expected by chance. Arguments that these results could be due to methodological flaws in the experiments are soundly refuted. Effects of similar magnitude to those found in government-sponsored research at Stanford Research Institute and Science Applications International Corporation have been replicated at a number of laboratories across the world.

Such consistency cannot be readily explained by claims of flaws or fraud."

Sources:

An Assessment of the Evidence for Psychic Functioning: http://anson.ucdavis.edu/~utts/air2.html

Fodor, Nandor: *Encyclopedia of Psychic Science*. London: Arthurs Press, 1933

Smyth, Frank: *The Supernatural: Ghosts and Poltergeists*. London: Aldus, 1975

Spence, Lewis: *An Encyclopedia of the Occult*. London: George Routledge & Sons, 1920

Psychography *see* Writing, Automatic

PSYCHOKINESIS (PK); TELEKINESIS

Abbreviated as PK, psychokinesis is the movement of objects without physically touching them, by using the power of the mind alone. It is a term that was adopted by Dr. **Joseph Banks Rhine** and his research team at Duke University in 1934, when they were experimenting with mentally influencing the roll of dice. Many **Spiritualists** who are **physical mediums** demonstrate psychokinesis in their **séances**.

Russian medium **Nelya Mikhailova** specializes in moving objects by concentrating on them, and is known in Russia as "the PK medium." She can pass her hands over a compass and set the needle spinning at high speed, she can cause cigarettes to roll across a table top, she can move a whole box of matches that have been emptied onto a table surface.

Similarly, Swedish **medium** Anna Rasmussen— whose powers first became obvious when she was twelve—has affected **pendulums**. Professor Winther of Copenhagen studied her intensively between 1922 and 1928. He designed a sealed glass case inside which hung a variety of pendulums. They were of different weights and supported on silk threads. Anna could concentrate on them and cause any one of them, as chosen by the professor, to swing in any direction requested. Anna had a **spirit guide** named Dr.

PSYCHOMETRY

Famous medium Stanislava Tomczyk demonstrates her psychokinetic influence on scales during Baron von Schrenck-Notzing's experiments in the 1920s. *Courtesy Fortean Picture Library.*

Lasaruz whom she claimed brought about the movements.

A similar phenomenon is Telekinesis, which is the movement of objects by **spirits**. An example would be the falling of a picture off a wall at the moment of someone's death. **Apportation** is similar, though the object there is usually moved from one dimension to another. There is a commonality between telekinesis and the movement of objects attributed to **poltergeists**. When objects are moved by spirit the object usually moves smoothly. Poltergeist energy is such that the object moves unpredictably and erratically.

Sources:

Holroyd, Stuart: *The Supernatural: Minds Without Boundaries.* London: Aldus, 1975

Rhine, J. B.: *Man, Myth & Magic: Psychokinesis.* London: BPC Publishing, 1970

P sychometry, also known as psychoscopy, is the ability to hold an object in the hands and to divine from it the history of that object. **Spiritualist** mediums, **psychics**, and others, can take a ring, watch, or similar object that has been in close contact with a person, and are able to "read" the past and present of the object itself and of those who have been in close contact with it for any length of time. The name (which is derived from the Greek *psyche* meaning "soul" and *metron* meaning "measure") was given by Dr. Joseph Rhodes Buchanan (1814–1899), a pioneer in psychometric research.

The theory is that everything that has ever existed has left its mark—some trace of its existence—on the ether. Lewis Spence suggests that **haunted** houses demonstrate this on a larger scale; events that took place left their impressions in the rooms, to be picked up by psychics. Impressions received through psychometry may vary in intensity, depending upon the acuteness of the atmosphere which has affected the object.

Everyone has the ability to psychometrize, though many need to practice at it in order to bring out what is latent. There is a well known story of Professor **William Denton**, a minerologist and researcher on psychometry, giving his wife and his mother meteoric fragments and other items, all carefully wrapped in paper so that they could not be seen. Denton's wife had done psychometry before. She held to her forehead a package containing carboniferous material, and immediately started describing swamps and trees with tufted heads and scaled trunks (palm trees). Denton then gave her lava from a Hawaiian volcanic eruption. She held it and described a "boiling ocean" of golden lava. Denton's mother, who did not believe in psychometry, was given a meteorite. She held it a moment then said, "I seem to be traveling away, away through nothing—I see what looks like stars and mist."

Spiritualist **mediums** say "**spirit** speaks first." What is meant by this is that first impressions are the most important. If too much thought is given, for too long, about the object being held, the mind starts trying to think logically and, whether consciously or unconsciously, to reason. If what first comes into the head is stated, no matter how outlandish it may seem at the time, it will invariably be the correct observation.

Psychics and sensitives have traced lost and stolen property and found missing people through the use of psychometry. **Gérard Croiset** frequently concentrated his energies on an object that had belonged to a missing person, in order to find them.

Sources:
Buchanan, Joseph R.: *Journal of Man.* Boston: Little, Brown, 1849

Buchanan, Joseph R.: *Manual of Psychometry.* Boston: Little, Brown, 1885

Buckland, Raymond: *The Fortune–Telling Book: The Encyclopedia of Divination and Soothsaying.* Detroit: Visible Ink Press, 2004

Butler, William E.: *How to Develop Psychometry.* New York: Samuel Weiser, 1971

Carrington, Hereward: *Your Psychic Powers: And How to Develop Them.* New York: Dodd, Mead, 1920

Spence, Lewis: *An Encyclopedia of the Occult.* London: George Routledge & Sons, 1920

PUHARICH, ANDRIJA HENRY KARL (1918–1994)

Andrija Henry Karl Puharich was born on February 19, 1918, in Chicago, Illinois. His parents were Yugoslavian. He obtained his B.A. from Northwestern University in 1942, and his M.B. and M.D. from the Northwestern University Medical School in 1947. In 1943, he married Virginia Jackson; she died in 1959. He had his internship and residency in medical research at Permanente Foundation Hospital in Oakland, California, from 1946 to 1948.

In 1948, Puharich became fascinated with **psychical research** and set up the Round Table Foundation in Glen Cove, Maine, to study the physico-chemical basis for paranormal phenom-

ena. There he designed and built a special Faraday Cage—a copper-sheathed, double box that enabled him to isolate a "sensitive" within an electrical field—demonstrating that electricity can be a significant aid to psychical research. As an inventor, Puharich held approximately fifty patents. Aldous Huxley described Puharich as "one of the most brilliant minds in parapsychology."

Puharich served in the U.S. Army Medical Field Service School and the Army Chemical Center in Edgewood, Maryland from 1953 to 1955. In June, 1954, he began studying a young Dutch sculptor named Harry Stone, who would go into deep **trance** and speak what was presumed to be the ancient **Egyptian** language. He would also write Egyptian hieroglyphics, of which he had no previous knowledge. Puharich studied him for three years.

Another of Puharich's subjects for psychical research was **medium Eileen Garrett**. He also studied **Peter Hurkos**. In 1960, Puharich led an expedition to Oaxaca, Mexico, to study the sacred mushroom rite of the Chatino Indians. He went on to examine psychic surgeon **José Arigó**, who removed a lymphoma from Puharich's arm in less than a minute. Puharich witnessed more than 200 surgeries performed by Arigó and filmed many of them. In 1971, Puharich visited Israel to study **Uri Geller**.

Among Puharich's books are *The Sacred Mushroom: Key to the Door of Eternity* (1959), *Beyond Telepathy* (1962), and *Uri: A Journal of the Mystery of Uri Geller* (1974).

Sources:
Fishley, Margaret: *The Supernatural.* London: Aldus, 1976

Fodor, Nandor: *Encyclopedia of Psychic Science.* London: Arthurs Press, 1933

Playfair, Guy Lion: *The Flying Cow: Research into Paranormal Phenomena in the World's Most Psychic Country.* London: Souvenir Press, 1975

Puharich, Andrija: *The Sacred Mushroom: Key to the Door of Eternity.* New York: Doubleday, 1959

Scientist Andrija Puharich, known for his efforts to bridge parapsychology and medicine. An experimental researcher and physician, he had numerous patents granted in medicine and electronics with some being used for the treatment of hearing loss. *Courtesy Fortean Picture Library.*

PURSEL, JACH

Jach Pursel was a Florida-based regional insurance supervisor. In October, 1974, he unexpectedly started **channeling** the entity known as Lazaris. This entity said it had never been in human form, but is a "group form" living in another dimension, where time and space as we know it do not exist.

Pursel originally had no great interest in **metaphysical** matters, though his wife Peny, had some knowledge. When Pursel constantly came home from work exhausted after long hours, Peny introduced him to **meditation**, assuring him that it would help him relax and feel better. One day he did his meditation, and as far as he knew, fell asleep during it. Pursel says that when he woke up he found his wife looking at him in astonishment. Apparently a strange voice had started speaking through Pursel. The voice was completely different from his own—a distinctive voice that was heavily accented. The voice also had different speech patterns from Pursel's. Peny had the presence of mind to write down what was said. When the couple found that the same thing happened every time Pursel meditated, Peny started running a tape recorder to capture the information. Pursel himself could not believe what he heard.

The session was the first of what developed into several thousands of hours of teachings by Lazaris. They followed similar lines to those given by **Jane Roberts's** Seth and others: that the universe is essentially spiritual; that souls are immortal; and that everyone has the power to create his or her own reality. In Lazaris's words, "The only way to get to God/Goddess/All-That-Is, is over the bridge of belief."

To make contact with Lazaris, Pursel simply relaxes, closes his eyes, and takes a few deep breaths. He almost immediately goes into a **trance** and his body is taken over by the **spirit/** entity. He has no memory of anything that happens until he opens his eyes again, much later, and wakes up. But as Lazaris himself describes it (he always speaks and refers to himself in the plural), there is more going on than appears to be. "We create thoughts as a mumbo jumbo and we then project those thoughts through the planes of reality. We project the conglomeration of all the thoughts and all the bleeps and blips we want to work with, and we project them down into a denser level and a denser level, and these enter in through the star system Sirius, to be quite specific with you, into the physical world." On *The Merv Griffin Show*, televised in July, 1986, Lazaris said, "We refer to ourselves in the plural, most definitely—not out of any imperial-ness, that's for sure, but rather we are aware of the multiplicity of ourselves."

Foreman said in *Mysteries of the Unknown: Spirit Summonings* (1989), "On their way to the physical world, Lazaris' thoughts reportedly pass through the so-called Mental Plane, Causal Plane, and **Astral Plane**—three of the levels of reality that supposedly separate the earthly plane from All That Is. Ultimately, the Lazaris thoughts reach the channel, or 'antenna,' in the form of signals that can then be decoded and articulated as words."

According to Jon Klimo, Pursel spends as much as forty hours per week in the unconscious state in order to channel Lazaris for public talks, lectures, private readings, and weekend workshops. All this is organized through a very successful corporation called Concept: Synergy.

Sources:

Buckland, Raymond: *Buckland's Book of Spirit Communications*. St. Paul: Llewellyn, 2004

Foreman, Laura (ed): *Mysteries of the Unknown: Spirit Summonings*. New York: Time-Life Books, 1989

Klimo, Jon: *Channeling: Investigations on Receiving Information from Paranormal Sources*. Los Angeles: Jeremy P. Tarcher, 1987

QABBALAH

Spelled variously Cabala, Kabbala, Qabbalah, and similar, this is a Jewish form of mysticism which originated in southern France and Spain in the twelfth century. The name has in more recent times come to be applied in reference to almost any mixture of occultism, Hermeticism, Gnosticism, Rosicrucianism, and exotic theosophy. Originally, however, it was a body of Jewish doctrines about the nature of man and his relationship to God. One fanciful story is that Moses received the Qabbalah at the same time that he received the Ten Commandments, but deemed it advisable to keep the Qabbalah secret and pass it on by word of mouth alone. It is said that he hid clues in the Pentateuch, the first five books of the **Bible**.

The *Sefer ha-Zohar*, or Book of Splendor, came into being sometime in the thirteenth century (probably between 1280 and 1286) and was written by a Spanish Jew named Moses de Leon. The idea of Moses receiving the Qabbalah along with the Ten Commandments may come from confusion with this Moses de Leon. The Zohar was a mystical commentary on the Pentateuch, containing a mixture of stories, poems, commentaries, and **visions** based on Qabbalistic ideas and symbols.

The meaning of the word Qabbalah is "receiving" or "that which is received." It was originally a secret tradition handed down orally from teacher to student. The Qabbalah was founded on a small book called the *Sepher Yesirah* or Book of Creation, dating from before the ninth century. It gives a discussion on cosmology and cosmogony, stating that the world was created by God using thirty-two secret paths of wisdom. These are made up of the *Sephiroth*, or *Sefirot* (divine emanations); ten Sephirah plus the twenty-two letters of the Hebrew alphabet, the letters being the Paths connecting the Sephiroth. Together they make up the Tree of Life, or *Otz Chiim*, with every Sephirah being a level of attainment in knowledge.

Each Sephirah emanates from the one above it, the top one being the first emanation, of the *Ein Soph Aur*, Kether. The centers are known as 1: the Crown, or Supreme Crown (*Kether*), 2: Wisdom (*Hokhmah*), 3: Understanding (*Binah*), 4: Love/Mercy (*Hesed*), 5: Strength (*Din* or *Giburah*), 6: Beauty (*Tifareth*), 7: Endurance (*Netsah*); 8: Splendor/Majesty (*Hod*), 9: Foundation (*Yesod*), and 10: Kingdom (*Malkuth*). The right hand side of the Tree—Hokhmah, Hesed, and Netsah—is regarded as male whilst the left hand side—Binah, Din, and Hod—is female. The central section—Kether, Tifareth, Yesod, and Malkuth—balances and unifies the two sides.

Each of the triads symbolizes a portion of the human body: the first the head, the second the arms, and the third the legs. The first is the Celestial Triangle: Kether, Hokhmah, Binah. The second is the Moral Triangle: Hesed, Tifareth, Din (Giburah). The third is the Mundane Triangle: Netsah, Yesod, Hod, with Malkuth below it.

Each Sephirah is, in turn, divided into four parts in which operate the Four Worlds. They are: *Atziluth*, the world of archetypes; *Briah*, or *Khorsia*, the world of creation; *Yetzirah*, the world of formation; and *Assiah*, the world of the material. In Atziluth, the Sephiroth manifest through the ten Holy Names of God. In Briah, the manifestation is through the ten Mighty Archangels. In Yetzirah, the manifestation is through various orders of Angels. In Assiah, the manifestation is through the "Planetary Spheres." The ten Sephiroth exist on each of the Four Worlds, but on a different level.

According to R. J. Zwi Werblowsky, in *Man, Myth and Magic* (1970), "the Mishna (a second century rabbinic collection of religious law) attests the existence of two subjects that should not be taught in public and which, therefore, were considered as esoteric disciplines intended for initiates only. These subjects were 'the work of creation' (based on Genesis, chapter 1) and the 'work of the chariot' (the mysteries of the Divine Throne, based on Ezekiel, chapter 1). The precise nature and contents of these mystical disciplines is a matter for conjecture but it seems certain that some of the early rabbis practiced an ecstatic contemplation which culminated in the vision of the Throne of Glory, the Merkabah."

The Merkabah, or "Throne Mysticism," is the earliest detailed mystical system accessible to the historian of Judaism and predates the Qabbalah. The main characteristic of Merkabah is the emphasis on the supernatural, mysterious aspect of God. The initiate "rises through the **spheres**, worlds, heavens and celestial mansions or 'palaces' (*hekhaloth*) guarded by all sorts of terrify-

ing **angelic** beings" to finally stand before the Divine Splendor.

The twenty-two Paths, which correspond to the letters of the Jewish alphabet, each have both an **occult** meaning and a **numerological** value, and have been equated to the twenty-two cards of the **tarot** deck's major arcana, otherwise known as the trumps.

The path between any two Sephiroth must be considered in the light of those Sephiroth; each having its own significance. The numerological value of that path, together with the meaning of the equivalent tarot card, also needs to be carefully considered in order to have full understanding of that Path. The Four Worlds, mentioned above, must also be taken into account.

Sources:

Albertson, Edward: *Understanding the Kabbalah*. Los Angeles: Sherbourne Press, 1973

Bardon, Franz: *The Key to the True Quabbalah*. Wuppertal: Dieter Rüggeberg, 1971

Epstein, Perle: *Kabbalah: The Way of the Jewish Mystic*. Boston: Shambhala, 1988

Fortune, Dion: *The Mystical Qabalah*. London: Ernest Benn, 1935

Guiley, Rosemary Ellen: *Harper's Encyclopedia of Mystical & Paranormal Experience*. San Francisco: Harper SanFrancisco, 1991

Kraig, Donald Michael: *Modern Magick: Eleven Lessons in the High Magickal Arts*. St. Paul: Llewellyn, 1988

Myer, Isaac: *Qabbalah: The Philosophical Writings of Avicebron*. New York: Samuel Weiser, 1970

Werblowsky, R. J. Zwi: *Man, Myth & Magic: Cabala*. London: BPC Publishing, 1970

QUAKERS AND SHAKERS

In the seventeenth century, the phrases "Children of Light" and "Friends of Truth" were applied to a group who were at the extreme left of the Puritan movement in Great Britain. The Quakers used the term "friend" when addressing anyone. "Quaker" itself was originally a cant name; a slang term applied derisively to the Society of Friends. It was used as early as 1647 and came about because of the physical manifestations of emotion, characteristic of many early Friends; the physical trembling and shaking.

The movement was founded by George Fox (1624–1691), the son of a Leicestershire, England, weaver. At age nineteen Fox had become disillusioned with the way in which professed Christians failed to live up to the standards they preached. He traveled for some years searching for spiritual help before eventually hearing **clairaudiently** a voice from **spirit** directing him. In 1649, he interrupted a preacher and was imprisoned for it. He was again imprisoned for six months in 1650, for alleged blasphemy. But by 1651, through his itinerant preaching, he started to gain a following. In June, 1652, he gathered many hundreds of people at meetings in Westmorland, and the Society of Friends was started (though the name "Society of Friends" did not appear until the late eighteenth century). In his preaching, Fox violently denounced all parish churches, calling them "steeple houses." Quakerism had no fixed creed, no liturgy, no priesthood. In addition, it admitted women on an equal footing with men. As Boddington points out (*The University of Spiritualism*, 1947), "This last item was peculiarly offensive to priesthoods, who regard Paul's statement, 'The women shall keep silent in the church,' as a divine command."

This was a time of great religious unrest in Great Britain with a variety of groups being formed, such as the Fifth Monarchy Men, Muggletonians, Ranters, Familists, and Seekers. The Seekers met together at set times, not to pray but to stand about in silence, waiting for divine inspiration. They would then begin **inspirational speaking**. Many of these Seekers responded to Fox and joined his group. John Lewis says that Fox "tried to draw men away from the 'dead letter' of scripture, and opposed the prevailing doctrine of the total depravity of man by asserting that in every man there was a divine spark ... it suggests that any man or woman can become a vehicle of the spirit to minister to and enlighten mankind."

In the eighteenth century, both in Great Britain and in America, Quaker thought was dominated by Quietism, which was a doctrine of immediate inspiration of the individual conscience. It was felt that it was not easy to know the will of God and the only true way to find it was to be totally "passive." In Quakerism, the insistence was on the inward and spiritual experience, with the operation of the spirit not limited to time, individual, or place. The early Friends claimed that "those who did not know 'quaking' or 'trembling' were strangers to the experiences of David, Moses, and the Saints." (*Encyclopedia Britannica*)

Trying to escape persecution in England, Quakerism entered America in 1656, in Massachusetts, though four of them were hanged there. In 1656, 1657, and 1658 laws were passed in Massachusetts to prevent the introduction of Quakers there. William Penn (1644–1718), who was an ardent Friend, secured a grant from Charles II for a new colony. He founded Pennsylvania and also sent many hundreds of Quakers to New Jersey. From the early nineteenth century, Friends took part in the increasing westward migration, moving from North Carolina and Virginia as well as from Pennsylvania.

A number of Quakers later turned to **Spiritualism**. For example, **Isaac and Amy Post** (Amy is known as "The Mother of Modern Spiritualism") were originally Hicksite Quakers; followers of Elias Hicks. Boddington points out that spirit manifestations, and **psychic** experiences were fairly common in the early days of Quakerism. As he says, "Warnings, **premonitions** and spiritual guidance were openly avowed and reported." George Fox, while in prison in the north of England, **prophesied** the Great Fire of London, which broke out two days after his release from prison. He also prophesied that "within two weeks the (Parliamentary) Speaker would be plucked from his chair;" an event that took place in that time frame when Cromwell dissolved Parliament.

An offshoot of the Quakers in their early days was known as the "Shaking Quakers." They

Society of Friends founder George Fox (1624–1691) preaching in a tavern, c. 1650. Followers of the movement later became known as Quakers because of their agitated movements while receiving revelations. *Hulton Archive/Getty Images.*

became notorious because of their trembling while indulging in inspirational speaking. They manifested all the **trance** states, with **visions** and prophetic utterances. Ann Lee was the founder of the Shakers; she was frequently imprisoned for breaking the Sabbath by dancing, shouting, and blasphemy. The "blasphemy" was repudiation of the orthodoxy of her time. She was often called "Mother Lee." She was born in Manchester, England, in 1736. She died in 1784.

The Shakers' main way of worshipping was through dance, with the men at one end of a hall and the women at the other end. They would dance or march toward each other, swinging their arms, advancing and retiring. They would then turn and face the side walls and do the same advancing and retiring. Then they would form into two concentric circles; the women in the inner one and the men in the outer one. There they would move rapidly round and round, singing and shouting. They would also dance independently, sometimes spinning round and round for up to half an hour or more. They would shake and tremble, and they would speak rapidly in unknown tongues (**glossolalia**). According to **Nandor Fodor**, "It seems clear that much of the very genuine joy and creativeness of the Shaker community arose from the intense energy of sexual sublimation."

In 1838, Philemon Stewart, a Shaker, arrived at a meeting so agitated that he needed help just to stand up. He suddenly started speaking; delivering a direct communication from spirit, in this instance from "the Heavenly Parents" Jesus and Ann Lee. Sometimes the "**medium**" delivering such a message would fall to the floor and go into trance, much as a **Vodoun** follower being possessed, or "ridden" by the *loa*. Some people, after giving their message, went into convulsions and suffered complete loss of speech. Many of the messages that came through came from the spirits of deceased Shaker Elders. The main leader of the Shakers in the Manchester area of England was James Wardley, who had previously been a member of the Society of Friends. Ann Lee was a follower of Wardley. At that time the Shakers were known as the United Society of Believers in Christ's Second Appearing.

In 1774, Mother Ann and eight other members of her group set out to establish the Shakers in America. They reached their greatest number in the decade before the Civil War (1861–1865), with 6,000 members. Fifty years later their numbers had sunk to only 1,000. With laws of strict celibacy, the Shakers were destined for extinction. But in 1847, the Shakers were warned several times through spirit communication that the manifestation would cease, but that a wider type of manifestation would soon appear. In 1848, the **Fox Family** experienced their phenomena, leading to Modern Spiritualism.

Sources:

Boddington, Harry: *The University of Spiritualism.* London: Spiritualist Press, 1947

Encyclopedia Britannica. Chicago: William Benton, 1964

Fodor, Nandor: *Encyclopedia of Psychic Science.* London: Arthurs Press, 1933

Lewis, John: *Religions of the World Made Simple.* New York: Doubleday, 1968

Symonds, John: *Man, Myth & Magic: Shakers.* London: BPC Publishing, 1970

Walker, Williston: *A History of the Christian Church.* New York: Scribners, 1970

QUEEN VICTORIA (1819–1901)

Alexandrina Victoria, queen of the United Kingdom of Great Britain and Ireland and (from 1876) empress of India, was born on May 24, 1819, the only child of Edward, duke of Kent. Edward was the fourth son of King George III. On February 10, 1840, she married her cousin, Prince Albert of Saxe-Coburg-Gotha (1819–1861).

It is not known how much of an interest in **Spiritualism** Queen Victoria had before her beloved husband Prince Albert died of typhoid fever, but with his death there was a very real connection made with the world of **spirit**. It was reported that the queen began indulging in **table tipping** at the royal residence at Osborne, on the Isle of Wight.

The same year that Albert died, and within days of his passing, a thirteen-year-old boy living in Leicester, named **Robert James Lees**, was taking part in a family **séance** when a spirit claiming to be the recently deceased Prince Albert came through. At a very early age Lees had exhibited mediumistic abilities. Before he was twelve years of age he was a deep **trance** medium. The spirit of Albert gave a message that he said was for the Queen. A local newspaper editor, who happened to be at the séance, published the message.

Seeing the report, Queen Victoria sent two representatives to visit the boy **medium**. The two used false names. Lees again **channeled** information from the Prince, who recognized the two visitors from the Royal Court and called them by their true names. The Prince went on to write a letter, through the entranced Lees, to the Queen. In the letter, he called her majesty by a pet name known only by the two of them. When the Queen received the letter, she immediately summoned Lees to the palace.

Lees was invited to give a séance at Windsor Castle and there he gave evidence that the deceased Prince Albert was still in attendance upon Victoria. A number of séances followed and the Queen offered Lees a permanent position at court. On the advice of his **spirit guide**, Lees declined, though he did visit the Queen on a few rare occasions.

John Brown, the Queen's personal servant at Balmoral (the Queen's estate in Scotland), was

Queen Victoria and Princess Beatrice at the Osborne House on the Isle of Wight. *Courtesy Fortean Picture Library.*

named as a substitute. Brown had been a medium for many years and, as a close servant, it is possible that he had conducted séances for her in the past. But now with Albert gone, those séances became very important to Victoria. Brown was described as being a "rough character" who had a strong influence with Victoria, somewhat reminiscent of the relationship between Rasputin and the Russian Czarina Alexandra, wife of Nicholas II. Brown was two years younger than the Queen. It is said that Victoria only tolerated Brown's rude and outspoken nature because he could make it possible for her to speak to her beloved husband.

Interestingly, although Brown is generally conceded to have been a medium and to have conducted séances for Queen Victoria, there seem to be no records of anything he produced and no details of his sittings.

When Brown died in 1883, Victoria wrote, "The shock—the blow, the blank, the constant missing at every turn of the one strong, powerful, reliable arm and head almost stunned me and I am truly overwhelmed." She erected a statue to Brown at Balmoral.

In 1997, a movie was issued starring Judy Dench as Queen Victoria and Billy Connolly as John Brown. The movie was directed by John Madden and focused on the relationship between the queen and the commoner. It did not touch on Brown's mediumship. The year after the movie's release, the film's producer claimed that he had seen a cache of "love letters" purportedly exchanged between the two. It seems extremely doubtful that they did become lovers but there was certainly an intimacy that developed between them to the point where Victoria's children would jokingly refer to their mother as "Mrs. Brown;" the name given to the movie.

After her death, Queen Victoria herself sent messages to her last surviving daughter, Princess Louise, through direct voice medium **Lesley Flint**. Supposedly her majesty also spoke with Canadian Prime Minister W. L. Mackenzie King, through the "medium" **William Roy**, though Roy was later exposed as one of the biggest frauds in the history of Spiritualism.

Sources:

Encyclopedia Britannica. Chicago: William Benton, 1964

Stemman, Roy: *The Supernatural: Spirits and Spirit Worlds.* London: Aldus, 1975

Radiesthesia *see* Pendulum

RAPPING; RAPS

In the chronicle *Rudolph of Fulda*, dated 858 CE, there is described a **spirit** rapping of the type experienced by the **Fox Family** in **Hydesville** in 1848. Elder C. Blinn, in *Spiritualism Among the Shakers*, describes rappings in an influx of spirit manifestations with the **Shakers** between 1837 and 1844. Rappings or tappings were also heard as early as 1661 in the case of the **Drummer of Tedworth**; these were sharp and loud taps on furniture and on the walls. The phenomena of raps on walls, windows, roofs, and furniture are usually accompanied by other **poltergeist** occurrences, though not in every instance. Such rappings are sometimes sharp but just as often heard as dull thumps or as loud bangs.

The case of the infamous "Cock Lane Ghost" in Smithfield, London, in 1762–1764, involved rappings like those at the Fox Cottage, that were used to spell out messages involving an accusation of murder. In the case of the Cock Lane ghost, however, it eventually came to light that the sounds were produced by Elizabeth Parsons, the twelve-year-old daughter of a parish clerk named Parsons. She faked the noises at the instigation of her father in order to persecute a stockbroker named Kent, to

whom Parsons owed money. Eventually, after investigation by such notables as Dr. Samuel Johnson and the Bishop of Salisbury, Parsons was taken to trial, found guilty, and sent to prison. However, the interesting point in the case was that the rappings—fraudulent though they were—were used as a means of communicating with the supposed spirit in order to get information (in this case leading to a false charge of murder). Such an exchange was not to be known again until 1848 and the "conversations" between the Fox Sisters and **Charles B. Rosna**, the murdered peddler. The rappings in the Fox Cottage at Hydesville helped launch the Modern **Spiritualist** movement and such rappings play a part in many **séances** today.

Sources:

Fodor, Nandor: *Encyclopedia of Psychic Science*. London: Arthurs Press, 1933

Guiley, Rosemary Ellen: *The Encyclopedia of Ghosts and Spirits*. New York: Facts On File, 1992

Grant, Douglas: *The Cock Lane Ghost*. New York: St. Martin's Press, 1965

RAUDIVE, DR. KONSTANTIN (1909–1974)

Over a number of years Dr. Konstantin Raudive, former professor of psychology at Uppsala and Riga universities, collected dozens of tapes of recorded **spirit** messages, totaling 72,000 voices. According to Worlditc.org,

> In 1967, (**Friedrich**) **Juergenson's** book *Radio Contact with the Dead* was translated into German, and Latvian psychologist Dr. Konstantin Raudive read it skeptically. He visited Juergenson to learn his methodology, decided to experiment on his own, and soon began developing his own experimental techniques. Like Juergenson, Raudive too heard the voice of his own deceased mother, who called him by his boyhood name: "Kostulit, this is your mother." Eventually he catalogued tens of thousands of voices, many under strict laboratory conditions.

At the eleventh annual conference of the **Parapsychological Association**, held at the University of Frieburg, Germany, in September, 1968, Dr. Raudive played some of these tapes to Dr. **Jules Eisenbud** (who worked with **Ted Serios** on thought photography, or "**thoughtography**"), Mrs. K. M. Goldney from the **British Society for Psychical Research**, Dr. Walter Uphoff of the University of Colorado, and others. Dr. Uphoff said,

> All we could do was listen and try to figure out what might explain what we were hearing. Some voices were clearer and more distinct than others; the level of static or background noise was high because the volume had to be turned to maximum level in order to reproduce the otherwise faint voices; and the cadence certainly suggested that these were not likely to be bits of stray radio signals.

Most of the received voices had been inaudible at the time of recording. The strategy was for the moderator—in this case Dr. Raudive—to announce the date and time and then to invite any spirits to communicate. Later playback called for increasing the volume and, in most instances, changing the speed. Raudive had published his results in a book (*Breakthrough*) which attracted publisher Colin Smythe, who wanted British rights to the book. But Smythe also wanted fresh proof before he published. He followed Raudive's instructions and succeeded in obtaining a voice himself—that of a colleague's (Peter Bander's) deceased mother. Bander was a psychologist who went on to translate Raudive's book into English. Bander also wrote his own book on the subject (*Carry On Talking: How Dead Are the Voices?* 1972) and appeared on more than twenty radio and television shows to discuss the subject. In his book, Bander reviewed how the Raudive voice phenomenon was investigated

In 1971, Raudive performed a controlled experiment with technicians at Pye Records. In the sound lab, special equipment was installed that would cut out any possible intrusion of outside radio or television signals. Raudive used one tape recorder, monitored by a control deck. He wasn't allowed to touch the equipment himself but could only speak into the microphone. This he did for twenty-seven minutes. The engineers were sure that no other sounds had been picked up, yet on playback they found more than 200 voices had been recorded over the time period. The voices spoke in various languages, many of them so faint that they were hard to decipher. This experiment was sponsored by the British newspaper, the *Daily Mirror*. Smythe later commented, "We were all amazed. The evidence was very clear—there was no way the voices could have been produced except by paranormal means. The engineers who supervised the experiment began with an attitude of healthy skepticism which changed to one of conversion."

Peter Hale, an expert trained in the suppression of stray electrical signals such as radio emissions, conducted further tests at the laboratories of Belling & Lee. Afterward Hale commented, "From the results obtained … something is happening which I can't explain in normal physical terms."

In the mid 1980s, Klaus Schreiber received on his television pictures of the faces of various deceased people—including Romy Schneider and Albert Einstein. He got the pictures by focusing a video camera onto the screen of the television and feeding the camera's output back into the television, forming a feedback loop. About this time a couple in Luxembourg started getting amazing voice contacts through their radio. The then deceased Konstantin Raudive spoke through the apparatus to them in 1994, saying, "It can only work when the vibrations of those present are in complete harmony and when their aims and intentions are pure."

Sources:

Buckland, Raymond: *Buckland's Book of Spirit Communications*. St. Paul: Llewellyn, 2004

Meek, George W.: *After We Die, What Then?* Columbus: Ariel Press, 1987

Randles, Jenny and Peter Hough: *The Afterlife: An Investigation into the Mysteries of Life after Death*. London: Piatkus, 1993

World ITC Organization: http://www.worlditc.org

RAYMOND

Raymond Lodge was the son of **psychical researcher** and world famous physicist Sir **Oliver Lodge**. He became the subject of a book by his father, titled simply *Raymond*. The book dealt with the apparent **spirit** return of Raymond after he was killed in World War I. It is regarded as one of the best-attested cases of spirit identity.

On August 8, 1915, the **medium Leonore Piper** had **Richard Hodgson**, the deceased psychical researcher, communicating through her. Hodgson said, "Now, Lodge, while we are not here as of old, i.e., not quite, we are here enough to give and take messages. [Frederick] **Myers** says you take the part of the poet, and he will act as Faunus. Faunus. Myers. Protect: he will understand. What have you to say, Lodge? Good work. Ask (Margaret) Verrall, she will also understand. Arthur says so."

According to **Nandor Fodor**, "The message reached Sir Oliver Lodge in early September, 1915. On September 17, the War Office notified him that his son Raymond had been killed in action on September 14. Before this blow fell, Sir Oliver Lodge wrote to Mrs. Verrall, a well known classical scholar, and asked her, 'Does the poet and Faunus mean anything to you? Did one pro-

tect the other?' She replied at once that 'The reference is to Horace's account of his narrow escape from death, from a falling tree, which he ascribes to the intervention of Faunus ... As bearing on your terrible loss, the meaning seems to be that the blow would fall, but would not crush; it would be 'lightened' by the assurance conveyed afresh to you by a special message from the still living Myers, that your boy still lives,'"

Raymond's mother, Lady Lodge, had a sitting with **Gladys Osborne Leonard** on September 25. Raymond contacted her and said, "Tell Father I have met some friends of his." He mentioned Myers, among others. Two days later another medium, Alfred Vout Peters, spoke of a photograph of a group of officers, with Raymond among them. A Mrs. Cheves—a complete stranger to the Lodges—wrote to say that she had a photograph of the officers of the South Lancashire Regiment, to which Raymond belonged. On December 3, Mrs. Leonard gave a full description of the photograph, describing exactly where Raymond was in it (he was described as sitting on the ground with another officer's hand on his shoulder). The photograph arrived on December 7 and was exactly as described.

A variety of other messages came from a number of different mediums. There was also cross correspondence on the Faunus issue. Sir Oliver Lodge included all the evidence in his book, which has become a classic of **Spiritualism**. In it Lodge wrote, "My conclusion has been gradually forming itself for years, though, undoubtedly, it is based on experience of the same sort of thing. But this event has strengthened and liberated my testimony. It can now be associated with a private experience of my own instead of with the private experience of others."

Sources:

Doyle, Sir Arthur Conan: *The History of Spiritualism*. New York: Doran, 1926

Fodor, Nandor: *Encyclopedia of Psychic Science*. London: Arthurs Press, 1933

Lodge, Sir Oliver: *Raymond, or Life and Death with Examples of the Evidence for Survival of Memory and Affection After Death*. London: Methuen, 1916

READING

A "reading" is material that is delivered to a sitter by a **medium** or a **psychic**. There are Spiritualist readings (sometimes referred to as "messages") and psychic readings. Either of these may be in the form of a private reading or a public reading. A Spiritualist private reading is one-on-one with the medium and usually allows the sitter to ask questions, give or ask for explanations (if necessary), and generally become more involved with the retrieval of the information. Public Spiritualist readings are more common, where the medium—often as a specific part of a Spiritualist church worship service—will stand on the platform and deliver messages to particular members of the congregation or audience. Here there is no opportunity for the recipient to ask questions. In both cases it may be necessary for the individual to follow up after the meeting to verify the information given.

Psychic readings are more generally private, with the psychic dealing with the past, present and probable future for the sitter. By definition these readings do not connect with spirit and the only way to gauge the accuracy of the future predictions is to wait and see. Some idea of the possible accuracy may be judged by what the psychic tells of the known past and present.

The **National Spiritualist Association of Churches** publishes a pamphlet titled *Hints for a Good Reading*. It offers the following advice for a reading from a **Spiritualist** medium.

1: Try to put your mind at ease and relax before you seek a medium's help. It creates a better atmosphere for the reading and makes it easier for **spirit** to make contact.

2: Let the medium proceed in his or her own manner. Don't expect your most pressing problems to be discussed at once.

3: Spirit provides evidence of identity in different ways. It may be by name, description, relationships, incidents, etc. Be willing to verify such evidential information so the medium can proceed to any message that is to be given.

4: Let the medium know when they are correct. Don't attempt to confuse them. Be fair.

5: Arguing or wanting things done your way makes it difficult for the medium to function effectively and may lead to failure.

6: Something may make more sense by the end of the reading, or understanding of the message may come at a later time — after you have had a chance to think about it. So don't be quick to say "No" to what is given by the medium.

7: The true success of a reading is not always measured by **prophecy** but by the guidance it provides. **Prediction** is possible, but you have the power to change coming events.

8: A good reading should explain the philosophy of harmonious living. Mediumship is not fortune-telling.

9: If you wish to ask a question, or questions, meditate on them in advance of the meeting. Give spirit ample time to get an answer. No spirit claims to have an answer on the spur of the moment. After all, you are communicating with people.

10: Don't try to prolong a reading. The medium realizes when the forces are gone. You are always welcome to come again.

Sources:

Faubel, Rita: *Hints for a Good Reading*. Lily Dale: NSAC, nd

RED CLOUD

Red Cloud was the **Native American spirit guide** for British **medium** Estelle Roberts. In life he had been a Sioux. According to **Maurice Barbanell**, Red Cloud once explained that he learned English "as part of the equipment for his mission through **Estelle Roberts**."

Red Cloud held a teaching **circle** every two weeks, "to propound the broader implications of the evidence which came at his **séances**." His talks revealed a versatility of knowledge far beyond the scope of the medium. He was able to discuss science with scientists and medicine with doctors. He was an expert on ancient empires, lost cities, and the customs of bygone times. He also had a considerable knowledge of past and contemporary religions. Barbanell said that there was never any confusion at circles because Red Cloud was "the perfect spirit master of ceremonies (who) spoke in between every communication."

There were many **trumpet** séances with Red Cloud, and he also specialized in **apports**. In fact he treated his apport séances like parties, often promising to bring to the sitters "anything within reason." At one, Kenneth Evett hesitantly asked for an apport from **Egypt**. He received a beautiful scarab edged in gold. Some days later Evett took it to the Department of Egyptian Antiquities at the British Museum where it was confirmed as genuine and from Abydos. At that same séance Red Cloud produced sixty-two apports. Each dropped from the end of the suspended trumpet; some from the small end and some from the large end.

Sources:

Barbanell, Maurice: *This Is Spiritualism*. Oxshott: The Spiritual Truth Press, 1959

Roberts, Estelle: *Fifty Years a Medium*. New York: Corgi Books, 1969

REGURGITATION

Many of the early **materialization** mediums were accused of fraud, with the explanation that the **ectoplasm** that they produced was, in fact, physical material that they had swallowed and then regurgitated. This theory was first propounded in 1922 by the **Society for Psychical Research** (SPR) in the case of **Eva C.**. The medium Eva Carriere was visiting London and being investigated by the SPR. Professor **Charles**

Richet said, "They [the SPR] admit that the only possible trickery is regurgitation. But what is meant by that? How can masses of mobile substance, organized as hands, faces, and drawings, be made to emerge from the oesophagus or the stomach? ... How, when the **medium**'s hands are tied and held, could papers be unfolded, put away and made to pass through a veil?"

At a **séance** on November 26, 1913, conducted by Baron von **Schrenck-Notzing**, a strong emetic was given to Eva to answer the charge that the ectoplasm was actually regurgitated material. It satisfied the researchers that she had swallowed nothing. A number of experiments took place at Dr. Gustav Geley's laboratories in 1917 and 1918. Nearly 150 scientists and others witnessed the sittings.

To state that the medium had "obviously regurgitated material" became a typical dismissal of a medium's performance by a researcher either too lazy to fully investigate or too skeptical to accept what was being proven before his eyes. However, there certainly were fraudulent mediums who did swallow cheesecloth and similar material and attempt to regurgitate it to create an ectoplasmic effect. One such was **Helen Duncan**, who was examined by the **National Laboratory of Psychical Research**. Following this, the *Morning Post* of July 14, 1931, carried an article claiming that Duncan had been caught out and exposed as a fraud. Researcher **Harry Price** called her "one of the cleverest frauds in the history of **Spiritualism**." It transpired that the "ectoplasm" was in fact a composition of wood pulp and egg white, which she was able to swallow and then regurgitate. On July 17, the *Light* carried a followup article also branding her as a fraud and carrying a confession from her husband.

Sources:

Fodor, Nandor: *Encyclopedia of Psychic Science*. London: Arthurs Press, 1933

The International Survivalist Society: http://www.survivalafterdeath.org

Psychic News, #3754, June 19, 2004. Stansted, Essex

Leonard, Sue (ed): *Quest For the Unknown—Life Beyond Death*. Pleasantville: Reader's Digest, 1992

REICHENBACH, BARON KARL VON (1788–1869)

Reichenbach was a well known Austrian industrial chemist who, in 1858, claimed to have discovered certain radiations coming from animals, **crystals**, plants, and magnets. He said that these emanations could be seen and felt in the dark by sensitive subjects, especially if they first acclimatized themselves for two or three hours. Reichenbach stated that the north end of a magnet would emit a blue glow while the south end would give off an orange hue. He also associated warmth with the south end and coolness with the north. The same conditions existed with crystals and with parts of animals. The human body was seen as orange and warm on the left while blue and cool on the right. Reichenbach's work *Physico-Physiological Researches* was translated into English in 1850.

Reichenbach postulated a quasi-magnetic emanation or fluid which he called Odyle, Od, or **Odic Force**, which radiated outward in varying degrees from all objects. Over a period of five years, he worked with more than 100 people, pursuing his theories. Those working with "animal magnetism" welcomed his work as complementary to theirs, though Reichenback did not work with **hypnotized**, or **mesmerized**, patients. This all developed into a whole study of what is more generally termed the "**aura**."

Sources:

Gauld, Alan: *Man, Myth & Magic: Magnetism*. London: BPC Publishing, 1970

Podmore, Frank: *Mesmerism and Christian Science*. (1909) New York: University Books, 1963

REINCARNATION

Reincarnation is the rebirth of the **spirit** or soul in successive bodies. It was originally a Christian tenet but was then rejected at the Second Council of Constantinople in 553 CE. Reincarnation is very much a part of Hindu and **Buddhist** beliefs, and according to Benjamin Walker (*Man, Myth & Magic* article, 1970), "is being increasingly adopted as an article of faith by a large number of people in other religious denominations." A U.S. Gallup Poll of October 2001 asked adults over 18 if they believed in "Reincarnation, that is, the rebirth of the soul in a new body after death." 25 percent said they did believe in it; 54 percent did not; 20 percent didn't know; and 1 percent had no opinion. Belief was slightly higher in males than in females while it varied considerably between age groups: belief amongst 28-29 year olds was at 25 percent; 30-49 year olds at 22 percent; and people over 50 were at 28 percent. Rosemary Ellen Guiley suggests that approximately two-thirds of today's population "accepts some form of reincarnation or rebirth as a fundamental belief."

The belief has certainly existed for thousands of years. The Orphics of ancient **Greece** held the doctrine from the Pythagoreans that a soul returned in a number of incarnations, each time gaining in purity by living a good life. This would continue until there was total purity, at which time divinity would be achieved. This is similar to the belief held in Wicca, where reincarnation is one of the primary tenets. Wiccans hold that the **spirit** goes through a number of incarnations, learning and experiencing in each until all things have been absorbed. At that time, the spirit becomes at one with the gods. The progression has been likened to passing through the grades in a school, where certain curricula have to be observed in order to graduate. Because the psycho-physical experience of a male is dissimilar to that of a female, then lives as both sexes must be experienced by the spirit in order to gain the full knowledge.

In the Hindu and Buddhist doctrines, the point of reincarnation is to return, in other lifetimes, in order to expiate one's transgressions. But in many doctrines, each individual life is not dependent upon the previous incarnation; each life is a separate experience with its own agenda.

Four-year-old Trulku-la, recognized by Tibetan Buddhists as the reincarnation of a high lama, is shown in January 1996. *AP/WideWorld Photos*.

In **Spiritualism** there is no fixed doctrine on the question of reincarnation. It is left to the individual's beliefs and feelings. Spiritualists seem evenly split on whether or not they believe in it. However, when **Allan Kardec** instituted **Spiritism**, he did make a belief in reincarnation one of the tenets of that particular branch of Spiritualism.

Sources:

Buckland, Raymond: *Buckland's Book of Spirit Communications*. St. Paul: Llewellyn, 2004

Dowling, Levi: *The Aquarian Gospel*. Los Angeles: Leo W. Dowling, 1925

Holzer, Hans: *Born Again—the Truth About Reincarnation*. New York: Doubleday, 1970

Kelsey, Denys and Joan Grant: *Many Lifetimes*. New York: Doubleday, 1967

Litvag, Irving: *Singer In the Shadows*. New York: Macmillan, 1972

Lutoslawski, W.: *Pre-Existence and Reincarnation*. London: Allen & Unwin, 1926

Stearn, Jess: *Yoga, Youth and Reincarnation*. New York: Doubleday, 1965

Stemman, Roy: *Reincarnation: True Stories of Past Lives*. London: Piatkus Books, 1997

Stevenson, Ian: *Twenty Cases Suggestive of Reincarnation*. Charlottesville: University of Virginia, 1974

Walker, Benjamin: *Man, Myth & Magic: Reincarnation*. London: BPC Publishing, 1970

Religious Society of Free Thinkers
see **Laona Free Association**

RESCUE CIRCLE

A rescue circle is a **circle** of **Spiritualists**—usually meeting on a regular basis—who spend their time connecting with **spirits** who are having difficulty adjusting to the transition from life on the physical plane to life on the spiritual plane. Some are unable to accept their own passing and remain in the locations with which they are familiar. Sometimes this is due to traumatic events such as a a sudden and unexpected death, or a variety of reasons tying them to their old life. If the sitters are able to connect with the spirit and explain what has transpired, and how spirits are meant to progress to the next level, then the "trapped" spirit can continue on.

Some Spiritualists believe that such rescue work should be left to those on the other side, who are normally there to greet a newly deceased person. Simply sending **prayers** from this physical plane is often felt to be all that is required or necessary. But according to **Nandor Fodor**, rescue circle adherents claim that "earthbound spirits are too gross to be reached by the influence of higher spirits from the other side. They stand closer to the material plane than to the spiritual."

The idea of rescue circles came from the **Shakers**, who saw the various Native American guides as being in need of "waking up" and wanted to proselytize and teach them. Records of various Shaker attempts are detailed in such books as D. E. Bailey's *Thoughts From the Inner Life* (1886) and W. Usborne Moore's *Glimpses of the Next*

State (1911). Similar work was carried on by medium Emilie S. French and was described in Edward C. Randall's *Frontiers of the After-Life* (1922). Karl A. Wickland's *Thirty Years Among the Dead* (1924) contains hundreds of recorded cases, while Sir **Arthur Conan Doyle**'s *Wanderings of a Spiritualist* (1921) details the work of the Tozer rescue circle in Melbourne, Australia.

Sources:

Doyle, Sir Arthur Conan: *The History of Spiritualism.* New York: Doran, 1926

Fodor, Nandor: *Encyclopedia of Psychic Science.* London: Arthurs Press, 1933

RETROCOGNITION; RETRODICTION

Retrocognition—also known as postcognition—is knowledge of an event *after* it happens, when the person would have no natural knowledge of that event. A better known term is **precognition**, which is knowledge of an event *before* it happens. (In the same way, retrodiction is the opposite of **prediction**.) J. M. Robertson, in *Buckle & His Critics* (1895), said, "Let us first put a little order in our conception of prediction and 'retrodiction' as they indisputably take place in the settled sciences." And **Frederick W. H. Myers**, in his 1901 work *Human Personality*, said, "Our retrocognitions seem often a recovery of isolated fragments of thought and feeling."

Most people who exhibit the ability to be retrocognitive are also precognitive. They have the ability to focus on people and events from either the past or the future. The information is frequently obtained through **clairvoyance**, **clairaudience**, or **clairsentience**. **Psychometry** is another one of the main ways of working with retrocognition. By handling an object, the **medium** is able to gain information about the past connections with that object, and the people and events that have come into contact with it.

One of the most famous cases of retrocognition was that of two English ladies who, on August 10, 1901, visited the Petit Trianon at Ver-

sailles, France. Annie E. Moberly and Eleanor M. Jourdain went through a side gate, just before getting to the main gate, and found themselves on a path which they followed, thinking it must lead to the main house. Instead, they found themselves back in the year 1770. In their perambulations, the ladies saw men in three-cornered hats, a woman with a large white hat, and others in the dress of the eighteenth century.

Sources:

Buckland, Raymond: *Buckland's Book of Spirit Communications.* St. Paul: Llewellyn, 2004

Holroyd, Stuart: *The Supernatural: Minds Without Boundaries.* London: Aldus, 1975

Myers, F. W. H.: *Human Personality and Its Survival After Bodily Death.* London: Longmans, 1903

Oxford English Dictionary, The. Oxford: Clarendon Press, 1989

Retrodiction *see retrocognition*

REVUE SPIRITE, LA

A monthly magazine founded by **Allan Kardec** in 1858. It was the official journal of French **Spiritism** published by Kardec's Parisian Society of Psychologic Studies in Paris, France. After Kardec's death, P. G. Leymarie became editor.

Sources:

Fodor, Nandor: *Encyclopedia of Psychic Science.* London: Arthurs Press, 1933

REVUE SPIRITUALISTE, LA

Published from 1858 until 1870, *La Revue Spiritualiste* was the rival magazine to **Allan Kardec**'s *La Revue Spirite.* It was started by M. Pierart. Pierart was the other great Spiritualist pioneer in France who, unlike Kardec, disbelieved in reincarnation and ran the oppositional school of French **Spiritualists**. For years there was intense rivalry between the two camps.

Sources:

Fodor, Nandor: *Encyclopedia of Psychic Science.* London: Arthurs Press, 1933

RHINE, JOSEPH BANKS (1895–1980)

Joseph Banks Rhine was one of the pioneers of **parapsychology**. He was the co-founder of the Parapsychology Laboratory, Duke University, Durham, North Carolina.

Rhine was born on September 29, 1895, in Juniata County, PA. In 1920, he married Louisa Ella Weckesser. Rhine studied at the University of Chicago, obtaining his B.S. in 1922, his M.S. in 1923, and his Ph.D. in 1925. He was an instructor in philosophy and psychology at Duke University in 1928, and a professor of psychology from 1929 to 1949. He was Director of the Parapsychology Laboratory from 1935 onward.

Rhine's interest in parapsychology developed after he investigated **Spiritualist mediumship** with Dr. **Walter Franklin Prince** at Harvard University in 1926. The following year he went to Duke University and studied **psychic** phenomena with Dr. **William McDougall**. Encouraged by McDougall, Rhine set up a program for the statistical validation of **extrasensory perception** (ESP), with emphasis initially on **clairvoyance** and **telepathy** using the **Zener** deck of test cards. He later also investigated **psychokinesis** (PK), originally known as telekinesis (TK).

In 1934, Rhine's work *Extrasensory Perception* was published by the **Boston Society for Psychic Research**. From 1937 onward, he published the *Journal of Parapsychology* at Duke. In 1960, Rhine established the Psychical Research Foundation as an independent center to study phenomena relating to the survival of human personality after death. It was sponsored largely by Charles E. Ozanne. Chester F. Carlson, the inventor of xerography, sponsored the **Foundation for Research on the Nature of Man**, founded in 1962.

Among Rhine's notable books were *New Frontiers of the Mind* (1937), *The Reach of the Mind* (1947), *New World of the Mind* (1953), *Parapsychology, Frontier Science of the Mind* (with J. G. Pratt, 1957), *Parapsychology Today* (1968), and *Progress In Parapsychology* (1971).

Sources:

Cavendish, Richard (ed.): *Encyclopedia of the Unexplained*. London: Routledge & Kegan Paul, 1974

Ellison, A. J.: *Mysteries of Mind, Space & Time; the Unexplained: Cause and Effect*. Westport: H.S. Stuttman, 1992

Rhine, Joseph Banks: *New Frontiers of the Mind*. New York: Farrar & Rinehart, 1937

Rhine, Joseph Banks: *New World of the Mind*. New York: William Sloane, 1953

Rhine, Louisa: *ESP in Life and Lab: Tracing Hidden Channels*. New York: Collier Books, 1967

Shepard, Leslie A: *Encyclopedia of Occultism & Parapsychology*. New York: Avon Books, 1978

Rhine Research Center
see **Foundation for Research on the Nature of Man**

RICHET, PROFESSOR CHARLES ROBERT (1850–1935)

Nobel Prize winner Charles Robert Richet was born in Paris, France, on August 26, 1850. His father was Louis Dominique Alfred Richet, Professor of Clinical Surgery in the Facility of Medicine, Paris. His mother was Eugenie (Renouard) Richet.

Richet studied in Paris and became a Doctor of Medicine in 1869 and Doctor of Sciences in 1878. He was Professor of Physiology at the University of Paris, Sorbonne, from 1887 to 1927. In 1877, he married Amélie Aubry; They had five sons, Georges, Jacques, Charles, Albert and Alfred, and two daughters, Louise and Adèle.

For twenty-four years, from 1878 to 1902, Richet was editor of the *Revue Scientifique* and from 1917 until his death in 1935, co-editor of the *Journal de Physiologie et de Pathologie Générale*. He published numerous papers in a wide variety of journals and wrote a large number of books. In 1913, he was the recipient of the Nobel Prize for physiology "in recognition of his work on anaphylaxis."

Richet was a man of many talents and many interests. He was attracted to aviation through

Professor Etienne J. Marey's experiments and publication of his *La Machine Animale* (1873). He also became greatly interested in **Spiritualism**, becoming one of the foremost **psychical researchers** of his day, coining the term *metaphysique* for **parapsychological** research. He sat with **William Eglinton** and **Madame d'Esperance**. He founded the *Annales des Sciences Psychique* in 1890 with Dr. Dariex, and took part in the investigation of the Milan Commission with **Eusapia Paladino** in 1892. In 1895, he was elected president of the **Society for Psychical Research**.

Experimenting with medium Marthe Beraud, in Algiers, Richet became convinced of the reality of **materialization**, though he called the phenomena of it "absurd." He explained,

> Spiritualists have blamed me for using this word "absurd;" and have not been able to understand that to admit the reality of these phenomena was to me actual pain; but to ask a physiologist, a physicist, or a chemist to admit that a form that has a circulation of blood, warmth, and muscles, that exhales carbonic acid, has weight, speaks, and thinks, can issue from a human body is to ask him of an intellectual effort that is really painful.

Richet became President of the **Institut Métapsychique**. He stated,

> Metaphysics is not yet officially a science, recognized as such. But it is going to be ... At Edinburgh, I was able to affirm before one hundred physiologists that our five senses are not our only means of knowledge and that a fragment of reality sometimes reaches the intelligence in other ways ... Because a fact is rare is no reason that it does not exist. Because a study is difficult, is that a reason for not understanding it? ... Those who have railed at metaphysics as an **occult** science will be as ashamed of themselves as those who railed at chemistry on the ground that pursuit of the philosopher's stone was illusory ... Greetings, then, to

the new science which is going to change the orientation of human thought.

In 1923, Richet's book *Traité de Métapsychique* summarized all of his experiments. He dedicated the book to Sir **William Crookes** and **Frederick W. H. Myers**. Richet died in Paris on December 4, 1935.

Sources:

Doyle, Sir Arthur Conan: *The History of Spiritualism*. New York: Doran, 1926

Charles Richet Biography: http://nobelprize.org/medicine/laureates/1913/richet-bio.html

Charles Robert Richet Biography: http://www.whonamedit.com/doctor.cfm/410.html

Shepard, Leslie A: *Encyclopedia of Occultism & Parapsychology*. New York: Avon Books, 1978

RICHMOND, CORA LODENCIA VERONICA (1840–1923)

Cora Richmond was also known as Miss Cora Scott, Mrs. Cora Hatch, Mrs. Cora L. V. Tappan, and Mrs. Cora L. V. Tappan-Richmond. She was born Cora Lodencia Veronica Scott, in Cuba, New York, in 1840. At age eleven, she spent some months in the Hopedale Community of **Adin Ballou**. At that community Cora went into **trance** and Ballou's deceased son came through her. At age thirteen she started doing **platform** work with her **inspirational speaking**, and by sixteen had earned a reputation as a public speaker, traveling about the country. She often lectured before scientists and other experts on randomly selected subjects including history, politics, science and philosophy. As a direct result of her experiences, other members of her family became interested in **Spiritualism** with some of them also developing **mediumship**.

Richmond traveled to England in 1873 and spent several years there. By then she had delivered more than 3,000 lectures on a wide variety of subjects. **Frank Podmore** said that her "trance utterances surpass those of almost every other **automatist** in that there is a fairly coherent argument throughout ... the speaker is never at a loss ... we find none of the literary artifices by which ordinary speakers are wont to give relief—there is no antithesis, no climax, no irony or humor in any form." It was through Richmond's influence that **Emma Hardinge Britten** became interested in Spiritualism.

Later in life Richmond became Pastor of the First Society of Spiritualists in Chicago, a position she held for fifty years. In 1893, Richmond was selected to address the World's Parliament of Religions in Chicago. The presentation—which was a discourse on Spiritualism as a science, philosophy, and religion—later became the basis of the principles adopted by the **National Spiritualist Association**.

Richmond assisted in founding the National Spiritualist Association and became its Vice President. She was also well known for her powers of **spiritual healing** and she was a prolific author. Her books included *My Experiments Out of the Body, Sciences and Their Philosophies* (1859), *The Soul in Human Embodiments, Soul—Its Nature, Relations and Expressions* (1897), *Psychosophy* (1890), and her trance addresses: *Discourses Through the Mediumship of Mrs. Cora L. V. Tappan* (1878). She died on January 3, 1923, in Chicago, Illinois.

Sources:

Doyle, Sir Arthur Conan: *The History of Spiritualism.* New York: Doran, 1926

Podmore, Frank: *Modern Spiritualism.* London: 1902; reprinted as *Mediums of the Nineteenth Century.* New York: University Books, 1963

RIDLEY, HAZEL (B. 1900)

Hazel Ridley was an American **direct voice** medium. Her psychic development began when she was eighteen. A **Native American spirit guide** named Grey Wolf suddenly manifested when she was in **trance** and predicted that she would develop voices. When she did, the voices had a strange whispering quality, issuing from her larynx with no function of her mouth. According to **Nandor Fodor**, Camden, New Jersey physician

Dr. Wilson G. Bailey testified in his book *No, Not Dead; They Live* (1923), saying, "I filled her mouth with water and then with salt, and still the voice came through without interruption or impediment and I also punctured her arm when in trance and although I drew blood she did not feel any pain."

Ridley visited England in 1926, and then again in 1931 and 1932. She also toured the United States. In the book *And After*, Dennis Bradley accused her of fraud, but without any real evidence for it. Will Goldston, one of the greatest professional stage magicians in Europe, testified to the genuineness of her performances. In *Death Unveiled*, Mrs. D. U. Fletcher, wife of a Florida Senator, gave details of positive **mediumship** by Ridley.

Sources:

Fodor, Nandor: *Encyclopedia of Psychic Science.* London: Arthurs Press, 1933

Rivail, Léon-Dénizard-Hippolyte *see* Kardec, Allan

ROBERTS, JANE (1929–1984)

Jane Roberts grew up in Saratoga Springs, New York, and attended Skidmore College. She later married artist Robert F. Butts and they took up residence in Elmira, New York. She said, "I was not 'born **psychic**' with a background of paranormal experience. Neither Rob nor I had any knowledge of such matters. Even after my first enthusiasm, I didn't accept these developments without serious self-questioning and intellectual analysis. I wanted to keep my experiences on as scientific a basis as possible."

Roberts first met Seth, indirectly, on September 9, 1963. Sitting at her desk, she went into a spontaneous **trance** and **automatically writing** extremely rapidly—began scribbling into her notebook. As she said later, "a fantastic avalanche of radical new ideas burst into my head with tremendous force, as if my skull were some sort of receiving station turned up to unbearable volume. Not only ideas came through this **channel**, but sensations, intensified and pulsating." From this wild accumulation of ideas, she was inspired to write her first nonfiction book *How to Develop Your ESP Power*. As part of her research, she and her husband borrowed a Ouija® **talking board** from their landlady and started using it. The first messages they got were from Roberts's grandfather but these soon gave way to other personalities, including one named Frank Withers who claimed to have lived in Elmira some years before. On December 2, 1963, Withers came through four times but the fourth was a very brief appearance. He was replaced by a personality calling itself Seth. Roberts said, "We found ourselves dealing with a personality who was of superior intelligence, a personality with a distinctive humor, one who always displayed outstanding psychological insight and knowledge that was certainly beyond our own conscious abilities."

Early in the sessions Seth insisted that **reincarnation** was "not only a possibility but a fact of human existence," and began listing previous incarnations of both Jane Roberts and her husband, giving names, dates, family relations, and other details. Roberts then found that she was hearing the words in her head, **clairaudiently**, as the **planchette** of the Ouija® board moved. Soon Seth came to speak through her fully, with her husband taking dictation and the Ouija board discarded. Eventually dozens of notebooks were filled with Seth's teachings, as he communicated for more than twenty years. The teachings were passed along in private classes, public lectures, in books, on radio and on television. The notebooks eventually were taken into the archives of Yale University.

Jane Roberts developed rheumatoid arthritis and died from its complications in September, 1984, at age fifty-three.

Sources:

Roberts, Jane: *How to Develop Your ESP Power*. New York: Frederick Fell, 1966

Roberts, Jane: *The Seth Material*. New Jersey: Prentice-Hall, 1970

Roberts, Jane: *Seth Speaks*. New Jersey: Prentice-Hall, 1972

Speaking with Spirits: http://www.speakingwithspirits.com

ROBERTS, MAY ESTELLE (1889–1970)

Born May 10, 1889, in Kensington, London, May Estelle Wills became one of England's leading twentieth century **mediums**. **Hannen Swaffer** called her "the most versatile British medium of her time." Her parents were Isobel and Edwin Blackstone Wills. She had four sisters and three brothers.

As early as seven years of age, Estelle and her sister Dolly saw the **apparition** of a knight in shining armor. Estelle soon claimed to see other **spirits** and to hear voices **clairaudiently**. At school she constantly saw apparitions and heard voices. One of her earliest spirit visitors was her brother Lionel, who had died before she was born. When she tried to describe her experiences, her parents scolded her, saying she had too vivid an imagination.

She had what she described as "an ordinary schooling in the local council school, which I left at the age of fourteen. I had continued without a break to meet my spirit people. They now started to warn me of events, which afterwards came to pass." At fifteen she took a job as a nursemaid to a family in Turnham Green, London, looking after three children. But still she heard voices and saw spirits. At seventeen she married Hugh Warren Miles. His stepmother was a sister-in-law to U.S. President Woodrow Wilson. After her husband fell ill with Bright's disease, Estelle worked long hous to support her family, which included three children—Ivy, Evelyn, and Iris. They moved to Hastings, for the health of all of them, but Hugh died on May 13, 1919. With the children, Estelle then moved to Hampton-on-Thames.

After a setback with her own health, Estelle took a job as a waitress at Victoria Station, but it involved long hours. She kept it until the end of 1920, when she married Arthur Roberts and was able to give up the job (she divorced him in 1938). One day her next door neighbor, Mrs. Slade, invited her to attend a **Spiritualist** meeting in Hampton Hill. Estelle went there three times and at each meeting whoever was the medium would address her and tell her she was destined to do Spiritualist work. At the third service she attended, the medium—Elizabeth Cannock—said, "You are a medium and have much work to do. Chosen by the **spirit world**, you must not ignore the call." She asked for proof and was told to go home and sit at a table and the spirits would give her physical proof. This she did for seven days. Nothing happened until she gave up. When she replaced the table at its normal position against a wall, and turned to walk away, the table rose up and pushed her in the back. It then pursued her as she retreated from it! She thanked spirit and then a voice spoke. It said, "I come to serve the world. You serve with me and I serve with you." It was her first encounter with Red Cloud, who was to be her long-time spirit guide.

Over more than fifty years, Roberts demonstrated **clairvoyance**, clairaudience, **trance**, **materialization**, **psychic healing**, **psychometry**, **automatic writing**, and the production of **apports**. One of the high points of her career was when she gave a demonstration of mediumship in the British House of Commons. She frequently appeared before sold out crowds at the Royal Albert Hall. Just before her eightieth birthday, she was given a celebratory dinner by *Psychic News* and *Two Worlds*; Britain's leading Spiritualist publications. More than six hundred guests attended. Estelle Roberts died in 1970, at her home in Poole, Dorset.

Sources:

Barbanell, Maurice: *This Is Spiritualism*. Oxshott: The Spiritual Truth Press, 1959

Roberts, Estelle: *Fifty Years a Medium*. London: Corgi Books, 1969

ROCHAS, LT.-COL. EUGENE AUGUSTE ALBERT D'AIGLUN (1837–1914)

Eugene Auguste Albert d'Aiglum Rochas was Administrator of the École Polytechnique of Paris. However, due to his great interest in **metaphysical** matters he was forced to resign. He became a prominent French **psychical researcher**, well known for his work with **hypnotism**, **reincarnation**, human emanations (**ectoplasm**), and **physical mediumship**.

Rochas was the first to acquaint the French public with the claims of Baron **Karl von Reichenbach**, and his theory of the exteriorization of motricity was regarded as an important contribution to the examination of **materialization**. He worked with **medium Eusapia Paladino** at his home at l'Agnelas, near Voiron. He also claimed to have exposed **Charles Bailey**, the Australian **apport** medium, but such exposure seems to have been uncertain. Certainly Sir **Arthur Conan Doyle** and others did not accept it.

Rochas wrote a number of books, including *La Science des Philosophes et l'Art des Thaumaturges dans l'Antiquité* (1882), *Les Forces non définies* (1887), *Le Fluide des Magnetiseurs* (1891), *Les États Profonds de l'hypnose* (1892), *Receuil de documents relatifs à la levitation du corps humain* (1897), *Les États Superficiels de l'hypnose* (1898), and *La Suspension de la Vie* (1913).

Sources:

Doyle, Sir Arthur Conan: *The History of Spiritualism*. New York: Doran, 1926

Fodor, Nandor: *Encyclopedia of Psychic Science*. London: Arthurs Press, 1933

Rochester rappings *see* **Hydesville**

ROGO, DOUGLAS SCOTT (1950–1990)

Douglas Scott Rogo was born on February 1, 1950, in Los Angeles, to John and Winifred Rogo. He earned a B.A. at California State University at Northridge in 1972 and then did graduate work in the psychology of music.

Rogo became interested in **psychical research** and became a **parapsychologist**. Working with **Raymond Bayless**, Rogo showed that hundreds of telephone calls from deceased friends and relatives are received each year. Together they wrote the book *Phone Calls From the Dead* (1979), the result of a two-year investigation into phantom phone calls. The authors were surprised to find that a large number of people had received phone calls from friends and relatives who had died, and that in some cases the call was received before the recipient knew of the death of the caller. In other cases, the caller had been long deceased. Usually the calls were of short duration and did not register on the telephone company's equipment. According to Tom and Lisa Butler, there were even "reports of calls coming through telephones that were not connected."

Rogo was a visiting research consultant for the Psychical Research Foundation and director of research for the former Southern California Society for Psychical Research. In 1978, he became a consulting editor for *Fate* magazine. Rogo authored nearly thirty books, including *Parapsychology: A Century of Enquiry* (1976), *In Search of the Unknown: The Odyssey of a Psychical Investigator* (1976), *Mind beyond the Body: The Mystery of **ESP** Projection* (ed. 1978), *The **Poltergeist** Experience: Investigations into **Ghostly** Phenomena* (1979), and *On the Track of the Poltergeist* (1986). He was murdered, stabbed to death at his home in Northridge on August 14 or 15, 1990.

Sources:

Butler, Tom and Lisa: *There Is No Death and There Are No Dead.* Reno: AA-EVP, 2003

Guiley, Rosemary Ellen: *The Encyclopedia of Ghosts and Spirits.* New York: Facts On File, 1992

Rogo, D. Scott: *Life After Death: The Case for Survival of Bodily Death.* Wellingborough: Aquarian Press, 1986

Rogo, D. Scott and Raymond Bayless: *Phone Calls From the Dead.* New Jersey: Prentice-Hall, 1979

ROME; ROMANS

The ancient Romans were steeped in magical practice and superstition. They had many deities of their own but did not hesitate to adopt deities from other nations, if they thought their powers would serve Rome. They incorporated into their own pantheon gods and goddesses of the **Egyptians**, **Greeks**, Persians, Etruscans, Sabines, and those of various indigenous tribes. Along with the gods, numerous **spirits** were honored with rites and rituals. Sacrifices were made, including human sacrifices. Magical rites were innumerable; festivals and sacred banquets were packed into the calendar throughout the year.

A major part of Roman religious practice was **divination**. Circa 300 BCE, a large priestly college was established by either Numa or Romulus, with three priest-augurs (those who read and interpreted the prophetic signs). By the time of Sulla, the number had been increased to fifteen augurs and then, in the time of Julius Cæsar, there were sixteen. The augurs wore a uniform toga, which had scarlet stripes and a purple border, known as the *trabea*. Since their pronouncements were unchallengeable, the augurs developed great political power. An augur would travel with armies and fleets and would interpret the flight of birds to gain knowledge of coming events before battle was enjoined. When doing a **reading**, the augur was accompanied by a magistrate who would verify the results. The magistrate was also the one who was officially entitled to ask the deities for signs. Rather than actually trying to see the future, the object was to ascertain whether or not the deities approved or disapproved of the course of action queried.

There was a manual that contained augural ritual and a collection of answers to questions that had previously been given to the college of the senate. The augur always announced his finding with a specific set of words, which were duly recorded by the magistrate. The complexity of interpretation of phenomena grew by degrees until it finally became so complex it was unmanageable, and the Roman college had to be abandoned.

Chaldean astrologers were much sought after in ancient Rome, as were **numerologists** and **soothsayers**. Most noble houses had their own astrologers. **Dreams** and their interpretation were considered especially important. There are many instances on record of **prophetic dreams**. There was recognition of **astral projection**; the Romans having a belief that dreams were the souls of individuals visiting one another during sleep. There was also a belief that the spirits of the dead could return to earth through dreams.

Pliny the Elder wrote, "The art of magic ... has brought in the arts of astrology and divination. For everyone desires to know what is to come to him and believes that certainty can be gained by consulting the stars."

Sources:

Buckland, Raymond: *The Fortune-Telling Book: The Encyclopedia of Divination and Soothsaying.* Detroit: Visible Ink Press, 2004

Encyclopedia Britannica. Chicago: William Benton, 1964

Hamilton, Edith: *The Roman Way to Western Civilization.* New York: W.W. Norton, 1932

Leach, Maria (ed): *Funk & Wagnalls Standard Dictionary of Folklore, Mythology and Legend.* New York: Harper & Row, 1984

Rose, H. J.: *Religion in Greece and Rome.* New York: Harper & Row, 1959

ROSNA, CHARLES B. (C. 1812–1843)

Charles B. Rosna was the murdered peddler whose body was buried in the basement of the **Hydesville**, New York, cottage where the **Fox Family** lived. It was his **spirit** that made contact with the Fox Family on March 31, 1848 and, through a "conversation" of spoken questions and **rappings** indicating answers, gave the details concerning his death. He had been killed about five years prior, by having his throat cut with a butcher knife. The residents of the cottage at the time were a couple named Bell.

John Bell and his wife had a maid named Lucretia Pulver. One day a peddler called at the house and the Bells invited him in. They gave their maid the evening off and when she returned the following morning she was told the peddler had left. But in fact the Bells had murdered him for what money he had—reportedly as much as five hundred dollars—and had bricked-up his body in the basement wall. His spirit thereafter haunted the cottage, driving out the next residents, a young couple named Michael and Hannah Weekman. The Foxes moved in on December 11, 1847.

According to Lucretia Pulver, Charles Rosna "carried a trunk—and a basket, I think, with vials of essence in it. He wore a black frock coat and light colored pants." She also said that on occasions afterward Mrs. Bell showed her some silver thimbles that she claimed she had got from the peddler.

When Rosna was describing his murder to the many people gathered in the Fox cottage in 1848, he claimed that his body was buried in the cellar. A number of the villagers, led by William Duesler and David Fox (the Fox's son), descended to the basement and began to dig. At a depth of three feet they hit water and had to stop. Some months later, in July, 1848, David Fox and Stephen Smith again dug and again hit water. But they also found smashed bits of pottery, bone fragments, and strands of hair. The bones and hair were claimed by skeptics to be from animals, so the discovery was inconclusive. It was not until 1904, when some school children were playing around the old Hydesville house, that the real evidence was discovered. As the children roamed the dark cellar, a wall crumbled and fell. Behind it was discovered a skeleton. The *Boston Journal* reported (November 23, 1904) that a doctor was consulted and he estimated that the bones were approximately fifty years old. It is said that a peddler's tin box was also discovered. This is now on view at the **Lily Dale Museum**.

Sources:

Doyle, Sir Arthur Conan: *The History of Spiritualism.* New York: Doran, 1926

Weisberg, Barbara: *Talking With the Dead.* HarperSanFrancisco, 2004

ROY, WILLIAM

William Roy, whose real name was William George Holroyd Plowright, has been described as the most audacious **Spiritualist** crook of modern times. He was first exposed in 1955, but not before he had become the best known **medium** in Great Britain. It was the Spiritualist publication *Two Worlds* (originally founded by **Emma Hardinge Britten**) that exposed Roy.

Roy claimed to produce the independent **direct voice** phenomenon. A voice, separate from his own, would issue from the region of his wrist and speak giving details of the sitters and their deceased. After his exposure, Roy admitted—being very well paid for a series of interviews, by the *Sunday Pictorial*—that he had devised a clever microphone relaying technique. An accomplice sat in an adjoining room and spoke into a microphone. The wires from it ran through the wall and under the carpet of the **séance** room. They terminated at two large brass tacks that looked as though they were there to hold the carpet in place. Roy himself was wired and had a metal plate on the sole of each shoe. When he stood on the tacks it completed a circuit that ran up his pants legs and then down his arm to what had been an old hearing aid, strapped to his wrist. The hearing aid had been adapted to become a miniature speaker. The voice of the accomplice would therefore come from the general region of Roy's wrist and could well be speaking even while Roy himself was speaking.

Roy researched possible clients very thoroughly, going to voters' lists and the National Registry of Births, Marriages, and Deaths. He pored over details of wills and property transfers. He kept a filing system with index cards filled with information on different people. He also claimed that he exchanged information with other fraudulent mediums. Among other things, he would have an accomplice go through the pockets and bags that clients had left in his hallway, and he listened in on their pre-sitting conversations through hidden microphones. Roy worked with fake **slates, trumpets** and, on occasion, used masks and cheesecloth for fake **materializations**. He claimed to have a **spirit guide** named Tinka, an **Native American**, and used another system of microphones to produce his voice.

As early as 1951 other Spiritualists became aware of Roy's fraud and, rather than give the whole of Spiritualism a bad name, it was agreed not to reveal him so long as he left the country. This Roy did. But he did not stay away long; he was soon back and continuing his practice. The British national Spiritualist magazine *Two Worlds* then published an article labeling him a fraud. Roy responded by suing the journal for libel. Once the matter went to court, *Two Worlds* was not allowed to make any further comments, which suited Roy very well. He kept the law suit pending for several years, but finally had to drop it in 1958. He agreed to pay the court costs to the editor of *Two Worlds*, but to do so in twenty-four monthly payments. Immediately afterward the journal published all of its evidence of fraud. The *Sunday Pictorial* offered Roy a substantial amount for his "story." By the time it was published Roy had once again left the country.

Roy's final words in the newspaper article were, "Even after this confession, I know I could fill séance rooms again with people who find it a comfort to believe I am genuine." He went on to prove this. In 1968, he was again exposed, this time by the Spiritualist newspaper **Psychic News** and its editor **Maurice Barbanell**. At that time Roy was using the name Bill Silver and was working as a medium under the patronage of a wealthy client. *Psychic News* revealed that indeed some of the sitters were aware of Roy's real identity and that he had previously been exposed, but they didn't seem to care. The sitters included a bishop and the Beatles.

Sources:

Edmunds, Simeon: *Spiritualism: A Critical Survey.* North Hollywood: Wilshire, 1960

Stemman, Roy: *The Supernatural: Spirits and Spirit Worlds.* London: Aldus, 1975

RYERSON, KEVIN

Kevin Ryerson was born in the 1950s. He is a **channeler** in California who hosts a large number of different entities. Most channelers are each a conduit for only one entity—as with **Jach**

Pursel's Lazarus and **Judy Knight**'s Ramtha—but Ryerson is different. His channeling started not long after joining an **Edgar Cayce**–based **meditation** group in the 1970s. Such groups were known as "Search for God" groups. A year after joining the group, Ryerson began to channel at will, tapping into what he termed "the universal mind." He claimed to connect with such entities as the Apostle John, a member of the Essene Hebrew sect incarnate at the time of Jesus; Obadiah, a Haitian; Tom McPherson, whose accent and language suggest an incarnation in Elizabethan Ireland; sages from ancient **Egypt** and from Japan. Ryerson claims that on awakening from **trance** he has no knowledge of what took place or of what the **spirit** had to say. "The spirits who speak through me," he says, "are human personalities who lived in another historical period ... They are merely in a discarnate state. Their motivation to speak when I'm in the trance state is to help facilitate both individual and collective well-being."

The success of his channeling over the years has made Ryerson one of the best known names in that field, although *Spirit Summonings (Mysteries of the Unknown: Spirit Summonings)*, (1989) observes, "His channeled information is fairly standard fare. Ryerson's entities expound, for example, on the reality of **reincarnation** and the need to look to the higher self for guidance." Klimo also says, "The content of Ryerson's channeling closely parallels that of other historical and contemporary channeled material. Although the messages vary somewhat according to which of his sources they supposedly come from, they generally concur on certain themes ... It reminds us that, beneath the appearance of the limited physical reality, we are essentially spiritual and immortal in nature, at one of the deepest levels of the universe, or God. From this relationship, we derive our power and our possibilities."

Ryerson received a boost when actress **Shirley MacLaine** described him in her bestselling books *Out On a Limb* and *Dancing in the Light*. In his lectures and demonstrations, he discusses the process of channeling and speaks on a wide range of similar topics. He has appeared on a large number of radio and television shows.

Sources:

Foreman, Laura (ed): *Mysteries of the Unknown: Spirit Summonings.* New York: Time-Life Books, 1989

Klimo, Jon: *Channeling: Investigations on Receiving Information from Paranormal Sources.* Los Angeles: Jeremy P. Tarcher, 1987

SCHNEIDER, WILLI (1903–1971) AND RUDI (1908–1957)

Willi and Rudi Schneider were from Braunau in Upper Austria. Their father was a lino-type compositor. They were **physical mediums** discovered by Baron Albert von **Schrenk-Notzing**, who tested them under stringent conditions and in the presence of a number of scientists. They had two brothers, Hans and Karl, who also had some slight **psychic** ability, and two other brothers who had none.

Willi was born in 1903. His **spirit guide** was named Olga Lintner. His **mediumship** began when he was sixteen, while the family was working a **planchette**. When Willi's hand was simply held over the planchette without actually touching it, the little platform moved by itself and spelled out words. In response to the question "Who is there?" it wrote, "Olga." Initially the spirit said she was also Lola Montez (Marie Dolores Eliza Rosanna Gilbert), the celebrated mistress of King Ludwig of Bavaria. She had died in 1861. However, after this initial contact there was no further mention of that personality and Olga continued.

At various family **séances**, Willi would fall into a **trance** and various phenomena were observed.

Olga would speak through him, objects moved without being physically touched, and ectoplasmic formations were observed. A retired Austrian warship commander named Fritz Kogelnik learned of Willi's abilities and, becoming convinced that they were genuine, introduced the boy to Dr. Albert von Schrenck-Notzing. Notzing in turn brought Willi to the Psychological Institute of the University of Munich, where he was tested by a group of doctors and scientists. All were favorably impressed. They worked with Willi between December 3, 1921, and July 1, 1922. Before a séance, the room would be carefully searched. Then Willi would be examined, sometimes being dressed in new clothes and sewn into the garments. Luminous bracelets were placed around his wrists and a number of luminous pins were attached to various points on his clothes, so that any movement could be seen, even in the dark. He sat outside a **cabinet** with a person on each side holding his hands and a third person immediately in front of him keeping Willi's legs firmly between his own. Objects to be moved **psychokinetically** were placed in a mesh cage. Despite these precautions, the results were positive, with many objects moved and with **ectoplasm** taking form. Von Schrenck-Notzing published the results in his book *Experimente der Fernbewegung* (1924).

In 1922, at Notzing's invitation, **Harry Price** and Dr. **Eric John Dingwall** (then research officer for the **Society for Psychical Research** in London) attended some sittings with Willi. Tables were moved, a handbell was rung, and a handkerchief and a bracelet were **levitated**. However, there was no ectoplasm. But both men signed statements attesting to the genuineness of the phenomena.

Willi wanted to become a dentist and moved to Vienna to study. There he lived with Dr. E. Holub, a psychiatrist and head of a large mental hospital in Stienhof. On Dr. Holub's death in 1924, séances were begun again, witnessed by university professors. Later in the year Willi and Dr. Holub's widow traveled to London at the invitation of the Society for Psychical Research and gave twelve sittings, from November 12 to December 13, 1924, on the society's premises. In Dingwall's report in the society's *Proceedings* he said, "The only phenomena clearly observed were telekinetic … the only reasonable hypothesis which covers the facts is that some supernormal agency produced the results."

Willi's abilities gradually diminished until one day Olga stated that his brother Rudi was a much more powerful medium and she wished to work with him from then on. The boys' mother protested that Rudi was too young but, at that moment, the door opened and Rudi walked in as though sleepwalking. Olga spoke through him and Willi then developed another personality named Mina. Olga remained with Rudi for the rest of his life.

Anita Gregory wrote in *Man, Myth & Magic* (1970),

Rudi was one of the most exhaustively investigated and carefully controlled mediums of all time. Apart from giving hundreds of sittings under more or less informal conditions in and about his home town of Braunau, Rudi was investigated over a number of years and with increasingly strict controls by Schrenck-Notzing in Munich. He trained him from boyhood as a "scientific medium", that is, one willing to accept any and every control and whatever test conditions the experimenters demanded. Rudi, according to the evidence of his investigators, never refused any condition imposed by researchers. The phenomena were similar to those reported in connection with Willi: the most frequent and best attested were movements of objects, whilst among the earlier phenomena, not often subsequently observed, were visible **materializations**. Levitations of the whole body of the medium were also reported, principally in the **home circle**, but also by Schrenck-Notzing and some of his medical and scientific collaborators.

Rudi was born July 27, 1908. His first independent séance was held in November, 1919, at Braunau, where the materialization of a small hand was observed. Rudi's career was checkered; he was charged with fraud on several occasions, yet on other occasions produced unusual interference of a complex system of **infrared** radiation. This infrared was intended to detect any physical interference. But the interference detected turned out to be produced by the spirit Olga, who would state that she was going to "go into the rays" and then would set off the alarm bells, flashlights, and other paraphernalia that had been carefully arranged as an anti-fraud precaution. These invisible intrusions by Olga were recorded in experiments in Paris, with Dr. Eugene Osty in 1930 and 1931, and in London, at the University of London Observatory and the **National Laboratory of Psychical Research** in 1932. However, a number of charges of fraud were brought against Rudi, though none of them proven. One such was published in Psyche, the German Spiritualist monthly magazine, in April, 1927. In the article, Warren Jay Vinton charged Rudi with fraud through confederacy. The article made a stir and Baron von Schrenck-Notzing decided to investigate and settle the matter. He arranged an elaborate investigation that was to take place in 1929, in Herr Krall's laboratory, using a system of partly electrical and partly tactual control. Unfortunately, early in 1929 both Krall and Schrenck-Notzing died.

Harry Price made arrangements for Rudi to visit the National Laboratory of Psychical Research in London in 1929. Karl Amereller, an electrician, installed a special indicator for the investigation. A number of electrical contacts were made so that if there was any movement of the medium's arms or legs, colored lights that were illuminated would go out. In the experiments, Harry Price himself controlled Rudi's hands and feet. The first séances were held April 12–22, 1929, with a second series lasting from November 14 until January 20, 1930. Harry Price described the results in his book *Rudi Schneider: A Scientific Examination of His Mediumship* (1930), "The fact remains that Rudi has been subjected to the most merciless triple control ever imposed upon a medium in this or any other country and has come through the ordeal with flying colors. The genuineness of the phenomena produced in his London séances has impressed nearly one hundred persons, including scientists, doctors, business men, professional magicians, journalists, etc." A wide variety of phenomena were experienced with much of it taking place inside the cabinet while Rudi was sitting outside. Well known stage magician Will Goldston said that a whole group of prestidigitators working under the same conditions could not have produced the same phenomena.

After the experiments, Harry Price, on behalf of the Council of the National Laboratory of Psychical Research, presented Rudi Schneider with a certificate attesting to his mediumship. Price said, "If the Laboratory issued a gold medal or a diploma for genuine mediumship under our own scientific conditions, we should have no hesitation in awarding it to Rudi." In October and November, 1930, Rudi sat at the French **Institut Métapsychique** with similar results and reactions: at the end of ninety sittings the Institut presented him with a gift of 5,000 francs in recognition of his mediumship.

In later years, Rudi's mediumship diminished. He eventually became an auto mechanic and married Mitzi Mangl. He died of a stroke on April 28, 1957, at Wyer, Austria.

Sources:

Fodor, Nandor: *Encyclopedia of Psychic Science.* London: Arthurs Press, 1933

Gregory, Anita: *Man, Myth & Magic: Schneider Brothers.* London: BPC Publishing, 1970

Gregory, Anita: *The Strange Case of Rudi Schneider.* Metuchen: Scarecrow Press, 1985

Guiley, Rosemary Ellen: *The Encyclopedia of Ghosts and Spirits.* New York: Facts On File, 1992

Price, Harry: *Rudi Schneider.* London: Methuen, 1930

SCHREIBER, KLAUS

In 1985, Klaus Schreiber invented a device that he called the Vidicom. It was inspired by **George Meek**'s Spiricom—a mechanical device that could be used to communicate with **spirits** of the dead. Where Meek's invention enabled the living to speak to the dead, Schreiber's enabled them to *see* the deceased on a television screen. He started with an experiment to try to hear voices of the dead, and eventually heard the voice of his deceased daughter Karin. These **Electronic Voice Phenomena (EVP)** voices suggested that he use video as well as audio to communicate. This he tried and eventually managed to distinguish faces on his television screen. He achieved this by recording blank channels with his video camera. He would aim his camera at the screen and then feed back the camera's output into the television to create a feedback loop. This created a swirling cloud-like appearance in which spirit images slowly appeared.

Tom and Lisa Butler report that although Schreiber's first pictures were blurred, his later ones were greatly improved, capturing a picture of his daughter and of other deceased relatives. The Butlers said, "His daughter became his research counterpart on the other side and assisted him with receiving further contacts from deceased family and friends." They add that **parapsychologist** professor Hans Bender declared that the phenomenon experienced by Schreiber was real.

Sources:

Butler, Tom and Lisa: *There Is No Death and There Are No Dead.* Reno: AA-EVP, 2003

Meek, George W.: *After We Die, What Then?* Columbus: Ariel Press, 1987

SCHRENCK-NOTZING, BARON ALBERT PHILLBERT FRANZ, FREIHERR VON (1862–1929)

Baron Albert Phillbert Franz von Schrenck-Notzing was born on May 18, 1862, in Oldenburg, Germany. As a young man he studied the treatment of nervous disorders and received his M.D. in 1888 for a study of the therapeutic use of hypnosis in a Munich hospital. One of his fellow students was Sigmund Freud. Schrenck-Notzing quickly established himself as an authority on the use of **hypnotism** and criminal pathology. Acquaintance with French physiologist **Charles Richet** introduced Notzing to the **psychic** field. He had met Richet at a conference in Paris in 1889.

In 1891, Notzing translated into German Richet's reports on **telepathy** experiments. The following year he married Gabrielle Siegle, who came from a wealthy industrial family. This gave Notzing the financial independence he needed to pursue his new interest in **psychical research**. He founded the *Gesellschaft für Metapsychische Forschung* (Society for **Metaphysical** Investigation). At Richet's invitation, he participated in the examination of Italian medium **Eusapia Paladino** at Richet's home on the Île de Ribaud in 1894. Paladino was a **physical medium** who produced **levitations**, **rappings**, and **psychokinesis**. Notzing followed Paladino all over Europe and twice had her as his guest in Munich. However, it was not until 1914 that he came to accept and believe in the reality of her phenomena. In 1920, he published his reports on her as *Physikalische Phenomena des Mediumismus* (*The Psychical Phenomena of Mediums*).

Notzing also studied **Eva C.** for four years, publishing a book *Materialisations Phenomene,*

1913 (*The Phenomena of Materialization*, English translation 1920), which included a number of photographs of her **materializations** and production of **ectoplasm**. Notzing also investigated **Willi and Rudi Schneider**, Stanislava P., Maria Silbert, Einar Nielsen, Stanislava Tomczyk, Franek Kluski, Linda Gazzera, Lucia Sordi, and many other **mediums** of all types. His book *Experimente der Fernbewegung* (Stuttgart, 1924) is considered one of the most important on the phenomenon of psychokinesis. In his later years Notzing concentrated on investigating **ghosts** and **hauntings**.

Baron Schrenck-Notzing died on February 12, 1929, in Munich, after an operation for acute appendicitis. René Sudre, wrote in a memorial article in *Psychic Research* (May, 1929) that Notzing never made any attempt to interpret the phenomena he observed. "He lacked the spirit of the philosopher," he said. But Notzing performed an immense service by establishing the physical phenomena of psychical research.

Sources:

Doyle, Sir Arthur Conan: *The History of Spiritualism.* New York: Doran, 1926

Fodor, Nandor: *Encyclopedia of Psychic Science.* London: Arthurs Press, 1933

Guiley, Rosemary Ellen: *The Encyclopedia of Ghosts and Spirits.* New York: Facts On File, 1992

Walther, Gerda: *Schrenck-Notzing: Pioneer Researcher.* New York: *Tomorrow* Magazine, Winter, 1958

SCOLE EXPERIMENTS

The central figure of the Scole Experiments is Robin Foy, a specialist in the paper industry. For more than twenty-five years he has dedicated himself to reviving the near-extinct practice of **physical mediumship**. He and his wife Sandra started a small research group in 1993. They met in the large basement of a rented house in Scole, Norfolk, England. In their sittings, they were contacted by a group of **spirits** led by an entity named Manu. Others in the group of spirits were John Paxton, Patrick McHenna, Raji, Edward Matthews, and Mrs. Emily Bradshaw. Communication was through Foy and his wife. As **mediums**, they would go into deep **trance** for the séances. These would last for two or three hours.

Near the end of 1994, word of the experiments became known outside the operating group. At that time the team of six people had started a newsletter titled the *New Spiritual Scientist*, to give details of what they were accomplishing. By 1995, the **Society for Psychical Research** (SPR) had become interested and began an investigation of the group and of the results so far obtained. These included **direct voice** communication, **apports**, and various **spirit photographs**, some taken by the members of the group, some by the spirits themselves, and some made without a camera.

The SPR investigators were Professor Arthur Ellison, Ralph Noyes (later replaced by Professor David Fontana, President of the society), and Montague Keen. It was quickly established that the spirit personalities were quite separate and distinct from the personalities of the mediums. There were constant demonstrations of floating lights or **orbs**, which "whirled around the room performing various manoeuvres. Occasionally, these lights would throw out beams, as well as pass through solid objects," and a striking example of the **materialization** and dematerialization of a crystal. There were also spirit hands that moved and touched people, floating semi-transparent figures, and **apports**. Included in the apports were original copies of newspapers from 1944 and 1945. Sittings continued for more than two years, convincing the investigators that there was no fraud taking place. One of the precautions taken was to use luminous Velcro wrist straps on every person present in the room, so that any and every movement of the hands could be seen. To attempt to remove the wrist straps would have entailed the use of both hands and, no matter how slowly and carefully done, would have been heard.

Keen reported,

The principle instrument was in the films. There were fifteen in all created during our investigation. Nearly all were attended by slightly different protocols. Most of the films were rolls of 35mm Polaroid which could be developed on the spot via an electrical development machine using chemical cartridges; some were Kodachrome, developed at Kodak's plant in Wimbledon. Normally films were bought and handled throughout by the investigators, sometimes sealed in a plastic security bag, which the spirit communicators found it difficult but not impossible to penetrate; more often in a padlocked box placed on the séance room table or held in an investigator's hand. Almost invariably the films remained untouched in their original tubes until taken out for development. The experiments were not always successful. Those which worked proved spectacular, the images being spread over most of the length of the roll. Some were deliberately aimed at setting us puzzles, and linking the message on the film with the preceding and succeeding discussions with the communicating "Team."

Among the first images was a clearly printed stanza of a poem by **Frederick W. H. Myers** along with references, in French and Greek, to his obituary notice by Sir **Oliver Lodge**. Results were so amazing that other investigators wanted to experience them. Dr. Hans Schaer, Dr. Ernst Senkowski, Piers Eggett, Keith Mcquin Roberts, Dr. Rupert Sheldrake, and Professor Ivor Grattan-Guiness were some of them. All had many years experience investigating the paranormal. In the United States, sessions were attended by scientists from NASA, the **Institute of Noetic Sciences**, and representatives from Stanford University. It is reported that some fifteen scientists from the NASA group later formed their own psychic group to communicate with the spirits.

A 300-page scientific report was prepared for the Society for Psychical Research, validating the phenomena. According to Montague Keen, "None of our critics has been able to point to a single example of fraud or deception."

Sources:
The Scole Debate Article: http://www.bufora.org.uk/archive/Scole.htm

The Scole Event Article: http://www.datadiwan.de/Sci MedNet/library/articlesN73+/N73Keen_Scoleevent. htm

The Scole Phenomena: http://www.afterlife101.com/ Scole_1.html

Solomon, Grant and Jane: *The Scole Experiment*. London: Piatkus, 1999

Victor Zammit site: http://www.victorzammit.com/ book/chapter05.html

Scrying; Skrying *see* **Crystal Gazing**

SÉANCE

The meaning of the word séance is "sitting." A séance is a sitting together of a group of people—usually including a **medium**—for a **Metaphysical** experiment. The people attending a séance are referred to as "sitters." Such a gathering can be of any size, though a group of six or eight people is most common. Two friends sitting with a **talking board** would be considered as having a séance; in this case both of them acting as mediums. The medium is the **channel** through whom the **spirits** communicate.

People attend séances for a variety of reasons. Usually, the object is to make contact with spirits of the deceased in order to obtain information from them. This may simply be a sitter looking for confirmation that indeed the spirit does continue existence after death, or it may be seeking more specific information concerning the quality of life in the afterworld, or to investigate some past, present, or possible future happening in this world.

Séances can be held at any time of the day or night, though the majority seem to be held in the late evening. Certainly at that time the "vibrations" are better for spirit communication. This may be something to do with the atmosphere; radio waves seem to travel farther and with less interruption in the evening. There is also a certain stillness and clarity that is missing during the day. Additionally, of course, a private séance held in the late evening is less likely to be open to interruption from unexpected callers.

A séance lifts the veil between this world and the next, so that the living and the dead may temporarily reunite and communicate with one another. With **physical mediumship**, phenomena such as **psychokinesis** (the moving of objects without physical contact), **levitation, materialization**, and similar may be experienced. With a **trance** medium there may be **clairvoyance, clairaudience**, and **direct voice** communication … the speaking of a spirit through the medium's vocal cords. The spirits speaking, either through the medium or by way of the medium's **spirit guide**, can impart knowledge of the past, present, or even of the future.

The question of lighting at a séance is often debated. Some groups work in complete or near total darkness while others work in bright light. The darkness is usually called for when there will be materializations, because production of **ectoplasm** seems to be restricted by light. However, many times a red light is permissible, and today events can be monitored with infrared light and film. Some mediums will work in candlelight while others just dim the lights. A lowered level of light does seem preferable, if only to cut down on distractions and as being conducive to shifting consciousness and entry into trance.

Many séances take place with the sitters around a table. It is then usual to place the hands on the table, at least initially, with some groups spreading their arms so that little fingers touch with neighbor's fingers, forming an unbroken circle of energy. Feet are usually kept flat on the floor, with legs uncrossed.

Whether or not there is a medium present, the group should have a leader. This person is responsible for everyone and, in a **development circle**, responsible for recognizing where talent is showing itself so that it may be encouraged. A brief **meditation** or the singing of a song at the start of the sitting is sometimes used as a relaxing and harmonizing tool, bringing everyone into accord.

As stated, the purpose of the séance can vary, as can the method of operating. **Table tipping** is sometimes part of a sitting, as is **automatic writing**,

Participants in a séance attempt to summon and communicate with the spirit world. *Courtesy Fortean Picture Library.*

clairvoyance, clairaudience, clairsentience, direct voice, psychokinesis, levitation and materialization. The aim may be to communicate with one or more specific spirits, perhaps related to sitters, or it may be to make contact with virtually any spirits.

There are also private séances. Someone with a strong desire to communicate with a deceased friend or relative may arrange a private sitting with an accomplished medium for this purpose. In this instance there is seldom input in the form of energy from the sitter, who is there to witness the phenomena produced by the medium and to acknowledge the material presented.

Sources:

Bentine, Michael: *The Door Marked Summer*. London: Granada, 1981

Bentine, Michael: *Doors of the Mind*. London: Granada, 1984

Buckland, Raymond: *Buckland's Book of Spirit Communications*. St. Paul: Llewellyn, 2004

Buckland, Raymond: *The Fortune-Telling Book: The Encyclopedia of Divination and Soothsaying*. Detroit: Visible Ink Press, 2004

Cowan, Tom: *The Book of Séance*. Chicago: Contemporary Books, 1994

Hollen, Henry: *Clairaudient Transmissions*. Hollywood: Keats Publications, 1931

Moses, William Stainton: *Direct Spirit Writing*. London: L. N. Fowler, 1878

Mühl, Anita M.: *Automatic Writing*. Dresden: Steinkopff, 1930

Owens, Elizabeth: *How to Communicate With Spirits*. St. Paul: Llewellyn, 2002

Second World War *see* World Wars

SEER; SEERESS

A seer is a "see-er;" a **clairvoyant**. It is one who is able to see the future; one to whom divine revelations are made in visions. In the **Bible**, I Samuel 9:9 reads, "Beforehand in Israel, when a man went to enquire of God, thus he spake, Come, and let us go to the seer, for he that is now called a Prophet was beforetime called a Seer." In Israel a seer was called *ro'eh*(meaning "visionary") or *hozeh* ("gazer"), while a prophet was *nabhi*.

Bletzer defines seer as "a male psychic specializing in clairvoyance, **clairsentience**, and **prophecy**. Female is called seeress."

Sources:

Bletzer, June G.: *The Encyclopedia Psychic Dictionary*. Lithia Springs: New Leaf, 1998

Buckland, Raymond: *The Fortune–Telling Book: The Encyclopedia of Divination and Soothsaying*. Detroit: Visible Ink Press, 2004

SEGRAVE, SIR HENRY (1896–1930)

Henry Segrave was born in 1896 in Baltimore, Maryland; his father was Irish and his mother was American. He is career in motor racing started immediately after World War I, and he had many successes over the years. On March 29, 1927, he became the first man to attain a speed of more than 200 mph, which he did with his 1000 horsepower, twin-engined, *Mystery Sunbeam* at Daytona Beach, Florida, establishing a world speed record of 203.79 mph. He later pushed that speed up to 231.44 mph in his *Golden Arrow*.

Turning his attention to the water speed record, Segrave hoped to break the 100 mph mark in his boat *Miss England II*, which was powered by two 2,000 horsepower Rolls Royce engines. He attempted the record on Britain's Lake Windermere. It was Friday June 13, 1930, and he did two runs—into the wind and with the wind—one of 96.41 mph and one of 101.11 mph. On a third run the boat apparently hit a small tree trunk floating on the surface of the lake. *Miss England II* flew up into the air, crashed down again, and sank. Segrave and his chief mechanic, Willcox, were rescued but his second mechanic, Halliwell, drowned. Segrave was rushed to a hospital but died of lung hemorrhages. Willcox survived.

According to Maurice Barbanell, shortly before Segrave had attempted to break the land speed record at Daytona, he had been advised of a message received at an English Spiritualist **séance**. The message advised him that a certain part of his car would break when a particular speed was attained. Segrave tested the part and found that, at that speed, it did indeed fail. The séance message prevented a probable tragedy. The incident aroused Segrave's curiosity and when he returned to England, after the successful land speed record attempt, he consulted journalist Hannen Swaffer about **Spiritualism**. Swaffer invited Segrave and Archie Emmett Adams to his London apartment. Adams was a **medium** who was, according to Barbanell, "more attracted to **Theosophy** than Spiritualism" and resented his own mediumship. But, "in the normal lighting of the flat ... Segrave witnessed the extraordinary feat of Swaffer's piano being **levitated** from the floor."

Segrave mentioned the levitating piano in an article he wrote for a newspaper. Two days after Segrave's death at Lake Windermere, the newspaper with his article in it was mysteriously moved about Hannen Swaffer's apartment; from one room to another. Swaffer wondered whether this was an indication that Segrave was trying to communicate, and wrote to tell Segrave's widow what he thought. It was some months later that Lady Segrave read one of Swaffer's books on Spiritualism and contacted the journalist again and asked him about possible communication with her deceased husband. Swaffer introduced her to Maurice Barbanell who, in turn, took her to one of **Estelle Roberts**'s voice séances. Lady Segrave became a regular sitter there, with her husband speaking to her on intimate terms, in his own voice by way of the spirit **trumpet**. Long after, when questioned about her feelings regarding the communication, Lady Segrave replied, "Again and again I have turned this evidence over in my mind, examined it critically and calmly. I have tried to explain it away. I have asked myself the questions: 'Can it be telepathy or the subconscious mind?' 'Have I been deceived?' Always the evidence stood every test."

Sources:

Barbanell, Maurice: *This Is Spiritualism*. Oxshott: The Spiritual Truth Press, 1959

Roberts, Estelle: *Fifty Years a Medium*. New York: Corgi Books, 1969

SEIDL, FRANZ

In 1967, Franz Seidl of Vienna, Austria, invented a device that would record **spirit** voices. It consisted of a tape recorder attached to a simple form of radio receiver and amplifier. The receiver had a wide range of frequencies. Theoretically any voices coming over the radio would be amplified and then recorded. He called the device a "psychophone" and described it in his book *The Phenomenon of Transcendental Voices* (1971).

Sources:

Butler, Tom and Lisa: *There Is No Death and There Are No Dead*. Reno: AA-EVP, 2003

Self-Realization Fellowship *see* Yogananda, Paramahansa

SELLERS, PETER (1925–1980)

Peter Sellers characterized his belief in **Spiritualism** "with respect that falls short of unction, with authority that is not dogmatic; he speaks with care because it is important, but the care does not become caution, for caution is the defence of the weak, the first barricade of the uncommitted." (*Peter Sellers: The Man Behind the Mask*, 1969)

Peter Sellers was born on September 8, 1925, in the coastal town of Southsea, England. His parents, Bill Sellers and Peg Welcome, were both in show business. Peter first appeared on stage—albeit he was carried on—within weeks of his birth.

At the outbreak of World War II, Peter Sellers met medium **Estelle Roberts**'s son Terry in Ilfracombe, England. They became friends and eventually Sellers asked if he could have a **séance** with Terry's mother. Estelle gave a sitting for both Sellers and his first wife Anne. At it, **Red Cloud** confirmed what Sellers had suspected—that the old British comedian Dan Leno's **spirit** was helping to shape Sellers' career.

On September 15, 1951, Sellers married Australian actress Anne Hayes. They were married for eleven years, while Sellers took his career from music hall comedian to radio actor/comedian, and then to movies. They had two children, Michael and Sarah, but ultimately divorced in April, 1963. For a time, Sellers' favorite **psychic** was **Maurice Woodruff**, who predicted that the next woman he married would have the initials B.E. Sure enough, Sellers met and fell in love with Swedish starlet Britt Ekland, whom he met in the lobby of the Dorchester Hotel, London, where he had gone to live after his divorce. After Sellers survived eight heart attacks, they married and had a daughter, Victoria, who was born in Paris.

Sellers' mother died in 1967, and he and Ekland separated the following year. For some years Sellers had what Derek Sylvester describes as "regular chats" with his mother by way of various **mediums**. After his mother's death, he again went to see Estelle Roberts. Peg related many things known only to herself and Sellers. Sellers continued to visit Estelle Roberts for many years.

In 1969, he married Miranda Quarry, the daughter of Lord Mancroft. By 1974, Miranda sued for divorce. Sellers said, "The real bliss I get out of life now comes directly from the **meditation** I do. There's no doubt about that. No woman has been able to give me that sense of inner peace and tranquility." By this time his life was governed by yoga and astrology. He had been introduced to Oriental discipline by Ravi Shankar, an Indian musician and friend of the Beatles. In 1976, he married his fourth wife, twenty-one-year-old

Lynne Frederick, a television actress. That same year, he had another minor heart attack and had a pacemaker installed. He went on to make more movies, and also to almost divorce his fourth wife. Finally, on July 24, 1980, at age fifty-five, Sellers died of a severe coronary at Middlesex Hospital, in London.

Sources:

Evans, Peter: *Peter Sellers: The Man Behind the Mask.* London: Frewin, 1969

Roberts, Estelle: *Fifty Years a Medium.* New York: Corgi Books, 1969

Sylvester, Derek: *Peter Sellers.* London: Proteus, 1981

SERIOS, TED

In the fall of 1963, Dr. **Jule Eisenbud** published a paper in a **parapsychological** journal, arguing that it was virtually impossible to devise a repeatable experiment in the field of paranormal phenomena. Eisenbud was a psychiatrist on the faculty of the University of Colorado Medical School. **Curtis Fuller**, then editor of **Fate** magazine and also President of the Illinois **Society for Psychical Research**, read the article and disagreed. He sent Eisenbud a copy of a *Fate* article about a man named Ted Serios. The article was written by Pauline Oehler, then Vice President of the ISPR. She said that Serios could impose his thoughts onto photographs and do it repeatedly, and copies of the photographs were published with the article as proof.

Serios was a bellhop in Chicago when the skeptical Eisenbud came in contact with him. On the insistence of Fuller and Freda Morris, Eisenbud met Serios and did some preliminary work that led to three photographs taken with a Polaroid camera. The photographs seemed to be paranormally produced. Serios worked with what he called a "gismo." This was always suspect by those who had not worked with him for any length of time, but it was repeatedly examined by Eisenbud and many others and was shown to be no more than a short section of plastic tube—initially with cellophane taped over one end—that

Serios held over the lens as the shutter was tripped. Examination had shown that there was no film transparency, or anything resembling that, on the end of the gismo. In later experiments, the gismo was no more than the short length of cardboard tube with nothing at all over either end.

Many of the attempted photos were failures, with totally black prints produced. But over a period of two years, Serios produced a wide range of photographs of vastly different subjects, all by concentrating his thoughts on the camera. Interestingly, some of the Serios photos were very similar to actual existing photographs ... but with small changes to show that they were not exact duplicates (e.g. a change of angles, changes of lighting/shadows, a window being to the left of a doorway instead of to its right.) Eisenbud said, "What Ted appeared to present was the missing link par excellence in a still only dimly discerned and poorly integrated panel of problems."

Serios moved to Denver, Colorado, and worked with Eisenbud in controlled experiments for two years. Every safeguard was taken to ensure there was no trickery, yet Serios produced photograph after photograph with his "thoughtography." Eisenbud sought the participation of the scientific community, and eventually more than twenty-five doctors of science—medicine, physics, chemistry, psychology, etc.—signed statements attesting to the validity of the experiments. At times the lens was completely removed from the camera; at other times all visible light sources were blocked; some experiments were carried out with Serios in five inch steel-and-lead-lined radiation shield chambers. Dr. John Beloff of the Edinburgh University Psychology Department in Scotland said that the phenomenon was "likely to prove the most remarkable paranormal phenomenon of our time."

Much earlier—in 1910—a Japanese woman was producing a type of thoughtography. Tomokichi Fukurai, Professor of Psychology at Tokyo University, tested **medium** Mrs. Ikuko Nagao to see if she could **clairvoyantly** identify an image on a photographic plate that had not been developed. He worked with photographs of geometric shapes, rather than actual scenes. Mrs. Nagao succeeded not only in identifying the figure but in putting the target image onto another unexposed film plate that was one of two sandwiching the target plate. This was done without using a camera. She then consistently imprinted a middle plate while leaving clear two other plates on either side of the one she affected.

Sources:

Eisenbud, Jule: *The World of Ted Serios: "Thoughtographic" Studies of an Extraordinary Mind*. New York: William Morrow, 1967

Holroyd, Stuart: *The Supernatural: Minds Without Boundaries*. London: Aldus, 1975

Shakers *see* Quakers and Shakers

SHAKESPEARE, WILLIAM (1564–1616)

The plays of William Shakespeare have many instances of **ghosts**, **prophesy**, and **spirit** communication. Best known, perhaps, are the **witches** of *Macbeth*. When they first meet Macbeth in Act I Scene III of the play, they immediately prophesy that he will be Thane of Glamis, Thane of Cawdor, and king. Later in the play (Act IV, Sc. I), they conjure up **materializations** of spirits of the dead to speak to Macbeth. In *Hamlet*, there is the appearance of the ghost of Hamlet's father. In *Cymbeline* there are words sung by Guiderius and Arvuragus, "No **exorciser** harm thee!" "Nor no witchcraft charm thee!" *The Tempest* is replete with magic, Prospero having many books of magic in his study and the very island on which he and his daughter Miranda live is bewitched by the witch Sycorax. Ariel is a spirit who appears **clairvoyantly** only to Prospero.

The **fairies** of *A Midsummer Night's Dream* are presented with obvious knowledge of fairy folklore and magic on Shakespeare's part. *The Merry Wives of Windsor* also contains fairies but, impor-

tantly, fairies who were acknowledged to be the same size as humans; Shakespeare has Mistress Page, a full-grown woman, not only dress as a fairy but expect to be accepted as one.

Julius Caesar has examples of prophesy, **dreams**, and the use of **omens**—for example when a **soothsayer** warns Caesar about the Ides of March, based on omens he has witnessed. There is also Act I, Scene III, in which Casca meets with Cicero in a street late at night in a raging storm. Casca comments on the many strange omens that are occurring. Dreams also feature in the play, with Caesar's wife Calpurnia herself dreaming of a variety of dire things which bode no good for her husband (Act II, Sc. II).

Sources:

Buckland, Raymond: *Witchcraft From the Inside*. St. Paul: Llewellyn, 1995

Shakespeare, William: *The Complete Works*. London: Odhams Press, 1938

SHAMANISM

A shaman is a priest/magician/**healer** especially as found in such areas as Siberia, Indonesia, Oceania, North and South America, Tibet, **China**, and Japan. Tools of the shaman usually include a specific costume and a drum. The shaman holds a type of **séance**, usually going into **trance**. The Altaic shaman ritually climbs a birch tree, into the trunk of which have been cut a number of steps. The birch symbolizes the World Tree and the steps are the various "heavens" through which the shaman must pass on his ecstatic journey to the highest heaven. There is an interesting parallel here with the various "**spheres**" or "levels" depicted in **Spiritualism** and detailed by **Emanuel Swedenborg**.

According to Mircea Eliade, "Shamanism in the strict sense is preeminently a religious phenomenon of Siberia and Central Asia. The word comes to us, through the Russian, from the Tungusic *saman* ... the magico-religious life of society centers on the shaman." Nandor Fodor suggests that the name also comes from the Sanskrit *sra-*

An Huichol Indian shaman performs a ritual in the desert of Wirikuta, Mexico; photographed in 1998. *Courtesy Fortean Picture Library.*

mana, meaning an ascetic. Fodor clarified, "As distinct from priests, shamans have no ritualistic knowledge but operate rather like Spiritualist **mediums.**"

There are three ways to become a shaman. The first is by spontaneous vocation; by realizing that one has been "called" to it. The second is by hereditary transmission of the profession. The

THE SPIRIT BOOK

third is by personal "quest." But as Eliade points out "By whatever method he may have been designated, a shaman is recognized as such only after having received two kinds of instruction. The first is ecstatic (for example, **dreams**, **visions**, trances); the second is traditional (shamanic techniques, names and functions of the **spirits**, mythology and genealogy of the clan, secret language)."

Sources:

Eliade, Mircea: *Shamanism: Archaic Techniques of Ecstasy*. Princeton University Press/Bollingen Series LXXVI, 1974

Fodor, Nandor: *Encyclopedia of Psychic Science*. London: Arthurs Press, 1933

SHERMAN, HAROLD MORROW (B. 1898)

Harold Morrow Sherman was born on July 13, 1898, in Traverse City, Michigan. He was educated at Traverse City High School and at the University of Michigan. In 1920, he married Martha Frances Bain.

Sherman conducted experiments in **clairvoyance**, **extrasensory perception**, **psychokinesis**, **precognition** and various forms of **mediumship**. He was head of the ESP Research Associates Foundation in Little Rock, Arkansas. In 1942, he wrote a book on long distance telepathy, *Thoughts Through Space: A Remarkable Adventure in the Realm of the Mind*. It was written in conjunction with Arctic explorer Sir Hubert Wilkins. Sherman said it was "reporting a day-to-day account of the impressions that had come to me, acting as receiver, of things that had happened to Wilkins and members of his crew while searching for lost Russian fliers near the North Pole." The recorded impressions were mailed each night by prearrangement to Dr. **Gardner Murphy**, then head of the psychology department of Columbia University. The experiment was conducted over a period of five and a half months, three nights per week, and resulted in an accuracy of approximately seventy percent.

Sherman was a pioneer in **Electronic Voice Phenomena**. His book *You Can Communicate With the Unseen World* (1974) examined the use of an ordinary tape recorder to record messages from departed spirits.

Sherman's books include: *Your Key to Happiness* (1938); *You Live After Death* (1949); *Know Your Own Mind* (1952); *The New TNT: Miraculous Power Within You* (1954); *Adventures in Thinking* (1955); *Your Key to Happiness* (1956); *Your Mysterious Powers of ESP* (1957); *How to Use the Power of Prayer* (1958); *How to Turn Failure into Success* (1958); *Your Power to Heal* (1973); *How to Make ESP Work for You* (1973); *How to Foresee and Control Your Future* (1973); *How to Work With the God Power Within You to Regain Health of Body and Mind* (1976); and *The Dead Are Alive: They Can and Do Communicate With You* (1981). His book *You Can Communicate With the Unseen World* (1974) contained a tribute to **medium Anne Gehman** and had chapters dealing with her work in **Spiritualism**.

Sources:

Fodor, Nandor: *Encyclopedia of Psychic Science*. London: Arthurs Press, 1933

Sherman, Harold: *The Dead Are Alive*. New York: Fawcett, 1981

Sherman, Harold: *You Can Communicate With the Unseen World*. New York: Fawcett, 1974

Sherman, Harold: *You Live After Death*. New York: Fawcett, 1972

SHOWERS, MARY

Mary Showers was a **materialization medium** who was born and grew up in Teignmouth, England. As a child she conversed with **spirits**. In the spring of 1872, she sat for the first time with her family's **circle** and produced **rappings** and **psychokinetic** phenomena. She also produced **direct writing**.

In 1874, her mother took her to London to give **séances** for established **Spiritualists**. At these, coils of rope and tape would be placed in the **cabinet**. Showers would go into the cabinet and shortly after, when the curtains were drawn back, she was discovered tightly bound and with tape over her mouth. Showers's **spirit guide** was a girl named Florence. She would materialize and was seen to be nearly eight inches taller than Showers.

On April 2, 1894, there was an attempt to expose Showers. At a séance held at the house of E. W. Cox, Serjeant-at-Law and well known **psychical researcher**, the materialization of Florence had just appeared issuing from the cabinet when Cox's daughter, Mrs. Edwards, opened the curtains wider. The spirit resisted and there was a struggle. In the struggle the headdress fell off, revealing Mary Showers the medium. Cox decided that she had "unconsciously impersonated the spirit".

Sources:

Fodor, Nandor: *Encyclopedia of Psychic Science.* London: Arthurs Press, 1933

SIBYLS

Legend has it that the ancient Sibyls could live for a thousand years. It seems more likely, however, that it was their *utterings* that were so long lived. Heraclitus, as quoted by Plutarch, said of them, "The Sibyl with raving mouth, uttering things without smiles, without graces and without myrrh, reaches over a thousand years because of the god."

The Sibyls were the **prophets** of ancient **Greece** and **Rome**. They seem to have originated in Greek Asia Minor and worked through **clairvoyance**, **clairaudience** and **clairsentience**, usually going into **trance**. They were always connected to Apollo, the god of prophecy, who also originated in Asia Minor. Where the Pythia of Delphi were controlled and protected by the priesthood, the Sibyls were in effect freelancers. The best known Sibyls were at Delphi, Erythræ, Marpessus, Phrygia, Sardis, and Thessaly. The majority of the prophesies uttered by the Sibyls dealt with war, famine, plague, and other disasters.

In Virgil's *Ænid* there is the story of the Sibyl of Cumæ who **predicted** the wars that would fol-

low Æneas's landing in Italy. Æneas had been told by the prophet Helenus to seek out the cave of the Sibyl of Cumæ as soon as he reached Italy. He was told that she was a woman of deep wisdom, who could foretell the future and advise him what to do. This she did and, in fact, traveled with him to guide him, eventually leading him to meet the **spirit** of his deceased father Anchises.

Sources:

Buckland, Raymond: *The Fortune-Telling Book: The Encyclopedia of Divination and Soothsaying.* Detroit: Visible Ink Press, 2004

Kaster, Joseph: *Putnam's Concise Mythological Dictionary.* New York: G.P. Putnam's, 1963

Parke, H. W.: *Sibyls and Sibylline Prophecy in Classical Antiquity.* New York: Routledge, 1988

Phillips, E.D.: *Man, Myth & Magic: Sibyls.* London: BPC Publishing, 1970

Potter, D.: *Sibyls in the Greek and Roman World.* Rhode Island: Journal of Roman Archaeology 3, 1990

SIDGWICK, PROFESSOR HENRY (1838–1900)

Born May 31, 1838, Henry Sidgwick became the first President of the **Society for Psychical Research** (SPR) in London, England. Sidgwick was Professor of Moral Philosophy at Cambridge University. He was described as "the most incorrigibly and exasperatingly critical and skeptical brain in England." On becoming President of the SPR in 1882, he said, "It is a scandal that the dispute as to the reality of these (**psychic**) phenomena should still be going on, that so many competent witnesses have declared their belief in them ... and yet the educated world, as a body, should still be simply in an attitude of incredulity." He worked with the society for eighteen years, contributing many important studies to the *Proceedings.* He once wrote to a friend, "I have actually heard the **raps** ... however, I have no kind of evidence to come before a jury." He was initially most impressed with the phenomena of the **medium Eusapia Paladino** but took a leading part in the sittings with her, held at Cambridge in 1895, which resulted in her exposure as a fraud. He had a number of sittings with **Leonora Piper**, in 1889–1890, and retained the keenest interest in her **trance** phenomena.

Sidwick had sittings with Henry Slade and Frank Herne, **séances** with the English **materialization** medium Miss C. E. Wood and **Annie Fairlamb Mellon**, but he never published his findings of these sittings. He died before he had a chance to recognize the validity of **psychokinesis** and **ectoplasm**.

After Sidwick's death on August 28, 1900, a number of mediums purported to bring word from his spirit. When English trance medium **Mrs. R. Thompson** channeled him on January 11, 1901, Mr. John George Piddington was present and said that the diction, manner of speech, and the voice itself were all astonishingly life like and he felt that he was indeed speaking with the man he had known.

Sources:

Buckland, Raymond: *The Fortune-Telling Book: The Encyclopedia of Divination and Soothsaying*. Detroit: Visible Ink Press, 2004

Fishley, Margaret: *The Supernatural*. London: Aldus, 1976

Spence, Lewis: *An Encyclopedia of the Occult*. London: George Routledge & Sons, 1920

SILVA, EDIVALDO OLIVEIRA (1930–1974)

Edivaldo Oliveira Silva was a Brazilian **psychic surgeon** and healer. He worked as a taxidermist and school teacher. In 1962, at age thirty-two, he discovered his **healing** powers after visiting a sick neighbor named Dona Zelita. He said "(Dona) had gone temporarily insane, so I went to sit with her while they went to fetch a doctor. When we were alone together I suddenly went mad myself for about an hour. I was completely unconscious; a **spirit** took me over and I became violent. When I recovered, there were broken things all over the

place, but the woman had got better." He went on to perform psychic surgery for people. This was of the invisible variety, where nothing is seen to happen physically as the surgeon moves his hands about in the air over the patient, yet the patient feels something and is subsequently cured. Silva, coming out of **trance**, would have no memory of what had been done. Silva's **spirit guide**, directing the surgery, was Dr. Calazans, a Spaniard. There were also other spirits: Pierre, a Frenchman; Johnson, a Londoner; and Dr. Fritz from Germany. Occasionally a Japanese, an Italian, and a Brazilian also put in an appearance.

In his twelve-year career as a psychic surgeon, Silva treated approximately 65,000 people and performed at least 10,000 operations. "I don't invoke anything," he said, "The spirits just come. I sit down and withdraw my own spirit, and Dr. Calazans takes over. There isn't room for two spirits in one body you see." His patients had included one marshal of the army, eight generals, and over fifty doctors. During his twelve years as a psychic surgeon, Silva studied both law and medicine, hoping to eventually qualify as a doctor.

Silva lived in Vitoria da Conquista in the state of Bahia, Brazil, but would drive 500 miles every other weekend to do his surgery in a **Spiritist** center in Rio de Janeiro. He once traveled to England to study taxidermy, and had also traveled to Argentina to demonstrate his **psychic** powers at La Plata University. He died in 1974 after a road collision with a truck.

Sources:

McGregor, Pedro: *The Moon and Two Mountains: The Myths, Ritual and Magic of Brazilian Spiritism*. London: Souvenir Press, 1966

Playfair, Guy Lion: *The Flying Cow: Research into Paranormal Phenomena in the World's Most Psychic Country*. London: Souvenir Press, 1975

SILVER CORD

It is said that the **astral body**, or etheric double, is connected to the physical body by a silver cord. Invisible to most people, the silver cord may be seen by a sensitive or **psychic** individual. The silver cord emerges from the position of the **Third Eye**, the spiritual center of the body. In the **Bible**, Ecclesiastes 12 describes the transition from life to death as the breaking of a silver cord: "ever the silver cord be loosed … (then) the spirit shall return unto God who gave it." In fact, that is what happens at death. During life—when the etheric double goes on astral journeys—the cord is infinitely elastic. At death it finally breaks, permanently separating the physical body from its astral counterpart.

In the **Spiritualist** journal *Light*, in 1935, Dr. R. B. Holt described his experience at the deathbed of an elderly aunt. He saw "a silver-like substance that was streaming from the head of the physical body to the head of the **spirit** double. This cord seemed alive with vibrant energy … At last the connecting strand snapped and the spirit-body was free. The spirit-body, which had been supine before, now rose and stood vertically."

The 1912 book *Speaking Across the Borderline* was received in the form of **automatic writing**, supposedly from a Scotsman named John Park. The writings were received by the **mediumistic** aunt of Parks's widow, Fanny Parks. In the writings, Parks described the transition from life to afterlife, "Generally the spiritual counterpart floats horizontally above the dying form. It may remain for some time in this position, for it is attached to the body by a fine, filmy cord. Death does not take place until this cord has been severed." An interesting point about this particular book is that John Parks, when alive, was unconvinced of Spiritualist ideas and teachings.

Sources:

Crookall, Robert: *The Techniques of Astral Projection*. London: Aquarian, 1964

Leonard, Sue (ed): *Quest For the Unknown—Life Beyond Death*. Pleasantville: Reader's Digest, 1992

SKOTOGRAPH

Skotograph is from the Greek meaning "writing in the dark." It is when writing is done by **spir-**
it on undeveloped film, so that it only becomes visible when the film is developed. The term was invented by Felicia Scatcherd as an alternative for the word "psychograph," used by **William Stainton Moses** for all forms of **direct writing**. Harry Boddington (*The University of Spiritualism*, 1947) said, "In the majority of experiments, it appears that the only purpose served by cameras is to focus the material setting. The further result is that cameras are now frequently dispensed with altogether. Unopened packets or light-proof plates are merely held in the hands. To cover this aspect of **psychic photography**, Felicia Scatcherd coined the term 'Skotograph,' the literal meaning being 'pictures obtained in darkness.'"

Sources:

Bletzer, June G.: *The Encyclopedia Psychic Dictionary*. Lithia Springs: New Leaf, 1998

Boddington, Harry: *The University of Spiritualism*. London: Spiritualist Press, 1947

Fodor, Nandor: *Encyclopedia of Psychic Science*. London: Arthurs Press, 1933

SLADE, HENRY (D. 1905)

Henry Slade was an America **medium** known best for his **slate writing**. He held slate writing **séances** for fifteen years. His phenomena divided skeptics and believers. British **psychical researcher Frank Podmore** was very impressed by what he read of Slade. Then, in 1876, Slade visited Britain en route for Russia. He had been invited to St. Petersburg to demonstrate before the investigators of the Imperial University, at the instigation of the Grand Duke Constantine of Russia, and had been especially selected by Mme. **Helena Blavatsky** and Colonel Henry Steel Olcott. Slade arrived in England on July 13, 1876, and stayed for six weeks, but his visit was brought to an abrupt end.

At his lodging in Russell Square, London, Slade produced his usual slate writing phenomena together with partial **materializations** and some **psychokinesis**. A table was moved and Slade himself was **levitated**. J. Enmore Jones, Editor of *Spiritual Magazine*, reported, "We have no hesitation in saying that Dr. Slade is the most remarkable medium of modern times." The magazine (under different editorship) later said that Slade had filled the place left by **Daniel Dunglas Home**. **William Stainton Moses** said that Slade "satisfied my desires entirely ... I have seen all these phenomena and many others several times before, but I never saw them occur rapidly and consecutively in broad daylight." Lord Rayleigh had a professional magician accompany him to a séance, but the man was unable to offer any explanation as to how Slade might be doing what he did. Lord Rayleigh then went on to convince Alfred Russel Wallace of Slade's genuineness and even to "finally" (as **Nandor Fodor** put it) solve Frank Podmore's doubts about **Spiritualism**.

Then, at one of Slade's séances, Professor Ray Lankester snatched the slate from the medium's hands and found that a message was already written on it. Slade gave an explanation for this but Lankester pressed charges against Slade for taking money under false pretenses. At the Bow Street Police Court on October 1, 1876, Slade was tried, found guilty, and sentenced to three months imprisonment with hard labor. Due to a technicality, the conviction was quashed and, before a fresh summons could be issued, Slade fled the country. It is not known whether or not Podmore witnessed any of Slade's sittings, or any of the trial, but the revelation of fraud had an effect on him and all his earlier doubts about mediums returned.

Professor Ray Lankester apparently had an axe to grind in that he had been out-voted as a member of the selecting Committee of the British Association for the Advancement of Science when Professor **William Fletcher Barrett**'s paper on Spiritualism was admitted. At that time, Lankester said, "The discussions of the British Association have been degraded by the introduction of Spiritualism." Lankester's attack on Slade was intended to strike a blow at the new phenomena and he proceeded with his charges despite Slade's offered explanations. Podmore summed up the feelings of many when he stated, "The Spiritualists were perhaps justified in not accepting the

Controversial American medium Henry Slade, whose phenomena had skeptics and believers bitterly divided both in America and Britain. *Courtesy Fortean Picture Library.*

incident as conclusive. Slade defended himself by asserting that, immediately before the slate was snatched from his hand, he heard the spirit writing, and had said so, but that his words were lost in the confusion which followed. If we grant that Slade's testimony was as good as Professor Lankester's or Dr. Donkin's it was difficult summarily to dismiss this plea." Sir **Arthur Conan Doyle** commented that the professor "was entirely without experience in psychic research, or he would have known that it is impossible to say at what moment writing occurs in such séances."

From the safety of Prague, Slade offered Lankester exhaustive private tests, but received no answer. With positive testimonies from many prominent Spiritualists, Slade went on to demonstrate for several months in The Hague, Berlin, and Denmark. In Berlin, after two or three sittings, the famous conjurer Samuel Bellachini testified on oath to Slade's powers. In December, 1877, experiments were conducted in Leipzig by professors Zöllner, Fechner, Scheiber and Weber, where writing was produced on sealed slates under the strictest test conditions, knots were tied on an endless string, and there were displays of force and penetration of matter through matter.

Later in Slade's career there were several charges of fraud. Fodor points out that the writing obtained on the slates "was generally of two kinds. The general messages were very legible and clearly punctuated, but when the communication came in answer to questions it was clumsy, scarcely legible, abrupt and vague. It bore traces of hasty work under difficult conditions as these impromptu messages could not be prepared in advance." More and more frequently Slade began to be caught out in fraud. He had, according to Fodor, fallen "victim to the drink habit" and what little genuine power he might have had seemed to have left him. He died penniless in a Michigan sanitorium in 1905, sent there by the American Spiritualists.

Sources:

Doyle, Sir Arthur Conan: *The History of Spiritualism.* New York: Doran, 1926

Fodor, Nandor: *Encyclopedia of Psychic Science.* London: Arthurs Press, 1933

Spence, Lewis: *An Encyclopedia of the Occult.* London: George Routledge & Sons, 1920

Slate Writing *see* Writing, Slate

SLATER, JOHN (1867–1932)

John Slater was an American **clairvoyant** who gave demonstrations of **mediumship** for over fifty years. He was born on September 24, 1867, in Philadelphia, Pennsylvania. His parents were Irish; his father Michael was a Roman Catholic and his mother Mary Killen a Baptist. Slater began showing **psychic** ability when he was only four years old. His four-year-old playmate Mary Powers died, and Slater spoke of seeing her in his back yard shortly after attending her funeral. By the age of twenty-one, he left home determined to devote his life to **Spiritualism**. His parents were not at all supportive of his interests and he suffered some self doubt. Slater and a friend—Spiritualist Elizabeth Holmes—had a séance with Leah Fox Underhill, one of the original **Fox Sisters**. At that sitting Slater was told, in effect, "You were born to do the work of the **spirit world**." He took the message to heart.

From the **platform**, Slater would read sealed letters and give names, addresses, dates, and all pertinent information regarding deceased people. He also excelled at **psychometry**. He traveled all over the United States, appearing before large audiences everywhere he went. He settled in San Francisco and married Eugenie Browell in 1890. Prior to that he had traveled to Hawaii, and been well received there.

Slater's **spirit guide** was his uncle William Killen, his mother's brother. His first spiritual camp work was at **Lake Pleasant**, Massachusetts, and shortly thereafter he went to **Lily Dale**, New York, which he then attended on a regular basis.

In 1930, Slater established his right to function as a medium in Detroit, Michigan. A clergyman there had him arrested for making **predictions**, which was a statutory offence. Slater won his case, with costs against the clergyman, and went on to do his work unchallenged until his death in 1932. In June of that year, Slater had been to the annual convention of the California State Spiritualists Association and died shortly after returning home from that event.

Sources:

Fodor, Nandor: *Encyclopedia of Psychic Science.* London: Arthurs Press, 1933

Spiritualism Mailing List: http://www.spiritualismlist.net

"Sleeping Prophet" *see* Cayce, Edgar

SLOAN, JOHN CAMPBELL

John Campbell Sloan was from Glasgow, Scotland. He worked for many years as a packer in a warehouse, and later became a shopkeeper. All his life, he was aware that supernormal occurrences took place around him. As a young man he frequently heard **rappings** and strange voices. Over a period of about thirty years, these gradually developed into manifestations of a specific nature. He would go into **trance**. He would experience **psychokinesis**, **apports**, **direct voice**, **materializations**, **clairvoyance** and **clairaudience**.

Sloan's **spirit guide** was a **Native American** named White Feather. The guide spoke through a **trumpet** and, on occasion, through Sloan himself, using his vocal cords. As **Arthur Findlay** put it (*On the Edge of the Etheric*, 1931), "When Sloan was in this state he speaks, but it would be more correct to say that his vocal organs vibrate the atmosphere, as no one can be with him long, while this is taking place, and think that his own personality is responsible for what is said. The voice is different and the accent is different, and much of what is said is quite outside his range of knowledge … In the **medium**'s presence, but quite apart from him, voices, claiming to be those of deceased people, speak, and, when replied to, answer back intelligently, which proves that there is not only a mind behind the voice but that the intelligence is able to hear as well as speak. … After twelve years' intimate experience of Mr. John C. Sloan, and having sat with most of the other leading mediums in this country and America, I can say with conviction that he is the best Trance, Direct Voice, Clairvoyant and Clairaudient medium with whom I have ever sat." The **British College of Psychic Science** also tested Sloan for five years.

After looking at 180 reports of Sloan's communications, Findlay stated, "An eminent mathematician on calculating the chances of correctly guessing all the facts recorded, answers that to have reached such accuracy represents the equivalent of 1 to 5,000,000,000,000, in other words the odds were 5,000,000,000,000 to 1 against chance being the explanation." Sir **Arthur Conan Doyle**, speaking of both Sloan and another Scottish medium named William Phoenix, said that both "have remarkable powers which cover almost the whole range of the spiritual gifts, and both are, or were, most unworldly men with a saintly disregard of the things of this life."

Sources:

Awtry-Smith, Marilyn: *"They" Paved the Way*. New York: Spiritualism & More, nd

Doyle, Sir Arthur Conan: *The History of Spiritualism*. New York: Doran, 1926

Findlay, J. Arthur: *Looking Back*. Stansted: Spiritualists' National Union, 1955

Findlay, J. Arthur: *On the Edge of the Etheric*. London: 1931

Fodor, Nandor: *Encyclopedia of Psychic Science*. London: Arthurs Press, 1933

SMITH, GORDON (B. 1962)

As a child, Scotsman Gordon Smith had many of the **psychic** experiences that seem to be common among psychics and **mediums**. His abilities didn't come to full bloom until he was twenty-five years old, with the **clairvoyant** and **clairsentient** contact of his friend's recently deceased brother. Smith is the seventh son of a seventh son—traditionally one who would have "the second sight." After the death of his friend's brother, he went with her to a **Spiritualist** service at the Glasgow Association of Spiritualists, in Somerset Place, where medium Mary Duffy told him he was going to become a medium himself and that he should join a **development circle**. It was some time before he found one on Glasgow's West Princes Street, run by Jean Primrose. He attended that for six years, gradually developing as a medium.

One Sunday when a scheduled medium failed to turn up at a Spiritualist church, Smith was urged to fill in. He did, and did very well. From then on, he worked for a while with Mrs. Primrose but soon was continuing alone, both at his own church and at others around the Glasgow area.

In January, 1995, Smith was invited to share the platform with Irish clairvoyant medium Albert Best, at the 130th anniversary celebration of The Glasgow Association of Spiritualists. Again he performed well and greatly impressed Best, who had a tremendous reputation. Consequently Best took Smith "under his wing" and taught and encouraged him until Best's death in 1997.

Over the years, Smith has made a name for himself as "the medium who provides exact names, dates, places, and even street names." Like his mentor Albert Best, Smith is outstandingly accurate. His extraordinary skills have attracted the attention of university scientists researching psychic phenomena, together with countless numbers of journalists and documentary film makers. **Psychic researcher** Professor Archie Roy of the University of Glasgow said that the information received from Smith has been "highly accurate" and that the probability of it being due to chance was "one in a hundred million million million." Despite his success, Smith has never given up his regular job as a Glasgow hairdresser. He says, "I am not an evangelist. I'm not out to change the world. This is a **healing** thing. I only want to prove it to those that need it … I don't just believe that life goes on after we die; I know it."

Sources:

Smith, Gordon: *Spirit Messenger: The Remarkable Story of a Seventh Son of a Seventh Son.* London: Hay House, 2004

Smith, Gordon: *The Unbelievable Truth: A Medium's Guide to the Spirit World.* London: Hay House, 2004

SOAL, SAMUEL GEORGE (1889–1975)

Samuel Soal was an author, lecturer, and mathematician who became a well known figure in British **parapsychology**. His image was later tarnished when it seemed evident that some of his results were fraudulent.

Soal was born in Kirby Moorside, Yorkshire, England, on April 29, 1889. He studied at London University where he obtained a bachelor degree in mathematics, with first class honors in 1910. He received his M.A. in mathematics in 1914, and D.Sc. in Psychology in 1945. He held a

number of prestigious teaching posts, and he was President of the Nottingham University **Society for Psychical Research** in 1938. He was a Perrott Student in Psychical Research at Cambridge from 1948 to 1949, and Fulbright Research Scholar in Parapsychology in 1951.

From 1919 onward, Soal conducted parapsychology studies, collaborating in quantitative research with Mrs. K.M. Goldney, Frederick Bateman, and J.G.Pratt. He lectured widely both in England and the United States. He was able to duplicate many of the results obtained by Dr. **Joseph Banks Rhine**. He wrote numerous articles and books, incluing *Modern Experiments in Telepathy* (with F. Bateman, 1954), and *The Mind Readers* (with H.T. Bowden, 1959).

Sources:

Buckland, Raymond: *The Fortune-Telling Book: The Encyclopedia of Divination and Soothsaying.* Detroit: Visible Ink Press, 2004

Shepard, Leslie A: *Encyclopedia of Occultism & Parapsychology.* New York: Avon Books, 1978

Society of Inner Light *see* Fortune, Dion

SOCIETY FOR PSYCHICAL RESEARCH (SPR)

In 1882, a group of Cambridge University scholars and others in the London area founded the Society for **Psychical Research**. Its purpose was to thoroughly examine paranormal subjects such as **clairvoyance**, **telepathy**, and **precognition**, to see whether or not there was any basis of fact. At the inaugural meeting, Professor **Henry Sidgwick** was elected President; he held that position for nine years. The first council included Professors **William Fletcher Barrett** and **Balfour Stewart**, **Edmund Gurney**, Richard Hutton, **Frederick W.H. Myers**, **William Stainton Moses**, E.T. Bennett, Dawson Rogers, Morell Theobald, and Dr. George Wyld.

Early activity was devoted to experimental investigation of **extrasensory perception**, which the society established as a fact. They also felt safe in confirming a connection existing between death and **apparitions**. The society collected and published a massive amount of research, finding a great deal of fraud among Spiritualist **mediums** but also finding many instances of unexplainable phenomena.

In 1885, the **American Society for Psychical Research** was founded in Boston by Sir William Fletcher Barrett of the British society. Barrett was visiting the United States at the time. Originally independent, the American society affiliated with the British one in 1889.

Led by Dr. **Richard Hodgson**, the SPR spent many years investigating the **trance** mediumship of Mrs. **Leonore Piper**. Hodgson was so impressed with her performances and the evidence she produced that he became converted to the cause of **Spiritualism** himself. E. Dawson Rogers, President of the London Spiritualist Alliance, said of this that he (Hodgson) had been "a very Saul persecuting the Christians." His conversion was seen as an achievement for Spiritualism.

The society built up a bias against **physical mediumship** and its phenomena, and refused to accept any evidence of it. Eventually the bias became so pronounced that in 1930, Sir **Arthur Conan Doyle** and a number of other prominent members resigned from the society. Over the past fifty years the society has spent most of its time with mass experiments evaluated by statistical methods, with most of its interest in extrasensory perception and in **psychokinesis**.

Sources:

Buckland, Raymond: *The Fortune-Telling Book: The Encyclopedia of Divination and Soothsaying*. Detroit: Visible Ink Press, 2004

Fodor, Nandor: *Encyclopedia of Psychic Science*. London: Arthurs Press, 1933

Guiley, Rosemary Ellen: *Harper's Encyclopedia of Mystical & Paranormal Experience*. San Francisco: HarperSanFrancisco, 1991

SOOTHSAYERS

A soothsayer is, literally, a "truth-sayer;" one who speaks the truth. It is, by extension, a person who foretells future events. **Shamans, seers**, astrologers, **tarot card** readers, cheiromancers, and **sibyls** are all soothsayers in that sense, because they provide information about what they perceive to be the truth of coming events. A soothsayer also deals in the interpretations of **dreams**.

Sources:

Buckland, Raymond: *The Fortune-Telling Book: The Encyclopedia of Divination and Soothsaying*. Detroit: Visible Ink Press, 2004

Soul *see* Spirit

SPHERES

B ased on information obtained by **mediums** through contact with **spirits**, the **spirit world** has been described as having seven spheres. Although there is some contradictory information, generally the first sphere is seen as the realm of "gross and ignorant" spirits, and that it is gloomy and desolate there. The thought is that such an atmosphere will bring about a desire to move on. The second sphere has scenery as natural as that on earth, and has harmony, love and kindness. The higher spheres cannot be seen by those on the lower levels and information about them can only be obtained from those spirits who make a point of visiting the lower levels. However, it is believed that there is much about the higher levels that is simply beyond the comprehension of those on the lower levels and cannot, therefore, be adequately described. According to **Nandor Fodor**, it is said that "beyond the spheres are the supernal heavens of boundless extent. This is the ultimate abode of the glorified and blest."

Hudson Tuttle, in *Arcana of **Spiritualism*** (1876), views these different areas as zones or levels, rather than spheres specifically. He claims that they are 120 degrees wide, in other words they extend for 60 degrees on each side of the equator. Tuttle said, "Whether spirits can pass to other globes depends on their degree of refinement. While some are very pure and ethereal, others are gross and unrefined. The sensualist, the depraved

Peruvian Andean soothsayer Erick Caceres inhales ayahuasca through a shell during a ceremony where sooth-sayers announce their visions. *AP/WideWorld Photos.*

debauchee, in many instances, are so gross that gravity chains them to the earth's surface as it does man. They are denser than the spirit ether, and hence have weight, and cannot rise from the earth. Others, who are more spiritual, can only rise to the first sphere; while others, still more refined, pass at will through the universal ocean of ether, visiting other globes and solar systems."

The first **trance** reference to spheres was made by Frederica Hauffe (1801–1829), who was known as the "**Seeress** of Prevorst." She also drew diagrams of the spheres. Many other mediums have produced information about the spheres; much of it contradictory. **Geraldine Cummins**, in her book *The Road to Immortality* (supposedly dictated by the spirit of the then deceased **Frederick W. H. Myers**), gives the

"Chart of Existence" which shows the journey of the soul. The seven spheres are listed as,

1. The Plane of Matter
2. Hades or the Intermediate State
3. The Plane of Illusion
4. The Plane of Color
5. The Plane of Flame
6. The Plane of Light
7. Out Yonder, Timelessness

"Between each plane," the spirit said, "or new chapter in experience, there is existence in Hades, or in an intermediate state, when the soul reviews his (or her) past experiences and makes his choice, deciding whether he will go up or down the ladder of consciousness."

Emanuel Swedenborg's descriptions of the world beyond death included details of a number of spheres, "representing various shades of luminosity and happiness." Swedenborg said that in these spheres the scenery and conditions of this present plane were closely reproduced; there were houses and temples, halls for assemblies, and palaces for rulers. Possibly because his views were tinged by his theological background, he spoke of angels and devils, though he did say that both such were the spirits of those who had previously lived on earth and were either highly developed souls or undeveloped souls. He gave many views of the afterlife, all in great detail. Many of his ideas have been absorbed into Spiritualist beliefs.

Sources:

Buckland, Raymond: *Buckland's Book of Spirit Communications*. St. Paul: Llewellyn, 2004

Doyle, Sir Arthur Conan: *The History of Spiritualism*. New York: Doran, 1926

Shepard, Leslie A: *Encyclopedia of Occultism & Parapsychology*. New York: Avon Books, 1978

Spiricon *see* Meek, George W.

SPIRIT

The majority of books on **Spiritualism** speak of **spirit world, spirit guides, spirit photography**, spirit contact, and similar, but gloss over any kind of definition of spirit itself. It seems to be taken for granted that everyone knows what is meant by the word "spirit." In the Declaration of Principles adopted by the **National Spiritualist Association of Churches**, Principle 2 states, "We believe that the phenomena of nature, both physical and spiritual, are the expression of **Infinite Intelligence**." The *NSAC Spiritualist Manual* interprets this to mean, "In this manner we express our belief in the immanence of Spirit and that all forms of life are manifestations of Spirit or Infinite Intelligence, and thus that all men are children of God." This is the closest that the *NSAC Spiritualist Manual* comes to actually defining Spirit. Its "Definitions" (adopted October 9, 1914; October 24, 1919; and October 24,

1951) do not include an actual definition of spirit, although they do speak of the "spirit world."

The word "spirit" implies indestructible life. **Nandor Fodor** describes it as "the inmost principle, the divine particle, the vital essence, the inherent actuating element in life" (*Encyclopedia of Psychic Science*, 1933). He says that spirit dwells in the **astral body** or the soul. In many religious philosophies the terms "spirit" and "soul" are used interchangeably. Thomas Grimshaw, in his *General Course of the History, Science, Philosophy and Religion of Spiritualism* (1973) said, "Spirits are real people, human beings—men, women and children stripped of their outer garment of flesh, but still possessed of a real, substantial body that we know as the spiritual body."

Andrew Jackson Davis said, "... the term spirit is used to signify the centermost principle of man's existence, the divine energy or life of the soul of Nature. In yet other language, soul is the life of the outer body and the spirit is the life of the soul. After physical death, the soul or life of the material body becomes the form or body of the eternal spirit" (*The Harmonical Philosophy*, 1917).

According to Spiritualism, the body constitutes of three principles: physical body, soul, and spirit. All three—referred to as Spiritualism's "triune being"—are animated by Universal Spirit ... Infinite Intelligence. The **Morris Pratt** Institute's *Educational Course on Modern Spiritualism* teaches that:

- Spirit is the highest or innermost principle.
- Soul is the spiritual body and the intermediate principle.
- (Physical) body is the material or outermost principle and the clothing and vehicle for the first two.

As the innermost core of a deceased personality, "spirit" is the term used for the intelligence contacted by a **medium** at a **séance**. Children with mediumistic abilities often claim spirit children as their invisible playmates. In her book *There Is No Death* (1920), Florence Marryat wrote about the little girl Mabel Williams, daughter of

Portrait of disembodied soul drawn by a spirit guide controlling the hand of 19th century medium Ferdnand Desmoulin. *Courtesy Fortean Picture Library.*

English **clairvoyant** and **healing** medium Bessie Williams, saying, "I have watched her playing at ball with an invisible child, and have seen the ball thrown, arrested half way in the air, and then tossed back again as if a living child had been Mab's opponent." Spirit can, therefore, manifest in various forms. It can actually appear through **materializations**, making use of a medium's **ectoplasm**, and it can make its presence felt through such tools as **automatic writing, psychokinesis, apports**, and the like. However it is defined, spirit is the proof of ongoing life.

There are also spirits in the sense of entities that inhabit trees, plants, rocks, lakes, springs, etc. Such Nature Spirits were encountered by **Peter Caddy** and his associates in Findhorn, Scotland, and contributed to their survival in a previously desolate area. The focus of the Caddy's work was love, and it was always acknowledged that what was achieved came about with the help of the spirits of the land: the **fairies** and elves. There is plenty of evidence for such spirits, including evidence that others have also successfully called on them for help when needed. Many gardeners will claim that they have seen such nature spirits among the flowers and vegetables.

Native Americans of most tribes believed in a wide variety of spirits, including spirits of the sun, moon, mountains, rain, lightning and thunder. In general they make no distinction between nature spirits and human spirits or **ghosts**.

Sources:

Bletzer, June G.: *The Encyclopedia Psychic Dictionary.* Lithia Springs: New Leaf, 1998

Boddington, Harry: *The University of Spiritualism.* London: Spiritualist Press, 1947

Fodor, Nandor: *Encyclopedia of Psychic Science.* London: Arthurs Press, 1933

Grimshaw, Thomas: *General Course of the History, Science, Philosophy and Religion of Spiritualism.* Milwaukee: Morris Pratt Institute, 1973

SPIRIT GUIDE

Sometimes referred to as a Spirit Control, a Spirit Guide is a personal connection with the **spirit world**. Rita Berkowitz said, "Spirit Guides are here to watch out for us, help us understand life lessons, and help us find joy and wonder as we journey through our earth plane existence … Spirit guidess are always with us, whether or not we realize it, and that they are there to *guide* not to control." This is why the term "spirit control" is something of a misnomer. Yet at a **séance** the **medium**'s guide is in control to the extent of acting as a master or mistress of ceremonies; contacting other spirits and arranging their access to the medium.

Some people have more than one guide. For example, if a person does **healing** he or she might have a guide who is specifically connected with healing; perhaps someone who was a doctor in their earthly existence. Someone who paints might have an artist guide for that aspect of their life.

Spirit guides once lived earthly lives. Some are, or were, related to the person for whom they now guide. It could be a deceased family member or close friend. It seems that many people have **Native American** guides, while others have Orientals. In *This Is Spiritualism* (1959), **Maurice Barbanell** wrote, "The North American Indians were masters of **psychic** laws, with a profound knowledge of supernormal forces and how they operated. This qualifies them, after their passing, to act as tutors and guides to their mediums." Certainly most **Spiritualists** acknowledge that by their very lifestyle, being close to nature and working with the earth, Native Americans were probably much more in tune with the forces of nature than most.

Sources:

Berkowitz, Rita S. and Deborah S. Romaine: *The Complete Idiot's Guide to Communicating With Spirits.* New York: Penguin/Alpha, 2003

Bletzer, June G.: *The Encyclopedia Psychic Dictionary.* Lithia Springs: New Leaf, 1998

SPIRIT LIGHTS

Spirit lights are frequently seen when a **physical medium** is operating, though they can occasionally be observed apparently independently of any person. They are often dancing globules or sparks of light that seem to fill the air, indicating that there is **spirit** presence in the room. French **psychical researcher** Dr. Gustav Geley (1868–1924) conducted a **séance** with the Polish **medium Franek Kluski** on May 15, 1921. He reported, "A large luminous trail like a nebulous comet, and about half a metre long, formed behind Kluski about a metre above his head and seemingly about the same distance behind him. This nebula was constituted of tiny bright grains broadcast, among which there were some specially bright points. This nebula oscillated quickly from right to left and left to right, and rose and

fell. It lasted about a minute, disappeared and reappeared several times."

There is a long tradition of people seeing spirit lights, often unexpectedly but more often connected with their **meditating** or **praying**. The **shamanic** tradition honors what are sometimes called the "sparkies;" little dots of light—often blue, purple, or silver—that appear in front of a healer when healing work is being done and the healer has the third eye open. They are also commonly seen by spiritual seekers and seem to be linked to moments when connecting with aspects of the Higher Self, God/Goddess/All-That-Is, Infinite Intelligence, angels and spirit guides.

Sources:

Bletzer, June G.: *The Encyclopedia Psychic Dictionary.* Lithia Springs: New Leaf, 1998

Fodor, Nandor: *Encyclopedia of Psychic Science.* London: Arthurs Press, 1933

SPIRIT PHOTOGRAPHY

Spirit photographs, sometimes called **psychic** photographs, are photographs that reveal pictures of the deceased. According to Sir **Arthur Conan Doyle** (*The History of Spiritualism,* 1926), the first spirit photographs were probably taken by the English photographer **Richard Boursnell** in 1851. However **William H. Mumler** of Boston, Massachusetts, is generally regarded as the first **spirit** photographer.

One day in 1861, William Mumler was at the studio of a friend and amusing himself with the equipment. He tried to take a photograph of himself and produced a picture that showed another figure beside him. It was a young girl sitting in a chair, with the chair itself visible through her body. Mumler's technique had been to set up the camera and focus it on a chair. He would then uncap the lens and jump into position, standing beside the chair and holding still while the camera mechanism tripped and took the photograph. On the back of that first photograph that was produced, he wrote,

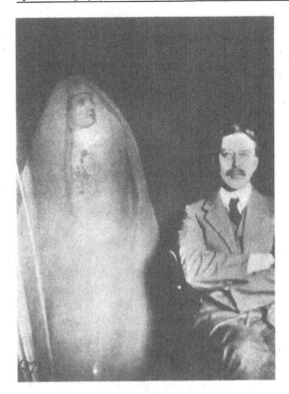

Psychic (or spirit) photograph taken by Richard Boursnell in October, 1904. *Courtesy Fortean Picture Library.*

"This photograph was taken of myself, by myself, on Sunday, when there was not a living soul in the room beside me— so to speak. The form on my right I recognize as my cousin, who passed away about twelve years since."

The **spirit world** had predicted the advent of spirit photographs. Thomas Slater, an optician, was holding a **séance** with Lord Brougham and Robert Owen in 1856, when the received **rappings** spelled out that Slater would one day take spirit photographs. Owen commented that if he was dead by the time such photographs were possible, then he would make a point of appearing in one himself. According to *The Spiritualist* of November 1, 1873, that is exactly what happened.

Unfortunately spirit photography was an area where it was easy for the unscrupulous to perpe-

trate fraud, through double exposures and similar. Many of the early spirit photographers kept a stock of photographic plates that had been exposed one time with a model posing. When a person then came, hoping for a true spirit photograph, the photographer would place such a prepared plate in the camera, pose the subject and take the picture. When it was then immediately developed it would show the subject *and* the extra—apparently a spirit.

One of the ways to ensure that a photograph was a true spirit photograph was if the extra figure could be identified as a deceased relative or close loved one of the sitter. If there was no way the photographer could have known that particular person was coming for a portrait, there was little likelihood that the accurate image could be planted ahead of time. However, if the photographer did not process the plate immediately, he could still superimpose a picture—or even a series of pictures around the sitter's image—when he later developed the plate, if he had access to a picture of the deceased.

This ease of making fake spirit photographs is the main reason that they fell out of favor. It does not mean, however, that spirit photographs are not possible. Today the trend is to concentrate on **infrared** still and video images, especially during séances and at allegedly **haunted** sites. Infrared is the electromagnetic radiation outside the color spectrum range of visibility, at the lower end and next to the red. Infrared film has been sensitized to this radiation. It can be used where the light is too dim to allow regular photography, making it possible to photograph things that cannot be seen under many séance conditions (e.g. ectoplasm, spirit forms).

Rosemary Guiley reports that the Ghost Research Society of Oak Lawn, Illinois, collects spirit photographs from around the world. The society analyzes the photographs received by scanning them into a computer and digitizing them. This produces images with far higher resolution than is usually the case, allowing minute details to be examined. The photographs can then be printed out on a laser printer. According to the society, some photographs that seem to be spirit photographs are actually the result of **thoughtography**, of the sort exhibited by **Ted Serios.**

Sources:

Doyle, Sir Arthur Conan: *The History of Spiritualism.* New York: Doran, 1926

Eisenbud, Jule: *The World of Ted Serios: "Thoughtographic" Studies of an Extraordinary Mind.* New York: William Morrow, 1967

Guiley, Rosemary Ellen: *The Encyclopedia of Ghosts and Spirits.* New York: Facts On File, 1992

SPIRIT WORLD

Thomas Grimshaw said in his *General Course of the History, Science, Philosophy and Religion of Spiritualism* (1973), "The Spirit World is a real world, just as real to **spirits** functioning through their spirit bodies as the physical world is to us who function through our physical bodies." It is the place where we make our homes after transitioning from the earth plane.

The spirit world is the level of existence where there are no boundaries, as we know them on earth; no boundaries of time, space, and tangibility. Also, there are no divisions, as in the Christian concept of "Heaven" and "Hell" (plus the Roman Catholics' "purgatory"). The spirit world is just one place; neither "good" nor "bad" and having neither rewards nor punishments. **Andrew Jackson Davis** named it "the **Summerland.**"

The view of Emanuel Swedenborg was that the world of spirit had been separated from the earthly world for good reason and that communication between the two was possible, but only for very cogent reasons—not simply out of mild curiosity.

Medium **Robert Lees** (1849–1931) produced a series of volumes of which he claimed were dictated to him. He said that one Christmas Eve, a stranger suddenly appeared before him, though the door was locked. The stranger proceeded to dictate the remarkable volume *Through the Mists* (London, 1898), outlining the nature of the spirit world. This book created tremendous interest and went through more than twenty editions.

Mediums have received many details of the spirit world by way of their **spirit guides**; the teachings of **Maurice Barbanell**'s Silver Birch are highly regarded. Further details have been found in the documentation of **near death experiences**, as noted by such researchers as **Raymond Moody** and **Elisabeth Kübler-Ross.** The *Spiritualist Manual*, issued by the **National Spiritualist Association of Churches**, contains a section titled "Nature of the Spirit World: Its Conditions and Employments," that was delivered in a trance address by medium Mary T. Longley, of Los Angeles, California.

In an interview with Ruth Brod, Maurice Barbanell expanded on his views of the spirit world, saying,

> What is called the spirit world is not some far-off geographically situated planet—it is part of the universe in which we live. There are no hard and fast boundaries between this world and what is wrongly called the next. They are both parts of one universe, and these aspects mingle and blend and merge all the time. But because of the constant, growing materialism in which man lives, he more or less automatically cuts himself off from the spiritual world, which is as much a part of his natural habitat as is the physical world. This is one of the reasons why so many primitive people remain naturally psychic—because they live close to nature. They haven't become town dwellers forced into materialistic pursuits in order to make a living, so they are normally accessible to the more subtle vibrations of the spirit world.

Sources:

Barbanell, Maurice: *This Is Spiritualism.* Oxshott: The Spiritual Truth Press, 1959

Berkowitz, Rita S. and Deborah S. Romaine: *The Complete Idiot's Guide to Communicating With Spirits.* New York: Penguin/Alpha, 2003

Buckland, Raymond: *Buckland's Book of Spirit Communications*. St. Paul: Llewellyn, 2004

Grimshaw, Thomas: *General Course of the History, Science, Philosophy and Religion of Spiritualism*. Milwaukee: Morris Pratt Institute, 1973

Robert James Lees Biography & Links: http://www.rjlees.co.uk

SPIRITISM; SPIRITIST

Spiritism is the French form of **Spiritualism** that was developed and promoted by **Allan Kardec** (Léon-Dénizard-Hippolyte Rivail—1804–1869).

Kardec was a member of the Society of Magnetism, which led to his investigation of somnambulism, **trance, clairvoyance**, and similar phenomena. In 1850, the phenomenon of **table tipping** came to France. Kardec recognized it as an important step in the communication between the worlds of the living and the dead. However, he was not himself a **medium** and so had to rely on others for all of his information. He was encouraged by the **spirits** to publish his findings. The title given to his first book of spirit teachings (again on the advice of the spirits themselves) was *Le Livre des Esprits* or *The Spirits' Book* (1857). The book sold extremely well throughout France and across the Continent. From later material, Kardec published *The Mediums' Book* (1861), which came to rank right alongside its precursor.

One of the teachings received by Kardec was the acknowledgement of **reincarnation** as a fact. This was—as it still is, with Spiritualists—a controversial subject. Kardec made a point of publishing only views that agreed with his acceptance of reincarnation. He also dismissed such things as **physical mediumship**, totally ignoring such famous physical mediums as **Daniel Dunglas Home**, for example, because Home did not believe in reincarnation.

Over the years Kardec's influence faded in his native France but flourished in South America—especially Brazil—and, to a lesser extent, in the Philippines. Kardec had adopted the terms "Spiritism" and "Spiritist" for his version of Spiritualism. These terms were used in South America along with the term "Kardecism" (*Kardecismo*). Today in Brazil there are Kardecist/Spiritist psychiatric hospitals in operation and fully accepted. The Instituto Brasileiro de Pesquisas Psicobiofisic, or the Brazilian Institute of Psycho-Biophysical Research, collects and studies Spiritist works. It was founded in 1963 by Hernani Andrade.

According to Guy Lion Playfair (*The Flying Cow*, 1975), "Members of Kardecist centres tend to come from the upper and middle classes, and they may be federal and state deputies, city mayors, police chiefs, surgeons, lawyers, bank managers, engineers, doctors—in fact, members of any profession you care to name." He also makes the point that Spiritists may also be Spiritualists but the reverse may not be true. Playfair said, "Followers of *umbanda* and *candomblé* may loosely be termed Spiritists as well, but when a Brazilian declares himself to be an *espírita*, he means that he is a believer in Kardecist Spiritism."

Sources:

Doyle, Sir Arthur Conan: *The History of Spiritualism*. New York: Doran, 1926

Fodor, Nandor: *Encyclopedia of Psychic Science*. London: Arthurs Press, 1933

Guiley, Rosemary Ellen: *The Encyclopedia of Ghosts and Spirits*. New York: Facts On File, 1992

Kardec, Allen: *The Spirits' Book*. (1857) New York: Studium, 1980

Playfair, Guy Lion: *The Flying Cow: Research into Paranormal Phenomena in the World's Most Psychic Country*. London: Souvenir Press, 1975

SPIRITUAL FRONTIERS FELLOWSHIP INTERNATIONAL

The Spiritual Frontiers Fellowship International was founded in 1956 by **Arthur Augustus Ford** (1897–1971), Paul Higgins, and Albin Bro. It is an interfaith, nonprofit movement. Although originating in the West, its spiritual orientation has long recognized the need to blend both Eastern and Western traditions. Its stated goal is, "Spiritual unfoldment within the individual, through the exploration of both old and new dimensions of human experience leading to a unity of body, mind and **spirit** ... It searches for eternal truths, explores cultural myths, investigates ancient secrets, and seeks experiential and intellectual (cognitive) ways to integrate these insights into daily living."

The Fellowship sought to express its goal philosophically through an emphasis on the exploration of mystical prayer and **meditation**, **spiritual healing**, and the survival of consciousness beyond the limits of bodily death. It maintains a library of several thousand volumes and publishes a monthly newsletter.

Sources:

Fodor, Nandor: *Encyclopedia of Psychic Science*. London: Arthurs Press, 1933

Encyclopedia of Religion and Society: http://hirr.hart sem.edu/ency/SFFI.htm

Spiritual Frontiers Fellowship International: http://www.spiritualfrontiers.org

SPIRITUAL HEALING

In spiritual healing it is frequently the **spirit** of a deceased doctor or surgeon who comes through the **medium** to give or suggest the necessary healing. Sometimes it is the **spirit guide** of the medium. **Gladys Osborne Leonard's Native American** guide, North Star, would work through her. She described it in *My Life In Two Worlds* (1931), "When North Star controlled me for **healing**, he always appeared to appeal to someone far higher than himself before commencing his treatment. He never spoke, but he used to hold his hands upward and outward as if he expected something to be put or poured into them. His attitude was so obviously one of **prayer**, or supplication, though he was usually in a standing position."

The **National Spiritualist Association of Churches** gives this definition of Spiritual Healing:

1. It is the sense of this convention that Spiritual Healing is a gift possessed by certain **Spiritualist** mediums, and that this gift is exercised by and through the direction and influence of excarnate spiritual beings for the relief, cure and healing of both mental and physical diseases of humankind; and that the results of spiritual healing are produced in several ways, to wit:

   (a) By the spiritual influences working through the body of the medium and thus infusing curative, stimulating and vitalizing fluids and energy into the diseased parts of the patient's body.

   (b) By the spiritual influences illuminating the brain of the healing medium and thereby intensifying the perception of the medium so that the cause, nature and seat of the disease in the patient become known to the medium.

   (c) Through the application of absent treatments whereby spiritual beings combine their own healing forces with the magnetism and vitalizing energy of the medium and convey them to the patient who is distant from the medium and cause them to be absorbed by the system of the patient.

2. It is further the sense of this convention that Spiritual Healing is recognized by the New Testament Scriptures and that it has been a tenet of ancient and modern religions and that it has been and is now a tenet of the religion of Spiritualism and is practiced by and among Spiritualists in conformity with their religious belief and knowledge of the power of spiritual agencies.

3. It is further the sense of this convention that great care and caution should be exercised in determining whether an applicant for a Healer's Commission really possesses any of the phases of the gift of Spiritual Healing to a sufficient degree to warrant the issuance of a commission.

4. That no person to whom a Spiritual Healer's Commission may be issued shall advertise other than as a "Spiritual Healer," unless legally entitled to do so.

Tibetan Buddhist Tenzing Lama (right) performs spiritual healing on a woman who lost her son and daughter-in-law to the tsunami that struck Southeast Asia on December 26, 2004. *AP/WideWorld Photos.*

5. That it is further the sense of this convention that any statute or ordinance which tends to resist or forbid the exercise of Spiritual Healing is an invasion of the religious rights, privileges and guarantees contained in the Federal Constitution.

Medium **George Chapman** works as a healer with deceased surgeon Dr. William Lang working through him. Munich-born Dr. Adolphus Fritz, who died in 1918, worked through Brazilian psychic healer **José Arigó**. Another Brazilian healer, **Edivaldo Silva**, has a number of different deceased doctors and surgeons working through him.

Sources:
Bletzer, June G.: *The Encyclopedia Psychic Dictionary*. Lithia Springs: New Leaf, 1998

Fodor, Nandor: *Encyclopedia of Psychic Science*. London: Arthurs Press, 1933

Kingston, Jeremy: *The Supernatural: Healing Without Medicine*. London: Aldus, 1975

Leonard, Gladys Osborne: *My Life in Two Worlds*. London: Two Worlds, 1931

National Spiritualist Association of Churches: *Spiritualist Manual*. Lily Dale: NSAC, 1911; 2002

SPIRITUALISM; SPIRITUALIST

Spiritualism is a movement that started in the mid-eighteenth century, sparked by the episode of the **Fox Family** in **Hydesville**, New York, in 1848. It has become a religion, a philosophy, and a science, though it tends to focus on communication with the world of **spirits** of the dead. Margaretta and Kate, later joined by Leah, Fox showed that such contact was possible and inspired thousands to try to renew communication with loved ones who had died.

In its early days, Spiritualism became a breeding ground for fraudulent **mediums** and those seeking fame and fortune. However, there were many who showed that true contact was possible. In its heyday, Spiritualism commanded more than two million followers on both sides of the Atlantic. Repeated exposés by **psychical researchers** and scientists quickly reduced that number, but a devoted core remains and is still active today. There have been some outstanding mediums never found to be fraudulent, such as **William Stainton Moses, Daniel Dunglas Home, Eileen Garrett, Ena Twigg, Estelle Roberts, George Anderson, Jean Cull**, and others.

Many enthusiasts made the movement into a religion, inspiring Spiritualist churches of various types. The movement became especially big in South America, in **Brazil** in particular, though there the focus was on what is termed **Spiritism**— inspired by the work of **Allan Kardec**. The focus of a lot of the Spiritualist groups, whether religiously affiliated or not, is **healing** of the sick through the agencies of departed medical experts, which is termed **spiritual healing**. The laying-on of hands, **auric** healing, Reiki, and similar are also very popular and effective.

Home circles, or **séances** (meaning "sittings"), allowed the movement to develop with groups of friends working together, with or without a professional medium, thus eliminating a controlling priesthood. From the use of **talking boards, automatic writing, clairvoyance, clairaudience, clairsentience**, etc., a true grassroots movement gave Spiritualism a foundation that it may never totally lose. In 1951, with the passing of the **Fraudulent Mediums Act** in England, Spiritualism there became legal as a religion. Today has seen something of a worldwide renaissance of Spiritualism, with outstanding mediums such as **John Edward, James van Praagh, Tony Stockwell, Colin Fry**, and **Gordon Smith** appearing not in semi-dark-

ened rooms but under the bright lights of television, with live audiences. A Gallup poll showed that in 1996, twenty percent of adults questioned expressed a belief that it was possible for the dead to communicate with the living. Another twenty-two percent believed it *might* be possible.

Figures published on the British Office of National Statistics' website at the end of 2004 showed that Spiritualism has emerged as Britain's eighth largest religious group, according to the ***Psychic News*** newspaper. The figures show that there are more Spiritualists in Great Britain than there are Roman Catholics.

Sources:
Brown, Slater: *The Heyday of Spiritualism*. New York: Hawthorn, 1970

Buckland, Raymond: *Buckland's Book of Spirit Communications*. St. Paul: Llewellyn, 2004

Edward, John: *Crossing Over: The Stories Behind the Stories*. New York: Princess Books, 2001

Owens, Elizabeth: *How to Communicate With Spirits*. St. Paul: Llewellyn, 2002

Psychic News, #3782, January 8, 2005. Stansted, Essex

Spiritualist Association of Great Britain
see **Marylebone Spiritualist Association**

SPIRITUALISTS' NATIONAL UNION

The British Spiritualists' National Union (SNU) is one of the largest **Spiritualist** organizations in the world and is the recognized national body of Spiritualism in the United Kingdom. It was founded in July, 1890, in Manchester, England, as the Spiritualists' National Federation. It was founded by **Emma Hardinge Britten**, who had started **Two Worlds** magazine three years earlier. The Union has been legally recognized by the British Home Office as an appointing body for Spiritualist Ministers since 1939. In 1948, the SNU merged with the British **Lyceum** Union. This had been founded in 1890 for the Spiritualist education of youth and children.

The Union is made up of affiliated Churches, individual members, and Mission Churches. The basis of the "Seven Principles of Spiritualism" adopted by the Union as its religious philosophy was communicated in 1871 by Robert Owen, through Emma Hardinge Britten's mediumship. The first President was W. Johnson, though in 1891—when it was still the Spiritualists' National Federation—the President was J. B. M'Indoe with **Hannen Swaffer** named Honorary President.

Sources:

Guiley, Rosemary Ellen: *The Encyclopedia of Ghosts and Spirits.* New York: Facts On File, 1992

Spiritualists' National Union: http://www.snu.org.uk

"SPLITFOOT, MR."

"**M**r. Splitfoot" was the name given by Katie Fox, one of the **Fox Sisters**, to the **spirit** that later came to be identified as **Charles B. Rosna**, the peddler who was murdered in the Fox Cottage. The name probably derives from the child's thoughts of the Christian devil with its cloven hooves. According to a statement made by the girl's mother, Mrs. Margaret Fox, on the night of Friday, March 31, 1848, "My youngest child, Cathie, said 'Mr. Splitfoot, do as I do,' clapping her hands. The sound instantly followed her with the same number of **raps**."

Sources:

Somerlott, Robert: *"Here, Mr. Splitfoot"—An Informal Exploration into Modern Occultism.* New York: Viking Press, 1971

Weisberg, Barbara: *Talking With the Dead.* San Francisco: HarperSanFrancisco, 2004

SPOKESPERSON

When working with a **talking board, table tipping, rappings,** or any of a number of the simpler methods of **spirit** communications, it is as well to appoint one of the sitters as "spokesperson." If anyone has a question, they should give it to the spokesperson to ask. Different people asking different questions—with sometimes more than one trying to speak at the same time—can be very confusing even in everyday life. It is therefore a good idea to have just one person dealing with the spirit(s).

Sources:

Buckland, Raymond: *Buckland's Book of Spirit Communications.* St. Paul: Llewellyn, 2004

SPRIGGS, GEORGE (1850–1912)

George Spriggs was a Welsh **materialization** medium. He discovered his abilities in 1877 and joined The Circle of Light in Cardiff, working as a **medium** for them. He had two main **spirit guides**, both of whom were **Native American**: Swiftwater and Shiwaukee.

What was special about Spriggs's materializations was that the **spirits** would move away from the medium, to walk about the house and even to be seen out in the garden. This would occur in the light of the late evening. As many as three figures would appear at the same time and sometimes change form into a different spirit. These wandering spirits were once observed by Spriggs's neighbors, who threatened to call the police and to charge him with "dealings with the devil."

In November 1880, Spriggs went to Melbourne, Australia, and produced similar materializations. One of the spirits held out at arms length a 14-pound stone. Another drank water, ate cookies, and wrote a letter. After six years, Spriggs's materialization powers seemed to fade, though he continued to hold **séances** with **clairvoyance** and **direct voice**. He also diagnosed disease and prescribed treatments through the spirits.

Spriggs returned to England in 1900, and from 1903 to 1905 gave free medical advice at the London Spiritual Alliance. The Psycho-Therapeutic Society was formed through his efforts. Spriggs died in 1912.

Sources:

Fodor, Nandor: *Encyclopedia of Psychic Science.* London: Arthurs Press, 1933

Estelle Stead, daughter of William T. Stead, whose image appears on her photograph taken by Ada Deane in October, 1915. W.T. Stead died in the Titanic shipwreck of 1912. *Courtesy Fortean Picture Library.*

STEAD, WILLIAM T. (1849–1912)

William T. Stead was a great British champion of **Spiritualism.** He edited the *Northern Echo* in Darlington, Yorkshire, and in 1883 took over the editorship of London's popular *Pall Mall Gazette.* In 1890, he founded the *Review of Reviews* where, at December, 1891, he published his *Real* **Ghost** *Stories.* This was the start of his demonstrated interest in **psychic** matters. The following year Stead discovered that he had the ability to do **automatic writing.** On March 14, 1893, he addressed the members of the **London Spiritualist Alliance** and told of his receipt of communications from a Chicago journalist, Julia Ames, who had died shortly before.

In 1893, Stead began publication of *Borderland,* a quarterly psychic magazine that ran for four years. In the Christmas, 1893, issue of the *Review of Reviews,* Stead published a story of his own, about the dangers of icebergs to shipping on the Atlantic Ocean. This theme cropped up a number of times in his writings. In the *Pall Mall Gazette* one year, he carried the story of a survivor from the sinking of a liner and in his editorial said, "This is exactly what might take place if liners are sent to sea short of (life) boats." More than twenty years later, he was invited to speak at Carnegie Hall, New York, on April 21, 1912. He set out aboard the *Titanic* to visit America. Before he left he wrote to his secretary, "I feel as if something was going to happen, somewhere, or somehow. And that it will be for good."

Sources:

Fodor, Nandor: *Encyclopedia of Psychic Science.* London: Arthurs Press, 1933

STELLA C. (CRANSHAW) (B. 1902)

Stella Crenshaw was a nurse and a **medium** discovered in 1923 by British **psychical researcher Harry Price.** Price met her on a train, and they conversed about psychical research. Stella was not greatly interested in her **psychic** powers and only reluctantly agreed to work with Price.

Known as "Stella C.," she sat for investigations at the **National Laboratory of Psychical Research** in London. One of the first things Price noticed was the drop in temperature when Stella was working. Tables of temperatures were kept that showed that on every occasion of a **séance** the temperature would fall anywhere from 1 degree to as much as 20.5 degrees. It was presumed that the energy was absorbed by the medium to produce the effects.

Stella was able to move things psychokinetically, leading Price to invent his "telekinetoscope;" described by Stuart Holroyd in *The Supernatural: Minds Without Boundaries* (1975), "(It) contained two electrical contacts that normally required a two-ounce pressure to bring them together. They were protected from physical interference by a soap bubble, a glass shade, and a cage. When the electrical contact was made a red bulb would light up." At her first attempt, Stella caused the bulb to light. Examination showed that the soap bubble and the glass shade were intact. Stella had caused the two electrical contacts to come together by the force of her mind. At another sitting, she **levitated** a heavy table and then allowed it to fall and be completely demolished.

Stella was subjected to a number of Price's inventions, all designed to prevent any sort of fraud on the part of the medium. He even had a system of **infrared** projectors in the walls and ceiling of the séance room and he designed and had built (by H. W. Pugh) a fraudproof table. This table could hold items such as musical instruments while keeping them inaccessible to the medium. Stella caused the instruments to play and she also produced **ectoplasm**. Roy Stemman described, "Stella Cranshaw sat at this table with other sitters, two of whom held her hands and feet throughout the proceedings. Soon after she went into **trance**, sounds were heard coming from within the table, such as the ringing of a bell or the playing of a harmonica. The trapdoor in the table top was pushed up from inside and when a handkerchief was placed over it sitters felt finger-like forms moving beneath it."

Stella worked with Price for five years but was never greatly interested in her own abilities. She never charged for any of her sittings and had no interest in any other psychic work. In 1928, she married Leslie Deacon and ceased to give séances altogether.

Sources:

Fodor, Nandor: *Encyclopedia of Psychic Science*. London: Arthurs Press, 1933

Holroyd, Stuart: *The Supernatural: Minds Without Boundaries*. London: Aldus, 1975

Stemmen, Roy: *Mysteries of Mind Space & Time; the Unexplained: Survival—The Solid Evidence?* Westport: H. S. Stuttman, 1992

Stemman, Roy: *The Supernatural: Spirits and Spirit Worlds*. London: Aldus, 1975

STEWART, BALFOUR (1827–1887)

Balfour Stewart was Professor of Natural Philosophy at Owens College in Manchester, England. He received the Rumford Medal of the Royal Society for his discovery of the law of equality between the absorptive and radiative powers of bodies. He was President of the **Society for Psychical Research** from 1885 to 1887, and joint author, with Professor Tait, of *The Unseen Universe*. This book created a stir in scientific circles since it was the first serious scientific attempt to oppose a **spiritual** view of the universe to the prevailing materialistic one.

Sources:

Fodor, Nandor: *Encyclopedia of Psychic Science*. London: Arthurs Press, 1933

STOCKWELL, TONY (B. 1969)

Anthony Stockwell was born on February 20, 1969, to Pat and Keith Stockwell. He was born in Walthamstow in the East End of London, England. When he was four years old, the family moved to Canvey Island, Essex, where he attended school. On leaving school at age sixteen, Stockwell attended his first meeting at a **Spiritualist** church and knew instantly that he had found his calling.

Stockwell took a job in sales at age seventeen, but continued to study Spiritualism and to attend Spiritualist churches. One night he was confronted by the **spirit** of a young Tibetan monk who said that Stockwell had lived a previous life in Tibet and that the **spirit world** hoped he would fulfill his destiny of becoming a **medium**. He began to sit on a regular basis with **trance** medium Marcia Ford, whose **spirit guide** was Ta Po, a Tibetan monk. Ta Po introduced Stockwell to his own spirit guide, a ninety-two-year-old Tibetan monk named Zintar. Then, at eighteen, Stockwell was invited to be a part of an exclusive development circle. It was two years before he gave his first messages in public, but was very accurate when he did. In a later address at a Spiritualist church, there were some physical manifestations, with flowers being moved and levitated. Stockwell also started to do some very successful spirit **healing**.

At age twenty-one, Stockwell formerly dedicated his life to spirit. Over the next year, he started leading his own development circles. He taught development groups at the **College of Psychic Studies** in South Kensington, London, and in Wickford, Essex. He also began to have private sittings with people who needed to contact dead loved ones. Stockwell founded the Avalon Project with his life partner Stuart, to promote mediumistic and spiritual learning. In 2002, he was approached by fellow medium **Colin Fry**, who had a successful television program called *6th Sense*. His production company wanted another similar program but with a younger, fresh psychic/medium. After a couple of successful pilot episodes, the production company

launched Stockwell as the *Street Psychic*. This was a success and was followed by *Psychic School*, where Stockwell taught people how to bring out their own **psychic** energies. On the heels of these successes, Stockwell was invited to America to do *Street Psychic in San Francisco*. He also made a number of guest appearances on Colin Fry's *6th Sense* and a variety of other television programs.

Stockwell has gone from success to success but never lost sight of the fact that he is doing a service to those who have lost loved ones. He has become one of the top British psychic mediums of modern times. He has taught for the **Spiritualist Association of Great Britain** and at the **Arthur Findlay** College at Stanstead Hall, home of the **Spiritualists' National Union**.

Sources:

Stockwell, Tony: *Spirited: Living Between Two Worlds—A Top Psychic Medium's Extraordinary Story.* London: Hodder and Stoughton, 2004

Tony Stockwell Homepage: http://www.tonystockwell.com

STOKES, DORIS (D.1987)

Doris Stokes was a British **Spiritualist medium** who became aware of her **psychic** gifts as a child, when she saw many deceased relatives. She had a special relationship with her father, who once told her, "All you've got to do is put out your hand and I'll be there to take hold." He was as good as his word and frequently came through to her after his passing, acting as her **spirit guide**.

Stokes came to prominence in 1978 when she undertook a series of tests on American television. She was a great success and did much to popularize mediumship. At the height of her popularity, she filled London's Royal Albert Hall to capacity and also filled the Sydney Opera House in Australia three nights in a row. Stokes claimed to communicate with the deceased John Lennon. Despite illness, she continued to tour extensively. She authored a number of books, including *Voices In My Ear* (1980), *More Voices In My Ear* (1981), *Innocent Voices In My Ear*, and *Whispering Voices*. Stokes died in 1987 after an extended illness.

Sources:

Doris Stokes Biography & Links: http://www.the-psychics.co.uk/doris-stokes.htm

STRATFORD, CONNECTICUT

In 1850, Stratford, Connecticut, was the scene of **poltergeist** phenomena. It started on March 10 of that year and continued for eight months, all at the home of Rev. Dr. Eliakim Phelps, a Presbyterian minister named.

As with most poltergeist occurrences, the phenomena seemed to center around a young child. In this case it was an eleven-year-old boy named Harry, one of four children in the house. In one instance, Harry's bed burst into flames; at another time his school books were destroyed; at another time his clothes were torn to shreds. **Rapping** was heard. **Andrew Jackson Davis** visited the house and commented that the raps were produced by electricity discharging from Harry. He said, "Young Harry frequently failed to discriminate during certain moments of mental agitation between the sounds and effects which he himself made and those sounds which were produced by **spiritual** presence."

Letters to the *New Haven Journal*, written by Phelps's neighbors, reported on the case. Initially various objects in the home were displaced while the family was at church. Then, on the family's return, objects would start to fly about the house. Many things in the house were broken due to this poltergeist activity. One of the most peculiar occurrences was the appearance of what have been described as "curious, stuffed effigies." A letter in the *New Haven Journal* said, "They were all female figures … Some of the figures were kneeling beside the beds, and some bending their faces to the floor in attitudes of deep humility. In the center of the group was a dwarf, most grotesquely arrayed; and above was a figure so suspended as to seem flying through the air." These effigies sometimes appeared in a room that had been locked and at a time when it was known no one had been there. The letter concluded that the whole assembly "was most beautiful and picturesque, and had a grace and ease and speaking effect that seemed the attributes of a higher creation."

Another time Rev. Phelps was writing, alone at his desk, when he turned away for a brief moment. When he turned back he found that a sheet of paper that had been blank was now covered with strange writing, with the ink still wet. This came to be the start of spirit correspondences, many of which came in hieroglyphs. The majority of the phenomena has never been explained.

Sources:
Fodor, Nandor: *Encyclopedia of Psychic Science*. London: Arthurs Press, 1933

SUMMERLAND

Summerland is the name given to the afterlife by **Andrew Jackson Davis** and adopted by most of **Spiritualism**. Sir **Arthur Conan Doyle** said that he believed "'the Summerland,' as Davis has named it,

is quite as real and objective to its inmates as our world is to us." Harry Boddington said, "Andrew Jackson Davis is often believed to have taught a fixed locality for his 'Summerland' and the various states he depicted. Each of these was described as adjoining the other in regular order, graduated to suit the type and quality of its inhabitants, with a radiant source of light at its center permeating the whole." **Frederick W. H. Myers** said that it is a "plane of illusion (which) appears to be a blissful land of rest and harmony, partly a creation of the inhabitant's own desires and the pleasures of earth-life, minus its drawbacks."

Sources:
Boddington, Harry: *The University of Spiritualism*. London: Spiritualist Press, 1947

Doyle, Sir Arthur Conan: *The History of Spiritualism*. New York: Doran, 1926

Myers, F. W. H.: *Human Personality and Its Survival After Bodily Death*. London: Longmans, 1903

SWAFFER, HANNEN (1879–1962)

Hannen Swaffer was a British Fleet Street journalist—known as "the Pope of Fleet Street"—who became a great advocate of **Spiritualism**. He wrote for the newspapers the *Daily Express* and the *Sunday Express* as theater critic, among other things. Swaffer created a lot of enemies with his blunt assessments of actors' performances. The actor Raymond Massey said, "Hannen Swaffer, a critic and theatre writer on the *Daily Express*, entered Noel Coward's dressing room after a fine performance in S. N. Behrman's *The Second Man* unannounced. He had been insufferable in his abuse of Noel (and of me too). 'Nowley,' he sneered in his assumed cockney accent, 'I've always said you could act better than you write.' 'And I've always said the same about you,' was Noel's instant reply."

Swaffer once said, of his own job, "Freedom of the press in Britain means freedom to print such of the proprietor's prejudices as the advertisers don't object to."

Swaffer was a good friend of **Maurice Barbanell** and many other prominent Spiritualists. Sir **Henry Segrave** went to talk with Swaffer about Spiritualism after receiving a lifesaving message from **spirit** by way of an anonymous sitter with a **home circle** group. The journalist arranged **séances** at his own apartment, which Segrave attended. At one of these, the **medium** Archie Emmet Adams caused a piano to **levitate** and produced other physical phenomena. Later in his racing life Segrave commented, "The only time I was ever frightened was when I saw a piano jump in Hannen Swaffer's flat."

Swaffer also introduced Lionel Logue to medium Lilian Bailey, at a time when Logue was desperate and considering suicide after the death of his wife. Logue was the Austalian speech therapist who cured England's King George VI of his stutter. Bailey was able to help Logue and he remained forever grateful to Swaffer for the introduction. Swaffer was one of the people most active in the **Spiritualists' National Union**, along with **Arthur Findlay**, Sir **Arthur Conan Doyle**, and Maurice Barbanell. He died in 1962.

Sources:

Barbanell, Maurice: *This Is Spiritualism*. Oxshott: The Spiritual Truth Press, 1959

Hannen Swaffer Quotations: http://www.saidwhat.co.uk/quotes/h/hannen_swaffer_1535.php

SWEDENBORG, EMMANUEL (1688–1772)

Emanuel Swedenborg was a Swedish engineer, philosopher, and mystic. He was a military engineer who turned the fortunes of a campaign for Charles XII of Sweden. He was an authority on astronomy and physics, and on the tides and latitudes. He was also a zoologist and anatomist. Swedenborg was a **Spiritualist** before there was such a term.

Regarded as one of the greatest and most learned men of his country, Swedenborg was born in Stockholm on January 29, 1688. He was the second son of Jesper Swedberg, a Lutheran pastor who was later appointed Bishop of Skara. Emanuel assumed the name Swedenborg when he was elevated to nobility by Queen Ulrica in 1719. He was educated at Uppsala University, and after graduating in 1710, he traveled throughout Europe for five years, pursuing scientific and mechanical knowledge.

In 1716, Swedenborg started the publication of a scientific periodical called *Dædalus hyperboreus*. Charles XII of Sweden was interested in the publication, and appointed Swedenborg as Assessor Extraordinary to the Royal College of Mines, a position Swedenborg held for thirty years. He finally resigned to devote the rest of his life to spreading the spiritual enlightenment for which he believed himself to have been especially chosen. Although he accepted the **Bible** as the work of God, he said that its true meaning was quite different from its seeming meaning, and that only he, Emanuel Swedenborg—with the help of the **angels**—could give its true meaning.

In 1734, Swedenborg published an important work, *Opera Philosophica et Mineralia*, about the formation of the planets. In the same year, he published *Prodomus Philosophiæ Ratiocinantrio de Infinte*, on the relationship between the finite and the infinite and between the **soul** and the body. He followed these with other major works on anatomy, geology, and mineralogy. Swedenborg believed he was in direct communication with heavenly **spirits** and in his books recorded conversations he had with them. He was an established **clairvoyant**. At one time—through **astral projection** or, as it was then known, "traveling clairvoyance"—he was able to describe a fire that was taking place in Stockholm, more than 250 miles away from where he was. This was attested to by the philosopher Immanuel Kant, who was present when Swedenborg described the fire and who followed up on it to check the facts. Swedenborg had shown similar **psychic** ability as a child.

Swedenborg had his first vision in 1744, at the age of fifty-six. He saw "a kind of vapor steaming from the pores of my body. It was a most visible watery vapor and fell downwards to the ground upon the carpet." To a modern-day Spiritualist, this was an apt description of **ectoplasm**. His later descriptions of the world beyond death included details of a number of **spheres**, "representing various shades of luminosity and happiness," according to Sir **Arthur Conan Doyle**. Swedenborg said that in these spheres, the scenery and conditions of this present plane were closely reproduced; there were houses and temples, halls for assemblies, and palaces for rulers. Possibly because his views were tinged by his theological background, he spoke of angels and devils, though he did say that both such were the spirits of those who had previously lived on earth and were either highly developed souls or undeveloped souls. He gave many views of the afterlife, all in great detail. Many of his ideas have been absorbed into Spiritualist beliefs.

At the death of his friend Polhern, Swedenborg reported, "He died on Monday and spoke with me on Thursday. I was invited to the funeral. He saw the hearse and saw them let down the coffin into the grave. He conversed with me as it was going on, asking why they had buried him when he was still alive." Doyle suggests that every Spiritualist should honor Swedenborg and that his bust should be in every Spiritualist temple.

The Swedenborg Church, also known as The Church of the New Jerusalem, was founded after his death in 1772. Many of his ideas influenced the later Spiritualist movement. Sir Arthur Conan Doyle suggested that it may have been the spirit of Swedenborg that influenced **Andrew Jackson Davis**.

Sources:

Buckland, Raymond: *Buckland's Book of Spirit Communications*. St. Paul: Llewellyn, 2004

Doyle, Sir Arthur Conan: *The History of Spiritualism*. New York: Doran, 1926

Ennemoser, Joseph (tr. William Howitt): *The History of Magic*. London: Henry G. Bohn, 1854

SYMBOLISM

The dictionary defines a symbol as "something that stands for something else, especially something concrete that represents or suggests another thing that cannot in itself be represented or visualized." Carl Jung said, "The inexpressible can only be expressed in terms of symbol or allegory." In **Spiritualism**, symbolism is regularly encountered. **Mediums** will receive **spirit** messages **clairvoyantly**, **clairaudiently**, or **clairsentiently**, and these **messages** will frequently be in symbolic form. Many times it is better for the medium to simply describe what is being received rather than to try to interpret it him- or herself, since the symbolism is sometimes pertinent to the sitter. However, there are also many instances of **spirit guides** developing symbols that they present to their mediums on a regular basis, quite separate from the "main text" of the message for the sitter. For example: a pink rose may always mean love; silver bells may always indicate a wedding; black ribbon may always mean a death.

In *One Last time* (1998), medium **John Edward** said, "Like other **psychics** and mediums, I hear sounds, see images, and—the most difficult to explain—feel thoughts and sensations that are put into my mind by spirits on the Other Side ... I must interpret the information so that the meaning is understood. I call the entire process 'psychic sign language.' What I've been able to do in the years since I started this work is to become more fluent in understanding the symbols, making it easier for me to validate the presence of spirits."

The symbolism used is most often the same symbolism that is found in **dreams**. For this reason, study of good books on dream symbolism can be a great help to the understanding of messages received at **séances**.

Sources:

Bletzer, June G.: *The Encyclopedia Psychic Dictionary*. Lithia Springs: New Leaf, 1998

Buckland, Raymond: *Gypsy Dream Dictionary*. St. Paul: Llewellyn, 1999

Edward, John: *One Last Time: A Psychic Medium Speaks to Those We Have Loved and Lost*. New York: Berkley Books, 1998

Merriam-Webster Dictionary, The. New York: Pocket Books, 1974

SYNCHRONICITY

Synchronicity is a term coined by Carl Jung to mean the simultaneous occurrence of two separate and dissimilar events which are then found to be related. The two events cannot be attributed to the cause and effect theory but are rather a simultaneous blending together in an inexplicable yet highly meaningful way. Jung explored the theory in his book (written with W. Pauli) *The Interpretation of Nature and the Psyche* (London, 1955). Synchronicity seems to be far more than just coincidence.

Sources:

Bletzer, June G.: *The Encyclopedia Psychic Dictionary*. Lithia Springs: New Leaf, 1998

Fodor, Nandor: *Encyclopedia of Psychic Science*. London: Arthurs Press, 1933

TRICKERY

TABLE TIPPING; TABLE TURNING

Nandor Fodor described table tipping, or table turning, as "the crudest form of communication with the subconscious self or with extraneous intelligences." Yet tables have been used since antiquity for purposes of **divination**. Ammianus Marcellinus (330–395 CE), the author of a history of the **Roman** Empire, described a table with a slab engraved with the letters of the alphabet, above which a ring was suspended from a thread. The ring would swing to a succession of letters and spell out words. However, table tipping was a little different from this and became very popular with the advent of **Spiritualism** in the mid-nineteenth century.

The usual method is for the sitters to be evenly spaced around a table and to sit with their fingertips placed lightly on the top edge of the table (*not* the underside). One of the sitters acts as **spokesperson** and calls out for a **spirit** to make contact. Very soon the table will start to move; sometimes quivering and shaking beforehand. It will often rise up on one or two legs and may actually turn, pivoting on one leg. The sitters invariably have to leave their seats and move around to keep up with the table. If questioned,

the table will rear up on one or two legs and then drop back down again. Taking one thump as the letter "A," two as "B," three as "C," and so on, messages can be laboriously spelled out. An alternate and faster method is for the spokesperson to call out the letters of the alphabet and the table will drop down at the specific letter. In the past, whole sermons have been dictated by a table, as have poems, and information about the **spirit world**.

Table tipping originated in America. It rapidly spread to Europe, reaching England in 1853, where it quickly became very popular. One of the attractions of it was that there was no need for a professional **medium**. It could be done with any group of people, and was usually done in someone's living room. Table tipping became such a phenomenon that scientists could not ignore it and felt they had to explain it. With the aid of the chemist Michael Faraday (1791–1867), they were able to show that the actual movement of the table was due to the unconscious muscular action of the people with their fingers on it. While honestly believing they pressed downward on the table, in fact their pressure was oblique, causing the rotation of the table. The scientists seemed satisfied to have explained that (even giving the force a name:

ectenic force), but neglected to address the question of who or what was utilizing and directing this muscle power. How was the "table" able to give answers, unknown to those present, to the questions asked?

When table tipping is done with a medium—especially one known for physical phenomena—it is not unknown for the table to not only tip but to **levitate**. There are many photographs, taken in **infrared** light, showing such levitation. Some of the photographs also show the **ectoplasmic** "rods" that emerge from the medium to do the lifting. Of his experiments with the medium **Eusapia Paladino**, the **psychical researcher Hereward Carrington** said that the table appeared to be somehow alive, "like the back of a dog." Paladino insisted on a table that was built entirely of wood, having no metal in it. She considered soft pinewood the best material. Rather than metal nails, the table should be fastened with wooden pegs. However, other mediums have no problem with metal, some modern circles even using metal folding card tables.

Although most table tipping **séances** are principally to communicate with the spirits of departed loved ones, they can also be for purposes of **divination**; to find out about future possibilities.

In his book *Psychic Force*, Gambier Bolton wrote of the medium **Florence Cook**,

> During any meal with Mrs. Elgie Corner (Florence Cook), in one's own house, and whilst she herself is engaged in eating and drinking—both of her hands being visible all the time— the heavy dining table will commence first to quiver, setting all the glasses shaking, and plates, knives, forks and spoons in motion, and then to rock and sway from side to side, occasionally going so far as to tilt up at one end or at one side; and all the time **raps** and tappings will be heard in the table and in many different parts of the room. Taking a meal with her in a public restaurant is a somewhat serious matter.

Sources:

Bolton, Gambier: *Psychic Force: An Investigation of a Little-Known Power*. London: Spiritualists' National Union, 1897

Buckland, Raymond: *Buckland's Book of Spirit Communications*. St. Paul: Llewellyn, 2004

Fodor, Nandor: *Encyclopedia of Psychic Science*. London: Arthurs Press, 1933

Owens, Elizabeth: *How to Communicate With Spirits*. St. Paul: Llewellyn, 2002

Spence, Lewis: *An Encyclopedia of the Occult*. London: George Routledge & Sons, 1920

TALKING BOARD

The "Talking Board" is a tool used by certain **Spiritualists** to communicate with **spirits** of the dead. It is also used by some people as a **divination** tool, to ascertain answers to questions about the past, present, and future. Various types of talking boards have been used for centuries. One of the earliest forms was known as *electromancy*, in which a cockerel picked up pieces of corn or wheat placed alongside letters of the alphabet arranged in a circle, thereby spelling out words in answer to questions asked by a diviner. In ancient **Greece** and in **Rome**, a small table on wheels moved about, to point to answers to questions. In China, c. 550 BCE, similar tools were used to communicate with the dead. The *squdilatc* boards used by various **Native American** tribes to obtain spiritual information and to locate lost people and objects were not unlike the modern Ouija® board. The name "Ouija" is taken from the French (*oui*) and the German (*ja*) words for "yes."

The board itself is flat and smooth with the letters of the alphabet marked on it, usually also with numbers and some short phrases. A small platform, or **planchette**, often heart shaped, slides over the board. The diviner sits with fingertips placed on the planchette and asks questions. The answers are given by the platform sliding about the board and stopping at a series of letters, to spell out words. Most boards include the letters of the alphabet, numbers from one to nine, the words "Yes" and "No," and sometimes "Goodbye" and/or other greetings. Although the diviner's fingers rest on the planchette, there is no conscious propelling of it. Supposedly, the platform moves as directed by spirits of the dead.

A very simple, yet very effective, **talking board** can be made by writing the letters of the alphabet on pieces of paper and laying them down in a circle, around the edge of a table. A wine glass can then be upturned and used as a planchette, the participants resting their fingers on the now-top edge of the glass. The glass will slide over the table surface to stop in front of appropriate letters.

There are a number of different boards commercially produced today. The first was patented by Elijah J. Bond in the late 1800s, who sold the patent to **William Fuld** in 1892. Fuld founded The Southern Novelty Company, in Maryland, which later became known as the Baltimore Talking Board Company. They produced the "Oriole Talking Boards," later labeled "Ouija®, the Mystifying Oracle." In 1966, the **Parker Brothers** toy and game manufacturer bought the rights to the board and marketed it to the point where it outsold their famous Monopoly® game. In its first year with Parker, more than two million Ouija® boards were sold. Understandably, many other companies started producing similar boards, though they were not allowed to use the name "Ouija."

The Fuld/Parker Brothers' recommended way of using the board is for two people to sit facing one another, with the board resting on their knees between them. At the outset, the planchette is in the center of the board and the two each have their fingers resting lightly on it. To avoid confusion, just one person acts as spokesperson. They enquire, "Is there anybody there?" This is repeated until the planchette starts to move. It should move across to "Yes" and then return to the center. It is possible to work the board with a number of participants sitting around a table. The more people, the more energy there is available to move the planchette. One person can also have success working alone.

The first time someone experiences a talking board, the feeling is that someone present is pushing the planchette when it moves. This can quickly be discounted when messages are spelled out which give information not known to anyone present: names, places, documents that need to be researched after the session. If the information received is known to any one person there, then it cannot be assumed that the message is coming from the **spirit world**. Even though no one may be pushing the pointer consciously, they may be doing so unconsciously. They may also be picking up the information through **extrasensory perception**. Although no one present is *directing* the planchette, the participants are in fact pushing it in the sense that their muscles are being used to cause it to slide across the surface of the board. The spirits are making use of their muscles to produce the physical movement. This is the same thing that happens with **table tipping**.

It is difficult to keep a finger on the planchette, observe to which letters it points and at the same time, write down everything. It is therefore a good idea to have a secretary for any extended talking board sessions. The **spokesperson**, as well as being the one to call out the questions, also calls out the letters received so that they can be recorded.

Many times what is recorded seems to make little sense when first studied. There is often confusion between similar looking letters: N, M and H; O and Q, P and R, I and J, and so on. Careful study of the written results should make it possible to correct any such substitutions. Another problem can be that words run into one another. This can easily be solved by requesting that the planchette make a quick circle of the board between each word, to indicate the break. Other possible problems might be receiving anagrams, or finding letters arranged as though by a person with dyslexia. It is frequently necessary to study a received message very carefully in order to make sense of it. One possible explanation for these difficulties is that the communicating spirit may not have had previous experience with this form of communication.

If the planchette sits still without moving, it may be that the question asked is ambiguous. Thought should be given to the phrasing of questions. Many messages do come through "loud and clear," perfectly spelled and making absolute sense. Record keeping is an important aspect of talking board use, if it is done seriously. Although many people use a talking board for fun, pushing the planchette for laughs, this is not tolerated among serious **psychical researchers**.

A list of questions to be asked may be prepared ahead of time, which will save time when actually dealing with the spirit. It is also a good idea to choose as many questions as possible that can be answered with a basic yes or no. This saves time and also avoids any misunderstanding of received information. But obviously not everything can be covered this way, so spelled-out answers are definitely part of the looked-for result.

A fear among novice talking board users is that they may become "possessed" through using the board. There are a thousand urban legends about people who have been so afflicted. There are stories of teenagers who have asked the board when they are going to die, and been told that it will happen the next week, month, or year. Needless to say, this can be a self-fulfilling prophesy having a terrible psychological effect on the person concerned. But this only points to the fact that the talking board is a serious tool; it is not a toy, despite being available in certain toy stores. Certainly the board can become addictive, but if handled sensibly it is no more a vehicle for possession than is the telephone.

There are certain precautions that beginners should take. First, if a lot of negative messages are received, especially messages directing the sitter to do certain things that go against the grain and that would not normally be done, then the sitter should simply stop using the board. It's as simple as that. If the board (or a particular "spirit" coming through the board) tells you to give away all your worldly possessions ... stop and think about it. Exactly who is telling you to do this and why? It may be a spirit calling itself Jesus, or describing itself as an

angel ... but what are the chances? And why, if they are who they say they are, would they tell you to do something that would harm you? Many overly religious people claim it is the Christian devil who speaks through the board. If this is what you believe, then "hang up the phone!"

Don't quit your job on the advice of, say, a long-dead relative. What do they know about today's labor market? Don't jump off a roof top on the direction of an unknown spirit. Why should you do so? In other words, use your head. Don't run to the board looking for answers to all of life's questions. Don't expect it to solve every little problem you have. The board is not an **oracle**; it cannot tell you the absolute future. Use it with common sense and don't abuse it. Enjoy it. If you don't enjoy it, don't use it.

Some extremely interesting information has been obtained through the talking board. The prime example is probably that of Patience Worth. On July 8, 1913, **Pearl Curran**, a St. Louis housewife, was persuaded by her friend Emily Hutchinson to try a Ouija® board. She did so and received the words, "Many moons ago I lived. Again I come; Patience Worth my name." This turned out to be the start of an avalanche of information that kept coming over a period of five years. Eventually moving on from the Ouija® board to **automatic writing**, Mrs. Curran produced 2,500 poems, short stories, plays, allegories, and six full-length novels, all authored by Patience Worth, who claimed to be an Englishwoman from the seventeenth century. In all, more than four million words were produced. What is interesting is that of all those millions of words, not a single anachronism has been found by experts; the vocabulary is consistent with that of the claimed time period, including ninety percent of Old English.

In *The History of Spiritualism* (1926), Sir **Arthur Conan Doyle** speaks of Sir **William Barrett** recording an evidential communication received in Dublin, Ireland, by Mrs. Travers Smith and her friend "Miss C." Doyle relates the case and concludes, "Both the ladies have signed a document they sent me ... Here there could be no explana-

Group attempting to communicate with spirits using a talking board. The spirit guides the participants' hands to move the planchette, spelling out messages. *Courtesy Fortean Picture Library.*

tion of the facts by subliminal memory, or **telepathy** or collusion, and the evidence points unmistakably to a telepathic message from a deceased officer (of the army in France at that time)."

With such evidence that the talking board can be used to communicate with the dead, it seems strange that the **National Spiritualist Association of Churches** has turned its back on the talking board while continuing to condone spirit **slates**, **trumpets**, automatic writing, and other similar tools.

Sources:

Buckland, Raymond: *Buckland's Book of Spirit Communications*. St. Paul: Llewellyn, 2004

Covina, Gina: *The Ouija® Book*. New York: Simon & Schuster, 1979

Guiley, Rosemary Ellen: *Harper's Encyclopedia of Mystical & Paranormal Experience*. San Francisco: Harper SanFrancisco, 1991

Hunt, Stoker: *Ouija®: The Most Dangerous Game*. New York: Harper & Row, 1985

Owens, Elizabeth: *How to Communicate With Spirits*. St. Paul: Llewellyn, 2002

TAPE RECORDER

A tape recorder can be a useful tool for receiving communications from the deceased. In *You Can Communicate With the Unseen World* (1974), **Harold Sherman** wrote, "By use of an ordinary tape recorder and/or a radio set attuned to unused frequencies, **spirit** voices of purported entities are being received." This is known as **Electronic Voice Phenomenon (EVP)**.

When setting out to record such **spirit** messages, many people start with either a short **prayer** or a brief period of **meditation**. The technique is to then set the tape recorder to "Record," to state the date and time, and then to leave it running. The recording is best done in an area where no sound would normally be picked up. Any spirit voices may be heard upon playing back the tape. The volume should be turned all the way up and the resulting background "noise" (e.g. possibly a hissing sound) listened to carefully. With a multi-speed tape recorder, it is recommended that the tape be played back at a different speed from that used for recording. Although spirit voices will speak at any time of the day or night, it is best—initially at least—to conduct experiments at the same time every day.

Some researchers will ask questions at intervals during the recording of the tape. This gives spirit a chance to address those questions. If this is done then it is suggested that the last question be an invitation for spirit to say something of his or her own choosing.

In *There Is No Death* (2003), Tom and Lisa Butler said, "There are no rigid rules for experimenting with EVP … EVP has been recorded on just about everything that will record voice frequencies." Reel-to-reel recorders were used at first, and later cassette recorders were used. Today there are personal note recorders, or digital note-takers, which are known as IC recorders. According to the Butlers, these perform even better than the cassette recorders, and produce results on par with reel-to-reel.

Sources:

Butler, Tom and Lisa: *There Is No Death and There Are No Dead*. Reno: AA-EVP, 2003

Sherman, Harold: *You Can Communicate with the Unseen World*. New York: Fawcett, 1974

TAROT CARDS

Although tarot cards are not a tool used by **mediums**, they can be useful in developing **psychic** abilities. Mediumship deals with communication between this world and the **spirit world** of the deceased. Psychism is basically of this physical plane, without contacting **spirits**.

The deck of cards known as the tarot is divided into two parts: the Major Arcana and the Minor Arcana (*Arcana* is from the Latin word for "secret"). The two parts are dissimilar. The Major Arcana is a set of twenty-two distinctive cards, each separately titled. The Minor Arcana is a combination of four suits, each suit comprised of cards numbered from one (or Ace) to ten, plus court cards: Page, Knight, Queen, and King. The Minor Arcana is the ancestor of the everyday playing cards, though the latter do not have the Knight and the Page has become known as the Jack.

The four suits of the Minor Arcana are most commonly known as Cups, Pentacles, Wands, and Swords (which became Hearts, Diamonds, Clubs and Spades, in the regular deck). However, on different decks they are variously known by other names such as cups, chalices, cauldrons, vessels, hearts; pentacles, coins, disks, wheels, deniers, stars, bells; wands, staves, batons, rods, scepters, leaves; swords, knives, blades, spears, acorns. Some decks are specialized in their art focus, thus producing yet other names for the suits. For **divinatory** reading of the tarot cards, the two Arcanas are usually intermixed; shuffled together and laid out in various spreads for interpretation.

The most common names for the twenty-two cards of the Major Arcana are: Fool, Magician, High Priestess, Empress, Emperor, Hierophant, Lovers, Chariot, Strength, Hermit, Wheel of Fortune, Justice, Hanged Man, Death, Temperance, Devil, Lightning-Struck Tower, Star, Moon, Sun, Judgement, World. The order of these can vary slightly (in some decks Strength and Justice are reversed). The Fool may be placed at either the beginning or the end, and consequently is unnumbered. (The Fool became the Joker of the regular playing card deck.) These cards depict symbolic figures, elements of nature, human experiences on the spiritual journey, and hopes, fears, joys, and sorrows. They are drawn from legend and myth, from universal symbolism, philosophies, religions, and magical beliefs. Some say they depict the

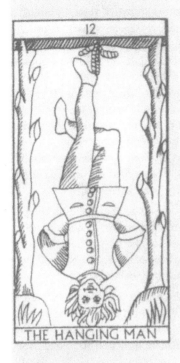

THE HANGING MAN

TEMPERANCE

Tarot cards based on the Marseilles deck: the Hanging Man, the unnamed Death Card, and Temperance. *Courtesy Fortean Picture Library.*

grades or stages of the journey of an initiate. Some authors equate the Major Arcana with the twenty-two letters of the Hebrew alphabet and work them with the Qabbalah and the Tree of Life. The French occultist known as Eliphas Zahed Lèvi (1810–1875), whose real name was Alphonse Louis Constant, was the first to do this.

In *A Complete Guide to the Tarot*, Eden Gray wrote, "Symbolic keys, like material ones, are expected to fit locks and open doors. Systems such as the Kabalah or the Tarot, however, do not accomplish this in a simple or direct manner. Here we find keys that fit more than one lock and locks that can receive more than one key. The correspondence between the twenty-two Major Arcana Keys and the twenty-two paths on the Tree of Life and the twenty-two letters of the

Hebrew alphabet, as well as astrological signs, evokes complex and subtle associations that can never be rigidly confined."

The first tarot cards were individually painted on thin sheets of ivory, parchment, silver and gold. Later they were produced on card stock, though still individually painted. There was a set of tarot cards painted especially for Charles VI of France, in 1392 (seventeen of these cards survive today in the Bibliothèque Nationale in Paris). With the coming of block printing in Nuremberg, c. 1430, they became more generally available and eventually quite popular. In fifteenth century England, King Edward IV forbade the importation of tarot cards, but soldiers fighting in Normandy, Touraine, Anjou, and Poitou smuggled cards from France, and the decks found their way into the homes of the nobility. By the time of the French Revolution, there was a grand revival of interest in esotericism, and with mystic lodges and secret societies springing up, the tarot came into fashion and more general use.

The actual origins of the tarot are lost in time. There is some evidence to show that the cards originated in the north of India and were brought out of that region by the Roma, or Gypsies, in their mass exodus. Certainly the Gypsies were responsible for much of the distribution across Europe. But there is also speculation that the cards originated in China, Korea, or Northern Italy.

The cards may be used as individual **meditation** tools. Some people draw a single card at the start of every day and meditate on it; obtaining an idea of what the coming day will hold. But the most common practice is to use the cards to answer questions, or to glean an idea of what the future might hold for oneself or for another. There is a traditional way of doing this, with a variety of spreads or layouts for the cards, with each position of a card having a specific meaning.

Sources:

Buckland, Raymond: *The Buckland Romani Tarot: The Gypsy Book of Wisdom*. St. Paul: Llewellyn, 2001

Buckland, Raymond: *The Fortune-Telling Book: The Encyclopedia of Divination and Soothsaying*. Detroit: Visible Ink Press, 2004

Donaldson, Terry: *Step-By-Step Tarot*. London: Thorsons, 1995

Gray, Eden: *The Tarot Revealed*. New York: Inspiration House, 1960

Gray, Eden: *A Complete Guide to the Tarot*. New York: Crown, 1970

Waite, Arthur Edward: *The Pictorial Key to the Tarot*. New York: University Books, 1959 (London 1910)

Telekinesis *see* **Psychokinesis**

TELEPATHY

From the Greek *tele*, "distance" and *pathos*, "to sense or feel from afar." The word was coined by **Frederick W. H. Myers** in 1882, who defined it as "transmission of thought independently of the recognized channels of sense." It therefore infers a communication between two or more individuals without use of the five regular senses. It usually involves one person sending information and another person receiving it. Sir **William Crookes** tried to explain telepathy as a physical process, saying, "It is known that the action of thought is accompanied by certain molecular movements in the brain, and here we have physical vibrations capable from their extreme minuteness of acting direct on individual molecules, while their rapidity approaches that of the internal and external movements of the atoms themselves."

Nandor Fodor observed that belief in telepathy is ages old and that **prayer** is actually telepathic communication between the petitioner and deity. He also suggests that the basis of sympathy and antipathy may be telepathy.

There is evidence that telepathy is not confined to humans but is also experienced by animals. For example, the novelist H. Rider Haggard told his wife of a **dream** in which their dog, Bob, appeared to him. The animal was lying on its side in brushwood near water, and was trying to let his master know that he was dying. Four days later the dog's body was found floating in a river. He had been struck by a train and knocked from the railroad bridge. Susan McGrath's book *How Animals Talk* (1993) includes examples of telepathy in animals as does Edmund Selous's *Thought Transference in Birds* (1931).

Professor **James Hervey Hyslop** thought it possible that **spirits** might be the cause of telepathy between the living. He claimed that Myers also saw this possibility at the start of his investigations into telepathy. In experiments conducted by Myers with Miss Miles and Miss Ramsden, Miles claimed that she could always tell when her telepathy had been successful because she heard **rappings**. (*Proceedings*, Vol. XXI).

Sources:

Fodor, Nandor: *Encyclopedia of Psychic Science*. London: Arthurs Press, 1933

Myers, F. W. H.: *Human Personality and Its Survival after Bodily Death*. London: Longmans, 1903

Spence, Lewis: *An Encyclopedia of the Occult*. London: George Routledge & Sons, 1920

TELEPORTATION

There are a number of examples of teleportation to be found in the **Bible** (e.g. Ezekiel 11.1). There are also many examples to be found in Modern **Spiritualism**. Teleportation was described by Leslie Shepard as "a composite phenomenon between **levitation** and **apports**." One of the classic cases was the teleportation of Mrs. **Agnes Guppy**, when she became a living apport at the **séance** given by **mediums Charles Williams** and **Frank Herne**. The two mediums specialized in apport séances. At one of their sittings someone jokingly suggested that they should apport Mrs. Guppy, who lived only a short distance from their séance room in High Holborn, London. This suggestion was greeted with laughter since Mrs. Guppy was a very large woman. But within a matter of minutes, a very large figure suddenly appeared, with a thump, on the top of the table. It was Mrs. Guppy, wearing a dressing gown, holding a pen wet with ink, and looking very startled. (*see* Apports) This was one of the best corroborated cases of teleportation.

Both Charles Williams and Frank Herne were themselves teleported at various times. Thomas Blyton wrote in his reminiscences, published in **Light** (April 11, 1931), "I was present on one occasion at a private home séance at Hackney, in London, when without warning or preparation, in total darkness, Mr. Frank Herne was suddenly placed in the midst of the sitters; and after recovering from our surprise and resuming the séance, Mr. Herne's overcoat, hat and umbrella were dropped on the table." Herne had been with friends, watching a play in another part of London.

The Sao Paolo medium **Carlos Carmine Mirabelli** was transported from the railroad station of Da Luz to Sao Vincenti, 90 kilometres away, in two minutes. He had been with friends at the railroad station, intending to travel to Santos. He suddenly disappeared just before the train was due to leave. A telephone call confirmed that he was in Sao Vincenti two minutes later.

Nandor Fodor recounts the teleportation of the medium the Marquis Centurione Scotto, on July 29, 1928 at Millesimo Castle. "The medium exclaimed, in a frightened voice, 'I can no longer feel my legs!' ... An interval of death-like silence followed. The medium was addressed, then felt for (it was a dark room sitting). His place was empty. They turned on the red light. The doors were still securely locked with the key on the inside but the medium had disappeared. All the rooms of the castle were searched but without result. Two and a half hours passed when it occurred to the sitters to ask Mrs. Gwendolyn Kelley Hack to try and get into communication, through **automatic writing**, with her **spirit guide** Imperator. After several attempts ... correct information came through: 'Go to the right, then outside. Wall and gate. He is lying–hay–hay–on soft place.' The place indicated a granary in the stable yard. The great entrance door was locked; the key was not in the lock. They ran back to fetch it and entering found a small door which had been previously overlooked. This door was also locked, the key being in the keyhole on the outside. They opened it with the greatest caution. On a heap of hay and oats the medium was comfortably lying, immersed in profound sleep."

Sources:

Bletzer, June G.: *The Encyclopedia Psychic Dictionary*. Lithia Springs: New Leaf, 1998

Shepard, Leslie A: *Encyclopedia of Occultism & Parapsychology*. New York: Avon Books, 1978

TENHAEFF, WILHELM HEINRICH CARL (1894–1981)

Wilhelm Heinrich Carl Tenhaeff was born in Rotterdam on January 18, 1894. He studied at the University of Utrecht and received a Ph.D. in 1933. His doctoral thesis was the first in the Netherlands on the subject of **parapsychology**.

Tenhaeff married Johanna Jacoba Hemmes in 1926. From 1933 to 1953, he was lecturer on parapsychology, and then from 1953 onward, Professor of Parapsychology and Director of the Parapsychology Institute, State University of Utrecht. He founded the institute, which is now known as the Parapsychological Division of the Psychological Laboratory. In 1928, Tenhaeff founded and edited the journal of the Dutch Society for Psychical Research and was Secretary (1929–1938) and Advisor (from 1945 on), interacting with the **Society for Psychical Research** in Britain.

Tenhaeff had been interested in parapsychology from an early age, investigating and writing reviews of reported examples of **psychometry, clairvoyance, precognition, psychic healing, radiesthesia** (the use of divining rods), and allied subjects. He spent many years investigating the powers of **psychic Gérard Croiset**. He lectured extensively on parapsychology in many different countries, and published articles in a variety of journals. He also authored a large number of books on the subject, among them *Short Textbook of Parapsychology—3 vols.* (1926), **Spiritism** (1936), *Parapsychological Phenomena and Speculations* (1949), *The Divining Rod* (1950), *Somnambulists and Healers* (1951), *Introduction to Parapsychology* (1952), **Telepathy** *and Clairvoyance* (1958), and *Precognition* (1961). Tenhaeff died in Utrecht on July 9, 1981.

Sources:

Fodor, Nandor: *Encyclopedia of Psychic Science.* London: Arthurs Press, 1933

THEOSOPHICAL SOCIETY

The Theosophical Society was founded on September 7, 1875, in an attempt to bring together eastern and western magical traditions. The founders were **Helena Petrovna Blavatsky**, Colonel **Henry Steele Olcott**, and W. Q. Judge. The Inaugural Address by President-Founder Colonel Olcott was delivered November 17, 1875, considered to be the official date of the founding of the Society. The stated aims of the society were:

1: To form a nucleus of the Universal Brotherhood of Humanity, without distinction of race, creed, sex, caste or color.

2: To encourage the study of Comparative Religion, Philosophy and Science.

3: To investigate unexplained laws of Nature, and the powers latent in man.

Blavatsky and Olcott had met the previous year in America, when Olcott was investigating the **Eddy Brothers** and their Spiritualist phenomena in Vermont. At that time Blavatsky was an ardent **Spiritualist**. She was also well read in most aspects of the **occult**. The two became firm friends, sharing an avid interest in a wide variety of occult subjects. They eventually lived together in New York and held evenings of discussions, lectures, and workshops with friends and acquaintances. One evening after a lecture on **Egyptian** art and magic, Olcott put forward the idea of forming a society. Blavatsky was all in favor and the word *Theosophy* was adopted as a name for the society. Theosophy means "knowledge of God or divine wisdom."

Blavatsky went on to write a book of this divine wisdom or body of truth concerning God, man, and the universe. It took two years to write and was published in New York in 1877 under the title *Isis Unveiled.* The book was written through **automatic writing, inspirational writing,** and—it was claimed—with writing that suddenly appeared on the paper while Blavatsky slept. It was something of an amalgam of eastern thought, western science, **witchcraft**, magic, alchemy; surveying the literature of the ages.

In February, 1879, Blavatsky and Olcott moved to India to establish the Theosophical Society there. In October of that year, they published the first of a monthly magazine titled *The Theosophist.* The driving force of the society were the Hidden Masters, or Secret Brothers, who existed in the Himalayas. Blavatsky claimed that she had been initiated by them in 1864. They provided the power for the seeming miracles that Blavatsky regularly performed. **Rappings** were frequently heard in her presence, as was the sound of tiny bells. **Apports** were common and so were many other mediumistic phenomena. Colonel Olcott traveled and established branches of the society throughout India and Ceylon. They purchased a large estate in southern India, in Adyar, near Madras, in May of 1882, which is still the headquarters of the Theosophical Society.

In 1884, a scandal broke when Alex and Emma Coulomb—a husband and wife who had been working for Blavatsky but had been fired—claimed that they had conspired with the medium to produce fraudulent phenomena. The Coulombs were working with a group of Christian missionaries. This happened at a time when Blavatsky and Olcott were in Europe and the medium was being investigated by the **Society for Psychical Research**. The society had been about to publish a glowing report on Blavatsky when the scandal broke. Blavatsky and Olcott hurried back to India and were prepared to sue the Couloms but were talked out of it by followers. Blavatsky finally left India, though the Theosophical Society continued its existence there. She went on to write *The Secret Doctrine*, an epic work on the root knowledge out of which all religion, philosophy, and science have grown. She died of Bright's disease on May 8, 1891. The Theosophical Society continued under the direction of Annie Wood Besant and Charles Leadbeater. Besant was the driving intellectual force and Leadbeater managed occult matters. W. Q. Judge, one of the original founders of the Theosophical Society, struggled with Besant for overall control and, on losing the fight, became leader of the American branch of the society, which seceded from the parent body.

Nandor Fodor said, "Whatever opinions may be held of the soundness of theosophical teaching, no doubt can be entertained of the extent and influence of the society, which has numerous members in lands so far apart and so different in **spirit** as America and India, besides every other civilized country in the world."

The Temple of Light at Adyar in the gardens of the Theosophical Society headquarters near Madras, India. *Courtesy Fortean Picture Library.*

Sources:

Cave, Janet (ed): *Mysteries of the Unknown: Ancient Wisdom and Secret Sects*. New York: Time-Life Books, 1989

Cranston, Sylvia: *H.P.B.: The Extraordinary Life & Influence of Helena Blavatsky, Founder of the Modern Theosophical Movement*. New York: G. P. Putnam's, 1993

Symonds, John: *Madame Blavatsky, Medium and Magician*. London: Yoseloff, 1960

Wilson, Colin: *The Supernatural: Mysterious Powers*. London: Aldus Books, 1975

THIRD EYE

The Third Eye is a spot between and slightly above the eyebrows, which coincides with the pineal gland. It is regarded as a mystical center and is the position of the sixth **chakra**. "Seeing" with the Third Eye is a form of **clairvoyance**. This spot is the focus for Oriental mystical meditation and is known in yoga philosophy as the *ajna chakra*, or center of command. In Tantric teachings, it is regarded as "the seat of the mental faculties; the abode of the individual consciousness; and the meeting place of the divine." Omar Garrison said, "**meditation** upon the *ajna* will result in *sadhaka's* (aspirant) being released from the consequences of actions in previous incarnations."

Sources:

Buckland, Raymond: *Buckland's Book of Spirit Communications*. St. Paul: Llewellyn, 2004

Garrison, Omar: *Tantra: The Yoga of Sex*. New York: Julian Press, 1964

THOMPSON, MRS. R.

Mrs. R. Thompson developed as a **medium** at the Delphic Circle organized by Frederic W. Thurstan at Hertford Lodge in Battersea, London. She was a **trance** medium and initially produced a wide variety of physical phenomena such as **rappings, psychokinesis, levitation,** psychic lights and **orbs,** elongation, **apports, direct voice,** scents and **materializations.** The earliest records of her sittings are found in *Light* magazine in 1897 and 1898.

Thompson came to the attention of the **Society for Psychical Research** and agreed to submit to experiments for them from 1898 onward. Unfortunately **Frederick W. H. Myers** discouraged her from continuing with **physical mediumship** and had her concentrate on working as a trance medium.

Thompson's **spirit guide** was her daughter Nelly, who had died in infancy. Another frequent communicator was Miss Cartwright, who had been a mistress at the school where Thompson was educated. Thompson's trances were not deep and it was reported that at times it appeared she was not in trance at all. Dr. **Richard Hodgson** was not impressed with her mediumship but others were, including the skeptic **Frank Podmore.**

Psychical researcher Margaret Verall had twenty-two sittings with Thompson and analyzed them as follows: 238 definite statements were made of past and present happenings. Of these, 33 were false, 64 were unidentified, and 141 (or fifty-nine percent) were true. Although Verall could see many of Thompson's own characteristics coming through, with her own speech patterns, the conclusion was that many of the personalities were easily recognized and acknowledged by the sitters. Dr. van Eeden came from Holland to test Thompson and received dramatic communication from a young suicide who spoke to the doctor in Dutch, a language unknown to Mrs. Thompson.

Frederick Myers' work with Mrs. Thompson convinced Myers of the survival of spirit after death. He and his friends had 217 sittings with her, about two thirds of which he attended himself. When Myers died on January 17, 1901, Thompson—although she had retired from mediumship at that time—contacted Sir **Oliver Lodge** and gave him two sittings. At both of these, communications were received that Lodge acknowledged were characteristic of Myers.

Sources:

Fodor, Nandor: *Encyclopedia of Psychic Science*. London: Arthurs Press, 1933

THOUGHTOGRAPHY

Thoughtography is a term for thought photography, coined by Dr. Tomokichi Fukurai, President of the Psychical Institute of Japan. In 1913, he published a book about his experiments with Ikuko Nagao and Chizuko Mifune, attesting to the validity of **clairvoyance.** This publication brought about his resignation from a professorship at the Imperial University of Tokyo. Fukurai continued working with a number of Japanese **mediums** and conducted experiments in thought photography. In 1921, he published *Clairvoyance and Thoughtography*.

Thoughtography has been more recently demonstrated by **Ted Serios,** working with Dr.

Jule Eisenbud. Serios would look into the lens of a Polaroid camera concentrating on a "target" image, the shutter being tripped when he gave the word. The resulting photograph would frequently show the picture that Serios had in his mind.

Sources:

Eisenbud, Jule: *The World of Ted Serios: "Thoughto-graphic" Studies of an Extraordinary Mind.* New York: William Morrow, 1967

Fukurai, Tomokichi: *Clairvoyance and Thoughtography.* London: Rider, 1931

Shepard, Leslie A: *Encyclopedia of Occultism & Parapsychology.* New York: Avon Books, 1978

Tomorrow see Garrett, Eileen

Tongues, Speaking In *see* Glossolalia

TRANCE

There are four different levels of brainwave activity that prescribe altered states of consciousness. These are designated *beta, alpha, theta* and *delta*. Normal wide awake consciousness is the beta state, with brainwaves ranging from 14 to 27 cycles per second. The next level down is the alpha level, and this is characterized by brainwaves of 8 to 13 cycles per second. Below this is theta at 4 to 8 cycles per second, and delta operates at 0 to 4 cycles per second.

Beta is the usual wide awake mode. During this mode, up to seventy-five percent of consciousness is spent monitoring physical functions. The next step down, alpha, is achieved in **meditation.** It is also the state for daydreaming, the *hypnagogic* state (just prior to falling asleep at night), and the *hypnopompic* state (just coming out of sleep in the morning). Alpha would be regarded as a "light trance" state.

The theta state is the equivalent of a light sleep, where there is a general unawareness of what is going on around the person. It is possible to achieve this state when in deep meditation. Delta, the deepest level, is sound asleep with no knowledge whatsoever of what is happening. It is the equivalent of somnambulism in **hypnosis.**

Trance in the **Spiritualistic** sense is the freeing of the spiritual perception, the freeing of those faculties which belong to the spiritual-being, and thereby suspending the physical-being. As the physical senses become dormant, there is a sinking sensation, or depending on the individual, it can be a soaring sensation. It is a sensation of freedom, of leaving the earthly restrictions on the physical body. Many **mediums** say that when going into trance it helps to be working in a **circle** of like-minded people. Whether or not they are all holding hands, there is a concentration of energies that can be enormously beneficial to the medium in passing into trance and establishing contact with the **spirit world.** The British medium **Ivy Northage** said,

> The medium's mind is taken over to a greater or lesser degree by the controlling **spirit.** In my own case this was a gradual process of complete withdrawal on my part and an increasing command on Chan's [her **spirit guide**]. Its purpose in psychic and spiritual terms is to extend the power of spiritual influence to reach and obtain more positive response in communication with the other world. Many would-be mediums believe trance work will automatically separate them from subconscious interference, but this is not so. Its first essential is a loose etheric body, together with a mental confidence in their own purpose and the ability of the guides who work with them. It is never a substitute for positive mediumship, but can reduce obstruction to spirit activity by creating a real dependence upon the guide, thus enabling him to work more freely. This must depend upon the depth of trance and the ability of the medium to control his own thoughts and emotions.

Not all Spiritualist mediums go into trance. **John Edward** is a good example of someone who operates in full consciousness (and in full light) and is extremely effective in his spiritual contact. But for every one that does not go into trance, there are many more who do, though the depth

A Thai man goes into a trance and races towards a stage area during an occult rite at Bang Phra Temple, 30 miles west of Bangkok. *AP/WideWorld Photos.*

of that trance may vary tremendously. For some phenomena—mostly physical—a deep trance does seem to be essential.

Trance may occur intentionally or spontaneously, and might be just a light trance or one of the deeper variety. In the lighter trance, the medium invariably has full memory after the event of all that transpired. In the deeper states, the medium has no knowledge of what took place the whole time he or she was in the altered state. Sometimes a medium is not even aware of being in trance because it is such a light one. For example, most mediums and **psychics** would swear they are not entranced when doing something like **psychometry** or simple **clairvoyance**, yet they have invariably slipped from the beta state into the beginnings of alpha.

Mediumistic trance can be induced hypnotically, but it is essentially different from plain hypnotic trance. When a hypnotist places a subject under hypnosis, that subject remains in rapport with the hypnotist, a living person. In a mediumistic trance, the medium loses all contact with the living and attunes to the spiritual realm, to the point where it is almost as though the spirit guide is the "hypnotist."

Nandor Fodor described Boston medium **Leonora Piper** (1859–1950) as "the foremost trance medium in the history of psychical research." She described her own trance, saying,

I feel as if something were passing over my brain, making it numb; a sensation similar to that experienced when I was etherised, only the unpleasant odour of the ether is absent. I feel a little cold, too, not very, just a little, as a cold breeze passed over me, and people and objects become smaller until they finally disappear; then, I know nothing more until I wake up, when the first thing I am conscious of is a bright, a very bright light, and then darkness, such darkness. My hands and arms begin to tingle just as one's foot tingles after it has been "asleep," and I see, as if from a great distance, objects and people in the room; but they are very small and very black.

Nandor Fodor said of Leonora Piper's trance,

On awakening from trance Mrs. Piper often pronounced names and fragments of sentences which appeared to have been the last impressions on her brain. After that she resumed the conversation at the point where it was broken off before she fell into trance.

In the earlier days of mediumship, the act of going into trance frequently seemed a painful one. Mediums would grimace and contort their faces and bodies, some even tearing their hair! Thankfully the process today seems much easier, with the medium slipping into unconsciousness as one slips into sleep.

Sources:

Buckland, Raymond: *Buckland's Book of Spirit Communications*. St. Paul: Llewellyn, 2004

Fodor, Nandor: *Encyclopedia of Psychic Science*. London: Arthurs Press, 1933

Northage, Ivy: *Mechanics of Mediumship*. London: College of Psychic Studies, 1973

Northage, Ivy: *Mediumship Made Simple*. London: College of Psychic Studies, 1986

Transcendental Meditation *see* Meditation

TRANSFIGURATION

Nandor Fodor described transfiguration as the "metamorphic power of the **medium** to assume bodily characteristics of deceased people for their representation." In *The National Spiritualist* journal, Rev. William J. Erwood reported on a 1931 **séance** with a medium named Mrs. Bullock. The sitting was conducted in sufficient light to show every movement of the medium, who presented more than fifty faces within a period of an hour and a half.

It was as though the medium's face were of plastic material being rapidly moulded from one form to another by some master worker in plastics. Oriental faces, Indians, calm, dignified, serious, spiritual, in short, almost every type of face was depicted during this most unusual séance. One of the most striking was the impersonation of a paralyzed girl whom I had known in the States. The medium's entire body, as well as face, was twisted out of all semblance of its normal state, to depict the condition of this victim of paralysis.

This is in sharp contrast to many so-called "red light transfiguration séances" often presented today. At these, the "medium" sits with a red light projected from below the level of his or her face—or even just holds a flashlight with a red filter over the lens—and by small movements of the facial muscles, gives the impression of different faces (for example, a slight curling of the upper lip can produce a shadow that looks like a mustache). These performances are no more than the equivalent of the antics children perform with a flashlight at summer camp to entertain each other. They are certainly not true transfigurations and not a part of **Spiritualism**. Yet there are some mediums who do demonstrate true transfiguration. One such is the young British medium **Tony Stockwell**.

In some transfigurations, **ectoplasm** covers the medium's face and changes the features. It can be dangerous to the medium for a strong light to be shone unexpectedly on the face, or for anyone to attempt to touch or interfere with the medium. Serious injury has been recorded, as in the instance of the medium Ada Besinnet when being examined by the **British College of Psychic Sci-**

ence in 1921. Sir **Arthur Conan Doyle**, speaking of **Florence Cook** (then Mrs. Corner) when she was seized by Sir George Sitwell and accused of impersonating a **spirit**, stated, "It is worthy of remark that upon this occasion the observers agreed that the figure was white, whereas when Mrs. Corner was seized no white was to be seen. An experienced investigator would probably have concluded that this was not a **materialization**, but a transfiguration, which means that the ectoplasm, being insufficient to build up a complete figure, has been used to drape the medium so that she herself may carry the simulacrum."

Sources:

Buckland, Raymond: *Buckland's Book of Spirit Communications*. St. Paul: Llewellyn, 2004

Doyle, Sir Arthur Conan: *The History of Spiritualism*. New York: Doran, 1926

Fodor, Nandor: *Encyclopedia of Psychic Science*. London: Arthurs Press, 1933

TREMBLERS

The eighteenth century Tremblers of Germany were among the Huguenots in the mountains of Cevennes. They had fled to the Cevennes under the continued persecution of Louis XIV. In their religious fervor they would enter *ekstasis*, reach an ecstatic state, and become seized with convulsions. They went into **trance**, spoke in tongues (**glossolalia**), communicated with **spirits**, and were able to **heal** the sick. The Tremblers gradually spread over most of Germany. In trance, they were insensitive to pain and impervious to the effects of jabs with pointed sticks and iron poles, or to having great weights laid on top of them. Men and especially children caught the contagion, though comparatively few women were affected. Trembling became so commong that they were called "The Tremblers of Cevennes."

In Roman Catholic countries such seizures often occurred in convents, in churches where young girls were brought for first communion, and at "miracle shrines." In Protestant countries they accompanied great religious excitement. In Cevennes they were attributed to the Spirit of the Almighty and not, as among the Catholics, to Satan.

Sources:

Cleveland, Catherine C.: *The Great Revival in the West 1797–1805*. Gloucester: Peter Smith, 1959

Ennemoser, Joseph (tr. William Howitt): *The History of Magic*. London: Henry G. Bohn, 1854

Shepard, Leslie A: *Encyclopedia of Occultism & Parapsychology*. New York: Avon Books, 1978

TRUMPET

In **Spiritualism** the trumpet is made of aluminum or occasionally of cardboard. It is a straight, cone-shaped device usually built in sections to allow it to collapse for ease of traveling. It is a **séance** tool, used to amplify the voices of **spirits**. The first **medium** to use one was **Jonathan Koons**, an early American medium who lived in Athens County, Ohio. According to Sir **Arthur Conan Doyle**, "It appears that **ectoplasm** coming chiefly from the medium, but also in a lesser degree from the sitters, is used by the spirit operators to fashion something resembling a human larynx. This they use in the production of the voice. In an explanation given to Koons by the spirits they spoke of using a combination of the elements of the spiritual body, and what corresponds to our modern ectoplasm, 'a physical aura that emanates from the medium'."

Nandor Fodor said, "Physically the phenomenon requires the supposition that some material, more solid than air, is withdrawn from the medium's or from the sitter's body to produce the necessary vibrations in the surrounding atmosphere. Indeed, séance room communications speak of improvisation of a larynx."

Arthur Findlay gives a description of the building of this artificial larynx in *On the Edge of the Etheric* (1931),

From the medium and those present a chemist in the spirit world withdraws certain ingredients which for want of a better name is called ectoplasm. To this the chemist adds ingredients of his own making. When they are mixed together a substance is formed which enables the chemist to **materialize** his hands. He then, with his materialized hands, constructs a mask resembling the mouth and tongue. The spirit wishing to speak places his face into this mask and finds it clings to him, it gathers round his mouth, tongue and throat. The etheric organs have once again become clothed in matter resembling physical matter, and by the passage of air through them your atmosphere can be vibrated and you hear his voice.

William Stainton Moses, speaking of a spirit voice box and **direct voice**, said "I did not observe how the sound was made, but I saw in a distant part of the room near the ceiling something like a box round which blue electric light played, and I associate the sound with that."

This artificial larynx is attached to the trumpet so that when the spirit places his or her face into the ectoplasmic mask and speaks, the voice is projected amplified by the trumpet. Usually the voice is heard from the larger, bell end of the trumpet but sometimes this is reversed and the sitter hears the voice issuing from the narrow end. The trumpet itself is moved about the séance room by rods of ectoplasm issuing from the medium. In **Harry Edwards's** book *The Mediumship of Jack Webber* (1940), there are a number of photographs taken in **infrared** light, which show a trumpet held up on such ectoplasm. It is the necessity of ectoplasm for the movement of the trumpet, and the initial building of the artificial larynx, that necessitates trumpet séances being held in darkness. Medium **Colin Evans**, at a Webber séance, described what happened immediately after Jack Webber had been securely tied into his chair.

The first movement of the trumpets occurred instantly on the light being put out … these trumpets— about two feet in height and two in number and very plenti-

fully daubed with luminous paint so that they were never lost sight of—had been standing on the floor well out of reach of the medium's hands where he was seated. First one trumpet soared swiftly up into the air, and then both trumpets simultaneously … Repeatedly the medium's control called for "light" and every time the light was switched on instantly, and as it was switched on the trumpets would sink with a fairly rapid movement, but not so rapid as a falling body, unsupported, towards the floor, and when the light was on the trumpets were usually just reaching the floor, but still in movement, and continued moving for a moment or two— once for almost half a minute— with gentle movements, obviously intelligently controlled, on the floor— not rolling on their curved sides, but "hopping" as it were on their broad flat ends.

Sources:

Doyle, Sir Arthur Conan: *The History of Spiritualism*. New York: Doran, 1926

Edwards, Harry: *The Mediumship of Jack Webber*. London: Rider, 1940

Fodor, Nandor: *Encyclopedia of Psychic Science*. London: Arthurs Press, 1933

TUTTLE, HUDSON (1835–1910)

Hudson Tuttle was born in Berlin, Ohio, in 1835. He received virtually no formal education. He recalled, "I had access to few books. I had attended school eleven months in all, six of which were at a district school, and five at a small academy." Itinerant Unitarian preachers would visit and stay at his father's house, and so he grew up in an atmosphere "burdened with dogmatic disputations." This soured him to the church.

One day he attended a **séance** at the home of a retired congregational minister who had heard the **rappings** in the **Fox Family** cottage and wanted to experiment. During the proceedings, Tuttle fell into a **trance** and began doing **automatic writing**.

As he wrote, raps were heard and the table moved. He joined regular sittings with the same group. In his trances, he received what was to be the majority of his education. He wrote an article on **prayer** that was published in *The Spiritual Telegraph*, and then began writing a story on life in the **spirit world**, titled *Scenes in the Spirit World* (this was published in England as *Life in Two Spheres*).

The **spirits** were frequently dissatisfied with the results of the automatic writing and Tuttle would do many rewrites of the material he produced. At the age of eighteen, he began a monumental work titled *Arcana of Nature*. When it was finally finished, the spirits were so dissatisfied that they insisted he burn it and start again. This he did. It took two years to produce the finished book, for which he claimed no personal merit, saying, "Mine has been the task of an amanuensis, writing that which has been given to me. I claim no honor, except honestly and faithfully attempting to perform my part of the task." He went on to write many more volumes on **Spiritualism**.

Tuttle married Emma Rood, a noted poet and journalist. She developed mediumistic abilities herself, and for many years worked with the Spiritualist **Lyceums**. With her husband Hudson, she wrote *Stories From Beyond the Borderland* (1910). Despite the success of his books, Tuttle never gave up his life as a farmer and breeder of horses. Sometimes there were long periods of waiting for the spirits to bring him new inspiration. He said, "Sometimes I have prolific periods, and, again, I go over a deserted country. For days, weeks, even months, I feel forsaken and alone. The very fountains of thought seem dried up." But invariably the spirits returned and Tuttle would write again. He produced many books including *Ethics of Spiritualism* (1878), *Philosophy of Spirit and the Spirit World* (1896), *Studies in Outlying Fields of Psychic Science* (1889), *Religion of Man and Ethics of Science* (1890), and *Mediumship and Its Laws* (1900). He died on December 15, 1910.

Sources:

Awtry-Smith, Marilyn: *"They" Paved the Way*. New York: Spiritualism & More, nd

Fodor, Nandor: *Encyclopedia of Psychic Science*. London: Arthurs Press, 1933

TWAIN, MARK (SAMUEL LANGHORNE CLEMENS) (1835–1910)

Samuel Langhorne Clemens was born November 30, 1835, in Florida, Missouri, the third son and fifth child of John Marshall Clemens and Sarah Lampton. When he was four years old, the family moved to Hannibal, Missouri. He received little schooling; attending a "dame school" and then two "common schools" for a while. His father died when he was twelve and his schooling came to an end when he started work as an apprentice to a printer. He later worked for his older brother Orion, who became a newspaper publisher. Clemens contributed some humorous pieces to Orion's *Journal*. In 1853, Clemens set out as an itinerant printer and started to work his way eastward, as far as New York City and Philadelphia.

In 1856, Clemens started on a trip down the Mississippi River, planning to travel to South America. On the riverboat, he became fascinated by Horace Bixby, the boat's pilot. He apprenticed himself to Bixby and gave up the idea of South America. Within eighteen months, Clemens became licensed as a riverboat pilot.

Less than a year later, in 1858, while piloting the steamboat *Pennsylvania*, Clemens had a **premonition**. He saw his younger brother Henry laid out in a metal coffin that rested on two chairs. There was a bouquet of white flowers in the coffin and a single red flower on the young man's chest. He was surprised that it was a metal coffin, for such were expensive and far more than he knew his family could afford. But so vivid was the dream that when Clemens awoke he was almost certain Henry had died. He later wrote in his autobiography, "I dressed and moved toward that door thinking I would go in there and have a look at it, but I changed my mind. I thought I could not yet bear to meet my mother ... (Then) it suddenly flashed upon me that there was nothing real about this—

it was only a **dream**." Although he told one or two people of the dream, he neglected to mention it to his brother Henry, who later came aboard the *Pennsylvania*. Then Clemens was transferred to another riverboat while his brother remained on the *Pennsylvania*. Two days later, the *Pennsylvania* unexpectedly exploded, killing 150 people. Henry Clemens was badly burned by the exploding boilers of the boat. Clemens rushed to his bedside and was there when his brother died. Waking from a sleep of exhaustion, Clemens found that Henry's body had been moved. When he found it, it was exactly as he had dreamed, in a metal coffin resting on the two chairs. It transpired that several ladies, who had been admirers of Henry, had taken up a collection and purchased the expensive coffin. As Clemens stood gazing at his brother's body in the coffin, an elderly lady approached and placed a white bouquet and a single red flower on his chest. The whole experience cemented in Clemens a belief in a sixth sense.

In 1862, Clemens accepted a post as a feature writer for the *Virginia City (Nevada) Territorial Enterprise* and adopted the pen name of Mark Twain, taken from the "two fathoms deep" soundings on the riverboats. After publication of his first book in 1867 (*The Celebrated Jumping Frog of Calaveras County, and Other Sketches*), Clemens/Twain traveled to Europe and the Middle East and then produced his second successful book, *Innocents Abroad* (1869).

As he became more successful, he met and befriended a wide variety of people. One was Helen Adams Keller who, although blind and deaf, achieved an education and training regarded as the most extraordinary accomplishment ever made in the education of handicapped persons. She entered Radcliffe College in 1900 and graduated *cum laude* in 1904. She wrote many books and articles. She and Twain became close friends. He was fascinated by her seemingly amazing **intuitive** abilities to know what other people were thinking and to be aware of her own surroundings. In fact, Twain experienced something of this **telepathy** on first meeting Keller. He said, "The girl began to deliver happy ejaculations, in her

Noted American writer Mark Twain (Samuel Clemens), c. 1885. *Hulton Archive/Getty Images.*

broken speech. Without touching anything, of course, and without hearing anything, she seemed quite well to recognize the character of her surroundings. She said, 'Oh, the books, so many, many books. How lovely!' I told her a long story, which she interrupted all along and in the right places, with cackles, chuckles, and carefree bursts of laughter. Then Miss Sullivan (Keller's teacher) put one of Helen's hands against her lips and said, 'What is Mr. Clemens distinguished for?' Helen answered, in her crippled speech, 'For his humor.' I spoke up modestly and said, 'And for his wisdom.' Helen said the same words instantly—'and for his wisdom.' I suppose it was mental telepathy for there was no way for her to know what I had said." Keller continued to amaze Twain by finishing his sentences for him as they conversed.

When **physical medium Daniel Dunglas Home** retired from public life, he refused to meet with most people. He did, however, agree to meet with Twain, who had been critical of him. Apparently Twain found Home convincing, and returned for several more private meetings with him. In 1879, Twain attended a series of private **séances** with the **medium** in Paris. The two men maintained a strong friendship until Home's death in 1886. Twain also became close friends with Count Louis Hamon, better known as "Chiero," the palm reader, **numerologist**, and astrologer. Cheiro's reading of Twain's palm was revealing. Twain wrote, "The past may leave its mark, I admit, and character may even be told even down to its finest shades of expression; all that I might believe—but how the future may be foreshadowed, that I cannot understand ... Cheiro has exposed my character with humiliating accuracy. I ought not to confess this accuracy, still I am moved to do it."

Twain joined the **Society for Psychical Research** and even contributed some articles to it, his first being a letter on the subject of mental telepathy or, to use his own term, "mental telegraphy." He wrote two articles for the *Journal*, "Mental Telegraphy" and "Mental Telegraphy Again." In these he outlined the latest research together with some of his own firsthand experiences.

Twain's hand-picked biographer Albert Bigelow Paine said of Twain, "**psychic** theories and phenomena have always attracted Mark Twain. In thought transference especially he had a frank interest, and an interest awakened and kept alive by certain phenomenon [sic], psychic manifestations we call them. In his association with Mrs. Clemens (he had married Olivia Langdon in 1870) it not infrequently happened that one spoke the other's thoughts or perhaps a long-procrastinated letter to a friend would bring an answer as quickly as it was mailed." In fact Twain experienced psychic events on such a regular basis that he was able to put his abilities to practical use. On a number of occasions, when he wanted someone to write to him he would himself compose a letter to the person requesting that he or she communicate. Twain would then destroy his letter without sending it. Invariably the next day he would receive the communication he wanted. Astrologer Sybil Leek said that there were numerous occasions when Twain did this and then received letters "that he opened in the presence of other people telling them exactly what was in the letter." On one occasion this happened when he received a letter from William Wright, a Virginia City, Nevada, journalist. Twain claimed that the (unopened) letter he held up to his friends, which he had just received, would contain comments concerning the possibility of Wright writing a novel about the Nevada silver mines. When the letter was opened it was almost word for word what Twain had written to Wright but had then destroyed and not mailed. Twain later commented, "Mr. Wright's mind and mine had been in close crystal clear communication with each other over three thousand miles of desert and mountains on this special morning in March."

Twain imagined that one day there would be a machine—which he dubbed the "phreno-phone"—that would be "a method whereby the communicating of the mind with mind may be brought under command and reduced to certainty and system." Preston Dennett said, "Mark Twain was ... profoundly psychic. Although his effect on the field of psychic research has often been overlooked, his research into the phenomenon of telepathy remains a significant contribution to our understanding of the potentials of the human mind." Samuel Clemens died April 21, 1910.

Sources:

Dennett, Preston: *The Psychic Adventures of Mark Twain*. Lakeville: FATE Magazine, June 2004

TWIGG, ENA (B. 1914)

On September 4, 1969, Ena Twigg and her husband Harry sat in their living room with close friend Canon John Pearce-Higgins. Suddenly a voice told Ena to turn on the tape recorder. She did so. Then she went into a **trance** and the voice continued to speak through her. It was the voice of Bishop **James Albert Pike**, who had been missing for seven days, lost in the Palestinian Desert. His voice advised that he was dead and had been for twenty-four hours. In detail, he gave the circumstances of his death and directions to the location of his body. This was the event that brought Ena Twigg to the attention of the general public. Ena Twigg was also the first **Spiritualist** minister ever featured on a religious program on the BBC in England, on Sunday March 12, 1967.

Ena was born in Gillingham, Kent, England, on January 6, 1914. She was the second of four children born to Harry and Frances Baker. According to Ena, the whole family was **psychic**. As a child, Ena enjoyed **astral projection** and often saw what she termed the "misty people". It was they who, one night, told her that her father was to leave the earth plane the following week. She adored her father and was devastated when, as predicted, he slipped and fell down the stairs, fracturing his skull and injuring his spine; injuries from which he died. When her mother remarried nearly two years later, Ena left home to marry the boy who lived across the street; Harry Twigg. Ena had many vivid experiences of **clairvoyance** and **extrasensory perception**. Her father's **spirit** came to her and acted as her **spirit guide**.

Harry Twigg joined the Royal Navy and for many years Ena and he were "globetrotting" from one naval depot to another. In Malta, she was operated on for acute appendicitis but complications led to her being sent back to England where she was advised that her heart was weak and she should look forward to life as an invalid. As she said, "I believe that before we are ready for a revelation, before we can make any big upward step, we are confronted with a terrific problem. It can be an emotional one, a material one, a spiritual one, or one of mental or physical suffering. How we deal with that situation determines how we are going to go on." One evening she was visited by three of her "misty people" who gave her injections and visited her on a regular basis for six months. This led to her complete recovery, and she determined to devote her life to helping others. Asking the "misty people" where she should start, she was given an address in a part of

town unknown to her. Ena and Harry went to the address and were greeted by a woman who said, "Do come in. It's our **circle** night." It transpired that a group meeting there had recently lost their **medium**. When Ena sat with them, she immediately went into trance. She was a natural medium. Not long after that, she found herself in a situation where she had to stand in for another medium as platform speaker and message-giver for the local Christian Spiritualist Church. It was at a later private home sitting that Harry was converted to Spiritualism; his deceased father came through Ena and exchanged with Harry various secrets of Freemasonry.

Throughout the war, Ena had visions and communications from the **spirit world**, advising her of the wellbeing of her husband. Her "misty people" had advised her that he would get through the war safely. She learned the details of the D-Day landing ahead of time and Harry learned that he would not have to go to the Far East for combat because the war would come to an end, which it did. In gratitude for their safety throughout the conflict, Ena and Harry dedicated the rest of their lives to helping others.

She subjected herself to any and all **psychical research** testing that was suggested, frequently being "trussed up with wires and electrodes like a chicken prepared for roasting." In one test done at the **College of Psychic Studies**, a registered package was brought into the room and opened for the first time. It was found to contain an eyeglass case. Ena immediately went into a trance and brought through so much valid information that the owner of the case became a convert to Spiritualism on the spot. Rosalind Heywood, then Vice President of the **Society for Psychical Research**, constantly urged Ena to always keep notes, make tape recordings, and have witnesses for all her séances. This she did. As a result, there was the later recording of Bishop Pike's first communication after his death in the Palestinian Desert.

Three years prior to that, in 1966, shortly after Bishop Pike's son committed suicide, Canon Pearce-Higgins, Vice-Provost of Southwark

Cathedral, arranged for the bishop to have a sitting with Ena. At that sitting, she brought through the son who desperately needed to explain things to his father. There was a lot of evidential material which was a great comfort to the grieving father. There followed a number of **séances** for the bishop over the next few years.

Ena became the first woman to speak in an Anglican cathedral. On Sunday, January 25, 1970, she spoke in Southwark Cathedral. She went on to speak at a large number of symposia before distinguished scholars and researchers. She was the medium to bring back Bert Lahr to his widow, and Edgar Cayce to discuss ARE affairs with Doctor Herbert Puryear.

Philip was a spirit who sometimes spoke through Ena, giving advanced teachings and enlightenment. In August 1970, he came through to give guidance and advice to the officers of the **Spiritual Frontiers Fellowship**. In due course, Ena Twigg opened her own **healing** clinic. She achieved a very high reputation as a healer, clairvoyant and trance medium.

Sources:

Barbanell, Maurice: *This Is Spiritualism*. Oxshott: The Spiritual Truth Press, 1959

Heywood, Rosalind: *Man, Myth & Magic: Mediums*. London: BPC Publishing, 1970

Lehmann, Rosamund: *The Swan in the Evening: Fragments of an Inner Life*. New York: San Francisco: Harcourt Brace Jovanovich, 1968

Stemman, Roy: *The Supernatural: Spirits and Spirit Worlds*. London: Aldus, 1975

Twigg, Ena: *How I Became a Medium*. New York: The Psychic Reader—World Publishing, 1969

Twigg, Ena with Ruth Hagy Bro: *Ena Twigg: Medium*. London: W. H. Allen, 1973

Two Worlds

Two Worlds is a **Spiritualist** magazine that was founded by **Emma Hardinge Britten** in 1887. It is published monthly and for many years was edited by **Maurice Barbanell**. Since the mid-1990s it has been edited by Tony Ortzen, who also edits the British weekly *Psychic News*. Britten founded the magazine when she had settled in Manchester, England, after spending many months lecturing in Australia, New Zealand, and America. She edited it herself for the first five years of the magazine's life.

Sources:

Fodor, Nandor: *Encyclopedia of Psychic Science*. London: Arthurs Press, 1933

Two Worlds magazine. London: Two Worlds Publishing

VICTORY

UV

Universal Brotherhood of Faithists
see Newbrough, Dr. John Ballou

UNIVERSAL
SPIRITUALIST ASSOCIATION

The Universal Spiritualist Association was founded in 1956 by Clifford Bias, Robert Chaney, and Lillian Dee Johnson after the disruption of the Spiritualist Episcopal Church earlier that year. It was formed by those who sided with Rev. Dorothy Flexer.

The earlier Spiritual Episcopal Church, which was based at **Camp Chesterfield**, Indiana, had become divided after a morals charge had been brought against one of the main mediums, who was also a candidate for a church office. Flexer moved the church headquarters to Lansing, Michigan, and the church's **mediums** were forbidden to work at Camp Chesterfield.

The Universal Spiritualist Association attempted **materializations**, but in 1960, the *Psychic Observer* published photographs showing outright fraud by mediums including Mabel Riffle and Penny Umbach. The association is today governed by a General Board composed of President, Vice President, Secretary and three Trustees. Churches within the association are autonomous,

though chartered by the association. Where the earlier Spiritual Episcopal Church did not acknowledge **reincarnation**, the present Universal Spiritualist Association does, and teaches classes and workshops on the subject. It describes itself as "a nondenominational association teaching, preaching, and practicing the great religions, including **Buddhism**, Christianity, Hinduism, Islam, and Judaism; as well as the esoteric faiths of Esotericism, Native American Spirituality, Rosicrucianism, **Spiritualism**, Sufism, and **Theosophy** as a Serene Way of Life in a troubled world—a Pathway for the devotees and adherents of the Mystic, the **psychic**, the New Age, the **Metaphysical**, and the Traditional."

Sources:

Melton, J. Gordon: *The Encyclopedia of American Religions*. Wilmington: McGrath, 1978

Universal Spiritualist Association: http://www.metareligion.com/New_religious_groups/Groups/Spiritual/universal_spiritualist_association.htm

VAN PRAAGH, JAMES

James Van Praagh was born on Long Island, New York, the youngest of four children. He grew up in Bayside. He was educated at Sacred

Heart Catholic School there and then, at fourteen, moved on to Eymard Preparatory Seminary in Hyde Park, New York. His introduction to psychism came when he was in grade school and had a premonition about his teacher's son. He told the teacher that her son had been struck by a car but that he had only broken his leg and was otherwise all right. The teacher quickly learned the truth of this statement and then had to explain to the bewildered Van Praagh that he had a "special gift." What he had exhibited was **clairsentience**—sensing something. When he was eight years old he exhibited **clairvoyance**—"clear seeing." He had been questioning the existence of God. In his bedroom, he felt a strong gust of cold wind and then saw a large hand descend from the ceiling and hover over him. He felt it to be the hand of God, letting him know that He did indeed exist.

When he was twelve, Van Praagh and his friend Scott decided to have a **séance**. They had previously used a **Ouija®** board, but typically, both had felt that the other was pushing the **planchette**. At their séance they sat quietly studying a lit candle. Since it was the anniversary of Janis Joplin's death, they called on her **spirit** to make itself known. The candle flame moved back and forth unnaturally and finally went out, greatly frightening them both. Van Praagh went on to have other **psychic** experiences, when investigating an old abandoned house with his friends and when going through a neighborhood cemetery.

Van Praagh's Irish Catholic mother wanted him to become a priest. He went to seminary, but realized during his first year that God was within him, as He was also a part of everyone. He left the seminary and went to New York City public high school. From there he went to San Francisco State College to major in broadcasting and communications. After graduation, Van Praagh moved to the west coast and got a job with the William Morris Agency. One day his supervisor invited him along to a sitting she was to have with **medium** Brian Hurst. Hurst told Van Praagh that he would one day be giving such readings himself.

Van Praagh started a self-imposed regimen of **psychic development** and soon found himself acting as regular psychic to his workmates. This led to him picking up on the details of one person's deceased grandmother. From there he went on to become a psychic medium. His **spirit guide** is a Chinese gentleman named Chang. There is also a Sister Theresa of the Sisters of Mercy order (his early schooling was at a school run by the Sisters of Mercy), an English doctor named Harry Aldrich, and a **Native American** named Golden Feather.

Once he turned his focus to mediumship, James Van Praagh made rapid progress, eventually becoming one of the best known mediums in America, with regular appearances on television talk shows. He did a daytime talk show titled *Beyond With James Van Praagh* which aired in the U.S. from September 2002 until September 2003. In April 2002, CBS-TV produced a miniseries starring actor Ted Danson, titled *Living With the Dead*. It was based on Van Praagh's first book, *Talking To Heaven*. A second mini-series is planned, titled *The Dead Will Tell*. Van Praagh does regular presentations and workshops at venues across the country, including at the **Spiritualist** community in **Lily Dale**, New York.

Sources:

James Van Praagh Homepage: http://www.VanPraagh. com

Van Praagh, James: *Talking To Heaven: a Medium's Message of Life After Death*. New York: Dutton, 1997

VASILIER, DR. LEONID L. (1891–1966)

Dr. Leonid Vasiliar was a **psychical research** pioneer in the Soviet Union. He was Chairman of Physiology at Leningrad University. In April 1960, he addressed a meeting of top Soviet scientists and told them that it was essential to research **extrasensory perception**, since the United States was testing **telepathy** on their submarines, as detailed in their *Nautilus* experiments. He said, "The discovery of the energy underlying ESP will be equivalent to the discovery of atomic energy." Within a year, Vasilier became head of a special **Parapsychology** Laboratory at Leningrad University.

Vasilier had begun experimenting with ESP in the 1930s under the Stalin regime, running hundreds of tests trying to "think people into action." For example, he would concentrate on making a person cross or uncross his legs. The results were too successful to be attributed to chance. He commented, "Out of thirteen tasks telepathically commanded, six were carried out with total accuracy; there are doubts about three; four weren't carried out." He also tried to mentally influence a person's body to feel well rather than sick and had some amazing results with a twenty-nine year old patient in a Leningrad hospital. For years she had suffered hysterical paralysis of the left side but, working with Vasilier and Dr. V. N. Finne, moved her paralyzed arm and leg from mental suggestions alone. These experiments were described in his 1962 book *Experiments in Mental Suggestion*. One of the most successful of Vasilier's experiments took place in a room that precluded the existence of electromagnetic radiation, thus eliminating any possible physical communication. Some of his experiments involved subjects who were several hundred miles away. One of Vasilier's test subjects was **Nelya Mikhailova**, the psychic who became known for her ability to "see" colors with her fingers.

Sources:

Fishley, Margaret: *The Supernatural*. London: Aldus, 1976

Ostrander, Sheila and Lynn Schroeder: *Psychic Discoveries Behind the Iron Curtain*. Englewood Cliffs: Prentice-Hall, 1970

VIETNAMESE SPIRITUALISM

Caodaism, or "High Palace," is the name given to a form of **Spiritualism** found in Vietnam since 1926. It is the third largest religion in Vietnam, after **Buddhism** and Roman Catholicism. *Cao* means "high" and *Dai* means "palace," refer-

ring to the supreme palace where God reigns. The word is also used as God's symbolic name. Caodaism is a fusion religion which combines elements from Buddhism, Christianity, Confucianism, Hinduism, Islam, Judaism, and Taoism, plus the indigenous religion of Vietnam known as Geniism.

The main religious center is in Tay Ninh, about sixty miles northwest of Saigon. In 2005, there were between seven and eight million followers in Viet Nam and 30,000 in Asia, Australia, Canada, Europe, and the United States. The Divine Teaching is dispensed in **spirit** messages obtained through "Ngoc Co", a "psychographic receptor" unknown to western occultism but used in the Orient for generations to communicate with the **spirit world**. According to the degree of spiritual evolution, the adept observes partial or integral vegetarianism and devotes him- or herself to simple **prayer** or daily **meditation** outside working hours.

Caodaism adopts "the norms of Confucian rigorism; the gentleness of Buddhism and its **Metaphysical** speculations; the code of ethics of Taoism and its esoteric conceptions; the morals of Christianity ... The **Spiritism** to which the adept has recourse has nothing in common—at least from the point of view of ceremonial and of result—with Western Spiritism and constitutes not an end in itself but a privilege of investigation of information and especially of study."

It is believed that due to the frailty of religious leaders such as Buddha, Lao Tse, Confucius, and **Jesus**, the truth became distorted. According to ReligiousTolerance.org,

A number of religions were formed but most flourished only in or near their countries of origin. Religions became adapted to the needs of individual cultures. Limitations in communication and transportation prevented the formation of a single, true universal religion which all of humanity could embrace. Followers of Caodaism believe that God was concerned that the multiplicity of religions prevented people from living together in harmony. God decided to initiate a third revelation, in which he communicated Caodaism by spiritist means ... Spiritism (called Spiritualism in England) is the method that God chose to transmit this new religion to humanity. Simple mechanical devices were used as a means of communication between spirit beings and humans. e.g.:

1. A small movable platform on a **Ouija®** board which is lightly touched by two or more **mediums**. During a **séance**, the platform is seen to move around the board and point to various letters, numbers and words.

2. A small table which the mediums touch lightly. During a séance, the table is observed to tip and tap on the floor. The number of taps would indicate a specific letter.

3. A *Ngoc co* (basket with beak), which consists of a wicker basket with a radiating stick about 26 inches long; a pen is attached near the end of the stick. In use, two mediums hold the basket; the apparatus moves and its pen writes out messages which are interpreted by a third person and written down by a secretary. This is a very efficient method of communication, because words are directly written. It is the preferred method in Caodism.

It is further stated that animals and humans have two components: a visible, physical body and an invisible component composed of "a spirit (conscience) which is part of God's spirit, and a soul (or perispirit) which is responsible for emotions and personality." There is a belief in **reincarnation** and in **karma**. In many respects Caodaism seems to be very similar to Spiritism or Kardecism; the Spiritualism that was promoted by **Allan Kardec**.

Sources:

Bui, Hum Dac: *Caodaism: A Novel Religion*. Redlands: Hum Dac Bui, 1992

Caodaism article: http://www.religioustolerance.org/caodaism.htm

University of Sydney, Australia: http://www-personal.usyd.edu.au

Vision *see* Apparition

VISUALIZATION

Visualization is the process of mentally picturing a particular person or thing. Bletzer said it is "to deliberately bring into manifestation a desire or need by an exercise of picturing the desire or need in the mind's eye; one sits and images the end result of the request in mundane form; the picture will eventually become a thought-form strong enough to manifest in the outer world."

Visualization is often a part of **meditation** and can be a useful tool in developing **mediumship**. It is a major part of **affirmations**, where actions, changes, or possessions are desired. To visualize a change in mental attitude, physical health, or abilities, is the first step to achieving what is desired. Exercises in visualization can include the study of, and concentration upon, an inanimate object followed by continuing to "see" it when the eyes are closed. Eventually it will be possible to not only see the surface of the object that was first apparent but to turn that object in the mind's eye and to see all angles and aspects of it. Such exercises in visualization can be useful steps toward the development of **clairvoyance**.

Sources:

Bletzer, June G.: *The Encyclopedia Psychic Dictionary*. Lithia Springs: New Leaf, 1998

Buckland, Raymond: *Buckland's Book of Spirit Communications*. St. Paul: Llewellyn, 2004

VODOUN; VOUDON

Voudon, or Voodoo, is a religion of initiation; a mystery religion stemming from the kingdom of Dahomey on the Ivory Coast of Africa. It was imported to the West Indies with the slaves in the late seventeenth century. The language of Dahomey was known as *fon*, meaning "king."

"Voudon" is the *fon* word for "spirit," "god," or a sacred object. It is not "black" magic and it does not consist of sticking pins into dolls.

A popular misconception of Voudon characterizes the religion as "black" magic that consists of sticking pins into dolls. This is not Voudon. In Voudon there are a number of gods, or *loa*. There is a priesthood and various festivals and ceremonies. The ceremonies are held at a sanctuary or temple known as a *hounfor* or *hunfo*. These sanctuaries vary greatly in size and style depending on the affluence of the immediate community. Some are very elaborate with a number of *peristyles* (covered altar areas) while others are small buildings with a rough cement block for an altar. The priest in Voudon is the *Houngan* and the priestess the *Mambo*. The many gods of Voudon have specific names and definite duties. They are invoked in ceremonies and make their presence known by possessing their worshippers.

There is one ritual in Voudon that is surprisingly similar to a **Spiritualist séance**. It is called *Retraite de l'esprit de l'eau* or "Retreat of the spirit of the water." A small canvas tentlike enclosure is erected in the hounfor, which serves much like a Spiritualist **cabinet**. Various offerings are placed inside, with a tub of water and a stool. The Mambo goes inside and the entrance flap is closed and secured. Several *hounsi* (initiated followers) then sit or lie on the ground beside the structure, holding *govi* jars. These are earthenware jars that contain the **spirits** of the dead. As the people assemble, the Mambo can be heard chanting in *langage*, the secret ritual language of the priesthood. There is a litany as she calls on the *loa* and the people respond. A sharp cry from the Mambo is the signal for the first *hounsi* to slip her *govi* under the canvas into the tent. After a moment the sound of rushing water is heard, soon followed by a strained, hoarse voice. The **spirit voice** will call the name of one of those assembled around the tent. It is invariably recognized as being the voice of a dead relative. A conversation will then ensure between the two, with the Mambo interjecting a word here and there. It is not unknown for the Mambo to be speaking *at the same time* that the dead ancestor is talking.

The ancestor may be consulted on family matters, or advice may be sought on a variety of things. He or she may have some vital message to impart, and there are sometimes warnings of future problems. All the while the voices are speaking, there is the sound of rushing water in the background. Although the Mambo has a bowl of water in the enclosure with her, this background noise is not something that can be reproduced using such a bowl. Occasionally during the ceremony, the Mambo will give an example of **glossolalia** (speaking in tongues) though this is not common. When a number of voices have been heard, the *govi* is returned to the *hounsi*, under the flap, and the next jar taken in. Should the voices begin to fade at any time, the Mambo will again chant in *langage* until the strength returns. When all *govi* have been used, there is a final song and then the Mambo emerges from the tent. As sometimes happens with a Spiritualist **medium** after a séance, the Mambo frequently appears exhausted and has to be helped away.

Voudon is found in places other than Haiti, though that seems to be the main area of its religious emphasis. In New Orleans, and many other large cities around the United States, there is a variety of Voudon that has more emphasis on the buying and selling of *gris-gris* (charms and spells), candles, baths, powders, and such. Many South American countries have variations of Voudon. In Brazil, the official religion is Roman Catholicism yet as with Haiti, it is only superficial for most people. Macumba, Umbanda, Qimbanda and Candomblé are the names of the varieties of Voudon found throughout Latin America. The followers of these different versions of Voudon are increasing in number. The reason for this could be the very personal nature of the relationship between the worshiper and the deities. In Voudon, the follower is not just a spectator but also a participant. The communion with divinity is absolute.

Sources:
Buckland, Raymond: *Anatomy of the Occult*. New York: Samuel Weiser, 1977

Buckland, Raymond: *The Fortune-Telling Book: The Encyclopedia of Divination and Soothsaying*. Detroit: Visible Ink Press, 2004

Deren, Maya: *Divine Horsemen*. London: Thames & Hudson, 1953

Lewis, John: *Religions of the World Made Simple*. New York: Doubleday, 1968

McGregor, Pedro: *The Moon and Two Mountains: The Myths, Ritual and Magic of Brazilian Spiritism*. London: Souvenir Press, 1966

Métraux, Alfred: *Voodoo In Haiti*. London: André Deutsch, 1959

St. Clair, David: *Drum & Candle*. New York: Bell, 1971

VOICES, SPIRIT

The voices of **spirits** may be heard in different ways. In *The History of Spiritualism* (1926), Sir **Arthur Conan Doyle** refers to the spirit voices heard by **Joan of Arc** and also comments on the many references in the **Bible** to such phenomena. Doyle also writes of the reports of ancient statues speaking—such as the statue of Apollo at Delphi—and suggests that the priests of the time were voice mediums.

Jonathan Koons seems to have been the first medium of Modern **Spiritualism** to have displayed the phenomenon of independent spirit voices, in 1852. The voices at Koons' **direct voice séances** were usually projected through a **trumpet**—again, the first recorded use of the mediumistic tool. A short time later, the **Davenport Brothers** produced spirit voices, as did Mrs. **Mary Marshall** and others. The production of such voices seems to have depended upon the building of a voice box or artificial larynx from **ectoplasm** produced by the **medium**.

Many times at séances, spirit voices will speak at the same time that the medium is speaking. General Boldero of Coupar, Fife, Scotland, described a sitting at his home with **Daniel Dunglas Home** in 1870, "Voices were heard speaking together in the room, two different persons, judging from the intonation. We could not make out the words spoken, as Home persisted in speaking

to us all the time. We remonstrated with him for speaking, and he replied, 'I spoke purposely that you might be convinced the voices were not due to any ventriloquism on my part, as this is impossible when anyone is speaking in his natural voice.' Home's voice was quite unlike that of the voices heard in the air."

Sometimes the spirit voices are mere whispers and need such an instrument as the trumpet to amplify them enough to be heard and understood. But at other times they can be very loud. **Elizabeth Blake**, an Ohio medium, specialized in direct voice séances. For these she used a long trumpet, two feet in length. The small end of this would be placed against her ear and the large, bell end at the sitter's ear. The voices which came from the trumpet were very loud and it has been said that they could be heard from as far away as a hundred feet.

Spirits speaking languages such as Welsh, Greek, Japanese, and Hindustani have been heard and even recorded. The strength of the direct voice can vary considerably. Sir Arthur Conan Doyle compared one voice to the sound of a roaring lion. David Duguid (1832–1907), a Scottish medium, on one occasion had the spirit voice so loud that it alarmed and frightened the sitters and they asked him to go away! George Valiantine's guides, Hawk Chief and Kokum, always spoke with tremendously booming voices. In relatively modern times, English medium **Leslie Flint** produced many spirit voices which seemed to originate from the region of his stomach.

Spirit voices are also projected from the throat and larynx of the medium. In fact this is far more common that direct voice. Spirits will speak through the medium, either in the medium's own voice or in the voice of the deceased.

Sources:

Burton, Jean: *Heyday of a Wizard: Daniel Home the Medium*. London: George G. Harrap, 1948

Doyle, Sir Arthur Conan: *The History of Spiritualism*. New York: Doran, 1926

Flint, Leslie: *Voices In the Dark*. New York: Bobbs-Merrill, 1971

W

WEBBER, JOHN BOADEN (JACK) (1907–1940)

John Boaden Webber was born in Loughor, South Wales, in 1907. He had an uneventful childhood and grew up to go to work in the Welsh coal mines. He worked there until 1936. In 1930, he married Rhoda Bartlett, who came from a staunch Spiritualist family. Webber considered **Spiritualism** to be "bunk," but to please his fiancée, he went with her to home **development circles**, where he invariably fell asleep. After two years of attending the circles, Webber began falling into **trance**. His **spirit guide** came through as Black Cloud, a Mohawk **Native American**. **Rappings**, slight movements of the table, and **levitation** of **trumpets** and other objects quickly followed. It was suggested that Webber sit inside a **cabinet** to focus the power, but he refused. He preferred to sit in a circle with the others.

Another spirit guide, a young **Egyptian** named Malodar, soon came through. His specialty was **healing**; Webber was led out to the marshlands in a semi-trance condition, to gather various herbs. The most effective healing technique for Webber was to stand beside the patient, in trance, and massage him or her. As he worked, thick oil would ooze from his hands. Spiritual healer **Harry Edwards** said, "So thick were these oils that his hands presented the appearance of having been immersed in a large can of Vaseline." Edwards was also the head of the Balham Psychic Research Society.

Other spirit guides were Paddy, a young boy, and Reuben, a South American schoolmaster. There were also Talgar, Rev. John Boaden (a deceased great-uncle of Webber's), Dr. Millar, and Professor Dale. Over the years of development, voices came both from trumpets and independently. Heads and hands **materialized**.

Many photographs have been taken of Webber's **mediumship**, mostly by **infrared** photography. Harry Edwards commented, "When the infrared ray first became practical for photographic use in the dark, it was said that it would expose **séance**-room trickery. Through Mr. Webber's mediumship it has proved the genuineness of physical phenomena, and, by doing so, has provided evidence of survival after 'death.'" Certainly the photographs reproduced in Harry Edwards's book *The Mediumship of Jack Webber*, are extraordinary, showing **ectoplasmic** "arms," levitating trumpets and tables, the appearance of **apports**, and the construction of ectoplasmic larynxes for use with the trumpets. The photographs have been taken in different places, frequently in surroundings that Webber had never previously visited. The photographers have included official press photographers representing national newspapers. The sitters were media representatives from the BBC, national newspapers, various Spiritual and psychical journals including **Psychic News**, **Two Worlds**, and the *Journal of Psychical Research*. There have been doctors, clergymen, scientists, university officials, and others. Webber's mediumship has been repeatedly tested by **psychical research** societies throughout Great Britain.

The medium **Colin Evans** gave what he described as a "critical analysis" of a Webber séance. The sitting was typical in that it contained a number of different phenomena including levitation, **direct voice**, materialization, trumpet work and more. Evans said,

> I scrutinized very closely the tying of the medium's arms and ankles to the chair by rope. Two men did this, and the knots tied and the tightness of the rope was such that no "escape" trickery was possible that would permit of getting back into the ropes without obvious disturbance of them. They cut closely into the flesh, and the muscles of arms and ankles were immovably secured to the solid wood of the chair ... Before he was tied in the chair, his coat was stitched all down the front so that it was an absolutely tight fit that could not possibly be taken off and put on again ... After the séance it took some minutes to cut away this stitching with scissors ... The first movement of the trumpets occurred instantly on the light being put out ... these trumpets—about two feet in height and two in number and very plentifully daubed with luminous paint so that they were never lost sight of—had been standing on the floor well out of reach of the medium's hands where he was seated. First one trumpet soared swiftly up into the air, and then both trumpets simultaneously ... Repeatedly the medium's control called for "light" and every time the light was

switched on instantly, and as it was switched on the trumpets would sink with a fairly rapid movement, but not so rapid as a falling body, unsupported, towards the floor, and when the light was on the trumpets were usually just reaching the floor, but still in movement, and continued moving for a moment or two—once for almost half a minute—with gentle movements, obviously intelligently controlled, on the floor—not rolling on their curved sides, but "hopping" as it were on their broad flat ends.

Evans further described the levitation of two luminous plaques, tambourines, bells, castanets (which played "in strict time and tempo, very strongly, to the rhythm of the sitters' singing"), the materialization of hands, multiple voices from the trumpets, and what in some ways was the highlight of the sitting: the removal and later reinstatement of the medium's jacket. The light was turned on at intervals so that Webber could be seen to be still tightly tied to his chair. But, as Evans said,

> After the medium had been inspected and his ropes and knots and stitched coat had been examined in full white light, the light was switched off and afterwards switched on again. The medium was seen to be still tightly and securely roped in his chair, the rope (including the evidentially exact angle at which these two loops crossed under one arm, which the medium himself could not have seen or rearranged even had the rope been loose enough for him to get his arms free and replace them) undisturbed—*his coat was off*. The stitching of the coat was examined and was undisturbed. The light was switched off again, and on being switched on again he was again wearing the coat, the sleeves being perfectly straight and smooth to a degree impossible if his arms with the coat on had been pushed through the loops of the rope which cut tightly into the arms through the coat sleeves. Intermittently, light rain of real objective cold water fell on sitters' faces.

This seemed typical of a Webber séance. His coat was removed and replaced at other séances as well. Infrared photographs even showed the coat at various stages, at one time with the back of the coat in front of the bound medium, in a normally impossible position. Reports in various publications included such comments as, "A bowl of water was placed on a locked piano and a jug of water on a gramophone cabinet. Despite the fact that both instruments were well beyond the medium's reach, Webber's Guides managed to place a record on the gramophone turntable and play it, and also play the piano." (*Psychic News*, July 8, 1939). "The Guide said he would dematerialize the medium, and before our eyes, in good red light, we saw the head, hands, and wrists vanish, leaving just the medium's clothes in the chair. It remained so for approximately a minute. We all then saw the rapid emergence of the medium." (*Two Worlds*, March 3, 1939).

Jack Webber died on March 9, 1940, after a short illness.

Sources:

Edwards, Harry: *The Mediumship of Jack Webber.* London: Rider, 1940

Stemman, Roy: *The Supernatural: Spirits and Spirit Worlds.* London: Aldus, 1975

WEST, MAE (1893–1980)

Mae West was born August 17, 1893, in working class Brooklyn, New York. She was her parent's first child. Her father was the boxer "Battlin' Jack West," and her mother Matilda was a corset model. Her mother exerted a profound influence on Mae, instilling generous amounts of self-confidence and ambition and pushing her onto the vaudeville stage at age seven as "Baby Mae—Song and Dance." Mae quit school after the third grade, and for the next two decades lived the rough-and-tumble life of a stage performer, appearing on Broadway and vaudeville and burlesque stages across the country. She gained national notoriety in 1928 for writing and staging her play *Sex* in New York, which led to

Mae West, film and stage actress, called on spirits for inspiration when writing her own scripts and plays. *Baron/Getty Images.*

her widely publicized trial on obscenity charges, culminating in one week of incarceration and a lifetime of fame. After several more controversial plays, she was signed by Paramount Pictures in 1932, where her phenomenal success is credited with keeping the studio solvent.

In 1948, West was appearing in *Diamond Lil* at the Prince of Wales Theater in London. She sent a note to British voice **medium Leslie Flint** asking for a sitting with him. The **séance** was to take place at her suite in the Savoy Hotel, after her evening performance. Mae West's business manager, Mr. Timonye, escorted Flint to the suite. As Flint described it, "[Mae West] came over to sit beside me and we talked about her films, all of which I had seen and enjoyed. Shortly Mr. Timoney shepherded the anonymous show business gentlemen out of the apartment and I was alone with her. Anti-climactic it may be but we went on talking and soon we were discussing psychic matters ... she had spent years reading widely in the fields of **psychic research** and comparative religion before finding her own truth in **Spiritualism** and then through **meditation** and self-discipline developing **psychic** power of her own."

A variety of **spirits** spoke to Mae West during the Flint séance, including her mother Matilda, who had died in 1930. She and her mother spoke affectionately for a long time during which Mae tested the spirit with mention of a particular pet she had. Her mother correctly named it and also gave Mae other evidential information, including her mother's maiden name of Doelger. After that initial sitting, Mae West had many other séances with Leslie Flint, several at his home in Hendon, London. In 1949, Leslie Flint went to America and again met with Mae West at her home in the Ravenswood Apartments, Hollywood, California

Mae West was an ardent Spiritualist and visited the Spiritualist community of **Lily Dale**, New York many times. Her favorite medium there was **Jack Kelly**. After Kelly's death, Mae claimed that his spirit appeared to her, dressed in a tuxedo. Another of her psychics was Kenny Kingston, in Hollywood, who said that he knew that the spirit world was Mae's first priority. Kingston recalls one occasion, "At the theatre, she'd invite me back to her dressing room for a brief séance ... She'd planned on the séance; wanted psychic messages about her career."

Emily Leider, author of *Becoming Mae West* (1997), acknowledged Mae's fascination with the spiritual. "Mae felt herself drawn back into the world of Spiritualism, which promised contact with the dead. At a resort called La Quinta, which was frequented by Paramount executives, she met Amelia Earhart, who shared this mystical bent. Mae had long admired Earhart for her courage and her mastery of the sky, 'a man's world' ... and the two pioneers—one in aviation, the other in sexuality—talked about their mutual interest in psychic explorations ... After the séance with Amelia Earhart, Mae concentrated on developing her psy-

chic powers. Each day she retreated to a dark room, where she sat, meditating, on a straight back chair, placing her hands on her knees."

Mae wrote the first five screenplays in which she starred, plus all of her stage shows. She wrote them by **inspirational writing**. She claimed that she had nothing to do with the formulation of the plots. Kenny Kingston explained, "She was a natural psychic. She went to the **spirit world** for all her answers. She had enormous depth of spirit. She could write screenplays in three or four days by dictating to stenographers while she lay in a **trance**." He went on to say, "When she was upset that no one had been able to come up with a script idea, she had walked about her room saying, 'Forces, Forces, come to me and help me write a script.' She would begin to hear voices and images, as the plot was revealed to her. Mae would summon stenographers to work with her around the clock, as she would lie in bed in a trance-like state, dictating as the spirits entered."

In August of 1980, Mae suffered a stroke. Friends tried to cheer her up by bringing her old movies and gramophone records to the hospital room. Later that year, she had a relapse, slipped into unconsciousness and died on November 22.

Sources:
Flint, Leslie: *Voices In the Dark*. New York: Bobbs-Merrill, 1971

Leider, Emily Wortis: *Becoming Mae West*. New York: Farrar Straus Giroux, 1997

Mae West Biography: http://www.bombshells.com/gallery/west/west_bio.php

Mae West Biography & Article: http://www.walnet.org/csis/news/toronto_2000/gandm-001125-3.html

Wicker, Christine: *Lily Dale: The True Story of the Town That Talks to the Dead*. San Francisco: HarperSanFrancisco, 2003

WHITE, STEWART EDWARD (1873–1946)

Born on March 12, 1873, in Grand Rapids, Michigan, Stewart Edward White studied at the University of Michigan. He obtained his Ph.D. in 1895 and M.A. in 1903. He married Elizabeth Calvert Grant in 1904. He became a member of the Royal Geographic Society, the American Association for the Advancement of Science, and the **American Society for Psychical Research.**

After writing a number of books about his life in mining and lumber camps, in 1937 White published *The Betty Book,* which contained statements made by his wife when in **trance.** These statements were supposed to have originated from entities calling themselves "The Invisibles." It started on March 17, 1919, when White, his wife Elizabeth, and some friends were working with a Ouija® board. The board became insistent that "Betty" use the **planchette** (though they had actually substituted an upturned wine glass, as an easier tool). The messages kept telling her to "get a pencil." Some days later, Elizabeth (Betty) experienced **automatic writing.** As she and White explained it, "The pencil moved very slowly, and it wrote curiously formed script, without capitals or punctuation, or even spacings, like one continuous word." They continued the experiment over several days. "After a time the words were divided one from the other. Betty blindfolded her eyes, or looked away from the paper so that she might separate herself as far as possible from what was to come next." The automatic writing continued for several months. Then, after White had read a book called *Our Unseen Guest* (by "Darby and Joan"), they tried with Betty going into a light trance. From there "the Invisibles" took over and it turned into full blown **channeling.** White believed that the messages received embodied a valuable philosophy and religious interpretation for daily life.

In 1939, a second book from the same source was published, titled *Across the Unknown.* White's wife died in 1939 and she communicated with him through a **medium**—the Joan of "Darby and Joan"—and the communications were published as *The Unobstructed Universe* (1940). Additional books were published by White in response to the many letters he received from readers of the earli-

er books. These later works were *The Road I Know* (1942), *Anchors to Windward* (1943), *The Stars Are Still There* (1946), *With Folded Wings* (1947) and *The Job of Living* (1948). The last two were published posthumously. White died at Hillsborough, California, on September 18, 1946.

Sources:

Joan and Darby: *Our Unseen Guest.* New York: Harper & Brothers, 1920

Shepard, Leslie A: *Encyclopedia of Occultism & Parapsychology.* New York: Avon Books, 1978

Stewart Edward White Biography: http://www.spiritwritings.com/stewartedwardwhite.html

White, Stewart Edward: *The Betty Book: Excursions into the World of Other-Consciousness, made by Betty between 1919 and 1936.* New York: E. P. Dutton, 1937

White, Stewart Edward: *The Unobstructed Universe.* New York: E. P. Dutton, 1940

Wicca *see* Witch; Witchcraft

WILDE, STUART (B.1946)

Stuart Wilde was born with a twin sister in Farnham, England, in 1946. His father was an officer in the British Navy; his mother was Sicilian and a professor of languages. His parents had met during the invasion of Sicily, in **World War** II.

Wilde left school and started a very successful business selling tie-dyed tee-shirts, which he discovered brought in a lot of money. In 1974, at twenty-eight, Wilde enrolled for a course in **Spiritual** mediumship at the **College of Psychic Studies.** He found that he had some **mediumistic** abilities and was able to contact **spirits.** His focus, however, turned to **meditation** and **trance.** After some years of training, Wilde said, "I developed the ability to enter into deep states of mind and not fall asleep. After five years of training, I found that I could hold concentration at the theta brain level (which is 4-6 cycles of brain rhythm per second) almost indefinitely."

Wilde wrote a number of books including a very successful "Taos Quintet": ***Affirmations,*** *The*

Force, Miracles, The Quickening, and *The Trick To Money Is Having Some.* Other books include *The Sixth Sense, Silent Power,* and *Miracles.*

Sources:

Stuart Wilde Biography & Links: http://cornerstone. wwwhubs.com/wilde.htm

WILLIAMS, CHARLES

Charles Williams was an English **materialization medium** who often sat with **William Stainton Moses.** Apparently Moses was in some doubt as to the genuineness of Williams' phenomena. In 1871, Williams joined forces with **Frank Herne** and together they presented some notable **séances.** The two of them began demonstrating at 61 Lamb's Conduit Street, London, and worked with a **spirit guide** who claimed to be a deceased buccaneer named John King. (In later years their protégée **Florence Cook** worked with King's daughter, Katie King.) Initially the pair produced **rappings** and **table tipping,** but when the lights were lowered their repertoire increased to include spirit voices, the touches of spirit hands, spirit lights, flowers and musical instruments floating in the air, and the movement of furniture. Their early séances were sponsored by **Agnes Nichol Guppy** (the very lady they were later to **apport**).

Psychical researcher Frank Podmore seemed unimpressed by the performances of Herne and Williams. He stated, "The sittings were nearly always held in the dark, or under illumination so faint as to preclude any possibility of accurate observation; active investigation on the part of any too curious sitters was discouraged by the linking of hands; suspicious sounds were drowned by the noise of the musical box or by the request on the part of the 'spirits' that all present should join in singing, so as to promote the harmony of the circle ... Finally, the phenomena presented under such conditions were as a rule palpably within the capacity of any fairly active and intelligent mortal who had acquired with practice some manual dexterity." In 1875, Mr. St. George Stock attempted to expose Herne but later, in 1877, wrote to *The Spiritualist* and apologized for the part he played in the attempted exposure.

In 1878, the Research Committee of the **British National Association of Spiritualists** constructed a **cabinet** with an automatic recording apparatus in it. During the séance, a spirit form appeared sometimes ten or twelve feet away from the cabinet. These appearances corresponded with fluctuations in the recording apparatus, with the medium registering a loss of weight as much as 100 pounds. A few months after this, in Amsterdam, Williams and a fellow medium, A. Rita, were exposed. They were caught with yards of white muslin, a false beard, brown silk ribbon, and a bottle of phosphorized oil.

Sources:

Doyle, Sir Arthur Conan: *The History of Spiritualism.* New York: Doran, 1926

Podmore, Frank: *Modern Spiritualism.* London: 1902; reprinted as *Mediums of the Nineteenth Century.* New York: University Books, 1963

Shepard, Leslie A: *Encyclopedia of Occultism & Parapsychology.* New York: Avon Books, 1978

WINGFIELD, KATE (D.1927)

Kate Wingfield was an English **medium.** **Frederick W. H. Myers** wrote enthusiastically about her in *Human Personality and Its Survival After Bodily Death* (1903) and in the *Proceedings* of the **Society for Psychical Research.** Myers referred to her as "Miss A." Sir Lawrence J. Jones, President of the Society for Psychical Research in 1928, told of a series of **séances** he and his wife had with Wingfield in 1900 and 1901. At that time she was doing **automatic writing** and **clairvoyance** and just developing into a **trance** medium. Jones said that he experienced **rappings, table tipping, physical mediumship, apports** and **levitation** at her séances. However, it was the trance speaking of Wingfield that convinced Sir Lawrence of survival. Deceased relatives proved their identity on a number of occasions.

Kate Wingfield's **spirit guide** was named Semirus, who claimed to be a doctor from

Witches invoking the Owlman near Falmouth in Cornwall, England, 1980. *Courtesy Fortean Picture Library.*

ancient **Egypt**. Wingfield's sittings gradually came to focus on being **rescue circles**. Eventually she had to give up having séances because of the objections of her parents, who did not want her to become known as a trance medium. Her automatic writings were published as *Guidance from Beyond* (1923) and *More Guidance from Beyond* (1925). Wingfield died in 1927.

Sources:

Myers, F. W. H.: *Human Personality and Its Survival After Bodily Death*. London: Longmans, 1903

Shepard, Leslie A: *Encyclopedia of Occultism & Parapsychology*. New York: Avon Books, 1978

WITCH; WITCHCRAFT

Many dictionaries and encyclopedias today still define the word "Witch" as a person who practices black magic and is associated with Satan, even though Witches do not, and never have, believed in the Christian devil. The so-called "Witch" of Endor, of the **Bible**, was actually a **Spiritualist** type of **medium**. The actual meaning of the word Witch is linked to "wisdom," and is the same root as "to have wit;" "to know." It comes from the Anglo-Saxon *wicce* (f) or *wicca* (m) meaning "wise one," Witches being both female and male. According to Dr. Margaret Alice Murray, who wrote the definition for the *Encyclopedia Britannica*, the word has been used almost exclusively from the fifteenth century onward for persons, male or female, who worked magic. She said, "**Divination** or foretelling the future is one of the commonest forms of witchcraft; when this is done in the name of the deity of one of the established religions it is called **prophecy**;

when, however, the divination is in the name of a pagan god it is mere witchcraft."

The word Witchcraft has been used and misused for hundreds of years. Christian missionaries, encountering native peoples in other lands whose beliefs differed from their own, automatically labeled those beliefs and practices as "witchcraft." There was, and is, reference to "African witchcraft," "Native American witchcraft," "Australian aboriginal witchcraft," and more, although none of these practices have any relationship to the ancient pre-Christian nature religions of western Europe.

In fact Witchcraft—*Wiccacræft*; the craft of the wise—dates from long before Christian times and is an ancient Pagan religion with a belief in both male and female deities, with a reverence for nature and all life, and recognition of a need for fertility among plants, animals, and humans. In western Europe, Witchcraft grew into a loosely formalized religion with its own priesthood. The followers worshiped at specific times of the year, at major festivals known as Sabbats, and at minor "working sessions" known as Esbats. The Sabbat festivals tie in with the agricultural year and also with the passage of the sun. The Esbats reflect the phases of the moon.

In the early days of Christianity, the Old Religion of the Pagans was tolerated by the new religion, but as Christianity grew and developed a desire to be the only religion, it aligned the ancient beliefs of the Witches with its own Satanism and with ideas of working evil and black magic. In fact Witches do not believe in the Christian Satan and it is against Witch beliefs to do harm to anyone or anything. *Wicca* is the preferred word for "Witchcraft" with most Witches today. It denotes the positive, nature-oriented, Pagan religion derived from pre-Christian roots. It is preferred since it does not carry the negativity associated with the stereotype witch promoted by Christianity.

In the rites of Wicca/Witchcraft, there is a celebration of the New Year at November Eve (on the ancient Celtic calendar). This is known as *Samhain*. Because of the change from the old year to the new, it is believed that the veil between the worlds becomes thin at this time and so it is possible to make contact with the **spirits** of deceased friends and loved ones. At the Samhain ritual, the witches would see (**clairvoyantly**) and hear (**clairaudiently**) the spirits and reunite with them, if only temporarily. In this sense, a Witchcraft/Wiccan Samhain ritual is very similar to a Spiritualist **séance**, with the leading priest and/or priestess serving as the medium.

Sources:

Buckland, Raymond: *Buckland's Complete Book of Witchcraft*. (Revised) Llewellyn: St. Paul, 2002

Buckland, Raymond: *The Witch Book: The Encyclopedia of Witchcraft, Wicca and Neo-Paganism*. Detroit: Visible Ink Press, 2002

Encyclopedia Britannica. Chicago: William Benton, 1964

Farrar, Janet and Stewart: *The Witches' Way*. London: Hale, 1985

Guiley, Rosemary Ellen: *The Encyclopedia of Witches and Witchcraft*. New York: Facts on File, 1989

Witchcraft Act *see* **Fraudulent Mediums Act**

WOODRUFF, MAURICE (D. 1973)

Maurice Woodruff was a **psychic** who frequently appeared on television making **predictions**. He was one of **Peter Sellers'** favorite psychics and predicted that the next woman Sellers would marry, after Anne Hayes, would have the initials B.E. Sellers met and fell in love with Swedish starlet Britt Ekland, whom he met in the lobby of the Dorchester Hotel, London, where he had gone to live after his divorce from Hayes.

Woodruff's syndicated newspaper column reached a circulation of nearly fifty million, and he received 5,000 letters per week from people looking for advice. Some of his predictions were extremely accurate, such as the death of President John F. Kennedy and the ending of the Viet Nam war. He died of a heart attack in 1973, in Singapore.

Sources:

Shepard, Leslie A: *Encyclopedia of Occultism & Parapsychology*. New York: Avon Books, 1978

WORLD WARS

The two World Wars and their aftermaths were times of great renewed interest in **Spiritualism**. With so many people killed, it was perhaps natural that many people would want to try to make contact with the **spirits** of their deceased loved ones. Additionally, this was a time when there were many instances of **apparitions, clairvoyance, extrasensory perception, near death experiences, premonitions**, and similar phenomena. Many parents, wives, and sweethearts sensed when a loved one was in danger, or was injured or killed. There are untold instances of a service member appearing or making some form of contact at the time of death or grave danger—what are known as "crisis apparitions."

In his book *Apparitions* (1953), G. N. M. Tyrrell points out that the spirits do not appear as they might at the actual moment of death itself—struck by bullets or blown to pieces by a bomb—but "adapt themselves almost miraculously to the physical conditions of the percipient's surroundings," so that the images may appear in mirrors or seem to have shadows (normally unusual in such cases) and appear as the recipient would best know them.

The time between the two World Wars was a time of great empowerment for Spiritualism. The bereavements of World War I provided a steady support for Spiritualism. As Kevin McClure says in *Mysteries of Mind, Space and Time; the Unexplained: War—What War?* (1992), "**Spirit guides** and communicators were powerful and important figures—in the 1930s, the pronouncements of guides were taken seriously by many, and they received excellent publicity." But interestingly, in 1939, both *Psychic News* and *Two Worlds*, the leading Spiritualist journals of Great Britain, continually emphasized that there would be no war, up until a day or so before the actual announcement that Britain had indeed gone to war.

On March 19, 1938, *Psychic News* ran a headline that said "No War for England!—a Spirit Prophecy." This was a promise apparently made by medium Kathleen Barkel's guide White Hawk. On August 18, 1939, *Two Worlds* had a lead story: "World Peace Not to be Broken! Will there be a World Peace Pact?" in which it gave the contents of a number of spirit messages, each claiming that there would be peace. Medium **Estelle Roberts'** guide Red Cloud said that the crisis of September, 1938 would pass; **Maurice Barbanell**, Spiritualist leader, **medium**, and publisher/editor of *Psychic News*, spoke at the Speaker's Corner in Hyde Park and assured everyone that the spirits spoke only of peace. As late as September 2, 1939, *Psychic News* contained a variety of messages from spirit guides, including from the **automatic writing** of **Geraldine Cummins**, all stressing that there would be no war. With the actual outbreak of war, the two journals did some fast backpedaling, acknowledging that although human personality survives bodily death, that does not give spirit knowledge of future events—a point that was obviously overlooked in the emotional time leading up to World War II.

Sources:

McClure, Kevin: *Mysteries of Mind Space & Time; The Unexplained: War—What War?* Westport: H. S. Stuttman, 1992

Tyrrell, G. N. M.: *Apparitions*. London: Society for Psychical Research, 1953

WORLD ITC

ITC stands for **Instrumental Transcommunication**. It represents the research of a few individuals working on **spirit** communication through technology. World ITC was founded in 2002 by Mark Macy of Windsor, Colorado, and Rolf-Dietmar Ehrhardt. Macy had previously founded the International Network for Instrumental Transcommunication. During the 1990s, he published a journal on the results of scientists and researchers from various countries who were studying instrumental transcommunication. The

World ITC was founded "to promote decency in human relationships, to sustain resonance among ITC researchers, and to forge a link with the light, **ethereal** realms of existence."

Sources:

Butler, Tom and Lisa: *There Is No Death and There Are No Dead*. Reno: AA-EVP, 2003

World ITC Organization: http://www.worlditc.org

Worth, Patience *see* **Pearl Curran**

WRITING, AUTOMATIC

see also **Art, Automatic**

Performing the tasks of writing, drawing, and/or painting without control by the conscious mind is called automatic writing/drawing/painting. **William Stainton Moses** (1839–1892) used the term "psychography" for this phenomena, which is common in **Spiritualism**. To focus on writing (drawing and painting follow the same procedures), the operator uses the same muscles that would normally be used, but in no way tries to govern what is actually written. The true "director" of the writing is believed to be a departed **spirit** attempting to communicate. Outside of Spiritualism, the practice is followed to gain possible knowledge of the future, with the governing force being thought of as a deity, disembodied spirit, alien or unknown force, depending upon the beliefs of the person acting as **medium** or **channel** for the writing.

In the Spiritualist form, the medium takes a pen or pencil and sits with a large sheet of paper on the table in front of, or beside, him or her. The writing produced is frequently voluminous and many mediums will use something like a roll of wallpaper or wrapping paper to ensure having enough paper available without having to look down or to turn pages.

Usually the medium will sit quietly at first, perhaps **meditating**. Then the hand holding the pen is rested on the paper and the medium directs his or her attention elsewhere. That might be to read a book, watch television, talk with another person, play a game of chess, or anything that will draw focus away from the hand holding the pen.

What usually happens is that the hand starts to move, initially in small movements, and seemingly of its own volition. The movements, of course, cause marking to appear on the paper. Initially these are no more than straight lines, developing into wavy lines, and then squiggles. Gradually it seems the force becomes aligned with the muscles of the hand and arm and able to direct the writing. Squiggles become circles and hooks, which slowly develop into letters. As the spirit hand–operator becomes more and more accustomed to the mechanics involved, the writing becomes clearer and is written much faster. Some automatic writing is done at incredible speed, with the medium's hand flying across the paper. Many times a normally right-handed medium will use the left hand for automatic writing, or vice versa. Usually the writing that is produced in no way resembles the normal handwriting of the medium.

While a neophyte needs to occupy the mind in order to disassociate from the writing, a medium who is skilled in automatic writing can separate from what is taking place sufficiently without needing outside stimulus, so that he or she does not influence what is written. This can be done to the point where it is then possible to look at the paper and to put questions and receive answers through the writing. If necessary, however, a second person may sit beside the medium and ask the questions, so that the medium cannot see what is written in reply.

There are instances of a medium going into a **trance** and producing writing, but actually no trance is necessary. A classic case was that of William Stainton Moses, who produced a large number of such writings from various spirits, which were published under the title *Spirit Teachings* (London 1883). Describing the procedure, Moses said,

> At first the writing was slow and it was necessary for me to follow it with my eye, but even then the thoughts were not my

thoughts. Very soon all the messages assumed a character of which I had no doubt whatever that the thought opposed my own. But I cultivated the power of occupying my mind with other things during the time that the writing was going on, and was able to read an abstruse book and follow out a line of close reasoning, while the message was written with unbroken regularity. Messages so written extended over many pages and in their course there is no correction, no fault in composition, and often a sustained vigour and beauty of style.

Another, perhaps better known, automatic writer—so far as the purported author is concerned—was **Pearl Curran** who produced the writings of an entity calling herself Patience Worth. Pearl Curran was a St. Louis housewife who was persuaded by a friend, Emily Hutchinson, to use a **Ouija®** board. On July 8, 1913, the **talking board** started spelling out a message which began, "Many moons ago I lived. Again I come; Patience Worth my name." The spirit identified itself as a seventeenth century Englishwoman. Pearl Curran progressed from the Ouija® board to automatic writing, and eventually produced 2,500 poems, short stories, plays, allegories, and six full-length novels all authored by Patience Worth. This amounted to a total of more than four million words within a period of five years.

Automatic writing has also been produced by such well known people as Victor Hugo, Goethe, Charles Linton, Professor **William James**, and **Mme. d'Esperance**. In Brazil automatic writing is known as "psychography.")

Sources:

Buckland, Raymond: *Buckland's Book of Spirit Communications*. St. Paul: Llewellyn, 2004

Ebon, Martin: *True Experiences in Communicating with the Dead*. New York: New American Library, 1968

Fodor, Nandor: *Encyclopedia of Psychic Science*. London: Arthurs Press, 1933

Moses, William Stainton: *Direct Spirit Writing*. London: L. N. Fowler, 1878

Mühl, Anita M.: *Automatic Writing*. Dresden: Steinkopff, 1930

Writing, Inspirational
see **Inspirational Speaking, Writing, Art**

Writing, Slate

Slate writing was very common in the early days of **Spiritualism**. It is a form of direct **spirit** writing, as opposed to **automatic writing** which is done using the **medium**'s hand. In slate writing, the writing appears without any physical contact with medium or sitters. It is sometimes termed "autography." The slates used for slate writing were pieces of rectangular slate set into a wooden frame, the same as the regular slates commonly used in schools many years ago. Today, a slate (or a pair of slates bound together) is placed in the center of the **séance** room and left there until the end of the sitting. A small piece of chalk, or slate pencil, may or may not be placed on the slate, or between the two slates. At the end of the séance, the slate is examined and may be found to have writing chalked onto it by a spirit.

Nandor Fodor described the older method, saying, "The medium and the sitter take their seats at opposite ends of a small table, each grasping a corner of an ordinary school slate, which they thus hold firmly pressed against the underside of the table. A small fragment of slate pencil is first enclosed between slate and table, for the use of the supposed spirit-writer. Should the séance be successful, a scratching sound, as of someone writing on a slate, is heard at the end of a few moments, three loud **raps** indicate the conclusion of the message, and on the withdrawal of the slate, it is found to be partly covered with writing—either a general message from the spirit world, or an answer to some question previously written down by the sitter."

One of the best known mediums who specialized in slate writing was the American **Henry Slade**. He did slate writing and other phenomena for nearly twenty years, impressing **William Stainton Moses** and skeptic **Frank Podmore**.

Other slate writing mediums included **William Eglinton**, Rev. **Francis Ward Monck**, and Mrs. Laura Pruden. Sir **Arthur Conan Doyle** was very favorably impressed by Mrs. Pruden, as were **psychical investigators Hereward Carrington** and **Harry Price**, and the **American Society for Psychical Research**.

Sources:

Doyle, Sir Arthur Conan: *The History of Spiritualism*. New York: Doran, 1926

Fodor, Nandor: *Encyclopedia of Psychic Science*. London: Arthurs Press, 1933

XAVIER, CHICO FRANCISCO CANDIDO (B. 1910)

Chico Xavier was a Brazilian **automatic writer** who produced well over 100 books. In Brazil, automatic writing is known as "psychography." By 1971, Chico Xavier's books had been published in twenty-three different languages.

Chico Francisco Candido Xavier was born on April 2, 1910, in the small town of Pedro Leopoldo in the central state of Minas Gerais, Brazil. He had eight brothers and sisters. His mother died when Chico was five; that same year she appeared to him in **spirit**. He quickly became accustomed to seeing and hearing spirits **clairvoyantly** and **clairaudiently**. As a young schoolboy, he won a prize for an essay on the history of Brazil which he produced by **inspirational writing**, dictated by a spirit who appeared to him.

Chico left school at age thirteen and began working as a **medium** at seventeen. One of his sisters appeared to go insane, but was completely and quickly cured by a Spiritist **healer**. This so impressed the family that they all renounced Roman Catholicism and became **Spiritists**. They joined the newly formed evangelical Spiritist center founded by the healing medium's wife,

Mrs. Carmen Perácio. A spirit voice kept telling Mrs. Perácio to give Chico pencil and paper, and every time she did he produced many pages of automatic writing. According to Guy Lion Playfair (*The Flying Cow*, 1975), "Chico soon proved to be an amazingly prolific automatic writer, and before long he began to produce a series of poems that made a profound impression on his fellow members of the center run by Mrs. Perácio. The poems kept on coming, signed by the names of most of Brazil's greatest deceased poets. In 1932, a selection of these poems was published by the Federacão Espírita Brasileira (FEB), or Brazilian Spiritist Federation. The 421-page volume is still in print today [1975] and has sold some 40,000 copies." It became a bestseller almost overnight, with no mistaking the styles of the famous poets.

Although Chico Xavier held a full time government job for nearly thirty years, he continued to produce books by automatic writing at the rate of three or four a year. Many of his books were written during public sessions. His sixtieth book was *Evolution in Two Worlds*, which was the first of a total of seventeen automatically written in collaboration with another medium, Waldo Vieira, a young doctor. Playfair said, "The interesting feature of this collaboration was that Chico, still in Pedro Leopoldo, would receive one chapter while Dr. Vieira would receive the next three days later and 250 miles away. In this way they produced the book's forty chapters at alternate sessions between January 15 and June 29, 1958. Upon completion of his half, Chico's **spirit guide** Emmanuel instructed him to contact Dr. Vieira and put the book together."

In 1958, Chico left his home town of Pedro Leopoldo and moved to Uberaba, 250 miles to the west. There he set about building up a small Spiritist center. This grew rapidly, funded by the royalties obtained from Chico's many books. He refused to use the royalties for himself—instead, he gave everything to pay for food, clothing and medical assistance for the poor. Playfair observed that Brazilian Spiritists make a clear distinction between *escrita automatica*, automatic writing which may or may not come from the unconscious mind, and what they call *psicografia*, which is the writing of a separate spirit entity. Chico said, "I have reached a state of certainty, an intimate certainty that is naturally personal and nontransferable, that if I were to say these books belonged to me, I would be committing a fraud for which I would have to answer in a very serious way after I left this world." Chico was the second most prolific writer in the Portuguese language, after Coelho Neto. Yet his formal education had only reached the primary level and he had, for most of his life, suffered from defective eyesight precluding him from further study.

Sources:

Playfair, Guy Lion: *The Flying Cow: Research into Paranormal Phenomena in the World's Most Psychic Country.* London: Souvenir Press, 1975

Xenoglossis *see* Glossolalia

X-RAY CLAIRVOYANCE

X-ray clairvoyance is **clairvoyance** that allows the **medium** to see inside things such as locked boxes, sealed envelopes, safes, or the human body. Natalia Demkina, a seventeen-year-old from Saransk, Russia, demonstrates excellent X-ray clairvoyance. In early 2004, she appeared on the British television program "This Morning." Faced with four complete strangers, she described their medical conditions in accurate detail, including the fact that one of them had only one kidney. Of another, Natalia said there had been surgery on the spleen—the woman showed the scar. Of a third, Natalia said, "There is damage to three areas of the spine. The major problem is where the chest part of the spine meets the waist part. Something is probably inserted there. It is something traumatic." The woman agreed, saying there were "metal rods in my back for many years. They were taken out but there was a broken screw which remained there. It was not removed because it would have caused damage." Of the last person, Natalia said that there was a right shoulder problem. The woman explained, "I smashed my shoulder into twelve pieces."

Natalia said, "It is like having double vision. I can switch from one to the other in no time. If I need to know a person's health problem, I see an entire human organism." Not knowing medical terms, she will often draw rough sketches of the human body and pinpoint problems. In Russia, she was shown a female patient in a hospital in Saransk. The doctor said, "The child had many ailments. Natalia diagnosed all of them."

Sir **Arthur Conan Doyle** reported that a doctor he met in Australia could walk along a street and diagnose the man who walked in front of him. He could see the relationships of the organs and note whether or not they were functioning correctly.

Many mediums, although unable to see inside the human body, are able to read messages sealed in envelopes and describe objects packaged in boxes. **Nandor Fodor** said, "X-Ray clairvoyance is a frequently observed manifestation of the power. There are many cases on record in which sealed letters were read when the contents were totally unknown to the experimenter or were couched in a language of which the seer was ignorant. The clairvoyant often has to handle the envelope but not necessarily; in pellet reading (or **billet reading**) the pellets may or may not be touched at all, they may even be burnt and the contents be revealed thereafter."

Sources:

Doyle, Sir Arthur Conan: *The History of Spiritualism.* New York: Doran, 1926

Fodor, Nandor: *Encyclopedia of Psychic Science.* London: Arthurs Press, 1933

Psychic News #3735, February 7, 2004. Stansted, Essex

YOGANANDA, PARAMAHANSA (1893–1952)

Paramahansa Yoganada was born Mukunda Lal Ghosh on January 5, 1893, in Gorakhpur, India, into an affluent and devout Bengali family. As a child he exhibited **psychic** powers and sought out many of India's sages, looking for a teacher who could guide him on what he felt was his spiritual quest. In 1910, he met Swami Sri Yukteswar Giri, a revered master, and became a disciple of his, entering Yukteswar's ashram. He took his final vows as a monk of the Swami Order in 1915, and also graduated from Calcutta University at that time. With his final vows, he took the name Yogananda, which means "bliss through divine union."

In 1917, Yogananda founded a school for boys where modern educational methods were combined with yoga training and instruction in spiritual ideals. It was headquartered in Dakshineswar, near Calcutta. Mahatma Ghandi said of the school, "This institution has deeply impressed my mind." By the 1930s, it had expanded to oversee 90 **meditation** centers, 21 educational institutions, and a variety of charitable facilities.

In 1920, Yogananda was invited to serve as India's delegate at an international congress of religious leaders to be held in Boston. That same year he founded the Self-Realization Fellowship, to disseminate his teachings on the science and philosophy of Yoga and meditation. In India it was known as Yogoda Satsanga Society. He lectured and taught on the East Coast of America, and in 1924 made a cross-country speaking tour. In 1925, he established the international headquarters for his Fellowship in Los Angeles, California. He con-

tinued to travel and lecture to capacity crowds, emphasizing the underlying unity of the world's great religions. He introduced Kriya Yoga, a "sacred spiritual science originating millennia ago in India, which had been lost in the Dark Ages and revived in modern times by his lineage of enlightened masters." According to **Nandor Fodor**, this yoga was based on the classic text *Yoga Sutras of Patanjali*, a form of **kundalini** yoga.

In 1935, Yogananda returned to India for an 18-month tour, speaking in cities throughout the subcontinent and meeting with such notables as Mahatma Ghandi, who requested initiation into Kriya Yoga. During this time, his guru Yukteswar bestowed on him India's highest spiritual title, *paramahansa* (meaning "swan"—a symbol of spiritual discrimination). In the late 1930s, he did less lecturing and concentrated instead on writing and on building and establishing his Fellowship. In 1946, his *Autobiography of a Yogi* was published and became a perennial bestseller. He died on March 7, 1952. It was said that his body remained free of decay for twenty days after his death.

Sources:

Fodor, Nandor: *Encyclopedia of Psychic Science.* London: Arthurs Press, 1933

Paramahansa Yogananda Homepage: http://www.yoga nanda-srf.org/py-life/index.html

Yogananda, Paramanhansa: *Autobiography of a Yogi.* Los Angeles: Self-Realization Fellowship, 1946

ZENER CARDS

Zener cards are a deck of twenty-five cards designed in the 1930s by Dr. **Karl E. Zener**, an associate of Dr. **Joseph Banks Rhine**. They are used in testing for **extrasensory perception** and are sometimes referred to simply as "ESP cards." The deck includes five each of five different designs: a circle, a cross, three wavy lines, a square, and a star.

The procedure as originally used by Rhine was to have a subject guess the sequence of the symbols in the deck, after it had been well shuffled to ensure a random order. The expected average of correct

Zener cards, a measurable, unambiguous way of testing for ESP. *Courtesy Fortean Picture Library.*

guesses was five. This is known as the "mean chance expectation," or MCE. The point of the experiment is to see if the subject can guess significantly higher, or significantly lower, than the MCE.

Sources:

Broughton, Richard S.: *Parapsychology: The Controversial Science.* New York: Ballantine, 1991

Buckland, Raymond: *The Fortune–Telling Book: The Encyclopedia of Divination and Soothsaying.* Detroit: Visible Ink Press, 2004

Guiley, Rosemary Ellen: *Harper's Encyclopedia of Mystical & Paranormal Experience.* San Francisco: Harper SanFrancisco, 1991

ZENER, KARL E.

D r. Karl E. Zener was an associate of Dr. Joseph Banks Rhine at Duke University,

North Carolina, in 1930. The two men created what became known as the **Zener Cards** as a means of simplifying **psi** tests that had previously been carried out with regular playing cards.

Sources:

Guiley, Rosemary Ellen: *Harper's Encyclopedia of Mystical & Paranormal Experience.* San Fransisco: Harper SanFrancisco, 1991

ZOLAR (BRUCE KING) (1897–1976)

B ruce King was born in Chicago, Illinois, on July 22, 1897. His parents were devout Roman Catholics who wanted King to be a priest. He dropped out of his freshman year of high school to study drama. Although he wrote and

Astrologer casts a horoscope with the Tables of Houses, Ephemerides and charts. *Courtesy Fortean Picture Library.*

acted in his own play at age sixteen, King ended up selling men's hats. He later worked as a travelling salesman, selling a line of men's wholesale clothing. By the age of nineteen, he was making $20,000 per year and driving a red Roamer, which at that time was comparable to a Rolls Royce. A year later, he was in the army during World War I.

When he came out of the army, King headed for California. He went from menswear to the securities business, and quickly becoming a successful broker. In 1931, the Great Depression had begun and King bought a radio station in Los Angeles. There he found that the only person who made any real money was an astrologer known as "Kobar." Kobar would give readings over the air and then sell horoscopes at one dollar each. King found that Kobar was selling more than 4,000 horoscopes per week. King made

Kobar the station manager, but later both of them decided to quit. King went to New York; not finding what he wanted there, he decided to go back to his hometown, Chicago. He went to the local radio station and purchased seven and a half hours per week of air time and wired for Kobar to join him. They became partners, with Kobar doing the show and King managing the business. After only a month, they were making $5,000 per week from selling horoscopes at a dollar each. Within a few months they had the third highest rated radio show in Chicago. This inspired them to expand to Detroit, St. Louis, Wheeling, Columbus, Pittsburgh, and Fort Worth. In each city, King would hire an actor, give him a mystical name such as "Ramar" or "Yogar", and have him read Kobar's old scripts. They had to hire thirty women in Chicago to ship the horoscope orders.

One day, quite unexpectedly, Kobar decided he was quitting and left the partnership. King himself then took over as "astrologer." He armed himself with Kobar's old scripts and starting reading astrology books. After only one show he knew he had found his niche. King later published the *Official Astrology Magazine* and started writing books on astrology, **dreams**, and other aspects of the **occult**.

In 1972, King met R. Donald Papon, who was editing *Sybil Leek's Astrology* magazine and teaching astrology courses at New York City's New School. They worked together for years on astrological projects and other ventures. In 1975, King was diagnosed with bone cancer and his health deteriorated. He died on January 15, 1976. In February 1979, King's widow Billie died and left the Zolar Publishing Company and all rights to the Zolar name to Papon. Papon picked up the banner and has been writing "Zolar" books ever since. *Zolar's Book of the **Spirits*** (1987) reviews **Spiritualism** and Spiritualist **mediums** around the country. It contains detailed summaries of many well known figures such as **Daniel Dunglas Home**, **Arthur Ford**, and the **Fox Family**, and reviews of **Lily Dale** and the **National Spiritualist Association of Churches**.

Sources:

The Hermetic Order Temple Heliopolis: http://www.zolar-thoth.org/

Zolar: *Zolar's Book of the Spirits: All the Most Famous and Fabulous Lore about Contacting the Spirit World.* New York, Prentice Hall, 1987

Resources

PRINT RESOURCES

Aarons, Marjorie: *The Tapestry of Life: Teachings Through the Mediumship of Lilian Bailey*. London: Psychic Press, 1979

Abbott, Arthur G.: *The Mysteries of Color*. Chicago: Aries Press, 1977

Accurso, Lina: *Mary Pickford: Superstitious Superstar*. Lakeville: *Fate* Magazine, October, 2004

Acorah, Derek: *The Psychic World of Derek Acorah*. London: Piatkus Books, 1999

Adare, Viscount: *Experiences of Spiritualism with Mr. D. D. Home*. London: privately printed, n.d. (c.1870)

Albertson, Edward: *Understanding the Kabbalah*. Los Angeles: Sherbourne Press, 1973

Alder, Vera Stanley: *The Fifth Dimension*. New York: Samuel Weiser, 1974

Alder, Vera Stanley: *The Finding of the Third Eye*. New York: Samuel Weiser, 1968

Alexander, C.: *The Life and Mysteries of the Celebrated Dr. "Q"*. Los Angeles: Alexander Publishing Company, 1921

Anderson, George: *Lessons from the Light*. New York: Putnam's, 1999

Anderson, George: *Walking in the Garden of Souls*. New York: Putnam's, 2001

Anderson, Mary: *Color Healing*. York Beach: Samuel Weiser, 1975

Anderton, Bill: *Fortune Telling*. North Dighton: JG Press, 1996

Angoff, Allan: *Eileen Garrett and the World Beyond the Senses*. New York: William Morrow, 1974

Arons, Harry: *The New Master Course in Hypnotism*. Irvington: Power Publishers, 1961

Arons, Harry and M. F. H. Bubeck: *Handbook of Professional Hypnosis*. Irvington: Power Publishers, 1971

Arya, Pandit Usharbudh: *Superconscious Meditation*. Glenview: Himalayan Institute, 1974

Ashby, Robert T.: *A Guide Book for the Study of Psychical Research*. New York: Samuel Weiser, 1972

Ashe, Geoffrey: *Man, Myth & Magic: Prophecy*. London: BPC Publishing, 1970

Asimov, Isaac: *Asimov's Guide to the Bible*. New York: Avon, 1968

Atkinson, William Walker: *Dynamic Thought*. Chicago: Yogi Publication Society, 1906

Atkinson, William Walker: *Psychic Healing*. Chicago: Yogi Publication Society, 1906

Atkinson, William Walker: *Reincarnation and the Law of Karma*. Chicago: Yogi Publication Society, 1908

Atwater, P. M. H.: *Coming Back to Life.* New York: Dodd, Mead, 1988

Auerbach, Lloyd: *ESP, Hauntings and Poltergeists: A Parapsychologist's Handbook.* New York: Warner Books, 1986

Awtry-Smith, Marilyn: *"They" Paved the Way.* New York: Spiritualism & More, n.d.

Babbitt, Edwin D.: *The Principles of Light and Color.* New York: Babbitt, 1878

Bagnall, O.: *The Origin and Properties of the Human Aura.* London: Routledge and Kegan Paul, 1957

Baker, Douglas: *The Opening of the Third Eye.* New York: Samuel Weiser, 1977

Baker, Douglas: *Practical Techniques of Astral Projection.* New York: Samuel Weiser, 1976

Baker, Douglas: *The Techniques of Astral Projection.* London: Douglas Baker, 1977

Bander, Peter: *Carry On Talking: How Dead Are the Voices?* Gerards Cross: Colin Smythe, 1972

Bander, Peter: *Voices From the Tapes: Recording From the Other World.* New York: Drake, 1973

Barbanell, Maurice: *Spiritualism Today.* London: Herbert Jenkins, 1969

Barbanell, Maurice: *This Is Spiritualism.* Oxshott: The Spiritual Truth Press, 1959

Bardens, Dennis: *Ghosts and Hauntings.* London: Taplinger, 1968

Bardon, Franz: *The Key to the True Quabbalah.* Wuppertal: Dieter Rüggeberg, 1971

Barnum, P. T.: *The Humbugs of the World: An Account of Humbugs, Delusions, Impositions, Quackeries, Deceits and Deceivers Generally, in All Ages.* New York: Carleton, 1866

Barrett, Francis: *The Magus, or Celestial Intelligencer; Being a Complete System of Occult Philosophy.* London: Lackington, Allen & Co., 1802

Barrett, W. P. (trans.): *The Trial of Jeanne d'Arc* New York: Gotham House, 1932

Barwisp, Mark A.: *A Preface to Spiritualism.* n.p.: National Spiritualist Association of U.S.A., 1937

Bassant, David: *The Truth About the Hereafter and Reincarnation.* Folkestone: Finbarr Books, 1982

Bassett, Jean: *100 Years of National Spiritualism.* London: Spiritualists' National Union, 1990

Bayles, Allison L.: *Essence of Religion.* St. Paul: Galde Press, 1993

Bechert, H. and R. Gombrich: *The World of Buddhism.* London: Thames & Hudson, 1984

Bentine, Michael: *The Door Marked Summer.* London: Granada, 1981

Bentine, Michael: *Doors of the Mind.* London: Granada, 1984

Bentov, Itzhak: *Stalking the Wild Pendulum.* New York: Bantam Books, 1979

Berger, A. S.: *Lives and Letters in American Parapsychology: A Biographical History, 1850–1987.* Jefferson: Scarecrow Press, 1988

Berkowitz, Rita S. and Deborah S. Romaine: *The Complete Idiot's Guide to Communicating With Spirits.* New York: Penguin/Alpha, 2003

Bernstein, Morey: *The Search for Bridey Murphey.* New York: Doubleday, 1956

Besant, Annie and Charles W. Leadbeater: *Thought Forms.* Wheaton: Theosophical Society, 1971

Besterman, T.: *Crystal-Gazing.* London: Rider, 1924

Bird, Malcolm J.: *"Margery" the Medium.* Boston: John Hamilton, 1925

Birren, Faber: *The Story of Color: From Ancient Mysticism to Modern Science.* Westport: Crimson Press, 1941

Birren, Faber: *Color Psychology and Color Therapy.* New York: University Books, 1961

Black, David: *Ekstasy: Out-of-the-Body Experiences.* Indianapolis: Bobbs-Merrill, 1975

Blackmore, Susan: *Beyond the Body: An Investigation of Out-of-the-Body Experiences.* London: William Heinemann, 1982

Blavatsky, Helena Petrovna: *Collected Writings,* Vol. *xii* Madras: Theosophical Publishing House, 1991

Blavatsky, Helena Petrovna: *Dynamics of the Psychic World.* Wheaton: Theosophical Society, 1972

Blavatsky, Helena Petrovna: *Isis Unveiled*. New York: J. W. Bouton, 1877

Blavatsky, Helena Petrovna: *The Secret Doctrine*. London: Theosophical Publishing Company, 1888

Blavatsky, Helena Petrovna: *The Theosophical Glossary*. London: Theosophical Publishing Society, 1892

Bletzer, June G.: *The Encyclopedia Psychic Dictionary*. Lithia Springs: New Leaf, 1998

Blunt, A.: *The Art of William Blake*. New York: Columbia, 1959

Bodian, Stephan: *Meditation for Dummies*. New York: Wiley Publishing, 1999

Boddington, Harry: *The University of Spiritualism*. London: Spiritualist Press, 1947

Bolton, Gambier: *Psychic Force: An Investigation of a Little-Known Power*. London: Spiritualists' National Union, 1897

Bonnell, Gary: *Your Book of Life: Accessing the Akashic Records*. Taos: Societas res Divina, 1996

Bord, Janet and Colin: *Ancient Mysteries of Britain*. London: Guild Publishing, 1986

Boston Courier: Spiritualism Shown As It Is! Boston Courier Report of the Proceedings of Professed Spiritual Agents and Mediums, in the Presence of Professors Peirce, Agassiz, Horsford, Dr. B. A. Gould, Committee, and Others, at the Albion Building, Boston, on the 25th, 26th, and 27th of June, 1857, Now First Published. Boston: Office of the Boston Courier, 1859

Bradbury, Will (ed): *Into the Unknown*. Pleasantville: Readers' Digest, 1981

Brandon, Ruth: *The Spiritualists*. New York: Knopf, 1983

Braude, Stephen: *The Limits of Influence: Psychokinesis and the Philosophy of Science*. London: Routledge and Kegan Paul, 1986

Brian, Dennis: *The Enchanted Voyager: The Life of J. B. Rhine*. New Jersey: Prentice-Hall, 1982

Briggs, Katharine: *Abbey Lubbers, Banshees & Boggarts: An Illustrated Encyclopedia of Fairies*. New York: Pantheon Books, 1979

Briggs, Katharine: *An Encyclopedia of Fairies: Hobgoblins, Brownies, Bogies, and other Supernatural Creatures*. New York: Pantheon, 1976

Bringle, Mary: *Jeane Dixon: Prophet or Fraud?* New York: Tower Books, 1970

Brinkley, Dannion: *At Peace in the Light: The Further Adventures of a Reluctant Psychic Who Reveals the Secret of Your Spiritual Powers*. New York: HarperCollins, 1995

Brinkley, Dannion: *Saved by the Light: The True Story of a Man Who Died Twice and the Profound Revelations He Received*. New York: Villard Books, 1994

Britten, Emma Hardinge: *Ghostland, or Researches into the Mysteries of Occultism*. Chicago: Progressive Thinker, 1909

Britten, Emma Hardinge: *Modern American Spiritualism*. (1870) New York: University Books, 1970

Bro, Harmon: *Edgar Cayce on Dreams*. New York: Warner Books, 1968

Broad, C.D.: *Man, Myth & Magic: F.W.H. Myers*. London: BPC Publishing, 1970

Broad, C. D.: *Man, Myth & Magic: Mrs. Willett*. London: BPC Publishing, 1970

Broad, C. D.: *Religion, Philosophy and Psychical Research*. New York: Humanities Press, 1969

Bromage, Bernard: *Tibetan Yoga*. Wellingborough: Aquarian Press, 1979

Broughton, Richard S.: *Parapsychology: The Controversial Science*. New York: Ballantine, 1991

Brown, Beth: *ESP With Plants and Animals*. New York: Simon & Schuster, 1971

Brown, Rosemary: *Unfinished Symphonies: Voices from the Beyond*. New York: William Morrow, 1971

Brown, Slater: *The Heyday of Spiritualism*. New York: Hawthorn, 1970

Browne, Sylvia: *Adventures of a Psychic*. Carlsbad: Hay House, 1990

Browne, Sylvia: *Conversations with the Other Side*. Carlsbad: Hay House, 2002

Browning, Elizabeth Barrett (ed. Leonard Huxley): *Letters to Her Sister*. New York: Dutton, 1918

Browning, Norma Lee: *The Psychic World of Peter Hurkos*. New York: Doubleday, 1970

Buchanan, Joseph R.: *Journal of Man*. Boston: Little, Brown, 1849

Buchanan, Joseph R.: *Manual of Psychometry*. Boston: Little, Brown, 1885

Buckland, Raymond: *Anatomy of the Occult*. New York: Samuel Weiser, 1977

Buckland, Raymond: *The Buckland Romani Tarot: The Gypsy Book of Wisdom*. St. Paul: Llewellyn, 2001

Buckland, Raymond: *Buckland's Book of Spirit Communications*. St. Paul: Llewellyn, 2004

Buckland, Raymond: *Buckland's Complete Book of Witchcraft*. (Revised) Llewellyn: St. Paul, 2002

Buckland, Raymond: *Color Magic–Unleash Your Inner Powers*. St. Paul: Llewellyn, 2002

Buckland, Raymond: *Doors To Other Worlds*. St. Paul: Llewellyn, 1993

Buckland, Raymond: *The Fortune-Telling Book: The Encyclopedia of Divination and Soothsaying*. Detroit: Visible Ink Press, 2004

Buckland, Raymond: *Gypsy Dream Dictionary*. St. Paul: Llewellyn, 1999

Buckland, Raymond: *Gypsy Witchcraft and Magic*. St. Paul: Llewellyn, 1998

Buckland, Raymond: *A Pocket Guide to the Supernatural*. New York: Ace Books, 1969

Buckland, Raymond: *Ray Buckland's Magic Cauldron*. St. Paul: Galde Press, 1995

Buckland, Raymond: *Scottish Witchcraft*. St. Paul: Llewellyn, 1992

Buckland, Raymond: *Signs, Symbols & Omens*. St. Paul: Llewellyn, 2003

Buckland, Raymond: *The Truth about Spirit Communication*. St. Paul: Llewellyn, 1995

Buckland, Raymond: *Wicca for Life*. New York: Citadel, 2002

Buckland, Raymond: *Wicca for One*. New York: Citadel, 2004

Buckland, Raymond: *The Witch Book: The Encyclopedia of Witchcraft, Wicca and Neo-Paganism*. Detroit: Visible Ink Press, 2002

Buckland, Raymond: *Witchcraft from the Inside*. St. Paul: Llewellyn, 1995

Buckland, Raymond and Hereward Carrington: *Amazing Secrets of the Psychic World*. New York: Parker Publishing, 1975

Budge, Sir E.A. Wallis: *Egyptian Magic*. New York: Bell Publishing, 1991

Bui, Hum Dac: *Caodaism: A Novel Religion*. Redlands: Hum Dac Bui, 1992

Burnham, Sophy: *A Book of Angels*. New York: Ballantine, 1990

Burr, George Lincoln: *Narratives of the Witchcraft Cases: 1648–1706*. New York: Barnes & Noble, 1914

Burroughs, H. Gordon: *Becoming a Spiritualist*. Lily Dale: NSAC, 1962

Burton, Jean: *Heyday of a Wizard: Daniel Home the Medium*. London: George G. Harrap, 1948

Butler, Tom and Lisa: *There Is No Death and There Are No Dead*. Reno: AA-EVP, 2003

Butler, William E.: *How to Develop Clairvoyance*. New York: Samuel Weiser, 1971

Butler, William E.: *How to Develop Psychometry*. New York: Samuel Weiser, 1971

Butler, William E.: *How to Read the Aura*. New York: Samuel Weiser, 1971

Cadwallader, M. E.: *Hydesville in History*. Stansted: Psychic Press, 1995

Caidin, Martin: *Ghosts of the Air: True Stories of Aerial Hauntings*. St. Paul: Galde Press, 1995

Campbell, J. B.: *Pittsburgh and Allegheny Spirit Rappings, Together with a General History of Spiritual Communications throughout the United States*. Allegheny: Purviance, 1851

Campbell, John Gregorson: *Popular Tales of the Western Highlands*. Edinburgh, 1890

Campbell, John Gregorson: *Superstitions of the Highlands and Islands of Scotland*. Glasgow, 1900

Cannell, J. C.: *The Secrets of Houdini*. New York: Bell, 1989

Capron, Eliab W.: *Modern Spiritualism: Its Facts and Fanaticisms, Its Consistencies and Contradictions; With an Appendix*. Boston: Bela Marsh, 1855

Capron, Eliab W. and Henry D. Barron: *Singular Revelations: Explanation and History of the Mysterious Communication with Spirits, Comprehending the Rise and Progress of the Mysterious Noises in Western New York*. Auburn: Capron and Barron, 1850

Carpenter, Sue: *Past Lives: True Stories of Reincarnation*. London: Virgin Books, 1995

Carrington, Hereward: *Eusapia Palladino and Her Phenomena*. New York: B. W. Dodge, 1909

Carrington, Hereward: *Modern Physical Phenomena*. New York: Dodd, Mead, 1919

Carrington, Hereward: *The Physical Phenomena of Spiritualism*. New York: Kegan Paul, 1920

Carrington, Hereward: *Your Psychic Powers: And How to Develop Them*. New York: Dodd, Mead, 1920

Carrington, Hereward and Nandor Fodor: *Haunted People*. New York: New American Library, 1968

Cave, Janet (ed): *Mysteries of the Unknown: Ancient Wisdom and Secret Sects*. New York: Time-Life Books, 1989

Cavendish, Marshall: *The Book of Fate & Fortune*. London: Cavendish House, 1981

Cavendish, Richard : *The Black Arts*. New York: G. P. Putnam's, 1967

Cavendish, Richard (ed.): *Man, Myth & Magic: An Illustrated Encyclopedia of the Supernatural*. London: BPC, 1970

Cavendish, Richard (ed.): *Encyclopedia of the Unexplained*. London: Routledge & Kegan Paul, 1974

Cavendish, Richard: *The Powers of Evil*. New York: G. P. Putnam's Sons, 1975

Cayce, Edgar: *Atlantis—Fact or Fiction?* Virginia Beach: A.R.E. Press, 1962

Cayce, Edgar: *Auras*. Virginia Beach: A.R.E. Press, 1973

Cayce, Edgar: *Edgar Cayce on the Akashic Records: The Book of Life*. Virginia Beach, A.R.E. Press, 1997

Cayce, Edgar: *Edgar Cayce on Atlantis*. New York: Paperback Library, 1968

Cayce, Edgar: *Gems and Stones*. Virginia Beach: A.R.E. Press, 1976

Cayce, Hugh Lynn: *Venture Inward*. New York: Paperback Library, 1969

Chambers, Howard V.: *An Occult Dictionary for the Millions*. Los Angeles: Sherbourne Press, 1966

Chaney, Robert G.: *Unfolding the Third Eye*. Upland: Astara, 1970

Chaney, Robert G.: *Mediums and the Development of Mediumship*. New York: Books for Libraries, 1972

Cheasley, Clifford W.: *Numerology*. Boston: Triangle, 1916

Cheiro (Louis Hamon): *Cheiro's Book of Numbers*. New York: Arc, 1964

Chinmoy, Sri: *Death and Reincarnation*. Jamaica, NY: Agni, 1974

Chrapowicki, Maryla de: *SpectroBiology*. Mokilumne Hill: Health Research, 1938

Christie-Murray, David: *Mysteries of Mind Space & Time: The Unexplained*. Westport: H.S. Stuttman, 1992

Christopher, Milbourne: *ESP, Seers & Psychics: What the Occult Really Is*. New York: Thomas Y. Crowell, 1970

Christopher, Milbourne: *Mediums, Mystics, and the Occult*. New York: Thomas Y. Crowell, 1975

Churchill, Winston: *The Second World War (6 vols.)* Boston: Houghton Mifflin, 1948–1954

The Church of England and Spiritualism: Majority Report of the Church of England Committee of Inquiry. London: Psychic Press, 1948

Clark, Adrian V.: *Psycho-Kinesis: Moving Matter with the Mind*. New York: Parker, 1973

Clébert, Jean-Paul: *The Gypsies*. New York: Penguin, 1967

Coggshall, William T.: *The Signs of the Times: Comprising a History of the Spirit-Rappings, in Cincinnati and Other Places; With Notes of Clairvoyant Revealments*. Cincinnati: William T. Coggshall, 1851

Cohen, Daniel: *The Encyclopedia of Ghosts*. New York: Dodd, Mead & Co., 1984

Collins, Terah Kathryn: *The Western Guide to Feng Shui*. Carlsbad: Hay House, 1996

Communication with the Dead. London: Smythe, 1971

Cook, Mrs. Cecil: *How I Discovered My Mediumship*. Chicago: Lormar, 1919

Cooke, Grace: *The New Mediumship*. Liss: White Eagle Publishing, n.d.

Corte, L. P.: *Sound and Vibration Measurement*. London: Medical Society for the Study of Radiesthesia, n.d.

Covina, Gina: *The Ouija® Book*. New York: Simon & Schuster, 1979

Cowan, Tom: *The Book of Séance*. Chicago: Contemporary Books, 1994

Cranston, Sylvia: *H.P.B.: The Extraordinary Life & Influence of Helena Blavatsky, Founder of the Modern Theosophical Movement*. New York: G. P. Putnam's, 1993

Crawford, W. J.: *Experiments in Psychical Science*. New York: E. P. Dutton, 1919

Crawford, W. J.: *The Psychic Structures at the Goligher Circle*. London: John M. Watkins, 1921

Crawford, W. J.: *The Reality of Psychic Phenomena: Raps, Levitations, etc*. New York: E. P. Dutton, 1918

Crenshaw, James: *Telephone between Two Worlds*. Los Angeles: DeVorss, 1950

Crookall, Robert: *The Study and Practice of Astral Projection*. London: Aquarian, 1960

Crookall, Robert: *The Techniques of Astral Projection*. London: Aquarian, 1964

Crookes, William: *Researches in the Phenomena of Spiritualism*. London: 1874

Crow, W. B.: *Man, Myth & Magic: Double*. London: BPC Publishing, 1970

Crowell, Eugene: *The Identity of Primitive Christianity and Modern Spiritualism*. New York: 1875

Cull, Robert: *More to Life Than This: The Story of Jean Cull, The Medium*. London: Macmillan, 1987

Cutlip, Audra: *Pioneers of Modern Spiritualism*. Milwaukee: NSAC, n.d.

Cyford, Janet: *The Ring of Chairs: A Medium's Story*. Baltimore: Thirteen-O-Seven Press, 2000

DaEl (Dale Walker): *The Crystal Book*. Sunol: The Crystal Company, 1983

D'Albe, E. E. Fournier: *The Life of Sir William Crookes*. London: T. Fisher Unwin, 1923

Davenport, Reuben Briggs: *The Death-Blow to Spiritualism: Being the True Story of the Fox Sisters, as Revealed by Authority of Margaret Fox Kane and Catherine Fox Jencken*. New York: G. W. Dillingham, 1888

Davidson, Thomas: *Rowan Tree & Red Thread*. Edinburgh: Oliver & Boyd, 1949

Davis, Richard Harding: *Vera the Medium*. New York: Charles Scribner's Sons, 1908

de Givry, Grillot: *A Pictorial Anthology of Witchcraft, Magic & Alchemy*. London: Spottiswoode, Ballantyne, 1931

De Haan, Richard W.: *The Spirit World*. Grand Rapids: Radio Bible Class, 1968

Dennett, Preston: *The Psychic Adventures of Mark Twain*. Lakeville: *Fate* Magazine, June 2004

Denning, Melita and Osborne Phillips: *The Llewellyn Practical Guide to Astral Projection*. St. Paul: Llewellyn, 1979

Denning, Melita and Osborne Phillips: *Vodoun Fire: The Living Reality of Mystical Religion*. St. Paul: Llewellyn Publications, 1979

Denning, Hazel M.: *True Hauntings*. St. Paul: Llewellyn, 1996

Derby, George H.: *Rochester Knockings! Discovery and Explanation of the Source of the Phenomena Generally Known as the Rochester Knockings*. Buffalo: George H. Derby, 1851

Deren, Maya: *Divine Horsemen*. London: Thames & Hudson, 1953

Dewey, D. M.: *History of the Strange Sounds or Rappings Heard in Rochester and Western New York, and Usually Called the Mysterious Noises! Which Are Supposed by Many to Be Communications from the Spirit World, Together with All the Explanation That Can as Yet Be Given of the Matter.* Rochester: D. M. Dewey, 1850

Dingwall, Eric J.: *Some Human Oddities.* New York: University Books, 1962

Dingwall, Eric J.: *Very Peculiar People.* London: Rider, 1950

Dingwall, Eric J. and John Langdon-Davies: *The Unknown—Is It Nearer?* New York: New American Library, 1956

Dingwall, Eric J., K. M. Goldney and Trevor Hall: *The Haunting of Borley Rectory.* London: Duckworth, 1956

Dixon, Jeane: *My Life and Prophesies.* New York: Bantam, 1970

Dixon, Jeane: *Yesterday, Today, and Forever.* New York: William Morrow, 1975

Dolfyn and Zu: *Bough Down: Praying with Tree Spirits.* Oakland: Earthspirit, 1986

Donaldson, Terry: *Step-By-Step Tarot.* London: Thorsons, 1995

Donnelly, Ignatius: *Atlantis, the Antediluvian World.* New York: Gramercy, 1949

Douglas, Alfred: *Extra-Sensory Powers: A Century of Psychical Research.* New York: Overlook Press, 1977

Dowding, Air Chief Marshall: *Many Mansions.* London: 1943

Dowling, Levi: *The Aquarian Gospel.* Los Angeles: Leo W. Dowling, 1925

Doyle, Sir Arthur Conan: *The Coming of the Fairies.* London: Hodder & Stoughton, 1922

Doyle, Sir Arthur Conan: *The Edge of the Unknown.* New York: G. P. Putnam's, 1930

Doyle, Sir Arthur Conan: *The History of Spiritualism.* New York: Doran, 1926

Doyle, Sir Arthur Conan: *The Wanderings of a Spiritualist.* London: Hodder & Stoughton, 1921

Dunne, J. W.: *An Experiment with Time.* New York: Hillary, 1967

Dunraven, Earl of: *Experiences in Spiritualism with D. D. Home.* Glasgow: University Press, 1924

Eadie, Betty J.: *Embraced by the Light.* Placerville: Gold Leaf Press, 1992

Earll, Tony: *Mu Revealed.* New York: Paperback Library, 1970

Eaton, William Dunseath: *Spirit Life, or Do We Die?* Chicago: Stanton & Van Vliet, 1920

Ebon, Martin (ed): *The Devil's Bride: Exorcism: Past and Present.* New York: Harper & Row, 1974

Ebon, Martin: *Psychic Discoveries by the Russians.* Bergenfield: New American Library, n.d.

Ebon, Martin: *Reincarnation in the Twentieth Century.* New York: New American Library, 1979

Ebon, Martin: *True Experiences in Communicating With the Dead.* New York: New American Library, 1968

Ebon, Martin: *True Experiences in Telepathy.* New York: Signet, 1967

Edge, Hoyt L., Robert L. Morris, John Palmer and Joseph H. Rush: *Foundations of Parapsychology.* Boston: Routledge & Kegan Paul, 1986

Edmonds, I. G.: *D. D. Home, the Man Who Talked With Ghosts.* Nashville: Thomas Nelson, 1978

Edmonds, John W. and George T. Dexter: *Spiritualism.* (2 volumes) New York: Partridge & Brittan, 1853, 1855

Edmunds, Simeon: *Hypnotism and Psychic Phenomena.* No. Hollywood: Wilshire, 1961

Edmunds, Simeon: *Spiritualism: A Critical Survey.* No. Hollywood: Wilshire, 1960

Edward, John: *After Life: Answers from the Other Side.* New York: Princess Books, 2003

Edward, John: *Crossing Over: The Stories Behind the Stories.* New York: Princess Books, 2001

Edward, John: *One Last Time: A Psychic Medium Speaks to Those We Have Loved and Lost.* New York: Berkley Books, 1998

Edwards, Harry: *A Guide for the Development of Mediumship*. Greenford: Con-Psy Publications, 2003

Edwards, Harry: *A Guide to the Understanding and Practice of Spiritual Healing*. Guildford: Healer Publishing Company, 1974

Edwards, Harry: *The Healing Intelligence*. London: Taplinger, 1971

Edwards, Harry: *The Mediumship of Jack Webber*. London: Rider, 1940

Edwards, Harry: *Spirit Healing*. London: Herbert Jenkins, 1960

Egby, Robert: *Parapsychic Journal*. E-journal #19, July 16, 2004

Egby, Robert: *Parapsychic Journal*. E-journal #22, October 14, 2004

Eisenbud, Jule: *The World of Ted Serios: Thoughtographic Studies of an Extraordinary Mind*. New York: William Morrow, 1967

Eliade, Mircea: *Shamanism: Archaic Techniques of Ecstasy*. Princeton University Press/Bollingen Series LXXVI, 1974

Ellis, D. J.: *The Mediumship of the Tape Recorder*. Pulborough: Ellis, 1978

Elliott, Charles Wyllys: *Mysteries: or, Glimpses of the Supernatural Containing Accounts of the Salem Witchcraft—The Cock Lane Ghost—The Rochester Rapping—The Stratford Mysteries—Oracles—Astrology—Dreams—Demons—Ghosts—Spectres, Etc., Etc*. New York: Harper & Bros., 1852

Ellison, A. J.: *Mysteries of Mind, Space & Time; the Unexplained: Cause and Effect*. Westport: H.S. Stuttman, 1992

Ellison, A. J.: *Mysteries of Mind, Space & Time; the Unexplained: Points of View*. Westport: H.S. Stuttman, 1992

Encyclopedia Britannica. Chicago: William Benton, 1964

Ennemoser, Joseph (tr. William Howitt): *The History of Magic*. London: Henry G. Bohn, 1854

Epstein, Perle: *Kabbalah: The Way of the Jewish Mystic*. Boston: Shambhala, 1988

Estabrooks, G. H.: *Hypnotism*. New York: E. P. Dutton, 1957

Estep, Sarah: *Voices of Eternity*. New York: Ballantine, 1988

Evans, Peter: *Peter Sellers: The Man Behind the Mask*. London: Frewin, 1969

Evans-Wentz, W. Y.: *The Fairy Faith in Celtic Countries*. New York: Carroll, 1990

Evans-Wentz, W. Y. (ed.): *The Tibetan Book of the Dead*. London: Oxford University Press, 1960

Evans-Wentz, W. Y.: *Tibetan Yoga and Secret Doctrines*. New York: Oxford University Press, 1961

Farraday, Ann: *The Dream Game*. New York: Harper & Row, 1974

Farrar, Janet and Stewart: *The Witches' Way*. London: Hale, 1985

Faubel, Rita: *Hints for a Good Reading*. Lily Dale: NSAC, n.d.

Feilding, Everard: *Sittings with Eusapia Palladino and Other Studies*. New York:

Ferguson, Rev. Robert A.: *Adventure in Psychic Development*. New York: Regency Press, 1972

Ferguson, Rev. Robert A.: *The Celestial Telegraph*. New York: Carlton Press, 1974

Ferguson, Rev. Robert A.: *Spiritual Progression after Death*. San Jose: Aquarian Fellowship, 1970

Ferguson, Rev. Robert A.: *Summerland*. San Jose: Aquarian Fellowship, 1969

Fields, Rick: *How the Swans Came to the Lake*. Boston: Shambhala, 1981

Findhorn Community: *The Findhorn Garden*. New York: Harper & Row, 1975

Findlay, J. Arthur: *On the Edge of the Etheric*. London: 1931

Findlay, Arthur: *Looking Back*. Stansted: Spiritualists' National Union, 1955

Finucane, R. C.: *Appearances of the Dead: A Cultural History of Ghosts*. Buffalo: Prometheus Books, 1984

Fishley, Margaret: *The Supernatural*. London: Aldus, 1976

Flammarion, Camille: *Haunted Houses*. London: T. Fisher Unwin, 1924

Flammarion, Camille: *Mysterious Psychic Forces*. London: Unwin, 1907

Flint, Leslie: *Voices in the Dark: My Life as a Medium*. New York: Bobbs-Merrill, 1971

Fodor, Nandor: *Between Two Worlds*. New York: Parker, 1964

Fodor, Nandor: *Encyclopedia of Psychic Science*. London: Arthurs Press, 1933

Fodor, Nandor: *The Haunted Mind*. New York: Helix Press, 1959

Fodor, Nandor: *Mind over Space*. New York: Citadel, 1962

Fodor, Nandor: *On the Trail of the Poltergeist*. New York: Citadel, 1958

Foli, Prof. P.R.S.: *Fortune-Telling by Cards*. Philadelphia: David McKay, 1902

Ford, Arthur: *Unknown but Known: My Adventure into the Meditative Dimension*. New York: Harper & Row, 1968

Ford, Arthur with Jerome Ellison: *The Life beyond Death*. New York: G. P. Putnam's Sons, 1971

Ford, Arthur with Margueritte Harmon Bro: *Nothing So Strange*. New York: Harper & Row, 1958

Forem, Jack: *Transcendental Meditation*. New York: E. P. Dutton, 1974

Foreman, Laura (ed): *Mysteries of the Unknown: Spirit Summonings*. New York: Time-Life Books, 1989

Forlong, J. G. R.: *Faiths of Man: Encyclopedia of Religions*. (3 vols.) New York: University Books, 1964

Forman, Henry James: *The Story of Prophecy*. New York: Tudor, 1940

Fortune, Dion: *The Mystical Qabalah*. London: Ernest Benn, 1935

Fortune, Dion: *Psychic Self Defence*. London: Aquarian Press, 1988

Fortune, Dion: *Spiritualism and Occultism*. Loughborough: Thoth Publications, 1999

Fortune, Dion: *Through the Gates of Death*. York Beach: Weiser Books, 2000

Fournier, D'Albe: *The Life of Sir William Crookes*. London: T. Fisher Unwin, 1923

Fox, Oliver: *Astral Projection: A Record of Out-of-Body Experiences*. London: Rider, 1939

Fraser, Angus: *The Gypsies*. Oxford: Blackwell, 1992

Freud, Sigmund: *The Interpretation of Dreams*. New York: Macmillan, 1913

Freyre, Gilberto (tr. Samuel Putnam): *The Master and the Slaves*. New York: Alfred A. Knopf, 1933

Frost, Gavin and Yvonne: *Astral Travel: Your Guide to the Secrets of Out-of-Body Experience*. London: Granada, 1982

Fukurai, T.: *Clairvoyance & Thoughtography*. New York, Arno, 1975

Fuller, Uriah: *Confessions of a Psychic: The Secret Notebooks of Uriah Fuller*. Teaneck: Karl Fulves, 1975

Gach, Gary: *The Complete Idiot's Guide to Understanding Buddhism*. Indianapolis: Alpha, 2002

Garfield, Laeh Maggie and Jack Grant: *Angels and Companions In Spirit*. Berkeley: Celestial Arts, 1995

Garfield, Laeh Maggie and Jack Grant: *Companions In Spirit*. Berkeley: Celestial Arts, 1984

Garfield, Patricia: *Creative Dreaming*. New York: Ballantine Books, 1979

Garrett, Eileen: *Adventures in the Supernormal: A Personal Memoir*. New York: Garrett Publications, 1949

Garrett, Eileen: *Many Voices: The Autobiography of a Medium*. New York: G. P. Putnam's, 1968

Garrett, Eileen: *My Life as a Search for the Meaning of Mediumship*. London: Rider, 1939

Garrison, Omar: *Tantra: The Yoga of Sex*. New York: Julian Press, 1964

Gaskell, George Arthur: *Dictionary of All Scriptures and Myths*. New York: Avenel, 1981

de Gasparin, Count Agenor: *A Treatise on Turning Tables*. New York: 1857

Gauld, Alan: *The Founders of Psychical Research.* London: Routledge & Kegan Paul, 1968

Gauld, Alan: *Man, Myth & Magic: Automatic Art.* London: BPC Publishing, 1970

Gauld, Alan: *Man, Myth & Magic: Magnetism.* London: BPC Publishing, 1970

Gauld, Alan: *Man, Myth & Magic: Psychical Research.* London: BPC Publishing, 1970

Gauld, Alan: *Mediumship and Survival: A Century of Investigations.* London: Heinemann, 1982

Gauld, Alan: *Proceedings, #55—A Series of Drop-In Communicators.* London: Society for Psychical Research, July 1971

Gauld, Alan and A. D. Cornell: *Poltergeists.* London: Routledge & Kegan Paul, 1979

Gauquelin, Michel: *The Cosmic Clocks.* New York: Avon, 1969

Geley, Gustave: *Clairvoyance and Materialization.* London: T. Fisher Unwin, 1927

Geller, Uri: *My Story.* New York: Praeger Publishers, 1975

Ghadiali, Dinshah P.: *Spectro-Chrome Metry Encyclopedia.* (Vols. 1, 2, 3) Malaga: Spectro-Chrome Institute, 1939

Gibson, Walter B. and Litzka R.: *The Complete Illustrated Book of the Psychic Sciences.* New York: Doubleday, 1966

Glanvill, Joseph: *Saducismus Triumphatus: or, Full and Plain Evidence concerning Witches and Apparitions.* (1689) Gainesville: Scholars' Facsimiles & Reprints 1966

Glass, Justine: *They Foresaw the Future: The Story of Fulfilled Prophecy.* New York: G. P. Putnam's Sons, 1969

Gluckman, M.: *The Allocation of Responsibility.* Manchester: Manchester University Press, 1970

Godwin, John: *This Baffling World.* New York: Hart Publishing, 1968

Godwin, Michael: *Angels.* New York: Simon & Schuster, 1990

Goldsmith, Barbara: *Other Powers: The Age of Suffrage, Spiritualism, and the Scandalous Victoria Woodhull.* New York: Alfred A. Knopf, 1998

Goleman, Daniel: *The Meditative Mind: The Varieties of Meditative Experience.* New York: Tarcher/Putnam, 1988

Grand Orient (A.E. Waite): *The Complete Manual of Occult Divination: Volume 1—Manual of Cartomancy.* London: William Rider, 1912

Grant, Douglas: *The Cock Lane Ghost.* New York: St. Martin's Press, 1965

Grant, Joan: *Winged Pharaoh.* London: 1937

Grant, Joan and Denys Kelsey: *Many Lifetimes.* New York: Doubleday, 1968

Grattan-Guiness, Ivor: *Psychical Research: A Guide to Its History, Principles and Practices* Wellingborough: The Aquarian Press, 1982

Gray, Eden: *A Complete Guide to the Tarot.* New York: Crown, 1970

Gray, Eden: *The Tarot Revealed.* New York: Inspiration House, 1960

Gray, Magda (ed.): *Fortune Telling.* London: Marshall Cavendish, 1974

Green, Celia: *Out-of-the-Body Experiences.* London: Hamish Hamilton, 1968

Green, Celia and Charles McCreery: *Apparitions.* London: Hamish Hamilton, 1975

Gregg, Susan: *The Complete Idiot's Guide to Spiritual Healing.* Indianapolis: Alpha Books, 2000

Gregory, Anita: *Man, Myth & Magic: Schneider Brothers.* London: BPC Publishing, 1970

Gregory, Anita: *The Strange Case of Rudi Schneider.* Metuchen: Scarecrow Press, 1985

Grimshaw, Thomas: *General Course of the History, Science, Philosophy and Religion of Spiritualism.* Milwaukee: Morris Pratt Institute, 1973

Guggenheim, Bill and Judy: *Hello From Heaven! A New Field of Research—After-Death Communication—Confirms That Life and Love Are Eternal.* New York: Bantam Books, 1995

Guiley, Rosemary Ellen: *The Encyclopedia of Ghosts and Spirits.* New York: Facts On File, 1992

Guiley, Rosemary Ellen: *The Encyclopedia of Witches and Witchcraft*. New York: Facts on File, 1989

Guiley, Rosemary Ellen: *Harper's Encyclopedia of Mystical & Paranormal Experience*. San Francisco: HarperSanFrancisco, 1991

Guiley, Rosemary Ellen: *Moonscapes: A Celebration of Lunar Astronomy, Magic, Legend and Lore*. New York: Prentice-Hall, 1991

Guiley, Rosemary Ellen: *Tales of Reincarnation*. New York: Pocket Books, 1987

Gurney, Edmund; Frederic W.H. Myers; and Frank Podmore: *Phantasms of the Living*. London: The Society for Psychical Research and Trubner & Co., 1886

Guthrie, John J. Jr., Phillip Charles Lucas, and Gary Monroe (eds): *Cassadaga: The South's Oldest Spiritualist Community*. University Press of Florida, 2000

Haddock, Joseph: *Psychology; or, The Science of the Soul, Considered Physiologically and Philosophically; With an Appendix, Containing Notes of Mesmeric and Psychical Experience*. New York: Fowlers and Wells, 1850

Haining, Peter: *A Dictionary of Ghost Lore*. New Jersey: Prentice-Hall, 1984

Halifax, Joan: *Shaman: The Wounded Healer*. New York: Crossroad, 1982

Hall, Angus: *The Supernatural: Signs of Things to Come*. London: Aldus, 1975

Hall, Manly P.: *Solving Psychic Problems and Submerged Personalities*. Los Angeles: Philosophical Research Society, 1956

Hall, Trevor H.: *The Enigma of Daniel Home*. Buffalo: Prometheus Books, 1984

Hall, Trevor H.: *The Medium and the Scientist: The Story of Florence Cook and William Crookes*. Buffalo: Prometheus, 1984

Hall, Trevor H.: *Search for Harry Price*. London: Duckworth, 1978

Hall, Trevor H.: *The Spiritualists*. London: Gerald Duckworth, 1962

Hall, Trevor H.: *The Strange Case of Edmund Gurney*. London: Duckworth, 1964

Halliday, W.R.: *Greek Divination*. London: William Rider, 1913

Hamilton, Edith: *The Roman Way to Western Civilization*. New York: W.W. Norton, 1932

Hamilton, Edith: *Mythology*. New York: Little, Brown, 1942

Hamilton, Margaret: *Is Survival a Fact?* London: Psychic Press, 1969

Hamilton-Parker, Craig: *Circle of Light*. New York: Sterling, 2005

Hamilton-Parker, Craig: *The Hidden Meaning of Dreams*. New York: Sterling, 1999

Hamilton-Parker, Craig: *Psychic Dreaming*. New York: Sterling, 2004

Hamilton-Parker, Craig: *What to Do When You Are Dead*. New York: Sterling, 2001

Hanh, Thich Nhat: *Peace Is Every Step: The Path of Mindfulness in Everyday Life*. New York: Bantam, 1991

Hanoka, N. S.: *The Advantages of Healing by Visible Spectrum Therapy*. Ghaziabad: Bharti Association, 1957

Hansen, Chadwick: *Witchcraft at Salem*. New York: George Braziller, 1969

Hapgood, Charles H.: *Voices of Spirit: Through the Psychic Experience of Elwood Babbitt*. New York: Delacourt Press, 1975

Harber, Francis: *The Gospel According to Allan Kardec*. New York: Original Publications, 1980

Harmony Grove Spiritualist Association: *2004 Summer Program*. Escondido: HGSA 2004

Harner, Michael: *The Way of the Shaman*. New York: Bantam Books, 1986

Harold, Edmund: *Focus on Crystals*. New York: Ballantine Books, 1986

Harris, Barbara and Lionel C. Bascom: *Full Circle: The Near-Death Experience and Beyond*. New York: Pocket Books, 1990

Harrison, Tom: *Life After Death—Living Proof: A Lifetime's Experience of Physical Phenomena*. London: Saturday Night Press, 2004

Harrison, Vernon: *H.P. Blavatsky and the SPR: An Examination of the Hodgson Report of 1885.* Pasadena: Theosophical University Press, 1997

Hart, Hornell: *The Enigma of Survival.* London: Rider, 1959

Hawken, Paul: *Findhorn—A Center of Light.* Boston: East/West Journal/Tao, 1974

Haynes, Renee: *The Society for Psychical Research, 1882–1982: A History.* London: Heinemann, 1982

Head, J. and S. L. Cranston (eds): *Reincarnation: An East-West Anthology.* Wheaton: Theosophical Publishing House, 1968

Headon, Deirdre (ed.): *Quest for the Unknown—Charting the Future.* Pleasantville: Reader's Digest, 1992

Heagerty, N. Riley: *The Physical Mediumship of the Bangs Sisters.* Swadlincote: Noah's Ark Society Newsletter, 1997

Helena, Theodore: *The American Indian.* La Canada: New Age Press, 1964

Heline, Corinne: *Healing and Regeneration Through Color.* La Canada: New Age Press, 1976

Heline, Corinne: *Healing and Regeneration Through Music.* La Canada: New Age Press, 1978

Heron, Laurence T.: *ESP in the Bible.* New York: Doubleday, 1974

Heywood, Rosalind: *Beyond the Reach of Sense: An Inquiry into Extra-Sensory Perception.* New York: E. P. Dutton, 1961

Heywood, Rosalind: *ESP: A Personal Memoir.* New York: E. P. Dutton, 1964

Heywood, Rosalind: *Man, Myth & Magic: Mediums.* London: BPC Publishing, 1970

Higham, Charles: *The Adventures of Conan Doyle: The Life of the Creator of Sherlock Holmes* New York: W. W. Norton, 1976

Hoffa, Helynn: *Animal Spirits.* San Leandro: Universal Church of the Master, n.d.

Hoffman, Enid: *Huna: A Beginner's Guide.* Gloucester: Para Research, 1976

Hogshire, Jim: *Life after Death.* Boca Raton: Globe Communications, 1991

Hole, Christina: *Haunted England.* London: Scribner, 1941

Hole, Christina: *Witchcraft in England.* New York: Charles Scribner's, 1947

Hollen, Henry: *Clairaudient Transmissions.* Hollywood: Keats Publications, 1931

Holroyd, Stuart: *The Supernatural: Dream Worlds.* London: Aldus, 1976

Holroyd, Stuart: *The Supernatural: Magic, Words, and Numbers.* London: Aldus, 1975

Holroyd, Stuart: *The Supernatural: Minds Without Boundaries.* London: Aldus, 1975

Holroyd, Stuart: *The Supernatural: Psychic Voyages.* London: Aldus, 1976

Holy Bible: various editions

Holzer, Hans: *Born Again—The Truth about Reincarnation.* New York: Doubleday, 1970

Holzer, Hans (ed. Raymond Buckland): *Ghosts, Hauntings & Possessions.* St. Paul: Llewellyn Publications, 1990

Holzer, Hans: *Psychic Photography: Threshold of a New Science?* New York: McGraw-Hill, 1970

Holzer, Hans: *Window to the Past: Exploring History through ESP.* New York: Doubleday, 1969

Holzer, Hans: *Yankee Ghosts.* New York: Ace Books, 1966

Home, Daniel Dunglas: *Incidents in My Life.* New York: A. J. Davis, 1864

Home, David Dunglas: *Incidents in My Life (Second Series).* London: Whittingham & Wilkins, 1872

Home, David Dunglas: *Lights and Shadows of Spiritualism.* London: Virtue, 1877–78

Hopkins, Albert A.: *Magic: Stage Illusions and Scientific Diversions Including Trick Photography.* (1897) New York: Arno, 1977

Houdin, J. E. Robert: *Memoirs.* London: Chapman & Hall, 1860

Houdini, Harry: *A Magician among the Spirits.* New York: Harper & Bros., 1924

Hudson, Thomas J.: *The Law of Psychic Phenomena.* New York: Samuel Weiser, 1975

Hughes, Pennethorne: *Witchcraft*. London: Longmans, Green, 1952

Hull, Rev. Moses & Prof. W. F. Jamieson: *The Greatest Debate Within a Half Century Upon Modern Spiritualism*. Chicago: Progressive Thinker, 1904

Hulme and Wood: *Ancient Egypt Speaks*. London: Rider, 1937

Hultkrantz, Ake: *Native Religions of North America*. San Francisco: Harper & Row, 1987

Hunt, Roland: *The Seven Keys to Colour Healing*. London: C. W. Daniel, 1971

Hunt, Stoker: *Ouija®: The Most Dangerous Game*. New York: Harper & Row, 1985

Hurwood, Bernhardt J.: *Passport to the Supernatural: An Occult Compendium from All Ages and Many Lands*. New York: Taplinger, 1972

Hyams, Ron: *Mysteries of Mind Space & Time; the Unexplained: Reach for the Stars*. Westport: H. S. Stuttman, 1992

Hyslop, James H.: *Contact With the Other World* New York: Century Company, 1919

Illustrated London News. London: n. p., June 6, 1936

Impartial Examiner, An: *Mesmeric and Spirit Rapping Manifestations Scripturally Exposed as Neither from Electricity nor Spirits of the Dead but Rather from Infernal Evil Spirits*. New York: R. T. Young, 1852

Inglis, Brian: *Science and Parascience: A History of the Paranormal 1914–1939*. London: Hodder and Stoughton, 1984

Iremonger, Lucille: *The Ghosts of Versailles*. London: Faber & Faber, 1957

Iverson, Jeffrey: *More Lives Than One? The Evidence of the Remarkable Bloxham Tapes*. London: Souvenir Press, 1976

Jackson, Herbert G., Jr.: *The Spirit Rappers*. New York: Doubleday, 1972

Jaegers, Beverly C.: *Practical ESP and Clairvoyance*. Richmond Heights: Aries Productions, 1974

Jaffé, Aniela: *Apparitions and Precognition*. New York: University Books, 1963

Jahn, Robert G. and Brenda J. Dunne: *Margins of Reality: The Role of Consciousness in the Physical World*. San Diego: Harcourt, Brace, Jovanovich, 1987

James, E.O.: *Prehistoric Religion*. New York: Barnes & Noble, 1962

James, William (eds. Gardner Murphy and Robert O. Ballou): *William James on Psychical Research*. New York: Viking, 1960

Joan and Darby: *Our Unseen Guest*. New York: Harper & Brothers, 1920

Jolly, W. P.: *Sir Oliver Lodge*. London: Constable, 1974

Judah, J. Stillson: *The History and Philosophy of the Metaphysical Movements in America*. Philadelphia: Westminster Press, 1967

Kalweit, Holger: *Dreamtime and Inner Space: The World of the Shaman*. Boston: Shambhala Publications, 1984

Kane, Margaret Fox: *The Love-Life of Dr. Kane*. New York: Carleton, 1866

Kardec, Allan: *The Book on Mediums: Guide for Mediums and Invocators*. (1874) York Beach: Samuel Weiser, 1970

Kardec, Allan: *Collection of Selected Prayers*. New York: De Pablo International, 1989

Kardec, Allan: *The Spirits' Book*. (1857) New York: Studium, 1980

Karlins, Marvin and Lewis M. Andrews: *Biofeedback; Turning on the Power of Your Mind*. New York: Lippincott, 1972

Kaster, Joseph: *Putnam's Concise Mythological Dictionary*. New York: G.P. Putnam's, 1963

Kautz, William H. and Melanie Branon: *Channeling: The Intuitive Connection*. San Francisco: Harper & Row, 1987

Keene, M. Lamar: *The Psychic Mafia*. New York: St. Martin's Press, 1976

Kelly, Penny: *The Elves of Lily Hill Farm*. St. Paul: Llewellyn, 1997

Kelsey, Denys & Joan Grant: *Many Lifetimes.* New York: Doubleday, 1967

Keyes, Ken.: *Handbook to Higher Consciousness.* Berkeley: Living Love Center, 1975

Keynes, Geoffrey (ed): *The Complete Writings of William Blake.* New York: Random House, 1957

Kilner, Walter J.: *The Human Aura.* New York, University Books, 1965

King, Francis: *The Supernatural: Wisdom From Afar.* London: Aldus, 1975

Kingston, Jeremy: *The Supernatural: Healing Without Medicine.* London: Aldus, 1975

Kirk, Eleanor: *The Bottom Plank of Mental Healing.* New York: Kirk, 1899

Klimo, Jon: *Channeling: Investigations on Receiving Information from Paranormal Sources.* Los Angeles: Jeremy P. Tarcher, 1987

Knight, Gareth: *Pytheness: The Life and Work of Margaret Lumley Brown.* Oceanside: Sun Chalice Books, 2000

Knight, Gareth: *Dion Fortune & the Inner Light.* Loughborough: Thoth, 2000

Kraig, Donald Michael: *Modern Magick: Eleven Lessons in the High Magickal Arts.* St. Paul: Llewellyn, 1988

Krippner, Stanley (ed.), et al: *Galaxies of Life: The Human Aura in Acupuncture and Kirlian Photography.* New York: Gordon & Breach, 1974

Kübler-Ross, Elizabeth: *On Death and Dying.* London: Tavistock, 1970

Kuhlman, Kathryn: *I Believe in Miracles.* New York: Prentice-Hall, 1962

Kuhn, Lesley and Salvatore Russo: *Modern Hypnosis.* New York: Psychological Library, 1947

Kung, Hans: *Eternal Life? Life After Death as a Medical, Philosophical, and Theological Problem.* New York: Doubleday, 1984

LaGrand, Louis E.: *After Death Communication: Final Farewells —Extraordinary Experiences of Those Mourning the Death of Loved Ones.* St. Paul: Llewellyn Publications, 1998

Lakhovsky, Georges (tr. Mark Clement): *The Secret of Life: Cosmic Rays and Radiations of Living Beings.* London: True Health, 1963

Lane, E.W.: *An Account of the Manners & Customs of the Modern Egyptians.* London: C. Knight, 1856

Lang, Andrew: *Cock Lane & Common Sense.* London: Longmans, 1894

Langley, Noel: *Edgar Cayce on Reincarnation.* New York: Paperback Library, 1967

Lawrence, Jodi: *Alpha Brain Waves.* New York: Avon, 1972

Lawson, John Cuthbert: *Modern Greek Folklore and Ancient Greek Religion.* New York: University Books, 1964

Leach, Maria (ed): *Funk & Wagnalls Standard Dictionary of Folklore, Mythology and Legend.* New York: Harper & Row, 1984

Leadbeater, Charles W.: *The Chakras.* London: Quest, 1972

Leadbeater, Charles W.: *Clairvoyance.* Adyar: Theosophical Publishing House, 1899

Leadbeater, Charles W.: *Man Visible and Invisible.* London: Theosophical Society, 1971

Leaf, Horace: *What Is This Spiritualism?* New York: George H. Doran, 1919

LeCron, Leslie M.: *Self-Hypnotism.* New Jersey: Prentice-Hall, 1964

Leek, Sybil: *Numerology: The Magic of Numbers.* New York: Collier, 1969

Lees, Robert James: *Through the Mists—Or Leaves from the Autobiography of a Soul in Paradise.* London: William Rider, 1920

Lehmann, Rosamund: *The Swan in the Evening: Fragments of an Inner Life.* New York: Harcourt Brace Jovanovich, 1968

Leland, Charles Godfrey: *Gypsy Sorcery & Fortune Telling.* London: Fisher-Unwin, 1891

Leonard, Gladys Osborne: *My Life in Two Worlds.* London: Two Worlds Publishing, 1931

Leonard, Sue (ed): *Quest For the Unknown—Life Beyond Death.* Pleasantville: Reader's Digest, 1992

LeShan, Lawrence: *Alternate Realities*. New York: M. Evans, 1967

LeShan, Lawrence: *The Medium, the Mystic, and the Physicist*. New York: Viking, 1974

Lewis, E. E.: *A Report of the Mysterious Noises Heard in the House of Mr. John D. Fox, in Hydesville, Arcadia, Wayne County, Authenticated by the Certificates, and Confirmed by the Statements of the Citizens of That Place and Vicinity*. Canandaigua: E. E. Lewis, 1848

Lewis, James R.: *The Death and Afterlife Book: The Encyclopedia of Death, Near Death, and Life After Death*. Detroit: Visible Ink Press, 1995

Lewis, John: *Religions of the World Made Simple*. New York: Doubleday, 1968

Leybrun, J.G.: *The Haitian People*. New Haven: Yale University Press, 1941

Lhermitte, J.: *True and False Possession*. New York: Hawthorne Books, 1986

Linson, Dr. H. Tom: *The Use of the Pendulum in Medicine*. London: Medical Society for the Study of Radiesthesia, n.d.

Lissner, Ivar: *The Living Past*. New York: Capricorn Books, 1961

Litvag, Irving: *Singer in the Shadows: The Strange Story of Patience Worth*. New York: Macmillan, 1972

Llewellyn Editorial Staff: *The Truth about Astral Projection*. St. Paul: Llewellyn, 1983

Lodge, Sir Oliver: *Raymond, or Life and Death with Examples of the Evidence for Survival of Memory and Affection after Death*. London: Methuen, 1916

Lodge, Sir Oliver: *Past Years: An Autobiography*. London: Hodder & Stoughton, 1931

Lopez, Vincent: *Numerology*. New York: Citadel, 1961

Lowie, Robert: *Primitive Religion*. New York: Boni and Liveright, 1923

Lutoslawski, W.: *Pre-Existence and Reincarnation*. London: Allen & Unwin, 1926

McAdams, Elizabeth and Raymond Bayless: *The Case for Life after Death*. Chicago: Nelson Hall, 1981

McClure, Kevin: *Mysteries of Mind Space & Time; The Unexplained: War—What War?* Westport: H. S. Stuttman, 1992

McConnell, R. A.: *E.S.P. Curriculum Guide*. New York: Simon & Schuster, 1971

McCoy, A. W.: *Cassadaga—Its History and Teaching*. New York: n.d.

McCoy, Edain: *A Witch's Guide to Faery Folk*. St. Paul, Llewellyn, 2000

McGregor, Pedro: *The Moon and Two Mountains: The Myths, Ritual and Magic of Brazilian Spiritism*. London: Souvenir Press, 1966

MacHovec, Frank J.: *Nostradamus: His Prophecies for the Future*. Mount Vernon: Peter Pauper Press, 1972

Mackay, Charles: *Extraordinary Delusions and Madness of Crowds*. (1841) New York: Farrar, Straus and Giroux, 1932

MacKenzie, Alexander (Commentary by Elizabeth Sutherland): *The Prophecies of the Brahan Seer*. (1877) London: Constable, 1977

MacKenzie, Andrew: *Hauntings and Apparitions*. London: Heinemann, 1982

McKenzie, James Hewart: *Spirit Intercourse*. London: 1916

Mallaz, Gitta (ed): *Talking with Angels*. London: Watkins, n.d.

Manning, Matthew: *The Link*. London: Holt Rinehart, 1974

Maple, Eric: *The Realm of Ghosts*. London: A. S. Barnes, 1964

Marryat, Florence: *The Spirit World*. London: F. V. White, 1894

Martin, Joel and Patricia Romanowski: *We Don't Die*. New York: Putnam's, 1988

Martin, Joel and Patricia Romanowski: *We Are Not Forgotten*. New York: Putnam's, 1991

Martin, Joel and Patricia Romanowski: *Love beyond Life*. New York: HarperCollins, 1997

Martin, Joel and Patricia Romanowski: *Our Children Forever: Messages from Children on the Other Side*. New York: Putnam's, 1994

Mattison, H.: *Spirit Rapping Unveiled!* New York: Mason Bros., 1853

Maury, Marguerite: *How to Dowse: Experimental and Practical Radiesthesia*. London: Bell, 1953

Mauskopf, Seymour and Michael McVaugh: *The Elusive Science*. Baltimore: Johns Hopkins, 1980

May, Antoinete: *Haunted Ladies*. San Francisco: Chronicle Books, 1975

Medhurst, R. G. and K. M. Goldney: *Crookes and the Spirit World*. New York: Taplinger, 1972

Meek, George W.: *After We Die, What Then?* Columbus: Ariel Press, 1987

Melton, J. Gordon: *The Encyclopedia of American Religions*. (2 vols.) Wilmington: McGrath, 1978

Melville, J.: *Crystal Gazing*. New York: Samuel Weiser, 1970

Mermet, Abbé: *Principles and Practice of Radiesthesia*. London: Watkins, 1975

Merriam-Webster Dictionary, The. New York: Pocket Books, 1974

Métraux, Alfred: *Voodoo in Haiti*. London: André Deutsch, 1959

Miller, Paul: *Born to Heal*. London: Spiritualist Press, 1962

Monroe, Robert A.: *Journeys Out of the Body*. New York: Doubleday, 1971

Montgomery, Ruth: *A Gift of Prophesy*. New York: Morrow, 1965

Montgomery, Ruth: *Here and Hereafter*. New York: Coward McCann, 1968

Montgomery, Ruth: *A Search for the Truth*. New York: Bantam Books, 1968

Montgomery, Ruth: *A World Beyond: A Message from Psychic Arthur Ford from Beyond the Grave*. New York: Coward, McCann & Geoghegan, 1971

Moody, Raymond: *Life after Life*. New York: Mockingbird Books, 1975

Moody, Raymond: *The Light Beyond*. New York: Bantam Books, 1988

Moody, Raymond: *Reflections on Life after Life*. New York: Bantam, 1977

Moody, Raymond and Paul Perry: *Coming Back: A Psychiatrist Explores Past-Life Journeys*. New York: Bantam, 1990

Moody, Raymond and Paul Perry: *Reunions: Visionary Encounters with Departed Loved Ones*. New York: Villard, 1993

Moore, R. Laurence: *In Search of White Crows: Spiritualism, Parapsychology and American Culture*. New York: Oxford University Press, 1977

Moore, W. Usborne: *Glimpses of the Next State*. London: Watts, 1911

Morris Pratt Institute: *Educational Course on Modern Spiritualism*. Milwaukee: M.P.I., 1981

Morse, J. J.: *A Brief History of Spirit Photography*. Manchester: Two Worlds, 1909

Moses, William Stainton: *Direct Spirit Writing*. London: L. N. Fowler, 1878

Moses, William Stainton: *More Spirit Teachings*. London: L. N. Fowler, n.d.

Mühl, Anita M.: *Automatic Writing*. Dresden: Steinkopff, 1930

Muldoon, Sylvan J. and Hereward Carrington: *The Case for Astral Projection*. Chicago: Aries Press, 1936

Muldoon, Sylvan J. and Hereward Carrington: *The Projection of the Astral Body*. London: Rider, 1929

Murphy, Gardner and Robert O. Ballou: *William James on Psychical Research*. New York: Viking, 1960

Murphy, G., Murphy, L.B., and Newcomb, T.: *Experimental Social Psychology: An Interpretation of Research upon the Socialization of the Individual*. New York: Harper, 1937

Murray, Margaret Alice: *The Witch Cult in Western Europe*. London: Clarendon Press, 1921

Myer, Isaac: *Qabbalah: The Philosophical Writings of Avicebron*, New York: Samuel Weiser, 1970

Myers, Frederick W. H.: *Human Personality and Its Survival After Bodily Death*. London: Longmans, 1903

Myers, Gerald E.: *William James: His Life and Thought*. New Haven: Yale University Press, 1986

Nagy, Ron: *Precipitated Spirit Paintings: Beyond the Shadow of Doubt*. Lakeville: Galde Press, 2005

National Spiritualist Association of Churches: *NSAC Spiritualist Manual*. Lily Dale: NSAC, 1911; 2002

The National Spiritualist Summit. Glendale: NSAC, No. 949; September 2004

Neech, W. F.: *Death Is Her Life*. London: Psychic Press, 1957

Neff, H. Richard: *Psychic Phenomena and Religion*. Philadelphia: Westminster, 1968

Neiman, Carol and Emily Goldman: *After Life: The Complete Guide to Life after Death*. London: Boxtree, 1994

Nelson, Geoffrey K.: *Man, Myth & Magic: Spiritualism*. London: BPC Publishing, 1970

Nelson, Geoffrey K.: *Spiritualism and Society*. New York: Shocken Books, 1969

Nelson, Robert A.: *The Art of Cold Reading*. Calgary: Mickey Hades Enterprises, 1971

Nelson, Robert A.: *A Sequel to the Art of Cold Reading*. Calgary: Mickey Hades Enterprises, 1971

Netherton, Morris and Nancy Shiffrin: *Past Lives Therapy*. New York: William Morrow, 1978

Nevius, John L.: *The Chinese*. Chicago: Revell, 1893

Newbrough, John B.: *Oahspe*. Los Angeles: n.p., 1935; London: Kosmon Press, 1960

Newhouse, Flower A.: *Rediscovering the Angels & Natives of Eternity*. Escondido: Christward Ministry, 1976

Nielsen, Greg and Joseph Polanski: *Pendulum Power*. New York: Warner Destiny, 1977

Northage, Ivy: *Mechanics of Mediumship*. London: College of Psychic Studies, 1973

Northage, Ivy: *Mediumship Made Simple*. London: College of Psychic Studies, 1986

Olcott, Henry Steel: *Inside the Occult: The True Story of Madame H. P. Blavatsky*. (originally *Old Diary Leaves, 1895-1931; 4 vols.*) Philadelphia: Running Press, 1975

Olcott, Henry Steel: *People From the Other World*. Hartford, Conn.: n.p., 1875

Oliver, Leroy: *Levitation*. London: n.p., 1928

Ophiel: *The Art and Practice of Astral Projection*. San Francisco: Peach Publishing, 1961

Opie, Iona and Moira Tatem: *A Dictionary of Superstitions*. Oxford: Oxford University Press, 1989

Oppenheim, Janet: *The Other World: Spiritualism and Psychical Research in England 1850–1914*. New York: Cambridge University Press, 1985

Ornish, Dr. Dean: *Dr. Dean Ornish's Program for Reversing Heart Disease*. New York: Ballantine, 1991

Ortzen, Tony: *The Psychic Life of Britain's Greatest Premier—Psychic News #3729, December 2003*. Stanstead: Psychic News Press, 2003

Ostrander, Sheila and Lynn Schroeder: *Psychic Discoveries behind the Iron Curtain*. Englewood Cliffs: Prentice-Hall, 1970

Ott, John N.: *Health and Light*. New York: Pocket Books, 1976

Ouseley, S. G. J.: *Color Meditations*. Essex: Fowler, 1949

Overlee, Vernon W.: *Psychics Past—Present; The Dead Speak*. Canaan, Mora Press, 1983

Owen, A. R. G.: *Can We Explain the Poltergeist?* New York: Garret/Helix, 1964

Owen, A. R. G.: *Man, Myth & Magic: Miracles*. London: BPC Publishing, 1970

Owen, A. R. G.: *Man, Myth & Magic: Poltergeists*. London: BPC Publishing, 1970

Owen, A. R. G.: *Man, Myth & Magic: Visions*. London: BPC Publishing, 1970

Owen, Iris M. with Margaret Sparrow: *Conjuring Up Philip*. New York: Harper & Row, 1976

Owen, Robert Dale: *The Debatable Land Between This World and the Next, with Illustrative Narrations*. New York: Carleton, 1872

Owen, Robert Dale: *Footfalls on the Boundary of Another World, with Narrative Illustrations*. Philadelphia: Lippincott, 1860

Owens, Elizabeth: *Cassadaga, Florida: Yesterday and Today.* Cassadaga: Pisces Publishing, 2001

Owens, Elizabeth: *Discover Your Spiritual Life.* St. Paul: Llewellyn, 2004

Owens, Elizabeth: *How to Communicate with Spirits.* St. Paul: Llewellyn, 2002

Owens, Elizabeth: *The Phenomena of Psychic Art.* Lakeville: *Fate* Magazine, April 2004

Oxford English Dictionary, The Oxford: Clarendon Press, 1989

Page, Charles G.: *Psychomancy: Spirit-Rappings and Table-Tippings Exposed.* New York: D. Appleton, 1853

Panati, Charles: *The Geller Papers.* Boston: Houghton Mifflin, 1976

Panchadasi, Swami: *A Course of Advance Lessons in Clairvoyance and Occult Powers.* Des Plains: Yogi Publication Society, 1916

Parke, H. W.: *Sibyls and Sibylline Prophecy in Classical Antiquity.* New York: Routledge, 1988

Pasricha, Satwant: *Claims of Reincarnation: An Empirical Study of Cases in India.* New Delhi: Harman, 1990

Pearsall, Ronald: *The Table-Rappers.* New York: St. Martin's Press, 1972

Peebles, J. M.: *The General Principles and the Standard Teachings of Spiritualism.* Mokelumne: Health Research, 1969

Peebles, J. M.: *Seers of the Ages.* Chicago: Progressive Thinker, 1903

Peebles, J. M.: *The Spirit's Pathway Traced: Did it Pre-Exist and Does it Reincarnate Again into Mortal Life?* Battle Creek: Peebles Institute, 1906

Perlmutt, Cyril: *Photographing the Spirit World: Images from Beyond the Spectrum.* Wellingborough: Aquarian Press, 1988

Phillips, E.D.: *Man, Myth & Magic: Sibyls.* London: BPC Publishing, 1970

Pickford, Mary: *Sunshine and Shadows.* New York: Doubleday, 1955

Picknett, Lynn: *Mysteries of Mind Space & Time; the Unexplained: Defying the Law of Gravity.* Westport: H. S. Stuttman, 1992

Picknett, Lynn: *Mysteries of Mind Space & Time; the Unexplained: A Gallery of Psychic Art.* Westport: H. S. Stuttman, 1992

Pierce, Marilyn Seal: *Lost Continents for the Millions.* Los Angeles: Sherbourne, 1969

Pike, James A. and Diane Kennedy: *The Other Side: An Account of My Experiences with Psychic Phenomena.* New York: Doubleday, 1968

Pike, Diane Kennedy: *Search: The Personal Story of a Wilderness Journey.* New York: Doubleday, 1970

Pike, S.N.: *Water-Divining.* London: Research Publications, 1945

Piper, Alta L.: *The Life and Work of Mrs. Piper.* London: Kegan Paul, Trench, Trubner, 1929

Playfair, Guy Lion: *The Flying Cow: Research into Paranormal Phenomena in the World's Most Psychic Country.* London: Souvenir Press, 1975

Playfair, Guy Lion: *Mysteries of Mind Space & Time; the Unexplained: "This Perilous Medium".* Westport: H. S. Stuttman, 1992

Pleasants, Helene (ed.): *Biographical Dictionary of Parapsychology.* New York: Helix Press, 1964

Podmore, Frank: *Mesmerism and Christian Science.* London: Methuen, 1909. 2nd ed.: New York, University Books, 1963

Podmore, Frank: *Modern Spiritualism.* London: 1902; reprinted as *Mediums of the Nineteenth Century.* New York: University Books, 1963

Podmore, Frank: *The Newer Spiritualism.* London: T. Fisher Unwin, 1910

Polidoro, Massimo: *Final Séance: The Strange Friendship between Houdini and Conan Doyle.* New York: Prometheus Books, 2001

Pollack, Jack Harrison: *Croiset the Clairvoyant.* New York: Doubleday, 1964

Pond, Enoch: *Familiar Spirits, and Spiritual Manifestations: Being a Series of Articles.* Boston: Bela Marsh, 1852

Pond, Mariam Buckner: *The Unwilling Martyrs—The Story of the Fox Family.* London: Spiritualist Press, 1947

Post, Eric: *Communicating With the Beyond*. New York: Atlantic Publishing, 1946

Post, Isaac: *Voices from the Spirit World: Being Communications from Many Spirits by the Hand of Isaac Post, Medium*. Rochester: Charles H. McDonell, 1852

Potter, D.: *Sibyls in the Greek and Roman World*. Rhode Island: Journal of Roman Archælogy 3, 1990

Powell, Arthur E.: *The Etheric Double*. Wheaton: Theosophical Publishing House, 1969

Price, Harry: *Confessions of a Ghost Hunter*. London: Putnam, 1936

Price, Harry: *The End of Borley Rectory*. London: Longmans, Green, 1946

Price, Harry: *Fifty Years of Psychical Research*. London: Longmans, Green, 1939

Price, Harry: *The Most Haunted House in England*. London: Longmans, Green, 1940

Price, Harry: *Rudi Schneider*. London: Methuen, 1930

Price, Harry and Eric J. Dingwall: *Revelations of a Spirit Medium*. London: 1922

Prince, Walter Franklin: *The Case of Patience Worth*. Boston: Boston Society for Psychical Research, 1927

Proskauer, Julien J.: *Spook Crooks! Exposing the Secrets of the Prophet-eers who conduct our wickedest industry*. New York: A. L. Burt Company, 1932

Psychic Magazine Editors: *Psychics*. New York: Harper & Row, 1972

Psychic News #3720, October 18, 2003. Stansted, Essex

Psychic News #3735, February 7, 2004. Stansted, Essex

Psychic News #3754, June 19, 2004. Stansted, Essex

Psychic News #3769, October 2, 2004. Stansted, Essex

Psychic News #3782, January 8, 2005. Stansted, Essex

Puharich, Andrija: *The Sacred Mushroom: Key to the Door of Eternity*. New York: Doubleday, 1959

Putnam, Betty L: *History of Lily Dale* Lily Dale: Lily Dale Historical Society, n.d.

Raine, Kathleen: *Man, Myth & Magic—Blake: Maker of Myths* London: BPC Publishing, 1970

Ram Dass, Baba: *The Only Dance There Is*. New York: Doubleday, 1970

Randi, James: *The Magic of Uri Geller*. New York: Ballantine Books, 1975

Randles, Jenny and Peter Hough: *The Afterlife: An Investigation into the Mysteries of Life after Death*. London: Piatkus, 1993

Randles, Jenny and Peter Hough: *Spontaneous Human Combustion*. New York: Robert Hale, 1992

Raudive, Konstantin: *Breakthrough: An Amazing Experiment in Electronic*

Rawcliffe, H. D.: *Illusions and Delusions of the Supernatural and the Occult*. New York: Dover, 1959

Rawlinson, George: *History of Ancient Egypt*. New York: Dodd, Mead, 1881

Reich, Wilhelm: *The Discovery of the Orgone*. New York: Orgone Institute Press, 1942

Rhine, J. B.: *Man, Myth & Magic: Psychokinesis*. London: BPC Publishing, 1970

Rhine, Joseph Banks: *Extrasensory Perception*. Boston: Bruce Humphries, 1934

Rhine, Joseph Banks: *New Frontiers of the Mind*. New York: Farrar & Rinehart, 1937

Rhine, Joseph Banks: *New World of the Mind*. New York: William Sloane, 1953

Rhine, Louisa: *ESP in Life and Lab: Tracing Hidden Channels*. New York: Collier Books, 1967

Richet, Charles: *Thirty Years of Psychical Research*. London: Rider, 1923

Rickard, Robert and Richard Kelly: *Photographs of the Unknown*. London: New English Library, 1980

Ridall, Kathryn: *Channeling: How to Reach Out to Your Spirit Guides*. New York: Bantam Books, 1988

Ring, Kenneth: *Life at Death* New York: Coward, McCann & Geoghegan, 1980

"Rita" (Mrs. Desmond Humphreys): *The Truth of Spiritualism*. Philadelphia: J. B. Lippincott, 1920

Roberts, C. E. Bechhofer: *The Truth about Spiritualism*. London: Eyre and Spottiswoode, 1932

Roberts, Estelle: *Fifty Years a Medium: The Autobiography of One of the World's Greatest Spiritualistic Mediums*. New York: Corgi Books, 1969

Roberts, Jane: *The Coming of Seth*. New York: Pocket Books, 1976

Roberts, Jane: *How to Develop Your ESP Power*. New York: Frederick Fell, 1966

Roberts, Jane: *The Seth Material*. New Jersey: Prentice-Hall, 1970

Roberts, Jane: *Seth Speaks*. New Jersey: Prentice-Hall, 1972

Roberts, Ursula: *The Mystery of the Human Aura*. New York: Samuel Weiser, 1950

Rogo, D. Scott: *On the Track of the Poltergeist*. Englewood Cliffs: Prentice-Hall, 1986

Rogo, D. Scott: *Life after Death: The Case for Survival of Bodily Death*. Wellingborough: Aquarian Press, 1986

Rogo, D. Scott: *The Infinite Boundary*. New York: Dodd, Mead & Co., 1987

Rogo, D. Scott and Raymond Bayless: *Phone Calls from the Dead*. New Jersey: Prentice-Hall, 1979

Roll, William George: *The Poltergeist*. New York: Nelson Doubleday, 1972

Roman, Sanaya and Duane Packer: *Opening to Channel: How to Connect With Your Guide*. Tiburon: H. J. Kramer, 1987

Rose, H. J.: *Religion in Greece and Rome*. New York: Harper & Row, 1959

Rose, L.: *Faith Healing*. London: Gollancz, 1968

Roy, Archie: *Mysteries of Mind Space & Time; the Unexplained: The Genius Within*. Westport: H. S. Stuttman, 1992

Salter, W. H.: *Trance Mediumship: An Introductory Study of Mrs. Piper and Mrs. Leonard*. London: S.P.R., 1962

Saltmarsh, H. F.: *Evidence of Personal Survival from Cross Correspondences*. London: G. Bell & Sons, 1938

Saltmarsh, H. F.: *Foreknowledge*. London: G. Bell & Sons, 1938

Sargent, Epes: *Planchette, or The Despair of Science. Being a Full Account of Modern Spiritualism, Its Phenomena, and the Various Theories Regarding It. With a Survey of French Spiritism*. Boston: Roberts, 1869

Sargent, Epes: *Proof Palpable of Immortality*. Boston: 1880

Sargent, Epes: *The Scientific Basis of Spiritualism*. Boston: 1880

Sauneron, Serge: *The Priests of Ancient Egypt*. New York: Grove Press, 1960

Schouten, Jack: *Spiritual Connections: Bringing to Consciousness Our Spiritual Interconnectedness*. Wooloongabba: Spiritual Books, 1996

Schrenck-Notzing, Albert, Baron von: *Phenomena of Materialization*. n.p.: Kegan Paul, Trench, Trubner, 1920

Schul, Bill and Pettit (ed.): *The Secret Power of Pyramids*. Greenwich: Fawcett, 1976

Schure, Edouard: *The Great Initiates: A Study of the Secret Religions of History*. San Francisco: Harper & Row, 1961

Schwartz, Gary E. with William L. Simon: *The Afterlife Experiments: Breakthrough Scientific Evidence of Life after Death*. New York: Pocket Books, 2002

Schwartz, Stephen A.: *The Secret Vaults of Time: Psychic Archaeology and the Quest for Man's Beginnings*. New York: Grossett and Dunlap, 1978

Scott's Bible: Old and New Testaments with Notes, Observations, and References. New York: Samuel T Armstrong, 1827

Scott, Ian (tr. and ed.): *The Lüscher Color Test of Dr. Max Lüscher*. New York: Random House, 1969

Scott-Elliot, W.: *The Story of Atlantis and the Lost Lemuria*. London: Theosophical Publishing House, 1968

Scott, Reginald: *Discoverie of Witchcraft*. London: n.p., 1584

Searcher after Truth, A: *The Rappers; or, The Mysteries, Fallacies, and Absurdities of Spirit-Rapping, Table-Tipping, and Entrancement*. New York: H. Long & Bro., 1854

Shakespeare, William: *The Complete Works*. London: Odhams Press, 1938

Shattuck, Louise and David James: *Spirit and Spa: A Portrait of the Body, Mind, and Soul of a 133-Year-Old Spiritualist Community in Lake Pleasant, Massachusetts*. Greenfield: Delta House, 2003

Shepard, Leslie A: *Encyclopedia of Occultism & Parapsychology*. New York: Avon Books, 1978

Sherman, Harold: *You Live after Death*. New York: Fawcett, 1972

Sherman, Harold: *You Can Communicate with the Unseen World*. New York: Fawcett, 1974

Sherman, Harold: *The Dead Are Alive*. New York: Fawcett, 1981

Shiffrin, Nancy and Morris Netherton: *Past Lives Therapy*. New York: Grossett & Dunlap, 1978

Shirley, Ralph: *The Mystery of the Human Double—The Case for Astral Projection*. New York: University Books, 1965

Sidgwick, Eleanor Mildred: *Phantasms of the Living*. (1923) New York: University Books, 1962

Sinnett, A.P.: *Incidents in the Life of Madame Blavatsky*. London: George Redway, 1886

Sitwell, Sacheverell: *Poltergeists: Fact or Fancy?* New York: Dorset Press, 1988

Smith, Alson J.: *Immortality: The Scientific Evidence*. New Jersey: Prentice-Hall, 1954

Smith, B.: *Meditation: The Inward Act*. London: McClelland, 1963

Smith, Gordon: *Spirit Messenger: The Remarkable Story of a Seventh Son of a Seventh Son*. London: Hay House, 2004

Smith, Gordon: *The Unbelievable Truth: A Medium's Guide to the Spirit World*. London: Hay House, 2004

Smith, Susy: *The Mediumship of Mrs. Leonard*. New York: University Books, 1964

Smith, Susy: *Prominent American Ghosts*. New York: World Publishing, 1970

Smith, Susy: *The Power of the Mind*. Radnor: Chilton Books, 1975

Smyth, Frank: *The Supernatural: Ghosts and Poltergeists*. London: Aldus, 1975

Snelling, John: *Elements of Buddhism*. Shaftsbury: Element Books, 1990

Solomon, Grant and Jane: *The Scole Experiment*. London: Piatkus, 1999

Somerlott, Robert: *"Here, Mr. Splitfoot"—An Informal Exploration into Modern Occultism*. New York: Viking Press, 1971

Spence, Lewis: *An Encyclopedia of the Occult*. London: George Routledge & Sons, 1920

Spence, Lewis: *The Fairy Tradition in Britain*. London: Rider, 1948

Spence, Lewis: *The Occult Sciences in Atlantis*. London: Rider, 1970

Spence, Lewis: *The Problem of Atlantis*. London: 1924

Spence, Lewis: *The Problem of Lemuria*. London: 1932

Spiritualist Lyceum Manual. Lily Dale: National Spiritualist Association of Churches, 1993

Spraggett, Alan: *Arthur Ford: The Man Who Talked with the Dead*. New York: New American Library, 1973

Spraggett, Allen: *Kathryn Kuhlman: the Woman Who Believes in Miracles*. New York: Thomas Y. Crowell, 1970

Spraggett, Alan: *The Unexplained*. New York: New American Library, 1967

St. Clair, David: *Drum and Candle*. New York: Bell, 1971

St. Clair, David: *Psychic Healers*. New York: Doubleday, 1974

St. Clair, David: *The Psychic World of California*. New York: Doubleday, 1972

Stearn, Jess: *Edgar Cayce: The Sleeping Prophet*. New York: Doubleday, 1967

Stearn, Jess: *The Search for the Girl with the Blue Eyes: A Venture into Reincarnation*. New York: Doubleday, 1968

Stearn, Jess: *Yoga, Youth and Reincarnation*. New York: Doubleday, 1965

Steiger, Brad: *Atlantis Rising*. New York: Dell, 1973

Steiger, Brad: *The Enigma of Reincarnation*. New York: Ace Books, 1967

Steiger, Brad: *Irene Hughes on Psychic Safari*. New York: Warner, 1972

Steiger, Brad: *Real Ghosts, Restless Spirits, and Haunted Places*. Detroit: Visible Ink Press, 2003

Steiger, Brad: *Voices From beyond: True Incidents Indicative of Life Beyond Death*. New York: Award Books, 1968

Steiger, Brad: *You Will Live Again: Dramatic Case Histories of Reincarnation*. New York: Dell Books, 1978

Steiner, Rudolf: *Atlantis and Lemuria*. London: Anthroposophical Publishing, 1923

Steiner, Rudolf: *Cosmic Memory*. San Francisco: Harper & Row, 1959

Stemmen, Roy: *Mysteries of Mind Space & Time, the Unexplained: In Search of the Sixth Sense*. Westport: H. S. Stuttman, 1992

Stemmen, Roy: *Mysteries of Mind Space & Time; the Unexplained: Survival—The Solid Evidence?* Westport: H. S. Stuttman, 1992

Stemman, Roy: *Reincarnation: True Stories of Past Lives*. London: Piatkus Books, 1997

Stemman, Roy: *The Supernatural: Atlantis and the Lost Lands*. London: Aldus, 1975

Stemman, Roy: *The Supernatural: Spirits and Spirit Worlds*. London: Aldus, 1975

Stemman, Roy: *The Supernatural: Visitors from Outer Space*. London: Aldus, 1976

Stevenson, Ian: *Twenty Cases Suggestive of Reincarnation*. Charlottesville: University of Virginia, 1974

Stevenson, Ian and John Beloff: *Proceedings, #427-447—An Analysis of Some Suspect Drop-In Communicators*. London: Society for Psychical Research, September 1980

Stockwell, Tony: *Spirited: Living Between Two Worlds—A Top Psychic Medium's Extraordinary Story*. London: Hodder and Stoughton, 2004

Storm, Stella (ed.): *Philosophy of Silver Birch*. London: Psychic press, 1969

Sugrue, Thomas: *There Is a River: The Story of Edgar Cayce*. New York: Dell, 1970

Summers, Montague: *The History of Witchcraft and Demonology*. New York: University Books, 1956

Sutphen, Dick: *You Were Born Again to Be Together*. New York: Pocket Books, 1976

Swann, Ingo: *Natural ESP*. New York: Bantam Books, 1987

Sylvester, Derek: *Peter Sellers*. London: Proteus, 1981

Symonds, John: *Madame Blavatsky: Medium and Magician*. London: Odhams, 1959

Symonds, John: *Man, Myth & Magic: Shakers*. London: BPC Publishing, 1970

Tabori, Paul: *Companions of the Unseen*. New York: University Books, 1968

Tabori, Paul: *Pioneers of the Unseen*. New York: Taplinger, 1973

Tallant, Robert: *Voodoo in New Orleans*. New York: Macmillan, 1946

Tanner, Amy and G. Stanley Hall: *Studies in Spiritualism*. New York: Appleton, 1910

Targ, Russell and Harold E. Puthoff: *Mind Reach: Scientists Look at Psychic Ability*. New York: Delacorte Press, 1977

Tarpey, Kingsley: *Healing by Radiesthesia*. London: Medical Society for the Study of Radiesthesia, n.d.

Taylor, John Gerald: *Science and the Supernatural*. New York: Dutton, 1980

Taylor, John Gerald: *Superminds: An Investigation into the Paranormal*. London: Granada, 1975

Taylor, Sarah E. L. (ed.): *Fox-Taylor Automatic Writing, 1869–1892, Unabridged Record*. Minneapolis: Tribune-Great West Printing, 1932

Taylor, W. G. Langworthy: *Katie Fox, Epochmaking Medium and the Making of the Fox-Taylor Record*. New York: G. P. Putnam's Sons, 1933

Thommen, George S.: *Is This Your Day?* New York: Crown Publishers, 1973

Thompson, C. J. S.: *Magic and Healing*. London: Rider, 1947

Thondup, Tulku: *The Healing Power of Mind: Simple Meditation Exercises for Health, Well-Being, and Enlightenment*. Boston: Shambhala, 1996

Thouless, Robert H.: *From Anecdote to Experiment in Psychical Research*. London: Routledge and Kegan Paul, 1972

Thurston, Rev. Herbert: *Ghosts and Poltergeists*. London: Regnery, 1950

Thurston, Mark A.: *Visions and Prophecies for a New Age*. Virginia Beach, A.R.E. Press, 1981

Tiertze, Thomas R.: *Margery*. New York: Harper & Row, 1973

Tomorrow Magazine, Vol. 1 No. 3; Spring 1953. New York: Garrett Publications

Tomorrow Magazine, Vol. 9 No. 1; Winter 1961. New York: Garrett Publications

Tompkin, Peter and Christopher Bird: *The Secret Life of Plants*. New York: Avon, 1974

Trethely, A. W.: *The 'Controls' of Stainton Moses*. London: 1923

Trobridge, George: *Swedenborg: Life and Teaching*. New York: Swedenborg Foundation, 1907

Turner, Gordon: *An Outline of Spiritual Healing*. London: 1963

Turner, Gordon: *A Time to Heal: The Story of a Healer*. London: Talmy, Franklin, 1974

Tuttle, Hudson: *Mediumship and its Law*. Wisconsin: National Spiritualist Association, 1890

Twigg, Ena: *How I Became a Medium*. New York: The Psychic Reader—World Publishing, 1969

Twigg, Ena with Ruth Hagy Bro: *Ena Twigg: Medium*. London: W. H. Allen, 1973

Two Worlds magazine. London: Two Worlds Publishing, n.d.

Tylor, Edward Burnett: *Religion in Primitive Culture*. New York: Harper & Row, 1956

Tyrrell, G. N. M.: *Apparitions*. London: Society for Psychical Research, 1953

Tyrrell, G. N. M.: *Science and Psychical Phenomena*. London: Methuen, 1938

Underhill, Leah A.: *The Missing Link in Modern Spiritualism*. New York: Thomas R. Knox, 1885

Underwood, Peter: *The Ghost Hunters*. London: Robert Hale, 1985

Underwood, Peter: *The Ghost Hunter's Guide*. Poole: Blandford Press, 1986

Underwood, Peter: *This Haunted Isle*. London: Harrup, 1984

Underwood, Peter: *Haunted London*. London: George C. Harrup, 1973

Underwood, Peter: *No Common Task: The Autobiography of a Ghost-hunter*. London: Harrup, 1983

Unger, Merrill F.: *The Mystery of Bishop Pike: A Christian View of the Other Side*. Wheaton: Tyndale House, 1971

Vander, Peter: *Voices from the Tapes: Recordings From the Other World*. New York: Drake Publishers, 1973

Van Praagh, James: *Healing Grief: Reclaiming Life after Any Loss*. New York: Dutton: 2000

Van Praagh, James: *Heaven and Earth: Making the Psychic Connection*. New York: Simon and Schuster, 2001

Van Praagh, James: *Looking Beyond: A Teen's Guide to the Spiritual World*. New York: Simon and Schuster, 2003

Van Praagh, James: *Meditations with James Van Praagh*. New York: Simon and Schuster, 2003

Van Praagh, James: *Reaching to Heaven*. New York: Dutton, 1998

Van Praagh, James: *Talking to Heaven: A Medium's Message of Life after Death*. New York: Dutton, 1997

Verner, Alexander: *Table Rapping and Automatic Writing*. London: L. N. Fowler, n.d.

Villoldo, Alberto and Stanley Krippner: *Healing States*. New York: Fireside, 1986

Vogt, Paula M.: *Historical Maplewood Hotel: Continuous Use Since 1880.* Lily Dale: Lily Dale Museum, n.d.

Vogt, Paula M. and Joyce LaJudice: *Lily Dale Proud Beginnings: A Little Bit of History* Lily Dale: Lily Dale Museum, 1984

Waite, Arthur Edward: *The Pictorial Key to the Tarot.* (London, 1910) New York: University Books, 1959

Walker, Benjamin: *Man, Myth & Magic: Karma.* London: BPC Publishing, 1970

Walker, Benjamin: *Man, Myth & Magic: Meditation.* London: BPC Publishing, 1970

Walker, Benjamin: *Man, Myth & Magic: Reincarnation.* London: BPC Publishing, 1970

Walker, Danton: *I Believe in Ghosts.* New York: Taplinger, 1969

Wallace, Alfred Russel: *On Miracles and Modern Spiritualism.* London: n.p., 1875

Wallace, Alfred Russel: *My Life.* London: Chapman and Hall, 1905

Wallis, E. W. and M. H.: *A Guide to Mediumship and Psychical Unfoldment.* Mokelumne Hill: Health Research, 1968

Wallis, E. W. and M. H.: *Mediumship Explained.* Summit: Stow Memorial Foundation, n.d.

Walter Franklin Prince: A Tribute to His Memory. Boston: Boston Society for Psychical Research, 1935

Walther, Gerda: *Schrenck-Notzing: Pioneer Researcher.* New York: Tomorrow Magazine, Winter, 1958

Ward, Charles A.: *Oracles of Nostradamus.* New York: Charles Scribner's Sons, 1940

Warrick, F. W.: *Experiments in Psychics.* New York: E. P. Dutton, 1939

Watkins, Alfred: *The Old Straight Track* London: Methuen, 1925

Watson, Lyall: *The Romeo Error.* New York: Anchor Press, 1975

Webster, Ken: *The Vertical Plane.* London: Grafton, 1988

Webster, Richard: *Spirit Guides & Angel Guardians.* St. Paul: Llewellyn, 1998

Weisberg, Barbara: *Talking with the Dead.* HarperSanFrancisco, 2004

Weiss, Brain: *Many Lives, Many Masters.* London: Piatkus Books, 1994

Werblowsky, R. J. Zwi: *Man, Myth & Magic: Cabala.* London: BPC Publishing, 1970

Wethered, Vernon D.: *The Practice of Medical Radiesthesia.* London: C.W. Daniel, 1967

Whitaker, Terence: *Haunted England.* Chicago: Contemporary Books, 1987

White, Rhea A. and Laura A. Dale: *Parapsychology: Sources of Information.* Metuchen: Scarecrow Press, 1973

White, Stewart Edward: *The Betty Book: Excursions into the World of Other-Consciousness, Made by Betty between 1919 and 1936.* New York: E. P. Dutton, 1937

White, Stewart Edward: *The Unobstructed Universe.* New York: E. P. Dutton, 1940

Wicker, Christine: *Lily Dale: The True Story of the Town That Talks to the Dead* San Francisco: HarperSanFrancisco, 2003

Wickland, Carl: *Thirty Years among the Dead.* Amherst: Amherst Press, 1924

Wiitala, Geri Colozzi: *Heather's Return: The Amazing Story of a Child's Communications from Beyond the Grave.* Virginia Beach: A.R.E. Press, 1996

Wilde, Stuart: *Affirmations.* Taos: White Dove, 1987

Wilkinson, Sir J. Gardner: *The Ancient Egyptians: Their Life and Customs.* New York: Crescent Books, 1988

Wilkinson, W. M.: *Spirit Drawings.* London: 1858

Williams, Gertrude Marvin: *Priestess of the Occult: Madame Blavatsky.* New York: Alfred A. Knopf, 1946

Wilson, Bryan R.: *Man, Myth & Magic: Enthusiasm.* London: BPC Publishing, 1970

Wilson, Colin: *Poltergeist! A Study in Destructive Haunting.* London: New English Library, 1981

Wilson, Colin: *The Supernatural: The Geller Phenomenon*. London: Aldus Books, 1976

Wilson, Colin: *The Supernatural: Healing Without Medicine*. London: Aldus Books, 1975

Wilson, Colin: *The Supernatural: Mysterious Powers*. London: Aldus Books, 1975

Wilson, Ernest C.: *Have You Lived Other Lives?* New York: Prentice-Hall, 1956

Wilson, Ian: *The After Death Experience: The Physics of the Non-Physical*. New York: William Morrow, 1987

Winer, Richard and Nancy Osborn: *Haunted Houses*. New York: Bantam Books, 1979

Wolfe, Bernard and Raymond Rosenthal: *Hypnotism Comes of Age*. New York: Bobbs-Merrill, 1948

Wolfman, Benjamin B. (ed.): *Handbook of Parapsychology*. New York: Van Nostrand Reinhold, 1977

Woolger, Dr. Roger: *Other Lives, Other Selves*. New York: Bantam Books, 1988

Yarbro, Chelsea Quinn: *Messages from Michael: On the Nature of the Evolution of the Human Soul*. New York: Playboy Press, 1979

Yarbro, Chelsea Quinn: *More Messages From Michael*. New York: Berkley, 1986

Yogananda, Paramanhansa: *Autobiography of a Yogi*. Los Angeles: Self-Realization Fellowship, 1946

Yost, Casper S.: *Patience Worth: A Psychic Mystery*. New York: Henry Holt, 1916

Zaleski, Carol: *Otherworld Journeys: Accounts of Near-Death Experience in Medieval and Modern Times*. New York: Oxford University Press, 1987

Zolar: *Zolar's Book of the Spirits: All the Most Famous and Fabulous Lore about Contacting the Spirit World*. New York, Prentice Hall, 1987

ONLINE RESOURCES

Abacci Books
http://www.abacci.com/books/

American Association of Electronic Voice Phenomenon
http://aaevp.com/

Andrew Jackson Davis Article
http://www.spirithistory.com/ajdavis.html

Angels Online
http://www.angels-online.com

An Assessment of the Evidence for Psychic Functioning
http://anson.ucdavis.edu/~utts/air2.html

Astrotheme (French)
http://www.astrotheme.fr/portraits/

Blavatsky Study Center
http://www.blavatskyarchives.com/

A Brief History of International Spiritualism
http://www.spiritualist.freeuk.com/History.htm

British Society of Dowsers
http://www.britishdowsers.org/

Camp Chesterfield
http://www.campchesterfield.net

Carlos Mirabelli Biography
http://www.fortunecity.com/roswell/seance/78/mirab.htm

Cecil Husk Biography
http://homepage.ntlworld.com/annetts/mediums/cecil_husk_physical_medium.htm

Charles Richet Biography
http://nobelprize.org/medicine/laureates/1913/richet-bio.html

Charles Robert Richet Biography
http://www.whonamedit.com/doctor.cfm/410.html

Church Universal and Triumphant
http://religiousmovements.lib.virginia.edu/nrms/cut.html

Circulo de Estudos Ramacharaca
http://www.ramacharaca.com.br/

Craig Hamilton-Parker Biography

http://www.psychics.co.uk/television/television_biog_craig.html

Derek Acorah Homepage

http://www.derekacorah.org/

Doris Stokes Biography and Links

http://www.the-psychics.co.uk/doris-stokes.htm

Dorothy Evelyn Begg Interview

http://www.ghostflowers.com/book2/interview.html

Edgar Cayce Homepage

http:///www.edgarcayce.org

Edgar Dean Mitchell Biography

http://www.jsc.nasa.gov/Bios/htmlbios/mitchell-ed.html

Electronic Voice Phenomena Article

http://members.tripod.com/cryskernan/electronic_voice_phenomena.htm

Elisabeth Kübler Ross Homepage

http://www.elisabethkublerross.com/

Elizabeth Clare Prophet Article

http://www.hcn.org/servlets/hcn.Article?article_id=4852

Encyclopedia of Religion and Society

http://hirr.hartsem.edu/ency/SFFI.htm

Ephemera—SpiritHistory.com

http://www.spirithistory.com

The Findhorn Foundation

http://www.findhorn.org

Fredrich Jurgenson Biography

http://www.paravoice.dk/friedrich%20jurgenson.htm

George Anderson Grief Support Programs

http://www.georgeanderson.com

The German Somnambules Article

http://www.survivalafterdeath.org/articles/podmore/german.htm

Hannen Swaffer Quotations

http://www.saidwhat.co.uk/quotes/h/hannen_swaffer_1535.php

Harry Edwards Spiritual Healing Sanctuary

http://www.harryedwards.org.uk

The Hermetic Order Temple Heliopolis

http://www.zolar-thoth.org/

Institute of Noetic Sciences

http://www.noetic.org

Instrumental Transcommunication—EVP & ITC

http://transcommunication.org

International College of Spiritual Science and Healing

http://www.colinscollege.com

The International Survivalist Society

http://www.survivalafterdeath.org

James Van Praagh Homepage

http://www.VanPraagh.com

Janet Cyphord Homepage

http://www.homecircles.com

Jeane Dixon Obituary

http://www.cnn.com/SHOWBIZ/9701/26/dixon/

Kathryn Kuhlman Biography & Links

http://nyny.essortment.com/kathrynkuhlman_rfbt.htm

Leslie Flint Homepage

http://www.leslieflint.com

Lilian Bailey Biography

http://website.lineone.net/~enlightenment/lilian_bailey.htm

Lois Barclay Murphy Biography

http://www.webster.edu/~woolflm/murphy.html

Llewellyn Worldwide

http://www.llewellyn.com

Mae West Biography
http://www.bombshells.com/gallery/west/west_bio.php

Mae West Biography and Article
http://www.walnet.org/csis/news/toronto_2000/gandm-001125-3.html

The Monroe Institute
http://www.monroeinstitute.org

Morris Pratt Institute
http://www.morrispratt.org/

The National Spiritual Alliance
http://www.thenationalspiritualallianceinc.org/

The New Church
http://www.newchurch.org

New Religious Group Index
http://www.meta-religion.com/New_religious_groups/Groups/Spiritual/universal_spiritualist_association.htm

Paramahansa Yogananda Homepage
http://www.yogananda-srf.org/py-life/index.html

Pesquisa Psi (Italian)
http://www.pesquisapsi.com/News/pesquisadorespsi/41/9/9/

Psychic Frontiers Article
http://www.mindreader.com/fate/articles/Fate1294.doc

Psychic News Bookshop Online
http://www.psychicnewsbookshop.co.uk

The Psychics and Mediums Network
http://www.psychics.co.uk

Robert James Lees Biography & Links
http://www.rjlees.co.uk

RootsWeb.com
http://archiver.rootsweb.com/th/read/NYBROOKLYN/2001-06/0991594736

ReligiousTolerance.org
http://www.religioustolerance.org/caodaism.htm

Shirley MacLaine Homepage
http://www.shirleymaclaine.com

Shirley MacLaine Interview
http://www.grandtimes.com/maclaine.html

The Scole Debate Article
http://www.bufora.org.uk/archive/Scole.htm

The Scole Event Article
http://www.datadiwan.de/SciMedNet/library/articlesN73+/N73Keen_Scoleevent.htm

The Scole Phenomena
http://www.afterlife101.com/Scole_1.html

The Sites of Ledash
http://www.cosmosite.net

Spark Online
http://www.spark-online.com

Speaking with Spirits
http://www.speakingwithspirits.com

Spirit Online
http://www.spiritonline.com

The Spirit Which Made a "Talkie" Article
http://www.survivalafterdeath.org/books/fodor/chapter25.htm

SpiritSite.com
http://www.spiritsite.com

Spiritual Frontiers Fellowship International
http://www.spiritualfrontiers.org

Spiritualism Mailing List
http://www.spiritualismlist.net

Spiritualists' National Union
http://www.snu.org.uk

Stewart Edward White Biography
http://www.spiritwritings.com/stewartedwardwhite.html

Stuart Wilde Biography & Links
http://cornerstone.wwwhubs.com/wilde.htm

The Susan B. Anthony House
http://www.susanbanthonyhouse.org

Sylvia Browne Homepage
http://www.sylvia.org

Tony Stockwell Homepage
http://www.tonystockwell.com

University of Sydney, Australia
http://www-personal.usyd.edu.au

Victoria Woodhull Biography
http://www.victoria-woodhull.com/tiltonbio.htm

Victor Zammit Article
http://www.victorzammit.com/articles/william.html

Voices from Space Article
http://www.fiu.edu/~mizrachs/voices-from-cspace.html

White Eagle Lodge
http://www.whiteagle.org/

World ITC Organization
http://www.worlditc.org

INDEX

Note: **Boldface** type indicates main entries and their page numbers; (ill.) indicates photos and illustrations.

A

Abdul (spirit guide), 14, 27–28
Aberfan, Wales, 318, 325
Abolitionists, 10, 315
"The Abraham Lincoln of Spiritualism." *See* Greeley, Horace
Absent healing, 107–8, 124
Academia de Estudos Psychicos, 259–60
Across the Unknown ("Darby and Joan"), 431
Adams, Archie Emmett, 366, 395
Adamson, Thomas (spirit guide), 28
Adare, Lord, **1–2**, 181
Adventists, 189–90
Ænid (Virgil), 372
Æschylus, 165
Æsculapius the Healer and Dream-sender, 164, 325
Aetherius Society, 136
Affirmations, **2**, 424
Afid (spirit guide), 82
After We Die, What Then? (Meek), 129, 252
Afterlife
    according to Swedenborg, Emmanuel, 396
    called Summerland, 115, 385, 394
    and Houdini, Harry, 186
    ITC communication with, 4, 130, 200, 252, 435
Agate, 90
Agpaoa, Tony, 328
Agricola, Georg, 110

Aino (Japan), 137
Ainslie, Sir Douglas, 261
Air elements (Âkâsa [Akasha]), 3
Ajna chakra, 410
Âkâsa (Akasha), 3
Akashic records, 3, **24**
Aksakof, Prof. Alexander, 104
Alais, ghost of, 330
Albert, Prince of Saxe-Coburg-Gotha, and Lees, Robert James, 224–25
Albert Edward, Prince of Wales (Edward VII), 148
Albert (spirit guide), 118
Alden, Theodore, 229–30
Alden, Willard, **3–4**, 229
Alden's Grove, 4, 229
Aldrich, Harry (spirit guide), 422
Alectromancy, 400
Alexandrina Victoria, Queen. *See* Victoria, Queen of the United Kingdom of Great Britain and Ireland
Aliens. *See* Extraterrestrials
Allison, Lydia Winterhalter, **4**
Alpha and Omega Lodge of the Stella Matutina, 146
Alpha waves, 36, 411
Alphabet
    Hebrew, 405
    in radiesthia, 301–2
    use of with talking board, 400–401
Altaic shaman, 369
Amber, 90

American Association of Electronic Voice Phenomena (AA-EVP), **4**
American Psychical Institute and Laboratory, **5**, 61
American Society for Psychical Research, 4, 33, 37, 330
    and Barrett, Sir William, 379
    and Hodgson, Dr. Richard, 177
    and Hyslop, James Hervey, 195
    and investigation of Crandon, Mina ("Margery"), 82–83, 84
    and James, William, 203–4
Amethyst, 90
Ammann, Inge, 102
Amphiaraus, Oracle of, 289
Amulets, of Scottish families, 91
Ancestor worship, 162
    in Chinese spiritism, 70
Ancestors, in Vodoun, 425
Anderson, George, **6–7**
Andrade, Hernani, 386
Andrews, Ellen, 314
Angel(s), **8–9**, 9 (ill.)
    encounters with, 9
    guardian, 166–67
Angelo of Manila, 328
Anglican Church, 420
Animal magnetism, 194, 254–55, 296, 346
Animals, and telepathy, 406
Anka, Darryl, **9–10**, 136
Annali Dello Spiritismo ("Annals of Spiritualism") (Italian journal), **10**. *See also* Italy

M

THE SPIRIT BOOK

S

CPSIA information can be obtained
at www.ICGtesting.com
Printed in the USA
LVHW060809010422
714790LV00014B/232